JURISDICTION OVER NON-EU DEFENDANTS

This book looks at the question of extending the reach of the Brussels Ia Regulation to defendants not domiciled in an EU Member State. The Regulation, the centre-piece of the EU framework on civil procedure, is widely recognised as one of the most successful legal instruments on judicial cooperation. To provide a basis for the discussion of its possible extension, this volume takes a closer look at the national rules that currently govern the question of jurisdiction over non-EU defendants in each Member State through 17 national reports. The insights gained from them are summarised in a comparative report and critically discussed in further contributions, which look at the question both from a European and from a wider global perspective. Private international lawyers will be keen to read the findings and conclusions, which will also be of interest to practitioners and policy makers.

Volume 36 in the series Studies in Private International Law

Studies in Private International Law

Recent titles in the series

Jurisdiction and Cross-Border Collective Redress: A European Private International Law Perspective
Alexia Pato

Rethinking Judicial Jurisdiction in Private International Law
Milana Karayanidi

Economic Sanctions in EU Private International Law
Tamás Szabados

Clawback Law in the Context of Succession
Jayne Holliday

Place of Performance: A Comparative Analysis
Chukwuma Okoli

Private International Law in Nigeria
Chukwuma Okoli and Richard Oppong

Planning the Future of Cross Border Families: A Path Through Coordination
Edited by Ilaria Viarengo and Francesca Villata

The Private International Law of Authentic Instruments
Jonathan Fitchen

The Hague Judgments Convention and Commonwealth Model Law: A Pragmatic Perspective
Abubakri Yekini

A Guide to Global Private International Law
Edited by Paul Beaumont and Jayne Holliday

Parental Child Abduction to Islamic Law Countries
Nazia Yaqub

The Application of Foreign Law in the British and German Courts
Alex Critchley

The HCCH 2019 Judgments Convention: Cornerstones, Prospects, Outlook
Edited by Matthias Weller, João Ribeiro-Bidaoui, Moritz Brinkmann and Nina Dethloff

Jurisdiction Over Non-EU Defendants: Should the Brussels Ia Regulation be Extended?
Edited by Tobias Lutzi, Ennio Piovesani and Dora Zgrabljić Rotar

Jurisdiction Over Non-EU Defendants

Should the Brussels Ia Regulation be Extended?

Edited by
Tobias Lutzi
Ennio Piovesani
and
Dora Zgrabljić Rotar

•HART•
OXFORD • LONDON • NEW YORK • NEW DELHI • SYDNEY

HART PUBLISHING

Bloomsbury Publishing Plc

Kemp House, Chawley Park, Cumnor Hill, Oxford, OX2 9PH, UK

1385 Broadway, New York, NY 10018, USA

29 Earlsfort Terrace, Dublin 2, Ireland

First published in Great Britain 2023

A catalogue record for this book is available from the British Library.

A catalogue record for this book is available from the Library of Congress.

Library of Congress Control Number: 2023930425

ISBN: HB: 978-1-50995-891-7
ePDF: 978-1-50995-893-1
ePub: 978-1-50995-892-4

Typeset by Compuscript Ltd, Shannon

FOREWORD

Should a future version of the Brussels Regulation unify equally the rules on jurisdiction applicable to defendants not domiciled in a Member State? So far, jurisdiction over such persons has been generally a matter for the Member States' own laws. Beyond the normative, and thus rather political issue of 'should we do it?', lies the seemingly more technical 'if yes, how?'

This volume is an excellent and timely contribution to both of these questions. It is exactly this type of sober, comparative groundwork that is frequently lacking prior to legislative endeavours in EU law today. With the membership of the EU increased to 27 jurisdictions, and time being a scarce resource, comparative input in new areas of law runs the danger of being replaced by axioms: either by an almost religious belief that there is a ready-made European solution out there (it just needs to be written down), or, even worse, that there is some global or transnational law (which is the same everywhere, is it not?). In both (and other similar) scenarios, what tends to be happening in reality are poorly veiled instances of legal and cultural self-projection, be they unintentional or, perhaps more often, very much desired.

It is therefore refreshing to see that there are representatives of young scholarship that are still ready to carry the proverbial torch of the more classic comparative law scholarship, which is not there to accept ready-made axioms or to engage in normative culture wars (with the one side making sweeping ideological statements and the other one immediately contradicting them by revealing the inherent post-whatever bias, with both of them being detached from and irrelevant to any actual law), but to discreetly inform our future legislative work by generating real knowledge and information. This type of scholarship provides not just an informed choice with regard to 'how to do it' technically: when seriously reflecting on the 'how', one might often go back to the 'should we?'. By looking in detail at what would be replaced, one might be for the first time, in fact, obliged to single out the genuine, practical need (or the absence thereof) for unifying something in the first place.

Finally, the comparative journey in this volume is enriched by being not purely horizontal, but equally diagonal in its scope and nature. It is not just a study of 17 more or less independent variables: the individual Member States. These samples themselves are embedded in, and react with, the system of EU law, or previously the respective Conventions standing outside the EU framework. The national approaches interact with it; they explore, to various degrees, the margins left by EU law. Thus, the added value of the volume is not in being just a bottom-up comparative study, but equally a study in different degrees of Europeanisation, or what might be called – somewhat heretically perhaps – Comparative European Law: how do the individual Member States react to the similar, legislative or judicial, impetus? Certainly, most of that interaction with regard to the specific question covered in this volume is happening outside the scope of EU law strictly considered. However, perhaps in contrast to referenda questions, the real life and interactions with EU law are not a binary 'in or out'. Not only might it be in reality difficult to ascertain what is exactly 'in' and what is 'out', but more importantly, there are some regimes, which are clearly governed by EU law, but where the Member States retain striking degree of autonomy. In other regimes, which are nominally outside the scope of EU law, one finds an enhanced degree of intended and implemented commonality amongst the Member States.

If I were the European Commission, I would happily consider a great part of my duty under Art 79 of the Brussels Ia Regulation discharged by this volume, at least in intellectual terms.

Michal Bobek

SERIES EDITORS' PREFACE

This is a book about the jurisdiction rules that apply to non-EU defendants (apart from defendants from the Lugano Convention 2007 States) in the EU Member States. These rules have not been harmonised by EU Law (currently in the Brussels Ia Regulation 2012). The key connecting factor which forms the basis of the general ground of jurisdiction is 'domicile', which has been harmonised for non-natural persons by Brussels Ia (in a broad way to include the place of incorporation, the principal place of business and the central administration) but which remains unharmonised for natural persons. Therefore, who is affected by this book – people who are not domiciled in an EU Member State or a Lugano Contracting State – is not a group entirely based on uniform EU law. As the group of natural persons covered by the Brussels Ia Regulation (and by the sister Lugano Convention 2007 which applies between Denmark, the rest of the EU, Iceland, Norway and Switzerland) depends on very diverse notions of domicile, establishing who is a person not domiciled in an EU Member State (or Lugano Contracting State) is an uncertain task requiring, in principle, a knowledge of the legal systems in all of those States. One of the exciting things about this book is the information it reveals about how domicile is defined for this purpose in the national laws of many, but not all, EU Member States. In fact, it is these national reports on the jurisdiction laws applying to non-EU domiciliaries in 17 Member States that lie at the heart of this book. UK readers, and others from common law jurisdictions elsewhere, will be fascinated to see that in many of the countries reported on in this book, the domicile of natural persons for the purposes of the Brussels Ia Regulation and the national rules applying to non-EU domiciliaries is like a domicile of choice familiar to the common law world, ie it is based on residence in a country with an intention to remain there indefinitely. This is, of course, in contrast to the UK statutory definition of domicile in the Civil Jurisdiction and Judgments Act 1982 (1982 Act) that was deliberately created to move away from the common law notion of domicile of choice and applied to these issues when the UK was a Member State of the EU. It still applies to the jurisdiction rules for intra-UK cases (the rules in Schedule 4 of the 1982 Act) and to the Scottish jurisdiction rules for cases where the defendant is not domiciled in another part of the UK (Schedule 8 to the 1982 Act) and the Hague Choice of Court Convention 2005 is not applicable. The UK statutory domicile in section 41 of the 1982 Act requires residence in the UK (or the relevant part of the UK) coupled with 'substantial connection' with the UK (or the relevant part of the UK) but the latter is presumed based on being 'resident for the last three months or more' in the UK or the relevant part of the UK. As is made clear by case law, notably an excellent early Sheriff Court decision in Scotland on the 1982 Act, *Daniel v Foster* 1989 SCLR 378, a natural person can be domiciled for these purposes in more than one country (in that case in Scotland where Foster was working and staying for 2–10 days at a time and in England where he had his home and stayed there when not working in Scotland). It is clear from the national reports that in some EU countries someone like Foster would be regarded as domiciled only in the country of his home and not in the country where he resided part of the time for work purposes. Therefore, if the fact scenario in Foster were today that his home was in the UK and he worked in an EU Member State it would depend on which Member State he was working in as to whether he would be regarded as domiciled there and therefore an EU domiciliary for the purposes of the Brussels Ia Regulation or a non-EU domiciliary. This distinction will determine whether an exorbitant jurisdiction can be used against him or not in an EU Member State (or in a Lugano Contracting State).

There is much to be said for being able to sue economically active natural persons on the basis of general jurisdiction in any place where they reside and have a substantial connection based on a liberally interpreted three months presumption. So perhaps the next round of the revision of Brussels Ia might adopt a uniform definition of domicile based on the UK statutory definition that was designed for that purpose now that the UK is not a party to Brussels Ia or the Lugano Convention. It would have the benefit that economically active people with a home base outside the EU who are working in the EU could be sure that they can only be sued in any EU Member State on a non-exorbitant basis of jurisdiction because it would be clear that they are domiciled in an EU State (as well as being domiciled in a non-EU State). This is much better than switching to habitual residence which has been hijacked by the CJEU into quite a rigid factual concept that says an adult person can only be habitually resident in one place (see Case C-289/20 *IB v FA* EU:C:2021:955), at least for the purposes of divorce jurisdiction. The Third Chamber in *IB* said:

> while it cannot be ruled out that a spouse may have several residences at the same time, he or she may have, at a given time, only one habitual residence [51].

Given that the Third Chamber then gave quite a weak test for habitual residence it is very difficult in a case where an adult resides in more than one country to know which is their habitual residence. The Chamber said:

> the concept of 'habitual residence' is characterised, in principle, by two factors, namely, first, the intention of the person concerned to establish the habitual centre of his or her interests in a particular place and, secondly, a presence which is sufficiently stable in the Member State concerned. [57].

But if this rule were adopted in a revised Brussels Ia Regulation it would not be clear where a person's habitual residence is (where they live and work, often alone, during the week or where they live, often with their family, at the weekend). In *IB v FA* the Third Chamber left that key decision to the national courts because habitual residence is 'essentially a question of fact' [52], and the CJEU in preliminary references is only empowered to determine questions of EU law. However, the Third Chamber seemed to hint that the person was habitually resident in the country where he was working because it said that both the tests in para 57 above were satisfied [59]–[60] while leaving it to the national court to decide if he had 'transferred his habitual residence' there from the country where his family home was which he went back to at the weekends [61].

The book has a very interesting contribution on US jurisdiction and on the use of exorbitant jurisdiction against non-EU defendants by the Brussels Ia Regulation from Professor Ron Brand of the University of Pittsburgh School of Law. I have had the privilege of working with Ron at the Hague Conference on Private International Law (HCCH) since 1996. His contribution demonstrates that the concerns that many States had, in the 1990's when we were negotiating the original Judgments Convention, about the potentially exorbitant character of US general doing business jurisdiction are no longer valid because of a series of reforming cases by the US Supreme Court greatly restricting the general jurisdiction applicable to companies and other non-natural persons. He encourages the EU to harmonise its rules applicable to non-EU defendants in a revised Brussels Ia without waiting for the harmonisation of direct jurisdiction rules at the HCCH. He rightly points out that the US is still not ready to adopt any (significant) harmonisation of direct jurisdiction rules in a Treaty at the HCCH. This may be partly because of the remaining US exorbitant jurisdiction against natural persons (service of a writ on a person while they are present in the jurisdiction) which is the foundation of jurisdiction in the Anglo-American common law world. It is very hard for those countries to abandon such a cornerstone of the basis on which jurisdiction has been constructed historically.

The issue for the EU is whether in the current Jurisdiction Project at the HCCH (see https://www.hcch.net/en/projects/legislative-projects/jurisdiction-project) it might be possible to persuade the HCCH to go ahead in the future (after a Convention on parallel proceedings is adopted with some priority jurisdictional connections – not direct grounds of jurisdiction) with a Convention or Principles on Direct Jurisdiction even if the US is reluctant to do so. This would require the HCCH Members at a Council meeting to adopt a constructive approach to 'consensus' decision making and not to block those States who want to negotiate a Convention/Principles on Direct Jurisdiction from doing so even though a number of Members may not be keen to negotiate such an instrument. Such a constructive approach to consensus was the only reason that the Hague Maintenance Protocol on Applicable Law of 2007 was ever adopted because the common law Members of the HCCH did not block the civil law Members from effectively negotiating that Protocol among themselves even though the common law States had (and still have) no interest in the Protocol.

This book is largely the work of early career and mid-career scholars in private international law. It is reassuring to see that the discipline is in good hands going forward. This is a worthy addition to the Hart Studies in Private International Law Series that should be of interest to all private international lawyers, not just those focusing on EU private international law, as it reveals the content of a remaining area of national private international law in 17 EU Member States.

Paul Beaumont FRSE
Professor of Private International Law and Head of Law
University of Stirling

PREFACE

This volume marks the end of a wonderful academic journey on which we embarked almost two years ago. It started with a somewhat naïve reading of Art 79 of the Brussels Ia Regulation, according to which the Commission was supposed to present a report on the application of the Regulation by 11 January 2022. This report should include 'an evaluation of the possible need for a further extension of the rules on jurisdiction to defendants not domiciled in a Member State'. While considering such an extension based on the practical application of the Regulation in the Member States and by the CJEU certainly seemed like a worthwhile endeavour, we felt that it would only paint half of the picture. How could an extension of the Regulation to non-EU defendants be sensibly discussed without a structured analysis of the national laws that currently govern third-state cases in these Member States?

The fact that the Commission Report seemed less and less likely to come out in 2022 only provided further motivation to use the resources of the EAPIL Young Research Network and start painting the second half of the picture. For this purpose, we put together a questionnaire with pertinent questions relating to the national provisions that an extended Brussels Ia Regulation would be most likely to replace. These questions were ultimately answered by 23 researchers from 17 EU Member States, providing a detailed picture of the status quo across the EU.

From the very first drafts we received, we were surprised both by the diversity of approaches in the different Member States – from traditional *double functionality* thinking in Germany and France to the tailored codifications of Croatia, Italy, or Poland (to name just a few) to the common-law inspired approaches of Cyprus and Malta – and by the structural similarities between them. We discussed these observations for the first time at a workshop in October 2021, on the basis of which we started to draft the Comparative Report, which constitutes the first chapter of this book. It is followed by the final versions of the national reports, which were repeatedly reviewed and amended as the project progressed.

The Comparative Report was first presented at the closing conference of the project, which took place in April 2022 at the University of Zagreb's Inter University Centre in Dubrovnik. The conference served to discuss both the Comparative Report and a number of more specific points which emerged as particularly interesting over the course of the project, and to link them to the wider policy discussion of whether or not to extend the Brussels Ia Regulation. For this latter purpose, we were fortunate to be joined by a number of internationally recognised experts, both from within and outside of the EU, many of whom kindly provided their contributions in writing, to be reprinted in the last part of this book.

No part of this book, nor of the research project on which it is based, would have been possible without the help of many others. First and foremost, we are deeply indebted to the members of the EAPIL Young Research Network who acted as national reporters and without whose tireless efforts the project would not have been able to succeed. We are also grateful to everyone else who attended the Dubrovnik Conference, most importantly to our guest speakers. The conference itself was sponsored by the Faculty of Law of the University of Zagreb and the European Commission in Zagreb, to whom we are equally grateful. We also thank the European Association of Private International Law for continuing to support the Young Research Network as well as Michal Bobek for kindly providing a foreword to this volume. Finally, the editors would like to thank Duygu Söztutar and Gordian Felix Schwarz, both research assistants at the University of Augsburg, as well as Tom Adams, Sasha Jawed, and Victoria Johnston from Hart Publishing for their diligent support in the editing of the manuscript for this book.

Tobias Lutzi
Ennio Piovesani
Dora Zgrabljić Rotar

CONTENTS

LIST OF CONTRIBUTORS

Ivan Allegranti, Research Fellow at the University of Camerino

Tess Bens, Research Fellow at the Max Planck Institute Luxembourg for International, European and Regulatory Procedural Law

Michal Bobek, Justice at the Supreme Administrative Court, Czech Republic, formerly Advocate General at the Court of Justice of the European Union

Katažyna Bogdzevič, Professor at Mykolas Romeris University

Ronald A Brand, Chancellor Mark A Nordenberg University Professor at the University of Pittsburgh

María Asunción Cebrián Salvat, Lecturer at the University of Murcia

Stefano Dominelli, Research Fellow at the University of Genoa

Paul Eichmüller, University Assistant at the University of Vienna

Aleksandrs Fillers, Assistant Professor at the Riga Graduate School of Law

Tena Hoško, Assistant Professor at the University of Zagreb

Marko Jovanović, Associate Professor at the University of Belgrade

Lydia Lundstedt, Senior Lecturer at Stockholm University

Tobias Lutzi, Junior Professor at the University of Augsburg

Vassiliki Marazopoulou, Teaching Fellow at the National and Kapodistrian University of Athens

Giedrius Ožiūnas, PhD Candidate at Mykolas Romeris University

Phuong Thao Phan, PhD Candidate at the Universities of Lorraine and Turin

Ennio Piovesani, Research Fellow at the University of Turin

Michiel Poesen, Lecturer at the University of Aberdeen

Ioannis Revolidis, Lecturer at the University of Malta

Konstantinos Rokas, Lecturer at the University of Nicosia

Anna Maria Ruiz Martín, Lecturer in Law and Research Fellow at the Geneva Business School and at the Open University of Catalonia

Dora Zgrabljić Rotar, Associate Professor at the University of Zagreb

Margherita Salvadori, Professor of Law at the University of Turin

Dafina Dimitrova Sarbinova, Senior Assistant Professor at the Sofia University "St. Kliment Ohridski"

Benjamin Saunier, Research Assistant at the University of Paris 1 Panthéon-Sorbonne

Ferenc Szilágyi, Assistant Professor at the Pázmány Péter Catholic University in Budapest

Johannes Ungerer, Erich Brost Lecturer at the University of Oxford

Felix M Wilke, Senior Lecturer at the University of Bayreuth

Anna Wysocka-Bar, Senior Lecturer at the Jagiellonian University in Kraków

Ning Zhao, Principal Legal Officer at the Permanent Bureau of the Hague Conference on Private International Law

TABLE OF CJEU CASES

(sorted by Case number)

Case	cited by
Case 22/70, *Commission of the European Communities v Council of the European Communities. European Agreement on Road Transport*, ECLI:EU:C:1971:32	Brand
Case 12/76, *Industrie Tessili Italiana Como v Dunlop AG*, ECLI:EU:C:1976:133	Germany, 5(a); Malta, 5(a); Netherlands, 5(a)
Case 14/76, *A. De Bloos, SPRL v Société en commandite par actions Bouyer*, ECLI:EU:C:1976:134	Malta, 5(a)
Case 21/76, *Handelskwekerij G. J. Bier BV v Mines de potasse d'Alsace SA*, ECLI:EU:C:1976:166	Comparative Report, 5(b); France, 5(b); Netherlands, 5(b); Sweden, 5(b); Brand
Case 133/81, *Roger Ivenel v Helmut Schwab*, ECLI:EU:C:1982:199	Belgium, 5(d)
Case C-189/87, *Athanasios Kalfelis v Bankhaus Schröder, Münchmeyer, Hengst & Co. et al.*, ECLI:EU:C:1988:459	France, 5(c); Spain, 4.3.2.
Case C-26/91, *Jakob Handte & Co. GmbH v Traitements Mécano-chimiques des Surfaces SA*, ECLI:EU:C:1992:268	France, 5(a); Germany, 5
Case C-68/93, *Fiona Shevill, Ixora Trading Inc., Chequepoint SARL and Chequepoint International Ltd v Presse Alliance SA*, ECLI:EU:C:1995:61	Comparative Report, 1(c); France, 5(b); Germany, 5(c); Sweden, 5(b)
Case C-364/93, *Antonio Marinari v Lloyds Bank plc and Zubaidi Trading Company*, ECLI:EU:C:1995:289	Comparative Report, 5(b); Germany, 5(b); Netherlands, 5(b); Sweden, 5(c)
Case C-383/95, *Petrus Wilhelmus Rutten v Cross Medical Ltd*, ECLI:EU:C:1997:7	France, 5(d)
Case C-412/98, *Group Josi Reinsurance Company SA v Universal General Insurance Company (UGIC)*, ECLI:EU:C:2000:399	Germany, 5(d)

I.

Questionnaire

1 Which rules of domestic law govern jurisdiction over non-EU defendants in matters regulated by the Brussels Ia Regulation? When answering this question, please address the following points:

(a) Specify the source of the domestic jurisdictional rules (indicate the name of said source in your national language and in English) and briefly introduce said rules.

(b) Specify whether the domestic jurisdictional rules apply specifically to transnational disputes, or whether they apply indistinctly to transnational and domestic disputes.

(c) Specify whether the jurisdictional rules of the Brussels Regime (ie the 1968 Brussels Convention, the Brussels I Regulation and the Brussels Ia Regulation) are extended by the domestic law of your Member State, either by reference or incorporation, to cases where the Brussels Ia Regulation applies only to non-EU defendants. When addressing this point, please also specify when those rules were enforced and which rules were applicable before the enforcement of such extension. If the jurisdictional rules of the Brussels Regime have not been (fully) extended to non-EU defendants yet, please mention whether scholars (or even lawmakers) in your Member State have considered the possibility of (further) extending the personal scope of said rules.

(d) Specify whether the information notified by your Member State pursuant to Art 76(1) Brussels Ia Regulation is exhaustive.

2 How is the notion of domicile of natural and legal persons defined in your Member State for jurisdictional purposes?

3 Does domestic law provide for a general rule on jurisdiction in matters regulated by the Brussels Ibis Regulation based on connecting factors other than domicile (eg the citizenship of the claimant or defendant, the residence or temporary stay of the defendant, the situation of property, etc.)? If the answer is in the affirmative, please explain how said connecting factors are defined in your Member State.

4 Does domestic law (including case law) envisage a forum necessitatis, ie the possibility for national courts of exercising jurisdiction in cases where no foreign forum would be available?

5 Which rules of domestic law govern jurisdiction over non-EU defendants in the corresponding cases considered in the Brussels Ia Regulation and listed below in points 5 (a)–(d)? When addressing each point, please describe the corresponding domestic jurisdictional rule(s), highlighting similarities and differences between the latter and those of the Brussels Ibis Regulation. Please mention also whether, when interpreting and applying the relevant rule(s) of domestic law, national courts refer to the rules of or principles enshrined in the Brussels Regime and/or to the preliminary rulings rendered by the ECJ on that Regime – if possible, please also provide some examples.

(a) Jurisdiction in matters relating to contract (cf Art 7 no 1 lit a) Brussels Ia Regulation)
(b) Jurisdiction in matters relating to tort, delict or quasi-delict (cf Art 7 no 2 Brussels Ia Regulation)
(c) Jurisdiction based on a close connection between defendants (cf Art 8 no 1 Brussels Ia Regulation)
(d) Jurisdiction over consumer, employment and insurance contracts (cf Arts 10–23 Brussels Ia Regulation). Please specify whether jurisdiction over said contracts is governed by special protective rules or ordinary rules governing jurisdiction over other contracts. Please also specify whether there exist protective rules on jurisdiction in matters regulated by the Brussels Ia Regulation and applicable in cases involving parties other than consumers, employees and insured (eg commercial agents).

II.

Comparative Report

TOBIAS LUTZI, ENNIO PIOVESANI AND DORA ZGRABLJIĆ ROTAR

The following report has been compiled on the basis of the national reports reprinted in chapter three of this book, also taking into account the results of an online workshop held in October 2021 and of the conference held in May 2022 in Dubrovnik. All references to national law have been verified by the respective national reporters, to whom the authors of this report wish to express their heartfelt gratitude.

The Comparative Report follows the same structure as the Questionnaire, reprinted in chapter one of this book.

Questions 1(a) and 1(b)

Broadly speaking, there appear to exist three approaches to international jurisdiction in the EU Member States. While some Member States still adhere to the principle of *'Doppelfunktionalität'* (double-functionality), by which the domestic rules on local jurisdiction (venue) are simply extended to questions of international jurisdiction, a growing number have enacted special acts on private international law that include rules on international jurisdiction. Cyprus and Malta are the only two Member States that follow an approach that appears to be distinctly rooted in the Common Law.

Rules on local jurisdiction extended to international jurisdiction (*'Doppelfunktionalität'*)	**Specific rules on international jurisdiction**	**Common Law approach**
- Austria - France - Germany - Greece - Latvia - Sweden	- Belgium - Bulgaria - Croatia - Hungary - Italy - Lithuania - Netherlands - Poland - Spain	- Cyprus - Malta

In the Member States belonging to the first group, where international jurisdiction is generally[1] governed[2] by rules on local jurisdiction, this approach has usually been developed by the courts. While some of the relevant sets of rules (such as the AUSTRIAN *Jurisdiktionsnorm*, in § 27a) nowadays acknowledge the extension to international jurisdiction, others (such as the FRENCH *Code de procédure civile* or the GERMAN *Zivilprozessordnung*)[3] still make no explicit reference to international jurisdiction. Although these systems generally follow the idea that a court with local jurisdiction according to national law necessarily also has international jurisdiction, the FRENCH and SWEDISH reports both emphasise that national courts will not necessarily construct the same norms identically for international and purely domestic cases; in fact, the SWEDISH courts appear to use the rules on local jurisdiction merely as an indication of the necessary connection to Sweden.

It should be noted that the FRENCH government currently considers codifying French private international law,[4] including its rules on international jurisdiction. Interestingly, though, the most recent proposal[5] contains a provision that would enshrine the principle of double functionality[6] and supplement it by more specific provisions.

This is in noticeable contrast to the Member States of the second group, which have often replaced the system of '*Doppelfunktionalität*' in its entirety by specific rules on international jurisdiction (usually as part of some more comprehensive legislation on private international law). With the oldest of these codifications – the POLISH *Kodeks postępowania cywilnego* – dating from 1965, they all tend to be relatively young,[7] especially when compared to the rules on venue still applied in AUSTRIA and GERMANY, which have essentially remained unchanged since 1898 and 1879, respectively. Those specific rules on international jurisdiction naturally require, either implicitly or explicitly,[8] the existence of a cross-border dispute.[9] In some cases

[1] Though Arts 14 and 15 of the FRENCH *Code civil* and Art 3 of the GREEK Κώδικας Πολιτικής Δικονομίας contain some rudimentary rules on international jurisdiction.

[2] See the FRENCH report, Question 1(b), for details on the development of the terminology used by the *Cour de cassation*.

[3] Interestingly, some individual provisions of the GERMAN ZPO and SWEDISH *rättegångsbalken* appear to be applicable only in cross-border cases (see the GERMAN report, Question 1(b), and the SWEDISH report, Question 1(b), for more detail).

[4] See G Cuniberti, 'Towards a French Code of Private International Law?', EAPIL Blog, 11 May 2022, www.eapil.org/2022/05/11/towards-a-french-code-of-private-international-law/.

[5] Available at www.cfdip.fr/offres/file_inline_src/717/717_pj_120422_114420.pdf.

[6] ibid, Art 15.

[7] The youngest comprehensive pieces of legislation appear to be the CROATIAN *Zakon o međunarodnom privatnom pravu* and the HUNGARIAN *törvény a nemzetközi magánjogról*, both from 2017.

[8] See, eg, Art 1(2) of the BULGARIAN *Кодекс на международното частно право*; Art 1 of the CROATIAN *Zakon o međunarodnom privatnom pravu*.

[9] But see the HUNGARIAN report, Question 1(b), and the DUTCH report, Question 1(b), for discussion of some possible extensions to domestic disputes.

(eg ITALY), they are still explicitly supplemented, in (civil and commercial) matters falling outside the material scope of the Brussels Regime, by the extension of rules on local jurisdiction.[10]

Regardless of whether or not a Member State has enacted specific legislation on international jurisdiction, its general rules tend to be supplemented by sectorial legislation governing specific types of disputes such as disputes in labour law,[11] over intellectual property,[12] or class actions.[13]

Finally, a third group of Member States, comprising only CYPRUS and MALTA, follows an approach rooted in the tradition of the English Common Law.[14] As such, they accept international jurisdiction on the basis of service (in the case of CYPRUS) or presence (in the case of MALTA), subject to a *forum (non) conveniens* test.[15]

Question 1(c)

Of the Member States that have enacted specific rules on jurisdiction applicable to non-EU defendants, the clear majority – with the exception of only LITHUANIA and POLAND – have reportedly taken the Brussels Regime[16] into account, either by incorporating it partly (such as ITALY) or even entirely (such as, in particular, CROATIA) through reference, or by using it as an inspiration for the domestic rules (such as BELGIUM, BULGARIA, the NETHERLANDS, or SPAIN). In the case of ITALY, the (partial) incorporation of the Brussels Convention raises the interesting problem of whether or not the references in question must nowadays be understood as references to the Brussels Ia Regulation; it is only recently that the *Corte di cassazione* appears to have answered this question in the positive.[17]

[10] See, eg, Art 3(2), second sentence, of the ITALIAN Law 218/1995. Until recently, CROATIA belonged to that group. Namely, Art 27 of the CROATIAN Civil Procedure Act allowed for jurisdiction of CROATIAN courts when no explicit rule allows it for cases with an international element, but jurisdiction stems from rules of territorial jurisdiction. This indirectly allowed for international jurisdiction in certain cases. In addition, Art 58 of the Civil Procedure Act contained rules of direct international jurisdiction. Both articles were revoked as a part of the legislative amendments of the Civil Procedure Act in 2022. See the CROATIAN report, Question 5(a).

[11] See §§ 4–9 ASGG, the AUSTRIAN *Arbeits- und Sozialgerichtsgesetz*; § 48(1a) of the GERMAN *Arbeitsgerichtsgesetz*.

[12] See Art 86 of the BELGIAN *Wetboek Internationaal Privaatrecht*; § 104(1) of the GERMAN *Urheberrechtsgesetz*.

[13] See Art R 632-2 of the FRENCH *Code de la consommation*.

[14] MALTESE law is in fact inspired by both common-law and civil-law traditions; although being codified, it largely relies on common-law institutions and principles.

[15] Although having codified rules on international jurisdiction, some other Member States (such as LITHUANIA) also accept very broad bases of (general) jurisdiction (such as permanent residence) but without counterbalancing them by a *forum non conveniens* test.

[16] The wording 'Brussels Regime' used in the text refers either jointly or indistinctly to the Brussels Convention, the Brussels I Regulation and/or to the Brussels Ia Regulation.

[17] See the references in the ITALIAN report, Question 1(c).

	Brussels Regime incorporated	Brussels Regime used as inspiration	little or no impact of Brussels Regime
Belgium		x	
Bulgaria		x	
Croatia	x		
Hungary		x	
Italy	x[18]		
Lithuania			x
Netherlands		x	
Poland			x
Spain		x	

Of the Member States that are still applying the rules on local jurisdiction to the question of international jurisdiction, many have seen a certain impact of the Brussels Regime and its interpretation by the CJEU on their national rules. While this impact could be most clearly identified for Germany and Sweden (where the national courts have even reversed their jurisprudence to better align it with the CJEU's interpretation of similar provisions in the Regulation), only the Austrian courts appear to have continued to interpret the national rules on jurisdiction in complete isolation from their European counterparts. Besides, the idea of transposing at least parts of the Regulation into national law seems to have been discussed in legal scholarship in all Member States.

	Interpretation of domestic rules influenced by the Brussels Regime	Interpretation of domestic rules not influenced by the Brussels Regime
Austria		x
France	x[19]	
Germany	x[20]	

(continued)

[18] Only to some extent, and with reference to the Brussels Convention.

[19] The French report specifically mentions the inspiration provided by the CJEU's decisions in Cases C-68/93 *Shevill* and C-170/12 *Pinckney* for the treatment of cyber-torts under Art 46 *Code de procédure civile* (French report, Questions 1(c), 5(b)).

[20] The German report refers to case law from the Bundesgerichtshof regarding the scope of the heads of special jurisdiction, the localization of the damage resulting from copyright infringements over the internet, and the scope of the national provisions on insurance contracts (German report, Questions 1(c), 5(a), 5(d)(3)).

(Continued)

	Interpretation of domestic rules influenced by the Brussels Regime	**Interpretation of domestic rules not influenced by the Brussels Regime**
GREECE	x[21]	
LATVIA	x[22]	
SWEDEN	x[23]	

Question 1(d)

Some reports have revealed exorbitant grounds of jurisdiction that have not been notified pursuant to Art 76(1) Brussels Ia – such as jurisdiction based on the location of property or other assets in POLAND. Others have also mentioned grounds that could have been included – such as the *forum arresti* in DUTCH law – but have been more hesitant to definitively qualify them as such.

Interestingly, MALTA, whose jurisdictional rules may be seen as particularly exorbitant due to their common-law origin, has notified its entire jurisdictional regime to the Commission.

Question 2

Even though, as reported *supra* under Question 1, the majority of the Member States have enacted special acts on private international law that include rules on international jurisdiction, and only a minority of the Member States still follow the principle of double-functionality, by which the domestic rules on local jurisdiction are simply extended to questions of international jurisdiction, the majority of member states still use the same definition of domicile for both national and international jurisdiction, while only three Member States have included a special definition of domicile in their respective private international law acts.

[21] The GREEK report refers to an explanatory report from the Greek parliament explicitly allowing the Greek courts to take into account the jurisprudence of the CJEU when interpreting the relevant rule for jurisdiction in tort (GREEK report, Questions 1(c), 5(b)).

[22] The LATVIAN report only refers to one decision on the interpretation of the concept of 'branch'.

[23] The SWEDISH report refers to several decisions by the Högsta domstolen according to which the Brussels and Lugano regimes constitute internationally recognised rules that provide an important inspiration for the interpretation of the equivalent SWEDISH provisions.

Definition of domicile used for national and international jurisdiction	**Specific definition of domicile in PILA**	**Common Law approach**
- Austria - Bulgaria - France - Italy - Latvia - Lithuania - Netherlands - Germany - Greece - Sweden - Poland - Spain	- Belgium - Croatia - Hungary	- Cyprus - Malta

The three Member States that do have a definition of domicile of natural and legal persons used exclusively for the purposes of international jurisdiction are the ones with the newest private international law acts in Europe. Namely, domicile of natural and legal persons is defined in Art 4 of the 2004 Belgian *Wetboek Internationaal Privaatrecht/Code de Droit International Privé*,[24] in arts 4 and 6 of the 2017 Croatian *Zakon o međunarodnom privatnom pravu*[25] and in Art 3 of the 2017 Hungarian *évi XXVIII. törvény a nemzetközi magánjogról*.[26]

In the Member States that use the same definition of domicile for both local and international jurisdiction, the definitions are usually integral parts of the respective Member State's civil code.[27] In Austria the definition is found in the § 66 of the *Jurisdiktionsnorm*, as the Austrian civil procedure is fragmented insofar as the *Jurisdiktionsnorm* covers the principal rules of when, by whom and under which conditions civil jurisdiction may be exercised, whereas the actual procedure of the court proceedings is set out in the *Zivilprozessordnung*.[28] In Sweden, the statutory definition of domicile for natural persons in the area of family law is, by analogy, used for jurisdictional purposes.[29]

However, notwithstanding whether the domicile of natural persons is defined in the Member State's private international law act or in other acts belonging to civil law, civil procedure law or family law, in almost all Member States the definition of the domicile of natural persons embodies two elements that need to be cumulatively present.

[24] The domicile of both natural and legal persons is defined in Art 4 of the Belgian *Wetboek Internationaal Privaatrecht/Code de Droit International Privé* (Belgian report, Question 2).

[25] The domicile of natural persons is defined in Art 4, while as the domicile of legal persons in Art 6 of the Croatian *Zakon o međunarodnom privatnom pravu* (Croatian report, Question 2).

[26] Art 3 of the Hungarian *évi XXVIII. törvény a nemzetközi magánjogról* provides a definition of the domicile of natural persons, while it should be interpreted together with the general jurisdictional rule in proprietary matters in Art 92 for a correct definition of the domicile of legal persons (Hungarian report, Question 2).

[27] France, Greece, Italy, Latvia, Lithuania, Netherlands, Poland, Spain and Germany.

[28] See the Austrian report, Questions 1(a) and 2.

[29] See the Swedish report, Question 2.

The first one is an objective prerequisite according to which a person has to live at that place (*corpus*) and the second criterion is a subjective one (*animus manendi*) according to which a person has to intend to reside at the place permanently.

Out of all civil law Member States, only three do not follow this definition. Namely, in BELGIUM and SPAIN domicile is defined as the place where the person is registered, while as in BULGARIA there is an ongoing debate whether the domicile of a natural person should be understood as the place where the person is registered or the place where they have their habitual residence.[30]

There are two significant outcomes of the unified definition of domicile of natural persons throughout the EU. Firstly, since the Brussels Ia Regulation does not contain an autonomous definition of domicile of natural persons, but a rule on the applicable law, the unanimity in defining the domicile of natural persons contributes significantly to a unified application of the rules of the Brussels Ia Regulation and, thus, indirectly to achieving the main aims of the Brussels Regime. Secondly, it leads to the conclusion that the majority of Member States do not add new bases of international jurisdiction through broadening the definition of domicile, ie they do not expand the international jurisdiction of their courts indirectly through a broader definition of domicile of natural persons.

However, in the case of the only two predominantly common-law Member States, the opposite might be concluded. Namely, both MALTA[31] and CYPRUS distinguish between two types of domicile of natural persons – domicile of origin and domicile of choice.[32] The domicile of origin does not always coincide with the traditional civil law understanding of the domicile which requires the objective and a subjective element. It is the domicile acquired by birth.[33] Under both systems it is possible to abandon a domicile of origin and acquire a domicile of choice if the person in question has chosen freely a new place as their domicile of choice. However, under both systems the burden of proof of a domicile of choice cannot be met easily. In both Member States it is the courts' decision whether a domicile of origin was abandoned and a domicile of choice acquired, and in both cases the courts have raised the threshold very high.[34]

[30] According to the BULGARIAN report the consensus on a definition of domicile of natural persons has not yet been reached. A summary of this problem may be found (in Bulgarian) in B Musseva, 'Action and Reaction between EU Law and Bulgarian Law in the Application of Brussels I Recast Regulation', in *Annual of the Law Faculty of Sofia University 'St. Kliment Ohridski'*, Sofia, 2019, 397–403 (BULGARIAN report, Question 2).

[31] Domicile is, modelled on ITALIAN law, a jurisdictional basis under Art 742(1)(a) and (b) of the Code of Organisation and Civil Procedure. However, MALTESE courts interpret the concept of domicile according to the jurisprudence of UK Courts. See the MALTESE report, Question 2.

[32] MALTESE courts also recognise the domicile of dependence, devised for minors and persons of diminished capacity as explained in the MALTESE report, Question 2.

[33] According to MALTESE law everybody is assigned her father's domicile at birth, which is the domicile of origin, and according to CYPRIOT law it is the domicile acquired at birth.

[34] In both MALTA and CYPRUS domicile of choice as a concept consists of two elements. The external element refers to the legal and social relationships as well as the activities of a person, and the internal element to the will of a person to establish a new domicile in a country other than the country of its birth. Case law shows that it is particularly difficult to prove the internal element and that clear and solid evidence is required to convince the court that a person wanted a change of permanent domicile and it is, thus, in practice very difficult to abandon one's domicile of origin in order to establish a domicile of choice. See the MALTESE report, Question 2; CYPRIOT report, Question 2.

This leads to a conclusion that by widening the notion of domicile, or making it very difficult to abandon the domicile of origin and acquire a domicile of choice, the courts of these two Member States have indirectly added a new connecting factor for establishing international jurisdiction and have added a possibility to retain their jurisdiction in a wider scope of cases.

On the other hand, Art 63 Brussels Ia provides a definition of the domicile of a legal person according to which a legal person is domiciled at the place of its statutory seat, central administration, or its principal place of business. All three connecting factors are defined autonomously. Thus, for the purposes of application of the Brussels Ia Regulation, the courts will determine the domicile of the legal person in cases over an EU defendant in accordance with the definition provided in the Regulation. The definitions of the domicile of legal persons found in national laws of Member States will only be applied in cases over third state defendants.

Even though in Croatia the rules on jurisdiction of the Brussels Ia Regulation are extended over non-EU defendants, the provision of the Croatian *Zakon o međunarodnom privatnom pravu* that extends the application of the Brussels I Regulation does not include the extension of the rules on domicile of natural and legal person. In the Croatian private international law act only statutory seat and the place of central administration are accepted as the seat of a legal person, thus the Croatian courts will not determine the seat of a legal person situated in a Member State in the same way as the seat of a person situated in a third state.[35]

Most Member States, apart from Malta, Greece and Sweden, which use only the real or actual seat as the connecting factors, and Germany, Latvia and Netherlands which ordinarily only use the statutory seat as a connecting factor (by reference to substantive law), adhere to a combination of two or three connecting factors, as found in the Brussels Ia Regulation, in their definition of the domicile of the legal person. In Poland the seat of a legal person is understood as the place where its managing body has the seat.[36] In Sweden a legal person is considered to reside at the place where the board has its seat or, if the board has no permanent seat or there is no board, at the place from which the administration is carried out,[37] however, there is a doctrinal stand that the definition of domicile in the Brussels Regime should be applied by analogy instead.[38]

Some of the Member States, eg Hungary, Bulgaria and Spain use all the connecting factors on equivalent grounds, but most of them specify a clear hierarchical order of application of the two or three connecting factors. In Belgium all three connecting factors are applied, but the statutory seat is a subsidiary connecting factor.

In Lithuania domicile of a legal person is the registered office which is the place where its permanent governing body is situated, however, according to a decision of the Lithuanian Supreme Court, the registered office could also be considered at its

[35] See the Croatian report, Question 2.

[36] M Wójcik, 'Comments to Article 1103' in A Jakubecki (ed), *Kodeks postępowania cywilnego Tom II Komentarz do Art 730–1217* (Wolters Kluwer, 2017) 613.

[37] Chapter 10, Section 1, para 3 of the Swedish Judicial Code.

[38] P Lindskoug, *Domsrätt och lagval vid elektronisk handel* (Juridiska fakulteten Lund, 2004) 50–53.

actual place of business.[39] In FRANCE the claimant can rely on both the statutory place of the seat and the place of the actual seat to establish national jurisdiction, however, it is uncertain whether this provision applies to international jurisdiction as well.[40]

Question 3

The majority of the Member States provide for additional grounds for international jurisdiction. The only three Member States that do not provide for any other grounds of general[41] international jurisdiction apart from the domicile of the defendant are GREECE, SPAIN and as of 2022 CROATIA,[42] while all others use at least one other connecting factor apart from the domicile of the defendant as grounds to establish international jurisdiction.

	General jurisdiction based on defendant's …				**General jurisdiction based on claimant's …**
	habitual residence	**presence/ establishment/ representative**	**property**	**nationality**	**nationality**
AUSTRIA	x	x[43]	x[44]		
BELGIUM	x	x[45]			
BULGARIA	x			x	x

(continued)

[39] Supreme Court of Lithuania, civil case No°3K-3-24/2012.

[40] Cf M Audit, S Bollée and P Callé, *Droit du commerce international et des investissements étrangers* 3rd edn (LGDJ, 2019) 55.

[41] By 'general', we understand rules that are not inherently limited to specific subject-matters (such as claims in contract or for rights in rem), but that apply to a wider range of civil and commercial claims (although not necessarily all of them).

[42] Namely, until 2022, the CROATIAN Civil Procedure Act included a provision that gives jurisdiction to CROATIAN courts when the defendant has property in CROATIA. The term 'property of the defendant' was understood in a very broad way. And under one other provision of the Civil Procedure Act, CROATIAN courts had jurisdiction based on the presence of the defendant on CROATIAN territory. CROATIAN courts were in no way reluctant to base their international jurisdiction on those provisions.

[43] It only applies if the defendant has neither a domicile nor a habitual residence in AUSTRIA or abroad. In these cases, general jurisdiction is granted to the AUSTRIAN courts on whose territory the defendant is physically present at the time when the lawsuit is filed. In the absence of *any* domicile or habitual residence, and only for obligations that arose during their presence, Austrian courts are competent if Austria was the place of last presence. See the AUSTRIAN report, Question 3.

[44] In the absence of general jurisdiction and it is restricted by its material scope: property jurisdiction applies only to monetary or monetarily measurable claims or to claims arising from a monetary relationship. See the AUSTRIAN report, Question 3.

[45] '[A]ctions relating to the exploitation of a secondary establishment of a body with separate legal entity, which has neither its domicile nor its habitual residence in Belgium, if the establishment is located in Belgium when the action is introduced' (Art 5(2) of the BELGIAN *Wetboek Internationaal Privaatrecht/Code de Droit International Privé*).

(Continued)

	General jurisdiction based on defendant's …				General jurisdiction based on claimant's …
	habitual residence	presence/ establishment/ representative	property	nationality	nationality
CROATIA					
CYPRUS	x	x[46]			
FRANCE				x	x
GERMANY			x[47]		
GREECE					
HUNGARY		x[48]			
ITALY	x	x			
LATVIA	x	x	x[49]		
LITHUANIA	x	x	x		
MALTA	x	x			
NETHERLANDS	x	x			
POLAND	x		x		
SPAIN					
SWEDEN		x	x		

One of the grounds that is traditionally considered an exorbitant jurisdictional ground is the nationality of the parties. FRANCE and BULGARIA are the only two Member States that allow the court to base international jurisdiction on the claimant's or respondent's nationality. This head of jurisdiction nowadays appears as controversial, especially in FRANCE where acquiring French citizenship is allowed for all descendants of French citizens without further requirement.[50]

Other additional grounds for establishing jurisdiction that are traditionally regarded as exorbitant should in many cases be examined carefully as their interpretation often depends on the respective Member States' courts and legislative interpretation. There are two such jurisdictional grounds still found in the legislation of a considerable number

[46] This head of jurisdiction is balanced out by a *forum non conveniens* test.

[47] In the absence of a domicile in GERMANY and provided that the case is sufficiently closely connected to GERMANY.

[48] '[A] branch or representation in Hungary and the legal dispute is related to their operations, including the case that the contract on behalf of the business having its seat abroad was concluded in Hungary' (Art 96 of the HUNGARIAN *évi XXVIII. törvény a nemzetközi magánjogról*).

[49] Location of immovable property is a subsidiary ground for natural persons only according to the Section 27(2) of the LATVIAN Civil Procedure Law.

[50] FRENCH citizenship can also be acquired when the child is born to foreigners on FRENCH soil, if one of his parents was also born there. Further, in case of dual citizenship, for the purposes of establishing jurisdiction the person shall be considered a FRENCH citizen. See the FRENCH report, Question 3.

of Member States. The mere presence of the defendant is a jurisdictional ground in Austria, Cyprus, Italy, Lithuania and Malta while the existence of the defendant's property on the territory of the Member State of the court in Austria, Germany, Latvia, Lithuania, Poland and Sweden.

In Hungary, Belgium, Latvia, Sweden and Netherlands courts have jurisdiction over a legal person not situated in their respective Member State, when that legal person has branch or representation there and the dispute is related to the operations of the branch or representation. In Italy courts have jurisdiction over a legal person that has a representative (with the power to stand in trial) in Italy.[51]

As to the presence of the defendant on the territory of the Member States' court, there are two groups of Member States. In the first group of Member States that include Austria and Lithuania this jurisdictional ground is interpreted narrowly. Namely, in Austria the defendant must be present when the lawsuit is filed, and if the defendant is not even present in Austria, the last presence may be the ground for jurisdiction but limited only to those obligations that came into existence during their presence in Austria or that must be performed in Austria. In Lithuania jurisdiction can be based on the presence of the defendant, however, given that the courts examine the substantial connection of the case with Lithuania proven by the existence of domicile, it could be argued that a brief presence in the country might not be enough to justify the jurisdiction of the courts.

On the other hand, the second group of Member States that includes Cyprus and Malta, where presence is also one of the connecting factors for establishing jurisdiction, traditionally takes a completely different approach by widening this jurisdictional ground. According to Maltese case law, any presence, even transient, will suffice to establish the court's jurisdiction. The threshold has been set very low in the case *of Angelo Cutajar and Sons Company Ltd v Cremona Anthony Dott*,[52] where the Maltese First Hall of the Civil Court held that the term 'presence' shall be interpreted widely and would even extend to a situation when a non-Maltese party has not been physically present in Malta, but has been represented there by a third person.[53]

Finally, although jurisdiction based on the presence of assets in a Member State is usually listed as one of the exorbitant grounds for jurisdiction, in all Member States this jurisdictional ground is restricted through legislation and case law. According to Art 23 of the German Civil Procedure Code (*Zivilprozessordnung*), German courts have jurisdiction over a defendant who owns assets in Germany, regardless of their value, but the *Bundesgerichtshof* has narrowed its interpretation significantly by interpreting it in a way that the case has to be sufficiently closely connected to Germany.[54] In Austria property jurisdiction applies only to monetary or monetarily measurable

[51] This refers to a 'general representative', whereas representatives appointed for specific transactions or specific tasks cannot stand in trial for the principal, unless this power has not been expressly conferred. See the Italian report, Question 3.

[52] *Angelo Cutajar and Sons Company Limited v Anthony Cremona Dott Et Noe*. First Hall, Civil Court, 16th October 2003.

[53] Maltese report, Question 3.

[54] See Bundesgerichtshof, 2 July 1991 – XI ZR 206/90, BGHZ 115, 90, sub II.1.b).

claims or to claims arising from a monetary relationship.[55] LITHUANIAN courts interpret this jurisdictional ground narrowly and only retain jurisdiction if the case is connected to LITHUANIA. In POLAND the property or property rights should be of significant value when compared to the value of the object of a dispute.[56] SWEDEN has a rule according to which three criteria must be satisfied for it to apply: the dispute concerns a debt obligation; the defendant is domiciled outside of SWEDEN (and States bound by the Brussels Regime); and the defendant owns property that is located in SWEDEN.[57] However, the courts have narrowed the scope of application of the rule. For instance, minimum value of the assets is not prescribed but the courts have found that the property must have more than mere symbolic value.[58]

Question 4

The possibility that jurisdiction be established in the exceptional case[59] of a 'denial of justice', the so-called *forum necessitatis*,[60] is envisaged in most Member States either in their written law (AUSTRIA; BELGIUM; CROATIA; NETHERLANDS; POLAND; SPAIN)[61] or by their courts (FRANCE; GERMANY; GREECE; ITALY; SWEDEN).[62] In the remaining Member States (BULGARIA; CYRPUS; HUNGARY; LATVIA; LITHUANIA; MALTA), even though it has neither been envisaged in written law nor by national courts so far, *forum necessitatis* is not an entirely alien concept either.[63]

[55] RIS-Justiz RS0045946. Under the last alternative, also declaratory relief may be covered, eg when the declaration of the invalidity of a monetary settlement (RIS-Justiz RS0046841) or of an acknowledgement of debt (OGH 28 February 1989, 10 Ob 501/87) is sought. See the AUSTRIAN report, Question 3.

[56] 2009 Amendments of the Civil Procedure Act. POLISH report, Question 3.

[57] 'In disputes concerning debt obligations, a person with no known residence in the Realm may be sued where property he owns is located' (Chapter 10, Section 3, first sentence of the Judicial Code). See the SWEDISH report, Question 3.

[58] See eg Högsta domstolen (SWEDISH Supreme Court), 15 September 1988, NJA 1988 s 440 (holding that a bill of lading for goods that had already been delivered lacked market value); Högsta domstolen, 10 June 1998 NJA 1998 s 361 (holding that an unprivileged claim in bankruptcy could found jurisdiction unless the defendant can show that the claim is obviously worthless because there will not be any distribution); Högsta domstolen, 30 December 2010, NJA 2010 s 734 (holding that the fact that the value of the asset that formed the basis for jurisdiction depended on the outcome of the claim did not prevent that asset from being a basis for jurisdiction, where the action does not appear to be unfounded).The Supreme Court held that a bank account with 888 crowns (approximately 89 euros) could not be the basis for jurisdiction over a dispute concerning debt of 40 million crowns (approximately 4 million euros) because the value was so limited that it had no practice significance from enforcement perspective (Högsta domstolen, 15 July 2016, NJA 2016 s 779, para 10). See the SWEDISH report, Question 3.

[59] Cf, in particular, the reports on BELGIUM; NETHERLANDS; SWEDEN.

[60] Cf, in particular, the reports on AUSTRIA; BELGIUM; FRANCE; SWEDEN.

[61] In AUSTRIA, § 28 Abs 1 Z 2 of the *Jurisdiktionsnorm*; in BELGIUM, Arts 7 and 11 of the *Wetboek Internationaal Privaatrecht*; in CROATIA, Art 58 of the *Zakon o rješavanju sukoba zakona s propisima drugih zemalja u određenim odnosima*; in the NETHERLANDS, Art 9 of the *Wetboek van Burgerlijke Rechtsvordering*; in POLAND, Art 1099 of the *Kodeks postępowania cywilnego*; in SPAIN, Art 22 *octies* 3 par 2 of the *Ley Orgánica del Poder Judicial*.

[62] It appears that, rather than having established jurisdiction based on *forum necessitatis*, GERMAN and ITALIAN courts have simply considered the existence of that head of jurisdiction so far.

[63] In BULGARIA, *forum necessitatis* is a matter of discussion among legal scholarship; in HUNGARY, the adoption of a rule on jurisdiction based on *forum necessitatis* was considered in the context of the reform which led

In contrast to its prominent position in legal scholarship, though, there appear to exist few reported decisions whereby the courts of the Member States have established jurisdiction (in civil and commercial matters) based on *forum necessitatis*.[64] The lack of practical relevance of *forum necessitatis* may be explained as follows. On the one hand, as mentioned below, a prerequirement of *forum necessitatis* is lack of jurisdiction of the seised court based on other heads of jurisdiction. On the other hand, most Member States envisage jurisdictional heads based on 'weak' links with the forum.[65] Therefore, in order to establish jurisdiction, it is often sufficient for national courts to resort to those exorbitant heads of jurisdiction without resorting to the much more opaque *forum necessitatis*.[66]

The rationale behind *forum necessitatis* of preventing a denial of justice may be traced back to constitutional and even supranational rules (arts 6 ECHR and 47 CFR) enshrining the fundamental rights to a fair trial and to an effective remedy.[67]

The requirements that must be met for a risk of denial of justice to be deemed existent, and thus to establish jurisdiction based on *forum necessitatis*, vary from one Member State to the other and are variously combined together.

As mentioned above, a common pre-requirement is lack of jurisdiction of national courts based on other heads of jurisdiction. In fact, *forum necessitatis* is generally construed as a 'subsidiary' head of jurisdiction.[68]

In addition to that pre-requirement, in most Member States (Austria; Belgium; Croatia; France; Germany; Netherlands;[69] Poland; Spain; Sweden), a first requirement is the existence of a sufficient link with the country of the seised court (which yet would not be sufficient to establish jurisdiction under other heads of jurisdiction).[70] What amounts to a sufficient link is often a matter of debate.[71] For example, in Austria, a sufficient link exists when the claimant is an EU citizen.[72]

to the *2017. evi XXVIII. törvény a nemzetközi magánjogról*; in Malta, the head of jurisdiction based on *forum necessitatis* contained in Art 793 of the Code of Organisation and Civil Procedure was repealed in 1995.

[64] Cf, in particular, the reports on Belgium; Greece; Netherlands.

[65] See above Question 3.

[66] Cf the reports on Cyprus; Germany; Greece; Malta. This may also explain why, as mentioned above, in some Member States *forum necessitatis* is not envisaged neither in their written law nor by their courts. In fact, for instance, among the latter Member States, in Bulgaria, Bulgarian nationality of one party is sufficient to establish jurisdiction; in Lithuania, jurisdiction may be established based defendant's mere presence in the country at the time of service of the claim; in Malta, people in need of judicial protection may bring their cases before courts based on their mere presence in the country.

[67] See the Bulgarian report, referring to Arts 56 of the Constitution of the Republic of Bulgaria, 6 ECHR and 47 CFR; the Cypriot report, referring to Art 6 ECHR; the Italian report, referring to the Italian Constitution and Art 6 ECHR.

[68] The subsidiary nature of *forum necessitatis* is underlined – either explicitly or implicitly – in the reports on Austria; Croatia; Italy; Netherlands; Poland; Spain; Sweden.

[69] Interestingly, in the Netherlands, a distinction is drawn between two forms *forum necessitatis*: so-called 'absolute' and 'relative' *forum necessitatis*, respectively envisaged in lits b) and c) of Art 9 of the *Wetboek van Burgerlijke Rechtsvordering*. The two forms of *forum necessitatis* apply when trial abroad is respectively impossible and unreasonable. That said, it appears that, a (sufficient) link with the Netherlands is required only with respect to the second (relative) form of *forum necessitatis*.

[70] Only the reports on Greece and Italy do not mention a sufficient link as a requirement.

[71] Cf, in particular, the Austrian report.

[72] Cf the Austria report; cf also the Belgian and German reports.

In most Member States, a second requirement, which must be met in addition to the first (ie that of a sufficient link), is that trial abroad be impossible.[73] In some Member States (AUSTRIA; BELGIUM; CROATIA; FRANCE; GREECE;[74] NETHERLANDS; POLAND), rather than impossible, trial abroad may 'simply' be unreasonable. As in the case of the requirement of a sufficient link, what amounts to impossibility or unreasonableness is also regularly debated. In any case, impossibility and unreasonableness are generally construed narrowly.[75] A dramatically current example of impossibility is that where the foreign court – which would in principle have jurisdiction over the dispute – belongs to a country whose judiciary is disrupted by armed conflict.[76] As a further and arguably more common example, in some Member States (FRANCE; GERMANY; ITALY; NETHERLANDS;[77] SPAIN),[78] impossibility is deemed to exist when the courts of no foreign country would have jurisdiction over the dispute.[79] However, lack of foreign jurisdiction is not a necessary requirement in all Member States (see AUSTRIA; BELGIUM; GERMANY; GREECE; NETHERLANDS).[80] In fact, as mentioned above, in order to establish jurisdiction based on *forum necessitatis*, rather than impossible, trial abroad may simply be unreasonable. Unreasonableness may be deemed to exist, eg, when the decision by the given foreign court would not be (eligible to be) enforced in the Member State of the seised court.[81] As a further, albeit controversial, example, unreasonableness may be deemed to exist even when trial abroad would entail significant additional legal costs (as compared to trial in the *forum necessitatis*).[82]

[73] Only the GREEK report does not mention – not even implicitly – impossibility as a requirement. Instead, even though the SWEDISH report does not mention explicitly impossibility as a requirement, that report mentions a decision rendered by the SWEDISH Supreme Court establishing jurisdiction based on *forum necessitatis* in a case where, on the one hand, national courts lacked jurisdiction based on other heads of jurisdiction and, on the other hand, the foreign court had previously refused jurisdiction.

[74] For the sake of completeness, the GREEK report does not mention explicitly unreasonableness as a requirement, but rather, more generally, cases where 'the claimant has no real ability to seek recourse before foreign courts'.

[75] Cf, in particular, the AUSTRIAN report.

[76] Cf the POLISH report.

[77] For the sake of completeness, in the NETHERLANDS (see above n 69), absolute *forum necessitatis* may be established when no foreign court has jurisdiction over the dispute. In turn, lack of foreign jurisdiction does not appear to be relevant in cases of relative *forum necessitatis*.

[78] For the sake of completeness, in SPAIN, Art 22 *octies* 3 par 2 of the *Ley Orgánica del Poder Judicial* requires that foreign courts have (previously) refused jurisdiction. However, SPANISH scholars hold that evidence that foreign courts would not have jurisdiction should suffice.

[79] An issue arises as to which law should be applied to determine whether foreign courts lack jurisdiction. That law may be either the *lex fori* of the seised court or that of the given foreign country. Cf the reports on GERMANY and SPAIN.

[80] Notably, in BELGIUM, jurisdiction based on *forum necessitatis* may be established even when a choice-of-court agreement designating a foreign court is applicable. Cf also the reference in the DUTCH report to a court decision, where jurisdiction was established based on (relative) *forum necessitatis* (see above n 68), irrespective of an applicable choice-of-court agreement designating a foreign court.

[81] See the AUSTRIAN report; cf the POLISH report.

[82] See the reports on AUSTRIA and BELGIUM; but see the POLISH report, where it is specified that the financial situation of the claimant alone is irrelevant.

	Requirements of *forum necessitatis*		
	Sufficient link	Trial abroad ...	
		impossible	unreasonable
AUSTRIA	x	x	x
BELGIUM	x	x	x
CROATIA	x	x	x
FRANCE	x	x	x
GERMANY	x	x	x
GREECE			x
ITALY		x	
NETHERLANDS	x	x	x
POLAND	x	x	x
SPAIN	x	x	
SWEDEN	x	x	

As mentioned above, *forum necessitatis* is envisaged in most Member States and its rationale may be traced back even to supranational rules (which, in the cases of arts 6 ECHR and 47 CFR, bind all Member States). Therefore, in principle, it appears that there would be no major obstacles to the adoption of *forum necessitatis* in a future recast of the Brussels Ia Regulation. In fact, the adoption of *forum necessitatis* within the context of the Brussels Regime was considered twice before, though without any success.[83] However, if the jurisdictional rules of Brussels Ia were (further) extended to non-EU defendants, and, at the same time, national rules on jurisdiction were consequently superseded, the adoption of *forum necessitatis* within the recast Regulation could be deemed appropriate, if not politically necessary. In this respect, during the Dubrovnik Conference Professor Burkhard Hess suggested that any discussion of a recast of the Brussels Ia should consider the adoption of *forum necessitatis*.[84] On the other hand, Professor Ronald Brand stressed that *forum necessitatis* might not be welcome from a non-EU perspective. In particular, in the US, *forum necessitatis* would be considered incompatible with the Due Process Clause of the Constitution. What is more, *forum necessitatis* does not appear to be a jurisdictional filter envisaged in the 2019 Hague Convention. Therefore, if *forum necessitatis* were adopted in the future recast of Brussels Ia,

[83] Cf Art 26 of the European Commission's Proposal for a Regulation of the European Parliament and of the Council on jurisdiction and the recognition and enforcement of judgments in civil and commercial matters Brussels, 14 December 2010, COM(2010) 748 final, 2010/0383 (COD); Committee on Legal Affairs of the European Parliament's Draft Report with recommendation to the Commission on corporate due diligence and corporate accountability, 2020/2129(NL)); cf also Art 11 Succession Regulation No 650/2012.

[84] Cf B Hess, 'Reforming the Brussels Ibis Regulation: Perspectives and Prospects' (Max Plank Institute Luxembourg for Procedural Law Research Paper Series No. 2021 (4)) 1, 6–7.

this might represent a liability for the coordination between the latter and the 2019 Hague Convention, but might also just be testimony to the exorbitant character of the concept.

Question 5(a)

In some Member States, the rules on jurisdiction in matters relating to contract of the Brussels Regime have been extended by national law to non-EU defendants, or have inspired the national jurisdictional rules applicable in the same matters (Croatia; Italy; Hungary; Netherlands; Spain).[85] In all other Member States, where the Brussels Regime was neither extended nor a source of inspiration, relevant differences (and similarities) exist between the respective national rules on jurisdiction applicable in matters relating to contract. In particular, those differences concern the material scope of, and the connecting factors employed by, the national rules in question.

As concerns the material scope, only in a few Member States (Lithuania; Malta; Sweden), there does not exist a special rule on jurisdiction in matters relating to contract; instead, those legal systems have a jurisdictional rule applicable to obligations in general.[86] In all other Member States except Latvia[87] (ie Austria; Belgium; Bulgaria; Cyprus; France; Germany; Greece; Poland), a special rule on jurisdiction applicable to contractual obligations exists,[88] usually with exceptions for obligations arising from specific contracts (in most cases, involving so-called 'weaker' parties).[89] In some of the latter Member States, the scope of the respective special rule is further limited to specific (contractual) claims (eg, in Austria, to claims brought by the creditor seeking a declaration on the existence, the performance or the avoidance of the contract, or compensation in cases of defective performance).[90] Incidentally, it is especially in those Member States where a special jurisdictional rule exists that the issue arises which law – either the *lex fori* or the *lex causae* – should determine whether or not the dispute actually concerns a contractual obligation.[91]

[85] Cf above Question 1(c).

[86] In Lithuania, Art 787 paras 1 and 3 of the *Lietuvos Respublikos civilinio proceso kodeksas*; in Malta, Art 742 para 1 of the Code of Organisation and Civil Procedure; in Sweden, Chapter 10, Section 4 of the Judicial Code.

[87] In Latvia it is unclear which jurisdictional rule should apply in matters relating to contract (Latvian report).

[88] In Austria, § 88 of the *Jurisdikitionsnorm*; in Belgium, Art 96 no 1 lits a) and b) of the *Wetboek Internationaal Privatreect*; in Bulgaria, Art 15 of the *Кодекс на международното частно право*; in Cyprus, 6.8 (η), (θ) and (ι) of the *Κανονισμοί Πολιτικής δικονομίας*; in France, Art 46 first indent of the *Code de procedure civil*; in Germany, § 29(1) of the *Zivilprozessordnung*; in Greece, Art 33 of the *Κώδικας Πολιτικής Δικον ομίας*; in Poland, Art 1103 sec 1 of the *Ustawa z 17 XI 1964 r Kodeks postępowania cywilnego*.

[89] See the reports on Austria; Belgium; France.

[90] See also the Cypriot report.

[91] See the Belgian report; cf the Greek report.

Rule on obligations in general	Special rule on contractual obligations
- LITHUANIA - MALTA - SWEDEN	- AUSTRIA - BELGIUM - BULGARIA - CROATIA - CYPRUS - FRANCE - GERMANY - GREECE - HUNGARY - ITALY - NETHERLANDS - POLAND - SPAIN

The connecting factors most frequently employed by the national rules on jurisdiction applicable in matters relating to contract appear to be those of place of performance or of contract (or obligation) formation.[92] In some Member States (BELGIUM; GREECE; LITHUANIA; MALTA), the two connecting factors are alternative. In other Member States, only one of them is employed: in AUSTRIA, BULGARIA, FRANCE, GERMANY and HUNGARY, place of performance; in CYPRUS, POLAND and SWEDEN, contract (or obligation) formation. Differences concerning the scope and determination of the place of performance exist among the Member States. Among such differences is that concerning the precise legal relationship for which this forum is available. In most Member States (BELGIUM; GERMANY; GREECE; LITHUANIA; MALTA), the courts at the place of performance are competent only for the disputed (contractual) obligation arising from the contract in question. The place of performance is determined in accordance with the *lex fori*[93] or with the *lex causae*.[94] In contrast, only in a few Member States, the place of performance is determined by taking into account the relevant contract, rather than the disputed obligation arising from it. For example, in BULGARIA, the only relevant place of performance is that where the contract's characteristic obligation should be performed. Similarly, in FRANCE, akin to Art 7(1) lit b) Brussels Ia, a single forum exists for all obligations arising out of contracts for the sale of goods and provision of services: in the first case, that where the goods were or had to be delivered; in the second case, that where the services were or had to be provided. However, unlike Art 7(1) Brussels Ia, the FRENCH rule on jurisdiction in matters relating to contract is not applicable if the contract is neither a sale of goods nor a provision of services.[95]

[92] For the sake of completeness, some national reports stress that further connecting factors may apply alternatively to those of place of contract formation and/or of performance, eg, that of the place where the defendant is either domiciled, habitually resident or has its place of business (see the reports on AUSTRIA; BULGARIA; FRANCE; POLAND), or where the latter has property or other assets (see the POLISH report).

[93] Cf the reports on GREECE, LITHUANIA, and SPAIN.

[94] Cf the GERMAN and MALTESE reports.

[95] On the other hand, it may be applicable even if the parties are not bound by a contract between them (see the FRENCH report for more detail).

	Most frequently employed connecting factors	
	Contract (or obligation) formation	**Place of performance**
Austria		x
Belgium	x	x
Bulgaria		x
Croatia		x
Cyprus	x	
France		x
Germany		x
Greece	x	x
Hungary		x
Italy		x
Lithuania	x	x
Malta	x	x
Netherlands		x
Poland	x	
Spain		x
Sweden	x	

Leaving aside the case of the Member States where the national rules on jurisdiction in matters relating to contract extend or are inspired by the rules of the Brussels Regime, the latter and the related decisions by the CJEU have had a considerable influence on the jurisdictional rules applicable in the same matters of some of the other Member States.[96] For instance, the Belgian courts have occasionally determined the place of performance, for the purposes of the relevant national rule on jurisdiction, in line with Art 7(1) lit b) Brussels Ia. By the same token, the French courts occasionally refer to the decisions of the CJEU when interpreting the national rule on jurisdiction in matters relating to contract – although the French *Cour de cassation* rejected the contractual characterisation of so-called 'abrupt termination of long-standing business relationship' endorsed by the CJEU in *Granarolo*.[97] In fact, during the Dubrovnik Conference, the French rapporteur stressed that the extension of the Brussels Ia jurisdictional rule in matters relating to contract would have an impact on the characterisation of the disputes in question by national courts. Of course, the extension would have an even greater impact in those few Member States (Austria; Cyprus; Germany) where EU law has not had any noticeable influence on the national rules of jurisdiction in matters relating to contract so far.

[96] See, eg, the reports on Belgium; France; Hungary; Sweden; cf the Polish report.

[97] See the French report; see also, most recently, C Maresca, 'La qualificazione della responsabilità derivante da rottura brusca di relazioni commerciali stabili: gli effetti delle sentenze della Corte di giustizia sulla giurisprudenza francese' (2022) *Riv dir in priv proc* 65 et seq.

Question 5(b)

Regarding the *forum delicti*, a distinction can be drawn between (a) those Member States that follow the wide interpretation adopted by the CJEU in *Bier*,[98] vesting jurisdiction both in the courts of the *locus delicti* and the *locus damni*, (b) those that limit jurisdiction to one of those places (such as GREECE (*locus delicti*) or SPAIN (*locus damni*)), and (c) those that have adopted (also) an entirely different connecting factor for torts. This last group consists only of MALTA, whose general rule on obligations appears to be a lot easier to apply to contractual than to non-contractual obligations as it raises the question of how to identify the place where a non-contractual obligation has been assumed or needs to be performed. The practical significance of this provision is drastically reduced, though, by the possibility of basing (general) jurisdiction on the mere presence of the defendant.

Interestingly, all legal systems that appear to distinguish between direct and indirect damage for jurisdictional purposes follow the CJEU[99] in limiting special jurisdiction to the direct or primary damage.[100]

<table>
<tr><th rowspan="3">Member State</th><th colspan="4">Connecting factor</th></tr>
<tr><th rowspan="2">Locus commissi delicti</th><th colspan="2">Locus damni</th><th rowspan="2">other</th></tr>
<tr><th>only direct damage</th><th>Direct and indirect damage</th></tr>
<tr><td>AUSTRIA</td><td>x[101]</td><td>(x)[102]</td><td></td><td></td></tr>
<tr><td>BELGIUM</td><td>x</td><td>x</td><td></td><td></td></tr>
<tr><td>BULGARIA</td><td>x</td><td colspan="2">x</td><td></td></tr>
<tr><td>CROATIA</td><td>x</td><td colspan="2">x</td><td></td></tr>
<tr><td>CYPRUS</td><td>x</td><td>x</td><td></td><td></td></tr>
<tr><td>FRANCE</td><td>x</td><td colspan="2">x</td><td></td></tr>
<tr><td>GERMANY</td><td>x</td><td>x</td><td></td><td></td></tr>
<tr><td>GREECE</td><td>x</td><td></td><td></td><td></td></tr>
<tr><td>HUNGARY</td><td>x</td><td colspan="2">x</td><td></td></tr>
<tr><td>ITALY</td><td>x</td><td>x</td><td></td><td></td></tr>
<tr><td>LATVIA</td><td>x</td><td colspan="2">x</td><td></td></tr>
<tr><td>LITHUANIA</td><td>x</td><td colspan="2">x</td><td></td></tr>
<tr><td>MALTA</td><td></td><td></td><td></td><td>x[103]</td></tr>
</table>

(continued)

[98] Case 21/76 *Bier*.

[99] See also Case C-364/93 *Marinari*.

[100] Which is in stark contrast to a recent decision by the UK Supreme Court, *FS Cairo (Nile Plaza) LLC v Lady Brownlie (Brownlie II)* [2021] UKSC 45.

[101] Only for damage to persons and physical property.

[102] Only for a small number of specific torts, namely for damage to forests and air pollution.

[103] According to the MALTESE report, claims in tort (and other non-contractual situations) are treated similarly to claims in contract with jurisdiction vested in the courts of the country in which the obligation has been assumed or must be performed.

(Continued)

Member State	**Connecting factor**			
	Locus commissi delicti	***Locus damni***		**other**
		only direct damage	**Direct and indirect damage**	
NETHERLANDS	x			
POLAND	x	x		
SPAIN		x		
SWEDEN	x	x		

As a final remark, it may be noted that several reports – namely those for FRANCE, GERMANY, and SWEDEN – have referred to the treatment of torts committed on the internet, noting both a certain alignment with the CJEU's interpretation of Art 7(2) Brussels Ia (in all three cases) but also significant differences (mainly in the case of GERMANY, where the courts have explicitly rejected the CJEU's centre-of-interests approach to online infringements of personality rights).[104]

Question 5(c)

In most Member States there are rules that are either fully aligned with Art 8(1) Brussels Ia which provides for the jurisdiction based on a close connection between defendants, eg CROATIA and HUNGARY, or can be interpreted as a variant of Art 8(1) of the Brussels Ia Regulation, eg AUSTRIA, BELGIUM, BULGARIA, FRANCE, NETHERLANDS and POLAND.

The member states that do not include a corresponding rule on the jurisdiction based on a close connection between defendants are GERMANY, LITHUANIA, MALTA and SWEDEN. In GREEK law, jurisdiction cannot be based on a close connection between defendants, but on a close connection between claims.

	Same or similar to Art 8(1) Brussels Ia Regulation	**No rule on jurisdiction based on connection between the defendants**
AUSTRIA	x	
BELGIUM	x	
BULGARIA	x	
CROATIA	x	
CYPRUS	x	

(continued)

[104] For references, see the GERMAN report, Question 5(d). The SWEDISH report refers to a decision by the Svea hovrätt (Svea Court of Appeal) from 18 October 2007, which also deviated from the CJEU's case law with regard to copyright infringements, although in a case that was only concerned with local jurisdiction – it appears unclear if SWEDISH courts would similarly deviate from the CJEU with regard to international jurisdiction.

(Continued)

	Same or similar to Art 8(1) Brussels Ia Regulation	No rule on jurisdiction based on connection between the defendants
France	x	
Germany		x
Greece		x[105]
Hungary	x	
Italy	x	
Latvia	x	
Lithuania		x
Malta		x
Netherlands	x	
Poland	x[106]	
Spain	x	
Sweden		x

In the Member States that do have a rule aligned with Art 8(1) of Brussels Ia, but not an entirely identical rule, there are different approaches to jurisdiction based on a close connection between defendants.

Belgium, for example, has taken a more generous approach for related actions: namely, even though the provision on jurisdiction based on the close connection was inspired by Art 6(1) Brussels I,[107] it does not require a connection between the actions, let alone the risk of irreconcilable judgments, for the Belgian courts to have jurisdiction over disputes involving multiple defendants, even though an important condition is that the action must not have been introduced solely to remove a defendant from the jurisdiction of his domicile or habitual residence abroad.[108]

A further example are the French courts, which make a difference depending on the degree of connection of the claims. For example, if the claims are indivisible, French courts will take jurisdiction notwithstanding a jurisdiction agreement between the plaintiff and one of the co-defendants giving jurisdiction to a foreign court.[109] If the claims are not indivisible, the foreign jurisdiction agreement constitutes a valid defence against jurisdiction of French courts.[110]

German law is one of the rare examples of a law that does not contain a general provision like Art 8(1) Brussels Ia. In civil and commercial matters, the rules of this

[105] The Greek Civil Code of Procedure provides for jurisdiction based on connection of claims, but not based on a close connection between the defendants.

[106] The Polish rule has a wider scope than Art 8(1) Brussels Ia, as it is not limited to cases when jurisdiction results from the domicile of the defendant: see T Ereciński 'Comments to Article 1103[10]' in T Ereciński (ed) *Kodeks postępowania cywilnego Komentarz Tom VI Międzynarodowe Postępowanie Cywilne Sąd polubowny* (arbitrażowy) (Wolters Kluwer, 2017) 131. See Polish report, Question 5(c).

[107] Wetsvoorstel houdende het Wetboek van internationaal privaatrecht, Toelichting, *Parl St Senaat* 2003, 3-27/1, 32.

[108] Belgian report, Question 5(c).

[109] Cour de cassation, civ 2e, 7 November 1994, 92-20.776, JCP G 1995, IV, 61, L'Alibi: claims 'on the same legal ground and for the same purpose'.

[110] Cour de cassation, soc, 26 June 1991, 88-40.170, D 1991, IR, 212, Sogexpat.

kind only exist for very specific scenarios, but that led some scholars to call for the analogous application of Art 8(1) to cases involving defendants not domiciled in a member state or for the introduction of a similar provision into German domestic law.[111]

Although SWEDEN is also one of the few Member States that do not have a provision on the jurisdiction based on a close connection between defendants, exceptionally, the rule used for domestic jurisdiction[112] can be applied if the reasons of procedural economy outweigh the inconvenience for the defendant.[113]

Question 5(d)

In several Member States (AUSTRIA; BELGIUM; BULGARIA; CROATIA; FRANCE; GERMANY; ITALY; LATVIA; NETHERLANDS; POLAND; SPAIN) there exist special rules on jurisdiction in matters relating to insurance, consumer contracts and/or individual contracts of employment. Those rules apply generally in the matters in question and/or in specific cases relating thereto. For example, in FRANCE, both a general rule on jurisdiction over consumer contracts and a specific rule on consumer class actions exist.[114] In GERMANY, there is no similar general rule, but a specific rule on off-premises contracts specifically focused on consumers.[115] Similarly, in AUSTRIA, there is no general rule in matters relating to insurance, but specific rules applicable in cases of claims brought by the insured against the insurer and arising from insurance contracts conveyed or concluded through an agent of the latter, or arising from contracts for the insurance of motor vehicles.[116]

	National rules on jurisdiction …		
	in matters relating to insurance	**over consumer contracts**	**over individual contracts of employment**
AUSTRIA	x[117]	x	x
BELGIUM		x	x
BULGARIA		x	x

(continued)

[111] See the GERMAN report, Question 5(c), n 61 and 62.

[112] Chapter 10, Section 14, first sentence, of the SWEDISH Judicial Code. As a rule, the provision cannot be applied *ex analogia* to international jurisdiction and that there should normally be an independent basis for jurisdiction against the defendant: see. See the SWEDISH report; Question 5(c)).

[113] S Dennemark, *Om domstols behörighet i internationellt förmögenhetsrättsliga mål* (PA Norstedt & Söners Förlag, 1961) 220; U Maunsbach, *Svensk domstols behörighet vid gränsöverskridande varumärkestvister – särskilt om Internetrelaterade intrång* (Juridiska fakulteten Lund, 2005) 245–247; C Thornefors, Lagkommentar Rättegångsbalk, (Karnov, 2018) 1942:740. In one case, the SWEDISH Supreme Court found that SWEDISH jurisdiction could be based on the rule when the defendant was domiciled in a third state but was a SWEDISH citizen, a foreign representative of a SWEDISH company and spent three months a year in SWEDEN (Högsta domstolen, 12 December 1986, NJA 1986 s 729). See the SWEDISH report; Question 5(c)

[114] ibid.

[115] See the GERMAN report.

[116] See the AUSTRIAN report.

[117] As mentioned in the text above, in AUSTRIA, there exists no general jurisdictional rule on insurance, but specific rules in matters relating thereto.

(Continued)

	National rules on jurisdiction …		
	in matters relating to insurance	**over consumer contracts**	**over individual contracts of employment**
CROATIA	x		
FRANCE	x	x	x
GERMANY	x	x[118]	x
ITALY	x	x	x
LATVIA			x
NETHERLANDS		x	x
POLAND	x	x	x
SPAIN	x	x	x

Moreover, in a few Member States, there exist special rules governing jurisdiction over disputes involving weaker parties other than those considered by the Brussels Regime (ie insured, consumers and employees). For instance, in BELGIUM, a special jurisdictional rule concerns commercial agents[119] and, in GERMANY, participants in distance learning.[120]

On the other hand, in a significant number of Member States (CYPRUS; GREECE; HUNGARY; LITHUANIA; MALTA; SWEDEN) it appears that special rules applicable in cases involving weaker parties do not exist at all.

In general terms, where existent, national rules on jurisdiction in cases involving weaker parties differ considerably from one Member State to the other, in particular as concerns their personal scope of application and the connecting factors employed. However, in equally general terms, as concerns the connecting factors employed, it appears that national rules may benefit the weaker parties by allowing them to sue the so-called 'stronger' parties in other fora, in addition to those made available under other (national) rules on jurisdiction.[121] For example, in the case of disputes arising from consumer contracts, these additional fora are those of the place where the consumer is domiciled and/or resident, or habitually resident.[122] In addition, the rules in question may also protect the weaker parties, by limiting the fora where they may be sued by the stronger party.[123] Incidentally, in AUSTRIA, national rules do not provide the weaker parties with additional fora, but only protect them from being sued by the stronger party before other fora.[124] For the sake of completeness, the protective nature of the jurisdictional rules in question also emerges in cases where of choice-of-court agreements

[118] As mentioned in the text above, in GERMANY, there exists no general jurisdictional rule on consumer contracts, but only a rule on off-premises contracts specifically focused on consumers (§ 29c ZPO).

[119] Also see the DUTCH report; cf the reports on GREECE and SPAIN.

[120] See the GERMAN report.

[121] See, eg, the reports on BELGIUM; BULGARIA; FRANCE; GERMANY.

[122] ibid.

[123] See, eg, with respect to jurisdiction over actions arising out of off-premises contracts, the GERMAN report.

[124] See the AUSTRIAN report.

apply. In fact, similar agreements are often deemed invalid when they purport to derogate jurisdiction from the forum or fora where the weaker party may sue the stronger party,[125] and/or when they are concluded before the relevant disputes have arisen.[126]

The Brussels Regime appears to have had a twofold impact on the national rules on jurisdiction over disputes involving weaker parties. On the one hand, the extension brought about by Brussels Ia of the EU-uniform rules on jurisdiction over consumer contracts and individual contracts of employment to non-EU defendants has superseded in most part, if not in full, the national rules of the Member States applicable in the same matters.[127] On the other hand, in any case, the national rules in question often appear to be close to, if not clearly inspired by, those of the Brussels Regime.[128]

Arguably, an extension of the rule on jurisdiction in matters of insurance of Brussels Ia to non-EU defendants would have a major impact in those (many) Member States where a similar rule does not exist (AUSTRIA,[129] BELGIUM, BULGARIA, CYPRUS, GREECE, HUNGARY, LATVIA, LITHUANIA, NETHERLANDS, SWEDEN). Moreover, if the extension entailed the abrogation of national rules on jurisdiction, the same extension would have an impact also in those Member States where special rules on jurisdiction apply to disputes involving weaker parties other than those considered by Brussels Ia.

Question 6

The answers to Question 6 are not reproduced in the national reports reprinted in this book, since they can be readily summarised as follows.

The national reports mention the following multilateral treaties in force between the Member States and third States, and containing so-called 'direct' jurisdictional rules in matters regulated by Brussels Ia:

- the (1868) Revised Convention for the navigation of the Rhine;[130]
- the (1951) Agreement between the Parties to the North Atlantic Treaty regarding the Status of their Forces;[131]
- the (1952) International Convention on Certain Rules concerning Civil Jurisdiction in Matters of Collision;[132]

[125] ibid.

[126] See the reports on BELGIUM and GERMANY.

[127] In this respect, it is illustrative comparing ITALY and CROATIA. In 1995, in ITALY, the scope of the jurisdictional rules of the Brussels Convention in matters relating to insurance (Arts 7 et seq), consumer contracts (Arts 13 et seq) and individual contracts of employment (Art 5 no 1) were extended by national law to non-EU defendants. That reference, however, was later partially superseded by the above-mentioned extension brought by the Brussels Ia with respect to jurisdiction in matters relating to consumer contracts and individual contracts of employment. In turn, in 2017, in CROATIA, the rules of the Brussels Ia were extended by national law to non-EU defendants, the legislature deemed it unnecessary to also extend the rules on jurisdiction in matters of consumer contracts and individual contracts of employment; only the rules of the same Regulation in matters relating to insurance were extended.

[128] Cf the reports on BELGIUM, the NETHERLANDS and POLAND.

[129] See above n 164.

[130] Adopted 17 October 1868. The text of the treaty can be consulted at www.ccr-zkr.org/11020200-en.html.

[131] Adopted 19 June 1951, entered into force 23 August 1953, 1999 UNTS 67.

[132] Adopted 10 May 1952, entered into force 14 September 1955, 439 UNTS 217.

- the (1952) International Convention relating to the Arrest of Seagoing Ships;[133]
- the (1956) Convention on the Contract for the International Carriage of Goods by Road (CMR);[134]
- the (1960) Convention relating to the Unification of Certain Rules concerning Collisions in Inland Navigation;[135]
- the (1960) Convention on Third Party Liability in the Field of Nuclear Energy;[136]
- the (1973) Convention on the Grant of European Patents (European Patent Convention);[137]
- the (1974) Athens Convention relating to the Carriage of Passengers and their Luggage by Sea;[138]
- the (1980) Convention concerning International Carriage by Rail (COTIF);[139]
- the (1999) Convention for the Unification of Certain Rules for International Carriage by Air (Montreal Convention);[140]
- the (2001) International Convention on Civil Liability for Bunker Oil Pollution Damage (Bunker Convention).[141]

As the number of contracting Member States varies from treaty to treaty and the data published online[142] has turned out not to be entirely reliable, we have decided not to include tables reflecting the state of adoption for each instrument. The only treaties that we have found to be in force in all Member States are: the European Patent Convention, the CMR,[143] the Bunker Convention,[144] the Montreal Convention,[145] and the COTIF.[146]

[133] Adopted on 10 May 1952, entered into force 24 February 1956, 439 UNTS 193.
[134] Adopted 19 May 1956, entered into force 2 July 1961, 399 UNTS 189.
[135] Adopted 13 March 1960, entered into force 13 September 1966, 572 UNTS 133.
[136] Adopted 29 July 1960, entered into force 1 April 1968, 956 UNTS 251.
[137] Adopted on 5 October 1973, entered into force 7 October 1973, 1065 UNTS 199.
[138] Adopted 13 December 1974, entered into force 28 April 1987, 1463 UNTS 19.
[139] Adopted 9 May 1980, entered into force 1 May 1985, 1396 UNTS 2, 1397 UNTS 2.
[140] Adopted 28 May 1999, entered into force 4 November 2003, 2242 UNTS 309.
[141] Adopted 23 March 2001, entered into force 21 November 2008, [2002] OJ L 256/9.
[142] The status of the (1868) Revised Convention for the navigation of the Rhine may be consulted at www.ccr-zkr.org/13020300-en.html#04, whereas that of the (1951) Agreement between the Parties to the North Atlantic Treaty regarding the Status of their Forces, of the (1952) International Convention on Certain Rules concerning Civil Jurisdiction in Matters of Collision, of the (1952) International Convention relating to the Arrest of Seagoing Ships, (1960) Convention on Third Party Liability in the Field of Nuclear Energy, of the (1960) Convention relating to the Unification of Certain Rules concerning Collisions in Inland Navigation, and of the (1974) Athens Convention relating to the Carriage of Passengers and their Luggage by Sea at www.treaties.un.org/.
[143] See Opinion of Advocate General Kokott, delivered on 28 January 2010 – Case C-533/08, *TNT Express Nederland BV v AXA Versicherung AG*, ERC 2010 I-04107, para 3.
[144] Cf status at www.imo.org/en/About/Conventions/Pages/StatusOfConventions.aspx, accessed 18 October 2021.
[145] 2001/539/EC: Council Decision of 5 April 2001 on the conclusion by the European Community of the Convention for the Unification of Certain Rules for International Carriage by Air (the Montreal Convention), OJ L 194, 18 July 2001, p 38.
[146] Agreement between the European Union and the Intergovernmental Organisation for International Carriage by Rail on the Accession of the European Union to the Convention concerning International Carriage by Rail (COTIF) of 9 May 1980, as amended by the Vilnius Protocol of 3 June 1999, OJ L 51, 23 February 2013, pp 8 et seq.

As concerns bilateral treaties concluded between the Member States and third States, and containing direct heads of jurisdiction in matters regulated by Brussels Ia, similar treaties are in force in Bulgaria, Cyprus, Germany, Hungary, Latvia, Lithuania, Poland and Spain.[147] In some of the latter Member States, the bilateral treaties in question even appear to have some practical relevance.[148] In contrast, in a significant number of Member States (Austria, Belgium, Croatia, France, Greece, Italy, Malta, Netherlands, Spain and Sweden) it appears that similar bilateral treaties do not exist.[149]

Most of the treaties mentioned above were concluded by the Member States before the date of entry into force of Brussels I. Considering the persistence of these treaties, it appears that subordination clauses such as those contained in Arts 71–73 of the latter Regulation should be maintained in a future recast of the Regulation in order to adequately address the issue relating to the interface between treaties in question and the recast Regulation.

[147] In particular, the bilateral treaties are concluded between: Bulgaria, on one side, and a number of unspecified third States, on the other side; Cyprus, on one side, and, respectively, Ukraine and China, on the other side; Germany and Norway; Hungary, on one side, and former Yugoslavian countries (namely, Bosnia and Herzegovina, Kosovo, Montenegro, North Macedonia and Serbia), on the other side; Latvia, on one side, and, respectively, Belarus, Kyrgyzstan, Moldova, Russia, Ukraine and Uzbekistan, on the other side; Lithuania, on one side, and, respectively, Armenia, Azerbaijan, Belarus, China, Kazakhstan, Moldova, Russia, Turkey, Ukraine and Uzbekistan, on the other side; Poland, on one side, and, respectively, Belarus, Russia, Ukraine, Vietnam, and former Yugoslavian countries (namely, Bosnia and Herzegovina, Montenegro, North Macedonia and Serbia), on the other side; Spain and El Salvador.

[148] The Lithuanian report mentions the existence of court decisions concerning the application of the bilateral treaty with Russia.

[149] Some of the reports on the latter Member States (Austria; Belgium; Italy) stress the existence of bilateral treaties with third States containing 'indirect', rather than direct, jurisdictional rules in matters regulated by Brussels Ia.

III.

National Reports

Austria

PAUL EICHMÜLLER

Question 1

(a)

The Austrian domestic jurisdictional rules are mainly set out in the Judicature Act (*Jurisdiktionsnorm*;[1] JN). Austrian civil procedure is thus fragmented insofar as the JN covers the principal rules of when, by whom and under which conditions civil jurisdiction may be exercised, whereas the actual procedure of the court proceedings is set out in the Civil Procedure Code (*Zivilprozessordnung*;[2] ZPO). Yet, both the JN and the ZPO were drafted simultaneously under the aegis of Franz Klein, who relied heavily on the earlier German ZPO in the drafting process.[3] Towards the end of the 20th century, the JN has undergone two major amendments for international jurisdiction. The first was the Civil Procedure Amendment (*Zivilverfahrens-Novelle 1983*;[4] ZVN), the second was the Extended Value Limit Amendment (*Erweiterte Wertgrenzen-Novelle 1997*; WGN). It reorganised and simplified international jurisdictional rules and decided the most controversial disputes that had arisen in both jurisprudence and literature.[5]

The JN is divided into three parts, the first of which covers the general principles of jurisdiction, such as the court structure and the impartiality requirements for judges, but also the rules on immunity from Austrian jurisdiction, general rules on international jurisdiction and delegation of jurisdiction within the courts of Austria. The second part of the JN covers the specific rules of jurisdiction for litigious litigation (*Streitsachen*) and includes rules on both subject-matter jurisdiction and territorial jurisdiction for specific categories of lawsuits. The third part is concerned with so-called non-litigious

[1] RGBl Nr 111/1895 idF BGBl I Nr 148/2020.

[2] RGBl Nr 113/1895 idF BGBl I Nr 148/2020.

[3] W Rechberger and D Simotta, *Zivilprozessrecht* 9th edn (Manz, 2017) para 3.

[4] BGBl Nr 135/1983; for more information see E Schalich, 'Überblick über die Zivilverfahrensnovelle 1983' [1983] *ÖJZ* 253.

[5] BGBl I Nr 140/1997; for more information see T Klicka, 'Die "Erweiterte Wertgrenzen-Novelle 1997"' [1998] *JAP* 260.

litigation (*Verfahren außer Streitsachen*) but falls – with the exception of commercial register and land register proceedings – outside of the Brussels Ia Regulation's scope of application.

Outside the JN, there are also jurisdictional rules for disputes arising out of employment contracts enshrined in §§ 4–6 Labour and Social Justice Act (*Arbeits- und Sozialgerichtsgesetz*;[6] ASGG).

(b)

The jurisdictional system of the JN is 'double-functional',[7] which means that it does not differentiate between domestic and international jurisdiction. Pursuant to § 27a JN, a court is automatically competent to hear an international case if domestic territorial jurisdiction for it is given – without any further requirements.[8] Yet, this general rule is limited to the extent that it only applies where the exercise of jurisdiction is not prohibited by international law.[9]

Under Austrian law, however, there are certain cases in which international jurisdiction extends further than domestic territorial jurisdiction. This is specifically the case where an international treaty obliges Austria to exercise international jurisdiction, in the case of a *forum necessitatis* (see below 4) and where Austria's international jurisdiction, but not the jurisdiction of a specific court has been agreed upon by the parties. In these constellations, the Austrian Supreme Court determines on application of the plaintiff which Austrian court may assume jurisdiction (so-called 'ordination').[10]

(c)

The jurisdictional rules of the Brussels Regime have not been adopted or extended by the Austrian legislator in any way. Neither has a general adoption been put forward by scholars as a proposal to replace the existing rules under the JN. However, Daphne-Ariane Simotta proposed that a *forum necessitatis* should be established (see below 4) as a matter of justice *on a case-by-case basis* in line with the Brussels Regime: In her opinion, actions in Austria against defendants in third countries should thus be possible if the European regulations granted Austria jurisdiction in analogous cases where the defendant is based in an EU member state, even if national jurisdictional rules do not. One example for her proposal would be the difference in tort jurisdiction under the (wider) Brussels Regime

[6] BGBl Nr 104/1985 idF BGBl I Nr 21/2021.
[7] GE Kodek and PG Mayr, *Zivilprozessrecht* 5th edn (Manz, 2021) para 211.
[8] T Klicka, 'Die "Erweiterte Wertgrenzen-Novelle 1997"', 260, 264.
[9] Cf § 27a Abs 2 JN.
[10] § 28 Abs 1, 4 JN.

and the (narrower) JN (for more detail see below 5(b)).[11] Yet, this approach has been criticised by other authors, as they regard it as the legislator's prerogative to implement such a change to the system of international jurisdiction of Austrian courts.[12] As of now, the Supreme Court has remained silent on this issue.

(d)

The Austrian rules property on jurisdiction pursuant to § 99 JN[13] were notified under Art 76(1)(a) Brussels Ia Regulation. Similarly, the third-party notice in § 21 ZPO and several superseded intra-European jurisdictional conventions were notified pursuant to Art 76(1)(b) and (c) respectively. These notifications are exhaustive.[14]

Question 2

In Austria, both the courts at the place of the defendant's domicile and of the defendant's habitual residence have general jurisdiction over the defendant pursuant to § 66 JN. Thus, two different notions have to be examined more closely, which are both defined in the JN:

The **domicile** ('Wohnsitz') is defined as the place where the defendant 'has settled with the demonstrable intention, or the intention evident from the circumstances, to take up continual residence there'. This means that a domicile is only established, if a subjective requirement – the intention to continually centre one's life's interests at this place – is fulfilled in addition to the objective requirement of factual presence.[15] It has to be noted, that under this definition, it is possible that a person has two or more domiciles at the same time.[16]

The requirement of factual presence does not mean that general jurisdiction is lost if a person leaves their domicile temporarily; yet, a longer period of absence may suffice to terminate the domicile.[17] As factual presence is required, the mere legal registration of a domicile in the Austrian central civil register is in itself not sufficient to constitute a domicile, yet it may have indicative effect.[18] There is, however, one important legal

[11] D Simotta, 'Die Neuregelung der internationalen Zuständigkeit durch die Wertgrenzen-Novelle 1997' in R Geimer (ed), *Wege zur Globalisierung des Rechts. Festschrift für Rolf A. Schütze zum 65. Geburtstag* (CH Beck, 1999) 850–851.

[12] PG Mayr, 'Die Reform des internationalen Zivilprozessrechts in Österreich' [2001] *JBl* 144, 159; T Garber, '§ 28 JN' in HW Fasching and A Konecny (eds), *Zivilprozessgesetze* 3rd edn (Manz, 2013) para 77.

[13] For more information see below 3.

[14] Cf K Binder and A Klauser, 'Art 76 EuGVVO 2012' in HW Fasching and A Konecny (eds), *Zivilprozessgesetze* 3rd edn (Manz, 2020) paras 4–6.

[15] RIS-Justiz RS0046600; D Simotta, '§ 66 JN' in HW Fasching and A Konecny (eds), *Zivilprozessgesetze* 3rd edn (Manz, 2013) para 4.

[16] RIS-Justiz RS0046688; PG Mayr, '§ 66 JN' in W Rechberger and T Klicka (eds), *ZPO* 5th edn (Verlag Österreich, 2019) para 2.

[17] ibid para 6.

[18] RIS-Justiz RS0046711; D Simotta, '§ 66 JN', para 19.

limitation to the factual nature of this objective requirement: Unlawful residence can never establish a domicile.[19] This is particularly relevant if a foreigner does not have a residence permit in Austria or is issued with a transfer decision.[20]

With respect to the intent to continually remain at the place of the domicile, it has to be noted that even though this requirement is of a subjective nature, it has to be outwardly apparent,[21] so that it contains an objective element as well. The intended residence at that place must be 'continual' ('*bleibenden Aufenthalt*'). Continual in this sense is, however, not understood as permanent: even a stay for a predefined limited duration does establish a domicile, if the place is made the centre of the person's life interests.[22]

The 'intent' to continually remain at the place of the domicile further presupposes a legally free disposition.[23] Thus, persons required by law to remain at a certain place (eg prisoners), persons without legal capacity[24] and minors[25] cannot establish a domicile for themselves. While they may not establish a domicile by themselves, they can still establish a domicile, but only by means of their legal guardian deciding for them.[26] For minors, there is a special rule altogether: minors always follow the general jurisdiction of their guardian.[27] For Austrian soldiers in foreign service, the place of the garrison acts as the soldier's fictitious domicile;[28] civil servants in service overseas are deemed to retain their previous domicile (if it cannot be determined, they assume a fictitious domicile at the place of the foreign office in Vienna).[29]

The other ground for establishing general jurisdiction under Austrian law, a person's **habitual residence** ('*gewöhnlicher Aufenthalt*'), is defined slightly differently. It is based exclusively on objective criteria,[30] which means that it does thus not require any intent.[31] As opposed to the domicile, it thus does not depend on free disposition.[32] Therefore, also prisoners establish a habitual residence at the place of the prison[33] and children and persons without legal capacity can have their own habitual residence.[34] Neither the lawfulness of the residence is relevant for habitual residence.[35]

The core question when determining a person's habitual residence is thus when a mere factual presence becomes a habitual residence. This habituality requirement is

[19] RIS-Justiz RS0046625.
[20] Cf D Simotta, '§ 66 JN', para 8.
[21] RIS-Justiz RS0046688.
[22] D Simotta, '§ 66 JN', para 15.
[23] PG Mayr, '§ 66 JN', para 2.
[24] D Simotta, '§ 66 JN', paras 11, 13.
[25] Verwaltungsgerichtshof (Higher Administrative Court), 22 December 2010, 2009/08/0016.
[26] § 257 Abs 2 ABGB.
[27] § 71 JN, which also applies for the habitual residence.
[28] § 68 JN.
[29] § 69 JN.
[30] § 66 Abs 2 S 2 JN.
[31] Oberlandesgericht Wien (Higher Regional Court of Vienna), 3 April 1987, 6 Nc 3/87; Oberlandesgericht Wien, 30 September 2003, 12 Nc 48/03-04; Landesgericht für Zivilrechtssachen Wien (Regional Civil Court of Vienna), 28 January 1988, 43 R 821/87; Landesgericht für Zivilrechtssachen Wien, 20 August 2002, 42 Nc 15/02c;
[32] § 66 Abs 2 S 2 JN.
[33] Landesgericht für Zivilrechtssachen Wien, 8 April 1999, 43 R 256/99m; A Klauser and G Kodek (eds), *JN – ZPO* 18th edn (Manz, 2018), § 66 JN E 26; D Simotta, '§ 66 JN', para 28.
[34] But only if the specific provision of § 71 JN is not applicable, cf D Simotta, '§ 66 JN', para 22.
[35] § 66 Abs 2 S 2 JN.

determined by a certain longer duration and continuity of the presence.[36] These two criteria further depend on whether the residence is the actual centre of the person's life, their economic interests and their social relations.[37] Generally, the necessary habituality can be assumed to be given if the residence exceeds 6 months.[38] However, this does not mean that a newly established residence cannot constitute a habitual residence.[39] In such cases, it has to be determined by the circumstances of the case, whether there are continuous connections between the person and their residence.[40] Among such connections are eg when a spouse moves to the other after getting married,[41] or – most importantly – the place of employment.[42]

When someone has more than one domicile or habitual residence, the courts of each one of those places have general jurisdiction.[43] This has the effect that the claimant can choose where to bring an action against the defendant.[44]

For legal persons, general jurisdiction follows the seat pursuant to § 75 JN. Unlike in Art 63(1) Brussels Ia Regulation, there is no alternative definition of the seat: it is primarily determined by compulsory rules of company law, secondarily by the statutory seat and only if the seat cannot be identified by these two factors by the place of factual administration.[45]

Question 3

In addition to the 'regular' general jurisdiction pursuant to § 66 JN, there is also a subsidiary general jurisdiction in § 67 JN. It is subsidiary to § 66 insofar as it only applies if the defendant neither has a domicile nor a habitual residence in Austria or elsewhere in the world – ie if the defendant is a vagabond without a place of general jurisdiction anywhere. In these cases, general jurisdiction is granted to the Austrian courts on whose territory the defendant is physically present at the time when the lawsuit is filed.[46]

[36] Oberlandesgericht Wien, 3 April 1987, 6 Nc 3/87.

[37] RIS-Justiz RS0046577.

[38] Oberster Gerichtshof (Supreme Court), 22 February 1989, 3 Ob 552/88; Landesgericht für Zivilrechtssachen Wien, 29 January 1991, 43 R 884/90; Landesgericht für Zivilrechtssachen Wien, 21 January 2001, 44 R 7/03k; Landesgericht für Zivilrechtssachen Wien, 20 September 2011, 42 R 436/11w; Landesgericht Salzburg (Regional Court Salzburg), 27 November 2015, 21 R 340/15v; D Simotta, '§ 66 JN', para 25.

[39] Landesgericht für Zivilrechtssachen Wien, 18 June 2002, 42 R 242/02y.

[40] Landesgericht für Zivilrechtssachen Wien, 6 June 2003, 43 R 413/03h; Landesgericht Krems and der Donau, 9 July 2003, 2 R 125/03z.

[41] Oberster Gerichtshof, 28 March 1996, 6 Ob 2021/96s.

[42] Oberlandesgericht Wien, 3 April 1987, 6 Nc 3/87; Landesgericht für Zivilrechtssachen Wien, 8 March 1984, 43 R 2031/84; Landesgericht für Zivilrechtssachen Wien, 21 March 1984, 44 R 1017/84; D Simotta, '§ 66 JN', para 29; PG Mayr, '§ 66 JN', para 3.

[43] § 66 Abs 3 JN.

[44] Landesgericht für Zivilrechtssachen Wien, 2 October 2008, 48 R 87/08m; D Simotta, '§ 66 JN', para 3; PG Mayr, '§ 66 JN', para 4.

[45] Which is counterintuitive, given that the text of § 75 JN mentions the factual place of administration as the connecting factor, but it only refers to cases "in doubt", cf PG Mayr, '§ 75 JN' in W Rechberger and T Klicka (eds), *ZPO* 5th edn (Verlag Österreich, 2019) para 1.

[46] PG Mayr, '§ 67 JN', para 1.

If the defendant is not even present in Austria, the courts at the place of their last domicile or their last presence in Austria may exercise jurisdiction. Yet, this is limited only to those obligations that came into existence during their presence in Austria or that must be performed in Austria – however, both limitations must be interpreted restrictively.[47]

Another rule that is not a rule of general jurisdiction by the Austrian national understanding – but in its effects comes close to it – is jurisdiction based on the situation of property pursuant to § 99 JN. The fact that it is not considered general jurisdiction, can already be drawn from the wording of § 99 JN, which declares itself subsidiary to general jurisdiction. Property jurisdiction can thus only be invoked if the defendant does not fall under general jurisdiction anywhere else in Austria. Furthermore, it is restricted by its material scope: property jurisdiction applies only to monetary or monetarily measurable claims or to claims arising from a monetary relationship.[48] The nationality of the parties is, however, not a criterion that influences whether Austrian courts have property jurisdiction or not. Both Austrians and foreigners can sue and can be sued in front of Austrian courts under the conditions of § 99 JN.[49]

Aside from these rules, there is no general jurisdiction in matters regulated by the Brussels Ia Regulation that are based on the parties' nationality, be it the claimant's or the defendant's.[50]

Question 4

As mentioned above, Austrian law stipulates the general rule that international jurisdiction is only given where there is domestic territorial jurisdiction for an Austrian court. However, in certain cases, the Austrian Supreme Court may determine a court which has jurisdiction pursuant to § 28 JN. This procedure is called 'ordination'. Ordination is not limited to cases of complete absence of jurisdiction anywhere in the world, but can also establish Austrian jurisdiction in parallel to a place of jurisdiction abroad. Among the cases enumerated in § 28 JN, the most important one is jurisdiction where legal action abroad is not possible or unreasonable pursuant to § 28 Abs 1 Z 2 JN.

The prerequisites for such a *forum necessitatis* under § 28 Abs 1 Z 2 JN are relatively strict: Firstly, there must not be an immunity arising from public international law and the matter must fall under the subject-matter jurisdiction of Austrian civil courts.[51] However, the latter is the case for all matters covered by the Brussels Ia Regulation.

[47] D Simotta, '§ 67 JN', para 6; this limitation places it somewhere as an intermediate jurisdictional rule between general and special jurisdiction. Although the Austrian Supreme Court explicitly calls it a case of special jurisdiction (Oberster Gerichtshof, 26 January 1966, 6 Ob 23/66), it is not limited to certain types of obligations, but only requires a sufficient connection to Austria and is hence in a sort of mezzanine position.

[48] RIS-Justiz RS0045946. Under the last alternative, also declaratory relief may be covered, eg when the declaration of the invalidity of a monetary settlement (RIS-Justiz RS0046841) or of an acknowledgement of debt (Oberster Gerichtshof, 28 February 1989, 10 Ob 501/87) is sought.

[49] D Simotta, '§ 99 JN', paras 11–12.

[50] The jurisdictional rules that make reference to the parties' nationalities, namely § 76 Abs 2 Z 1, § 108 Abs 3, § 110 Abs 1 Z 1, § 113b Abs 1 Z 1 and § 114 Abs 4 JN are exclusively within the field of family law and thus do not fall within the scope of the Brussels Ia Regulation.

[51] PG Mayr, '§ 28 JN', para 1.

The second requirement is that there is no jurisdiction for an Austrian court by virtue of any other jurisdictional rule – international jurisdiction is thus created constitutively by the ordination.[52]

As Austria cannot be a *forum necessitatis* for all claims in the world, there must thirdly be a certain link to Austria for Austrian courts to adjudge the case in question. In detail, it is disputed when such a link is given.

In the past, the majority view adhered strictly to the wording of § 28 JN that Austrian nationality of the claimant was supposed to be a sufficient link. However, this view has been extended to include EU citizens in the meantime.[53] The Austrian legislator considered that in any case, the habitual residence or domicile of the claimant in Austria also establishes such a link.[54] Recourse solely to the person of the claimant is, nevertheless, in general seen critically in the literature.[55]

Fourthly and most importantly, the action before Austrian courts must be necessary to avoid a denial of justice, which means that legal action abroad is (objectively) impossible or (subjectively) unreasonable.[56] This has to be determined on a case-by-case basis.[57] Nevertheless, as an exception to the general rules of jurisdiction, this requirement needs to be interpreted restrictively, as it should not lead to a general *forum actoris*.[58] Cases where the Supreme Court found unreasonable difficulties in bringing the action abroad include where the foreign judgment could not be enforced in Austria,[59] where urgent proceedings abroad would take too long,[60] cases of a factual standstill of

[52] Ibid para 6; but seen differently by F Matscher, 'Die Neuregelung der inländischen Gerichtsbarkeit durch die WGN 1997' [1998] *JBl* 488, 494.

[53] On the incompatibility of this approach with Art 18 Treaty on the Functioning of the European Union [2012] OJ C 326/47 see T Garber, '§ 28, para 65; PG Mayr, 'Die Reform des internationalen Zivilprozessrechts in Österreich', 159; W Jelinek, 'Liegenschaftsbezogene Konkursanfechtung vor österreichischen Gerichten nach Konkurseröffnung in Deutschland', in Kaan, Cronenberg & Partner (eds), *Recht betrachtet* (Linde, 1998) 31, 37; D Simotta, 'Die Neuregelung der internationalen Zuständigkeit durch die Wertgrenzen-Novelle 1997', 848–849; raising but not discussing this issue Oberster Gerichtshof, 29 September 2008, 3 Nc 50/08w. However, the government bill (898 BlgNR 20. GP 33–34) explicitly supports the view that § 28 Abs 1 Z 2 JN and what is now Art 18 TFEU are compatible; see also Oberster Gerichtshof, 30 August 2017, 3 Nc 16/17h; but not for nationals of mere EEA Member States, cf Oberster Gerichtshof, 20 September 2013, 5 Nc 13/13a; see also M Slonina, 'Ordinationsantrag für Bestandstreitigkeiten betreffend ein in Liechtenstein gelegenes Mietobjekt' [2014] *Wobl* 60, 62–63.

[54] T Garber, '§ 28 JN', para 63.

[55] ibid para 64; D Simotta, 'Die Neuregelung der internationalen Zuständigkeit durch die Wertgrenzen-Novelle 1997', 849; in this sense probably also Oberster Gerichtshof, 17 October 2008, 3 Nc 66/08y; 3 March 2010, 3 Nc 8/10x.

[56] PG Mayr, '§ 28 JN', paras 6–7.

[57] H Heiss and PG Mayr, 'Neuerungen im österreichischen internationalen Verfahrens- und Vertragsrecht' [1999] *IPRax* 305, 307; F Matscher, 'Die Neuregelung der inländischen Gerichtsbarkeit durch die WGN 1997', 494; T Garber, '§ 28 JN', paras 11–12.

[58] Oberster Gerichtshof, 27 May 2005, 10 Nc 19/05h; 26 January 2001, 10 Nc 44/06m; 22 October 2010, 7 Nc 21/10p.

[59] RIS-Justiz RS0046148; Oberster Gerichtshof, 25 August 2011, 5 Nc 14/11w; R Loewe, 'Erneuerung des österreichischen internationalen Zivilverfahrensrechts' [1983] *ZfRV* 180, 186; T Garber, '§ 28 JN', para 75 also supports ordination for new proceedings, if there already is a foreign judgment, but it cannot be enforced in Austria.

[60] RIS-Justiz RS0046148; W Rechberger and D Simotta, *Zivilprozessrecht*, para 89; R Loewe, 'Erneuerung des österreichischen internationalen Zivilverfahrensrechts', 186 also supports an ordination if the general duration of proceedings is excessive, which is criticised by M Schwimann, '§ 28 JN und die Grenzen der inländischen Ziviljurisdiktion in Vermögens- und Wirtschaftsstreitigkeiten' [1984] *ÖZW* 97, 107.

judicature in the respective country,[61] severe doubts regarding the independence of the courts abroad[62] and where one of the parties would be subject to political persecution abroad.[63] Where bringing the action abroad would lead to significant additional costs compared to litigation in Austria, a *forum necessitatis* may also be available,[64] but only in exceptional circumstances: these costs have to exceed the usual (travel) costs, as shifting the proceedings to Austria would otherwise just mirror the costs at the defendant's expense;[65] such additional costs include the lack of legal aid,[66] the lack of reimbursement of legal costs by the winner of the proceedings[67] or high deposits when bringing the claim.[68] In contrast, a less favourable position in the substantive law abroad is insufficient to justify an ordination of an Austrian *forum necessitatis*.[69] In relation to Member States of the Brussels Ia Regulation and the 2007 Lugano Convention, the ordination of a *forum necessitatis* is usually impossible, since bringing a claim in these countries will not normally be considered impossible or unreasonable.[70] Nevertheless, the Austrian Supreme Court made exceptions in the past for enforcement proceedings of injunctions issued in Austria, particularly in relation to Germany, but also to countries following the system of '*astreinte*' like France and Belgium.[71] The reason for an ordination in these cases lies in the nature of Austrian injunctions that do not set a penalty in the original judgment, but simply states a prohibition in the style of 'The defendant is owed to refrain from …'.[72] The questions whether a penalty should be set and the amount of such a penalty are then decided during the enforcement proceedings.[73] In line with criticism in literature that such an injunction should be enforced without problems

[61] Oberster Gerichtshof, 28 May 1991, 6 Nd 506/91; M Schwimann, '§ 28 JN und die Grenzen der inländischen Ziviljurisdiktion in Vermögens- und Wirtschaftsstreitigkeiten', 107.

[62] Oberster Gerichtshof, 16 May 2002, 6 Nd 512/01; cf also Oberster Gerichtshof, 13 January 1988, 3 Nd 511/87.

[63] RIS-Justiz RS0046148.

[64] RIS-Justiz RS0046148; also emphasised in the government bill (898 BlgNR 20. GP).

[65] RIS-Justiz RS0046420; Oberster Gerichtshof, 23 November 2006, 8 Nc 25/06b; 26 January 2007, 10 Nc 44/06m; T Garber, '§ 28 JN', para 78; but a bit more lenient: Oberster Gerichtshof, 22 October 2010, 7 Nc 21/10p.

[66] Oberster Gerichtshof, 14 April 2004, 2 Nc 11/04x.

[67] D Czernich, 'Österreichisch-Amerikanisches Zivilprozessrecht' [2002] *JBl* 613, 616–17, who formulates this as a general rule which does, however, not always apply, eg not to damage claims in the USA due to the possibility to award punitive damages in lieu of reimbursement of costs.

[68] Which cannot be assumed for Member States of the Hague Convention on Civil Procedure [1954], cf Oberster Gerichtshof, 4 March 2004, 2 Nc 8/04-05; 10 February 2010, 5 Nc 21/09x.

[69] RIS-Justiz RS 0117751; Oberster Gerichtshof, 12 May 1003, 9 Nc 109/02g; PG Mayr, '§ 28 JN', para 7. An exception is only made where the foreign substantive law amounts to a violation of Austrian *ordre public*, cf Oberster Gerichtshof, 28 March 2003, 10 Ob 17/06g; A Burgstaller and M Neumayr, 'Beobachtungen zu Grenzfragen der internationalen Zuständigkeit: Von forum non conveniens bis Notzuständigkeit' in B Bachmann et al (eds), *Grenzüberschreitungen. Beiträge zum Internationalen Verfahrensrecht und zur Schiedsgerichtsbarkeit. Festschrift für Peter Schlosser zum 70. Geburtstag* (Mohr Siebeck, 2005) 132–33.

[70] RIS-Justiz RS0112108; GE Kodek and PG Mayr, *Zivilprozessrecht*, para 215; H Heiss and PG Mayr, 'Neuerungen im österreichischen internationalen Verfahrens- und Vertragsrecht', 307.

[71] Oberster Gerichtshof, 18 December 2002, 3 Nc 104/02b; 1 March 2006, 4 Nc 7/06a; more generally RIS-Justiz RS0053178; however, there was a case concerning the Netherlands, where this impossibility was not regarded as given: Oberster Gerichtshof, 3 March 2010, 3 Nc 8/10x.

[72] Cf eg Oberster Gerichtshof, 27 June 2019, 6 Ob 6/19d.

[73] § 355 Abs 1 Exekutionsordnung RGBl Nr 79/1896 idF BGBl I Nr 147/2021.

under the regime of Art 54 Brussels Ia Regulation,[74] the Supreme Court slowly made a turn regarding the possibility of enforcement of injunctions in Germany and does not confer jurisdiction in those cases anymore.[75] The relevance of the ordination of a *forum necessitatis* is thus declining, and has recently to a large extent been limited to claims arising from Regulation No 261/2004.[76]

Question 5

(a)

The Austrian jurisdiction for contractual matters is enshrined in § 88 JN, which assigns jurisdiction to the courts of the place of performance of the contract in question. Similar to Art 7 no 1 lit a Brussels Ia Regulation, the national jurisdictional rule covers all contracts independently from their type (eg sales, service, barter, custody or loan contract) and independently of whether the involved parties are professionals or private individuals.[77] Only employment contracts[78] and rental contracts of immovable properties[79] are regulated separately (see below 5(d)). As under the Brussels Ia Regulation, it also establishes only alternative jurisdiction, meaning that it does not replace the general jurisdiction at the domicile or habitual residence of the defendant.[80]

While it does thus prima facie look very similar to the Brussels Regime, § 88 JN is in fact more restrictive in several ways: First and foremost, the main difference lies in the fact that the place of performance has to be agreed upon in the contract. It is insufficient to establish jurisdiction pursuant to § 88 JN if the place of performance is only determined by statute or commercial custom.[81] Even a mention of the place of performance in a waybill or a bill of lading does not suffice.[82] Whether such an agreement of the place of performance has been validly concluded, is to be determined by the substantive *lex causae* of the underlying contract.[83]

[74] J Rassi, 'Art 55 EuGVVO 2012' in HW Fasching and A Konecny (eds), *Zivilprozessgesetze* 3rd edn (Manz, 2020) para 11.

[75] The first indication of a turnaround was made in Oberster Gerichtshof, 23 October 2019, 3 Nc 28/19a; since Oberster Gerichtshof, 23 September 2020, 3 Nc 20/20a, this new line of jurisprudence has been consistent case-law.

[76] Regulation (EC) No 261/2004; cf recently eg Oberster Gerichtshof, 19 April 2021, 10 Nc 5/21y.

[77] D Simotta, '§ 99 JN', paras 6–7; the restrictions of § 14 KSchG (BGBl Nr 140/1979 idF BGBl I Nr 175/2021) apply for consumer contracts nevertheless, see below 5(d).

[78] Cf §§ 4–6 ASGG.

[79] § 83 JN takes precedence as the more specific provision (*lex specialis*).

[80] D Simotta, '§ 88 JN', para 1.

[81] RIS-Justiz RS0046717.

[82] Oberster Gerichtshof, 20 June 2018, 7 Ob 173/17t.

[83] PG Mayr, '§ 88 JN', para 1; HW Fasching, 'Abgrenzungs- und Anwendungsprobleme beim Gerichtsstand des Erfüllungsortes nach österreichischem Recht' in WJ Habscheid and KH Schwab (eds), *Beiträge zum internationalen Verfahrensrecht und zur Schiedsgerichtsbarkeit. Festschrift für Heinrich Nagel zum 75. Geburtstag* (Aschendorff, 1987) 29–30.

While this agreement may be concluded without any formal requirements,[84] it needs to be proven to the court by documentary evidence, if jurisdiction pursuant to § 88 JN is contested by the defendant.[85] This means that also a document that has been signed only by the defendant fulfils this requirement, like an order form.[86] However, the Austrian Supreme Court has established relatively strict requirements as to the discernible intent of the signor that the agreement of the place of performance is encompassed by the signature. While such a clause below the line of signature is regularly unproblematic – at least if it would normally be noticed by the average person[87] – a clause on the back side of the order form is insufficient.[88] Whether a place of performance set out in standard terms to which the contract refers suffices, is still disputed by scholars.[89]

Another difference to Art 7 no 1 lit a Brussels Ia Regulation is that § 88 JN does not encompass all disputes arising from the contract, but only four specific cases: actions for the declaration of (non-) existence of a contract, actions for performance, actions for avoidance and actions for compensation in cases of non-performance or faulty performance.[90] Although it encompasses the most important contractual claims, there are specific cases – like restitution after a mutually agreed termination of the contract – which are not covered by this provision.[91]

Finally, a further restriction compared to the Brussels Regime is that jurisdiction pursuant to § 88 JN can only be drawn on by the creditor, but not by the debtor (eg seeking declaratory relief that he does not owe money from a sales contract anymore, because he has already paid). This effect is, however, mitigated by the fact that in synallagmatic contracts, both parties are creditors (the debtor in the example above could claim the delivery of the goods from the sales contract or seek declaratory relief that the contract never existed).[92] Due to these stark differences, courts as well as scholars generally do not refer to the Brussels Regime when interpreting § 88 JN.

(b)

Tort jurisdiction under Austrian law is both broader and narrower than its European counterpart in Art 7 no 2 Brussels Ia Regulation. On the one hand, § 92a JN is broader because it does not only cover tort claims, but also claims for damages in general,

[84] PG Mayr, '§ 88 JN', para 2; D Simotta, '§ 88 JN', para 12.

[85] Oberster Gerichtshof, 24 April 1997, 6 Ob 36/97-98; W Rechberger and D Simotta, *Zivilprozessrecht*, para 247; D Simotta, '§ 88 JN', paras 19–20.

[86] RIS-Justiz RS0046994.

[87] RIS-Justiz RS0046736.

[88] Oberster Gerichtshof, 7 July 1971, 5 Ob 150/71. But not in agreements of entrepreneurs, who can also be expected to read the back side, cf Oberster Gerichtshof, 18 February 1981, 6 Ob 539/81.

[89] G Iro, M Kellner and O Riss, 'Grundregeln für die Beziehung zwischen Kunde und Kreditinstitut' in R Bollenberger and M Oppitz (eds), *Bankvertragsrecht I. Geschäftsbeziehung, Bankgeheimnis, Bankauskunft* 3rd edn (Verlag Österreich, 2019) para 1/201.

[90] D Simotta, '§ 88 JN', para 33.

[91] ibid para 14.

[92] PG Mayr, '§ 88 JN', para 4.

ie including contractual damage claims.[93] The – at times difficult – differentiation between contractual claims and tort claims in EU law[94] is thus irrelevant under the Austrian national jurisdictional provisions. On the other hand, jurisdiction is limited by the type of damage for which compensation is claimed: Only damage to persons (including illegal restraint) and to physical objects can establish jurisdiction[95] – contrarily, damage of immaterial rights (copyrights, name rights, etc) or pure financial loss do not fall under § 92a JN.[96]

As opposed to the Brussels Regime, the Austrian domestic tort jurisdiction is based purely on the place where the harmful conduct took place – the place of damage is irrelevant.[97] For conduct consisting of several acts in different places, jurisdiction for the entire damage claim is created for every court in whose area one of the acts was conducted.[98] For claims arising from omissions, the relevant connecting factor is the place where the required act should have been performed.[99] However, this approach has been criticised by some authors, who support the view that § 92a JN should be interpreted analogously to Art 7 no 2 Brussels Ia Regulation and that the theory of ubiquity should also apply to national jurisdictional rules.[100] Such a wide interpretation of § 92a JN was certainly not intended by the legislator[101] and is thus rejected by the majority of scholars.[102]

There is also specific tort jurisdiction for damage claims resulting from accidents involving motor vehicles or trains[103] and electricity or gas[104] – each at the place of the accident – and for forest-damaging air pollution at the place of damage.[105]

(c)

Similar to Art 8 no 1 Brussels Ia Regulation, there is jurisdiction pursuant to § 93 JN for cases in which there is a multitude of defendants that do not have general jurisdiction at the same place. Both provisions allow for an action against all defendants at the place of general jurisdiction of one of them. It is important to note that this only applies for the place of *general* jurisdiction (see above 2 and 3), but not for specific alternative

[93] RIS-Justiz RS0046705.
[94] Cf eg Case C-59/19 *Wikingerhof* or the cases concerning the delineation of the Rome I and Rome II Regulations, such as Case C-359/14 *ERGO Insurance*.
[95] PG Mayr, '§ 92a JN', para 1.
[96] D Simotta, '§ 92a JN', paras 2–3.
[97] Oberster Gerichtshof, 23April 1992, 7 Ob 541/92; 5 November 2003, 9 Ob 130/03p; 1 July 2004, 2 Ob 157/04h.
[98] Oberster Gerichtshof, 5 November 2003, 9 Ob 130/03p.
[99] Oberster Gerichtshof, 19 December 2002, 2 Ob 308/02m.
[100] D Simotta, '§ 92a JN', para 9/1; MJ Maxl, 'Produkthaftung, Internationales Zivilprozessrecht und Internationales Privatrecht' [1992] *JBl* 156, 158–160.
[101] Cf ErläutRV zur ZVN 1983, 669 BlgNR 15. GP 39.
[102] W Lorenz, 'Internationale Zuständigkeit österreichischer Gerichte für Klagen gegen ausländische Produzenten' [1993] *IPRax* 193; E Schalich, 'Überblick über die Zivilverfahrensnovelle 1983', 256; PG Mayr, '§ 92a JN', para 2.
[103] § 20 EKHG (BGBl Nr 48/1959 idF BGBl I Nr 19/2017).
[104] Art V Verordnung zur Einführung des Reichshaftpflichtgesetzes (dRGBl I S 713/1940 idF BGBl Nr 48/1959).
[105] § 57 Abs 2 ForstG (BGBl Nr 440/1975 idF BGBl I Nr 56/2016).

jurisdiction (eg for tort or contract) that is only given for one of the defendants.[106] Differently to the Brussels Regime, however, § 93 JN is only applicable if there is no other common specific (alternative, exclusive or agreed) jurisdiction that is common to *all* defendants.[107] It is important to note that there is an ongoing dispute both in literature and in jurisprudence whether the consumer protection of § 14 Consumer Protection Act (*Konsumentenschutzgesetz*; KSchG) (see below 5(d)) is applicable in cases of § 93 JN or not. Recently, the majority opinion seems to follow the approach that § 93 JN is not affected by the consumer protection rules,[108] but the Supreme Court has not yet changed its older line of judicature that § 14 KSchG prohibits suing a consumer pursuant to § 93 JN.[109]

As concerns the required connection between the defendants, the European provision necessarily has to define it itself and does so as 'so closely connected that it is expedient to hear and determine them together to avoid the risk of irreconcilable judgments resulting from separate proceedings'.[110] However, § 93 JN refers to a legal concept that is known from general Austrian civil procedure law: the joinder of parties (*Streitgenossenschaft*). § 11 Z 1 ZPO defines it as two parties who 'share a shared legal position with regard to the subject-matter of the claim or have been entitled or obliged for the same factual reason or jointly and severally'. Examples include among others co-owners, partners of a company, co-heirs or persons committing an intentional tort together.[111] The Austrian definition is thus a bit narrower than the European definition,[112] which is why generally no reference is made to the European case law on this issue.

Similar to Art 8 no 1 Brussels Ia Regulation,[113] the prerogatives of § 93 JN only have to be fulfilled at the time when the action reaches the court. If the action against the defendant on whose general jurisdiction the claim is based is later rejected as inadmissible or withdrawn, jurisdiction for the other defendants is thus not affected. Yet, if the claim against this defendant is refused by the court due to an immunity arising from public international law or if the matter falls outside the subject-matter jurisdiction of Austrian civil courts in general, jurisdiction is automatically also lost for all connected claims against the other defendants.[114]

[106] D Simotta, '§ 93 JN', para 10.

[107] Yet, if only one of a multitude of defendants does not share the specific jurisdiction, jurisdiction pursuant to § 93 JN is given for all defendants, cf PG Mayr, '§ 93 JN', para 2; D Simotta, '§ 93 JN', para 6.

[108] Arguing for this solution is particularly D Simotta, '§ 93 JN', paras 8/1–8/3; 'Der Verbraucher als Streitgenosse – § 14 Abs 1 KSchG versus § 93 Abs 1 JN' in B König (ed), *Historiarum ignari semper sunt pueri. Festschrift Rainer Sprung zum 65. Geburtstag* (Manz, 2001) 359 et seq; PG Mayr, '§ 93 JN', para 3; M Roth, 'Neuerungen der Zivilverfahrensnovelle 1983 im Bereich der Klagenhäufung' in W Buchegger and R Holzhammer (eds), *Beiträge zum Zivilprozeßrecht II* (Springer, 1986) 233–234; E Schalich, 'Überblick über die Zivilverfahrensnovelle 1983', 256; in case law Landesgericht Innsbruck, 4 February 2011, 2 R 303/10p.

[109] RIS-Justiz RS0046739; also H Krejci, '§ 14 KSchG. Gerichtsstand' in P Rummel, *ABGB* 3rd edn (Manz, 2002), para 6.

[110] Cf Art 8 no 1 Brussels Ia Regulation.

[111] B Schneider, '§ 11 ZPO' in HW Fasching and A Konecny (eds), *Zivilprozessgesetze* 3rd edn (Manz, 2013) para 10.

[112] Cf W Rechberger and D Simotta, *Zivilprozessrecht* 9th edn (Manz, 2017) para 139; H Heiss, 'zu Artikel 8' in D Czernich, GE Kodek and PG Mayr, *Europäisches Gerichtsstands- und Vollstreckungsrecht* 4th edn (LexisNexis, 2015) para 14; Landesgericht Feldkirch, 8 June 2004, 1 R 175/04i.

[113] Cf Case C-103/05 *Reisch/Kissel*.

[114] Oberster Gerichtshof, 8 February 1956, 2 Ob 747/55; D Simotta, '§ 93 JN', para 4.

(d)

The domestic system of jurisdiction for consumer, employment and insurance contracts differs substantially from the Brussels Regime. Art 18 Brussels Ia Regulation is both of a facilitating and a protective nature, as it offers the consumer as a claimant specific jurisdiction at their place of domicile and shields the consumer as a defendant from being sued at any place other than their domicile. In contrast, the consumer jurisdiction in Austria is only of a protective nature.

The central provision, § 14 KSchG, does not create specific jurisdiction for consumers to facilitate an enforcement of their claims.[115] However, it limits the places in which the consumers can be sued. The other party may only rely on the specific jurisdiction against the consumer pursuant to §§ 88 (contracts), 89, 93 Abs 2 (bills of exchange) and § 104 JN (choice of court agreements) if the place of jurisdiction coincides with their domicile, habitual residence or place of employment.[116] However, this does not mean that consumers can only be sued in those places as a general rule: the claimant can rely on all other provisions of specific jurisdiction (eg tort jurisdiction pursuant to § 92a JN) in an action against a consumer.[117]

Furthermore, if the consumer acts as the claimant in the proceedings, choice of court agreements are subject to an important condition. They are void insofar as they deprive the consumer of an option to bring the action in a place that would otherwise have jurisdiction according to the default jurisdictional provisions.[118] Thus, the consumer may rely on additional jurisdiction created by a choice of court agreement, but the agreement cannot prevent the consumer from accessing jurisdiction given by law.[119]

Austrian domestic international jurisdiction over individual employment contracts is regulated in § 4 Abs 1 Z 1 ASGG and is far broader than jurisdiction over individual contracts of employment under art 21 and 22 Brussels Ia Regulation. While the Brussels Regime differentiates between actions brought by the employer and those by the employee, the domestic provisions apply equally to both situations.[120] In addition, they are not exclusive, but additional jurisdiction provisions, that apply alongside the defendant's general jurisdiction or other specific jurisdiction.[121] The specific connecting factors for employment contracts include the employee's domicile or habitual residence (both during and at the time of termination of the employment contract), the seat of the employer's enterprise, the place where (at least part of) the work is/was performed and the place where the remuneration is to be paid.[122] Finally, § 6 ASGG goes one step further and stipulates that if no Austrian jurisdiction is given pursuant to § 4 ASGG, also the courts at the place where a branch of the enterprise is situated.

[115] Cf § 14 Abs 1 and 3 KSchG.
[116] G Kathrein and T Schoditsch, '§ 14 KSchG' in H Koziol, P Bydlinski and R Bollenberger, *ABGB* 6th edn (Verlag Österreich, 2020) para 2. On the discussion whether § 14 KSchG also applies to the jurisdiction pursuant to § 93 Abs 1 JN, see above 5©.
[117] H Krejci, '§ 14 KSchG. Gerichtsstand', para 6.
[118] Cf § 14 Abs 3 KSchG.
[119] H Krejci, '§ 14 KSchG. Gerichtsstand', para 11.
[120] Cf M Neumayr, '§ 4 ASGG.' in M Neumayr and GP Reissner (eds), *Zeller Kommentar zum Arbeitsrecht* 3rd edn (Manz, 2018) paras 8–12.
[121] ibid para 1 and 8; for more information about general jurisdiction see above 2 and 3.
[122] § 14 Abs 1 Z 1 JN.

For insurance contracts, there is no general jurisdictional provision in Austrian domestic law, so general provisions (§ 65–67 JN) apply.[123] However, for insurance contracts concluded by consumers, the regular rules for consumer contracts apply. Additionally, there is specific additional jurisdiction for actions against the insurer in all cases where an insurance agent conveyed or concluded the contract with the insurer. The courts at the insurance agent's place of establishment (or subsidiarily their domicile) at the time of the conveyance or conclusion of the insurance contract thus also have jurisdiction over disputes against the insurer.[124] This specific jurisdiction cannot be excluded by means of a choice of court agreement.[125]

Furthermore, there is specific jurisdiction for cases relating to the insurance of motor vehicles: for such contracts, there is also jurisdiction for actions brought by the insured person at their place of domicile or habitual residence.[126]

[123] D Simotta 'Art 9 EuGVVO', in HW Fasching and A Konecny (eds), *Zivilprozessgesetze* 2nd edn (Manz, 2008), para 4.

[124] § 48 Abs 1 VersVG (BGBl Nr 2 /1959 idF BGBl I Nr 51/2018).

[125] § 48 Abs 2 VersVG.

[126] § 23 KHVG (BGBl Nr 651/1994 idF BGBl I Nr 19/2017); H Salficky, 'Prozessuale Aspekte der Kfz-Haftpflichtversicherung' [2015] *ZVR* 456, 459.

Belgium

MICHIEL POESEN

Question 1

(a)

The rules on the international jurisdiction of the Belgian courts are laid down in the 2004 Code of Private International Law (*Wetboek Internationaal Privaatrecht/ Code de Droit International Privé* – hereafter 'PIL Code'). An official German translation of the PIL Code was enacted by Royal Decree of 12th October 2005.[1] The Code was translated into English by Ms Caroline Clijmans and Professor Paul Torremans in 2013.[2] The PIL Code is by far the most important source of jurisdictional grounds in the domestic law of Belgium.[3] Note that the PIL Code has been modified a few times since its adoption, the most recent and important one being the reform of the private-international-law aspects of company law.[4] Sectorial legislation, such as the Code of Economic Law, might contain rules that relate to specific matters, such as pre-contractual liability in commercial cooperation or commercial agency.[5] It is safe to say that those rules are not as significant as the rules contained in the PIL Code.

The PIL Code is the product of a codification project under the auspices of leading Belgian academics in the field. This is reflected in the highly detailed and structured text of the Code. It starts by setting out the general rules and definitions of key terms (Chapter I). Here, the PIL Code confirms that the Belgian courts have general jurisdiction over claims brought against defendants who are domiciled (ie registered or incorporated) or habitually resident (ie have their main residence or seat) in Belgium.[6]

[1] Belgian State Gazette, (10 November 2005, 48274) www.ejustice.just.fgov.be/eli/besluit/2005/10/12/2005000620/staatsblad.

[2] C Clijmans and P Torremas, 'Law of 16 July 2004 Holding the Code of Private International Law' (2004) 6 *Yearbook* of Private International Law 319–75.

[3] Belgian State Gazette 27 July 2004, 57344.

[4] Inserting a new Art 109 and 111 PIL Code: see M Poesen, 'So Long, Savigny? The Case of Jurisdiction over External Directors' Liability in Belgian Private International Law' (*EAPIL Blog*, 10 December 2020) www.eapil.org/2020/12/10/so-long-savigny-the-case-of-jurisdiction-over-external-directors-liability-in-belgian-private-international-law/.

[5] Art X.25 of the Code of Economic Law allocates exclusive jurisdiction to the Belgian courts over all activities of a commercial agent who has its principal establishment in Belgium. In a similar vein Art X 33 of the Code of Economic Law allocates jurisdiction to the Belgian courts if the person acquiring the right to exploit an activity is mainly active in Belgium.

[6] Art 5, § 1 PIL Code.

Furthermore, the rules on choice of court agreements are contained here, as well as rules on jurisdiction over multiple defendants and provisional measures.[7] Interestingly, Art 9 PIL Code elevates relatedness between actions to the status of a ground of jurisdiction in Belgian private international law, in contrast to Art 31 Brussels Ia that deals with related actions through a stay of posterior proceedings.[8] This means that the Belgian courts have jurisdiction over actions that are related to actions over which they normally have jurisdiction under the PIL Code (see Question 5 below). Chapter I of the PIL Code also contains a *forum necessitatis* provision, which is aimed at avoiding denials of justice (Art 11; see Question 4 below). Chapters II–XI then lay out rules of applicable law and jurisdiction concerning specific subject matters such as civil status, marriage, cohabitation, filiation, maintenance obligations, inheritance, property, obligations, legal persons, insolvency, and trusts. Most of these subject-specific rules apply over and above the general rules contained in Chapter I, which is then confirmed in the subject-specific rule's phrasing. Chapter IX on obligations, to illustrate, applies over and above the general rules laid down in Chapter I. However, Chapter X on legal persons (including the rule of jurisdiction on disputes concerning the validity and internal functioning of legal persons) applies in derogation of the general rules of Chapter I, in close resemblance to the exclusive ground of jurisdiction in Art 24(1) Brussels Ia. In a similar vein, disputes concerning the validity of intellectual property rules are governed by Art 86(2) PIL Code in Chapter VIII on property, which also displaces the rules of Chapter I by according jurisdiction to the Belgian courts insofar as the intellectual property right at stake is registered in Belgium. This approach echoes the one taken in Art 24(2) Brussels Ia.

The Belgian courts are required to verify their international jurisdiction of their own motion (Art 12 PIL Code).[9]

(b)

The rules of the PIL Code only 'regulates in an international situation the jurisdiction of Belgian courts', as confirmed by Art 2 PIL Code.[10] The relative territorial competence of the Belgian courts is laid down in the 1967 Code of Civil Procedure and particular legislation on civil procedure, unless otherwise provided. In reality, the PIL Code

[7] Arts 6–7 PIL Code; Art 5, § 2 PIL Code; Art 9 PIL Code: Art 10 PIL Code.

[8] cf Hof van Beroep Antwerpen (Antwerp Higher District Court), 12 May 2014, (2014) *Nieuw Juridisch Weekblad Primary Industries Trading GmbH/Kowa Shipping*, 893), which misconstrued Art 9 PIL Code as not containing a ground of jurisdiction despite the provision's clear wording. In fact, the court seemed to read Art 9 PIL Code in analogy to Art 28 Brussels I, which deals with related actions through the stay of proceedings instead of through the allocation of jurisdiction.

[9] As a result, defendants are not required to raise the lack of jurisdiction of the Belgian courts *in limine litis*: Rechtbank van Koophandel Gent (Ghent Commercial Court), 18 February 2004, Tijdschrift voor Gentse en West-Vlaamse Rechtspraak 2004, 217.

[10] The present statute regulates in an international situation the jurisdiction of Belgian courts, the designation of the applicable law and the conditions for the effect in Belgium of foreign judgments and authentic instruments in civil and commercial matters without prejudice to the application of international treaties, the laws of the European Union or provisions of special statutes.

only regulates relative territorial competence for enforcement proceedings. Art 23 PIL Code allocates jurisdiction to the first instance courts over these proceedings and hence supplants the Code of Civil Procedure. Art 13 PIL Code expressly confirms this.[11] In the exceptional situation where the Belgian courts have jurisdiction pursuant to the gateways in the PIL Code but neither the Code of Civil Procedure nor the PIL Code point towards an internally competent court, the district court (*rechtbank van eerste aanleg/tribunal de première instance*) of Brussels has jurisdiction.

(c)

Before the entry into force of the PIL Code, Arts 635–638 of the 1967 Belgian Code of Civil Procedure and Art 15 of the Civil Code governed the international jurisdiction of the Belgian courts vis-à-vis international disputes.[12] These rules too reflected some of the principles contained in the Brussels Regime, such as *actor sequitur forum rei* (Art 4(1) Brussels Ia) and anchor defendants (Art 8(1) Brussels Ia).

The PIL Code retained many of those rules as well as further incorporated certain rules of the Brussels I Regulation and 1968 Brussels Convention. This is the case for the regime of recognition and enforcement, which was explicitly informed by the provisions of the 1968 Brussels Convention and Brussels I Regulation.[13] As to jurisdictional gateways, many rules of the Brussel I Regulation inspired the drafters of the PIL Code, as was confirmed in the Parliamentary Preparations of the PIL Code. In this sense, the rules of the Brussels Regime were 'extended' to non-EU defendants by the PIL Code. Art 2 Brussels I (*actor sequitur forum rei*) informed the general rule of jurisdiction of Art 5(1) PIL Code.[14] For cases involving multiple defendants, Art 6(1) Brussels I (anchor defendants) informed Art 5(2) PIL Code, which allocates jurisdiction to the Belgian courts over cases involving multiple defendants insofar as one of them is domiciled or habitually resident in Belgium.[15] Furthermore, Art 6(2) Brussels I (counterclaims) inspired the insertion of Art 8 PIL Code.[16] The protective provisions Arts 13–14 1968

[11] Art 13 Internal jurisdiction; when Belgian courts have jurisdiction by virtue of the present statute, the territorial jurisdiction of the court will be established according to the relevant provisions of the Code of Civil Procedure and special statutes, except in the case provided for in Art 23 [note of author: this provision concerns jurisdiction for recognition and enforcement proceedings]. In the absence of a provision that determines the territorial jurisdiction of the court, the latter will be established according to the provision of the present statute regarding the international jurisdiction. If these provisions do not allow designating the court that has territorial jurisdiction, the action may be brought before the court of the district of Brussels.

[12] Art 15 Civil Code governed jurisdiction when the defendant was a Belgian whereas the provisions in the Code of Civil Procedure governed jurisdiction when the defendant was a 'foreigner': A Heyvaert, *Belgisch International Privaatrecht* (Mys en Breesch, 1999) 59–60.

[13] Proposition de loi portant le Code de droit international privé/Wetsvoorstel houdende het Wetboek van internationaal privaatrecht, (Parl.st. Senaat/Doc.parl. Sénat, nr. 3-27/1, 2003, 51) www.senate.be/www/webdriver?MItabObj=pdf&MIcolObj=pdf&MInamObj=pdfid&MItypeObj=application/pdf&MIvalObj=50331657; G Van Calster, 'Tien jaar Wetboek Internationaal Privaatrecht: Eigen Belgische koers of Europees kielzog?' in *Recht in beweging – 22ste VRG Alumnidag 2015* (Maklu, 2015) 97–98.

[14] ibid 32.

[15] ibid.

[16] ibid 35.

Brussels Convention (consumer contracts) as well as the case law of the CJEU under Art 5(1) for employment contracts informed similar protective provisions laid down in Art 97 PIL Code.[17] The rules in Art 22(2) Brussels I on intellectual property, Art 24 Brussels I on jurisdiction by voluntary appearance, and Art 31 Brussels I on jurisdiction for provisional measures also informed similar provisions in respectively Arts 86, 6, §1, para 2, and 10 PIL Code.[18]

Moreover, the Belgian courts (including the *Hof van Cassatie/Cour de Cassation*, the highest court in ordinary) have read the PIL Code against the backdrop of the Brussels Ia Regulation in a good number of cases. There appears to be an assumption that the PIL Code, where possible, should be interpreted in line with Brussels Ia, particularly in those cases where the provisions of the PIL Code were inspired by Brussels I. This could be seen as a praetorian incorporation of Brussels Ia into Belgian private international law, over and above the already fairly extensive statutory incorporation. Instances of such praetorian incorporation are mentioned throughout this report when they occurred (see fn 10 above, and Question 5(a) and (b) below).

(d)

Yes, the information is exhaustive insofar as the bilateral conventions under Art 69 Brussels Ia Regulation are concerned. As to the grounds of jurisdiction in Arts 5(2) and 6(2) Brussels Ia, and the rules on third-party proceedings under Art 65 Brussels Ia, Belgium seemed to have opted to not notify any domestic provisions to the European Commission.

Question 2

Art 4 PIL Code does not only define 'domicile' (*woonplaats/domicile*) but also 'habitual residence' (*gewoonlijke verblijfplaats/residence habituelle*) as follows:

> Art. 4. Domicile and habitual residence
>
> §1. For the purposes of the present statute, *domicile* means:
>
> 1 the place where a natural person has his main residence according to the civil register of the population, the register of foreigners or the "waiting register";
>
> 2 the place in Belgium where a body with separate legal personality has its statutory seat.
>
> §2. For the purpose of the present statute, *habitual residence* means:
>
> 1 the place where a natural person has established his main residence, even in the absence of registration and independent of a residence or establishment permit; in

[17] ibid 122.

[18] ibid 133 (intellectual property), 34 (voluntary appearance), 35 (provisional measures).

order to determine this place, the circumstances of personal or professional nature that show durable connections with that place or indicate the will to create such connections are taken into account.

2 the place where a body with separate legal personality has its main establishment;

§3. For the purposes of the present statute the main establishment of a body with separate legal entity is determined by taking into account primarily the place of administration, as well as the centre of its business and activities, and in subsidiary order the statutory seat.

(emphasis added)

Question 3

In addition to domicile, which is a formal notion that centres on the registration of a natural or legal person in Belgium, *the PIL Code allocates jurisdiction to the Belgian courts over claims brought against defendants who are* habitually resident *in Belgium* (Art 5, § 1 PIL Code). Habitual residence is defined in Art 4, § 2 PIL Code (see Question 2 above). The jurisdiction of the Belgian courts also extends to 'actions relating to the exploitation of a secondary establishment of a body with separate legal entity' (ie a legal person) that is not domiciled or habitually resident in Belgium insofar as the secondary establishment is in Belgium (Art 5, § 2 PIL Code). This jurisdictional gateway is contained in Art 5 PIL Code.[19]

A general rule of jurisdiction, in the strict sense of the word, can perhaps not be found in Art 9 PIL Code. This provision contains a rule of jurisdiction for related actions that creates an extensive jurisdictional basis for actions related to actions over which the Belgian courts have jurisdiction. Therefore, it is akin to a ground of general jurisdiction. Art 9 PIL Code allocates jurisdiction to the Belgian courts if an action over which the Belgian courts have jurisdiction is so closely related to another action over which such jurisdiction does not exist that it is expedient to hear and determine them together to avoid the risk of irreconcilable judgments if the actions were heard separately. This is indeed a fully-fledged ground of jurisdiction that was inserted in Chapter I of the PIL Code.[20] Therefor, it applies regardless of the subject matter involved, unless a specific rule in Chapter II et seq excludes its application.

[19] Art 5 International jurisdiction based on the domicile or habitual residence of the defendant, § 1 except when otherwise provided for by the present statute, the Belgian courts have jurisdiction if the defendant has his *domicile or habitual residence* in Belgium when the action is introduced. In the event of multiple defendants, the Belgian courts will have jurisdiction if one of them has his domicile or habitual residence in Belgium, unless the action has been introduced solely to remove a defendant from the jurisdiction of his domicile or habitual residence abroad. § 2 the Belgian courts have also jurisdiction to hear actions relating to the exploitation of a secondary establishment of a body with separate legal entity, which has neither its domicile nor its habitual residence in Belgium, if the establishment is located in Belgium when the action is introduced (emphasis added).

[20] B De Groote, 'Artikel 9' in J Erauw, M Fallon, E Guldix et al (eds), *Het wetboek internationaal privaatrecht becommentarieerd – Le code de droit interational privé commenté* (Intersentia, 2006) 51.

The presence of property in Belgium only is a subject-specific jurisdictional ground for property-related disputes (Art 85 PIL Code).

Question 4

The PIL Code contains two provisions relating to *forum necessitatis*. The first one is Art 11 PIL Code. This is a proper rule on jurisdiction by necessity, which allows Belgian courts to assume jurisdiction in exceptional circumstances where the case has close connections with Belgium:

> Art. 11. Exceptional attribution of international jurisdiction
>
> Notwithstanding the other provisions of the present statute, the Belgian courts will exceptionally have jurisdiction when the matter presents *close connections with Belgium* and proceedings abroad seem *impossible* or when it would be *unreasonable* to demand that the action be brought abroad.
>
> (emphasis added)

This provision was inspired by the aim to *avoid a denial of justice*. The parliamentary preparations of the PIL Code explicitly reserve the application of the provision to 'emergencies', ie cases in which it is impossible or unreasonable to demand the claimant to litigate abroad.[21] The legislature aimed to remedy the undesirable consequences of a system of jurisdiction that is based on strict rules of jurisdiction. In particular, the legislature noted it 'could be unreasonable to require a party to litigate abroad, taking into account financial costs and the elements that localise the dispute, if the contested financial stakes are not proportionate to the additional costs.' The *forum necessitatis* provision in the Belgian PIL Code was inspired by Art 3 of the Swiss Law on Private International Law.[22] That being said, *forum necessitatis* was not entirely unknown until the enactment of the PIL Code. In the past, Belgian courts accepted that a Belgian national could have recourse to the Belgian courts in civil status matters despite a lack of any other relevant connection to the Belgian territory apart from its nationality.[23] The *forum necessitatis* provision, however, does not elevate the nationality of the claimant as a decisive element in assessing necessity.[24]

In practice, Art 11 PIL Code is mainly relevant in divorce cases.[25] Another example – given by the drafters of the PIL Code – in which *forum necessitatis* might be applied is where the Belgian-domiciled rightful owner of a good claims restitution of stolen

[21] Proposition de loi/Wetsvoorstel, www.senate.be/www/webdriver?MItabObj=pdf&MIcolObj=pdf&MInamObj=pdfid&MItypeObj=application/pdf&MIvalObj=50331657, 35–36.

[22] ibid 36.

[23] A Nuyts, 'Article 11' in J Erauw, M Fallon, E Guldix et al (eds), *Het wetboek internationaal privaatrecht becommentarieerd – Le code de droit interational privé commenté* (Intersentia, 2006) 68.

[24] ibid 36.

[25] Tribunal de la famille Bruxelles (Brussels Family Court), 6 March 2019, Tijdschrift@IPR.be 2019, 146; Rechtbank Brussel (Brussels District Court), 9 December 2011, (2012) *Revue trimestrielle de droit familial*, 364; C Henricot, 'Le "for de nécessité" de l'article 11 du Code de DIP: premières illustrations jurisprudentielles en divorce' [2012] *Revue trimestrielle de droit familial* 369.

property that was taken abroad.[26] In one case, which demonstrates the subsidiary and exceptional nature of Art 11 PIL Code, the commercial court of Brussels was asked to apply Art 11 PIL Code to a dispute concerning a licencing agreement between a Belgian licensor and a Chinese licensee. The Belgian company pursued the Chinese company to obtain payment of licence fees. The former argued that it would be unduly burdensome to commence proceedings in China (Hong Kong) since under the applicable law, the Belgian claimant would be required to offer collateral of up to 20,500.00 EUR. The Brussels commercial court held that the claimant did not prove that it was effectively required to pose such collateral, which lead it to conclude that there was no impossibility or undue burden preventing the Belgian claimant from pursuing the defendant abroad.[27] Indeed, mere allegations of the impossibility or unreasonableness of proceedings abroad will not suffice for the application of Art 11 PIL Code.[28]

The second provision – Art 7 PIL Code – governs the relationship between Art 11 and choice of court agreements in favour of a foreign court. Art 7 provides that *forum necessitatis can trump choice of court agreements in favour of foreign courts*. In others words, this provision confirms expressly that the Belgian courts can put aside such a choice of court agreement under the conditions spelled out by Art 11 PIL Code.[29]

Question 5

(a)

The Belgian courts have jurisdiction over contracts if either the place of performance of a contractual obligation (Art 96, 1, b) PIL Code) or the place where the contractual obligation came into existence (Art 96, 1, a) PIL Code) are located in Belgium.[30]

The Belgian provision on contract jurisdiction differs from the head of jurisdiction 'in matters relating to a contract' in Art 7(1) Brussels Ia in a number of aspects. First of all, the text of Art 96, 1°, a) PIL Code does not distinguish between general contracts and sale-of-goods or provision-of-services contracts, in contrast to Art 7(1)(a) and

[26] Proposition de loi/Wetsvoorstel, www.senate.be/www/webdriver?MItabObj=pdf&MIcolObj=pdf&MInamObj=pdfid&MItypeObj=application/pdf&MIvalObj=50331657, 133.

[27] Tribunal de commerce Bruxelles, 31 August 2015, (2018) *Tijdschrift voor Belgisch Handelsrecht/Revue de Droit Commercial*, 83.

[28] A Nuyts, 'Article 11', 69.

[29] Art 7 Exclusion of international jurisdiction by agreement; when in a matter in which, according to Belgian law, the parties can freely dispose of their rights, the parties validly agreed to confer jurisdiction on foreign courts or on a foreign court to hear the disputes which have arisen or may arise in connection with a legal relationship; and the case is pending before a Belgian court, the latter must stay its proceedings, unless it is anticipated that the foreign judgment is not amenable to recognition and enforcement in Belgium *or unless the Belgian courts have jurisdiction according to article 11*. The Belgian courts must decline jurisdiction when the foreign decision can be recognized according to the present statute (emphasis added).

[30] Art 96 International jurisdiction regarding contractual and non-contractual obligations; in addition to the cases provided for in the general provisions of the present statute, the Belgian courts have jurisdiction to hear actions with respect to obligations regarding: 1° a contractual obligation, a) if the latter came into existence in Belgium; or b) if the latter is or has to be executed in Belgium. […]

(b) Brussels Ia, which contains a gateway for the provision of services or the sale of goods. The Belgian legislature concluded that the application of the Belgian provision of Art 96, 1, a) PIL Code would prove less complicated than its EU counterpart would, since the Belgian domestic rules are not concerned with the allocation of jurisdiction within the EU.[31]

Be that as it may, some courts have interpreted Art 96, 1°, b) PIL Code in line with Art 7(1)(b) Brussels Ia. The Antwerp court of appeals has interpreted the place of 'execution' of a contractual obligation under Art 96, 1°, b) PIL Code – in this case: the obligation of a principal to pay damages to a commercial agent in case of recession of a concession agreement – as referring to 'the place where the service was provided'.[32] In this case, the commercial agent was deemed to deliver the service. Note that the court of appeals did not refer to the applicable law to locate the place of provision of the service. Moreover, the court did not refer to the Brussels I(a) Regulation in defining the place of performance autonomously. In an earlier case, the Antwerp court of appeals dealt with the question of jurisdiction over a dispute arising out of a contract for maritime transport from China to the port of Antwerp. The court held that it had jurisdiction, since the agreement was 'not only performed in China but also in Belgium, since the goods were shipped from China to Antwerp and were delivered in Antwerp'.[33] Once again, this decision echoed CJEU case law such as *Rehder*, in which the place of performance received a similar under Art 7(1)(b) Brussels Ia.[34] In another case before the commercial court of Ghent, it was unclear how the court located the place of 'execution' of the contractual obligation for the purpose of Art 96, 1°PIL Code. The dispute before it concerned the quality of goods delivered under a sale of goods agreement. The court, without reverting to the applicable law, found that the obligation to deliver was to be performed in Belgium. From other elements of the judgment, it appears that the goods were to be physically made available to the purchaser in Belgium.[35] It is noteworthy that in all three cases that were discussed here, the Belgian courts located the place of execution without reverting to the law applicable to the contract, which signals an aversion towards the conflicts method that was developed by the CJEU in *Tessili*.

Moreover, Art 96, 1°PIL Code does not only accord jurisdiction to the Belgian courts if the contractual obligation was or should have been performed in Belgium. In addition to said *locus executionis*, it uses the *place where the contractual obligation came into existence*. This ground was deemed especially relevant for disputes concerning the existence (*ontstaan/existence*) or validity of a contractual obligation.[36] It may also be relevant where a dispute relates to a negative obligation to refrain from certain acts, such

[31] Proposition de loi/Wetsvoorstel www.senate.be/www/webdriver?MItabObj=pdf&MIcolObj=pdf&MInamObj=pdfid&MItypeObj=application/pdf&MIvalObj=50331657, 170.

[32] Hof van Beroep Antwerpen (Antwerp Higher District Court), 19 May 2016, (2017–2018) *Rechtskundig Weekblad*, 705.

[33] Hof van Beroep Antwerpen (Antwerp Higher District Court), 12 May 2014, (2014) *Nieuw Juridisch Weekblad*, 893, *Primary Industries Trading GmbH/Kowa Shipping*.

[34] C-204/08 *Redher*; confirmed in Joined Cases C-274/16, C-447/16 and C-448/16 *flightright*.

[35] Ondernedmingsrechtbank Gent (Ghent Commercial Court), 15 April 2021, Tijdschrift@ipr.be 2021, 85.

[36] Proposition de loi/Wetsvoorstel, www.senate.be/www/webdriver?MItabObj=pdf&MIcolObj=pdf&MInamObj=pdfid&MItypeObj=application/pdf&MIvalObj=50331657, 121.

as a non-compete clause.[37] The place where the obligation came into existence should be determined under the law applicable to the obligation as designated by the Rome I Regulation.[38] However, it does not seem easy to apply in cases where the validity of an entire contract is at stake as opposed to the validity of a single contractual obligation. Therefore, this rule does not resolve the difficulty of applying the place-of-performance gateway to cases concerning the validity of a contract.[39]

The final element of interest is characterisation. Unlike other national codifications of private international law, *the Belgian PIL Code does not specify under which law characterisation should be conducted* nor what the object of characterisation ought to be. As to the object, Lenaerts argued that 'substantive rules of law' are to be subsumed under the categories of private international law. As to the law that should be applied to characterise those substantive rules for the purposes of Belgian private international law, he proposed the use of the *lex fori*, ie Belgian law.[40] Unfortunately, there is no record of Belgian cases where characterisation was at issue in the context of the PIL Code. It should be added that some Belgian courts have indeed been prone to applying the *lex fori*, ie Belgian law, when characterising claims under the Brussels Ia Regulation or the Rome I/II Regulations.[41]

(b)

Under Art 96, 2° PIL Code, the Belgian courts have jurisdiction over non-contractual obligations if either the damage or the event causing damage are (partially)[42] located in Belgium.[43] This double rule is explicitly inspired by the *Bier* case law of the CJEU.[44] The localisation of the connecting factors under Art 96, 2° PIL Code has attracted attention recently. Recent case law of the Belgian supreme court in ordinary (*Hof van Cassatie/Cour de Cassation*) has adopted the case law of the CJEU in interpreting A96, 2° PIL Code.[45] More particularly, in a case about financial loss suffered by

[37] T Kruger, 'Artikel 96' in J Erauw, M Fallon, E Guldix et al (eds), *Het wetboek internationaal privaatrecht becommentarieerd – Le code de droit interational privé commenté* (Intersentia, 2006) 493.

[38] Proposition de loi/Wetsvoorstel, www.senate.be/www/webdriver?MItabObj=pdf&MIcolObj=pdf&MInamObj=pdfid&MItypeObj=application/pdf&MIvalObj=50331657, 172; ibid 492.

[39] See Case C-366/13 *Profit Investment SIM*, Opinion of AG Bot, para 83 et seq.

[40] K Lenaerts, 'Systeemschets van het internationaal privaatrecht' [1983–84] Jura Falconis 465, 467–69.

[41] T Kruger and E Ulrix, 'Belgium' in P Beaumont and others (eds), *Cross-Border Litigation in Europe* (Hart Publishing 2017), 15; see Cour d'appel Mons (Mons Higher District Court), 8 May 2014, (2015) *Droit de la Consommation* 157 (note E Ulrix); Hof van Beroep Brussel (Brussels Higher District Court), 3 March 2009, (2009) *Jaarboek Handelspraktijken & Mededinging* 374.

[42] T Kruger, 'Artikel 96', 493–94.

[43] Art 96 International jurisdiction regarding contractual and non-contractual obligations. In addition to the cases provided for in the general provisions of the present statute, the Belgian courts have jurisdiction to hear actions with respect to obligations regarding: […] 1 […] 2° an obligation resulting from a tort, a) if, the fact giving rise to the obligation occurred or is likely to occur entirely or partially in Belgium; or b) if and to the extent that the damage occurred or is likely to occur in Belgium. 3° a quasi-contractual obligation, if the fact from which the obligation results took place in Belgium.

[44] Proposition de loi/Wetsvoorstel, www.senate.be/www/webdriver?MItabObj=pdf&MIcolObj=pdf&MInamObj=pdfid&MItypeObj=application/pdf&MIvalObj=50331657, 121.

[45] Hof van Cassatie, (Tijdschrift@IPR.be, 24 May 2018, 43) www.ipr.be/sites/default/files/rechtspraak/20183_20180524.pdf. See also Hof van Cassatie, (Tijdschrift@IPR.be 2016, 7 November 2016, 26) www.ipr.

a shareholder, the court readily applied the *Kolassa* ruling in answering the question whether a bank account can be regarded as the place where the damage occurred. That being said, it is unclear whether the case law of the CJEU should inform the application of Art 96, 2°PIL Code as a matter of principle. There most certainly appears to be a tendency to take into account the case law of the CJEU when applying the PIL Code. To illustrate, the president of the commercial court of Ghent, faced with an action aimed at obtaining an injunction to remove online advertising, held that the Belgian courts had jurisdiction over such a claim under Art 96, 2°PIL Code since the information was accessible in Belgium and therefore could have caused harm here.[46] While a reference to the case law of the CJEU is lacking, this decision clearly echoes CJEU judgments concerning the autonomous interpretation of Art 7(2) Brussels Ia such as *Wintersteiger* or *eDate advertising*. In another case, the Antwerp court of appeals applied the CJEU's *Réunion européenne* ruling on Art 7(2) Brussels Ia in a case involving Art 96, 2°PIL Code.[47] The ruling allowed the court to conclude that the port of destination is the place where the damage occurred in a non-contractual dispute concerning maritime transport between the owner of cargo and the ship owner. The court considered that a certain influence of the case law of the CJEU on the interpretation of Belgian private international law is inevitable, even though said case law is only relevant strictly speaking when applying EU private international law.[48]

Of particular note is the unclear relationship between the contract gateway of Art 96, 1° PIL Code and the tort gateway of Art 96, 2° PIL Code. In a case before the commercial court of Ghent, a claim relating to the delivery of goods was based concurrently on the seller's contractual and non-contractual liability. The court briefly held that it had jurisdiction over the contractual claim under Art 96, 1° PIL Code and over the non-contractual claim under the gateway for non-contractual claims under Art 96, 2°PIL Code.[49] Unfortunately, it did not entertain the impact of concurrent liabilities on the question of characterisation or on the relationship between the contract and tort gateway more specifically. Most likely, the solution would be sought in domestic Belgian substantive law.[50]

Moreover, Art 96, 3°PIL Code contains a jurisdictional basis for quasi-contractual obligations. The Belgian courts have jurisdiction over these obligations if the fact from which the obligation resulted took place in Belgium. Under Belgian law, such obligations comprise *negotiorum gestio*, restitution in case of undue payment and unjust

be/sites/default/files/rechtspraak/20164_20161107_1.pdf; G Van Calster, 'Lodi Trading, a lotta fog: Kolassa in the Belgian Supreme Court' (*GAVC*, 13 February 2017) www.gavclaw.com/2017/02/13/lodi-trading-a-lotta-fog-kolassa-in-the-belgian-supreme-court/.

[46] Voorz. rechtbank van koophandel Gent (Gent Commercial Court, summary proceedings), 8 October 2010, Thomas Electronics BVBA/Impact TEC Ltd, (2010) *Jaarboek Marktpraktijken*, 682. For a similar case, see Voorz. Brussel (Brussels District Court, summary proceedings), 24 May 2006, (2007) *Auteursrecht/Droit d'auteur*, 180.

[47] Hof van Beroep Antwerpen (Antwerp Higher District Court, 12 May 2014, (2014) *Nieuw Juridisch Weekblad*, 893, *Primary Industries Trading GmbH/Kowa Shipping*.

[48] ibid 895.

[49] Ondernemingsrechtbank Gent (Ghent Commercial Court), 15 April 2021, Tijdschrift@ipr.be 2021, 85.

[50] J Erauw, *Internationaal Privaatrecht* (Wolters Kluwer, 2009) 353.

enrichment.[51] This approach stands in stark contrast to that of the Brussels Ia Regulation, where such obligations may fall under Art 7(1) and 7(2) Brussels Ia or are sometimes not subjected to a rule of special jurisdiction altogether (as the recent *Hrvatske Šume* decision of the CJEU indicated).[52]

(c)

The Belgian courts have jurisdiction over actions brought against multiple defendants insofar as one defendant is domiciled or habitually resident in Belgium, unless the action has been introduced solely to remove a defendant from the jurisdiction of his domicile or habitual residence abroad (Art 5, § 1, para 2 PIL Code). Even though this provision was inspired by Art 6(1) Brussels I,[53] it does not require a connection between the actions let alone the risk of irreconcilable judgments for the Belgian courts to have jurisdiction over disputes involving multiple defendants.[54] Moreover, the PIL Code contains a particularly generous rule for related actions, including related actions involving multiple defendants. Under Art 9 PIL Code, Belgian courts with jurisdiction to hear an action also have jurisdiction to hear an action so closely related to it that it is expedient to hear and determine them together to avoid the risk of irreconcilable judgments if the actions were heard separately. In a maritime transport case, the Antwerp court of appeal held that under Art 9 PIL Code, there is no risk of irreconcilable judgments if claims concerning the loss of cargo are brought against multiple defendants on contractual and non-contractual bases.[55] Legal scholarship observed that Art 9 PIL Code may be construed in line with Art 28 Brussels I.[56]

(d)

Art 97 PIL Code contains provisions pertaining to the jurisdiction of the Belgian courts over employment contracts and consumer contracts:

> Art. 97. International jurisdiction with respect to consumer relationships and individual employment relationships
>
> § 1. In addition to the cases provided for in article 96 of the present statute, Belgian courts have jurisdiction to hear actions regarding an obligation referred to in article 96, brought by a natural person who acted with a purpose other than his professional

[51] T Kruger, 'Artikel 96', 494.
[52] Case C-242/20 *Hrvatske Šume*.
[53] Proposition de loi/Wetsvoorstel www.senate.be/www/webdriver?MItabObj=pdf&MIcolObj=pdf&MInamObj=pdfid&MItypeObj=application/pdf&MIvalObj=50331657, 32.
[54] B De Groote, 'Artikel 5' in J Erauw, M Fallon, E Guldix et al (eds), *Het wetboek internationaal privaatrecht becommentarieerd – Le code de droit interational privé commenté* (Intersentia, 2006) 29.
[55] Hof van Beroep Antwerpen (Antwerp Higher District Court), 12 May 2014, (2014) *Nieuw Juridisch Weekblad*, 893, *Primary Industries Trading GmbH/Kowa Shipping.*
[56] B De Groote, 'Artikel 9', 51–54.

activity, namely as consumer, against a party that has supplied or had to supply a good or service within the framework of its professional activities, if:

1 the consumer completed the actions required to execute or conclude the agreement in Belgium and had his habitual residence in Belgium at that time;

2 the good or service is supplied or should have been supplied to a consumer who had his habitual residence in Belgium upon placing the order, if the order was preceded by an offer or by publicity in Belgium.

§ 2. With respect to the individual labor relationship the contractual obligation is performed in Belgium in the sense of article 96 if the employee habitually carries out his duties in Belgium at the time of the dispute.

§ 3. An agreement that attributes international jurisdiction will only produce effects vis-à-vis the employee or consumer if entered into after the dispute has arisen.

Firstly, Art 97, § 3 PIL Code is stricter vis-à-vis choice of court agreements than the Brussels Ia Regulation, as it only allows choice of court after the dispute has arisen. The Brussels Ia Regulation also allows choice of court agreements that elaborate the available fora for the weaker party.

Secondly, the gateway for employment contracts ('individual labour relationships') in Art 97, § 2 PIL Code was informed by Art 5(1) Brussels Convention and the CJEU's *Ivenel* decision accompanying this provision.[57] In keeping with the spirit of this case law, Art 97, § 2 PIL Code defines the 'place of execution' under the gateway for contracts in Art 96, 1, b) PIL Code as the place of habitual employment. In so doing, the PIL Code does not provide for a bespoke, 'self sufficient' jurisdictional regime for employment contracts the likes of Arts 21–23 Brussels Ia.[58]

Thirdly, the consumer provision of Art 97, § 1 PIL Code was informed by Arts 13 and 14 of the 1968 Brussels Convention. This is apparent in the definition of 'consumer' (ie a natural person who acted with a purpose other than his professional activity). Under Art 97, § 1 PIL Code, the Belgian courts have jurisdiction if (1) the consumer completed the actions required to execute or conclude the agreement in Belgium and had his habitual residence in Belgium at that time or if (2) the good or service is supplied or should have been supplied to a consumer who had his habitual residence in Belgium upon placing the order, if the order was preceded by an offer or by publicity in Belgium. Once again Art 97, § 1 PIL Code is not self sufficient, since it applies 'in addition to the cases provided for in article 96 of the present statute' which in turn applies over and above the general rules contained in Chapter I of the PIL Code.[59]

Fourthly, the PIL Code does not contain a special rule of jurisdiction for insurance contracts. The only provision relating to insurance specifically is Art 106 PIL Code, which governs the law applicable to direct actions against insurers and therefore is akin to Art 18 Rome II.

[57] Case C-133/81 *Ivenel*, para 15.

[58] Confirmed in cour de travail Bruxelles (Brussels Higher Labour Court), 1 April 2009, RG no°49.521, Royaume d'Arabie Saoudite c/SA, (2011) *Sociaalrechtelijke Kronieken*, 335, para III.2.2.

[59] J Erauw, *Internationaal Privaatrecht* (Wolters Kluwer, 2009) 660.

Interestingly, Belgian domestic private international law sometimes extends protection to economically weaker parties who are not protected under Brussels Ia. The best-known example is the exclusive jurisdiction accorded to the Belgian courts by Art X.25. of the Code of Economic Law over commercial agents who have their principal establishment in Belgium.[60]

[60] See G Rühl, 'The Protection of Weaker Parties in the Private International Law of the European Union: A Portrait of Inconsistency and Conceptual Truancy' (2015) 10 *JPrivIntlL*, 343, who questions the lack of protection of agents under Brussels Ia.

Bulgaria

DAFINA SARBINOVA

Question 1

(a)

The main Bulgarian domestic piece of law governing Bulgarian courts' jurisdiction in cross-border civil and commercial matters (as per the Brussels Ibis Regulation's terminology) is the Private International Law Code of 2005 (*Кодекс на международното частно право*) ('PIL Code').[1] This legislative act represents the first Bulgarian private international law codification. It was adopted before Bulgaria's accession to the European Union ('EU') in 2007 with an ambition to regulate in a comprehensive manner the applicable law to private law relations with an international element, as well as the international jurisdiction of Bulgarian courts and the recognition and enforcement of foreign judgments in Bulgaria.[2] Such special legislative act was deemed necessary with a view to the accession of Bulgaria to EU. The operation of the four EU freedoms (of movement of goods, people, services, and capital) was considered impossible without clear and uncontradictory regulation of cross-border private law relations. In this line of reasoning, the adoption of PIL Code was a part of the process of preparing the national legislation for the accession of Bulgaria to the EU.[3]

Article 1(1) of the PIL Code outlines the scope of the act which encompasses: 1. the international jurisdiction of the Bulgarian courts (as well as of other authorities), and general rules for international civil procedures; 2. the law applicable to private law relationships with an international element; and 3. the recognition and enforcement of foreign judgments and authentic instruments in the Republic of Bulgaria. Conflict of laws rules are necessary for regulating private law relationships with an international

[1] Promulgated in State Gazette No 42 from 17 May 2005, as amended subsequently.

[2] Before the adoption of the PIL Code, separate conflict of laws provisions featured in several legislative acts including in the Family Code 1985 (repealed), the Contracts and Obligations Act 1950, the Commerce Act 1991, the Commercial Maritime Code 1970, and the International Commercial Arbitration Act 1988, while jurisdictional rules, including for cross-border disputes, could be found in the Civil Procedure Code 1952 (repealed).

[3] This is the explanation given in the Reasons for the Adoption of the PIL Code cited in Nikolay Natov, *Komentar na Kodeksa na mezhdunarodnoto chastno pravo* (Kniga 1, Ciela, 2006), 21. This reasoning represents part of *travaux preparatoires* of the act.

element. In accordance with the definition in Art 1(2) PIL Code – 'a private law relationship with an international element' is a 'a relationship involving two or more States'. The leading doctrinal study defines the legal relationship with international element as such affecting – personally, territorially, or both personally and territorially – the sovereignty of two or more States.[4] Such international element is also required in the context of determination of the international jurisdiction of the Bulgarian court. Disputes concerning purely domestic private law relationships do not invoke the issue of international jurisdiction and only trigger the application of internal domestic procedural rules contained in the Civil Procedure Code of 2007.[5]

The PIL Code is influenced by the modern continental private international law rules – in particular the Italian law of 1995 and the Belgian code of 2004 as well as the conventions adopted under the auspices of the Hague Conference of Private International Law. Further it was meant to harmonise Bulgarian law with EU law in the field of private international law which was applicable at the time of drafting of the Code – like 1980 Rome Convention, the draft Rome II Regulation and Regulation 44/2001.[6] To the extent domestic laws on jurisdiction may be binding solely on Bulgarian courts (as opposed to foreign courts), the relevant PIL Code jurisdictional rules are classified as unilateral.

The jurisdictional rules are situated in Chapter 2, Part 2, Articles from 4 to 28 (inclusive) of the PIL Code. The provision of Art 4(1) provides for a general competence of Bulgarian courts when the *defendant has habitual residence, statutory seat, or principal place of business in Bulgaria, or either the claimant or defendant is a Bulgarian national or a legal person registered in Bulgaria*. The latter jurisdictional rule is premised on the *forum actoris* principle and represents a basis for exorbitant jurisdiction of Bulgarian courts which only applies to the extent that the defendant is not domiciled in a Member (or Contracting) State under the meaning of the Brussels Ibis Regulation or the Lugano Convention of 2007. Pursuant to Art 4(2), actions against a legal person, where the dispute has arisen out of direct relationships with a branch of the said legal person, may be brought before Bulgarian courts if the branch is registered in Bulgaria.

[4] Vladimir Koutikov, *Private International Law of the Peoples' Republic of Bulgaria* 3rd edn (Nauka i Izkustvo, 1976) 14–18; this position is also shared in the practice of the national courts which hold that private relationships with an international element are relationships 'between independent parties standing on equal footing, connected with two or more States' and further accept that 'the international character of a private relationship triggers the applicability of the private international law rules for the competent authority' – Judgment No 223 from 22 January 2013, commercial case No 924/2011, of the Supreme Court of Cassation, Commercial Chamber.

[5] Promulgated in State Gazette No 59 from 20.07.2007, effective as of 1 March 2008, as amended subsequently.

[6] V Stancheva-Mincheva, *Commentary on Private International Law Code. Comparison with European Union Acts* (Sibi, 2010), 23–24. Y Zidarova and V Stancheva-Mincheva from Sofia University "St. Kliment Ohridski" are the Bulgarian scholars who were involved in the preparation of the draft of PIL Code – mainly its general and conflict of laws part. In this process, they were helped by the Max Planck Institute for Comparative and International Private Law in Hamburg. V Stancheva-Mincheva, 'The Reform of the Bulgarian Private International Law Implemented with Codification of 2005', in B Musseva and V Pandov (eds), *Changes in the Bulgarian Legal System in the Light of International Relations, International Law and EU Law, Essays Collection in honor of Prof. Dr. Yordanka Zidarova*, (Sofia University Publishing 2021), 35–64.

The PIL Code provides also for jurisdictional grounds concerning *specific type of civil and commercial law matters*, applied *in addition* to the rules of general jurisdiction. Bulgarian courts have *special jurisdiction over contractual matters* if the place of performance of the obligation is within Bulgaria or where the defendant has a principal place of business within Bulgaria (Art 15 PIL Code).

Bulgarian courts have *special jurisdiction over claims on damage sustained as a result of a tort or delict* where the harmful event was committed in Bulgaria or where the damage or part thereof occurred in Bulgaria (Art 18(1) PIL Code). In these circumstances direct action taken by the party who has suffered the damage against the insurer of the person claimed to be liable shall also be subject to the jurisdiction of Bulgarian courts (Art 18(2)).

Bulgarian courts are given *exclusive jurisdiction* under Art 12(1) in disputes concerning *in rem* rights in immovable property situated in the Republic of Bulgaria, the matters relating to enforcement or to security which such property constitutes, as well as the matters relating to transfer or establishment of rights *in rem* in such property. This provision should be considered derogated by Art 24(1) Brussels Ibis Regulation to the extent the personal scope of application of this provision is universal, ie regardless of the domicile of the parties to the dispute. Article 12(2) PIL Code grants Bulgarian courts special jurisdiction over actions on rights in rem in movable property if the property is located in Bulgaria in addition to the general jurisdiction under Art 4.

Article 13(1) provides Bulgarian courts with jurisdiction over disputed on copyrights and neighbouring rights where protection is sought for the territory of Bulgaria while Art 13(2) grants exclusive jurisdiction of Bulgarian courts in proceedings concerning industrial property rights, where the patent has been issued or the registration has been made in the Republic of Bulgaria. While the first jurisdictional basis is applicable to the extent the defendant is not domiciled in a Member (Contracting) State of the Brussels Ibis Regulation or the Lugano Convention, the second one is derogated in full by Art 24(4) Brussels Ibis Regulation.

Article 19 PIL Code grants exclusive jurisdiction to Bulgarian courts in matters relating to the legal status of legal persons registered in the Republic of Bulgaria. Bulgarian courts have exclusive jurisdiction over actions for establishing the inadmissibility, the voidness or the non-existence of the circumstances concerning corporate registration when such are required by law; as well as over disputes which have as their subject the nullity or the dissolution of a corporation or another legal person, or the revocation of acts of the corporate bodies, the protection of membership and the challenge of the transformation of a commercial corporation, where the corporation or the other legal person is registered in the Republic of Bulgaria. This provision should be considered derogated by Art 24(2) of Brussels Ibis Regulation.

Pursuant to Art 22 PIL Code the international jurisdiction of Bulgarian courts and other authorities is exclusive only in case this has been expressly said in the respective provision. The above mentioned exclusive jurisdictional rules coincide to a great extent with the scope of application of Art 24 of the Brussels Ibis Regulation, which expressly provides that the domicile of both parties to the dispute is irrelevant for the purposes of this provision. The matters which fall under the exclusive jurisdiction of the Bulgarian court under PIL Code concern: *in rem rights* in immovable property;

the validity of the constitution, nullity or dissolution of companies or other legal persons or the validity of acts/resolutions of their bodies; the validity of entries in public registers; the registration or validity of industrial property rights; and the enforcement of judgments. Article 22 PIL Code may be applicable to the extent it covers matters excluded from the scope of the Brussels Ibis Regulation and no other jurisdictional basis applies under the Regulation.

Bulgarian courts are granted jurisdiction when *the parties have submitted expressly or tacitly to their competence*. Express submission to Bulgarian courts is possible under the conditions laid down in Art 23 PIL Code with a written agreement of the parties. In case nothing on the contrary is stated, it is presumed that the court has been granted exclusive jurisdiction. This provision should be considered as derogated in full by Art 25 Brussels Ibis Regulation.

Article 23(1) PIL Code also provides for the *preconditions for the submission to the jurisdiction of a foreign court*. This is possible if the legal proceedings are brought to assert a proprietary right and the dispute does not fall within the exclusive jurisdiction of the Bulgarian courts. Such action may be submitted to a foreign court by agreement in writing between the parties. Where the Bulgarian court has been seized while such an agreement is in place, the defendant must raise an objection to the exercise of such jurisdiction within the time limit for response to the statement of claim and before the court has ruled on the merits of the dispute. This provision is not a ground for establishing the jurisdiction of the foreign court, but for recognition of a choice of court agreement in favour of the court of a third State, ie it may be relevant to the extent this state is not a Member (Contracting) State to Brussels Ibis Regulation and/or 2007 Lugano Convention and is not a party to 2005 Hague Choice of Court Convention.

The court practice takes the position that the choice of court agreements in favour of third states should be considered in line with its national jurisdictional rules and in particular Art 23 PIL Code. The Bulgarian court judgments which deal with this matter have been issued in proceedings for recognition and enforcement of foreign court judgments originating from third states where the jurisdictional issue is boiled down to the examination of indirect competence with regard to the derogative effect of the choice of court clauses. In one of the cases – Judgment No 260632 from 30.12.2020 under commercial case No 1743/2019 of Sofia City Court,[7] the choice of court agreement in favour of the Israeli court in Tel Aviv is found to be binding and effective in an exequatur proceeding under Art 117 PIL Code. This was also the case with the examination of a choice of court clause in favour of a Russian court in Judgment No 3978 from 6.07.2020 under civil case No 15843/2018 of Sofia City Court in the course of the proceedings for recognition and enforcement of a Russian court decision under the bilateral legal aid treaty with Russia.[8] Pursuant to Art 24 PIL Code where the jurisdiction of the Bulgarian

[7] Confirmed by the higher instance court, Judgment No 376 from 23 June 2021, commercial case No 418/2021 of Appellate Court Sofia.

[8] Art 117 et seq PIL Code provides for the prerequisites for the recognition and enforcement of foreign court judgments (outside the Brussels regime) in case no special bilateral treaty exists with respect to a specific country. To the extent there is a specific bilateral treaty of legal aid with Russia, the rules of this treaty are applied, while the relevant rules of PIL Code find subsidiary application – Judgment No 101 from 9.02.2010 r. under court case No 919/2009 of the Supreme Court of Cassation, Civil Law Chamber.

courts may be stipulated by an agreement, the said jurisdiction may be established even without any such agreement if the defendant accepts such jurisdiction expressly or tacitly through acts on the merits of the dispute within the time limit for response to the statement of claim.

The Bulgarian courts also have *jurisdiction to secure a claim* for which in substance they do not have international jurisdiction if the subject matter of the conservatory attachment is situated in Bulgaria and the foreign court judgment is entitled to recognition and enforcement in Bulgaria (Art 25 PIL Code).

(b)

The jurisdictional rules in the PIL Code apply only to transnational disputes to the extent the legal relation subject to dispute has to have an international element as defined in Art1(2) PIL Code, ie a relationship involving two or more Sates.

(c)

The jurisdictional rules of the Brussels Regime have not been expressly extended to non-EU defendants. However, the jurisdictional rules of the Brussels Regime have been taken into consideration in the process of drafting of the jurisdictional rules in Part Two, Chapter II of PIL Code 'Jurisdiction of Bulgarian Court and Other Authorities'. As it has been clarified already *most of the jurisdictional rules in the PIL Code follow closely the Brussels Regime but do not fully coincide with these rules*. In the process of drafting of the Code it was taken into account by the legislator that at the time of accession of Bulgaria to the EU, the respective EU legal instruments shall derogate the application of the PIL Code to a great extent and its provisions on the jurisdiction of the Bulgarian court shall remain *relevant only for relations involving third states, respectively non-EU defendants*. A notable departure of the Brussels Regime represents the *re-introduction of the exorbitant basis of general jurisdiction* of Bulgarian courts in Art 4(1) when *the claimant is a Bulgarian national or a legal person registered in Bulgaria*. PIL Code does not abandon the citizenship of the natural persons and the nationality of the legal entities in their capacity of claimants as a valid basis for jurisdiction.[9]

It is admitted in the *travaux preparatoires* (the Reasons for the Adoption of the PIL Code)[10] that such exorbitant basis for jurisdiction is internationally undesirable and a Bulgarian court judgment based on such a ground eventually shall not be recognised and enforced abroad. The relevance and the efficiency of this jurisdictional ground is left to the judgement of the claimant, ie it may be estimated as useful in case the defendant has assets on the territory of Bulgaria against which enforcement may be undertaken. The applicability of the Brussels Regime on the stage of the enforcement of a Bulgarian judgment grounded on exorbitant jurisdictional base against a non-EU defendant

[9] As it was present before the adoption of the PIL Code in Art 7(2) of the Civil Procedural Code (repealed).
[10] Published in N Natov, *Komentar na Kodeksa na mezhdunarodnoto chastno pravo*, 24.

even strengthens the effectiveness of this type of jurisdiction to the extent that such judgment becomes enforceable in all Member States.

As a rule, Bulgarian courts under the PIL Code do not have discretion whether to exercise their competence in case such competence derives from the provisions of the code. The court is obliged to check the existence of its international jurisdiction on its own motion (Art 28 PIL Code) to the extent the rules on jurisdiction are mandatory. The court ruling on the existence – or the lack of – jurisdiction is subject to appeal both to appellate and third instance court of cassation (if such third instance appeal is admissible to the dispute in question under the national rules of civil procedure). The lack of competence of the court makes the claim inadmissible while the resulting judgment (if any) is void. This statement finds argumentation also in Art 117 PIL Code pursuant to which the foreign judgment rendered by a court without competence is not subject to recognition and enforcement in Bulgaria (as a rule of indirect jurisdiction).[11]

(d)

The information notified under Art 76(1) Brussels Ibis Regulation and available at the website of the European Judicial Atlas in Civil Matters is exhaustive.[12]

The exorbitant rules of jurisdiction referred to in Art 5(2) and 6(2) of the Brussels Ibis Regulation may be found in Art 4(1), item 2 PIL Code according to which Bulgarian courts have jurisdiction when the applicant or the plaintiff is a Bulgarian national (citizen) or a legal person registered in the Republic of Bulgaria.

Below is the list of the conventions referred to in Art 69 of the Brussels Ibis Regulation, which cover the same matters as those to which the Regulation applies:

- the Convention between Bulgaria and Belgium on certain Judicial Matters, signed at Sofia on 2 July 1930,
- the Agreement between the People's Republic of Bulgaria and the Federal People's Republic of Yugoslavia on Mutual Legal Assistance, signed at Sofia on 23 March 1956, still in force between Bulgaria, Slovenia and Croatia,
- the Treaty between the People's Republic of Bulgaria and the Romanian People's Republic on Legal Assistance in Civil, Family and Criminal Matters, signed at Sofia on 3 December 1958,
- the Agreement between the People's Republic of Bulgaria and the People's Republic of Poland on Legal Assistance and Legal Relations in Civil, Family and Criminal Matters, signed at Warsaw on 4 December 1961,
- the Agreement between the People's Republic of Bulgaria and the People's Republic of Hungary on Legal Assistance in Civil, Family and Criminal Matters, signed at Sofia on 16 May 1966,

[11] T Todorov, *Private International Law. EU and the Republic of Bulgaria* 3rd edn (Sibi, 2010), 70.
[12] www.e-justice.europa.eu/350/EN/brussels_i_regulation_recast?BULGARIA&init=true&member=1.

- the Agreement between the People's Republic of Bulgaria and the Hellenic Republic on Legal Assistance in Civil and Criminal Matters, signed at Athens on 10 April 1976,
- the Agreement between the People's Republic of Bulgaria and the Czechoslovak Socialist Republic on Legal Assistance and Regulation of Relations in Civil, Family and Criminal Matters, signed at Sofia on 25 November 1976,
- the Agreement between the People's Republic of Bulgaria and the Republic of Cyprus on Legal Assistance in Civil and Criminal Matters, signed at Nicosia on 29 April 1983,
- the Agreement between the Government of the People's Republic of Bulgaria and the Government of the French Republic on Mutual Legal Assistance in Civil Matters, signed at Sofia on 18 January 1989,
- the Agreement between the People's Republic of Bulgaria and the Italian Republic on Legal Assistance and the Enforcement of Judgments in Civil Matters, signed at Rome on 18 May 1990,
- the Agreement between the Republic of Bulgaria and the Kingdom of Spain on Mutual Legal Assistance in Civil Matters, signed at Sofia on 23 May 1993,
- the Agreement between the People's Republic of Bulgaria and the Republic of Austria on Legal Assistance in Civil Matters and Documents, signed at Sofia on 20 October 1967.

Question 2

The Notion of Domicile Defined for the Purposes of Brussels Ibis Regulation

The provision of Art 63 of Brussels Ibis Regulation provides for autonomous definition of the notion of domicile when the party is a legal person. The domicile is the place where it has in the alternative its (a) statutory seat; (b) central administration; (c) principal place of business. This is the reason why it is certain and predictable what criteria the national court should use for the purposes of the qualification of the domicile of a legal person. In this regard, no notable problems are detected in the case law of Bulgarian courts.

On the other hand, there is no unitary criteria for the definition of the notion of domicile when it comes to natural persons. The Brussels Ibis Regulation (Art 62) refers to the internal law of the court seised for the purpose of determining whether the domicile of the natural person is in that Member State, while if the party is not domiciled in the Member State whose courts are seised of the matter, then, in order to determine whether the party is domiciled in another Member State, the court applies the law of that Member State.

To determine whether the court has jurisdiction to hear the dispute (and in case no universal jurisdictional basis under the Regulation is present), the Bulgarian court needs to define whether the defendant is domiciled in Bulgaria pursuant to its internal law.

This approach of the Regulation may potentially lead to different ultimate results in different Member States and may cause uncertainties and unpredictability in the process of the application of the Regulation.

The Bulgarian court practice and scholarship until this moment *has not reached a consensus on a single relevant definition for domicile of the natural person in Bulgaria* under the Regulation.[13] Three different criteria may be outlined as relevant. Pursuant to the first group of authors, the domicile shall relate to the so-called 'present residential address' (*настоящ адрес*) as defined under Art 94 of the Civil Registration Act, ie the address where the person resides. It is said that each person has only one present residential address. This criterion is adequate for determination of the domicile of the natural person because it represents a formal and easily ascertainable connection between the person and the State and has the purpose to be a proof of the fact that said person truly resides at this address. If the person relocates abroad this address should be no longer registered as an address on the territory of Bulgaria and shall be replaced by the name of the state where the person resides. The present residential address is deemed to express the maxim *actor sequitur forum rei* in the sense that the claimant should follow the defendant at the place where he actually resides. On the other hand, the competing criterion 'permanent residential address' (*постоянен адрес*) is related to an administrative requirement which applies to each Bulgarian citizen and does not always coincide with his actual residence. *De facto* it is equal to citizenship and may be of fictitious character.

A group of scholars argue that the domicile under the Regulation should be the *permanent* residential address of the natural person under the Civil Registration Act. The reasoning for this conclusion is grounded on the fact that the notion of permanent residential address replaces the previous legislative term 'place of residence' (*местоживеене*) which was equal to the notion of domicile for jurisdictional purposes. A third group of authors define the notion of domicile as equal to the term 'habitual residence' (*обичайно местопребиваване*) in Art 48(7) PIL Code. The argument for their position is that the PIL Code was adopted just before the accession of Bulgaria to EU and is in compliance with EU law. 'Habitual residence of a natural person' denotes the place where this person has settled predominantly to live. Habitual residence is determined without regard to any requirement for registration or authorisation of residence. In determining the place of habitual residence, special regard must be placed to circumstances of personal or professional nature arising from connections maintained between the person and the said place or from the intention of the person to establish such connections (Art 48(7)).

The practice of the Bulgarian courts also differs in the interpretation of the domicile of natural person under domestic law. Pursuant to some of the acts of the court of highest instance – the Supreme Court of Cassation – the domicile is equated to the habitual residence to the extent this is the definition given in Bulgarian domestic law under

[13] A summary of this problem may be found (in Bulgarian) in B Musseva, 'Action and Reaction between EU Law and Bulgarian Law in the Application of Brussels I Recast Regulation', (2019) Annual of the Law Faculty of Sofia University "St. Kliment Ohridski", 397–403.

Art 48(7) PIL Code,[14] while others argue that it should follow the notion of present residential address.[15] In accordance with a third line of reasoning of the Supreme Court of Cassation, the domicile should be determined as the place where the person truly resides regardless of any formal requirement for registration.[16]

This approach solves the problem with the identification of the domicile of Bulgarian citizens residing *de facto* in other Member States without complying with their administrative obligation under Bulgarian law to make the relevant de-registration of their present residential address in Bulgaria. This latter understanding is reaffirmed in recent *Ruling No 1166 of 30.04.2022 under civil case No 810/2022 of Appellate Court – Sofia.* The court takes the view that the notion of domicile of a natural person under the Regulation stays closer to the term 'habitual residence' under the PIL Code compared to the notion of administrative address defined under the Civil Registration Act.

The Notion of Domicile Defined for the Purposes of Application of Domestic Law Jurisdictional Rules

The notion of 'domicile' which from a perspective of comparative law is one of the leading criteria for determination of the jurisdiction of the court and the applicable law to personal status (specifically in the countries belonging to the Anglo-American legal tradition), is not recognised as such under Bulgarian PIL.

Relevant criteria for determination of the general jurisdiction of the Bulgarian courts concerning natural persons is the habitual residence of the defendant and the citizenship of the claimant; while for legal persons these are the statutory seat or the place of the management of the defendant, as well as the registration (which is equal to incorporation) of the applicant in Bulgaria. Broadly speaking, the criteria used for defining the domicile of the legal persons falls into the notion of domicile of a legal person under Art 63 Brussels Ibis Regulation.

Question 3

Bulgarian domestic law provides for several different connecting factors other than domicile in the rules for general jurisdiction for matters regulated by the Brussels Ibis Regulation. General jurisdiction is normally defined in opposition to special jurisdiction, as the jurisdictional basis where the court finds itself competent to hear the case regardless of the particular type in substance of the dispute; it may be a dispute related to contractual or quasi-contractual relation, commercial law, labour law, a dispute related to IP rights, etc. This type of jurisdiction is predominantly based on the connection

[14] Court Statement No 9 from 13.01.2010, private civil case No 435/2009, Civil Chamber of the Supreme Court of Cassation.

[15] Court Statement No 886 from 9.11.2011, private commercial case No 130/2011, Commercial Chamber of the Supreme Court of Cassation.

[16] Court Statement No 543 from 16.06.2016, private civil case No 1754/2016, Civil Chamber of the Supreme Court of Cassation.

(direct or indirect) between the case and the parties to the dispute while the subject matter of the dispute is irrelevant. The PIL Code includes rules on general jurisdiction grounded, on one hand, on the connection with the defendant, which reflects the principle *actor sequitor forum rei*, and on the other, on the connection with the claimant, which reflects the principle *forum actoris*. Article 4 PIL Code (entitled 'General jurisdiction') envisages the basis for establishing general jurisdiction of the Bulgarian courts. Firstly, they are competent if the defendant has a habitual residence, statutory seat or principal place of business in the Republic of Bulgaria (Art (4)(1), item 1). The notion of habitual residence refers to defendants who are natural persons, while the connecting factors related to the statutory seat, or the principal place of business, relate mostly to legal persons.

The provision of Art 48(7) PIL Code gives *ex lege* definition of the term 'habitual residence' (*обичайно местопребиваване*) of a natural person in the sense that this is the place where the 'person has settled predominantly to live without this being related to a need of registration or authorization of residence or settlement'. Habitual residence is considered as factual and informal situation. For the purpose of determining this place 'special regard must be given to circumstances of personal or professional nature arising from sustained connections of the person with the said place or from the intention of the said person to establish such connections'. What is required are genuine connections of the person with place which have been created by way of personal and professional connections[17] This definition of habitual residence is given for the use of this notion both for jurisdictional and choice of law purposes when the rules of PIL Code apply. As it has been explained in the answer to question 2 above, according to some authors in Bulgarian scholarship and the prevailing case law, this criterion is also used for determining the domicile of the defendant when it is a natural person under Art 62 of the Brussels Ibis Regulation. Nevertheless, this use of the term is still under debate and there are also arguments (in scholarship and court practice) that the domicile of the natural person under the Regulation should be his/her present/current (or permanent) residential address pursuant to the Civil Registration Act.

Another connecting factors for establishing general jurisdiction of the Bulgarian courts related to legal persons are the place of their (a) *statutory seat* and (b) *principal place of business*. The statutory seat (*седалище по устав*) is normally a circumstance which may be found in the charter, the articles of incorporation or anther document evidencing the formation of the organisation. The statutory seat of the defendant (which coincides with the place of incorporation under Bulgarian law) may relate not only to legal persons but also to a sole merchant. The latter is a natural person who performs commercial activity and is subject to registration with the Commercial Registry and the Registry for Non-Profit Entities at the Bulgarian Registration Agency (held electronically and publicly available registry) in the same way as the other merchants under Bulgarian law which are legal persons. The non-profit organisations (including the circumstances concerning their statutory seat) are also subject to registration with the registry held by the Registration Agency.

[17] Y Zidarova and V Stancheva-Mincheva, 'Gesetzbuch über das Internationale Privatrecht der Republik Bulgarien', *RabelsZ* 71 (2007), 414.

In addition, the real place of business (*действително управление*) of the defendant may be used as a connecting factor if it does not coincide with the statutory seat in Bulgaria, ie in case the legal entity is not registered in Bulgaria. The place of business of the defendant should be based on the existence of economical connection of the legal entity with the territory of the State. This is normally the place where the management bodies of the entity adopt resolutions concerning the activities of the entity, ie the place where the administrative centre of the entity is.[18] To a large extent, the notion of real place of business should relate with the term for 'central administration' under Art 63(1)(b) Brussels Ibis Regulation. Further, Bulgarian courts have general jurisdiction if the defendant has a branch registered in Bulgaria where the dispute has arisen out of direct relationships with that branch of the legal person (Art 4(2) PIL Code).

Bulgarian courts also have general type jurisdiction on an exorbitant (extended) ground premised on the *forum actoris* principle when the claimant is (1) a Bulgarian citizen or is (2) a legal person registered in the Republic of Bulgaria (Art 4(1), item 2 PIL Code). The *Bulgarian citizenship of the claimant* is kept as a connecting factor of personal connection with the territory of the state of the court in the PIL Code deliberately and knowingly from the side of the legislator that after the accession of Bulgaria to EU it shall be used only vis-à-vis non-EU defendants. The Bulgarian legislator leaves to the discretion of the claimant to decide whether to use this jurisdictional ground with a view to the probable impossibility for recognition and enforcement of such Bulgarian judgment abroad.[19] In case the claimant has a double nationality, the relevant citizenship is the Bulgarian one – Art 3 Bulgarian Citizenship Act.

If the claimant is a legal person than the relevant connecting factor is *the registration of that person in the Republic of Bulgaria*. As already explained all commercial and non-profit entities are registered in the publicly available Commercial Registry and Registry for Non-Profit Entities at the Bulgarian Registration Agency for the purposes of their incorporation. The use of this connecting factor from such applicants has an effect similar to the one outlined for the applicants when they are Bulgarian citizens.

This exorbitant jurisdictional rule is used rarely in the court practice of Bulgarian courts and may serve the purpose of the missing *forum necessitatis* rule in Bulgarian law: *Judgment No 852 of 21.04.2020 under civil case No. 1025/2019 of Appellate Court – Sofia*. It was applied as a jurisdictional ground for a tort claim initiated by Bulgarian citizens against Libyan nationals who were also employees of the Libyan Chief Investigation Office. The claim stands for compensation of pecuniary and non-pecuniary damages suffered by the Bulgarian citizens (medical specialists) during their detention in the process of a criminal trial in Libya where the Bulgarian medical specialists were humiliated and tortured by the Libyan nationals (the Libyan HIV Trial). The unlawful behaviour was conducted on the territory of Libya in the period 09.02.1999–24.07.2007 and expressed itself in caucusing isolation, traumatic injuries, torture, humiliating and inhuman treatment to the Bulgarian citizens.

[18] V Zheliazkova, *Commercial Companies in Private International Law* (Ciela, 2009), 117.

[19] The PIL Code itself in Art 117 introduces the requirement – the jurisdiction of the foreign court not to be grounded only on the nationality of the plaintiff or its registration in the State of the court seised, as a condition for recognition and enforcement of a foreign judgment in Bulgaria (applicable to judgments originating from non-EU Member States).

Question 4

Forum necessitatis is not envisaged as a jurisdictional base in Bulgarian domestic law. Neither does the court practice refer to this notion. Domestic rules on international jurisdiction provide a broad base for the competence of the Bulgarian court, including on exorbitant grounds (like the Bulgarian citizenship or the corporate registration of the claimant in Bulgaria) which may in fact be used instead of the missing *forum necessitatis* rule vis-à-vis defendants domiciled in non-EU Member States.

Forum necessitatis is examined in the Bulgarian legal scholarship in the broader terms of the constitutional principle of *effective defence before the court* of the rights and the legitimate interests of the individuals and the legal persons embedded in Art 56 of the Bulgarian constitution.[20] This constitutional text has been elaborated in the interpretation given by the Constitutional Court of Bulgaria in its Judgment No 9 from 1998[21] pursuant to which 'It [the right of defence under Art 56] has a broad scope of application, but above all it presupposes a duty of the State through the adopted legislation and its application to guarantee a right of legal defence (adequate legal remedies) for the citizens to protect their rights or legitimate interests if violated or endangered in front of the court or the administrative bodies'.[22]

In the field of international jurisdiction of the court, the principle of effective court defence is also seen in its negative reflection and a reason for jurisdictional self-restriction in the sense that (1) Bulgarian courts should not exercise their jurisdiction if the court of another State has exclusive jurisdiction to hear the case (*principium non interventionis*) and/or (2) Bulgarian courts should not exercise their jurisdiction if the resulting Bulgarian judgment shall not be recognised or enforced abroad (*principium respectus ipsius*).[23]

Theoretically, in addition to Art 56 of the Bulgarian constitution, normative justifications for *forum necessitatis* are also sought in the right to a fair trial under Art 6 of the European Convention on Human Rights and the right to an effective remedy and to a fair trial under Art 47 of the EU Charter of Fundamental Rights.[24]

Question 5

(a)

Under national law, Bulgarian courts have special jurisdiction over contractual matters if the place of performance of the obligation is within Bulgaria or where the defendant has a principal place of business within Bulgaria (Art 15 PIL Code).

[20] Art 56 of the Constitution of the Republic of Bulgaria reads the following: 'Every person shall have a right to legal defense whenever his rights or legitimate interests are violated or endangered. He shall have the right to be accompanied by legal counsel when appearing in front of a State body'.

[21] Promulgated in State Gazette No 45/1998.

[22] Relevant here is also Judgment No 14 from 04 November 2014 of the Constitutional Court of Bulgaria.

[23] T Todorov, *Private International Law. EU and the Republic of Bulgaria*, 71–72.

[24] V Pandov, *Mezhdunarodna kompetentnost po grazhdanski i targovski dela* (Ciela, 2018), 296.

As a rule, special jurisdiction under the PIL Code is not an alternative to the general jurisdiction in Art 4 PIL Code in the sense that it may exist as a single standing ground even when neither of the conditions under Art 4 PIL Code is present. Bulgarian courts follow the principle that in interpreting provisions of domestic law origin, they should follow *lex fori*. Although the jurisdictional rules of the PIL Code have been drafted with a view to the rules of the then existing Brussels Regime, they were specifically tailored in the eyes of the law makers as rules operating towards non-Member States.

There is no official or generally accepted interpretation of the notion 'the place of performance of the obligation in Bulgaria' – whether it should be considered in each case depending on the ground on which the claim is based, or it should be defined in autonomous manner. Nevertheless, there are suggestions in case law that the place of performance of the obligation is the place of delivery of the goods pursuant to the agreed between the parties, ie the place where the characteristic performance of the contract should be effected – Judgment No 260135 from 9.10.2020 under commercial case No 2075/2019 of Sofia City Court.

(b)

In addition to the grounds envisaged in Art 4 PIL Code, the Bulgarian courts have special jurisdiction over actions on damage sustained as a result of a tort or delict where *the harmful event was committed in Bulgaria* or where *the damage or part thereof occurred in Bulgaria* (Art 18(1) PIL Code). In these circumstances a direct claim taken by the party who has suffered the damage against the insurer of the person claimed to be liable shall also be subjected to the jurisdiction of Bulgarian courts (Art 18(2)).

(c)

Article 20 PIL Code provides for the jurisdiction of the Bulgarian court in claims brought against a number of defendants. The Bulgarian courts have jurisdiction over claims brought against several defendants if the grounds for jurisdiction exist in respect of one of them.

(d)

There are special protective jurisdictional rules with respect to consumer and employment contracts, but no such rules exist for insurance contracts or other matters (eg contract for commercial agency) where it may be seen fit to have rules for protective jurisdiction.

According to Art 16(1), in addition to the jurisdictional grounds in Art 4, the Bulgarian courts have jurisdiction over claims brought by a consumer where the consumer is habitually resident in the Republic of Bulgaria and the conditions for application of the conflict of law rule for determining the applicable law to consumer contracts under Art 95(2) are present. These conditions are as follows: (1) the conclusion of the contract in the State of the habitual residence of the consumer was preceded by a specific invitation addressed to the consumer or by advertising, and the consumer had taken in that State all the steps required for the conclusion of the contract, or (2) the other party or an agent of the said party received the consumer's order in that State, or (3) the contract is for the sale of goods and, for the purpose of inducing the consumer to buy goods, the seller arranged the consumer's journey to another State where the consumer gave his or her order. As it can be noticed, these conditions under the PIL Code follow the conditions in the Brussels Convention. There is no mention of 'directing' the activities of the commercial party to the State of the habitual residence of the consumer. Further, an agreement on choice of court is admissible solely if entered into after the dispute has arisen.

According to Art 16(1), in addition to the jurisdictional grounds in Art 4, the Bulgarian courts have jurisdiction over employment disputes, where the employee habitually carries out his or her work in the Republic of Bulgaria. An agreement on choice of court is admissible solely if entered into after the dispute has arisen.

The scope of application of the protective jurisdictional rules under PIL Code is extremely limited due to the fact that the Brussels Ibis Regulation has introduced universal grounds for jurisdiction regardless of the domicile of the commercial party.

Croatia

TENA HOŠKO AND DORA ZGRABLJIĆ ROTAR

Question 1

(a)

Croatia does not have a civil code or a commercial code. Instead, the dominant sources of private law are statutes governing individual fields of law such as the law of obligations, property law, inheritance law, private international law, etc.[1]

Private international law has been codified in Croatia since 1982 when the 'Act concerning the resolution of conflicts of laws with the provisions of other countries in certain matters' (*Zakon o rješavanju sukoba zakona s propisima drugih zemalja u određenim odnosima*)[2] (hereinafter: 1982 PILA) came into force. The name of this Act is somewhat misleading, since the Act does not govern only conflict of laws, but also other aspects of private international law in the wider sense, such as international jurisdiction and recognition and enforcement of foreign judgments.

The 1982 PILA was originally enacted as a federal statute of the former Socialist Federative Republic of Yugoslavia.[3] The original text of the law was taken over as the law of Croatia in 1991, when the country declared independence.[4] The 1982 PILA has not been affected by the major legislative reforms carried out in 1990s, when Croatia underwent a transition from a socialist economy to a market-based economy.

Rules of international jurisdiction were found primarily in the 1982 PILA. However, additional rules were also incorporated into the Croatian Civil Procedure Act (hereinafter: CPA).[5]

[1] H Ernst, 'General Introduction' in T Josipović (ed), *Introduction to the Law of Croatia* (Wolters Kluwer, 2014) 4.

[2] Zakon o rješavanju sukoba zakona s propisima drugih zemalja u određenim odnosima, Narodne novine no 53/91.

[3] Službeni list SFRJ nos 43/82, 72/82.

[4] D Babić 'Private International Law' in T Josipović (ed), *Introduction to the Law of Croatia* (Wolters Kluwer, 2014) 439. The only major change since 1982 was that the rules on recognition and enforcement of arbitral awards were abolished and replaced by the Arbitration Act of 2001 (Narodne novine no 88/01, Art 50).

[5] Narodne novine nos 53/1991, 91/1992, 58/1993, 112/1999, 88/2001, 117/2003, 88/2005, 02/2007, 84,123/2008, 57/2011, 148/2011, 25/2013, 89/2014.

With the need for reform of private international law, the bill for a new Private International Law Act was passed by the Croatian Parliament on 4 October 2017 and came into effect on 29 January 2019 (hereinafter: 2017 PILA).[6]

Both the 1982 PILA and the 2017 PILA are comprehensive codifications of private international law. Although the codifications are comprehensive, some areas of private international law governing certain specific areas are codified in special laws. Thus, for example, private international rules relating to maritime law are codified in the Maritime Code.[7]

Croatia joined the European Union on 1 July 2013. Since that date, EU regulations take precedence over national rules on international jurisdiction that coincide with their scope of application. For the purpose of the Regulations' transitory provisions, the date of Croatia's accession is treated as the day of the entry into force of the Regulations.[8]

The Brussels I Regulation[9] applies to determination of jurisdiction in legal proceedings instituted and to documents formally drawn up or registered as authentic instruments after 1 July 2013 (Art 66 Brussels I Regulation).[10] Thus, in proceedings commenced after 1 July 2013, Croatian courts examine its jurisdiction by applying the private international law rules from Brussels I Regulation. In 2012, the Regulation was replaced by its new and amended version, the Brussels Ibis Regulation,[11] which came into effect on 10 January 2015. Consequently, in proceedings commenced after 10 January 2015, Croatian courts apply the Brussels Ibis Regulation to examine jurisdiction in civil and commercial matters.

Rules applicable to international jurisdiction over non-EU defendants are a part of the 1982 PILA in legal proceedings instituted before 29 January 2019. Some additional rules for those cases are also found into the CPA. In cases instituted after the 2017 PILA came into force on 29 January 2019, the rule on international jurisdiction over non-EU defendants is found in the 2017 PILA. The 2017 PILA extends the rules of Brussels Ibis Regulation to cases over a non-EU defendant. The additional rules found in the CPA were also applicable until they were revoked by CPA amendments adopted by the Croatian Parliament in April 2022.

(b)

According to Art 1 of the 2017 PILA the rules on jurisdiction contained in the Act apply specifically to cross-border disputes. A similar provision is found in the 1982 PILA as well, thus the rules of that Act also apply only to disputes with an international element.

[6] Zakon o međunarodnom privatnom pravu, Narodne novine no 101/17.

[7] Pomorski zakonik, Narodne novine nos 181/04, 76/07, 146/08, 61/11, 56/13, 26/15.

[8] Art 2 Act Concerning the Conditions of Accession of the Republic of Croatia to the Treaty on European Union, the Treaty on the Functioning of the European Union and the Treaty Establishing the European Atomic Energy Community.

[9] Council Regulation (EC) no 44/2001 of 22 December 2000 on jurisdiction and the recognition and enforcement of judgments in civil and commercial matters [2001] OL L12/1.

[10] D Babić, 'Vremenske granice primjene uredaba 44/2001 i 1215/2012 u Hrvatskoj' in J Garašić(ed), *Europsko građansko procesno pravo* (Narodne novine, 2013) 140.

[11] Regulation (EU) no 1215/2012 of the European Parliament and of the Council of 12 December 2012 on jurisdiction and the recognition and enforcement of judgments in civil and commercial matters (recast) [2012] OJ L351/1.

The additional rules on international jurisdiction that were a part of the CPA applied primarily to domestic disputes, but were also applicable to cross-border disputes when certain conditions have been fulfilled. The CPA regulated international jurisdiction indirectly in Art 27, by prescribing the application of the rules of territorial jurisdiction to determine the international jurisdiction of the Croatian courts, and directly in Art 58 of the CPA.[12]

Art 27 of the CPA stated that international jurisdiction of Croatian courts can be established through the application of the rules of territorial jurisdiction when no express provisions on international jurisdiction are provided in law or international agreement.[13] Art 58 para1 and 58 para3 of the CPA regulated the rules of special international jurisdiction over defendants over which there is no general jurisdiction in Croatia.[14]

(c)

The new Croatian 2017 PILA that came into force on 29 January 2019, and applies in cases instituted after that date, has explicitly extended the rules of Brussels Ibis Regulation to cases in which the defendant is not domiciled in the EU.

Article 46 of the 2017 PILA regulates the application of the Brussels Ibis Regulation. The first subparagraph directs the courts to apply the Brussels Ibis Regulation when determining jurisdiction in civil and commercial matters (Art 46 para 1 PILA). The provision only serves as a reminder and, as other similar provisions in the 2017 PILA, aims at providing guidelines to the courts regarding the application of various sources of private international law.[15]

The second paragraph explicitly extends the rules of the Brussels Ibis Regulation over non-EU defendants. It reads: 'Jurisdiction of the court of the Republic of Croatia is governed by the rules of Chapter II, sections 2 and 3 of the Regulation mentioned in subparagraph 1 of this Article in all cases when the defendant, within the meaning of that Regulation, is not domiciled in a Member State of European Union'.

The ratio behind widening of the scope of application of the Brussels regime lies in avoiding the dualism of jurisdictional rules which would make the application of private international law rules easier for courts.[16]

[12] D Babić, *Međunarodna nadležnost za ugovorne sporove u europskom, hrvatskom i američkom pravu* (PhD Thesis, Zagreb 2005) 210.

[13] 'A court in the Republic of Croatia shall have jurisdiction over a trial when its jurisdiction over disputes with an international element is explicitly laid out in the law or international agreement. If the law or international agreement does not contain any explicit provision on the jurisdiction of a court in the Republic of Croatia over specific types of disputes, the court in the Republic of Croatia shall also have jurisdiction over trials in this type of disputes when its jurisdiction originates in the provisions on territorial jurisdiction of courts in the Republic of Croatia'.

[14] The Act states general territorial jurisdiction. Even though general international jurisdiction would be nomotechnically better, it has no practical significance. Babić, *Međunarodna nadležnost za ugovorne sporove u europskom, hrvatskom i američkom pravu* 220.

[15] T Hoško, 'Novo uređenje međunarodnog privatnog prava u RH – Zakon o međunarodnom privatnom pravu' 1 (2018) 1 *Zakonitost* 19, 23.

[16] H Sikirić, 'Zakon o međunarodnom privatnom pravu' *Tradicionalno XXXIII. savjetovanje – Aktualnosti Hrvatskog zakonodavstva i pravne prakse, Godišnjak 25* [2018] 61, 111–112.

The third paragraph extends the scope of the Brussels Ibis Regulation to choice-of-court agreements in favour of courts of non-EU MS. Namely according to Art 46 para 3 'the parties are free to choose a court of a non-EU MS as the competent court, unless a Croatian court or another EU MS court has exclusive jurisdiction. That choice-of-court agreement will be governed by the rules of section 7 of the Regulation mentioned in subparagraph 1 of this Article'.

The 1982 PILA, which was applicable before 29 January 2019, provides a rule on general jurisdiction in Art 46. Primary rule is enshrined in para 1 which provides for jurisdiction of Croatian courts if the defendant has its domicile or seat in Croatia.

Except from general jurisdiction, the 1982 PILA also included rules on subsidiary general jurisdiction. Under Art 46 para 2 of the 1982 PILA, Croatian courts are competent over a defendant who has no domicile in Croatia or any other state, but has a residence in Croatia. Also, according to Art 46 para 3 of the 1982 PILA, subsidiary general jurisdiction is given to Croatian courts if all the parties are Croatian nationals and the defendant has residence in Croatia.

The general jurisdiction may also attract jurisdiction for other co-defendants, even if they have no seat in Croatia.

Attraction of jurisdiction is foreseen in Art 46 para 4 of the 1982 PILA which states that if there are several material co-defendants, the court of the Republic of Croatia has jurisdiction also when one of the co-defendants is domiciled or has its seat in the Republic of Croatia.

The Croatian court will have jurisdiction based on Art 46 para 4 1982 PILA if two conditions are fulfilled: firstly, one of the co-defendants has its domicile (for natural persons) or seat (for legal persons) in the Republic of Croatia and secondly, the co-defendants are material co-defendants. Both conditions need to be fulfilled cumulatively. This is also confirmed in the Croatian court practice.[17] The effect is that if one of the conditions is not fulfilled, the court will remain competent over the defendant it has been competent from the outset, but its jurisdiction will not be expanded to other defendant(s).[18] In other words, there will be no attraction of jurisdiction.

Besides general international jurisdiction, Croatian courts may also have special international jurisdiction over a certain defendant under 1982 PILA. Such special jurisdiction exists for the claims arising out of laws of obligation in Art 55 of the 1982 PILA.[19] Art 55 of the 1982 PILA specifies that special jurisdiction over a certain defendant that has no domicile or seat in the Republic of Croatia exists if several conditions are fulfilled. Jurisdiction will exist for obligations that have arisen or must be performed in the Republic of Croatia if the defendant with domicile or seat abroad has

[17] Vrhovni Sud (Supreme Court), Judgment no Rev 17/07-2, 10 May 2007; Judgment no Rev 285/04-2, 7 June 2005; Judgment no Gr1 580/04-2, 31 January 2005; Judgment no II Rev-49/1998-2, 8 March 2000; Judgment no II Rev-84/1994-2, 22 May 1996; Judgment no Rev 3667/1993-2, 20 January 1994; Judgment no II Rev 103/1992-2, 4 February 1993.

[18] Supreme Court, Judgment no Rev 3667/1993-2, 20 January 1994 determined that no jurisdiction towards the second and third defendant exists because they are not material co-defendants with the first defendants.

[19] M Dika, G Knežević, S Stojanović, *Komentar Zakona o međunarodnom privatnom i procesnom pravu* (Nomos 1990) 202; P Bosnić, *Hrvatsko međunarodno privatno i procesno pravo, Knjiga II* (Pravni fakultet Sveučilišta u Splitu 2003) 44; T Varadi, B Bordaš, G Knežević, V Pavić, *Međunarodno privatno parvo* 15th edn (Univerzitet u Beogradu – Pravni fakultet, 2016) 506–507.

its representative or agency in the Republic of Croatia or if the seat of the organisation of associated labour to which the discharge of business has been entrusted is in the Republic of Croatia.

There are therefore three conditions that need to be fulfilled cumulatively:[20]

1. obligations in question have arisen in or must be performed in the Republic of Croatia and
2. the defendant has domicile or seat abroad and
3. the defendant has its representative or agency in the Republic of Croatia or the seat of the organisation of associated labour to which the discharge of business has been entrusted is in the Republic of Croatia.

(d)

The information provided pursuant to Art 76 para 1a Brussels Ibis Regulation is now, as of the latest legislative amendments of the Civil Procedure Act in 2022, exhaustive.

The only information provided is on the application of the provisions of 2017 PILA. The available information concerns Art 46 of the 2017 PILA which explicitly states that the Brussels Ibis Regulation applies within the scope of that Regulation, and extends its application to include situations involving residents of third countries.

It should be mentioned that the provisions on the additional rules on international jurisdiction found in the Croatian CPA were not mentioned. Although the rules of CPA apply primarily to domestic disputes, the CPA regulated international jurisdiction indirectly in Art 27, by prescribing the application of the rules of territorial jurisdiction to determine the international jurisdiction of the Croatian courts, and directly in Art 58 of the CPA.[21]

The information provided pursuant to Art 76 1b and 1c Brussels Ibis Regulation is exhaustive.

Question 2

Autonomous definitions of a domicile of a natural person and the seat of a legal person have been for the first time introduced in the Croatian private international law with the entry into force of the 2017 PILA.

Domicile of natural persons is defined in Art 4 of the 2017 PILA as 'the place where a natural person has settled with the intent to permanently live at that place'. The definition embodies two elements that need to be cumulatively present. The first one is an objective prerequisite according to which a person has to live at that place *(corpus)*. The second criterion is a subjective one *(animus manendi)* according to which a person has to intend to reside at the place permanently. This definition corresponds to the

[20] Also confirmed in Croatian court practice, see Supreme Court, Judgment no II Rev 79/91, 21 January 1992.

[21] Babić, *Međunarodna nadležnost za ugovorne sporove u europskom, hrvatskom i američkom pravu*, 210.

definition that is commonly found in the Croatian legal doctrine.[22] It also corresponds to the definition found in the Croatian Foreigners Act (*Zakon o strancima*)[23] that is used as the relevant definition for the purpose of private international law cases where the courts apply the 1982 PILA.

Domicile of a legal person is defined in Art 6 of the 2017 PILA. According to that provision 'the seat of a legal person is the place established as such by its statute or other corresponding act. When the seat cannot be determined in accordance with that definition, it will be held that the seat is in the place where central administration of the legal person is situated'. The 1982 PILA did not include a definition of the seat of a legal person.

When it comes to the application of the Brussels Ibis Regulation over EU defendants, the court will apply Art 62 of the Brussels Ibis Regulation, which does not provide an autonomous definition of the notion of domicile for natural persons but a rule on the applicable law. In the case when the court will have to decide whether a person is domiciled in Croatia for the purposes of application of the Brussels Ibis Regulation, it will use the definition provided in Art 4 of the 2017 PILA. On the other hand, the Brussels Ibis Regulation provides a definition of the domicile of a legal person in Art 63 as the statutory seat, central administration, or principal place of business of the legal person. Thus, the Croatian court will determine the domicile of the legal person in cases over an EU defendant in accordance with the definition provided in the Regulation.

However, when the Croatian court applies the rules of the Brussels Ibis Regulation over non-EU defendants in accordance with the extension provided in Art 46 para 2 2017 PILA, the courts will not determine the domicile in the same way it would have in a case over an EU defendant. Namely, the provision of the Croatian PILA that extends the application of the Brussels I Regulation over non-EU defendants does not include the extension of the rules on domicile of natural and legal person, ie Arts 62 and 63 of the Brussels Ibis Regulation.

When it comes to the application of Art 62 of the Brussels Ibis Regulation on the domicile of natural persons that is not surprising since the rule on applicable law to determine a person's domicile is construed in a way that it should only be applicable when the courts determine whether a party is domiciled in the Member State whose courts are seised of a matter or determine whether the party is domiciled in another Member State. Thus, the wording of the article already suggests that it should only be used to determine the domicile in a Member State. This is also confirmed in the Jenard report which explicitly explains that the article is not applicable if the person is domiciled in a non-EU state and that in that case the court seised of the matter must apply its rules of private international law.[24] Thus in the case of deciding on the domicile of a non-EU defendant, Croatian courts will apply the same provision of the 2017 PILA as in cases over EU-defendants, namely Art 4.

On the other hand, since the Brussels Ibis Regulation does, in Art 63, provide a definition of the domicile for a legal person, and since that definition differs from the one

[22] Sikirić, 'Zakon o međunarodnom privatnom pravu', 75.

[23] Narodne novine nos 130/11, 74/13, 69/17, 46/18.

[24] P Jenard, 'Report on the Convention of 27 September 1968 on jurisdiction and the enforcement of judgments in civil and commercial matters' [1979] OJ C 59/2, 16.

provided in the Croatian 2017 PILA, the Croatian court will not determine the seat of a legal person situated in a Member State in the same way as the seat of a person situated in a third state. Namely, the Regulation defines the seat of a legal person as the place of its statutory seat, its central administration, or its principal place of business. The three criteria are hierarchically equal so the defendant can be sued in any one of the three places.[25] In the Croatian 2017 PILA only two of those three are accepted as the seat of a legal person – statutory seat and the place of central administration. This clearly is not in line with the main aim of the extension of the Brussels Ibis Regulation and could presumably lead to problems in practice.

Question 3

Other connecting factors were provided by domestic law until recently. Namely, Art 27 of the CPA stated that international jurisdiction of Croatian courts can be established through the application of the rules of territorial jurisdiction when no express provisions on international jurisdiction are provided in law or international agreement. Art 58 para 1 and Art 58 para 3 of the CPA regulated the rules of special international jurisdiction over defendants over which there is no general jurisdiction in Croatia. This is fully explained in the answer to the question under 5(a) of this questionnaire. However, the rules are out of force as of 2022, thus they no longer serve as the basis for jurisdiction over non-EU defendants.

Question 4

Under the new 2017 PILA the *forum necessitatis* rule was for the first time introduced in the Croatian legal order. This novelty is considered to be a modernisation of the private international law of Croatia as it furthers avoidance of denial of justice in cases with an international element.[26] The rule contained in Art 58 of the 2017 PILA provides for jurisdiction of Croatian courts over non-EU defendants in cases when jurisdiction cannot be based on other national rules or rules stemming from international treaties. Croatian courts shall have jurisdiction if the proceedings cannot be conducted abroad or that is not reasonably expected, but only if the subject matter of the proceedings is sufficiently connected with the Republic of Croatia that it would be purposeful to conduct the proceedings in Croatia. The twofold criterion of purposefulness and connection will have to be interpreted in the court practice. It surely should not lead to exorbitant jurisdiction so a certain level of restrictive interpretation is necessary. The criterion of impossible or unreasonable foreign proceedings will most probably be invoked and proved by the plaintiff which will surely enable swiftness in decision-making of the court when deciding on *forum necessitatis*.

[25] P Vlas, 'Article 63' in U Magnus and P Mankowski (eds), *European Commentaries of Private International Law, Volume I, Brussels Ibis Regulation* (Sellier, 2016) para 3.

[26] Hoško, 'Novo uređenje međunarodnog privatnog prava u RH – Zakon o međunarodnom privatnom pravu', 28.

Question 5

Prior to entry into force of the PILA 2017 a separate set of rules on the issues described existed for the non-EU defendants. However, Art 46 para 2 PILA 2017 widened the scope of application of the Brussels regime to non-EU defendants in case of special jurisdiction, jurisdiction over co-defendants as well as for insurance contracts (ie sections 2 and 3 of the Chapter II of the Brussels Ibis Regulation). These rules thus apply from its entry into force on 29 January 2019. The ratio behind widening of the scope of application of the Brussels regime lies in avoiding the dualism of jurisdictional rules which would make the application of private international law rules easier for courts.[27]

Given the recent commencement of application of the Brussels regime to non-EU defendants, the older rules will also be described as they were in force for the first five and a half years of Croatia's membership in the EU and it is still possible that some proceedings in which they were applied are pending.

(a)

The scope of application of Art 7 para 1 of the Brussels Ibis Regulation has been widened by Art 46 para 2 of the 2017 PILA to defendants domiciled outside the EU.

Until 2022, Art 27 of the CPA allowed for jurisdiction of Croatian courts when no explicit rule allows it for cases with an international element, but jurisdiction stems from rules of territorial jurisdiction. This indirectly allowed for international jurisdiction in certain cases. In addition, Art 58 of the CPA contained rules of direct international jurisdiction.

Article 58 no 1 CPA provided for jurisdiction when defendant has property in Croatia or the object requested by the claim is situated in Croatia. This rule is more or less a verbatim copy of Art 54 para 1 1982 PILA so further considerations will primarily focus on the interpretation of that 'old' rule in legal theory. According to Art 54 para 1 of the 1982 Croatian PILA jurisdiction for property claims (excluding rights in rem) existed if the property of the defendant or the object for which the proceedings were instituted is situated in the territory of Croatia. So the basis for jurisdiction could have been either the property of the defendant situated in Croatia or the object requested by the claim. The term 'property of the defendant' should be understood in a broad way. The property can be a real estate or a movable property, it can be a claim that the defendant has towards a third person or any other belonging of the defendant. Most importantly, the property does not have to be related to the claim, nor does it have to be of the same value as the claim.[28] The reason it was included into the PILA was the protection of the creditors, with the aim to provide for jurisdiction of the Croatian courts if there is property in Croatia that could be used for enforcement. However, according to the understanding of the provision that is accepted in the doctrine, the property

[27] Sikirić, 'Zakon o međunarodnom privatnom pravu', 111–112.

[28] Dika/Knežević/Stojanović, *Komentar Zakona o međunarodnom privatnom i procesnom pravu*, 199; Varadi/Bordaš/Knežević/Pavić, *Komentar Zakona o međunarodnom privatnom i procesnom pravu*, 507.

in question does not in fact have to be adequate to satisfy the creditor (if he wins the case) or proportionate to the value in dispute. This jurisdictional ground was, for those reasons, subject to malpractice and, thus often criticised.[29] In line with the prevailing view that the provision is subject to misuse, Croatian legal theory took the stand that it should be interpreted narrowly based on the good faith principle.[30] The grounds for a narrow interpretation lie in the provision of the CPA according to which the parties are obligated to use its procedural right with scrutiny.[31] Thus, it can be argued that the term 'property' has to be understood as 'property enforceable by the creditor, ie the winning plaintiff'. This is predominantly important for the interpretation of establishing jurisdiction based on the fact that the defendant has a claim over a debtor situated in Croatia. A jurisdiction on that basis could be established only if defendant's claim is enforceable. Otherwise, establishing jurisdiction on any unenforceable claim could be interpreted as a misuse of procedural rights and a breach of the good faith principle.

Article 58 para 2 of the CPA determined territorial jurisdiction in cases when international jurisdiction was based on the fact that the dispute arises out of an obligation that arose while the defendant was in Croatia. Basically, that rule was used to determine territorial jurisdiction in case international jurisdiction was based on Art 54 para 2 of the 1982 PILA. Such rule on international jurisdiction does not exist anymore and did not exist from the time of the entry into force of the 2017 PILA until 2022. The applicability of Art 58 para 2 of the CPA was thus, during that period, questionable.

Article 58 para 3 of the CPA provided a completely new basis of international jurisdiction.[32] Under that provision: 'In disputes against a person regarding whom there is no general territorial jurisdiction in the Republic of Croatia, with respect to obligations to be performed in the Republic of Croatia, a complaint may be filed with the court in whose territory these obligations are to be fulfilled'. Therefore, the rule provides for jurisdiction of the court of *loci solutionis*, ie the place of performance of the obligation.

Croatian courts were in no way reluctant to base their international jurisdiction on that provision which is evidenced in case law.[33] There have been some discrepancies in the case law regarding the application of that rule. Namely, the High Commercial Court has found that Art 58 para 3 of the CPA cannot be applied to contractual obligations given that international jurisdiction for obligations is expressly regulated by Arts 54 and 55 of the 1982 PILA.[34] This logic could easily be transferred to the new 2017 PILA that for contractual disputes widens the scope of application of the Brussels Ibis Regulation, ie expressly regulating international jurisdiction in those cases. Still, courts

[29] Dika/Knežević/Stojanović, *Komentar Zakona o međunarodnom privatnom i procesnom pravu*, 199; Bosnić, *Hrvatsko međunarodno privatno i procesno pravo, Knjiga II*, 43; Varadi/Bordaš/Knežević/Pavić, *Međunarodno privatno parvo*, 497, 507.

[30] Dika/Knežević/Stojanović, *Komentar Zakona o međunarodnom privatnom i procesnom pravu*, 199.

[31] Art 9 of the CPA: 'Before the court, the parties and the intervenor shall be obliged to speak the truth and avail themselves of the rights granted to them by this Act in a conscientious manner'.

[32] Dika/Knežević/Stojanović, *Komentar Zakona o međunarodnom privatnom i procesnom pravu*, 201; Babić, *Međunarodna nadležnost za ugovorne sporove u europskom, hrvatskom i američkom pravu*, 211–212.

[33] High Commercial Court, Judgment no Pž 537/04-3, 12 December 2006; Judgment no Pž 2136/03-3, 23 August 2006; Judgment no Pž 2622/99, 6 July 1999; Judgment no Pž-2698/96, 14 January 1997; Judgment no Pž-2826/93, 1 February 1994; Judgment no Pž-7739/93, 6 July 1993; Judgment no Pž-1028/92, 30 March 1993.

[34] Visoki trgovački sud (High Commercial Court), Judgment no Pž-6941/06, 12 October 2009.

have predominantly applied Art 58 para 3 of the CPA to establish international jurisdiction without any obstacles.

What turned to be rather problematic is the case when the obligation that needs to be performed is payment as it in the end leads to establishing of *forum actoris*. Namely, when interpreting the place of payment courts apply Croatian Act on Obligations. According to Croatian Act on Obligations payment is performed in the seat of the creditor, ie plaintiff.[35] Such stance is contrary to the idea of the substantive law concept of the place of performance which leads to deviation of the widely accepted *actor sequitur forum rei* principle and acceptance of the forum of the plaintiff in a wide number of cases.[36] The place of performance of the obligation should be determined under the law applicable to the obligation in question (*lex causae*). This is accepted in Croatian academic writings[37] and is identical to the solution in the EU law.[38] However, Croatian case law follows a different reasoning and applies Croatian law as *lex fori* to the issue.[39]

Finally, prior to application of the new 2017 PILA under the 1982 PILA special jurisdiction for claims arising out of law of obligations existed in Arts 54 (which was already thoroughly explained in connection to Art 58 CPA) and 55 CPA.

Article 55 provided for jurisdiction for obligations that have arisen or must be performed in the Republic of Croatia if the defendant with domicile or seat abroad has its representative or agency in the Republic of Croatia or if the seat of the organisation of associated labour to which the discharge of business has been entrusted is in the Republic of Croatia.

(b)

Given the rule contained in Art 46 para 2 of the PILA 2017 the rule contained in Art 7 para 2 of the Brussels Ibis regulation also applies to non-EU defendants in non-contractual cases.

It is questionable whether the rule of Art 58 para 3, that was in force in the Croatian legal system until 2022, could have been applied in non-contractual cases – it provided for the *forum solutionis* as explained above. When 1982 PILA was in force the prevailing opinion was that the rule covers all types of obligations – contractual obligations as well as non-contractual obligations.[40] That stance has been confirmed in the court practice of the High Commercial Court, which found that Croatian courts have jurisdiction on the basis of Art 58 para 3 of the CPA in a dispute over a non-contractual obligation.[41]

[35] Art 179 of the Act on Obligations, Narodne novine nos 35/05, 41/08, 125/11, 78/15.

[36] Babić, *Međunarodna nadležnost za ugovorne sporove u europskom, hrvatskom i američkom pravu*, 231–32.

[37] Dika/Knežević/Stojanović, *Komentar Zakona o međunarodnom privatnom i procesnom pravu*, 200; V Tomljenović, 'Pravila o mjesnoj nadležnosti u funkciji pravila o međunarodnoj nadležnosti – kada i kako?', 2 (1998) 3–4 *Vladavina prava = Rule of the law: časopis za pravnu teoriju i praksu*, 93, 107–08; Babić, *Međunarodna nadležnost za ugovorne sporove u europskom, hrvatskom i američkom pravu*, 230–32.

[38] Peter Mankowski 'Article 7', in U Magnus and P Mankowski (n 25), paras 205–10.

[39] High Commercial Court, Judgment no Pž 537/04-3, 12 December 2006; Judgment no Pž 2136/03-3, 23 August 2006; Judgment no Pž-2698/96, 14 January 1997; Judgment no Pž-2826/93, 1 February 1994.

[40] Babić, *Međunarodna nadležnost za ugovorne sporove u europskom, hrvatskom i američkom pravu*, 221–23.

[41] High Commercial Court, Judgment no XV Pž 3092/97-2, 9 December 1997; Judgment no XV Pž 2468/96-2, 25 November 1997.

There was, however, a dissenting scholarly opinion according to which Art 58 para 3 of the CPA is applicable only to contractual and not to non-contractual obligations.[42] Under that view Art 58 para 3 of the CPA is a rule that indirectly determines international jurisdiction by virtue of Art 27 of the CPA. Accordingly, rule of Art 58 para 3 of the CPA could only be relevant for determination of special jurisdiction in contractual relations since neither the 1982 PILA nor any international agreement provided a special rule for international jurisdiction in contractual obligations. On the other hand, the rule could not have been used to establish jurisdiction for non-contractual obligations since specific jurisdictional rule for such situations was provided in Art 53 of the 1982 PILA. Such stance did not have many supporters; most probably due to the fact that Art 58 para 3 of the CPA by its wording applies in cases when Croatian courts have no general jurisdiction over the defendant which leads to the conclusion that it provides for a direct international jurisdiction. Nevertheless, scholars agree that *forum solutionis* is an unacceptable forum for non-contractual obligations due to weak connection between the forum and the circumstances of the case.[43] Moreover, on the comparative level *forum solutionis* is predominantly used only as a way to establish jurisdiction for contractual obligations.[44] Even more important, *forum solutionis* is accepted as a basis only for jurisdiction for contractual obligations on the EU level as well, namely in Art 7 para 1a of the Brussels Ibis Regulation.

Prior to entry into force of 2017 PILA Croatian courts had special jurisdiction over non-contractual matters when the damage occurred in Croatia.[45] That rule was applied by virtue of an express rule to insurers' direct responsibility and to regress claims.

There is no clear standpoint in legal theory as to the interpretation of the place where the damage occurred. Some authors restrained it to *locus damni* where others thought it would also encompass locus *delicti commissi*.[46] However, the rule of Art 27 CPA leads to possible application of rules on territorial jurisdiction as well. Under those rules territorial jurisdiction was elective – both the court of the place where the act causing damage and the place of damage had jurisdiction.[47]

[42] Tomljenović, 'Pravila o mjesnoj nadležnosti u funkciji pravila o međunarodnoj nadležnosti – kada i kako?', 104–109.

[43] Babić, *Međunarodna nadležnost za ugovorne sporove u europskom, hrvatskom i američkom pravu*, 223; Tomljenović, 'Pravila o mjesnoj nadležnosti u funkciji pravila o međunarodnoj nadležnosti – kada i kako?', 105.

[44] Tomljenović, 'Pravila o mjesnoj nadležnosti u funkciji pravila o međunarodnoj nadležnosti – kada i kako?', 103–104.

[45] '1. As regards proceedings for non-contractual liability the court of the Republic of Croatia has jurisdiction if that jurisdiction exists by virtue of the provisions of Article 46 and Articles 50–52 of this Act or if the damage occurred in the territory of the Republic of Croatia. 2. Paragraph 1 of this Article shall also be applied to proceedings against the cooperative for insurance of property and persons for third-party liability on the basis of the rule of direct liability of that cooperative, and to proceedings involving a right of recourse against debtors on basis of the liability for damages'. Art 53 of the 1982 PILA. This rule allows for application of general international jurisdiction as well as jurisdiction based on the acceptance of the defendant and the case when Croatian workers that are defendants who live aborad where they were sent abroad by their employers, but have their domicile in Croatia.

[46] See more in V Tomljenovic, 'Posebna međunarodna nadležnost u sporovima izvanugovorne odgovornosti za štetu – neka otvorena pitanja tumačenja i kvalifikacije' (1998) 19 *Zb Prav Fak Sveuc Rij* 867, 907–08.

[47] Art 57 para 1 of the CPA.

(c)

As with special jurisdiction in contracts and torts, Croatian PILA 2017 widens the scope of application of the Brussels Ibis Regulation to non-EU domiciled co-defendants. It is worth noting here that the general rule of the Brussels Ibis Regulation, ie jurisdiction based on the defendant's domicile, also applies to non-EU defendants in Croatia.[48] Thus the rule contained in Art 8 para 1 of the Brussels Ibis Regulation should apply without any hurdles.

The old 1982 PILA also contained a specific rule applicable to co-defendants. Article 46 para 3 of the 1982 PILA provided for jurisdiction over material co-defendant in case one of them had domicile or seat in Croatia, ie when Croatian courts had general jurisdiction over one of them. In order for the attraction of jurisdiction to occur one of the co-defendants had to have domicile (or seat) in Croatia and co-defendants had to be material co-defendants. Both conditions need to be fulfilled cumulatively. This is also confirmed in the Croatian court practice.[49] The prerequisite that the co-defendants are material co-defendants ensures that the claims are closely connected. The question whether the co-defendants are considered material was determined under Croatian civil procedure law.[50] Material co-defendants are defined in Croatian legal theory as those that are 'before and outside the lawsuit in a certain legal or real connection in relation to the (indirect) subject matter of the dispute'.[51]

The conditions set for attraction of jurisdiction under the Brussels Ibis Regulation seem to be more flexible as court is not given a strict definition of close connection between the co-defendants but is to assess whether 'the claims are so closely connected that it is expedient to hear and determine them together to avoid the risk of irreconcilable judgments resulting from separate proceedings'.

(d)

The scope of application of jurisdictional rules relating to insurance contracts contained in the Brussels Ibis Regulation has been widened to non-EU defendants in Croatia.[52] These rules are thus the same. The application of the rules provided for consumer and individual employment contracts has not been widened. The reason lies in the fact that these rules apply to employers and professionals domiciled outside the EU by virtue of

[48] Art 55 of the PILA 2017.

[49] Supreme Court, Judgment no Rev 17/07-2, 10 May 2007; Judgment no Rev 285/04-2, 7 June 2005; Judgment no Gr1 580/04-2, 31 January 2005; Judgment no II Rev-49/1998-2, 8 March 2000; Judgment no II Rev-84/1994-2, 22 May 1996; Judgment no Rev 3667/1993-2, 20 January 1994; Judgment no II Rev 103/1992-2, 4 February 1993.

[50] Dika/Knežević/Stojanović, *Komentar Zakona o međunarodnom privatnom i procesnom pravu*, 170;Bosnić, *Hrvatsko međunarodno privatno i procesno pravo, Knjiga II* 33; Supreme Court, Judgment no Rev 17/07-2, 10 May 2007; Judgment no Rev 285/04-2, 7 June 2005; Judgment no II Rev-49/1998-2, 8 March 2000; Judgment no Rev 3667/1993-2, 20 January 1994; Judgment no II Rev 103/1992-2, 4 February 1993.

[51] S Triva, M Dika, *Građansko parnično procesno pravo* (Narodne novine 2004) 441, Varadi/Bordaš/Knežević/Pavić, *Međunarodno privatno parvo*, 498.

[52] Art 46 para 2 of the 2017 PILA.

the Brussels Ibis Regulation anyway. The Croatian legislator found no reason to widen the scope of application of the protective rules to weaker parties, ie employees and consumers domiciled abroad, outside the EU. On the other hand, the rules in insurance contracts are dependent of the domicile of the defendant and have thus be widened.

Under the old rules contained in 1982 PILA no specific rule existed as to the jurisdiction in consumer, employment and insurance contracts and general rules applied.

Cyprus

KONSTANTINOS A ROKAS*

Question 1

(a)

Cyprus applies the common law for determining international jurisdiction where EU law rules are not applicable. The rules determining domestic territorial jurisdiction also affect international jurisdiction.[1] Domestic jurisdiction rules also determine the jurisdiction in international cases. The source of the domestic jurisdiction rules is to be found in the Civil Procedure Law, Ch 6 (hereinafter CPL, Ch 6; 'O peri politikis dikonomias nomos, kefalaio 6 – Ο περί πολιτικής δικονομίας νόμος, κεφάλαιο 6'), the Civil Procedure Rules (hereinafter CPR; 'Thesmoi Politikis Dikonomias – Θεσμοί Πολιτικής δικονομίας') and in the Courts of Justice Law 14/60 ('O peri dikastirion nomos – Ο περί Δικαστηρίων νόμος του 1960'). The Court of Justice law provides that the principles of common law and equity apply as a source of Cypriot law.[2] Given that the system of Cyprus is substantially codified, judges will apply common law principles every time there is no legislation in force and provided that the existing legislation is not contradicted.[3] The Civil Procedure Rules have recently been modified (19 May 2021) but the acts required for their implementation have yet to be adopted.[4] However, the reform of the Civil Procedure Rules introduces no major changes regarding the rules that affect the determination of international jurisdiction.

* The author would like to thank Anna Plevri, Nikolas Kyriakides, and Agis Georgiades for their help and their valuable comments.

[1] A Emilianides, 'Cyprus (up-to-date as of October 2019)', in W Vandenbussche (ed), *Kluwer IEL Civil Procedure* (2020) 80; A Emilianides and A Plevri, 'Cyprus', in *Regulation BIa: a standard for free circulation of judgments and mutual trust in the European Union (JUDGTRUST)*, research conducted by the TMC Asser Instituut, Universität Hamburg, University of Antwerp, Internationaal Juridisch Instituut, project coordinators Prof Vesna Lazic and Prof Peter Mankowski, (JUDGTRUST, August 2019) 4–5, www.asser.nl/media/795645/cyprus_report.pdf.

[2] A Emilianides and A Plevri, 'Cyprus', in *Regulation BIa: a standard for free circulation of judgments and mutual trust in the European Union (JUDGTRUST)*, research conducted by the TMC Asser Instituut, Universität Hamburg, University of Antwerp, Internationaal Juridisch Instituut, project coordinators Prof Vesna Lazic and Prof Peter Mankowski, (JUDGTRUST, August 2019) 6.

[3] S Symeonides, 'The Mixed Legal System of the Republic of Cyprus' 78 *Tulane Law Review* (2003) 441; A Emilianides, 'Cyprus: Everything Changes and Nothing Remains Still' in S Farran et al (eds), *A Study of Mixed Legal Systems: Endangered, Entrenched or Blended*, (Aldershot: Ashgate, 2014) 215.

[4] The new rules are expected to enter into force in September 2023.

Article 21 of the Courts of Justice law provides that a Court has jurisdiction to hear a case 'whenever the subject matter of the action has arisen, wholly or partly, within the areas of the district in which the District Court was constituted, or whenever the plaintiff, or any of the defendants, resides or works within the district of the court'.[5] In principle, a District court ('Eparhiako Dikastirio – Επαρχιακό Δικαστήριο') has jurisdiction whenever there is some connection with Cyprus.[6] Such connection can be identified either because the plaintiff or the defendant reside or work within a court's area of jurisdiction or, even, because the subject-matter of the case has arisen within this area, in whole or in part. Therefore, the requirements for the establishment of domestic territorial jurisdiction are wide in scope and the jurisdiction of Cypriot courts is determined and understood in broad terms. This broad understanding and perception of jurisdiction is mitigated by the acceptance of the *forum non conveniens* doctrine, which is also accepted within the Cypriot legal order.

The Supreme Court of Cyprus has adopted the principles[7] set out by English courts as regards the *forum non conveniens* doctrine and, in particular, the criteria set out in the *Spiliada Maritime Corpn* case.[8] A court has discretion to stay an action, if it concludes that it is not the appropriate forum to hear the case. In principle, a stay will only be granted if the court is persuaded that there is another forum which has competence and which will be available to hear the case, provided that the latter is more appropriate to hear the case in such a way that both the interests of all parties and the purpose of justice will be thus better served.[9] It is the defendant who bears the burden of proving that the Cypriot court is not the appropriate forum. If the judges are convinced that there is another court available to hear the case, then the plaintiff has the burden of proving that the court before which the case has been brought should, nonetheless, hear the case because there are special circumstances that justify such exercise of its jurisdiction. In general, there is a twofold test for the application of the *forum non conveniens* doctrine: the defendant has to prove, on the one hand, that the Cypriot court is not the natural or appropriate forum to hear the case and, on the other hand, that there is another court which is clearly better placed to do so. A forum is considered as the natural forum to hear a case when it has a substantial and real connection with the case.[10] Among other criteria, the following will be taken into consideration for the purpose of deciding on the appropriateness of the Cypriot courts to hear an action: the availability of witnesses; the place of residence or the place where the parties conduct their business; the law governing the dispute.[11] The judges will have to provide an answer to the question whether justice can be rendered by another court with substantially less inconvenience

[5] A Emilianides, S Laulhé Shaelou, A Solomou, 'Cyprus', in B Verschraegen (ed), *Kluwer IEL Private International Law* (Suppl 46, 2015) 109.

[6] ibid.

[7] Anotato Dikastirio-Ανώτατο Δικαστήριο (Supreme Court of the Republic of Cyprus), 22 June 1995, [1995] 1 *The Cyprus Law Reports* 621, *Shehata v Elias*; also Anotato Dikastirio, 18 May 2000, [2000] 1 *The Cyprus Law Reports* 707, *Zeeland Navigation Co Ltd v Banque Worms*; Anotato Dikastirio, 27 March 2012, Civil Appeal 13/2009, *Hampton Advisory Group SA v Papadopoulos*; cited by A Emilianides, S Laulhé Shaelou, A Solomou, 'Cyprus', 111.

[8] UK House of Lords, 19 November 1986, *Spiliada Maritime Corpn v Cansulex Ltd* [1987] AC 460.

[9] A Emilianides, S Laulhé Shaelou, A Solomou, 'Cyprus', 111.

[10] ibid 112.

[11] ibid.

or expense for the parties.[12] However, even when this is the case, special circumstances can lead the court to retain its jurisdiction. For instance, this can occur when a plaintiff shows that they will not be able to obtain justice in a foreign court.[13]

In addition to the aforementioned rules and principles, the establishment of international jurisdiction for defendants not domiciled in the EU is dependent on a claimant's possibility to serve the defendant.[14] In *Philippou v Philippou*, the Supreme Court of Cyprus underlined the importance of the possibility to serve a defendant for the needs of the establishment of international jurisdiction of the courts:

> The summons is essential as the foundation of the Court's jurisdiction. When a writ cannot legally be served upon a defendant, the Court can exercise no jurisdiction over him. Jurisdiction, according to the English Law and the system of law … in this country, is based on the act of personal service. It is far otherwise in other systems where service is in no sense a foundation of jurisdiction, but merely a sine qua non before effective action is allowed.[15]

In order for an action to start, a writ of summons – as it has been traditionally called[16] – or claim form – as it is called today – has to be served on the defendant. A defendant can be served if they are present in Cyprus, even when their presence is only temporary. If the defendant is abroad, the claimant has to seek leave by the district court in order to serve the claim form. The grounds on which a court can grant leave to serve abroad are set out in Order 6 CPR on Service out of the jurisdiction. In any case, the claimant has to request leave to serve a claim form every time they want to file an action against a defendant who is abroad. As stated in *Nisiotis v Azman*,[17] if the acceptance and sealing of a claim form takes place without prior leave by the court, the lawsuit is rejected. As further stated in the same decision, non-observance of the criteria for leave to serve out of the jurisdiction may lead the court to dismiss the lawsuit. The courts assume jurisdiction over persons who are abroad and do not have the Cypriot citizenship in general with thoughtfulness in the exercise of their discretion.

It should be stressed that leave to serve abroad is sought by the claimant in ex parte proceedings. In this framework, the court carries out merely a prima facie verification of whether one of the conditions of Order 6, Rule 1 CPR (hereinafter 'O.6 R.1 CPR') is met. Naturally, the defendant can at a later stage apply for an annulment of the claim form (writ of summons) and eventually of its service as well. At that stage, the defendant may raise the issue of the *forum non conveniens*. The *forum non conveniens* test is as crucial as in English common law for the establishment of jurisdiction.

To some extent, therefore, the grounds on which someone can, under O.6 R.1 CPR, seek leave to serve a claim form/writ of summons abroad can indeed be seen as indirectly and complementarily important in the determination of the international

[12] ibid.

[13] ibid.

[14] Anotato Dikastirio, 1 December 1986, (1986) *The Cyprus Law Reports* 689, *Philippou v Philippou and others*.

[15] ibid.

[16] The term 'claim form' is a synonym for the term 'writ of summons'; the latter has been replaced by the former in the 1998 reform of the Civil Procedure Rules of England and Wales; C Mittleton, *Jurisdiction and Service out of Cyprus of a Writ of Summons, United Kingdom & Russia*, 29–30 (in Greek).

[17] Anotato Dikastirio, 21 September 2001, (1986) *The Cyprus Law Reports* 689, *Philippou v Philippou and others*.

jurisdiction of Cypriot courts. Consequently, the rules that provide such grounds are decisive for the establishment of the international jurisdiction of Cypriot courts;[18] these grounds function indirectly as connecting factors for the purposes of establishing international jurisdiction.

The criteria set out in O.6 R.1 CPR (I shall hereinafter use the new numbering of this rule, as recently amended, is expected to enter into force in September 2023; hereinafter 'Art 6.8.1 … CPR') allow a claimant to have recourse to a Cypriot court against a defendant not domiciled in an EU Member State with regard to disputes connected with contracts, non-contractual liability, rights in rem or other rights linked with immovable property, when there is a connection between the court and the action. They also permit Cypriot courts to exercise their jurisdiction with regard to claims against persons which would normally fall outside their jurisdiction when they do have jurisdiction for another claim which is closely connected to the former.

The criteria which show a connection between a trust-related claim and the Cypriot courts are equally broad; this allows Cypriot courts to assert jurisdiction. The plaintiff will be granted leave to serve a claim form out of the jurisdiction, and thus establish the jurisdiction of Cypriot courts, where a claim is brought in relation to: '6.8 … (ν) … a trust that has been created under the law in force, either in writing or orally, and is proven in writing, and which is governed by the law of Cyprus' or '(ξ) a trust that has been created by virtue of the law, either in writing or orally, and is proven in writing, and which provides that jurisdiction over such a claim shall be conferred to the courts of Cyprus', as well as where '(ρ) A claim is brought against the defendant as a trustee in a constructive trust, or as a trustee in a resulting trust, when the claim arises from acts committed or facts which occurred within the jurisdiction or is related to assets situated within the jurisdiction'.

Moreover, in accordance with common law rules, a Cypriot court is also competent to hear a case when a defendant submits to its jurisdiction.[19] A defendant can submit to the Cypriot courts either implicitly or explicitly through a choice of court clause.[20] When a defendant appears before a Cypriot court, that court is considered to have jurisdiction if the defendant did not raise an objection as to its competence. The defendant will also be considered to have submitted to the jurisdiction of a Cypriot court where they have initiated an action before a Cypriot court, where they have instructed their lawyer to accept service within the jurisdiction so as to fight a claim on the merits or where they have acknowledged service without filing a motion to challenge the jurisdiction of the court.[21]

Finally, in Cyprus there are two types of specialised tribunals which have jurisdiction precisely over matters covered by the Brussels Ibis Regulation, namely: the Industrial Disputes Tribunals ('Dikastirio Ergatikon Diaforon – Δικαστήριο Εργατικών

[18] N Koulouris, *Cypriot Civil Procedure* (Nomiki Bibliothiki, 2017) 17.

[19] A Emilianides and A Plevri, 'Cyprus', in *Regulation BIa: a standard for free circulation of judgments and mutual trust in the European Union (JUDGTRUST)*, research conducted by the TMC Asser Instituut, Universität Hamburg, University of Antwerp, Internationaal Juridisch Instituut, project coordinators Prof Vesna Lazic and Prof Peter Mankowski, (JUDGTRUST, August 2019) 5, www.asser.nl/media/795645/cyprus_report.pdf.

[20] A Emilianides, S Laulhé Shaelou, A Solomou, 'Cyprus', 110.

[21] ibid.

Διαφορών'), which rules on specific issues of labour law, and the Rent Control Tribunal ('Dikastirio Eleghou Enoikiaseon – Δικαστήριο Ελέγχου Ενοικιάσεων'), which mainly hears cases concerning the recovery of possession of rented property and the setting of fair rents.[22] However, the general rules on international jurisdiction are not supplemented by specific rules proper to these tribunals.

(b)

There is no clear distinction between transnational and domestic disputes. Thus, domestic jurisdictional rules also apply to transnational disputes.

(c)

The national legislature has not extended the personal scope of jurisdictional rules of the Brussels Regime (ie the 1968 Brussels Convention, the Brussels I Regulation and the Brussels Ibis Regulation) to defendants not domiciled in the EU.

There have been some suggestions to move towards an alignment of national jurisdictional rules with the Brussels Regime. In particular, it has been suggested that the notions of domicile and residence, as used by domestic rules, be interpreted in accordance with the same terms in the Brussels Regime, in order to achieve a minimum level of coordination between domestic and EU rules on international jurisdiction.[23] Still, no explicit proposal has been made by courts or scholars to extend the Brussels Regime to defendants not domiciled in an EU Member State either through legislative reform or through application by analogy.

(d)

The information provided is exhaustive as regards Art 76(1)(a) and (c); however, it has changed as regards Art 76(1)(b).

Question 2

'Domicile' is a legal notion. As is the case in several countries, the domicile of natural and legal persons is also used in Cyprus for jurisdictional purposes. Article 6.8(1) CPR provides that a claimant can seek to have a claim form served on a person out of the

[22] N Hatzimihail, 'Cyprus as a Mixed Legal System', 6 *J Civ L Stud* (2013) 37, 62 www.digitalcommons.law.lsu.edu/jcls/vol6/iss1/3.

[23] C Mittleton, *Jurisdiction and Service out of Cyprus of a Writ of Summons, United Kingdom & Russia*, 43 (in Greek).

Cypriot jurisdiction and thus establish the jurisdiction of domestic courts where a claim is brought:

> … (b) … against any person domiciled or habitually resident within the jurisdiction …

The meaning of 'domicile' in Cypriot law is influenced by common law, but the perception of domicile in civil law countries also plays a role in the establishment of the international jurisdiction of Cypriot courts and in the evaluation of the *forum non conveniens* doctrine. The traditional perception of domicile requires both an objective and a subjective element. According to this understanding, which mostly prevails in civil law countries, a person has their domicile in the country where they are established with the intention of staying for an indefinite period of time.

The Cypriot legal order also adopts the distinction known to common law countries between *domicile of origin* and *domicile of choice*. The *domicile of origin* may, in certain circumstances, not coincide with domicile as perceived in civil law countries. The distinction between domicile of origin and domicile of choice can be found in the Wills and Succession Law (Ch 195), in Art 6.

> Categories of domicile
>
> 6. Each person has at any given time–
>
>   (a) the domicile which they acquired at the time of birth (which in this Part is referred to as the 'domicile of origin') or
>
>   (b) a domicile (other than the domicile of origin) acquired or maintained by the person by his own actions (which in this Part is referred to as the 'domicile of choice').
>
> Domicile of origin of a child born in wedlock
>
> 7. In the case of a child born in wedlock during the lifetime of the child's father, the domicile of origin shall be the domicile of the father at the time of the child's birth.
>
> How to acquire a domicile of choice
>
> 9. A person shall acquire a domicile of choice by taking up residence in any place in the Republic with the intention of permanent or indefinite residence in that place, but not otherwise.
>
> No person shall be deemed to have acquired a domicile of choice in the Republic for the sole reason that they reside in the navy, military, air force or in the public sector services of the United Kingdom.
>
> The domicile of origin is predominant
>
> 10. The domicile of origin prevails and shall be maintained until a domicile of choice has actually been acquired.
>
> Maintaining a domicile of choice
>
> 11. A domicile of choice shall be maintained until abandoned when either–
>
>   (a) a new domicile of choice is acquired, or
>
>   (b) the domicile of origin is restored.

The criteria for the acquisition of a domicile of choice were set by the Supreme Court of Cyprus in *Schwartz v Republic*.[24] It is possible to abandon a domicile of origin and

[24] Anotato Dikastirio, 11 July 1995, [1995] 3 CLR 1359 (in Greek).

acquire a domicile of choice if the person in question has freely chosen a new place as their domicile of choice. Article 9 of the Wills and Succession Law determines how a person can acquire a domicile of choice. In that regard, two separate conditions have to be met. Firstly, there is an objective requirement, namely that a person has to be established in a specific place. The settlement in that place must be real and not merely ostensible. Secondly, a subjective requirement is also necessary. The person concerned must have freely chosen the place in question as their permanent residence for an indefinite period of time. Judge Scarman observes, in *In the Estate of Fuld decd*,[25] that:

> a domicile of choice is acquired only if it can be affirmatively shown that the propositus is resident within a territory subject to a distinctive legal system with the intention, formed independently of external pressures, of residing there indefinitely. If a man intends to return to the land of his birth upon a clearly foreseen and reasonably anticipated contingency, e.g., the end of his job, the intention required by law is lacking; but, if he has in mind only a vague possibility, such as making a fortune … or some sentiment about dying in the land of his fathers, such a state of mind is consistent with the intention required by law. But no clear line can be drawn: the ultimate decision in each case is one of fact – of the weight to be attached to the various factors and future contingencies in the contemplation of the propositus, their importance to him, and the probability, in his assessment, of the contingencies he has in contemplation being transformed into actualities.

The domicile of origin continues to exist until it is proven that a new domicile of choice has been acquired.[26] The burden of proof regarding the existence of a domicile of choice cannot be satisfied easily. Clear and solid evidence is required for a court to be satisfied that, on the balance of probabilities, there has been a permanent change of domicile. To this end, independent testimony is required to prove one's intention to change their domicile permanently.[27]

According to the aforementioned case law (and rules), there are two categories of domicile, ie the domicile of origin and the domicile of choice. Depending on the circumstances and on the general principles of private international law, the court determines the domicile of the person in question. This means, for example, that, in order to serve a claim form, by virtue of Art 6.8.1b CPR, on a person who stays permanently in Russia but whose domicile of origin is Cyprus, we have to verify that they have not acquired a domicile of choice in the Russian Federation. However, as already pointed out, the acquisition of a domicile of choice cannot be lightly inferred.

We are of the opinion that the understanding of domicile of civil law countries also plays a role in the establishment of the international jurisdiction of Cypriot courts, since the applicable rules allow for the service of a claim form on a person who is physically present in the Cypriot Republic even where that person's domicile of origin is in another

[25] Probate Divorce & Admiralty Division of the High Court of Justice, 1 November 1965, (No 3) [1966] 2 WLR 717 also reported at [1968] P 675, 684.

[26] Anotato Dikastirio, 8 April 2020, Civil Appeal No 259/2013, 260/2013, *Islamic Republic of Pakistan v KHAN and others* (in Greek).

[27] Probate Division of the High Court of Justice, 20 October 1964, *Henderson v Henderson* [1965] 2 WLR 218; UK House of Lords, 19 June 1974, *Steadman v Steadman* [1976] AC 536; Family Division of the High Court of Justice, 22 May 2000, *Irvin v Irvin* [2001] 1 FLR 178, and UK House of Lords, 27 May 1930, *Bowie or Ramsey v Liverpool Royal Infirmary and others* [1930] AC 588.

country. In addition, the evaluation of the *forum non conveniens* doctrine by Cypriot courts is conditional upon a determination of the appropriateness of Cypriot courts to hear a case. In this context, it is reasonable to think that, among other elements, a judge has to take into consideration the domicile of the person in question as it is usually perceived in civil law countries. This is imperative in cases where the judge wants to examine whether a different court has jurisdiction to hear the same case.

The meaning of 'residence' has not been subject to extensive analysis for the needs of application of the rules on international jurisdiction. Therefore, it can be submitted that this term can be understood in this context to indicate both a temporary stay in a country as well as a more permanent one. The latter would be closer to the understanding of the notion of 'habitual residence'.

Question 3

As already explained, domestic law on international jurisdiction adopts a broad understanding of criteria that allow for the establishment of international jurisdiction of Cypriot courts. The provision of Art 21 of the Courts of Justice law, which provides that a court has jurisdiction to hear a case 'whenever the subject matter of the action has arisen, in whole or in part, within the areas of the district in which the District Court was constituted, or whenever the plaintiff, or any of the defendants, resides or works within the district of the court'[28] is to be considered as a general rule on jurisdiction. However, the establishment of the international jurisdiction of Cypriot courts is, as already stated, influenced by the grounds on which a claimant can seek leave to serve a claim form out of jurisdiction. Given that these criteria are defined in a very broad manner, they may allow Cypriot courts to exercise their jurisdiction even in cases where the link with the Cypriot legal order is tenuous. In such a situation, a defendant will be able to challenge the jurisdiction on the basis of the forum non conveniens test.

Contrary to common practice in most continental law countries, there has so far been no in-depth scholarly analysis of the different criteria that serve to establish the jurisdiction of Cypriot courts. Having a system that allows for the establishment of international jurisdiction in broad terms partly explains the reason why connecting factors have not been the object of an extensive analysis. An additional explanation is offered by the fact that connecting factors have not led to any noteworthy problems as regards the establishment of international jurisdiction.

Question 4

Domestic law doesn't explicitly envisage a *forum necessitatis*. The fact that Cypriot rules that determine international jurisdiction are extremely wide in scope allows the Cypriot

[28] UK House of Lords, 19 November 1986, *Spiliada Maritime Corpn v Cansulex Ltd* [1987] AC 460.

courts to exercise their jurisdiction in cases where no other court would be reasonably available. Nonetheless, in some exceptional circumstances *forum necessitatis* can serve as a basis to avoid an instance of denial of justice and to guarantee access to justice in accordance with Art 6 ECHR. Although the international jurisdiction of Cypriot courts is determined in terms so broad that it can be accepted even in the presence of a tenuous connection to the Cypriot legal order, *forum necessitatis* could still constitute an *ultimum refugium* in exceptional sets of circumstances.

Question 5

As already explained above, there are no specific rules on international jurisdiction similar to the ones of Member States of the continental tradition. However, the grounds on which a claimant can obtain leave to serve a claim form on a defendant who is out of the jurisdiction (Art 6.8.1 CPR), do influence the determination of the international jurisdiction of Cypriot courts. Without service of the claim form on the defendant who is abroad, it will be impossible to gain access to the Cypriot court system. We explain below the criteria adopted by Art 6.8.1 CPR, which present the closest affinity with the criteria adopted by the Brussels regime in matters relating to contracts, tort, delict or quasi-delict, jurisdiction based on a close connection between defendants and jurisdiction over consumer, employment and insurance contracts. It should be noted that the criteria in Art 6.8.1 CPR are all of equal standing. Therefore, a court can establish its jurisdiction based on the ground that it considers the most appropriate, on a case-by-case basis. Mittleton observes that judges tend to rely on the grounds of Art 6.8.1 CPR without providing an appropriate and satisfactory interpretation of the scope of each of those grounds.[29] Furthermore, she recommends that it would be advisable for Cypriot courts to adopt the approach of the CJEU in its efforts to justify recourse to the rules of international jurisdiction under the Brussels I Regime.[30]

It results from the aforementioned analysis that a comparison between Cypriot legislation and the equivalent provisions of the Brussels Ibis Regulation is rather difficult. Even though several Cypriot provisions are similar to the relevant provisions of the Brussels Ibis Regulation, the whole underlying logic and philosophy of the Cypriot system is diametrically opposed to that of the Brussels Ibis Regulation. Thus, the Cypriot domestic rules on international jurisdiction also differ significantly in practice from domestic rules on international jurisdiction adopted by Member States of the continental tradition. Under the Cypriot system, courts are granted a wide margin to decide on their jurisdiction, contrary to what is the case under the rules of the Brussels Ibis system. Thus, the presentation of the following provisions is of an indicative value only and cannot be used to draw more general conclusions.

[29] C Mittleton, *Jurisdiction and Service out of Cyprus of a Writ of Summons, United Kingdom & Russia*, 152–53 (in Greek).

[30] ibid 153.

(a)

In contractual disputes a claimant can have recourse to Cypriot courts under Art 6.8.1 CPR in a wide set of circumstances. A plaintiff can ask for leave to serve a defendant abroad where:

> … η) A claim is brought in respect of a contract, when the contract …:
>
> (i) was entered into within its jurisdiction;
> (ii) was entered into by or through an agent trading or residing within the jurisdiction;
> (iii) is governed by Cypriot law; or
> (iv) contains a provision under which the court has jurisdiction to decide on any claim in respect of the contract.
>
> (θ) A claim is brought in respect of a breach of contract, which has taken place within the jurisdiction,
>
> (ι) A claim is brought seeking a declaration that a contract does not exist for the case where if it was established that this contract existed, it would conform with the requirements set out in Regulation 6.10 (1).

Thus, the criteria pursuant to which Cypriot courts can exercise their jurisdiction in matters relating to contract are worded in broader terms in comparison with those included in Regulation Brussels Ibis. There has been no case law revealing significant difficulties in the application of these criteria. Given the wide margin of appreciation of judges in the evaluation of the aforementioned criteria, and the criticism of the relevant provisions of the Brussels regime, the Cypriot legal order might be reluctant to extend the EU rules on international jurisdiction in matters relating to contract to defendants not domiciled in an EU Member State.

(b)

For actions based on non-contractual liability, the plaintiff can establish the jurisdiction of Cypriot courts for claims based on a civil wrong where '6.8 … (κ) … (i) damage has occurred or will occur within its jurisdiction; or (ii) the damage which has occurred or will occur results from an act which was committed or is likely to be committed within the jurisdiction' and for a recovery claim '6.8 … (σ) … where: (i) the defendant's alleged liability arises from acts committed within the jurisdiction; or (ii) the enrichment takes place within the jurisdiction; or (iii) the claim is governed by the law of Cyprus'.

It results that the grounds based on which Cypriot courts exercise jurisdiction in matters relating to tort, delict or quasi-delict constitute a close reproduction of the wording of Art 7(2) of Brussels Ibis Regulation. A Cypriot court will be in a position to hear a claim for a civil wrong where 'damage has occurred or will occur within its jurisdiction'; or where 'the damage which has occurred or will occur results from an act which was committed or is likely to be committed within its jurisdiction'.[31] The existing

[31] District Court of Nicosia, 17 April 2018, App No°6075/15, ECLI:CY:EDLEF:2018:A246, *Vaimicus Estates Limited v Bank of China (Hong Kong) Limited and Khoo Kim Guang.*

case law is not sufficient to demonstrate that significant differences would arise in practice. And there is no analysis in case law differentiating between the different limbs of Art 6.8.1 CPR relating to non-contractual liability. This conclusion is corroborated by the fact that Cypriot courts accept their jurisdiction to a great extent.

(c)

Concerning jurisdiction based on a close connection between defendants, Art 6.8.1 CPR allows Cypriot courts to exercise their jurisdiction under the following terms.

> Article 6.8(1) CPR
>
> …
>
> (δ) A claim is brought against a person ('the defendant') on whom the claim form has been served or will be served (but not by virtue of this paragraph) and–
>
> (i) there is a real issue between the plaintiff and the defendant which is reasonable for the Court to hear; and
>
> (ii) the claimant wishes to serve the claim form on another person who is a necessary or proper party to that claim.
>
> (ε) The claim is an additional claim by virtue of Part 21 and the person on whom the claim has to be served is a necessary or proper party to the claim or to the additional claim.
>
> (στ) A claim is brought against the defendant following the application of one of the Regulations 6.8 (1)(γ) and (η-(στ) and an additional claim is brought against the same defendant which is based on the same facts or on facts which are closely connected to them.

(d)

There are no criteria specifically relevant to consumer, employment and insurance contracts.

No cases have been identified where the Cypriot judiciary has had recourse to the rules of or principles enshrined in the Brussels Regime, and/or to the preliminary rulings rendered by the CJEU on that Regime, when applying the relevant domestic rules.

France

BENJAMIN SAUNIER AND PHUONG THAO PHAN

Question 1

(a)

The French law of international jurisdiction as such has never caught the attention of the French legislator. Lacking a specific code or statute on the matter, and although there is now a recent draft for a French code of private international law, of which references will be made throughout this report, sources for jurisdictional rules in the French system are very diverse. Some have been adopted through legislation, some have been developed by case-law. Because of their practical significance and mixed origins, jurisdictional rules based on the extension of internal rules of venue deserve a separate mention.

Legislative rules on international jurisdiction. There are very few jurisdictional rules of legislative origin specifically designed to apply to transnational disputes. The most famous ones are to be found in Arts 14 and 15 of the civil code (*code civil*), which give jurisdiction to French courts if either the claimant (Art 14) or the defendant (Art 15) is a French citizen, regardless of his or her domicile or place of residency.

Judge-made rules on international jurisdiction. Case-law has developed rules specific to international disputes. *Forum necessitatis* and extension of internal rules are discussed further in this report. Most notable examples of judge-made rules of jurisdiction in the field of civil and commercial matters are enforcement orders and interim measures sought on French territory.[1]

Rules based on the extension of internal rules of jurisdiction. Rules of venue within the French judicial system for civil and commercial matters are provided chiefly in Arts 42 to 48 of the Civil Procedure Code (*code de procédure civile*; CPC). These rules have been extended to transnational disputes by French courts. The scope and results of this extension, which is the same as double functionality, is explained below.

[1] Cour de cassation, civ 1re, 11 February 1997, no°94-21.500, Grands arrêts, Strojexport, 548; Cour de cassation, civ 2e, 10 December 2020, ECLI:FR:CCASS:2020:C201368, Bulletin, *A v USA*, 253; Cour de cassation, civ 2e, 10 December 2020, ECLI:FR:CCASS:2020:C201366, Bulletin, *Standard Chartered Bank*, 255.

(b)

Art 14 and 15 civil code, as well as the few rules designed specifically for international jurisdiction, apply only to international disputes. As for the third mentioned category, it would be improper to state that French written rules of jurisdiction apply to both domestic and transnational disputes, as the Cour de cassation, the highest French court for civil matters, has repeatedly referred to their 'extension' to international matters.[2] On some other instances however, it has ruled that they 'govern international jurisdiction'[3] or simply are 'applicable in the international order'.[4] In recent decisions, the Cour de cassation has again qualified the reference to domestic rules in international matters not as a mere application, but rather as an extension of them.[5] The consequences are twofold. First, there is not one set of rules, remotely applicable to all disputes, be they domestic or international, but two different sets of rules, one on venue in a domestic context, the other on international jurisdiction.[6] Second, while the domestic rules provide guidance for the criterion the disputes must fulfil for the French courts to have international jurisdiction over them, adaptations might be made in order to adjust to international litigation.[7] To this day, such adaptation has always resulted in giving jurisdiction to French courts in absence of a domestic rule to be usefully extended,[8] never in a waiver of jurisdiction in spite of the requirements of a domestic rule being met. An example is given by Art 44, which deals with actions related to real, immovable property (*actions réelles immobilières*). It provides that only the courts within whose jurisdiction the immovable property is located may rule on any action in rem dealing with it. The rule is extended to international disputes where the immovable property is located in France but with a wider understanding of what constitutes an in rem legal action as in domestic matters. As long as part of the action tends, in the end, to grant ownership of an immovable asset located in France, or more generally in rem rights to it, French courts will consider that they can rule over it.

Article 42 CPC as extended to international disputes provides for the French courts to be competent, if the defendant inhabits France, if he has his 'domicile' in the sense of French law (see below for the exact definition). It is seen as an application of the *actor sequitur forum rei* principle. As mentioned above, Art 44 CPC deals with actions relating to immovable property. Article 45 CPC is outside the scope of Brussels Ibis Regulation (successions). Article 46 CPC, for contracts and delict claims, has also been

[2] Cour de cassation, civ, 19 October 1959, no°58-10.628, D 1960, 37, *Pelassa*; Cour de cassation, civ, 30 October 1962, Grands arrêts, *Scheffel*, 319; this decision having been rendered outside what is today Brussels Ibis Regulation's material scope. Cour de cassation, civ, 30 October 1962, Grands arrêts, *Scheffel*, 319.

[3] Cour de cassation, civ 1re, 26 October 1982, no°81-13.380, JCP G 1983, IV, *Bank Saderat Iran*, 17; see also Cour de cassation, civ, 19 October 1959, no°58-10.526, D 1960, *Ranft*, 37.

[4] Cour de cassation, com, 13 April 2010, no°09-11.885, D 2010, *Mitsui*, 1152.

[5] Cour de cassation, civ 1re, 4 March 2020, ECLI:FR:CCASS:2020:C100175, D 2020, *Metelmann & Co GmbH*, 601.

[6] Cf P Mayer, V Heuzé and B Remy, *Droit international privé* 12th edn (LGDJ, 2019) 202.

[7] Cf B Ancel and Y Lequette, *Les grands arrêts de la jurisprudence française de droit international privé* 5th edn (Dalloz, 2006) 325.

[8] Cour de cassation, civ 1re, 4 March 2020, ECLI:FR:CCASS:2020:C100175, D 2020, 601, *Metelmann & Co GmbH* (matrimonial property between spouses).

extended to transnational disputes (see below). Article 48 CPC gives the possibility to enter into a choice of court agreement.[9] Various rules to be found elsewhere have been extended to international disputes, but are not encompassed by civil and commercial matters in the sense of Brussels Ia Regulation.

(c)

Brussels rules on international jurisdiction have not been extended to non-EU defendants. Discrete inspiration from them can be identified in the case-law on cyber-torts (see below). Article 42 CPC as extended to international disputes has the same practical effect as Art 4 Brussels Ibis Regulation. The issue of Brussels I rules extension over non-EU defendants has been addressed in legal literature, though not extensively.[10] It has also been suggested not to incorporate the rules themselves but to adopt the subject-matter definitions given by the CJEU in its preliminary rulings, in order to harmonise domestic rules with EU rules.[11]

The latest development in the French law of international jurisdiction is the release of the aforementioned draft for a code of private international law. The draft has been authored by a working group commissioned by the French ministry of justice and composed of academics and practitioners (lawyers, judges). The draft comes with a report explaining the choices made by the working group.[12] Given the repeated failures of similar projects in the past, this initiative can only be met with a healthy scepticism. However, it does offer some insights into what the French law of international jurisdiction could look like if the project was to go through. References to the draft will be made in this report. The approach to international jurisdiction is not to change French law, but to reaffirm the current practice ('*consolider les acquis*'),[13] so it would not bring about major changes in the law of international jurisdiction. It does extend some of the rules of the Brussels Ibis Regulation in specific extracontractual liability cases.[14]

(d)

The information provided by France pursuant to Art 76(1) Brussels Ibis Regulation is exhaustive.

[9] Cour de cassation, civ 1re, 17 December 1985, no°84-16.338, Grands arrêts, *Compagnie de signaux et d'entreprises électriques*, 645.

[10] Cf N Castell and P de Lapasse, 'Les révisions du règlement Bruxelles I à la suite de la publication du livre vert de la Commission. Perspectives et opportunités' (2010) 148 *La Gazette du Palais* 26 (favourable); H Gaudemet-Tallon, 'La refonte du règlement Bruxelles I' in Mélina Douchy-Oudot and Emmanuel Guinchard (eds), *La justice civile européenne en marche* (Dalloz, 2012) (with great reservations); C Kessedjian, 'Commentaire de la refonte du règlement n° 44/2001' [2011] *Revue trimestrielle de droit européen* 117 (opposed); É Pataut, 'Le domaine spatial des règles de compétence', (2012–2014) *Travaux du comité français de droit international privé* (favourable).

[11] Cf M Minois, *Recherche sur la qualification en droit international privé des obligations* (LGDJ, 2020), 339.

[12] Groupe de travail pour la codification du droit international privé français, 'Rapport du groupe de travail présidé par Jean-Pierre Ancel' (2022).

[13] Cf ibid 15.

[14] Art 93 of the draft code ; cf ibid 14 and further in this report.

Question 2

Domicile of natural persons for jurisdictional purposes is defined by reference to the general notion of domicile, which is used in substantial rules and domestic civil procedure.[15] Pursuant to Art 102 civil code, a natural person has her domicile where she has her 'main establishment' ('*principal établissement*'). While the applicability of this provision to international jurisdiction cases is disputed, it does not seem to make any difference as the standards used by French courts in international litigation are the same as in domestic matters.[16] There is no requirement of duration for a domicile to be characterised, but an intention to stay (Art 103 civil code), a residence and a lasting settlement ('*installation durable*').[17] Without a real intention of having one's domicile at a given place, it can only be considered a residence at best. Owners of a house in France are not considered and not even presumed to have a domicile there if they only spend a few periods of time in the country.[18] French courts on some occasions also satisfied themselves with an appearance of domicile in France, when the claimant had been led on to believe that the defendant had his domicile in France, even if this was in fact not the case.[19]

Domicile of legal persons for jurisdictional purposes[20] is, pursuant to Art 43 civil procedural code, the place where the legal person is 'established' ('*établie*'). Pursuant to Art 1837 civil code and L 210-3 commercial code, a third person to a company can rely on both the statutory place of the seat and the place of the actual seat while dealing with the company. It is uncertain whether this provision applies to international jurisdiction.[21] The result would be that a choice be given to the claimant between the courts of the real seat and those of the statutory seat, if those two were to differ. While the statutory seat is the one chosen in the statutes, the actual seat of a company is the location where the main decisions are made.[22]

In any case, it must be noted that the 'main stations doctrine' ('*jurisprudence des gares principales*', because it was first developed in cases involving railway companies) ie the possibility for the plaintiff to go before the court within whose jurisdiction the defendant company has an important settlement,[23] has been put to use in international cases.[24] Therefore, a legal person can be sued in French courts, if it has a place of business in France and the facts of the case are in connection with its activities there.

[15] See Art 3 in the draft code.

[16] Cf H Gaudemet-Tallon, 'Compétence internationale: matière civile et commerciale' (2019) *Répertoire de droit international*, para 24.

[17] See eg in a domestic case: Cour de cassation, civ 2e, 19 April 1984, no°84-60.160, (1984) IV *JCP G* 197, *Dugain*.

[18] Cour d'appel de Paris (Paris Court of Appeal), 4 November 1991, D 1994, *Al Saud v Transcontal*, 351.

[19] Cour de cassation, civ 1re, 13 May 2020, ECLI:FR:CCASS:2020:C100280, (2021) *Rev crit DIP* 137, *Huawei*. Brussels Ibis Regulation might have been applicable but has been overseen by the parties: see the commentary by M Minois, (2021) *Rev crit DIP* 139.

[20] See Art 4 for a 'general' definition and Art 16 for jurisdictional purposes ; cf Groupe de travail pour la codification du droit international privé français, 'Rapport du groupe de travail présidé par Jean-Pierre Ancel', 15–16.

[21] Cf M Audit, S Bollée and P Callé, *Droit du commerce international et des investissements étrangers* 3rd edn (LGDJ, 2019) 55.

[22] Cf M Menjucq, *Droit international et européen des sociétés* 5th edn (LGDJ, 2018) 102.

[23] Cour de cassation, civ 2e, 6 April 2006, no°04-17.849, Bulletin II, *GAN*, 96.

Question 3

Jurisdiction Based on French Citizenship of One of the Parties

Pursuant to Art 14 and 15 civil code, French courts have a general jurisdiction, except on a few matters, most notably real immovable property located abroad,[25] if the claimant (Art 14) or the defendant (Art 15) has French citizenship. This couple of rules has always been highly controversial. They are still applied in civil and commercial matters. French citizens may renounce this 'privilege', either by entering into a formal agreement to give jurisdiction to a foreign court or becoming a party to a foreign litigation.[26] In the draft code, the principle underlying the rules is maintained,[27] somewhat surprisingly.[28]

French citizenship is defined in and its criterion set by French law.[29] Suffice it here to say that descendants of a French citizen acquire French citizenship without further requirement, and that a child born to foreigners on French soil is granted French citizenship,[30] if one of his parents was also born there. Dual citizenship is recognised and permitted by French law, but it will never be an obstacle to the jurisdiction of French courts if the provisions mentioned are applicable.[31]

Legal persons, which for jurisdictional purposes can be considered citizens of a particular state, can be subject to both articles.[32] French case-law considers that the 'citizenship' of a company is that of the state in which it has its real seat.[33]

Absence of Jurisdiction Based on Sole Residence

Article 42 civil procedure code as extended to international disputes gives jurisdiction to French courts if the defendant inhabits France. Although the text itself speaks of '*demeurer*', which would best be translated as 'to reside, to live (somewhere), to inhabit

[24] Cour de cassation, com, 21 March 1995, no°92-20.477, LPA 1995, no°44, *Mobil North Sea Ltd*; Cour d'appel de Versailles (Versailles Court of Appeal), 27 February 1997, no°4403/95, (1997) *BJS* 543, *Maaldrift v Comilog*.

[25] Cour de cassation, civ 1re, 27 May 1970, no°68-13.643, Grands arrêts, 445, *Weiss*; see also Cour de cassation, civ 1re, 14 April 2010, no°09-11.909, D 2010, 1087, *BIC-CI*, for enforcement abroad.

[26] Cour de cassation, civ 1re, 22 May 2007, no°5-20.473, D 2007, 1569, *Fercométal*; Cour de cassation, civ 1re, 1 July 2009, no°08-15.955, D 2009, 1899, *Valavia v Cessna Aircraft Company*.

[27] Art 17 of the draft code.

[28] The working group held that, although the rules did not longer serve a purpose inside the European Union, they still were of relevance for other parts of the world: cf Groupe de travail pour la codification du droit international privé français, 'Rapport du groupe de travail présidé par Jean-Pierre Ancel', 17.

[29] Cf C Bertossi and A Hajjat, 'Country Report: France', in EUDO Citizenship Observatory, 2010/14, Country Reports 2013/14.

[30] At least in theory, French nationality can therefore be passed on through generations indefinitely. However, French law provides for loss of French nationality by judgement, if an individual who could be a French national has in fact no relation to France and his family has cut ties with France for 'half a century', Art 23-6 civil code. Cf P Lagarde, *La nationalité française*, 4th edn (Dalloz, 2011), 83.

[31] Cour de cassation, civ 1re, 25 March 2015, ECLI:FR:CCASS:2015:C100411, AJ Fam. 2015, 289 (divorce case).

[32] Cour de cassation, civ 1re, 30 September 2009, no°08-17.587, (2010) *Rev crit DIP* 134, *Thinet*.

[33] Cour de cassation, ass, 21 December 1988, no°88-15.744, D 1991, 305, *Roval*.

(a place)', pursuant to Art 43, the defendant needs to have his or her domicile ('*domicile*') within the court's jurisdiction (by extension, in France). Residence will only constitute a ground for jurisdiction in domestic cases if the defendant has no known domicile in France. Although there is to this day no conclusive example on this point, a simple residence of the defendant in France would only justify international jurisdiction of the French courts, if the defendant has no domicile in France nor abroad.[34]

Question 4

French courts have taken jurisdiction on the basis of a risk of denial of justice (*déni de justice*), precisely where it can be safely assumed that either no foreign forum would be available[35] or that it would be overly burdensome for the claimant to go before the ones that come to mind.[36] It is difficult to provide an exhaustive account of the exact requirements, as decisions on this issue differ in their motivation.

The latest policy of the Cour de cassation seems to be the following: for French courts to have international jurisdiction as *forum necessitatis*, there needs to be a legal dispute (a) with no possibility of a foreign forum being available to the defendant and (b) a genuine contact with France. The second criterion was interpreted restrictively in a recent decision.[37] It ruled that the fact that a French-based company owned the foreign defendant company did not tie the situation to France enough to urge French courts to hear the dispute.

Article 18 of the draft code provides for a *forum necessitatis* under the same conditions.[38]

Question 5

(a)

Article 46 first hyphen CPC provides that 'in addition to the court of the place where the defendant resides, the plaintiff may also choose to bring an action in contractual claims, before the court of the place of the actual delivery of the goods or of the place of performance of the service'.

[34] Cf P Mayer, V Heuzé and B Remy, *Droit international privé*, 203.

[35] Cour de cassation, civ 1re, 1 February 2005, no°01-13.742, D 2005, 2727, NIOC.

[36] See Cour de cassation, soc, 10 May 2006, no°03-46.593, D 2006, 1400, *Moukarim*; however, there is a controversy as to whether French courts have taken jurisdiction in this case to avoid a denial of justice; while the decision itself makes no mention of it, the Cour de cassation released a press statement making comparisons with decisions explicitly relying on the risk of a denial of justice: www.courdecassation.fr/jurisprudence_2/chambre_sociale_576/communique_8860.html.

[37] Cour de cassation, soc, 14 September 2017, ECLI:FR:CCASS:2017:SO02024, (2018) *Rev crit DIP* 267, *Comilog*.

[38] Cf Groupe de travail pour la codification du droit international privé français, 'Rapport du groupe de travail présidé par Jean-Pierre Ancel', 16.

This provision gives the plaintiff an option: besides the court of the place where the defendant resides, he may lodge the claim with the court of the place of actual delivery of the goods or of the place of performance of the services. This article has been extended to international matters. It is therefore sufficient that one of the connections to which they refer be located in France for the French courts to have jurisdiction; and in their absence, the article extended to international disputes does not offer a ground for French jurisdiction.

For example, an action for compulsory enforcement of a sale can be brought before the French courts if the goods were to be delivered in France, even though they were not delivered to the buyer directly but to a freight forwarder.[39] Conversely, in a case where the incoterm 'EXW' was used in the contract, the seller had the buyer ship the goods from its headquarters in Hungary. French courts did not have jurisdiction over the dispute arising out of the contract.[40] An architect living in France cannot bring an action against a client living abroad for which he was designing villas in a foreign country before French courts, if the building plans were not to be delivered in France.[41]

The two criteria are very similar to those used in Art 7 no 1 lit a and b. However, Art 46 first hyphen refers only to place of delivery of goods and place of delivery of services. Therefore, it can only be applied for claims in relation with a contract where such performance can be localised.[42] Specific rules exist for leases (Art R 213-9 code of the judiciary), commercial leases (Art R 145-23 commercial codes) and the contracts mentioned further in this text under letter (d).

One interesting difference between Art 7 no 1 lit a and French law on jurisdiction over contractual claims is the possibility to use Art 46 in the absence of a contractual relation between the claimant and the defendant. Such action is permitted where the claimant can make a case from a contract the defendant has concluded with another party. It is called 'direct action' ('*action directe*'). The action is available, in particular, in liability insurance cases (the victim of a tort can bring a claim against the wrongdoer's insurance company) and sales (the sub-buyer of goods can make the claim the buyer would have been able to make against the original seller). In these cases, the claimant can lodge an application with French courts, even though she was not party to the contract giving rise to French jurisdiction. Such an extension of jurisdiction in contractual claims in sales was dismissed within the Brussels Convention by the ECJ in a 1992 decision,[43] but there is no reason it should not be allowed under French law.[44]

[39] Cour de cassation, civ 1re, 23 January 2007, no°04-12.760, D 2007, 586, Diffusion des ébénistes contemporains.

[40] Cour d'appel de Lyon, 16 September 2004, no°203/07413, www.legifrance.gouv.fr/juri/id/JURITEXT000006944386, *Shopguard*; see also Cour de cassation, com, 19 February 2013, ECLI:FR:CCASS:2013:CO00169, *Yaknoo*.

[41] Cour de cassation, civ 1re, 20 May 2003, no°01-03.121, www.legifrance.gouv.fr/juri/id/JURITEXT000007463898.

[42] Cour de cassation, civ 2e, 13 January 1982, no°80-14.663, www.legifrance.gouv.fr/juri/id/JURITEXT000007009586.

[43] Case C-26/91 *Handte*.

[44] Cf H Gaudemet-Tallon, 'Compétence internationale: matière civile et commerciale' (2019) *Répertoire de droit international*, para 34.

Another difference is the approach to the action for damages for 'abrupt termination of a long-standing business relationship', peculiar to French substantial law (Art L. 442-1 commercial code). While the CJEU, under certain conditions, regards it as a contractual action,[45] the Cour de cassation considers this action a matter relating to a delict.[46] Even though the Cour de cassation hasn't had the occasion, since the *Granarolo* ruling, to either to stand by its previous qualification or to adjust to the CJEU ruling in order to follow the same category in domestic, autonomous law as under the Brussels Ia Regulation, there is, just as for 'actions directes', no particular reason for the Cour de cassation to do the latter.[47]

(b)

Pursuant to Art 46 CPC third hyphen, the claimant may bring the dispute 'in matters relating to tort or delict, to the court of the place where the damage occurred or the court in whose jurisdiction the damage was suffered'.

Extension of this provision to international cases results in the French courts having jurisdiction when the tort, delict or quasi-delict has been at least in part realised in France: either if the harmful event (ie the event giving rise to the damage or the 'causal event') occurred in France, while the damage was suffered abroad; and if the damage occurred in France, while the harmful event happened abroad. There is no example comparable to the *Bier* case[48] in French case-law, but the distinction and resulting option open to plaintiff do exist.[49]

French courts have not expressly referred to the Brussels Ia Regulation while extending Art 46 to international disputes, but they did have the occasion of applying both simultaneously. This was the case in an unfair competition claim brought by French companies against a British company and an Indian one. The Orleans court of appeal had to assess its jurisdiction for both defendants. In doing so, it gave Art 46 extended to international disputes a very similar interpretation as the one given by the ECJ to Art 5 no 3 Brussels Convention in the *Shevill* case, with a limitation of jurisdiction to the damage suffered in France.[50] While this interpretation allowed for French courts to have jurisdiction over the Indian company, Art 5 no 3 was applied in that case to deny jurisdiction with regards to the British company, as it did not offer to purchase its goods on the accessible website online.[51] In cyber-torts cases, French courts have localised

[45] Case C-196/15 *Granarolo*.

[46] Cour de cassation, civ 1re, 25 March 2014, ECLI:FR:CCASS:2014:CO00326, D 2014, 1250, *Guerlain*.

[47] See recently Cour d'appel d'Aix-en-Provence, 30 June 2022, no°22/00843, www.courdecassation.fr/decision/62be906655cf2069b366186d. This decision applies Art 46 as extended to international litigation to a dispute between a French and a Chinese company concerning the alleged abrupt termination of longstanding business relationship, but it does not conclusively say whether it considers the suit a contractual or a civil liability matter, perhaps because French courts would have jurisdiction either way with respect to the facts of the case.

[48] Case 21/76 *Bier*.

[49] Cour de cassation, civ 1re, 16 April 1985, 83-16.195, (1987) *Rev crit DIP* 586, *MAAF*.

[50] Case C-68/93 *Fiona Shevill*.

[51] Cour d'appel d'Orléans (Orleans Court of Appeal), 6 May 2003, (2004) *Rev crit DIP* 139, *Les Jolies Céramiques*.

the damage in the sense of Art 46 'where the website is accessible'[52] with the result that French courts can rule on the action arising out of it if the website is accessible in France.

There is another example. The CJEU in the *Pinckney* case considered that accessibility of a website in a given member state was a ground sufficient to justify jurisdiction of this member state's courts for IP infringement claim, provided the infringed right is protected in this member state. The ruling was requested by the French Cour de cassation (France's highest court) and this court subsequently ruled that French courts had jurisdiction for damages suffered in France in this particular case, because the website where the infringed goods were sold was accessible in France.[53] On the same day, the Cour de cassation delivered another decision on article 46 extended of the French code of civil procedure, in another IP case concerning the sales of photographs, whereby it took the exact same wording as in its *Pinckney* decision, and decided that accessibility of a website in France could ground jurisdiction of the French courts for damages suffered there because of an IP infringement.[54]

In other cases however, the damage had been localised in France only on the condition that the activity of the website was 'directed' towards a French audience.[55] To that extent, French case-law applying domestic rules to international jurisdiction is not very different from the CJEU case-law on cyber-torts, in the sense that they share the same hesitations as to the best way to localise a damage suffered because of online activities.[56] The draft code aims at aligning French national law on international jurisdiction with the caselaw of the CJEU for personality right infringement cases.[57]

(c)

Pursuant to Art 42§2, 'If there are several defendants, the plaintiff shall bring the matter before the court of the place where one of them resides ["*demeure*"], at his option'.

Under French law, the forum of co-defendants provided for in Art 42§2 CPC is extended to international disputes,[58] provided that there is a strong connection between the claims brought against the defendants, and that the one against the co-defendant domiciled in France is 'real and serious'.

For example, the connection between the claim for price fixing in a construction contract and the claim for nullity of guarantees for the same contract was not deemed strong enough for Art 42 § 2 CPC to be extended to an international dispute where only the construction company, of all parties, had its seat in France.[59]

52 Cour de cassation, civ 1re, 18 October 2017, ECLI:FR:CCASS:2017:C101110, CCC 2018, comm 7, *Royal de Luxe*.

53 Case C-170/12 *Pinckney*; Cour de cassation, civ 1re, 22 January 2014, ECLI:FR:CCASS:2014:C100033.

54 Cour de cassation, civ 1re, 22 January 2014, ECLI:FR:CCASS:2014:C100060, *Korda*.

55 Cour de cassation, com, 9 March 2010, no°08-16.752, D 2010, 1183, Delticom; Cour de cassation, com, 3 May 2012, no°11-10.508, (2013) *Rev crit DIP* 192, eBay.

56 See the recent case C-251/20 *Gtflix*.

57 Art 93; see Groupe de travail pour la codification du droit international privé français, 'Rapport du groupe de travail présidé par Jean-Pierre Ancel', 55.

58 Cour de cassation, civ 1re, 12 November 2009, no°08-15.269, (2010) *Rev crit DIP* 372, *Gulfair*.

59 Cour de cassation, civ 1re, 24 February 1998, no°95-20.627, (1999) *Rev crit DIP* 309, *Intertour*.

The 'seriousness' criterion seems to serve the purpose of avoiding 'tricks' to bring a defendant before court by relying on a loose connection with another dispute: Art 42 § 2 'does not allow a defendant living abroad to be brought before a French court when the claim against it and a co-defendant domiciled in France is not serious as far as the latter is concerned, even if it is related to another claim against the same defendants'.[60] It is the same concern that underlies the interpretation of Art 8 no 1 Brussels Ia Regulation by the CJEU.[61]

There is a difference between Art 42§2 CPC extended to international disputes and Art 8 no 1 Brussels Ia Regulation. While the latter cannot apply to a co-defendant who has entered a jurisdiction agreement with the plaintiff giving jurisdiction to another court,[62] French courts make a difference depending on the degree of connection of the claims. If the claims are 'indivisible', ie if the connection between them go beyond the requirement for art 42 § 2 CPC to be applied to the dispute, then French courts will take jurisdiction notwithstanding a jurisdiction agreement between the plaintiff and one of the co-defendants giving jurisdiction to a foreign court.[63] If the claims are not indivisible, the foreign jurisdiction agreement constitutes a valid defence against jurisdiction of French courts.[64]

(d)

Consumer Contracts

Article R 631-3 of the Consumer Law Code (*code de la consummation*; CCons) provides that the consumer may bring an action, at his option, in addition to one of the courts having territorial jurisdiction under the CPC (Arts 42 and 46), 'before the court of the place where he resided at the time of the conclusion of the contract or the occurrence of the harmful event'. This provision should be extended to international disputes if need be. As a result of Brussels Ia Regulation rules on consumer contracts being applicable to extra-EU defendants, there is no case-law on the subject.

With respect to consumer class actions, Art R 623-40 CCons grants jurisdiction to the court of the defendant's residence or, if the defendant lives abroad or its domicile or residence is unknown, to Paris first instance tribunal.

Insurance Contracts

The rules of territorial jurisdiction set forth in Art R 114-1 of the Insurance Code (*code des assurances*) are extensible to international disputes.[65] Thus, with regard to the

[60] Cour de cassation, com, 13 April 2010, no°09-11.885, D 2010, 1152, *Mitsui*.

[61] Case 189/87 *Kalfelis*, at 9; Case C-103/50 *Reisch Montage*, at 32.

[62] Case C-352/13 *CDC*, at 59.

[63] Cour de cassation, civ 2e, 7 November 1994, no°92-20.776, (1995) IV *JCP G* 61, *L'Alibi*: claims 'on the same legal ground and for the same purpose'.

[64] Cour de cassation, soc, 26 June 1991, no°88-40.170, D 1991, IR, 212, *Sogexpat*.

[65] Cour de cassation, civ 1re, 31 January 1995, no°92-20.224, www.legifrance.gouv.fr/juri/id/JURITEXT000007033688, *Couach*: while jurisdiction is based on Art 14 civil code, this decision also rules

determination and settlement of compensation due, the French courts have jurisdiction when the insured person, whether plaintiff or defendant, has her domicile in France. However, French courts have no international jurisdiction, at least under French law, if the connecting factors referred to in Art R 114-1 Insurance Code are located abroad.

Employment Contracts

French courts have jurisdiction, pursuant to Art R 1412-1 French Labour Law Code (*code du travail*), either when the work is performed in an establishment of the employer located in France,[66] or when the employee, working outside of any establishment or at home, is domiciled in France.[67] French jurisdiction is also justified if the employer has its seat in France.

French courts have made rather wide interpretations of these connecting factors, favourable to the employee. For example, a series of extended business trips to France has been deemed sufficient to locate the performance of the contract there, prompting French courts to hear the dispute over a dismissal of the employee.[68] It is doubtful such a decision could be made under the Brussels Ibis Regulation relevant provisions.[69]

Other Types of Contracts

The research has not shown other sets of jurisdictional rules designed to protect a presumably weak party to an international dispute.

that the jurisdictional rules of *codes des assurances* (Insurance code) still apply in international disputes, even if the insurer is being sued subsidiarily.

[66] Cour de cassation, civ 1re, 26 October 1982, no°81-13.380, (1983) IV *JCP G*, 17, *Bank Saderat Iran*.

[67] Cour de cassation, soc, 9 April 1987, no° 84-42.669, www.legifrance.gouv.fr/juri/id/JURITEXT000007018395 *Cofras*.

[68] Cour de cassation, soc, 9 January 2012, no°10-25.985, (2012) *Rev crit DIP* 620, *Teksid Aluminio do Brasil*.

[69] See eg Case C-383/95 *Rutten*.

Germany

TOBIAS LUTZI AND FELIX M WILKE

Question 1

(a)

In German law, local (and international, see (b)) jurisdiction is governed by the Code of Civil Procedure (*Zivilprozessordnung*; ZPO).[1] The relevant section (Book 1, Section 1, Titles 2 and 3; §§ 12–40) contains a set of provisions on general jurisdiction (§§ 12–19), followed by a number of heads of special jurisdiction (§§ 20–34), some provisions on the relationship between the different heads of jurisdiction (§§ 35–37) and the rules governing the choice of court (§§ 38–40).

The provisions of the ZPO are supplemented by individual provisions contained in more specific pieces of legislation that govern specialised courts – such as the Act on Labour Courts (*Arbeitsgerichtsgesetz*; ArbGG) – or regulate specific areas of law – such as the Act on Insurance Contracts (*Versicherungsvertragsgesetz*; VVG).

(b)

Generally speaking, German law contains no specific rules on international jurisdiction. Instead, courts apply the principle of double functionality (*Doppelfunktionalität*; codified (only) for family courts)[2] to extend the rules on local jurisdiction (venue) to the question of international jurisdiction.[3] Thus, whenever a German court has local jurisdiction, it also has international jurisdiction.

Still, a small number of provisions contain rules that presuppose the existence of a transnational dispute. For instance, § 23 ZPO creates a head of jurisdiction at the

[1] Official translation provided by the Ministry of Justice, www.gesetze-im-internet.de/englisch_zpo/englisch_zpo.html.

[2] See § 105 Act on Proceedings in Family Matters and in Matters of Non-contentious Jurisdiction (*Gesetz über das Verfahren in Familiensachen und in den Angelegenheiten der freiwilligen Gerichtsbarkeit*; FamFG).

[3] See Bundesgerichtshof (Federal Court of Justice), 2 July 1991, XI ZR 206/90, BGHZ 115, 90, sub I; 18 April 1985, VII ZR 359/83, BGHZ 94, 156, sub 2 a); see also H Linke and W Hau, *Internationales Zivilverfahrensrecht*, 8th edn (Cologne, Otto Schmidt, 2021), paras 4.2–3, 4.63.

place where the defendant holds assets that is only available if the defendant has no domicile in Germany. Similarly, § 38(2) ZPO relaxes the requirements for a choice-of-court agreement if German courts do not have general jurisdiction over at least one of the parties.

(c)

As far as the aforementioned legal framework on jurisdiction is concerned, German law has remained independent from the Brussels Ia Regulation.

In a small number of cases, however, German courts have referred to the Regulation (as interpreted by the CJEU) to support their interpretation of the parallel provisions of domestic law,[4] or even changed[5] their interpretation in order to ensure the alignment of the two systems.

Scholars have also occasionally suggested applying specific provisions from the Brussels Ia Regulation, such as its Art 8(1),[6] by analogy.

(d)

As far as the reporters can tell, the information notified by Germany is both accurate and exhaustive.

Question 2

As a matter of terminology, the ZPO distinguishes between the 'domicile' (*Wohnsitz*) of natural persons and the 'seat' of legal persons as the relevant jurisdictional connecting factors.[7]

§§ 12, 13 ZPO state that a *natural person* can generally be sued before the courts of her domicile. It has long been held that 'domicile' must be interpreted by reference to the respective provisions of substantive law – § 7 et seq of the German Civil Code (*Bürgerliches Gesetzbuch*; BGB) – which are applied in this context for nationals, foreigners and stateless persons alike.[8] A few special provisions (§§ 15, 16 ZPO) supplement these rules.

[4] See, eg, Bundesgerichtshof, 28 February 1996, XII ZR 181/93, BGHZ 132, 105, sub I.3.b), discussed in more detail below, at n 42; Bundesgerichtshof, 8 November 2017, IV ZR 551/15, BGHZ 216, 358, discussed in more detail below, at n 96.

[5] See, eg, Bundesgerichtshof, 21 April 2016, I ZR 43/14, GRUR 2016, 1048 (*An Evening with Marlene Dietrich*), para 18, discussed in more detail below at n 60.

[6] See, eg, H Linke and W Hau, *Internationales Zivilverfahrensrecht*, para 5.65; see also below, under 5(c).

[7] This can lead to uncertainty with regard to provisions that contain only one of the two terms, see below 5(d)(3).

[8] Reichsgericht (Imperial Court), 9 December 1907, VI 276/07, RGZ 67, 191, 193; 10 October 1929, VIII 244/29, RGZ 126, 8,9; Bundesgerichtshof, 25 March 1987, IVb ARZ 6/87, (1988) *NJW-RR* 387; H Roth, '§ 13', in R Bork, H Roth, F Stein and M Jonas (eds), *Kommentar zur Zivilprozessordnung* (Mohr Siebeck, Vol 1, 2014), para 2; M Pagenstecher, 'Gerichtsbarkeit und internationale Zuständigkeit als selbständige Prozeßvoraussetzungen', (1938) 11 *RabelsZ* 337, 362 (in footnote 8a).

Pursuant to § 7(1) BGB, a person establishes her domicile where she settles permanently. This requires both a factual presence and a will to take domicile.[9] Abandoning the place with the intention to give it up means the termination of domicile at that place (§ 7(3) BGB). A person can have more than one domicile as § 7(2) BGB expressly sets forth. This translates to the jurisdictional rules so that the person can be sued at all places where she has a domicile.[10] People lacking full capacity to contract (such as minors) require the consent of their legal representative in order to take up a domicile (§ 8 BGB). Typically, a minor shares the domicile of her parents (who have the right to care for her) under § 11 BGB; if the parents separate, the minor thus has two domiciles.[11]

Germans enjoying immunity abroad as well as German public servants working abroad keep their last domicile in Germany for jurisdictional purposes pursuant to § 15(1) cl 1 ZPO. If they never had a domicile in Germany, they can be sued before the Local Court of Schöneberg (Berlin) pursuant to § 15(1) cl 2 ZPO. In the rare case that a person has no domicile at all,[12] she can be sued at the place of her current residence in Germany or, if this is not known, at the place of her last domicile (§ 16 ZPO).

As regards *legal persons*,[13] § 17(1) ZPO sets forth that they can be sued at the place of their 'seat'. Again, this is a reference to the relevant substantive law, eg company law, and in particular to the statutory seat (not the 'real seat').[14] Although the concept of double functionality applies in this context as well,[15] the provision is of very limited practical relevance for the international jurisdiction of German courts.[16] Whenever a defendant legal person has a statutory seat, its central administration or its principal place of business in Germany, the Brussels Ia Regulation will determine international jurisdiction pursuant to Art 5(1), 63(1) Brussels Ia. This includes limited-liability companies registered in third states that German law treats as (mere) partnerships if they move their principal place of business to Germany.[17] In case of summary proceedings for a payment order (*Mahnverfahren*), however, § 17(1) ZPO is still of practical relevance because jurisdiction in this context depends on the domicile/seat of the applicant, not of the respondent (§ 689(2) ZPO).[18]

[9] Bundesgerichtshof, 14 January 2010, IX ZB 76/09, *ZEV* 2010, 528; M Beurskens, '§ 7', in: G Dannemann and R Schulze (eds), *German Civil Code – Bürgerliches Gesetzbuch (BGB)* (Beck/Nomos, Vol I, 2020), para 7.

[10] Roth, '§ 13', para 5.

[11] Bundesgerichtshof, 30 November 1983, IVb ARZ 50/83, (1984) *NJW*, 971.

[12] For an example see Bundesgerichtshof, 14 January 2010 (n 12), (2010) *ZEV* 528.

[13] With the exception of the German State itself, see §§ 18–19 ZPO.

[14] H Schack, *Internationales Zivilverfahrensrecht: mit internationalem Insolvenzrecht und Schiedsverfahrensrecht* 8th edn (Beck, 2021) 303; Roth, '§ 17', para 2.

[15] Bayerisches Oberstes Landesgericht (Highest Regional Court of Bavaria), 20 February 2003, 12 AR 160/02, RIW 2003, 387.

[16] C Kern, 'Anerkennungsrechtliches Spiegelbildprinzip und europäische Zuständigkeit' (2007) 120 *ZZP* 31–71, 34–35.

[17] See in particular the famous '*Trabrennbahn*' decision in which the *Bundesgerichtshof* treated a Swiss company by shares as a German partnership after it had moved its principal place of business to Germany: Bundesgerichtshof, 27 October 2008, II ZR 158/06, (2009) *NJW* 289. Also eg Bundesgerichtshof, 22 November 2016, II ZB 19/15, *RIW* 2017, 303, 305, concerning a company from the Bahamas.

[18] See Roth, '§ 17', para 15.

Question 3

German domestic law only contains one general head of jurisdiction, which is generally based on domicile (as defined above, under 2) and defined more specifically for different types of defendants in §§ 12–19 ZPO.

§ 23 ZPO could be seen as a subsidiary general head of jurisdiction as it renders the courts of the place in which the defendant's assets are located competent for all claims in economic matters, which includes all claims falling within the scope of the Brussels Ia Regulation, provided that the defendant has no domicile in Germany and that the case is sufficiently closely connected to Germany.[19]

Question 4

German statutory law does not contain any rules on a *forum necessitatis* in civil and commercial matters,[20] nor is there any case law on this point. The *Bundesgerichtshof* and some *Oberlandesgerichte* (Higher Regional Courts) have entertained the idea of a *forum necessitatis* on several occasions, but never actually had to rely on such a ground of jurisdiction.[21]

Scholarly opinion seems to uniformly favour some way of establishing German international jurisdiction in cases where no[22] other forum would be available.[23] The main approach lies indeed in the assumption of an unwritten *forum neccesitatis* that a judge must rely upon if its conditions are met.[24] The biggest problem[25] then becomes identifying the special nexus (connecting factor) tying a case to Germany specifically. *Neuhaus's* oft-quoted seemingly sweeping proposition that every country can exercise international jurisdiction where no country has international jurisdiction[26] is generally rejected; it was not meant to imply limitless jurisdiction, anyway, as it presupposes the claimant's need for protection in the particular forum.[27] One factor that is typically

[19] See Bundesgerichtshof, 2 July 1991, XI ZR 206/90, BGHZ 115, 90, sub II.1.b).

[20] However, as regards eg matters of parental responsibility, visitation rights, guardianship, see § 99(1) cl 2 FamFG (above 1(b)), which de facto is an instance of a *forum necessitatis*. Further examples are provided by M Kübler-Wachendorff, *Das forum necessitatis im europäischen Zuständigkeitsrecht* (Mohr Siebeck, 2021) 13.

[21] Eg Bundesgerichtshof, 21 June 2006, IX ZR 39/06, *EuZW* 2007, 582, 584; Oberlandesgericht Rostock (Higher Regional Court of Rostock), 11 November 1999, 1 U 31/98, IPRspr 1999, No 132, 312, 317.

[22] It is considered to be sufficient that no foreign forum is available whose decision could be recognised in Germany: Kübler-Wachendorff, *Das forum necessitatis im europäischen Zuständigkeitsrecht*, 39; T Pfeiffer, *Internationale Zuständigkeit und prozessuale Gerechtigkeit: Die internationale Zuständigkeit im Zivilprozess zwischen effektivem Rechtsschutz und nationaler Zuständigkeitspolitik* (Frankfurt, Klostermann, 1995) 451.

[23] In more detail Kübler-Wachendorff, *Das forum necessitatis im europäischen Zuständigkeitsrecht*, 14–39.

[24] Kübler-Wachendorff, *Das forum necessitatis im europäischen Zuständigkeitsrecht*, 44; also J Kropholler, 'Kapitel III – Internationale Zuständigkeit' in *Handbuch des Internationalen Zivilverfahrensrechts I* (Mohr Siebeck, 1982), para 187.

[25] A second issue arises once one relies on an unwritten *forum necessitatis* to establish Germany's international jurisdiction: There is no obvious rule determining *local* jurisdiction in such a situation.

[26] P Neuhaus, 'Internationales Zivilprozessrecht und Internationales Privatrecht: Eine Skizze', (1955) 20 *RabelsZ*, 201, 265; also J Schröder, *Internationale Zuständigkeit* (Opladen, Westdeutscher Verlag, 1971), 216.

[27] P Neuhaus, 'Internationales Zivilprozessrecht und Internationales Privatrecht: Eine Skizze', 265.

considered sufficient is the expectation that a judgment could also be enforced in Germany.[28] At the same time, this explains why the issue has so far not played any role in practice: if the claimant (later) wants to seize assets of the defendant's located in Germany, German courts can usually assume international jurisdiction under the 'exorbitant' rule of § 23 ZPO (above, under 3).[29] Further links to Germany that may be considered sufficient may be derived from a person's[30] German nationality or even her mere (ie not habitual) residence in Germany as well as from a prejudicial effect of the case on another case in Germany or from the (desired)[31] applicability of German law.[32]

In the 1970s, an alternative solution was suggested that, in spite of being mentioned quite a lot, has not gained much traction since. It consists in allowing *renvoi* in the law of jurisdiction.[33] This 'jurisdictional *renvoi*' would mean to analyse whether another country that would have international jurisdiction under the *German* rules for international jurisdiction would, in applying *its own* jurisdictional rules, consider Germany to have international jurisdiction (or would consider a third country to have international jurisdiction which in turn would assume itself or Germany to have international jurisdiction).[34] Even if one accepted this approach, it would still leave claimants effectively unprotected who might have access to a foreign forum by law but could not reasonably expect any success for factual, including political, reasons.[35] Moreover, a jurisdictional *renvoi* would inevitably conflict with the need for predictable, clear grounds of jurisdiction.[36]

Question 5

At the outset, it might be worth noting that the special heads of jurisdiction in German law and under the Regulation share two important similarities. First, they each define

[28] Kübler-Wachendorff, *Das forum necessitatis im europäischen Zuständigkeitsrecht*, 41 (with further references).

[29] Schack, *Internationales Zivilverfahrensrecht: mit internationalem Insolvenzrecht und Schiedsverfahrensrecht*, para 503; see also Kübler-Wachendorff, *Das forum necessitatis im europäischen Zuständigkeitsrecht*, 13.

[30] The *Bundesgerichtshof* was wary of potential manipulations in the past, considering the claimant's domicile in Germany to be insufficient for the establishment of a *forum necessitatis* where the claim in question had only been assigned to the claimant. Rather, the claimant should have turned to the courts of the country of the assignor's seat in order to try to establish a *forum necessitatis*: Bundesgerichtshof, 17 January 1995, XI ZR 182/94.

[31] It may seem to be circular reasoning to derive the competence of German courts from the application of German substantive law as the applicable conflict of laws rules depend on the forum in the first place. What is meant, however, is a desired legal consequence that only German law provides, Kübler-Wachendorff, *Das forum necessitatis im europäischen Zuständigkeitsrecht*, 43–44.

[32] Kübler-Wachendorff, *Das forum necessitatis im europäischen Zuständigkeitsrecht*, 42–44 (with further references); Kropholler, 'Kapitel III – Internationale Zuständigkeit', para 192.

[33] The main proponents of the jurisdictional *renvoi* are E Milliker, *Der Negative Internationale Kompetenzkonflikt* (Bielefeld, Gieseking, 1975) 81 et seq and Schröder, *Internationale Zuständigkeit*, 789 et seq.

[34] See the concise explanation by J Kropholler, 'Kapitel III – Internationale Zuständigkeit', para 197.

[35] Kübler-Wachendorff, *Das forum necessitatis im europäischen Zuständigkeitsrecht*, 16.

[36] Pfeiffer, *Internationale Zuständigkeit und prozessuale Gerechtigkeit: Die internationale Zuständigkeit im Zivilprozess zwischen effektivem Rechtsschutz und nationaler Zuständigkeitspolitik*, 460.

the relevant categories (of contract, tort, etc) autonomously, ie without reference to the *lex causae*.[37] Second, each head of special jurisdiction is limited (as regards the international dimension)[38] to the specific types of claims that it covers; thus, a parallel claim in tort cannot be brought in the *forum contractus*, unless it is also the *forum delicti*, and vice versa.[39] In 1996, the *Bundesgerichtshof* upheld this jurisprudence, expressly referring to the need for uniformity with the CJEU's interpretation of the Brussels Convention.[40]

(a)

According to § 29(1) ZPO, '[f]or any dispute arising from a contractual relationship and disputes regarding its existence, the court of that location shall have jurisdiction at which the obligation is to be performed that is at issue'.[41]

Just like Art 7(1) Brussels Ia, the provision not only refers to the place of performance but also requires to determine it for the specific obligation in question rather than identifying a single forum for the contract as a whole.[42] Also like Art 7(1) Brussels Ia,[43] § 29(1) ZPO does not include a definition of the 'place of performance' but rather refers to the *lex contractus*.[44]

Still, there is a number of significant differences between the two heads of jurisdiction.

Maybe most importantly, § 29(1) ZPO does not emulate letter (b) of Art 7(1) Brussels Ia, which subjects two practically significant types of contracts entirely to the law of a specific place, independently of the obligation in question. Thus, while all obligations arising from a contract of sale can be adjudicated in the court of the Member State of delivery under Art 7(1)(b) Brussels Ia, German law will limit this forum to claims against the seller. The forum for claims against the buyer, on the other hand, will depend on where the buyer's obligation is supposed to be performed under the applicable contract law. This approach has been criticised for creating arbitrary results that do not depend on any consideration of jurisdiction but only on how the applicable contract law qualifies the relevant obligation.[45]

[37] See Bundesgerichtshof, 28 February 1996 (n 7), sub I.2.a); Schack, *Internationales Zivilverfahrensrecht: mit internationalem Insolvenzrecht und Schiedsverfahrensrecht*, para 313. As to the Regulation, see, eg, Case C-26/91 *Jakob Handte*, para 11.

[38] The Bundesgerichtshof changed its position with regard to local jurisdiction, however. A court with local jurisdiction over tort claims (§ 32 ZPO) can also rule on a parallel claim under contract law, Bundesgerichtshof, 10 December 2002, X ARZ 208/02, (2003) NJW 828. The respective scopes of international and local jurisdiction diverge in such a situation, sub III.3.d.

[39] See Bundesgerichtshof, 8 January 1971, V ZR 125/67, (1971) *NJW* 564, sub II.1; 6 November 1973, IV ZR 199/71, (1974) NJW 410, 411, sub B.II.1.; Schack, *Internationales Zivilverfahrensrecht: mit internationalem Insolvenzrecht und Schiedsverfahrensrecht*, para 426. As to the Regulation, see Case 189/87 *Kalfelis*, para 19.

[40] Bundesgerichtshof, 28 February 1996 (n7), sub I.3.b).

[41] In the official translation of the Ministry of Justice (n 2).

[42] See Schack, *Internationales Zivilverfahrensrecht: mit internationalem Insolvenzrecht und Schiedsverfahrensrecht*, para 317.

[43] See Case C-12/76 *Industrie Tessili Italiana Como v Dunlop AG*; but see also F Wilke, 'Is Tessili still good law?' (conflictoflaws.net, 9 March 2021); F Wilke, 'Autonome Auslegung und kein Ende?', *GPR* 2021, 57, 59 et seq.

[44] See Bundesgerichtshof, 7 November 2011, VIII ZR 108/12, BGHZ 195, 243, para 15; 18 January 2011, X ZR 71/10, BGHZ 188, 85, para 29; H Linke and W Hau, *Internationales Zivilverfahrensrecht*, para 5.33.

[45] See Schack, *Internationales Zivilverfahrensrecht: mit internationalem Insolvenzrecht und Schiedsverfahrensrecht*, paras 321–24.

Finally, it should be noted that Art 7(1) Brussels Ia and the jurisprudence of the CJEU do not seem to have had any noticeable influence on the interpretation of § 29(1) ZPO by the German courts so far.

(b)

According to § 32 ZPO, '[f]or complaints arising from tort, the court in the jurisdiction of which the tortious act was committed shall have jurisdiction'.[46]

As far as the wording is concerned, § 32 ZPO differs more noticeably from its corollary in Art 7(2) Brussels Ia than § 29 ZPO differs from Art 7(1) Brussels Ia. Yet, both the place in which 'the tortious act was committed' in § 32 ZPO and the place of the 'harmful event' in Art 7(2) Brussels Ia are understood by the *Bundesgerichtshof* and the CJEU, respectively, as referring to both the place of the causal event (*Handlungsort*) and the place of the direct damage (*Erfolgsort*)[47] but not the place of any incidental or indirect damage.[48]

Whether, and if so, to what degree, German case law on § 32 ZPO differs from the CJEU's interpretation of Art 7(2) Brussels Ia in specific situations is not always easy to tell, as the different courts have not necessarily had opportunities to decide similar cases. The CJEU, for instance, has rendered multiple decisions on how to locate purely economic loss, allowing claimants to bring a claim for prospectus liability at the seat of the bank holding the relevant bank account.[49] There is no analogous German decision, although German courts seem similarly inclined to consider the place of a bank account a sufficient basis for jurisdiction in cases of fraud (where the special rule of § 32b ZPO does not apply).[50]

A particularly insightful example can arguably be found in the area of online torts. Long before the internet, both the German courts and the CJEU held that torts committed by publishing infringing material must be understood as taking place 'in any place in which the material has been published'.[51] Yet, while the German courts have always considered this fact to provide a basis for territorially unlimited jurisdiction,[52] the CJEU adopted the so-called mosaic approach, according to which the courts of each Member State will only have jurisdiction for the damage caused by publication in that State.[53] When confronted with the first cases of online defamation, the two lines of case law

[46] See also § 14(2) cl 2 Act Against Unfair Competition (*Gesetz gegen den unlauteren Wettbewerb*; UWG).

[47] See Bundesgerichtshof, 25 November 1993, IX ZR 32/93, (1994) *NJW*, 1413, sub III.4.a) (and already Reichsgericht, 18 October 1909, Rep II 96/08, RGZ 72, 41, 42–44) for § 32 ZPO and Case C-21/76 *Bier*, para 19, for Art 7(2) Brussels Ia.

[48] See Bundesgerichtshof, 3 May 1977, VI ZR 24/75, (1977) *NJW* 1590, sub II.1.b) for § 32 ZPO and Case C-364/93 *Antonio Marinari v Lloyds Bank plc und Zubaidi Trading Company*, paras 14–15, for Art 7(2) Brussels Ia.

[49] Case C-304/17 *Löber*, para 28; Case C-375/13 *Kolassa*, para 55.

[50] See Bundesgerichtshof, 25 November 1993, IX ZR 32/93, (1994) *NJW*, 1413, 1415; Bundesgerichtshof, 6 February 1990, XI ZR 184/88, (1990) *NJW-RR*, 604, 605.

[51] Bundesgerichtshof, 3 May 1977 (n 51), sub II.1.a). See also Case C-68/93 *Fiona Shevill*, para 29.

[52] See already Reichsgericht, 18 October 1909 (n 50), 44–46; see also Lutzi, 'Private International Law Online' (2020) *OUP*, para 4.102.

[53] Case C-68/93 *Fiona Shevill*, para 30; recently confirmed in Case C-251/20 *Gtflix Tv*, para 30.

diverged even further. The *Bundesgerichtshof* restricted the international jurisdiction of the German courts to publications that are objectively connected to Germany,[54] whereas the CJEU effectively created an additional *de facto forum actoris* by allowing the claimant to sue at her centre of interests.[55] Interestingly, the German courts used to also be more restrictive with regard to other online torts, requiring that a website be directed at Germany for the German courts to have international jurisdiction for infringements of IP rights;[56] the requirement was dropped, though, with explicit reference to the jurisprudence of the CJEU that considered mere accessibility a sufficient basis for jurisdiction.[57]

(c)

German law does not contain a general provision like Art 8 No 1 Brussels Ia, which allows the establishment of international jurisdiction over one defendant merely on the basis of their connection to another.[58] In civil and commercial matters, rules of this kind only exist for very specific scenarios, such as § 603(2) ZPO, which allows the suing of all defendants allegedly liable under a bill of exchange in each court (and thus state) that has general jurisdiction over at least one of them, and § 56(2) cl 2 of the Air Traffic Act (*Luftverkehrsgesetz*; LuftVG), which allows the suing of the other party to a contract for carriage of cargo by air jointly with their subcontractor in the same forum.

In domestic cases, this lacuna can usually be overcome by application of § 36(1) No 3 ZPO, which allows a superior court to designate one of the fora with general jurisdiction for one of several joint defendants to hear a claim against all of them if no common forum exists. The provision also applies to international cases – where courts even use some additional flexibility[59] – but requires that the German courts have international jurisdiction for every single defendant.[60]

The lack of a provision similar to Art 8 No 1 Brussels Ia has led some scholars to call for its analogous application to cases involving defendants not domiciled in a member state,[61] and/or for the introduction of a similar provision into German domestic law.[62]

[54] Bundesgerichtshof, 2 March 2010, VI ZR 23/09, BGHZ 184, 313 (*New York Times*), para 20.

[55] Joined Cases C-509/09 and C-161/10 *eDate Advertising*, para 48; later refined in Cases C-194/16 *Bolagsupplysningen* and C-800/19 *Mittelbayerischer Verlag*.

[56] Bundesgerichtshof, 29 April 2010, I ZR 69/08, BGHZ 185, 291, para 14.

[57] See Bundesgerichtshof, 21 April 2016 (*An Evening with Marlene Dietrich*) (n 8), para 18, referring to Case C-170/12 *Pinckney*.

[58] See also Schack, *Internationales Zivilverfahrensrecht: mit internationalem Insolvenzrecht und Schiedsverfahrensrecht*, para 439; H Linke and W Hau, *Internationales Zivilverfahrensrecht*, para 5.66.

[59] See Bayerisches Oberstes Landesgericht, 22 March 1988, AR 1 Z 12/88, (1988) *NJW*, 2184, applying the provision although another (foreign) forum had been available.

[60] See Bundesgerichtshof, 6 November 1970, I ARZ 228/70, (1971) *NJW*, 196; Schack, *Internationales Zivilverfahrensrecht: mit internationalem Insolvenzrecht und Schiedsverfahrensrecht*, para 440.

[61] See, eg, H Linke and W Hau, *Internationales Zivilverfahrensrecht*, para 5.65; Schack, *Internationales Zivilverfahrensrecht: mit internationalem Insolvenzrecht und Schiedsverfahrensrecht*, para 443.

[62] See Schack, *Internationales Zivilverfahrensrecht: mit internationalem Insolvenzrecht und Schiedsverfahrensrecht*, para 443; P Mankowski, (2017) *EWiR*, 415, para 3.3; F Rieländer, 'Dje verkappte Streitgenossenszuständigkeit am Verbrauchergerichtsstand des Art 18 Abs. 1 EuGVVO' (2021) *IPRax*, 512, 521.

(d)

Consumers

German law does not contain a general ground of consumer jurisdiction.[63] Legal scholars have occasionally called for the introduction of such a provision,[64] but the German legislator has not paid heed to this proposal thus far. There are some special grounds of jurisdiction that *also* benefit consumers among the rules to be expounded below. Still, only § 29c ZPO, which governs actions arising out of off-premises contracts, has a specific focus on consumers.

Under § 29c(1) ZPO, the court in whose district the consumer has her domicile (above, under 2) at the time the court is seised has jurisdiction over an off-premises contract. Because of the idea of double functionality (above, under 1(b)), this translates to German courts having international jurisdiction in these cases if the consumer has her domicile in Germany. If the consumer has no domicile at all,[65] the consumer's habitual residence in Germany suffices (§ 29c(1) cl 1 2nd alternative). Where the consumer is the defendant, this ground of jurisdiction is exclusive (§ 29c(1) cl 2 ZPO);[66] conversely, where the consumer brings the action, § 29c(1) ZPO only serves as an additional ground of jurisdiction.

Since 2018, § 29c(2) ZPO contains a definition of 'consumer' that is independent from substantive law. The only relevant point is whether the natural person did not predominantly act in the context of her trade or profession when acquiring the respective right,[67] whereas, unlike in the context of § 13 BGB, the purpose of the transaction does not matter. Somewhat paradoxically, however, this definition does not have any effect on the application of § 29c ZPO itself[68] because the provision requires an off-premises contract as defined under substantive law, including the respective definition of the term 'consumer'.[69]

§ 29c(4) ZPO allows for choice-of-court agreements designating a court different from the one determined by § 29c(1) ZPO in cross-border cases specifically. They may

[63] The respective statement by the Oberlandesgericht Karlsruhe (Higher Regional Court of Karlsruhe) from more than two decades ago is still correct: OLG Karlsruhe, 22 September 1999, 19 AR 14/99, (2000) *NJW-RR* 353.

[64] In particular with further references G Vollkommer and M Vollkommer, 'Empfiehlt sich ein (ggf. subsidiärer) allgemeiner oder besonderer Verbrauchergerichtsstand in der ZPO?' in Schütze (ed), *Einheit und Vielfalt des Rechts* (Beck, 2002) 1367, 1367; against this position eg Roth, '§ 29c', para 2.

[65] Not only not in Germany, see Roth, '§ 29c' para 10.

[66] Since Art 18(2) Brussels Ia applies to actions against consumers domiciled in an EU Member State, § 29c(1) cl 2 ZPO has a very limited scope of application.

[67] See R Koch and LM Friebel, 'Inhalt, Reichweite und Auswirkungen des prozessrechtlichen Verbraucherbegriffs (§ 29c Abs. 2 ZPO)' (2019) *GPR* 280, 282–83.

[68] R Koch and LM Friebel, 'Inhalt, Reichweite und Auswirkungen des prozessrechtlichen Verbraucherbegriffs (§ 29c Abs. 2 ZPO)', 284.

[69] It appears that the legislator created § 29c(2) ZPO with a view to model declaratory actions (*Musterfeststellungsklagen*) in §§ 606 (!) et seq ZPO and only chose this location in the ZPO because the Code makes mention of 'consumers' for the first time here. Indeed, the change to § 29c ZPO was part of the Act Introducing a Civil Model Declaratory Action of 12 July 2018, Federal Gazette 2018 I No 26, 1151.

only be concluded in order to take precautions against the consumer taking up a new domicile or habitual residence outside Germany after conclusion of the off-premises contract (or that the consumer's domicile/habitual residence is not known at the time the court is seised). The reverse case of the trader relocating to another country requires no special rule. For one, choice-of-court agreements for this situation are allowed anyway (§ 38(3) No 2 ZPO)[70] – for another, the consumer could and most likely would still rely on § 29c(1) ZPO.

Thus, German law differs from Art 17 et seq Brussels Ia in many respects, mainly because the two regimes have diverging approaches to consumer jurisdiction. § 29c ZPO only encompasses one kind of situation in which consumer contracts are *concluded* (namely: off premises). By contrast, Art 17(1)(c) Brussels Ia is limited to certain *commercial settings*: the trader must have pursued the commercial or professional activities in the Member State of the consumer's domicile or have directed them at that Member State, and the contract has to fall within the scope of such activities. Additionally, Art 17(1)(a), (b) Brussels Ia covers two *types* of contracts (independently from the setting or circumstances of their conclusion): contracts for the sale of goods on instalment credit terms and loan contracts if made to finance the sale of goods.

As regards choice-of-court agreements in the consumer context, the similarities are more pronounced, but far from ubiquitous. Art 19(3) Brussels Ia renders permissible (subject to the law of the respective Member State) choice-of-court agreements where consumer and trader are at the time of the conclusion of the contract domiciled or habitually resident in the same Member State and jurisdiction is conferred on the courts of that Member State. This provision has the same effect as § 29c(4) and § 38(3) No 2 ZPO. Choice-of-court agreements entered into after the dispute has arisen are accepted in principle both by Art 19(1) Brussels Ia and (the general rule of) § 38(3) No 1 ZPO. Under German law, however, this does not apply for proceedings against the consumer because choice-of-court-agreements may not derogate from grounds of exclusive jurisdiction, § 40(2) No 2 ZPO. Finally, unlike Art 19(2) Brussels Ia, German law does not allow choice-of-court agreements prior to the dispute arising even if they increase the consumer's options.

Employment Matters

In addition to the rule for international jurisdiction in § 15 of the German Posting of Workers Act (*Arbeitnehmerentsendegesetz*: ArbEntG),[71] § 48(1a) ArbGG[72] provides for special rules of local jurisdiction for labour courts in certain employment matters. It has long been accepted that, on principle, the concept of double functionality (above, under 1(b)) applies in labour matters as well,[73] so that one must read 'district' as

[70] Roth, '§ 29c', para 13.

[71] As this rule is based on Art 6 Directive No 96/71/EC, Brussels Ia does not prejudice its application pursuant to Art 67 Brussels Ia.

[72] Above 1(a).

[73] Bundesarbeitsgericht (Federal Labour Court), 19 March 1996, AZR 656/94, (1997) *NZA* 334, 335; also Schack, *Internationales Zivilverfahrensrecht: mit internationalem Insolvenzrecht und Schiedsverfahrensrecht*, para 347.

'Germany' for this purpose. Pursuant to § 48(1a) cl 1 ArbGG, the labour court *in* whose district the employee habitually carries out her work, or most recently habitually carried out her work, has jurisdiction. If this one habitual place of work cannot be determined (because no place is truly 'central'), the labour court *from* whose district the employee habitually carries out her work or most recently habitually carried out her work has jurisdiction under § 48(1a) cl 2 ArbGG. The wording ('also') clearly indicates that § 48(1a) ArbGG does not supersede other grounds of jurisdiction. In particular and among others, jurisdiction at the place of performance (§ 29 ZPO; above, under 5(a)) or jurisdiction in tort matters (§ 32 ZPO; above, under 5(b)) can be relevant in employment disputes.[74]

By its reference to certain parts of § 2(1) ArbGG, § 48(1a) ArbGG only covers individual employment disputes, not least those concerning claims arising out of an employment contract (§ 2(1) No 3(a) ArbGG) and those concerning the (non-)existence of an employment contract (§ 2(1) No 3(b) ArbGG). The personal dimension of the provision extends to employees and employers. Pursuant to § 5(1) ArbGG, employees for the purposes of jurisdiction are workers (*Arbeiter*) and employees in the narrow sense (*Angestellte*) including outworkers as well as people employed for the purpose of their vocational training.

It will have become apparent that the connecting factors of § 48(1a) ArbGG are very similar to the ones used in Art 21(1)(b)(i) Brussels Ia. The similarity is even more striking with regard to the German version of Brussels Ia. This is no accident. The proposal for § 48(1a) ArbGG expressly referred to Art 19 Brussels I.[75] By contrast, unlike Art 21(1)(b)(ii) Brussels Ia, § 48(1a) ArbGG does not use the place of the business that engaged the employee as a connecting factor. Similar results can be reached under German law by applying § 21 ZPO (special jurisdiction at a place of business),[76] however. This ground of jurisdiction differs from its counterpart in Brussels Ia in that it exists in addition to jurisdiction at the habitual workplace, not only as a subordinate option. Conversely, German law does not contain a ground of exclusive jurisdiction like Art 22(1) Brussels Ia for actions against an employee.

The personal dimension of the jurisdictional rules is quite similar, but, due to slightly different definitions, not perfectly congruent. § 5(1) ArbGG is based on the general understanding of 'employees' in substantive German law as codified in § 611a BGB since 2017.[77] Thus, an employee is a person under an obligation to provide labour in the service of another in personal dependency (subordination). The employee is subject to the other person's directives that can extend to the type of work, the manner in which it is to be carried out, its time and its place. According to § 5(1) cl 3 ArbGG, however, persons who by law, by charter or by the articles of association[78] have the authority to represent

[74] B Reinhard and S Böggemann, 'Gesetz zur Änderung des Sozialgerichtsgesetzes und des Arbeitsgerichtsgesetzes – Änderungen des ArbGG', (2008) *NJW* 1263–64.

[75] See BR-Drs. 820/07, 31. The 'from where' alternative now found in Art 21(1)(b)(i) Brussels Ia was added in the Recast, creating a parallel to Art 8(2) Rome I.

[76] See Bundesarbeitsgericht, 19 March 1996, 9 AZR 656/94, (1997) *IPRax*, 335, 336, for an example.

[77] Bundesarbeitsgericht, 9 April 2019, 9 AZB 2/19, (2020) *NZA* 67, 68.

[78] Power of representation conferred on a person by way of a legal transaction does not suffice. Such a representative would not be exlcuded by § 5(1) cl 3 ArbGG.

a company will not be considered employees for the purposes of the ArbGG – even if the contractual relationship between the company and the respective person indeed is an employment contract under substantive law.[79] Commercial agents can be considered employees for the purposes of the ArbGG, but only under the narrow conditions of § 5(3) ArbGG, including the one that they do not earn more than 1,000 EUR per month on average.

Both issues just mentioned could be resolved differently under Brussels Ia. The CJEU has defined an employment relationship for the purposes of the Lugano II Convention as implying 'the existence of a hierarchical relationship between the worker and his employer', to be assessed on the basis of all circumstances of the relationship between the parties.[80] The court has also identified several characteristics of employment contracts: that 'they create a lasting bond which brings the worker to some extent within the organisational framework of the business of the undertaking or employer, and they are linked to the place where the activities are pursued, which determines the application of mandatory rules and collective agreements'.[81] Moreover, 'the essential feature of an employment relationship is that for a certain period of time one person performs services for and under the direction of another in return for which he receives remuneration'.[82] Hence, the director and manager of a corporation could be considered an employee for the purposes of Brussels Ia.[83] Depending on the individual circumstances, commercial agents can also meet the requirements set forth by the CJEU.[84]

Insurance Matters

§ 215 VVG[85] contains a special rule concerning local jurisdiction that, in line with the concept of double functionality (above, under 1(b)), also applies to international jurisdiction.[86] Following the model of § 29c(1) ZPO[87] (above, under 5(d)(2)), § 215(1) cl 2 VVG provides for exclusive jurisdiction for actions arising out of an insurance contract or relating to insurance agents/brokers (see § 59 et seq VVG) against the insured at the place of her domicile or, if she has no domicile, habitual residence. For actions against

[79] Bundesarbeitsgericht, 3 December 2014, 10 AZB 98/14, (2015) *NZA* 180, para 15.

[80] Case C-603/17 *Bosworth*, para 26.

[81] Case C-47/14 *Holterman*, para 39.

[82] Case C-47/14 *Holterman*, para 41.

[83] Case C-47/14 *Holterman*, paras 33–47. Indeed, the director of a German company with limited liability ('GmbH') will always have to be considered an employee if she is not a shareholder – and even if she is, she still might be treated as an employee under Brussels Ia; see J Lüttringhaus, 'Die Haftung von Gesellschaftsorganen im internationalen Privat- und Prozessrecht' (2015) *EuZW* 904, 906; P Mankowski, 'Organpersonen und Internationales Arbeitsrecht' (2004) *RIW* 167, 169 et seq.

[84] The CJEU, however, in Case C-19/09 *Wood Floor*, apparently did not spare any thought on whether the commercial agency agreement at issue could be characterised as an employment contract. German cases on the Brussels regime seem to have been concerned thus far only with commercial agents too independent from their contractual partner to consider them employees, eg Bundesarbeitsgericht, 20 October 2015, 9 AZR 525/14, (2016) *NZA* 254, para 20 et seq; Oberlandesgericht Hamburg (Higher Regional Court of Hamburg), 14 April 2004, 13 U 76/03, (2004) *NJW*, 3126, 3127 et seq.

[85] Supra 1(a).

[86] Bundesgerichtshof, 1 June 2016, IV ZR 80/15, (2016) *NJW*, 3369, 3370.

[87] Indeed, the German legislator had § 29c ZPO in mind when creating § 215 VVG: BT-Drs. 16/3945, 117.

the insurer, § 215(1) cl 1 VVG sets forth an additional forum at this place. Whether insured/beneficiaries can also rely on this provision, either in direct or analogous application, is subject to debate among courts and scholars.[88] There seems to be unanimity, however, that the first clause of § 215(1) VVG cannot be used against an insured/beneficiary.[89] The insurer can also be sued, inter alia, at its domicile pursuant to §§ 12, 17 ZPO (under 2). Choice-of-court agreements designating a court different from the one determined by § 215(1) VVG are only allowed to a limited extent under § 215(3) VVG. This provision corresponds to § 29c(4) ZPO (above, under 5(d)(2)).

§ 215 VVG applies to insurance contracts, ie agreements by which one party (the insurer), in return for payment, assumes a duty to perform certain services when an uncertain event occurs, with the risk being spread over a large number of people who face the same danger.[90] It does not apply to reinsurance and marine insurance contracts (§ 209 VVG). As the wording of § 215 VVG is somewhat ambiguous,[91] there was some academic debate over whether this provision only applied if the insured party was a natural person or even only a consumer. The *Bundesgerichtshof*, however, has held that it extends to legal persons, as well. The court mainly relied on the legislative history and the purpose of the rule, noting that the provision is more concerned with the respective court's access to evidence and its local vicinity to the relevant factual situation than with a (perceived) need for protection of the insured party.[92] Moreover, it stated that it could not be assumed that the German legislator wanted to offer less protection to legal persons than under Art 9 Brussels I Regulation.[93]

It can be assumed that Section 3 of Brussels Ia likewise applies to legal persons as policyholders (and as insured[94]/beneficiaries). It appears from Recital (18) Brussels Ia that policyholders, insured and beneficiaries must be considered weaker parties regardless of their legal nature (or indeed economic power). As regards the substantive scope of application, however, the CJEU has held that the jurisdictional rules for insurance contracts, even without an express indication to this effect, do not cover disputes between a reinsurer and a reinsured in connection with a reinsurance contract.[95] In this respect, German law and EU law are aligned. As far as we can tell, the court has not yet provided a definition of 'matters relating to insurance'. It certainly must be independent from concepts of national law. Moreover, it extends to co-insurance contracts, liability insurance, insurance of immovable property as well as marine – excluded from the scope of § 215 VVG, see § 209 VVG – and aviation insurance because Art 11(1)(c), Art 12 and Art 16 No 1 Brussels Ia expressly mention them.[96] The connecting factors of

[88] See only D Looschelders, '§ 215', in T Langheid and M Wandt (eds), *Münchener Kommentar zum VVG*, 2nd edn (Beck, 2017) para 16.

[89] See only Looschelders, '§ 215', para 17.

[90] See only Bundesgerichtshof, 29 September 1994, I ZR 172/92, (1995) *NJW*, 324, 325.

[91] As mentioned before, § 215 VVG refers to the 'domicile' (*Wohnsitz*) of a person. Usually, this term would not be applied to legal persons (above, under 2).

[92] Bundesgerichtshof, 8 November 2017, IV ZR 551/15, (2018) *NJW* 232, 233 et seq (with many references for the different views).

[93] Bundesgerichtshof, 8 November 2017 (n 96), (2018) *NJW* 232, 234.

[94] The CJEU seems to have implicitly based its decision upon this assumption in Case C-112/03 *Société financière et industrielle du Peloux*.

[95] Case C-412/98 *Group Josi*, para 76.

[96] See Case C-412/98 *Group Josi*, para 62.

Brussels Ia are quite similar to German law. The supposedly weaker parties can sue the insurer both at its own and at the insurer's domicile (Art 11(1)(a) and (b) Brussels Ia) whereas the insurer, in principle, must sue before the courts of the defendant's domicile (Art 14(1) Brussels Ia).

Other (Arguably) Protected Categories

German law contains a plethora of further grounds of jurisdiction both in the ZPO and in more specialised legislation, some of which arguably aim to protect certain structurally disadvantaged parties.

§ 30(2) ZPO contains a special ground of jurisdiction for contracts of carriage of passengers and their luggage on a ship. Here, the place of departure or the destination, as provided for in the contract of carriage, serves as the connecting factor for the exercise of (international)[97] jurisdiction. As regards contracts for carriage of passengers by aircraft, § 56(2) cl 1 LuftVG[98] contains an additional ground of jurisdiction for damage claims regarding personal injury, delay, and damaged luggage. Here, (only) the place of destination is the relevant connecting factor. § 56(3) LuftVG clarifies that certain conventions, namely the Montreal Convention, take precedence over this rule.

The German rules of international jurisdiction do not clearly favour tenants of residential property. § 29a ZPO does contain a rule for exclusive local jurisdiction over tenancies concerning 'rooms' (ie not just living space). Theoretically, as always (above, under 1(b)), this would imply German international jurisdiction for rooms situated in Germany.[99] But this does not actually mean much in practice, as even in relation to defendants in third states, Art 24(1) Brussels Ia takes precedence.

§ 32b ZPO concerns exclusive jurisdiction in cases of wrong, misleading or missing public capital market information. It only applies to certain parties with a seat in Germany – and thus has no relevance for the determination of Germany's international jurisdiction, as a seat in Germany would lead to the application of Brussels Ia (see above, under 2). It is disputed, however, whether it follows from § 32b ZPO that a respective judgment from a third state cannot be recognised in Germany (§ 328(1) No 1 ZPO).[100]

Pursuant to § 319(2) cl 1 of the Capital Investment Code (*Kapitalanlagegesetzbuch*; KAGB), the domicile or seat of the representative of an EU alternative investment fund or a foreign alternative investment fund is an additional relevant connecting factor for actions against the fund itself, its management or distributing company. This only applies to actions that have a relation to the marketing of shares to private customers. Derogation by a choice-of-court agreement is not allowed (§ 319(2) cl 2 KAGB).

For disputes arising out of a distance learning contract or concerning the existence of such a contract, § 26(1) of the Act on the Protection of Participants in Distance

[97] Expressly Roth, '§ 30', para 3.
[98] Above, 5(c).
[99] Roth, '§ 29a', para 4.
[100] For this proposition eg J von Hein, 'Der ausschließliche Gerichtsstand für Kapitalanleger-Musterverfahren – eine Lex Anti-Americana?' (2004) RIW 602, 608; against eg Roth, '§ 32b', para 5.

Learning (*Fernunterrichtsschutzgesetz*; FernUSG) sets forth the exclusive jurisdiction of the court in whose district the participant can generally be sued, ie in which she has her domicile or seat (above, under 2). Clearly, this provision considers the 'participant' to be worthy of special protection. Interestingly, there are no further personal requirements, ie no limitation to consumers or even to natural persons.[101]

For copyright actions brought against a natural person using protected material outside her profession, the courts in whose district that person has her domicile (or, failing that, her habitual residence) have exclusive jurisdiction (§ 104a(1) of the Copyright Act (*Urheberrechtsgesetz*; UrhG)). The German legislator introduced this provision in 2013 in order to protect consumers against forum shopping by claimants on the basis of § 32 ZPO (above, under 5(b)) in cases of (alleged) copyright violations on the internet.[102] If the defendant has neither her domicile nor her habitual residence in Germany, the German court in whose district the act was committed has jurisdiction pursuant to § 104(1) cl 2 UrhG.[103]

§ 22 of the Regulation on the Basic Supply of Electricity (*Stromgrundversorgungsverordnung*: StromGVV) and § 22 of the Regulation on the Basic Supply of Natural Gas (*Gasgrundversorgungsverordnung*; GasGVV), applicable to the relationship between electricity/gas providers and households, state that local jurisdiction over the mutual duties arising out of a contract about the basic supply of electricity/natural gas lies with the courts at the place where the customer receives the electricity/gas.

[101] G Vollkommer and M Vollkommer, 'Empfiehlt sich ein (ggf. subsidiärer) allgemeiner oder besonderer Verbrauchergerichtsstand in der ZPO?', 1377.

[102] BT-Drs 17/13429, 9.

[103] As to which see also above, under 5(b).

Greece

VASSILIKI MARAZOPOULOU

Question 1

(a)

Greek (domestic) jurisdictional rules are set out in the Greek Code of Civil Procedure (hereinafter 'GCCP'; «*Κώδικας Πολιτικής Δικονομίας*» in Greek; *Kodikas Politikis Dikonomias*).[1] The applicable provisions of the GCCP include Art 3 and Arts 22–34 thereof; while jurisdictional rules in matters falling within the material application scope of the Brussels Ia Regulation are provided for in Arts 22, 23, 31, 33, 35 and 40 of GCCP. GCCP is the only legal act including jurisdictional rules that fall within the material scope of Brussels Ia.

The Greek jurisdictional system as established under the GCCP is based on the principle of (i) territoriality,[2,3] i.e. the principle that both Greek as well as foreign nationals are submitted to the jurisdiction of Greek courts, provided that said courts have territorial competence, along with (ii) the principle of 'Doppelfunktionalität', the principle pursuant to which jurisdictional rules serve the double function of both establishing territorial competence of the national courts as well as establishing international jurisdiction of the Greek courts.[4]

Both these fundamental principles are enshrined in Art 3 GCCP pursuant to which: '§1. Greeks and foreigners are subject to the Greek Courts' jurisdiction, in case of competence of a Greek Court. §2. Foreigners who enjoy immunity are exempted from the Greek courts' jurisdiction, except for the disputes that are submitted to the provisions of Art 29'.[5] Furthermore, Art 22 GCCP establishes the general jurisdiction of the defendant's domicile by providing that: 'The court in the district of which the defendant has his/her domicile is competent unless otherwise provided by law'.[6] In addition, Art 23 GCCP provides for the case of defendants who do not have a known domicile,

[1] Greek Presidential Decree, no°503/1985.

[2] Since the introduction of the GCCP as in force. It is noted that under the former Greek Code of Civil Procedure (called 'old Civil Procedure' under Greek legal doctrine) the main criterion was initially the nationality of the litigant party; analytically explained by K Kerameus, *Civil Procedural Law - General Part* (Sakkoulas Editions, 1997), 2–4.

[3] With the exception of immunity as provided for under para 2 of Art 3 GCCP.

[4] See more analytically answer under question 2 of this questionnaire.

[5] Translation of C Taliadoros, *Greek Civil Code* (Ant N Sakkoulas Publishers, 2000).

[6] Translation of C Taliadoros, *Greek Civil Code*.

thus complementing the aforementioned rule of general jurisdiction. Pursuant to Art 23 GCCP: '§1. If the defendant is not domiciled in Greece nor abroad, then the court where the defendant is habitually resident competent is competent. If the place of residence is not known, then the court is competent in the district of which the defendant had his last domicile in Greece and if the defendand did not have his domicile in Greece, his last habitual residence. §2. If the defendant has a special domicile then the court at the district of which such domicile is situated is competent'.[7]

The jurisdictional rule of domestic Greek law with respect to contractual disputes is established by Art 33 GCCP, pursuant to which: 'Disputes with respect to the existence or the validity of an inter vivos contract as well as any and all rights arising therefrom may be introduced before the court at the district of which the place where the contract was concluded or the place where the performance is to be fulfilled. Disputes concerning loss of profit as well as for compensation due to fault during negotiations'.[8]

The jurisdictional rule of domestic Greek law with respect to disputes arising out of tort is established by Art 35 GCCP, pursuant to which: 'Disputes arising from tort may be introduced before the court of the place where the harmful event took place or the place where occurrence of such harmful event is imminent'.[9]

Greek law includes a forum arresti provision, Art 40 GCCP, pursuant to which: 'Proceedings against individuals who do not have their domicile in Greece may be brought before the court in the district of which the defendant has assets or where the object of the proceedings is situated, if the object of the proceedings is pecuniary'.[10]

(b)

As already explained, the principle of '*Doppelfunktionalität*'[11] is fundamental under the jurisdictional system of the GCCP. Jurisdictional rules under the GCCP do apply indistinctly to transnational and domestic disputes. As already explained, this means that pursuant to the Greek civil procedure the jurisdictional rules serve the double function of both establishing territorial competence of the national courts as well as establishing international jurisdiction of the Greek[12] courts. This also explains why the wording of the relevant provisions is not orientated to disputes with an international element; despite this, they undoubtedly fall within the application scope of such provisions.

(c)

The jurisdictional rules of the Brussels regime were not extended by the (domestic procedural) Greek law, neither by reference; nor by incorporation. To the best of our

[7] Translation of C Taliadoros, *Greek Civil Code*.
[8] Translation of C Taliadoros, *Greek Civil Code*.
[9] Translation of C Taliadoros, *Greek Civil Code*.
[10] Translation of C Taliadoros, *Greek Civil Code*.
[11] See on the principle of Doppelfunktionalität under Greek law among others, V Marazopoulou, *Extraterritorial enforcement in civil and commercial matters under European law* (Nomiki Vivliothiki Ed, 2015) 71.
[12] See also preliminary analysis under answer to question 1 of this questionnaire.

knowledge, no specific propositions have been articulated in Greek legal doctrine to support extension of the personal scope of the Brussels regime jurisdictional rules; nor are there until this day specific legislative initiatives to this effect. However, in year 2011 (ie relatively recently compared to the introduction of the Brussels regime in the Greek legal order), the Greek legislator did pave the way for construction of the (domestic) jurisdictional provision for disputes arising out of tort to take into consideration the construction of the respective jurisdictional rule of Brussels I, by virtue of specific reference in an explanatory report.[13] To the best of our knowledge, this is the sole example to this effect; there are no other known examples of judgments in which the Greek courts construed domestic jurisdictional provisions based on the respective jurisdictional provisions of Brussels Ia.

(d)

Greece notified the European Commission that the Greek legal system contains one exorbitant jurisdictional basis, ie, Art 40 GCCP pursuant to Art 76(1) Brussels Ia. This indication from the part of Greece is in truth exhaustive, since the sole domestic provision that establishes an exorbitant jurisdictional basis in the sense of the Brussels regime is actually the aforementioned Art 40 GCCP.

Question 2

Pursuant to the absolutely dominant stance in Greek case-law[14] and doctrine[15] the notion of domicile of natural persons (individuals) is determined for the purposes of Art 22 GCCP in accordance with Arts 51–56 of the Greek Civil Code (hereinafter 'GCC'), ie, the respective provisions of Greek substantive civil law.[16] Pursuant to Art 51 of GCC:[17]

> A person has his/her domicile in the place of his principal and permanent establishment. No one has principal and permanent establishment. No one may have at the same time more than one domicile. In so far as transactions are concerned which arise from the exercise of a profession shall be considered a special domicile of a person, the place where he exercises his/her profession.[18]

As 'domicile' in Greek substantive law in the sense of Art 51 GCC is meant the place where the natural person has his/her main and permanent establishment, ie the place

[13] See more analytically answer to question 5(b) of this questionnaire.

[14] See already Athens Court of Appeal judgment, date unknown, no°5774/1976, *Nomiko Vima*, 397; see also Thessaloniki Court of Appeal judgment, date unknown, no°485/1999, 2001, *Armenopoulos*, 480.

[15] See among others M Margaritis and A Margariti, *Code of Civil Procedure-Commentary: doctrine-case law* (Ed PN Sakkoulas, 2018), Article 22, no 2, 73.

[16] Although it is notable that this refers only to jurisdictional bases; it does not hold true in order for instance to determine domicile for the purposes of the GCCP rules on service.

[17] Translation of C Taliadoros, *Greek Civil Code.*

[18] See also Art 52 of GCC: 'The domicile shall be maintained until the acquisition of a new domicile', as well as Art 53 of GCC: 'If it is not possible to establish the last domicile of a person his place of residence shall be deemed to be his last domicile'; C Taliadoros, *Greek Civil Code.*

that has become at the will of such individual the permanent centre of his/her viable relations. Therefore, in order for an individual to establish domicile in a certain place, both (i) the 'corpus' element, ie a permanent (although not necessarily through an entire lifetime) establishment in said place, as well as (ii) the 'animus' element, ie the actual will of a person to live permanently in said place, are necessary. Such place is the centre of a person's socioeconomic life and it does not necessarily equate to a person's current residence (or to other legal terms used by other legal provisions for their purposes, such as the tax domicile/residence of a person). As concerns the domicile of legal persons (seat of the legal person) for the purposes of the rule of Art 22 GCCP, it is meant in the sense of Art 10 CC. Pursuant to said provision the capacity of a legal person is governed by the law of its seat, while under established Greek case-law[19] the seat of the legal person in the sense of Art 10 of CC is in principle the real seat of the legal person.

Question 3

No, the general jurisdictional rule in matters regulated by the Brussels Ia Regulation is based on domicile as the connecting factor under domestic Greek law. Habitual residence is only used as an alternative connecting element for jurisdictional purposes for defendants who do not have a known domicile as provided for in Art 23 GCCP.[20]

Question 4

There is no specific provision in Greek law envisaging a *forum necessitatis* for matters that fall within the material application scope of Brussels Ia. The issue does not seem to have been discussed at all during the preparatory works for the introduction of the GCCP. It is however supported in legal doctrine that Greek courts courts may[21] or have to[22] assume jurisdiction based on public policy. It has been suggested that public policy shall intervene in cases that (i) it is impossible for the state that would regularly have international jurisdiction to adjudicate the dispute (which is determined by application of the Greek jurisdictional rules) to actually exercise jurisdiction, taking also into consideration objective or subjective grounds that concern the specific litigant parties, or (ii) the claimant has no real ability to seek recourse before foreign courts and if therefore Greek courts were not to assume jurisdiction, then the said claimant (litigant party) would practically be deprived of legal protection and recourse to justice.[23] This latter

[19] The most fundamental judgment being Greek Supreme Court judgment, 21 January 2003, no°2/2003, *Epitheorisi Emporikou Dikaiou*, 60; see detailed analysis on the construction of Art 10 GCC, the principle of the real seat under Greek law and its exceptions, Ch Pamboukis, *Private International Law – General Part-Special Part-International Procedural Law* (Nomiki Vivliothiki Ed, 2020), 486–87, with further references.

[20] See also reference in answer to question 1 of this questionnaire.

[21] N Nikas, *Handbook of Civil Procedure* (Sakkoulas Editions, 2018) 60.

[22] The view that the Greek courts are obliged to assume jurisdiction in case of forum necessitatis has been supported in a legal opinion provided for the purposes of judgments Gesiou-Feltsi and G Mitsopoulos, 'International jurisdiction of Greek courts by virtue of a prorogation clause. International jurisdiction on public policy grounds as well as on relatedness' (1997) *Elliniki Dikaiosini* 517.

[23] ibid.

legal construction seeks a concrete legal basis upon Art 24 GCCP pursuant to which: 'In case the claimant has residence neither in Greece nor abroad, then the court in the district of which the claimant has his/her residence is competent'.[24]

Despite the fact that the feasibility to apply *forum necessitatis* is not contested in Greek legal doctrine, to the best of our knowledge there is no such precedent in matters that fall with the material application scope of Brussels Ibis. There are only two reported judgments in the field of succession law.[25] In order to explain this, one could take into consideration that Greek law includes a specific jurisdictional basis of *forum arresti* in matters that fall within the material application scope of Brussels Ibis[26] which (*forum arresti*) does not qualify as *forum necessitatis* under domestic Greek law. In addition, the fact that public policy intervenes most often in matters of family or succession law may also be taken into consideration in this context.

Question 5

(a)

As already mentioned,[27] pursuant to Art 33 GCCP, jurisdiction in contractual disputes is conferred to the courts of the place where the contract was concluded or the place where the contractual performance is to be fulfilled.

As to the material application scope of Art 33 GCCP, from a general point of view the following are noted. The material application scope of Art 33 GCCP is wider than Art 7 no 1 lit a Brussels Ia, as in force, since it definitely includes all disputes of any material scope in the wider sense of civil disputes, such as civil (in the strict sense of the term) disputes; commercial disputes; disputes arising from legal transactions in rem; family disputes; succession disputes. On the other hand, when it comes to Brussels Ia, in order for Art 7 no 1 lit a thereof to be applied, any dispute at hand will necessarily have to fall within the (general) material application scope of the said Regulation; in this context a need for delineation with Regulation No 2201/2003 and Regulation No 650/2012 may always arise.

A concrete example of the different approach between Art 33 GCCP and Art 7 no 1 lit a Brussels Ia is drawn from the maintenance disputes; although they do fall within Art 33 GCCP they are now explicitly excluded from Brussels Ia.[28]

[24] See also to this effect Patras Single Member Court of Appeals judgment, date unknown, no°137/2019; such construction also acknowledged in Greek legal doctrine; see M Margaritis and A Margariti, *Civil Code Commentary*, 2nd edn (PN Sakkoulas publications, 2018) art 3, n 1–2.

[25] Athens Multimember Court of First Instance judgment, date unknown, no°9970/1997, *Dikaiosyni*, 677, and Athens Multimember Court of First Instance judgment, date unknown, no°9971/1997, 1998 *Dikaiosyni*, 692. These judgments arose out of the very same factual and legal background; therefore, in essence reference is made to one case of *forum necessitatis* application. The Athens Multimember Court of First Instance established jurisdiction of Greek courts on a *forum necessitatis* basis, on the grounds that one of the heirs (who sought recourse before Greek courts) was under a legal inability to file an action-at-law before the courts of any other jurisdiction and hence on public policy grounds; added to public policy the Athens Multimember Court of First Instance ruled that the fact that the nationality of the deceased was Greek is a crucial element for the purposes of establishing jurisdiction.

[26] Article 40 GCCP; see more analytically answer to question 1(d) of this Questionnaire.

[27] See above answer to question 1 of this questionnaire.

[28] Compare previous Art 5 §2 Brussels I.

As to whether claims from unjust enrichment fall within the provision, pursuant to dominant Greek case-law[29] disputes arising from unjust enrichment are to be considered as disputes related to rights arising out of a contract provided that they are related to non-performance of the contractual obligations and in such case they do fall within the application scope of Art 33 of GCCP. The ratio of the relevant Greek case-law consists in that the examination of the validity of the contract, as well as the examination of the issue whether such contract and the rights arising therefrom are in force are necessary prerequisites in order for the court to rule on the unjust enrichment claim as well. This, regardless to the fact that the unjust enrichment claims are undoubtedly non-contractual claims under Greek law. It seems that this approach is not fundamentally different than the one followed in the context of Brussels Ia, Art 7 no 1 lit a.[30]

Another difference when examining the application scope of the domestic (Greek) provision and Art 7 Brussels Ia is that unilateral acts actually do fall under Art 33 GCCP,[31] in contradistinction to Art 7 no 1 lit a Brussels Ia.

Furthermore, as to the connecting factors, it becomes apparent already from the wording of Art 33 GCCP that includes one additional connecting factor, compared to Art 7 of Brussels Ia. In particular, except for the connecting factor of the place where the contractual performance is to be fulfilled, the place where the contract was concluded is also employed as a connecting factor by virtue of Art 33 GCCP.[32] It is the claimant's choice which of the two connecting factors to establish jurisdiction upon pursuant to Art 33 GCCP.

Furthermore, for the purposes of construing the connecting factor 'place of contractual performance' in the sense of Art 33 GCCP, the respective articles of the GCC are taken into consideration (Arts 320–321 GCC). Pursuant to Art 320 GCC (*Place of performance*):

> If the place of performance cannot be deduced from the transaction or from the circumstances and especially from the nature of the contractual relationship the performance shall be furnished at the place where the debtor had his domicile at the time the obligation arose. If the obligation has arisen from the exercise of the debtor's profession the performance shall take place at the debtor's professional establishment in lieu of his domicile.[33]

[29] See among others the recent judgment of the Single Member Court of First Instance of Messologi, date unknown, no°21/2019, published in legal database NOMOS; see also Single Member Court of Appeals of Piraeus, date unknown, no°320/2015, Larissa Court of Appeals, date unknown, no°77/2004, published in legal database NOMOS; see from rare and earlier case-law to the contrary Thessaloniki Court of Appeals, date unknown, no°2402/1996, published in legal database NOMOS.

[30] See among others U Magnus, P Mankowski, *Brussels Ibis Commentary* (Verlag Dr Otto Schmidt, 2016) Art 7 para 61, explaining that claims of unjust enrichment also fall within the scope of Art 7 no 1 lit a, provided that they purport to cover a contractual exchange, also referring to relevant German case-law. See in any case the recent groundbreaking CJEU judgment C-242/20, *Hrvatske Šume*, by virtue of which it was ruled that an action for restitution based on unjust enrichment does not fall within the scope of the jurisdictional basis of Art 5(3) of Brussels I, while leaving room for it to fall within the scope of the jurisdictional basis of Article 5(2) thereof; see comments on the 'Online symposium on Hrvatske Sume', eapil.org, 9 January 2022, www.eapil.org/2022/01/09/online-symposium-on-hrvatske-sume/.

[31] Ibid, P Arvanitakis, 'EU Regulation 1215/2012', in P Arvanitakis/E Vassilakakis (eds), *Commentary* (Sakkoula Editions, 2020), Art 7 para 8, with further references to case-law under Art 33 GCCP to this effect.

[32] See also P Arvanitakis, 'EU Regulation 1215/2012', Art 7 paras 7–8.

[33] Translation of C Taliadoros, *Greek Civil Code*.

Pursuant to Art 321 GCC:

> If the performance consists in monetary payment, in case of doubt a debtor shall be obliged to effect payment at the place where the creditor has his domicile at the time of payment. If the claim has arisen from the exercise of the creditor's profession the performance shall take place at the place of the creditor's professional establishment in lieu of his domicile.[34]

Finally, on the question at what contractual performance reference is made to, it is noted that, under Art 33 GCCP reference is made to the litigious contractual performance/the contractual performance at stake; as is the case also under Art 7 no 1 lit a[35] Brussels Ia.

(b)

Pursuant to Art 35 GCCP as in force: 'Disputes arising from tort may be introduced before the court of the place where the harmful event took place or the place where occurrence of such harmful event is imminent'.

First of all, when comparing the said Greek (national) provision with Art 7 Brussels Ia, it should be noted that the formulation of the legal category thereunder is narrower ('disputes arising from *tort*', emphasis added) as compared to the formulation of the respective legal category under Art 7 no 2 Brussels Ia (in matters relating to *tort, delict or quasi-delict*).

In addition, the history of the domestic provision is enlightening as to the relation between the (domestic) Greek law provision and Art 7 no 2 Brussels Ia. More in particular, the previous version of the provision that stated: 'Disputes arising from a criminal act may also be introduced before the court at the district of which the criminal act was committed, even if the claim is made against an individual who does not bear criminal liability' was amended[36] mainly in order for the domestic Greek law provision to be harmonised with the provision of Art 5.3 of the (at the time of such amendment applicable) Brussels I. Therefore, by virtue of the new version of Art 35 GCCP, the Greek legislator on the one hand (i) extended the material scope of the provision in order for it to encompass all and an disputes arising from tort[37] and on the other hand (ii) added the connecting factor 'place where the harmful event is imminent to occur' in order for it to specifically include preventive injunctions in matters relating to tort. It is in this respect that the Greek legislator specifically referred to the Schlosser Report by virtue of the respective Explanatory Report.[38]

[34] Translation of C Taliadoros, *Greek Civil Code*.

[35] But not Art 7 para 1 lit b Brussels Ia.

[36] The amendment of the provision was made by virtue of Art 5 of Law no°3994/2011, *Official Gazette A*, no°165/, 25 July 2011. At the same time previous Art 40A of the GCCP was also abolished (previous Art 40A GCCP stated: 'Disputes concerning compensatory claims of any kind for damages caused by car may also be introduced before the court at the district of which the damage was caused').

[37] As explicitly stated in the Explanatory Report the ratio that the court that is situated at the place where the harmful event took place is the most appropriate to adjudicate the dispute is the forum convenient holds true for all and any torts and not only criminal acts.

[38] Explanatory Report to the draft legislative act 'Rationalization and amelioration to the administration of civil justice and other provisions', www.hellenicparliament.gr/UserFiles/2f026f42-950c-4efc-b950-340c4fb76a24/e-expol-eis.pdf, 3.

The Greek legislator further explicitly stated in the relevant Explanatory Report its will for the connecting factor 'place where the harmful event took place' to be construed (i) in the same manner as previous Art 35 GCCP was construed, ie encompassing the 'place where the harmful effect occurred' and (ii) at the same time in accordance with the respective construction of the homonymous connecting factor by the CJEU.[39] As to (ii), it was specifically stated in the Explanatory Report that the CJEU case-law is still under formulation.[40]

As to the delineation of the jurisdictional basis for disputes arising from contract from the jurisdictional basis for disputes arising from tort, both under the Brussels Ia scheme, as well as under the domestic Greek law provisions, they are distinct. Under the Greek law regime, it seems that the jurisdictional basis for disputes arising from contract is examined by means of priority, since the latter is construed widely, including in principle also disputes arising out of *ex lege* obligations.[41]

(c)

There is no comparable jurisdictional basis as to the one envisaged under Art 8 no 1 Brussels Ia under (domestic) Greek law. GCCP does provide for jurisdiction based on connection of claims, but not based on a close connection between the defendants.

More in particular, by virtue of the provision of Art 31 GCCP jurisdiction may be established based on connection between main and ancillary claims. Article 31 GCCP states:

> §1. Disputes that are related by way of main and ancillary, especially incidental actions-at-law, actions for guarantee, interventions and other similar cases are submitted to the exclusive competence of the court of the main proceedings.
>
> §2. The ancillary cases normally submitted to the competence of the Single Member Court of First Instance are submitted to the competence of the Multimember Court of First instance adjudicating the main dispute and the ancillary cases of the district court are submitted to the competence of the Single Member Court of First Instance.
>
> §3. In case of main proceedings related to one another the court, the court that was first seized has exclusive jurisdiction and the provision of paragraph 2 applies by way of analogy.

In addition, by virtue of the provision of Art 218 GCCP jurisdiction for more claims of the same claimant against the same defendant may be established. Article 218 GCCP reads:

> §1. More claims of the same claimant against the same defendant arising from the same or from a different cause that concern the same or a different object and are based on the same or on different grounds may be joined in the same legal deed if a) they are not contradictory, b) if they are submitted as a whole to the competence of the court before which they are introduced in terms of amount, c) if they are submitted to the local competence of the same court,

[39] ibid.
[40] ibid.
[41] See M Margaritis and A Margariti, *Code of Civil Procedure-Commentary: doctrine-case law*, Art 33, para 12, 80.

d) if they are submitted to the same procedure, e) if their simultaneous adjudication does not cause confusion.

§2. If more claims are joined without fulfillment of the prerequisites of paragraph 1 their separation is ordered either in sequence to a relevant petition or ex officio (…).

(d)

Domestic Greek procedural law does not include specific protective jurisdictional rules for the establishment of jurisdiction either for weaker parties in general, nor for specific categories of such parties, such as those provided for in the Brussels Ia (consumer, employment and insurance contracts). Moreover, Greek law does not include any specific protective jurisdictional law provisions for other parties that may be considered weak parties, such as commercial agents, distributors et alia.

There is, however, Greek case-law (applying domestic Greek procedural law) concerning the validity of prorogation clauses with respect to certain types of banking agreements (such as housing loans; agreements for the issuance of credit cards; car leasing et alia) that have been concluded between credit institutions and credit beneficiaries. Such prorogation clauses had been included in non-negotiable general terms and conditions in said banking agreements. It is, however, worth mentioning that Greek courts tend to rule on the validity of such prorogation clauses either (i) by considering the relevant prorogation clause as abusive and therefore invalid or (ii) by invoking Art 42§1 GCCP pursuant to which: 'A first instance court that is not locally competent may by rendered competent by virtue of an explicit or an implicit agreement of the litigant parties, unless the disputes in hand do not have a disputed property right as its object' and by judging that the prerequisites of the said article are not complied with.[42]

Finally, it has been supported in Greek legal doctrine[43] that protection from a procedural point of view, as such is granted by Brussels Ia to prorogation clauses included in consumer, employment and insurance contracts should also be provided to other weaker parties by virtue of a proper construction of prorogation clauses that they conclude. Such construction is proposed based on what may be called as an 'acquis' of Art 10–23 Brussels Ia. To the best of our knowledge, however, there does not seem to be Greek case-law to this effect insofar.

[42] See A Anthimos, 'Exclusive and asymmetric choice of forum clauses between credit institutions and debtors', (2019) *Armenopoulos*, 454.

[43] Ch Pamboukis and G Nikolaidis, (2008), 'Especially as to the validity of prorogation clauses pursuant to EC Regulation 44/2001 and the applicable law that seemingly deprive the exclusion of a distributor from indemnity in respect of customers and terms under which the distributor is entitled to said indemnity' (legal opinion), 2008 Nomiko Vima 2568.

Hungary

FERENC SZILÁGYI

Question 1

(a)

The domestic jurisdictional rules in matters regulated by the Brussels Ia Regulation are included in §§ 92–100 of *new* PIL Code [2017]. The group of jurisdictional rules in §§ 92–100 bears the title '[Title] 36. Cases in property' (*36. Vagyonjogi ügyek*), a category which covers the matters regulated by the Brussels Ia Regulation applicable to EU defendants only (not falling under one of the exceptions). The term 'vagyonjogi ügy', ie 'case in property' is broader than the term 'civil and commercial matters' in the sense of the Brussels Ia Regulation. In his article on the *new* Hungarian PIL Code [2017] Tamás Szabados refers to 'cases in property' as 'matters involving economic interest', which might better describe or explain the nature of the cases falling under this category, compared to the mere translation of Hungarian into English.[1]

As the general jurisdictional rule, § 92 *new* PIL Code [2017] – identical with Brussels Ia Regulation – stipulates the defendant's domicile or seat. Specific jurisdictional rules, establishing concurrent (alternative) jurisdiction,[2] concern contracts (§ 93); non-contractual obligations (§ 94); property rights in movables (§ 95); disputes pertaining to the operations of foreign enterprises carried out by branches or representations of such enterprises in Hungary, also including the case of a dispute concerning a contract concluded in Hungary on behalf of the foreign company (§ 96); defendants not domiciled in Hungary if they have assets located in Hungary which may be subjected to enforcement (§ 97); and jurisdiction based on the parties' agreement (§ 99).

For clarity it should be added that § 98 *new* PIL Code [2017] establishes the jurisdiction of the Hungarian court as regards the succession proceedings of Hungarian citizens, and stipulates the competence of a Hungarian notary public to conduct inheritance proceedings if the deceased is a Hungarian citizen or the estate is located in Hungary. Furthermore § 100 *new* PIL Code [2017] establishes jurisdiction of Hungarian

[1] T Szabados, 'The New Hungarian Private International Law Act: New Rules, New Questions' (2018) 82 *Rabels Zeitschrift für ausländisches und internationales Privatrecht* 972, 998.

[2] F Mádl and L Vékás, *Nemzetközi magánjog és nemzetközi gazdasági kapcsolatok joga* (ELTE Eötvös Kiadó, Budapest, 2018) 535.

courts in insolvency proceedings if the legal person debtor has its seat indicated in the articles of association in Hungary, or has a site of operation (branch or other establishment) in Hungary and if its activity carried out in Hungary is not only temporary. If the Hungarian court has jurisdiction to conduct insolvency proceedings it may also proceed in claims arising from and closely connected with the insolvency proceedings. § 100 only applies, of course, if the debtor's centre of main interests is outside the EU, otherwise the Insolvency Regulation applies.

(b)

The domestic jurisdictional rules apply to transnational disputes only. This follows from § 1 *new* PIL Code [2017] which defines its scope of application: 'This Act shall determine (…), b) upon which rules the Hungarian courts establish their jurisdiction and which procedural rules they follow (…) in private law relationships containing foreign elements.' As explained in the commentary,

> The jurisdiction answers the question of which state's judiciary body, court or authority is entitled to conduct legal proceedings in a case containing a significant foreign element. The issue of jurisdiction designates the country, its reason is the international distribution of cases (among the states), and its rules cover so-called jurisdictional grounds.[3]

Nevertheless, Tamás Szabados argues that under the *new* PIL Code [2017], an agreement on jurisdiction might be possible also in purely domestic matters. He criticises the unclear wording of the relevant provision (§ 99 *new* PIL Code [2017]). A problem may arise where, in a purely domestic matter, the parties agree to the jurisdiction of a court of a third country. If a Hungarian court is seised, the question arises whether such an agreement is permissible under the *new* PIL Code [2017] or not, since the Brussels I Regulation and the Hague Convention on Choice of Court Agreements do not apply to this case. As highlighted by Szabados, relevant case law and some authors require the existence of a foreign element for accepting the choice of a foreign court (prorogation of jurisdiction). In contrast, Szabados's view is that for the choice of court agreement to be valid it is sufficient that the prorogated and derogated courts differ: the foreign element is created by the choice of the foreign court by the parties living in the same country. Szabados further argues that requiring an additional foreign element would require courts to evaluate the significance of the existing foreign elements and would also require them to make a distinction between less and more significant foreign elements that justify the application of § 99 on the choice of court agreement of the *new* PIL Code [2017]. Acting in this way only causes uncertainty since it is relative which foreign elements are significant. The prohibition of such an agreement is meaningless, because if a designated court's own law does not preclude its jurisdiction, what is to stop the designated court from deciding the dispute? In connection with this, however, it is also true that concerning the same dispute, proceedings before a Hungarian court could be initiated, based on the exclusive or concurrent jurisdiction of the latter. And beside

[3] G Palásti, 'I. Fejezet: A nemzetközi magánjog általános szabályai', in Z Csehi (ed), *Magyarázat a nemzetközi magánjogról* (Wolters Kluwer Hungary, 2020) 45, 49. Translation by the author of this report.

this, arguments, as also remarked by Szabados, allowing the choice of a foreign court in purely domestic matters, would be also more in line with Art 25 Brussels Ia Regulation as it is possible to designate the court of a Member State in a purely domestic matter of another Member State.[4]

(c)

No, since Hungary has recently adopted the *new* PIL Code [2017]. When drafting the *new* PIL Code [2017], the Hungarian legislator tried to adapt itself as much as possible to the EU legal context, which determined to great extent the scope for national legislation. In doing so, the Hungarian legislator sought to establish a uniform legal practice for legal practitioners.[5]

(d)

The information notified by Hungary pursuant to Art 76(1) Brussels Ia Regulation is exhaustive. Claimants domiciled in an EU Member States might resort to the jurisdictional rules of that state without regard to their citizenship, and, as such, also to the jurisdictional rules notified by that state pursuant to Art 76(1) lit a Brussels Ia Regulation. In accordance with the option provided in Art 76(1) lit a Brussels Ia Regulation, Hungary notified § 57[6] of the *old* PIL Code [1979] repealed, as from 1 January 2018, by the *new* PIL Code [2017], and, while slightly different in wording nevertheless with the same content, is now included in § 97 *new* PIL Code [2017].[7] As explained in a commentary, by the jurisdiction based on assets located within the territory of Hungary which may be subject of judicial enforcement, the law shall enable the claimant's domestic enforcement of their claim as against a non-domestic defendant (having no domicile in or having no seat in Hungary). The application of this rule does not require there to be

[4] T Szabados, 'The New Hungarian Private International Law Act: New Rules, New Questions', 972, 999–1000.

[5] K Gombos, 'Rules of jurisdiction in the new Hungarian private international law' (2020) 61 *Hungarian Journal of Legal Studies* 52, 64; K Gombos, 'A joghatóság hazai szabályozása', in A Menyhárd and I Varga (eds), *350 éves az Eötvös Lóránd Tudományegyetem Állam- és Jogtudományi Kara I. kötet* (ELTE Eötvös Kiadó, Budapest 2018) 729, 738.

[6] § 57 *old* PIL Code [1979]: 'Hungarian courts shall have jurisdiction in property actions [*vagyonjogi per*; in German: Vermögensstreitigkeiten] where the defendant has no domicile or habitual residence in Hungary but does have enforceable assets in Hungary. Any claim due a defendant shall be considered as the defendant's asset in Hungary if the residence of the person owing the claim is in Hungary or if the claim is secured by a thing situated in Hungary'. The term 'actions in property' (vagyonjogi per) is defined in § 7(1) no 18 of the Civil Procedure Code [2016] (2016. évi CXXX. törvény a polgári perrendtartásról/Act CXXX of 2016 on the Code of Civil Procedure), ELI: www.njt.hu/eli/v01/TV/2016/130: '"action relating to property" shall mean actions where the claim enforced is based on the party's property rights or whose value can be expressed in money'. An unofficial English translation provided by the Ministry of Justice is available at the Website of the National Legislation Database www.njt.hu/translations/-:-:2016:130/1/10.

[7] § 97 *new* PIL Code [2017]: 'Hungarian courts may also proceed in property actions [in German: Vermögensstreitigkeiten] against a defendant having no domicile or seat in Hungary, provided that the defendant has enforceable assets in Hungary. A due claim of the defendant shall be deemed part of the defendant's assets in Hungary, if the domicile of the debtor is in Hungary, or if the claim is secured by a thing located in Hungary'.

no prospect of enforcement of the domestic judgment in another country in the case of the claim being successful, for example because the defendant has their domicile or has assets located in a country in which the judgment of a Hungarian court might not be enforced for lack of respective bilateral treaty or reciprocity.[8]

Question 2

Pursuant to § 3 lit c *new* PIL Code [2017]: 'domicile is the place where the individual person resides permanently or with the intention of permanent settlement'. In conjunction with the application of the general jurisdictional rule in proprietary matters (§ 92 *new* PIL Code [2017], see above) as regards legal persons the correspondent jurisdictional ground is the seat or central place of administration.[9]

It is important to note that the concept of domicile under the *new* PIL Code [2017] is not based on the administrative act of registering an address with the competent authority. In most cases, the domicile under the *new* PIL Code [2017] will coincide with the address registered in the relevant state register, but, nevertheless, for the purposes of the application of the PIL Code, the existence of the domicile should be assessed separately.[10]

Under Hungarian law, the seat of a legal person is its registered office, where the legal person *receives legal declarations* addressed to it and where the documents of the legal person as defined by law must be accessible.[11] The central administration may take place somewhere other than the seat of the legal person, which must be indicated in the articles of association.[12] In the case of a legal person operating under the law of another country, the seat of the legal person is the place indicated in the articles of association, or, if the legal person has no registered seat or has more than one registered seat, respectively, the place of central administration should be taken into account when assessing jurisdiction.[13] Seat of the legal person and place of central administration are equivalent grounds of jurisdiction under the PIL Code.[14]

Question 3

With a view to matters regulated by the Brussels Ia Regulation, the *general rule* connecting factor is the domicile, and, in case of legal persons, respectively, the seat of the defendant in Hungary (§ 92 *new* PIL Code [2017]).

[8] A Osztovits, 'X. Fejezet: Joghatóság' in Z Csehi (ed), *Magyarázat a nemzetközi magánjogról* (Wolters Kluwer Hungary, 2020) 843, 856.

[9] F Mádl and L Vékás, *Nemzetközi magánjog és nemzetközi gazdasági kapcsolatok joga*, 535; K Gombos, 'X. fejezet: Joghatóság', in L Vékás, Z Nemessányi and A Osztovits (eds.), *A nemzetközi magánjogról szóló törvény kommentárja* (HVG-Orac, Budapest 2020) 396, 413; K Raffai, 'XVI. fejezet: Joghatósági szabályok, eljárásjogi kérdések, és a külföldi határozatok végrehajtása' in L Burián, K Raffai and S Szabó, *Nemzetközi magánjog* (Pázmány Press, Budapest 2018) 439, 454.

[10] K Gombos, 'X. fejezet: Joghatóság', 413.

[11] K Gombos, 'X. fejezet: Joghatóság', 413.

[12] K Gombos, 'X. fejezet: Joghatóság', 413.

[13] K Gombos, 'X. fejezet: Joghatóság', 413.

[14] K Gombos, 'X. fejezet: Joghatóság', 413.

§ 96 *new* PIL Code [2017] might be identified as a general jurisdictional rule other than domicile (or seat) not inherently limited to specific subject-matter:

> Hungarian courts may proceed in procedures initiated against a business having its seat abroad, if the business has a branch or representation in Hungary and the legal dispute is related to their operations, *including the case that the contract on behalf of the business having its seat abroad was concluded in Hungary.*[15]

Question 4

Although Paragraph 70 of the codification (regulatory) concept of the *new* PIL Code [2017] explicitly envisaged that the new code would also provide a rule on *forum necessitatis*,[16] this institution was not codified in the end. The *new* PIL Code [2017] does not include it because it cannot be fitted into the system of jurisdiction of Hungarian law. The former Hungarian law (before the *new* PIL Code [2017]) did not know it either, and jurisdictional rule cannot be created by case law.

Question 5

(a)

§ 93 *new* PIL Code [2017]:

> Hungarian courts shall also have jurisdiction in contract disputes if the place of performance of the disputed obligation is in Hungary. For the purposes of this §, the place of performance of the disputed obligation is a) the place that the parties agreed upon in the contract as the place of performance, otherwise b) with regard to the sale of a movable property [thing], the place where the given thing was delivered or should have been delivered pursuant to the contract, c) with regard to the provision of services, the place where the service was or should have been provided pursuant to the contract, or *d) with regard to other contracts, the place determined by Hungarian law as the place of performance of the disputed claim.*

Comparison with Art 7(1) lit a – lit b Brussels Ia Regulation: Identical except § 93 lit d) which is a typical (and functionally desirable) catch-all rule 'with regard *to other contracts*, the place determined by Hungarian law as the place of performance of the disputed claim'. Apparently the Hungarian legislator was inspired by the relevant provision of the Brussels Ia Regulation.

The Explanatory Statement to the legislative proposal on the *new* PIL Code [2017][17] delivers the following explanation: § 93 of the *new* PIL Code [2017] is based on the rule

[15] Unofficial English translation, www.njt.hu/translations/-:-:2016:130/1/10.

[16] 673/2016. (XI. 29.) Korm. határozat az új nemzetközi magánjogi törvény koncepciójáról/Government Decision No°673/2016. (XI. 29.) (29 November 2016) on the regulatory concept of the *new* PIL Code; ELI: www.njt.hu/eli/v01/H/2016/Korm/1673.

[17] 2017. évi XXVIII. törvény [nem hivatalos] indokolása a nemzetközi magánjogról/[Unofficial] Explanatory Statement to Act XXVIII of 2017 on the Private International Code, source: commercial legal sources database 'Jogtár' (2017), www.uj.jogtar.hu, operation and rights holder of the database: Wolters Kluwer Hungary Kft.

on jurisdiction for contractual disputes from the *old* PIL Code, while its wording was brought in line with Art 7(1) Brussels Ia Regulation. As a result, § 93 clarifies that the place of performance of the disputed obligation, which is not necessarily the primary obligation (duty) under the contract, is the decisive factor in determining jurisdiction. The place of performance is determined primarily by the contractual agreement of the parties. If such an agreement is missing, the law sets out the criteria for determining the place of performance.[18] *There is no substantive difference compared to the Brussels Ia Regulation, as the Hungarian rule was drafted in line with it.*

'Contract disputes' include claims for a declaration of non-existence of a contract, unless circumstances clearly exclude that the contract has been concluded. But it also includes claims arising out of the performance, breach or termination of a contract, as well as questions of formation, invalidity or ineffectiveness of a contract.

As the commentary by Katalin Gombos points out, the wording of § 93 *new* PIL Code [2017] is very close to Art 7(1) Brussels Ia Regulation. She therefore considers it appropriate that the interpretation should take into account the relevant case law of the CJEU: the autonomous interpretation of 'a matter relating to a contract or a contractual claim' shall be followed while interpreting the wording 'contract disputes' of § 93 *new* PIL Code [2017].[19] Gombos advocates the interpretation of the wording of § 93 'contract disputes' *along the lines of the relevant CJEU case law*. Thus, the following claims fall under this wording: the claimant's dispute over a legal obligation freely assumed by one of the parties; different claims in the same case where the connecting factor applies to all claims under the same contract; obligations arising out of a contract where the claimant pleads non-performance of the contract; claims of an *actio pauliana* nature fall under this wording; joint and several debtors' or indirect debtors' internal redress claims as the special jurisdiction is based on the legal cause of the claim in relief.[20] On the one hand, if the claim against the former manager of the company is based on breach of duty, as it is usually a contractual claim, it also falls under the wording 'contract disputes' of § 93 *new* PIL Code [2017]. On the other hand, it is considered to be non-contractual liability if the manager's act does not constitute a breach of a contractual obligation under company law.[21] This can help to distinguish between a contract claim and a non-contractual liability claim.

The understanding of the place of performance under Hungarian law should be elucidated in connection with § 93 lit d: 'with regard to other contracts, the place determined by Hungarian law as the place of performance of the disputed claim'. This provision applies where the contract is not for the sale of a movable property [thing] or the provision of services and the parties have not agreed on the place of performance. The rules on the place of performance are included, as far as non-monetary obligations are concerned, in § 6:37 Hungarian Civil Code[22] (hereafter 'HunCC'), and, as far as

[18] [Unofficial] Explanatory Statement to § 93 *new* PIL Code [2017].
[19] K Gombos, 'X. fejezet: Joghatóság', 415.
[20] K Gombos, 'X. fejezet: Joghatóság', 415–16.
[21] K Gombos, 'X. fejezet: Joghatóság', 416.
[22] 2013. évi V. törvény a Polgári Törvénykönyvről/Act V of 2013 on the Civil Code (2013), as amended; ELI: www.njt.hu/eli/v01/TV/2013/5; An English translation 'for informational purposes only' is available at the Website of the National Legislation Database www.njt.hu/translations/-:0000:2013:5/1/10.

monetary obligations are concerned, in § 6:44 HunCC. These are default rules: they apply only to the extent that the parties have not agreed on the place of performance.

As regards *non-monetary obligations*, unless otherwise provided in the HunCC, § 6:37 HunCC applies: subsection (1) 'the place of performance shall be the obligor's establishment at the time when the obligation was created; in the absence of such, its seat or, for a natural person, his place of domicile or, in the absence of such, his place of habitual residence'; subsection (2) '[i]f the obligor has more than one establishment, the establishment with the closest connection to the obligation shall be considered the place of performance'; subsection (3) '[i]f the place of performance changes after the obligation has been created, and the obligor notifies the obligee of this fact, the place of performance shall be the new establishment or seat, or, for a natural person, the new place of domicile or habitual residence'. Subsection (3) also states that '[a]dditional costs arising from the change in the place of performance shall be advanced and borne by the obligor'.

As regards *monetary obligations*, § 6:44 HunCC applies. Subsection (1) stipulates that '[t]he place of performance of a monetary obligation as a cash payment shall be the obligee's establishment at the time when the obligation was created; in the absence of such, its seat or, for a natural person, his place of domicile or, in the absence of such, his place of habitual residence'. If the monetary obligation is not performed in cash payment '[t]he place of performance of the monetary obligation shall be the establishment of the bank maintaining the obligee's payment account at the time of creating the obligation; in the absence of such, its seat'. Furthermore subsection (1) provides that '[i]f, upon the creation of the obligation, the obligee had several payment accounts, the obligor shall have a right of choice with respect to the place of performance'. According to subsection (2) '[i]f the obligee has more than one establishment, the establishment with the *closest connection* to the obligation shall be considered the place of performance'. Pursuant to subsection (3) '[i]f the place of performance changes after the monetary obligation has been created, and the obligee notifies the obligor of this fact, the place of performance shall be the new establishment or seat, or, for a natural person, the new place of domicile or habitual residence', while subsection (4) provides that '[a]dditional costs arising from the change in the place of performance shall be advanced and borne by the obligee'.

(b)

§ 94 *new* PIL Code [2017]:

(1) Hungarian courts may also proceed in legal disputes concerning noncontractual obligations if the legal fact giving rise to the obligation or its effect occurred or could occur in Hungary. This provision shall apply accordingly to claims arising from violation of rights relating to personality.
(2) Hungarian courts may proceed in matters of compensation for damage caused by criminal offences and of civil law claims enforced in criminal procedures, if the criminal offense giving rise to the procedure falls within the scope of Hungarian criminal jurisdiction.
(3) Hungarian courts may also proceed in actions brought for establishing or raising the amount of compensation paid in annuities, if the domicile of the person entitled to compensation is in Hungary.

Comparison with Art 7(2) Brussels Ia Regulation: § 94(1) corresponds to Art 7(2) Brussels Ia Regulation. § 94(2) corresponds to Art 7(3) Brussels Ia Regulation. § 94(3) apparently has no equivalent under the Brussels Ia Regulation. There is no substantive difference compared to the Brussels Ia Regulation, as the Hungarian rule was drafted in line with it.

Similar to the interpretation of the wording 'contract disputes' in § 93 *new* PIL Code [2017], Katalin Gombos again proposes to follow the interpretation of the CJEU case law in connection with the application of § 94 *new* PIL Code [2017], when assessing the meaning of the place of the damage.[23] The following principles are developed by Gombos based on the CJEU's relevant case law.

- The place of the damage includes both the place where the damage occurred and the place where the damaging act took place. Depending on the claimant's choice, the claimant can therefore sue the defendant in the court of the place where the damage occurred as well as in the court where the damaging act happened.
- The place where damage has occurred should not be interpreted so broadly as to mean any place where the consequences of an act causing damage which has already occurred elsewhere may be present.
- Damage suffered as an indirect consequence of damage suffered by other persons who are the direct victims of the damage suffered, in a place other than that in which the indirect victim subsequently suffered damage, won't give rise to jurisdiction.
- In the case of damage resulting from a competition infringement under Article 101 TFEU, the place of damage is the relevant market where the distorted prices were applied and where the victim claims the damage occurred; it is irrelevant that the claim is against a participant in the cartel with whom the victim did not have a contractual relationship.
- In the area of product liability, the place of the act causing the damage is the place of manufacture of the product.[24]

A case regarding non-contractual obligation falls within the scope of § 94 *new* PIL Code [2017], but does not necessarily involve damages. The category of non-contractual obligation includes *all cases that are not governed by a contract*. In addition to non-contractual liability, it also covers unjust enrichment (§§ 6:579–6:582 HunCC), benevolent intervention into someone else's affairs (*negotiorum gestio*) (§§ 6:583-6:586 HunCC), 'implied conduct' (§ 6:587 HunCC),[25] promise of reward (§ 6:588 HunCC) and commitment for a purpose of public interest (§§ 6:589-6:592 HunCC). § 94 *new* PIL Code [2017] covers not only the actual occurrence of the conduct causing the damage or its consequences, but also its possible occurrence (imminent damage or other non-contractual

[23] K Gombos, 'X. fejezet: Joghatóság', 420.
[24] K Gombos, 'X. fejezet: Joghatóság', 420–21.
[25] It is a special non-contractual obligation of Hungarian law, which differs from non-contractual liability in that the sanctioned conduct does not reach the level to qualify as 'unlawful', and therefore cannot be dealt with under non-contractual liability. § 6:587 [Implied conduct] 'The person whose intentional conduct has, for a reasonable cause, led another person acting in good faith to show conduct which caused damage to that person without any fault on his part, may be obliged by the court to compensate for the damage in whole or in part'.

obligation). The second sentence of § 94 (1) *new* PIL Code [2017] states by way of a rule of reference that it shall also apply to non-pecuniary claims if the relevant event giving rise to the obligation occurred in Hungary or its result occurred in Hungary. As pointed out, this makes it possible for pecuniary and non-pecuniary claims arising from an infringement of a personality right or a right relating to a person to be dealt within one proceeding. In addition, *Gombos* bases the criteria applicable to non-contractual obligations (infringement of personality rights, infringement of copyright, trademark infringement, damaging the reputation of a business legal person) on the CJEU case law.[26] The jurisdiction of the Hungarian court is established if the centre of interests of the party whose personality rights have been infringed is in Hungary.[27] With regard to damage caused as a result of a criminal offence, § 94(2) *new* PIL Code [2017] covers not only civil claims in criminal proceedings, but also other proceedings for compensation for damage caused as a result of a criminal offence.[28] The jurisdiction rule applies if the offence falls under Hungarian criminal jurisdiction,[29] which is defined in § 3 Hungarian Criminal Code.

The rule on compensation paid in annuities has been codified in § 94(3) *new* PIL Code [2017] with a view to the equitable interests of the annuitant.[30]

(c)

§ 90 *new* PIL Code [2017]:

> (1) If more than one defendant is sued simultaneously, the Hungarian court may have jurisdiction over all defendants if at least one of the defendants is domiciled in Hungary, or, for legal persons or legal entities without legal personality, has its seat or central place of administration (for the purposes of this chapter hereinafter jointly 'seat') in Hungary, provided that there is a close relationship between the actions so that it is practical to assess and decide on them jointly in order to avoid contradictory decisions rendered in separate procedures.[31]

Comparison with Art 8(1) Brussels Ia Regulation: § 90(1) *new* PIL Code [2017] corresponds to Art 8(1) Brussels Ia Regulation. The Explanatory Statement to the legislative proposal of the *new* PIL Code [2017] states explicitly that although § 90 of the *new* PIL

[26] K Gombos, 'X. fejezet: Joghatóság', 422–23.

[27] Applying § 56/A of the *old* PIL Code [1979], the Debrecen Court of Appeal held that the Hungarian court has jurisdiction to hear an action for damages based on infringement of personality rights if the centre of the interests of the injured party is in Hungary and the television programme complained of, broadcast from abroad, can also be received in Hungary, or the programme is available on websites with foreign domain names (Debreceni Ítélőtábla Gf. I. 30741/2012/3, no.°BDT2013.2884 in the commercial legal sources database 'Jogtár' www.uj.jogtar.hu).

[28] K Gombos, 'X. fejezet: Joghatóság', 424.

[29] K Gombos, 'X. fejezet: Joghatóság', 424–25.

[30] K Gombos, 'X. fejezet: Joghatóság', 425.

[31] On the basis of this provision, the Kúria (Hungary's highest judicial body) confirmed, for example, the jurisdiction of the Hungarian court in a case of infringement of personality rights (right of personal portrayal), where the author and publisher of the infringing publication were non-EU defendants and the distributor of the book in Hungary was a defendant from Hungary. (Kúria Pfv.IV.20.937/2021/8, no BH2022.125 in the commercial legal sources database 'Jogtár' www.uj.jogtar.hu.)

Code [2017] is based on the relevant jurisdictional rule of the *old* PIL Code [1979], the conditions for its application had been aligned to Art 8(1) of the Brussels Ia Regulation.[32]

§ 90(2) *new* PIL Code [2017] corresponds to Art 8(2) Brussels Ia Regulation:

> If the primary and secondary obligors are sued simultaneously, Hungarian courts shall have jurisdiction regardless of the domicile or the seat of the secondary obligor, provided that the domicile or seat of the primary obligor is in Hungary.

§ 90(3) *new* PIL Code [2017] corresponds to Art 8(3) Brussels Ia Regulation:

> If a Hungarian court has jurisdiction to decide on a claim, it shall also have jurisdiction in respect of the counter-claim.

(d)

There are no such provisions in the *new* PIL Code [2017]. Insurance contracts are governed by ordinary rules governing jurisdiction over contracts (§ 93 *new* PIL Code [2017]). There are no protective rules on jurisdiction in matters regulated by the Brussels Ia Regulation.

[32] [Unofficial] Explanatory Statement to §§ 88–91 *new* PIL Code [2017].

Italy

ENNIO PIOVESANI AND STEFANO DOMINELLI[1]

Question 1

(a)

National rules on jurisdiction are mostly[2] found in Law 31 May 1995 no 218, the 'Reform of the Italian system of private international law' (hereafter, 'Law 218/1995').[3]

The 'general' rule on jurisdiction is found in Art 3 Law 218/1995, which contains three separate rules.[4] Pursuant to Art 3 para 1 Law 218/1995,[5] Italian jurisdiction exists when the defendant is domiciled, resident, or has a representative authorised to stand in trial in accordance with Art 77 Code of Civil Procedure (*Codice di procedura civile*; CPC) in Italy,[6] or when it exists under (national laws implementing) international treaties, special rules found in Law 218/1995, or other special laws. If Italian jurisdiction does not exist pursuant to Art 3 para 1 Law 218/1995, the latter may nevertheless exist under the following Art 3 para 2 of that Law, which, in turn, is composed of two sentences, containing two separate rules. In particular, pursuant to the first sentence of Art 3 para 2 Law 218/1995, Italian jurisdiction may additionally exist 'based on the criteria set forth in Sections 2, 3 and 4 of Title II of the [1968 Brussels Convention]

[1] For academic purposes only, it is specified that the answer to Question 5 is attributable to Stefano Dominelli, whereas the others are attributable to Ennio Piovesani.

[2] Cf P Franzina, *Introduzione al diritto internazionale privato* (Torino, Giappichelli, 2021) 129 et seq.; M Castellaneta, 'Competenza giurisdizionale' in R Baratta (ed), *Diritto internazionale privato* (Giuffré, 2011) 52.

[3] Legge of 31 May 1995 no 218, Riforma del Sistema italiano di diritto internazionale private, Gazzetta Ufficiale no 128 of 3 June 1995 – Supplemento Ordinario no 68. For English translations of Law 218/1995, see A Montanari and VA Narcisi, 'Italy' in J Basedow, G Rühl, F Ferrari, P de Miguel Asensio (eds), *Encyclopedia of Private International Law*, (Vol IV, Edward Elgar, 2017) 3329; A Russo and RE Rains, 'The Reform of the Italian System of Private International Law with Particular Regard to Domestic Relations Issues' (2000) 25 *NCJ Int'l L & Com Reg* 271, 310; A Giardina, 'Italy: Law Reforming the Italian System of Private International Law' (1996) 35 *Int'l Legal Materials* 760, 765.

[4] Cf B Barel and S Armellini, *Diritto internazionale privato*, 14th edn (Giuffrè, 2019) 157.

[5] See F Mosconi and C Campiglio, *Diritto internazionale privato e processuale*, 9th edn (Vol I, Utet, 2020) 158; F Salerno, *Lezioni di diritto internazionale privato* (Milanofiori Assago, Wolters Kluwer, 2020) 119; Barel and Armellini, *Diritto internazionale privato*, 359; A Bonomi and T Ballarino, 'Italy' in Basedow, Rühl, Ferrari and de Miguel Asensio (eds), *Encyclopedia of Private International Law*, (Vol III, Edward Elgar, 2017) 2209 and Castellaneta, 'Competenza', 55.

[6] Regio Decreto of 28 October 1940 no 1443, Codice di procedura civile, Gazzetta Ufficiale no 253 of 28 October 1940.

and following amendments in force for Italy, even if the defendant is not domiciled in the territory of a Contracting State, insofar as one of the matters falling within the scope of said Convention is concerned'. The latter provision thus extends, by reference, the personal scope of application of specific jurisdictional criteria set forth in the 1968 Brussels Convention. If neither the conditions of Art 3 paras 1 and 2, first sentence, Law 218/1995 are met, Art 3 para 2, second sentence, of that Law applies. Pursuant to the latter provision, Italian jurisdiction may be established based on national rules on venue jurisdiction.[7]

While Art 3 Law 218/1995 sets forth a number of general rules on jurisdiction, other jurisdictional rules are found in the same Law or in other special laws. As concerns the other jurisdictional rules found in Law 218/1995, the latter have a broader scope of application, such as those on prorogation and derogation of jurisdiction (Art 4); actions concerning rights in rem in immovable properties located in Italy (Art 5); preliminary questions (Art 6); *lis pendens* (Art 7); voluntary jurisdiction (Art 9); protective measures (Art 10). Today, the latter rules mostly overlap[8] with those of the Brussels Ia Regulation. Moreover, other rules found in Law 218/1995, which do not overlap with the Brussels Ia Regulation, have a much more limited material scope of application, such as those on disappearance, absence and presumed death (Art 22); annulment of marriage, legal separation and divorce (Art 32); dissolution of civil union (Art 32-*quarter*); filiation (Art 37); adoption (Art 40); measures protecting minors (Art 42) or adults (Art 44), and succession (Art 50).[9] Incidentally, some of the latter rules might still present some exorbitant nature.[10]

As mentioned above, pursuant to Art 3 para 2, second sentence, Law 218/1995, national rules on venue jurisdiction may be applied to establish Italian jurisdiction. Some of the latter rules are found in the CPC and in the Code of Navigation (*Codice della navigazione;* COD NAV).[11] For instance, Art 18 para 2 CPC[12] provides that if the

[7] See Corte di cassazione, Sezioni Unite, 27 November 1998, no°12056 (1993) Giust civ 2383, (1999) Riv dir int priv proc 601; G Conetti, S Tonolo and F Vismara, *Manuale di diritto internazionale privato,* 4th edn (Giappichelli, 2020) 20, 23; Mosconi and Campiglio, *Diritto internazionale privato*, 160; Salerno, *Lezioni di diritto internazionale privato*, 119; Castellaneta, 'Competenza', 57; G Conetti, S Tonolo and F Vismara, *Commento alla riforma del diritto internazionale privato italiano,* 2nd edn (Giappichelli, 2018) 15; G Broggini, 'Art 3 I', in S Bariatti (ed), *Legge 31 maggio 1995, n. 218, Riforma del sistema italiano di diritto internazionale privato* (Cedam, 1996) 909–10.

[8] See with respect to Arts 4 and/or 5 Law 218/1995, Conetti, Tonolo and Vismara, *Manuale*, 33; Mosconi and Campiglio, *Diritto internazionale privato*, 164; Barel and Armellini, *Diritto internazionale privato*, 375.

[9] See Barel and Armellini, *Diritto internazionale privato*, 357; M Torsello (ed), *Commento alla Legge 31 maggio 1995, n. 218 di riforma del sistema italiano di diritto internazionale privato*, e-book linked to M Franzoni, R Rolli (eds), *Codice civile commentato con dottrina e giurisprudenza* (Turin, Giappichelli, 2018) 6; Conetti, Tonolo and Vismara, *Commento*, 13; Broggini, 'Art 3 I', 907.

[10] See P Picone, *La riforma italiana del diritto internazionale privato* (Cedam, 1998) 105 et seq.

[11] See, on the growth of special rules on venue jurisdiction in the COD NAV, from a private international law persepective, SM Carbone, P Celle and M Lopez De Gonzalo, *Il diritto marittimo attraverso i casi e le clausole contrattuali* 6th edn (Giappichelli, 2020) 7; P Ivaldi, 'La riforma della legge n. 218/95: un'occasione per il riordino del diritto internazionale privato della navigazione' in C Campiglio (ed), *Un nuovo diritto internazionale privato* (Cedam, 2019) 131.

[12] See Conetti, Tonolo and Vismara, *Manuale*, 23; Mosconi and Campiglio, *Diritto internazionale privato*, 160; Castellaneta, 'Competenza' 57; F Pocar, 'Das neue italienische internationale Privatrecht' (1997) *IPRax* 145, 148.

defendant is not resident nor domiciled in Italy, or if his place of stay in that country is unknown, the (Italian) courts of the place where the claimant resides have (venue) jurisdiction. The latter provision, when combined with Art 3 para 2, second sentence, Law 218/1995, may considerably extend Italian jurisdiction against natural persons,[13] thereby establishing an exorbitant head of jurisdiction.[14] As concerns the COD NAV, eg, pursuant to its Art 14, in case of claims arising from the collision of vessels or aircrafts or the assistance, salvage or recovery in high waters or spaces not subject to the sovereignty of any State, Italian courts have jurisdiction, if the vessel or aircraft involved, or the one salvaging, flew the Italian flag; or, additionally, if the salvaged persons or goods are in Italy.[15]

(b)

The jurisdictional rules found in Law 218/1995 apply specifically to cross-border disputes.[16] For sake of completeness, as mentioned above, in accordance with Art 3 para 2, second sentence, Law 218/1995 national rules on venue jurisdiction may become relevant to establish Italian jurisdiction in matters falling outside the scope of the Brussels Regime.

(c)

Article 3 para 1 Law 218/1995 replaced the connecting factor based on nationality employed by the former general rule on jurisdiction (Art 4 no 1 CPC)[17] with that of domicile, residence or legal representative authorised to stand in trial in accordance with Art 77 CPC.[18] That replacement was made in order to avert discrimination between nationals and foreigners[19] and to uniform the general rule on jurisdiction to that of

[13] Cf Corte di cassazione, Sezioni Unite, 9 May 2018, no°11178 (2019) Corr giur 549.

[14] See Conetti, Tonolo and Vismara, *Manuale*, 23; Mosconi and Campiglio, *Diritto internazionale privato*, 160; Salerno, *Lezioni*, 119; Conetti, Tonolo and Vismara, *Commento*, 15; Pocar, *Das neue*, 148; Broggini, 'Art 3 I', 910.

[15] See Castellaneta, 'Competenza', 58–59; Broggini, 'Art 3 I' 907–908; see also, on jurisdiction in maritime employment matters, SM Carbone, 'Conflit de lois en droit maritime' (2010) 340 *Recueil des cours* 214 et seq; A Zanobetti, *Il rapporto internazionale di lavoro marittimo* (Bologna, BUP, 2008).

[16] Cf Conetti, Tonolo and Vismara, *Manuale*, 20; Castellaneta, 'Competenza', 53.

[17] See Art 73 Law 218/1995.

[18] See Corte di cassazione, Sezioni Unite, 5 May 2006, no°10312 (2006) 1 Foro it col 3388; Corte di cassazione, Sezioni Unite, 11 February 2003, no°2060 (2003) Riv dir int priv proc 547; Corte di cassazione, Sezioni Unite, 24 March 2006, no°6585 (2008) Il diritto dei trasporti 564; Corte di cassazione, Sezioni Unite, 27 November 1998, no°12056; F Pocar, *Il nuovo diritto internazionale privato,* 2nd edn (Giuffré, 2002) 278; Conetti, Tonolo and Vismara, *Manuale*, 21–22; Mosconi and Campiglio, *Diritto internazionale privato*, 158; Salerno, *Lezioni*, 119 and 125–126; Torsello, *Commento*, 4; Conetti, Tonolo and Vismara, *Commento*, 14; Pocar, *Das neue*, 147; Broggini, 'Art 3 I', 906.

[19] See Corte di cassazione, Sezioni Unite, 24 March 2006, no°6585; Corte di cassazione, Sezioni Unite, 27 November 1998, no°12056; Castellaneta, 'Competenza', 55; Broggini, 'Art 3 I', 906.

Art 2 para 1 1968 Brussels Convention.[20] In order to further uniform national rules on jurisdiction to the 1968 Brussels Convention,[21] as mentioned above, Art 3 para 2, first sentence, Law 218/1995, extends, by 'incorporation through reference' ('*incorporazione mediante rinvio*'),[22] the personal scope of application of the special and protective jurisdictional criteria (rather than the jurisdictional rules *stricto sensu*)[23] found in Title II, Sections 2–4 of the 1968 Convention to non-EU defendants.[24]

A lively debate concerns the question as to whether the reference made in Art 3 para 2 first sentence, Law 218/1995 should be interpreted as being in favour of the Brussels I Regulation, and, today, of the Brussels Ia Regulation. The answer to that interpretative question is crucial if one considers the differences between the mentioned instruments (eg those concerning the rule on jurisdiction in matters of contract,[25] as well as the fact that the Brussels Ia Regulation introduces new provisions, eg those on actions concerning the restitution of looted cultural goods).[26] In particular, the question revolves around the interpretation of the wording of Art 3 para 2, first sentence, Law 218/1995 '[1968 Brussels Convention] and following amendments in force for Italy'. With respect to the reference to the 1968 Brussels Convention, some stress that, pursuant to Arts 68 Brussels I and Ia Regulations, the latter Regulations replace the said Convention.[27] However, another question is whether the Regulations may actually

[20] See Corte di cassazione, Sezioni Unite, 5 May 2006, no°10312; Conetti, Tonolo and Vismara, *Manuale*, 22; Torsello, *Commento*, 4–5; Conetti, Tonolo and Vismara, *Commento*, 14; Broggini, 'Art 3 I', 907.

[21] See Conetti, Tonolo and Vismara, *Manuale*, 22; Mosconi and Campiglio, *Diritto internazionale privato*, 159–60; Conetti, Tonolo and Vismara, *Commento*, 14–15; N Trocker, 'La disciplina dell'àmbito della giurisdizione italiana nella legge di riforma del diritto internazionale privato', in Quaderni della Rivista trimestrale di diritto e procedura civile, *La riforma del sistema di diritto internazionale privato e processuale* (Giuffrè, 1996) 35.

[22] Trocker, 'La disciplina', 35.

[23] See Franzina, *Introduzione*, 131.

[24] See Conetti, Tonolo and Vismara, *Manuale*, 22; Mosconi and Campiglio, *Diritto internazionale privato*, 159; Castellaneta, 'Competenza', 56.

[25] See F Bortolotti, *Il contratto internazionale*, 2nd edn (Cedam, 2017) 214–15.

[26] See, on looted cultural goods in international civil procedure, Z Crespi Reghizzi, 'A New Special Forum for Disputes Concerning Rights in Rem over Movable Assets: Some Remarks on Article 5(3) of the Commission's Proposal' in F Pocar, I Viarengo and F Villata (eds), *Recasting Brussels I* (Cedam, 2012) 173; F Francioni, 'Public and Private in the International Protection of Global Cultural Goods' (2012) 23 *EJIL* 719; P Franzina, 'The Proposed New Rule of Special Jurisdiction Regarding Rights in Rem in Moveable Property: A Good Option for a Reformed Brussels I Regulation?' (2011) 25 *Dir comm int* 789; M Gebauer, 'A New Head of Jurisdiction in Relation to the Recovery of Cultural Objects' in F Ferrari and F Ragno (eds), *Cross-border Litigation in Europe: the Brussels I Recast Regulation as a Panacea?* (Giuffré, 2016) 31; LE Gillies, 'The Contribution of Jurisdiction as a Technique of Demand Side Regulation in Claims for the Recovery of Cultural Objects' (2015) 11 *JPIL* 295; A Leandro, 'Prime osservazioni sul Regolamen-to (UE) n 1215/2012 ("Bruxelles I bis")' (2013) *Giust proc civ* 583; P Mankowski, 'Article 7' in U Magnus and P Mankowski (eds), *European Commentaries on Private International Law*, Brussels Ibis Regulation (Vol I, Otto Schmidt, 2016) 121; F Marrella, 'Proprietà e possesso di beni mobili di interesse culturale nel diritto internazionale privato italiano' in F Marrella (ed), *Le opere d'arte tra cooperazione internazionale e conflitti armati* (Cedam, 2006) 107, and T Szabados, 'In Search of the Holy Grail of the Conflict of Laws of Cultural Property: Recent Trends in European Private International Law Codifications' (2020) 27 *Int J Cultural Property* 323.

[27] See Mosconi and Campiglio, *Diritto internazionale privato*, 54; Barel and Armellini, *Diritto internazionale privato*, 361; Torsello, *Commento*, 6; cf Corte di cassazione, Sezioni Unite, 25 June 2021, no°18299 (2021) Riv dir int priv proc 1008; Tribunale di Bergamo 15 April 2021, no°673, unpublished; Corte di cassazione 24 November 2021, no°36371, unpublished; Corte di cassazione, Sezioni Unite, 10 November 2021, no°33002, unpublished; Corte di cassazione, Sezioni Unite, 10 November 2021, no°33003, unpublished; Tribunale di Bergamo 12 December 2020, no°1787, unpublished.

qualify as 'following amendments' to the 1968 Brussels Convention.[28] In fact, if one takes a formalistic approach, the latter question should be answered in the negative, since a Regulation cannot 'amend' an international treaty. An additional question is that of whether the 1968 Brussels Convention may be still considered as being 'in force for Italy'.[29] With the latter respect, in 2009, the Court of Cassation took the view that the 1968 Brussels Convention was still in force for Italy with Denmark.[30] This view is questionable, because at the time of the Cassation's decision the 2005 EC–Denmark Agreement had already been concluded.[31] At most, at that time, the 1968 Brussels Convention could have been considered in force with the non-EU territories of the Member States referred to in Art 355 TFEU.[32] However, in light of Art 69 para 7 of the 2007 Lugano Convention, the latter later superseded the 1968 Brussels Convention in the relations between the Member States and the non-EU territories of the same States.[33] Therefore, the conclusion that, today, following the 2007 Lugano Convention, the 1968 Brussels Convention may no longer be considered as being in force for Italy,[34] raises the further question as to whether the reference made by Art 3 para 2, first sentence, Law 218/1995 should be considered as being 'receptive' ('*recettizia*') or 'mobile' ('*mobile*'). If it is held that, on the one hand, the reference is mobile – and thus does not 'crystallise' the content of the 1968 Brussels Convention – and that, on the other hand, the latter Convention is no longer in force for Italy, Art 3 para 2, first sentence, Law 218/1995 would have to be considered as having been substantially repealed. The resulting gap could be filled by applying Art 3 para 2, second sentence, Law 218/1995, thereby leading to the application of exorbitant rules on jurisdiction.[35]

While most scholars agree that the reference made by Art 3 para 2, first sentence, Law 218/1995 should be interpreted as being in favour of the Brussels I and Ia Regulations,[36] case law witnessed different approaches: some courts have referred to

[28] See Conetti, Tonolo and Vismara, *Commento*, 15; Castellaneta, 'Competenza', 56

[29] See Mosconi and Campiglio, *Diritto internazionale privato*, 52 et seq.

[30] Corte di cassazione, Sezioni Unite, 21 October 2009, no°22239 (2010) Riv dir int priv proc 481.

[31] Agreement between the European Community and the Kingdom of Denmark on jurisdiction and the recognition and enforcement of judgments in civil and commercial matters [2005] OJ L 299/61 (2005 EC–Denmark Agreement); see Mosconi and Campiglio, *Diritto internazionale privato*, 52; PA Nielsen, 'Brussels I and Denmark' (2007) *IPRax* 506.

[32] See recital (9) Brussels Ia Regulation; Mosconi and Campiglio, *Diritto internazionale privato*, 52–53.

[33] See Franzina, *Introduzione*, 133 et seq; B Cortese, 'Brexit e diritto internazionale privato tra Roma, Bruxelles e Lugano: "How Can I Just Let You Walk Away"?' (2021) 13 *CDT* 153, 163.

[34] Incidentally, according to the prevailing view, following Brexit, the 1968 Brussels Convention should not 'revive' between Italy and the United Kingdom. See Tribunale di Torino 29 July 2021, unpublished; A Malatesta, 'Circolazione delle sentenze tra Unione euorpea e Regno Unito: a favore di una cooperazione in seno alla Conferenza dell'Aja' (2021) *Riv dir int priv proc* 878, 884–85; Cortese, 'Brexit', 162–63; C Tuo, 'The Consequences of Brexit for Recognition and Enforcement of Judgments in Civil and Commercial Matters: Some Remarks' (2019) *Riv dir int priv proc* 302, 308–09; P Bertoli, 'La "Brexit" e il diritto internazionale privato e processuale' (2017) *Riv dir int priv proc* 599, 608–10.

[35] See Picone, *La riforma*, 107.

[36] See F Marongiu Buonaiuti, 'Il rinvio della legge italiana di riforma del diritto internazionale privato alle convenzioni, tra adeguamento al mutato contesto normativo e strumentalità alla tutela dei valori ispiratori' (2021) 57 *Riv dir int priv proc* 266, 271–72; Conetti, Tonolo and Vismara, *Manuale*, 22; Barel and Armellini, *Diritto internazionale privato*, 361; Torsello, *Commento*, 6; Conetti, Tonolo and Vismara, *Commento*, 15; *contra* Castellaneta, 'Competenza', 56.

the 1968 Brussels Convention,[37] others to the Brussels Regulations,[38] in most cases without (thoroughly) discussing the reasons for referring to one rather than the other instrument.[39] More recently, the Court of Cassation seems to have settled the issue, by stating that the reference made in Art 3 para 2, first sentence, Law 218/1995 must be interpreted as being in favour of the Brussels Ia Regulation.[40]

For sake of completeness, as of today, to the best of our knowledge, there does not seem to exist any legislative proposal to further extend[41] the reference contained in Art 3 para 2, first sentence, Law 218/1995, to other jurisdictional criteria of the Brussels Ia Regulation,[42] even though, occasionally, Italian courts have referred to the Brussels Regime when interpreting national rules on jurisdiction at large.[43]

[37] See eg Corte d'appello di Venezia 6 October 2021, no°2513, unpublished, in matters relating to contract; Tribunale di Teramo, 15 June 2021, no°601, unpublished, in matters relating to contract; Tribunale di Teramo, 15 January 2021, no°691, unpublished, in matters relating to contract; Tribunale di Vicenza, 12 January 2021, no°30, unpublished, in matters relating to contract; Corte d'appello di Genova, 27 July 2019 (2020) Riv dir int priv proc 151, in matters relating to employment; Corte di cassazione, Sezioni Unite, 22 June 2019, no°15748 (2020) Riv dir int priv proc 400, in matters relating to contract; Corte di cassazione, 12 March 2019, no°7007 (2020) Riv dir int priv proc 108, in matters relating to contract, tort and close connection between defendants; Tribunale di Brescia, 4 April 2018, no°613, unpublished, in matters relating to close connection between defendants; Tribunale di Trieste, 3 October 2017 (2020) Riv dir int priv proc 693, in matters relating to contract; Corte di cassazione, Sezioni Unite, 21 July 2015, no°15200 (2016) Fall 489, in matters relating to insolvency; Corte di cassazione, Sezioni Unite, 1 April 2015, no°6603 (2015) 1 Foro it col 2405, in matters relating to contract; Corte di cassazione, Sezioni Unite, 2 December 2013, no°26937, unpublished; Corte di cassazione, Sezioni Unite, 23 July 2013, no°17866 (2014) Fall 475, in matters relating to tort and close connection between defendants; Corte di cassazione, 12 April 2012, no°5765 (2013) Riv dir int priv proc 156, in matters relating to contract and close connection between defendants; Tribunale di Como, 22 February 2011 (2011) Riv dir int priv proc 782, in matter relating to contract; Corte d'appello di Napoli, 4 January 2010, unpublished, in matters relating to tort; Corte di cassazione 21 October 2009, no°22239, in matters relating to contract; Corte di cassazione, 22 February 2008, no°5090 (2008) Riv dir int priv proc 1090, in matters relating to contract; Tribunale di Bologna, 26 September 2007, unpublished, in matters relating to contract; Tribunale di Genova, 23 February 2007, unpublished, in matters relating to tort; Tribunale di Genova, 7 August 2006, unpublished, in matters relating to contract; Tribunale di Genova, 5 September 2005, unpublished, in matters relating to contract.

[38] See eg Tribunale di Chieti, 25 May 2021, no°181, unpublished, in matters relating to employment; Tribunale di Bergamo, 15 April 2021, no°673, in matters relating to contract; Tribunale di Roma, 3 May 2021, no°7620, unpublished, in matters relating to tort; Tribunale di Bergamo, 12 December 2020, no°1787, in matters relating to contract; Tribunale di Palermo, 6 October 2020, no°2993, unpublished, in matters relating to tort; Corte di cassazione, Sezioni Unite, 13 December 2018, no°32362 (2019) Dir mar 580, in matters relating to contract; Tribunale di Milano, 11 January 2016, unpublished, in matters of trademark infringement and close connection between defendants; Tribunale di Roma, 7 Feburary 2014 (2014) Società 973, in matters relating to contract and tort; Corte di cassazione, Sezioni Unite, 20 February 2013 no°4211, unpublished, in matter relating to consumers contract; Tribunale di Monza, 30 January 2013 (2014) Riv dir int priv proc 174, in matter relating to contract and related actions; Corte di cassazione, Sezioni Unite, 22 May 2012, no°8076 (2013) Riv dir int priv proc 431, in matter relating to tort; Corte di cassazione, Sezioni Unite, 18 May 2011, no°10862 (2012) Riv dir int priv proc 217, in matters relating to contract; Tribunale di Roma, 28 October 2011, unpublished, in matters relating to tort; Tribunale di Tolmezzo, 27 March 2008, unpublished, in matter relating to contract; Tribunale di Genova, 22 February 2008, unpublished, in matters relating to contract.

[39] Bortolotti, *Il contratto*, 215.

[40] See Corte di cassazione, Sezioni Unite, 25 June 2021, no°18299; Corte di cassazione, Sezioni Unite, 10 November 2021, no°33002; Corte di cassazione, Sezioni Unite, 10 November 2021, no°33003; Corte di cassazione, 24 November 2021, no°36371; G Zarra, 'La Cassazione si pronuncial sul rinvio alla Convenzione di Bruxelles nell' art. 3, comma 2, della Legge 218 del 1995: fine dell'epoca' (2022) *Dir comm int* 197.

[41] See Marongiu Buonaiuti, 'Il rinvio', 283–84.

[42] See A Malatesta, 'Origini, obiettivi e caratteri' in Malatesta A (ed), *La riforma del regolamento Bruxelles I* (Giuffrè, 2016) 7; P Franzina, 'L'universalisation partielle du régime européen de la compétence en matière civile et commerciale dans le Règlement Bruxelles I *bis*: une mise en persepctive' in E Guinchard (dir),

(d)

The information provided by Italy pursuant to Art 76 para 1 Brussels Ia Regulation appears to be overall exhaustive, considering that it mentions, in particular, Art 3 Law 218/1995.

Question 2

For the purposes of Art 3 para 1 Law 218/1995, the notion of 'domicile' must be interpreted in accordance with the *lex fori*.[44] Pursuant to Art 43 para 1 Civil Code (*Codice civile;* CC),[45] the domicile of a person is at the place where it has established its main seat of business and interests. Italian courts have specified that: domicile refers to a factual situation;[46] a foreigner may be domiciled in Italy even when he resides abroad;[47] a foreigner residing abroad is domiciled in the Italian municipality where he has notified public authorities that he holds firearms, where he applied to stay and where the bank where he chose to deposit his savings is situated;[48] an Italian national residing in a foreign country is presumed as being domiciled in that country,[49] and that presumption may not be rebutted by the simple fact that he often returns to Italy;[50] the existence of a 'elective domicile' ('*domicilio elettivo*')[51] in Italy is sufficient to establish Italian jurisdiction.[52]

Le nouveau règlement Bruxelles I bis (Brussels, Bruylant, 2014) 39 et seq; R Luzzato, 'On the proposed application of jurisdictional criteria of Brussels I Regulation to non-domiciled defendants' in F Pocar, I Viarengo and F Villata (eds), *Recasting Brussels I* (Cedam, 2012) 111 et seq; F Pocar, 'Révision de Bruxelles I et ordre juridique international: quelle approche uniforme' (2011) Riv dir int priv proc 591 et seq.

[43] See eg, with respect to Art 4 Law 218/1995, Tribunale di Roma, 5 April 2021, no°7820, unpublished.

[44] Cf Corte di cassazione, Sezioni Unite, 5 May 2006, no°10312, quoting Corte di cassazione, Sezioni Unite, 27 May 1999, no°309, unpubished; Conetti, G; Tonolo, S and Vismara, *Manuale*, 22; A Rizzieri, 'Domicilio e residenza' in G Cian and A Trabucchi (founded by), *Commentario breve al codice civile*, 14th edn (2020) 104 I para 9; Salerno, *Lezioni*, 126; Barel and Armellini, *Diritto internazionale privato*, 360; Torsello, *Commento*, 5; Castellaneta, 'Competenza', 54–55; Broggini, 'Art 3 I', 907.

[45] See Rizzieri, 'Domicilio e residenza', para 9; Torsello, *Commento*, 5, quoting Corte di cassazione, Sezioni Unite, 29 November 2006, no°25275, unpublished; Castellaneta, 'Competenza', 55.

[46] Tribunale di Perugia, 28 May 1954, in F Capotorti, B Conforti, L Ferrari Bravo and V Starace, *La giurisprudenza italiana di diritto internazionale privato e processuale, Repertorio 1942–1966* (Bari, De Donato editore Leonardo da Vinci, 1967) 156–57.

[47] Corte di cassazione, 14 October 1976, no°3438 (1976) Rep Foro it col 458 para 87; Corte di cassazione, Sezioni Unite, 27 May 1999, no 309 (1999) Rep Foro it col 1152 para 53, quoted in Rizzieri, 'Domicilio e residenza', 105 II para 18.

[48] Corte di cassazione, 14 October 1976, no°3438, quoted in Rizzieri, 'Domicilio e residenza', 105 II para 18, and in R Villani, 'Domicilio e residenza' in G Cian (ed), *Codice civile e leggi collegate*, 2nd edn (Cedam, 2016) 175 II para 2.

[49] Torsello, *Commento*, 5, quoting Corte di cassazione, Sezioni Unite, 11 February 2003, no°2060.

[50] Tribunale di Pordenone, 21 July 2016 (2018) Riv dir int priv proc 738.

[51] Elective domicile is at the place where a person has designated expressly and in writing its seat with reference to determined acts or business. See Art 47 CC; P Zatti and V Colussi, *Lineamenti di diritto privato*, 15th edn (Cedam, 2015) 148; A Torrente and P Schlesinger, *Manuale di diritto privato*, 21st edn (Giuffré, 2013) 114.

[52] See, though with reference to former Art 4 CPC, Corte d'appello di Napoli 28 May 1948, in Capotorti, Conforti, Ferrari Bravo and Starace, *La giurisprudenza italiana*, 156.

The notion of domicile in Art 3 para 1 Law 218/1995 includes that of the seat of legal persons, which, in turn, is derived from Art 19 CPC.[53] Pursuant to the latter provision, seat is the 'legal seat': that determined by law, by the order instituting the legal person, or that specified in the deed of incorporation. If the legal seat is not the effective seat (ie that where most of the relevant transactions take place) pursuant to Art 46 CC and consistent case law, third parties may bring their claims at the place where the latter is situated.[54] Alternatively,[55] venue jurisdiction is also with the courts of the place of establishment (ie any secondary legal or effective seat), insofar as in that place there is a person authorised to stand in trial in accordance with Art 77 CPC with respect to the relevant claim.[56] Moreover, pursuant to Art 19 para 2 CPC, companies without legal personality, non-recognised associations and committees are deemed to have their seat at the place where they pursue their activities on a regular basis.

Question 3

In matters governed by the Brussels Ia Regulation, as mentioned above, Art 3 para 1 Law 218/1995 provides for three connecting factors: domicile, residence and the existence of a representative authorised to stand in trial in accordance with Art 77 CPC. These connecting factors are alternative between them and thus may, at least virtually, largely broaden the scope of Italian jurisdiction.[57]

The notions of 'residence' and of 'representative authorised to stand in trial in accordance with Art 77 CPC', like that of 'domicile', must be interpreted in accordance with the *lex fori*.[58] In particular, pursuant to Art 43 para 2 CC, residence is at the place where a person has their habitual place of stay.[59] With respect to the notion of residence, Italian courts have specified that: Italian students studying abroad, but belonging to families residing in Italy, are not considered as residing in a foreign country if they are not

[53] On Art 19 CPC, see M Marinelli and P Widmann, 'Foro generale delle persone giuridiche e delle associazioni non riconosciute' in C Consolo (dir), *Codice di procedura civile, Commentario*, 6th edn (Wolters Kluwer, 2018) 377, 378 I para 1; L Passante, 'Foro generale elle persone giuridiche e delle associazioni non riconosciute' in F Carpi and M Taruffo (founded by), *Commentario breve al codice di procedura civile*, 9th edn (Cedam, 2018) 102 I para 2; L de Propris (adjourned by), 'Foro generale elle persone giuridiche e delle associazioni non riconosciute' in N Picardi, B Sassani and A Panzarola (eds), *Codice di procedura civile* 6th edn (Giuffré, 2015) 165; F and A Panzarola, 'Della competenza per materia e valore, della competenza per territorio' in *Commentario al codice di procedura civile* (Bologna, Zanichelli, 2015) 215, 216 et seq.

[54] See Marinelli and Widmann, 'Foro generale', 378 I para 2; Passante, 'Foro generale', 102 I para 2; Auletta and Panzarola, 'Della competenza', 219.

[55] See Marinelli and Widmann, 'Foro generale', 378 I paras 2 and 3; Passante, 'Foro generale', 102 I paras 2 and 7; de Propris, 'Foro generale', 166; Auletta and Panzarola, 'Della competenza', 225.

[56] See Marinelli and Widmann, 'Foro generale', 378 I para 3; Auletta and Panzarola, 'Della competenza', 225 et seq.

[57] See Salerno, *Lezioni*, 122.

[58] See, with reference to the notion of representative to stand in trial in accordance with Art 77 CPC, Corte di cassazione, Sezioni Unite, 5 May 2006, no°10312; with reference to the notion of residence, see Corte di cassazione, Sezioni Unite, 16 June 1948, no°933, in Capotorti, Conforti, Ferrari Bravo and Starace, *La giurisprudenza*, 156.

[59] See, on Art 43 CC, Rizzieri, 'Domicilio e residenza', 104 et seq; Villani, 'Domicilio e residenza', 175 et seq; L Montuschi, 'Art 43', in A Sicaloja and G Branca, *Commentario del codice civile* (Bologna, Zanichelli, 1970) 1 et seq.

employed and have no other interests in that foreign country;[60] residence in Italy exists when private and professional connections with the Italian territory clearly prevail over any returns to foreign territory.[61] As concerns the notion of 'representative',[62] pursuant to Art 77 para 1 CPC, the general representative and the representative appointed with respect to specific business[63] cannot stand in trial for the principal, unless the related power is not expressly conferred upon them in writing, except for urgent acts and protective measures. Pursuant to the following paragraph of Art 77 CPC the power in question is presumed to be conferred upon the general representative of who is not resident nor domiciled in Italy and upon the manager.[64] With respect to the notion of representative, Italian courts have specified that it is presumed that the consignee is a representative of the ship-owner or charterer (pursuant to Art 288 COD NAV)[65] and that the accredited ambassador is a representative of his State, in the case of claims against the latter arising from *acta iure gestionis*.[66]

Question 4

There is no express rule of Italian positive law providing for *forum necessitatis*.[67] However, in a decision rendered in 2008, the Court of Cassation held that, a 'Constitution-oriented' interpretation of Art 3 Law 218/1995 requires to conform the latter with Art 6 ECHR, with the result that Italian jurisdiction residually exists under the former article in those (exceptional) cases where neither Italian nor foreign jurisdiction exists.[68] Yet, as proven by the very same decision,[69] practical recourse to *forum necessitatis* in civil and commercial matters truly appears to be a choice of last resort.

Question 5

Considering that Art 3 para 2 Law 218/1995 refers to specific (special and protective) jurisdictional criteria set forth in the 1968 Brussels Convention – and, today, according

[60] See Consiglio di Stato, 10 January 1968, no°2828 (1968) 3 Foro it col 519.

[61] See Corte di cassazione, 28 October 1985, no°5292 (1985) Rep Foro it col 1109 para 28.

[62] See, on Art 77 CPC, P Nappi 'Rappresentante del procuratore e dell'institore' in C Consolo (dir), *Codice di procedura civile, Commentario*, 6th edn (Wolters Kluwer, 2018) 848 et seq; E Zucconi Gallo Fonseca, 'Foro generale elle persone giuridiche e delle associazioni non riconosciute' in F Carpi and M Taruffo (founded by), *Commentario breve al codice di procedura civile* 9th edn (Cedam, 2018) 308 et seq; G Romano (adjourned by), 'Foro generale elle persone giuridiche e delle associazioni non riconosciute' in N Picardi, B Sassani and A Panzarola (eds), *Codice di procedura civile*, 6th edn (Giuffré, 2015) 640 et seq.

[63] See Torsello, *Commento*, 5, quoting Corte di cassazione, 7 May 2003, no°6899, in (2003) 1 Foro it col 2698.

[64] The manager is the person is appointed by the businessman to manage a business, or a secondary seat, or a particular branch of the same business. See Zatti and Colussi, *Lineamenti*, 720; Torrente and Schlesinger, *Manuale*, 971; Corte di cassazione, Sezioni Unite, 5 May 2006, no°10312.

[65] Corte di cassazione, 8 April 1975, no°1269 (1975) Rep Foro it col 1135 para 24.

[66] Corte di cassazione, Sezioni Unite, 22 November 1984, no°5982 (1986) Riv dir int priv proc 134; Corte di cassazione, Sezioni Unite, 26 April 2012, no°6489 (2013) Riv dir int priv proc 181; Torsello, *Commento*, 5.

[67] Cf Salerno, *Lezioni*, 153 et seq.

[68] Corte di cassazione, Sezioni Unite, 17 July 2008, no°19595 (2010) Riv dir int priv proc 93, quoted in Barel and Armellini, *Diritto internazionale privato*, 360.

[69] In that decision Italian jurisdiction was established under Art 603 COD NAV.

to the better view, in the Brussels Ia Regulation – those criteria should be interpreted and applied consistently with preliminary rulings rendered by the ECJ.[70]

(a)

Among the specific jurisdictional criteria set forth in the Brussels Regime extended by Art 3 para 2, first sentence, Law 218/1995 to non-EU domiciled defendants, is that concerning jurisdiction in matters relating to contract. In this case, the question as to whether the reference made by Art 3 para 2, first sentence, Law 218/1995 should be made in favour of the 1968 Brussels Convention rather than to the Brussels Regulations becomes relevant, considering that, in matters relating to contract, the instruments in question set forth different rules on jurisdiction. A recent decision of 15 April 2021 by the Tribunale of Bergamo is illustrative. In that case, an Italian company was awarded by the Tribunale with an *ex parte* order against a San Marino company for the payment of the price of sold goods delivered (and assembled) in the latter country. The defendant challenged the existence of Italian jurisdiction. If the 1968 Brussels Convention applied, Italian jurisdiction would have existence (since, under Art 1182 para 3 CC payments must be made at the creditor's domicile). Instead, if the Brussels Ia Regulation applied, considering that the place of delivery was in San Marino, Italian jurisdiction would have not been given. The Tribunale held that the reference made by Art 3 para 2, first sentence, Law 218/1995 should today be interpreted as being in favour of Brussels Ia Regulation, and, accordingly, declared the lack of Italian jurisdiction. For sake of completeness, should contractual claims fall outside the material scope of the Brussels Regime, other national rules could come into play, including Art 18 para 2 CPC.[71]

(b)

Among the specific jurisdictional criteria set forth in the Brussels Regime extended by Art 3 para 2, first sentence, Law 218/1995, to non-EU defendants, are also those in matters relating to non-contractual claims. For sake of completeness, should similar claims fall outside the material scope of the Brussels Regime, other national rules may come into play, such as that contained in Art 20 CPC,[72] whereby claims relating to obligations may also be brought before the courts of the place where the disputed obligation arose or where the latter must be performed.

[70] Cf Conetti, Tonolo and Vismara, *Manuale*, 27; Mosconi and Campiglio, *Diritto internazionale privato*, 160; see, with reference to the 1968 Brussels Convention, Castellaneta, 'Competenza', 56–57; A Bonomi, 'The Italian Statute on Private International Law' (1999) 27 *Int'l J Legal Info* 247, 251; Pocar, *Das neue*, 146; Broggini, 'Art 3 I', 907.

[71] Corte di cassazione, Sezioni Unite, 9 December 1996, no°10954, unpublished.

[72] See eg Tribunale di Bologna, 1 June 2017, unpublished; Tribunale di Reggio Emilia, 30 June 2007, unpublished.

(c)

The jurisdictional criteria set forth in the Brussels Regime in matters concerning multiple defendants are also extended by Art 3 para 2, first sentence, Law 218/1995, to non-EU domiciled defendants. In cases not falling within the material scope of application of the Brussels Regime, Art 22 CPC provides that, in the case of claims against multiple defendants, concerning the same object and based on the same legal ground, the Italian court that has jurisdiction over one of the defendants also entertains jurisdiction over the others.

(d)

Preliminarily it must be noted that, in general terms, jurisdiction over claims brought by weaker parties domiciled in the EU against stronger parties not domiciled in the EU are governed by the Brussels Ia Regulation, with the exception of jurisdiction in matters relating to insurance where no 'EU exorbitant' head of jurisdiction exists. National rules on jurisdiction come into play to the extent that the Brussels Ia Regulation is not applicable. For instance, the latter case may be that of the claim brought by the policyholder against the insurance company domiciled outside the EU. That said, to the best of our knowledge, there do not exist express rules of Italian positive law providing for heads of jurisdiction in cases involving parties other than the insured, the consumer or the employee.

Latvia

IVAN ALLEGRANTI AND ALEKSANDRS FILLERS

Introductory Remarks

In Latvia, the domestic rules for international jurisdiction are codified in the Latvian Civil Procedure Law (*Civilprocesa likums*)[1] (further – 'CPL').[2] The CPL does not contain special rules for international jurisdiction, the international jurisdiction of Latvian courts is determined using the exact same rules that determine local jurisdiction in domestic cases.[3] This means that rules that are primarily aimed at domestic situations are likewise determining international jurisdiction. Unsurprisingly, the CPL establishes precedence of civil procedural rules found in international agreements (Section 5(2) CPL) and European Union instruments (Section 5(3) CPL) over national rules. Hence, domestic jurisdictional rules apply only so far as there are no applicable European or international rules.[4]

Before we start to discuss Latvian jurisdictional rules, it is necessary to clarify that only in a very few cases Latvian courts, particularly, the Latvijas Republikas Augstākā tiesa (Republic of Latvia Supreme Court; hereinafter: 'Supreme Court'), have interpreted the CPL rules on jurisdiction. This may be due to the fact that Latvia is a small country and parties are rarely concerned whether their case will be heard by one or another local court. Moreover, to some degree, the relevance of jurisdictional rules might be diminished by Section 32^1(1) CPL that allows the court of first instance to initiate a transfer of the case to another court of first instance for the reasons of expediency. This option is not without important restrictions. Firstly, pursuant to Section 32^1(1) CPL the transfer is impossible if the court was chosen in the choice of court agreement concluded in compliance with Section 30 CPL. Secondly, Section 32^1(3) CPL further provides that if the jurisdiction is determined pursuant to Sections 28 or 29[5] CPL, then the transfer can be initiated only upon a written request from the plaintiff. Nevertheless, such 'mobility'

[1] Civil Procedure Law of the Republic of Latvia, adopted 14 October 1998, in force on 1 March 1999, published in Latvijas Vēstnesis [Herald of Latvia] No 326/330, 03 November 1998, available at www.likumi.lv/ta/en/en/id/50500-civil-procedure-law#_ftn1&pd=1.

[2] B Rudevska, 'Latvia' in J Basedow, G Rühl, F Ferrari and P de Miguel Asensio (eds), *Encyclopedia of Private International Law* (Edward Elgar, 2017), 2252.

[3] ibid, 2253. See also: K Torgāns (ed), *Civilprocesa likuma komentāri. I daļa (1.-28.nodaļa)* (Tiesu namu aģentūra, 2016), 102.

[4] K Torgāns (ed), *Civilprocesa likuma komentāri. I daļa (1.-28.nodaļa)*, 102.

[5] Section 29 CPL contains rules on exclusive jurisdiction.

of the disputes might also obstruct the perception of the relevance of jurisdictional rules in domestic cases. Irrespective of the exact cause, court practice on jurisdictional rules remains scarce. As a result, most of the relevant CPL jurisdictional rules have ambivalent content.

Question 1

(a)

Section 26(1) CPL provides that 'actions against natural persons shall be brought before a court based on their declared place of residence'. Section 26(2) further specifies that 'actions against legal persons shall be brought before a court based on their legal address'. On the basis of these provisions, the Supreme Court has observed that under the CPL the general rule is that an action is brought at the defendant's declared place of residence (further – 'DPR') or legal address.[6] This general rule needs further elaboration.

Firstly, let us focus on jurisdiction in actions against legal persons. For these actions, jurisdiction will be established on the basis of legal address of the defendant. In practice the legal address is a synonym of the statutory seat in the Brussels Ia Regulation;[7] hence companies incorporated in Latvia will have legal address therein. The CPL, unlike the Brussels Ia Regulation (Art 63), does not allow for any alternative connecting factors like central administration and principal place of business.

When the defendant is a natural person, the general rule is more complex. Normally, the connecting factor is the defendant's DPR.[8] Section 3(1) of the Declaration of Place of Residence Law (*Dzīvesvietas deklarēšanas likums*)[9] (further – 'DPRL') defines the DPR as 'A place of residence is any place (with an address) connected with immovable property freely selected by a person, in which the person has voluntarily settled with an intention to reside there expressed directly or implicitly, in which he or she has a lawful basis to reside and which has been recognised by him or her as a place where he or she is reachable in terms of legal relations with the State or local government'. The place of residence becomes the DPR once the person has informed the state authorities that this specific address is the DPR.[10]

In some cases, natural persons might lack the DPR. On the one hand, natural persons living in Latvia are obliged to inform state authorities about their place of residence

[6] Latvijas Republikas Augstākās tiesas Civillietu departaments 20 June 2014, No. C31391709, para. 6.2.1.

[7] U Magnus & P Mankowski (eds), *European Commentaries on Private International Law ECPIL. Commentary: Volume I. Brussels Ibis Regulation* (Otto Schmidt, 2016), 994.

[8] Section 26(1) CPL.

[9] Declaration of Place of Residence Law, adopted 20 June 2002, in force on 1 July 2003, published in Latvijas Vēstnesis [Herald of Latvia] No 104, 10 July 2002, available at www.likumi.lv/ta/en/en/id/64328-declaration-of-place-of-residence-law.

[10] This follows from Section 2(1) DPRL: 'This Law determines the obligation of a person to declare his or her place of residence, as well as the quantity of information to be declared and procedures for the registration thereof. [...]'. Further Section 4(1) specifies that 'In case of change of the place of residence, the relevant person has a duty to declare it at the institution for the declaration of a place of residence within one month from the day he or she permanently resides at the new place of residence'.

that will be treated as the DPR.[11] If such a person moves abroad, then it is obliged to inform state authorities about their foreign address.[12] Hence, for example, Kurzemes rajona tiesa (Kurzeme District Court) found that the person that had informed Latvian authorities about its address in Norway had place of residence therein.[13] On the other hand, some people are homeless and thus cannot have the DPR. Likewise, foreigners who have moved to Latvia, but have failed to inform state authorities about their place of residence will lack the DPR.

A more pertinent problems is that the DPR is a formal connecting factor as many people do not actually live at the place of their declared residence.[14] Some natural persons might have moved abroad without informing state authorities about their departure, thus preserving the DPR in Latvia. The formal nature of the DPR is evident in one domestic case where the Rīgas apgabaltiesa (Riga Regional Court) rejected the argument brought up by the defendant, who argued that it was not actually living at the DPR.[15] In the court's view, the ratio behind the DPR is for the person to assent that he/she will be reachable for state or municipality at the specific address. Hence, a person could not argue that it was not reachable at that address.[16] In fact, practice (and language) of courts often indicates that they share the 'informative approach' to jurisdiction: a defendant has a duty to be reachable at the DPR and since he/she is reachable he/she is presumed to be informed about the litigation. In other words, it seems that many courts look at the main jurisdictional rules for natural and legal persons through the lens of their rights to be informed about proceedings.

Section 27(1) CPL provides that if the defendant does not have a declared address in Latvia, then the place of residence will be used to establish the jurisdiction.[17] The precise meaning of the concept of place of residence is not entirely clear. On the one hand, one of the opening definitions of the Citizenship Law (*Pilsonības likums*)[18] states that 'Permanent place of residence [is] a place which has been declared by a person as

[11] Section 6(1) DPRL. See also, K Torgāns (ed), *Civilprocesa likuma komentāri. I daļa (1.-28.nodaļa)*, 106.

[12] Section 6(5) DPRL.

[13] Kurzemes rajona tiesa 12 November 2018, ECLI:LV:KURT:2018:1112.C69228418.2.S, No. C69228418. In fact, the decision poses many questions. Firstly, the court should have considered the application of the Lugano Convention. It was never mentioned. Secondly, the court mixed together place of residence (domicile) under Art 7 LCL and place of residence under the DPRL, but this is a general tendency in court practice. Following another general tendency: the court regarded the question of jurisdiction through the lens of defendant's rights to be informed about litigation.

[14] See, A Mieriņa, *Starptautiskās privāttiesības: ģenēze un sintēze* (Latvijas Universitāte, 2015) 170. Eg, because one person could own multiple immovable objects or own one object and rent another or be declared at the immovable owned by parents or a spouse but rent/own another immovable. Moreover, municipalities often grant rebates on immovable property tax if the owner has the DPR in the given municipality. This encourages the person owning an immovable in the given municipality to declare the place of residence there even if the person lives elsewhere (eg, as a tenant).

[15] Rīgas apgabaltiesas Civillietu tiesu kolēģija 26 October 2015, No C29641509.

[16] This follows from the DPRL. Its Section 1 states that: 'The purpose of this Law is to ensure that every person is reachable in terms of legal relations with the State or local government'. The definition of the DPR provided in Section 3 of the said law expressly mentions that the DPR is a place that the natural person recognises 'as a place where he or she is reachable in terms of legal relations with the State or local government'.

[17] Section 27(1) CPL: 'An action against a defendant who does not have a declared place of residence shall be brought based on their place of residence'.

[18] Citizenship Law, adopted 22 July 1994, in force on 25 August 1994, published in Latvijas Vēstnesis [Herald of Latvia] No 93, 10 August 1994, available at www.likumi.lv/ta/en/en/id/57512-citizenship-law.

his or her place of residence in Latvia where he or she actually resides and he or she can prove it by submitting a statement of the State, local government or merchant, or other evidence that confirms the fact that the person is living in Latvia'. The already recited Section 3(1) DPRL further describes the concept of place of residence, but the purpose of that description is to determine which address is suitable to be communicated to state authorities and registered as the DPR. On the other hand, Art 7(1) of Latvian Civil Law (*Civillikums*)[19] (further – 'LCL') states that 'Place of residence (domicile) is that place where a person is voluntarily dwelling with the express or implied intent to permanently live or work there'. Therefore, there are three approaches that can be used to construe Section 27(1) CPL. The first approach is to construe place of residence in accordance with the DPRL but bearing in mind that the defendant has neither declared the place of residence nor informed state authorities about his/her address abroad.[20] This approach then would be used both for domestic and cross-border cases. The second approach is premised on the view that Section 3(1) DPRL is clearly meant to determine the specific address for persons living in Latvia to ensure communication with state and municipal authorities and thus is not appropriate for cross-border cases.[21] Hence, for cross-border cases the concept of place of residence should be construed pursuant to Art 7 LCL. The third approach is to construe place of residence in Section 27(1) CPL always pursuant Art 7 LCL,[22] provided the person has no DPR. At the moment, there seems to be no clear position on which approach is preferable and what are the advantages and disadvantages of each of them.

Finally, if a natural person does not have the place of residence in Latvia or it is unknown, then the action can be brought either at the last known place of residence or at the place where an immovable belonging to the person is located (Section 27(2) CPL). The provision does not establish any hierarchy between the criteria and the plaintiff can choose the more convenient option. In practice, this means that the location of the defendant's immovable is in and of itself sufficient ground to establish jurisdiction of a Latvian court. Interestingly, the CPL does not provide such an option against foreign legal person (companies) owning immovables in Latvia.[23]

[19] Civil Law of the Republic of Latvia has been adopted on the 28.01.1937, in force on 1.09.1992, published in Valdības Vēstnesis [Government Herald], No. 41, 20 February 1937, available at www.likumi.lv/ta/en/en/id/225418-the-civil-law.

[20] For example, in a domestic case, one court observed that the defendant does not have the DPR. Hence, the court established jurisdiction on the basis of the information provided by the plaintiff – the defendant did not participate in the litigation – about the defendant's actual place of residence. As is often the case, the court referred in its reasoning to both Section 3 DPRL and Art 7 LCL to justify its decision without actually explaining the concept of place of residence (domicile). Zemgales rajona tiesa 23 September 2020, ECLI:LV:ZRT:2020:0923.C73545319.4.S, No C73545319.

[21] B Rudevska 'Eiropas maksājuma rīkojuma procedūra: piemērošana un problēmjautājumi' (2009) 567/568 Jurista Vārds; I Kačevska, B Rudevska, V Mizaras, A Brazdeikis, M Torga, *Practical Application of European Union Regulations Relating to European Union Level Procedure in Civil Cases: the Experience in Baltic States* (2012), 57 available at www.kacevska.lv/f/baltic%20FINAL%20en.pdf.

[22] For a somewhat unclear position on the question whether place of residence in the CPL ought to be determined in conformity with Art 7 LCL, see K Torgāns (ed), *Civilprocesa likuma komentāri. I daļa (1.-28. nodaļa)*, 103.

[23] Probable cause of this omission is the domestic policy behind jurisdictional rules. A natural person living in Latvia might have no DPR and its place of actual residence might be unknown to the plaintiff. However, it is assumed that any legal person incorporated in Latvia will have a legal address. As a consequence, there is no perceived need for subsidiary jurisdictional rules. Had the legislator kept in mind the possible 'cross-border

These general rules are supplemented by rules on exclusive jurisdiction (Section 29 CPL), rules on choice of court agreement (Section 30 CPL) and specific jurisdictional grounds (Section 28 CPL). Finally, Section 31(1) provides that a counterclaim shall be brought before the court where the initial claims is brought. Some of the jurisdictional grounds provided in Section 28 CPL will be described below.

(b)

As stated above, in Latvia rules on local jurisdiction simultaneously determine jurisdiction of Latvian courts in cross-border cases.

(c)

Currently, Latvia has no rules that would extend the application of the Brussels Ia Regulation to situations when defendants are not domiciled within the EU. In cases that are not covered by the Brussels Ia Regulation, jurisdiction might be established on the basis of international treaties. Outside cases covered by international treaties, jurisdiction will be allocated pursuant to the CPL. While certain rules of the CPL are similar to those of the Brussels Ia Regulation, most are different. As stated above, the general rule for jurisdiction: the DPR or legal address[24] is rather different from the concepts of domicile of a natural[25] and legal person used by the Brussels Ia Regulation. Also, alternative jurisdictional grounds mostly differ from their Brussels Ia counterparts. Thus, we cannot speak of incorporation of the Brussels rules into the Latvian legislation.

The idea of substituting the current CPL by the Brussels rules in cross-border cases has not been advocated by scholars. However, it is important to bear in mind that the Latvian community of private international law scholars is very small.[26] Most scholars in the field focus their attention on interpreting current private international law rules. In other words, *de lege lata* analysis dominates the field. Moreover, usually private international law scholars have a strong interest in EU legal instruments, while the CPL rules on jurisdiction are deemed a part of domestic civil procedure, analysed by scholars whose area of interest is civil procedure. As a result, scholars dealing with private international law rules are less keen on discussing the merits and flaws of the CPL, while

dimension', it might have come to a conclusion that it seems illogical to allow litigation in Latvia against a natural person, having no other connection with Latvia except a location of an immovable, while denying it if the defendant, under the same circumstances, was a foreign legal person.

[24] The legal address of the legal person corresponds to the concept of the statutory seat under the Brussels Ia Regulation. But the Brussels Ia Regulation provides two additional connecting factors for the domicile of a legal person.

[25] Even though it is not entirely clear how a Latvian court should construe the concept of domicile of a natural person under the Brussels Ia Regulation. Once again it is possible to argue that this should be done using the concept of the DPR, since this concept is central for local jurisdictional rules. Nevertheless, it seems that Art 7 LCL is considered to be the appropriate means of determining domicile under the Brussels Ia Regulation. This approach is hard to oppose because Art 7 LCL explicitly mentions 'domicile' even if only in brackets, while the DPRL never does.

[26] Cf, B Rudevska, 'Latvia', 2256.

scholars dealing with the CPL are far less concerned with cross-border cases and have lesser expertise in the Brussels Ia Regulation.

(d)

Article 76(1) imposes upon Member States an obligation to notify the Commission about three different issues: (a) the rules of jurisdiction referred to in Arts 5(2) and 6(2); (b) the rules on third-party notice referred to in Art 65; (c) the conventions referred to in Art 69.

Performing its obligation under Art 76(1)(a), Latvia informed the Commission that the relevant jurisdictional rules are: 'Articles 27(2), 28(3), 28(5), 28(6) and 28(9) of the Law on Civil Procedure'.[27] This list is not exhaustive as not all relevant CPL rules are described. Firstly, Section 26(1) CPL currently contains the main jurisdictional rule for natural persons: the DPR of the defendant. This rule is not mentioned. It is possible that the author of the text assumed that a person with a DPR in Latvia will have the domicile in the EU for the Brussels Ia Regulation purposes. But this conclusion is not necessarily the right one.[28] Secondly, Art 28(7) CPL is also not mentioned, and this is a variation of the previous problem. Pursuant to this provision '[a]n action against several defendants who reside at or are located in various places may be brought based on the declared place of residence or legal address of one defendant'. The text of the provision is ambiguous: it is not clear what the term 'reside' exactly means: place of residence or the DPR? However, under the most likely interpretation, the provision could be used to consolidate actions against natural persons with DPRs in different parts of Latvia. This would seemingly also apply if all those natural persons with DPRs in Latvia had domiciles in third states. Thirdly, Latvian notice does not mention Section 28(4) CPL, which will be described below, that uses the place where the damage to the property occurred as a connecting factor.

Information provided under Art 76(1)(b) seems exhaustive. Latvia has notified the Commission that the relevant provisions are: 'Articles 78, 79, 80, 81 and 75 of the Law on Civil Procedure'. This is adequate information as it refers to the section of the CPL that describes the procedural status of third parties.

Information provided under Art 76(1)(c) is exhaustive. Latvia is a party to two international treaties with other Member States whose scope overlaps with that of

[27] The information referring to Art 76 of Regulation (EU) No 1215/2012 of the European Parliament and of the Council on jurisdiction and the recognition and enforcement of judgments in civil and commercial matters (OJ C 4, 9.1.2015).

[28] At least if we follow the approach that under Art 62(1) Brussels Ia, the domicile is not determined on the basis of DPRL, but Art 7 LCL. This approach seems the correct one since the very term 'domicile' is found only in Art 7 LCL and not in the Citizenship Law or DPRL. For the support of the use of Art 7 LCL see: B Rudevska 'Eiropas maksājuma rīkojuma procedūra: piemērošana un problēmjautājumi' (2009) 567/568 Jurista Vārds; I Kačevska, B Rudevska, V Mizaras, A Brazdeikis, M Torga, *Practical Application of European Union Regulations Relating to European Union Level Procedure in Civil Cases: the Experience in Baltic States*. In fact, the contrary approach would allow Latvian courts to circumvent the very purpose of Art 62(1) to subject the natural person to his/her home jurisdiction. Eg, a natural person living for years in France that has failed to inform Latvia authorities about its address abroad would be considered to be subject to Latvian jurisdiction just because its name appears in the 'Register of Natural Persons'.

the Brussels Ia Regulation and that are not devoted to particular matters. These treaties are: the Agreement of 11 November 1992 on Legal Assistance and Legal Relations between the Republic of Lithuania, the Republic of Estonia and the Republic of Latvia and Agreement of 23 February 1994 between the Republic of Latvia and the Republic of Poland on Legal Assistance and Legal Relations in Civil, Family, Labour and Criminal Matters.

Question 2

In Latvia the concept of place of residence (domicile) is defined by Art 7 LCL. This provision primarily serves the purposes of conflict of laws. As described above, there is some uncertainty whether Art 7 LCL should be consulted to establish jurisdiction under the CPL over natural persons that do not have DPR or to determine domicile under the Brussels Ia Regulation. Nevertheless, the approach to use Art 7 LCL when determining jurisdiction pursuant to Art 62(1) Brussels Ia seems particularly appropriate as only Art 7 LCL explicitly mentions the term 'domicile', even if only in brackets. Hence, it would seem that Art 7 LCL should be used to examine the domicile in Latvia under Art 62(1) Brussels Ia, irrespective of whether the defendant has the DPR in Latvia. Hence, we will describe the concept of domicile as it is understood in the LCL. For sake of brevity, answering this question, we will refer mostly to the concept of Art 7 LCL as 'domicile', even though it is important to bear in mind that the provision puts an equals sign between place of residence and domicile, while the CPL jurisdictional rules do not refer to domicile, but only to place of residence.

Pursuant to Art 7 of the LCL 'place of residence (domicile) is that place where a person is voluntarily dwelling with the express or implied intent to permanently live or work there. A person may also have more than one place of residence. Temporary residence does not create the legal consequences of a place of residence and shall be adjudged not on the basis of duration, but in accordance with intent'. As evident from the text, Art 7 LCL identifies the place of residence with the domicile.[29] The concept of domicile as such is only used for natural persons.[30] Article 7 LCL allows one person to have multiple domiciles and it does not require the court to weigh which domicile is more important.

Pursuant to Art 7, domicile is usually understood to have two elements: actual presence in certain territory (Latin: *habitatio*) and an intention to permanently settle in that territory (Latin: *animus manendi* or *animus remanendi*),[31] while the motive for choosing to settle in the given territory is irrelevant.[32] However, since the intention is a necessary element of the domicile then, eg, an exchange student temporarily living in

[29] A Mieriņa, *Starptautiskās privāttiesības: ģenēze un sintēze* (Latvijas Universitāte, 2015) 165.

[30] V Sinaiskis, 'Civīllikuma principi un ģimenes tiesības' (1938) 1 *Tieslietu Ministrijas Vēstnesis* 42; A Mieriņa, *Starptautiskās privāttiesības: ģenēze un sintēze* (Latvijas Universitāte, 2015) 172.

[31] B Berent, H Blaese, H Ehlers, C von Schilling & T Zimmermann, *Lettlands Zivilgesetzbuch vom 28 Januar 1937 in Einzeldarstellungen. Band I Einleitung, Familienrecht, Erbrecht* (Verlag der A/G Ernst Plates, 1938) 63.

[32] ibid, 65–66.

Latvia will not acquire domicile. The need for an intention also prevents persons with limited capacity (minors and persons with mental limitations) to determine their own domicile; their domicile can be determined only by their representatives.[33]

One peculiar characteristic of Art 7 LCL is that it uses an alternative: intent to permanently live or work in a given territory. It is clear that the intention to work is not *a conditio sine qua non* and persons without employment can acquire domicile.[34] However, the exact significance of this alternative is not well understood in academic literature or court practice. A number of older cases have tried to analyse the interaction between the intention to live and to work. In the 1937 decision, the Supreme Court stated that not in every situation a place of work would amount to a domicile, eg, when an engineer works on a certain object, he/she might have no intention to remain permanently in the given territory.[35] However, in an earlier 1932 decision,[36] the Supreme Court was following a different approach – emphasising the importance of the place of employment. After two Latvian theatres commissioned stage productions from a foreign stage director, the latter arrived in Riga and rented an apartment. He also obtained a work permit and rented a summer house and moved some of his personal belongings to Latvia. Around the same time, a litigation against him was initiated. Fifty-five days later, the court had the first hearing. The court established that up to that date, the defendant had resided in Latvia only for seven days as in the meantime he visited Berlin, Stockholm and other foreign cities. The case reached the Supreme Court. The Supreme Court observed that the seven-day term was sufficient to establish the domicile, because it was evident that the defendant had an intention to move his economic (professional) activity to Riga and this intention was sufficient to establish the domicile at the very moment when he moved to Latvia. The Supreme Court also analysed whether the fact that the defendant had extensive travels affected this conclusion. The Supreme Court thought that this fact was irrelevant. The defendant was an internationally recognised stage director and foreign trips were the necessary part of his profession. Finally, the fact that the defendant preserved his domicile in Germany was likewise irrelevant; a person could have multiple different domiciles: eg, one domicile for personal life and one (or even multiple) professional domiciles. Some scholars had observed that both judgments convey different line of reasoning: while, in 1932, the Supreme Court was willing to recognise the professional activity (even if temporary) as a crucial element for establishing domicile, in 1938 the Supreme Court wanted to diminish its importance and give more weight to the intention to live permanently in the given territory.[37] Unfortunately, the further elaboration of the concept of domicile is not found in the recent case law of the Supreme Court.

From the procedural point of view, Section $54^1(1)$ CPL states that '[i]f a defendant does not have a declared place of residence in Latvia, the plaintiff has an obligation

[33] ibid, 62–63.

[34] F Konradi & A Valters, *XIV Izvilkumi no Latvijas Senāta Civilā Kasacijas departamenta spriedumiem* (Tieslietu Ministrijas izdevums, 1938), 76–77.

[35] ibid, 77.

[36] F Konradi & A Valters, *VIII Izvilkumi no Latvijas Senāta Civilā Kasacijas departamenta spriedumiem* (Autoru izdevums, 1933), 32–36.

[37] A Rūsis, 'Internacionalo privattiesību pamatprincipi jaunā Civillikuma gaismā', (1939) 1 *Tieslietu Ministrijas Vēstnesis*, 93.

to indicate the address of the place of residence of the defendant to the court, if he or she knows it'. The second part of the same section states that: '[i]f due to objective reasons the plaintiff has not been able to determine the place of residence of the defendant which is not in Latvia, the court, upon a reasoned request from the plaintiff, may use the procedures provided for in international agreements binding to the Republic of Latvia or legal acts of the European Union for ascertaining the address of the defendant'. However, scholars have argued that the judge could verify the place of residence (domicile) of the defendant even if the place of residence (domicile) alleged by the plaintiff is in Latvia.[38] Thus, in one case,[39] the plaintiff informed the court that the last known place of residence (domicile) of the defendant was in Latvia. The judge, however, performed a search through state databases only to find that the defendant had informed state authorities about his departure to Cyprus and his official address therein. Thus, the judge concluded that the defendant's last known place of residence (domicile) was not in Latvia.

Question 3

As stated above, the general rule for jurisdiction in proceedings against a natural person is its DPR. The concept of DPR is described by the DPRL. Section 3(1) defines the place of (declared) residence as 'any place (with an address) connected with immovable property freely selected by a person, in which the person has voluntarily settled with an intention to reside there expressed directly or implicitly, in which he or she has a lawful basis to reside and which has been recognised by him or her as a place where he or she is reachable in terms of legal relations with the State or local government'. The concept of 'lawful basis to reside in an immovable exists if the person owns the immovable or has obtained the rights to use the immovable on the basis of rental or lease contract or has the right to use that property on the basis of marriage, kinship, affinity or on another legal or contractual basis' (Section 3(2) DPRL). In particular, the place of residence of a minor is that of his/her parents (guardians), provided they have not declared his/her place of residence to be elsewhere.[40]

Section 6 DPRL imposes an obligation to declare the place of residence on: Latvian citizens and non-citizens, citizens of Member States of EU, EEA and Swiss Confederation and their family members who have received a registration certificate or permanent residence certificate issued in the Republic of Latvia, foreigners and stateless persons who have received a residence permit. These persons must also inform the state authorities about the change of the place of residence within one month (Section 4(1)). Similarly, these persons are obliged to inform state authorities if relocating abroad (Section 6(5)). This, of course, does not ensure that the DPR always corresponds to the actual place of residence.

[38] K Torgāns (ed), *Civilprocesa likuma komentāri. I daļa (1.-28.nodaļa)*, 196, 197.
[39] The decision is not published, but is recited ibid, 197.
[40] Section 3(3) DPRL.

As stated above, Section 27(2) CPL provides that '[a]n action against a defendant whose place of residence is unknown or who has no permanent place of residence in Latvia shall be brought before a court based on the location of their immovable property or their last known place of residence'. It follows that the location of defendant's immovable is an alternative connecting factor to the last known place of residence of the defendant for defendants who do not have the DPR or place of residence in Latvia. It might also be the unique ground for jurisdiction if the defendant never had DPR and place of residence in Latvia and other grounds of jurisdiction (eg, under Section 28 CPL) are not applicable. The determination of the place of the immovable is elementary – the location of the immovable is checked through the Land Register or the Cadastre Register. This connecting factor does not require further analysis.

As we have already explained, in Latvia the concept of place of residence (domicile) is not used for legal persons. For them Section 26(2) CPL uses legal address as a connecting factor. According to Section 139(1) of the Latvian Commercial Law (*Komerclikums*):

> The address entered in the Company Register shall be the legal address of the company. The board shall submit an application to the Commercial Register Office in case of change of the legal address for making the relevant record.[41]

The Commercial Register Office is obliged to make this information publicly available, and any person is able to easily find it via a simple search in the register.[42] Legal persons (eg, associations or foundations) that are not classified as companies also have legal addresses that are initially determined upon registration (incorporation).[43]

Question 4

The Latvian law does not envisage *forum necessitatis*. In cross-border cases, the jurisdiction can be determined on the basis of the EU private international law, international treaties or domestic jurisdictional rules. However, domestic rules do not provide a possibility for national courts to exercise jurisdiction simply because no foreign *fora* would be accessible to the plaintiff.

Question 5

General Remarks

There is no observed general tendency for national courts and scholars to use the Brussels Ia Regulation to interpret domestic jurisdictional rules, although, in a few publications, scholars have referred to the Brussels Ia (or its predecessor's) rules and the Court of Justice of the European Union as a source for better understanding of

[41] Commercial Law, adopted 14 April 2000, in force on 1 January 2002, published in Latvijas Vēstnesis [Herald of Latvia] No 158/160, 5 May 2000, available at www.likumi.lv/ta/en/en/id/5490-commercial-law.

[42] cf K Torgāns (ed), *Civilprocesa likuma komentāri. I daļa (1.-28.nodaļa)*, 105.

[43] cf: ibid.

the CPL jurisdictional rules.[44] Similarly, there have been a few tentative attempts to use this methodology in court practice. One case of the Supreme Court is particularly interesting.[45] Two companies registered in the British Virginia Islands brought an action against two companies registered in the Netherlands and a natural person domiciled in Switzerland. Assessing jurisdiction under the Brussels Ia Regulation, the Supreme Court observed that neither of the defendants were domiciled in Latvia, thus, in principle, the court did not have jurisdiction. Nonetheless, it also addressed an argument of the plaintiff that the plaintiff's branch in Latvia served as a basis for jurisdiction. Strictly speaking, the court should have proceeded with the analysis of other grounds of jurisdiction in the Brussels I Regulation and the Lugano Convention. In practice, the court did not analyse the Lugano Convention whatsoever. However, the court did refer simultaneously to Section 28(1) CPL and Article 5(5) Brussels I Regulation. Seemingly the court interpreted the notion of the branch in both provisions based on the practice the CJEU,[46] thus implying that the understanding of the concept would be similar in domestic law. Nevertheless, such reliance on the CJEU case law seems rather singular and does not illustrate any well-established trend.[47]

(a)

The CPL does not contain a special connecting factor for contractual actions. However, Section 28(5) provides that an action for the recovery of property or compensation for the value thereof may also be brought based on the declared place of residence of the plaintiff.[48] The scope of this provision is ambiguous. It might be assumed that it was meant to cover a vindicative or a possessory action over a movable object. The reference to 'compensation for the value' could have been meant to cover a situation described in Arts 1046 and 1047 LCL. Article 1046(2) provides that an owner may bring a vindicate action against someone who 'prior to the commencement of trial, [...] alienate[d] property in bad faith, in order to divert an action from himself or herself [...]'. Article 1047 then clarifies that such a defendant may be adjudged to pay the monetary value of the property sought to be recovered, and all losses and expenses.

If this restrictive interpretation of Section 28(5) is preferred, then it would seem that the provision does not apply to contractual actions. However, the wording of the

[44] Eg, L Rasnačs, 'Civillietu teritoriālā jurisdikcija un atsevišķu šīs jurisdikcijas noteikšanas principu piemērošana' (2010) 1 *Juridiskā Zinātne*, 125–40; L Rasnačs, *Jurisdikcijas un tās noteikšana civiltiesiska rakstura lietās* (PhD dissertation) (2009), retrievable at dspace.lu.lv/dspace/bitstream/handle/7/5043/14214-Lauris_Rasnacs_2009.pdf?sequence=1.

[45] Latvijas Republikas Augstākās tiesas Civillietu departaments 20 June 2014, No. C31391709.

[46] The court referred to: Case C-154/11 *Mahamdia*.

[47] In fact, the reference to Section 28(1) CPL seems redundant to begin with, as the defendants' domiciles were in the Netherlands and Switzerland, making the said provision inapplicable.

[48] Section 28(5) CPL: 'An action for the recovery of property or compensation for the value thereof may also be brought based on the declared place of residence of the plaintiff'. It is important to mention that based on Section 28(10) CPL adds that 'If a plaintiff does not have a declared place of residence in the cases referred to in this Section, he or she may bring an action according to his or her place of residence'. Thus, for all those jurisdictional rules mentioned in Section 28 CPL where the connecting factor is the DPR of the plaintiff, it can be substituted by place of residence, provided the plaintiff does not have the DPR.

provision does not necessarily support this. In fact, it remains to be seen whether Section 28(5) could be likewise applied to contractual actions on the recovery of movable (and immovable)[49] property. For example, in a loan for use, the creditor requests that the debtor return the car he/she has been allowed to use. If Section 28(5) is read extensively then actions for recovery of property based on contracts (deposit, loan for use, lease, etc) could be covered by this alternative jurisdictional ground. However, to the best knowledge of the authors there is neither definite case law thereupon nor doctrinal interpretation thereof.

(b)

Section 28 CPL contains two connecting factors that are similar to that found in Art 7(2) Brussels Ia. Firstly, Section 28(3) specifies that an action arising from a private delict can be also brought at the place of the declared address of the plaintiff or the place where the delice was inflicted.[50] The term 'private delict' is meant to cover the following actions arising from: (1) death (of the relative) or bodily injury; (2) unlawful deprivation of freedom; (3) injury to reputation and dignity; (4) a rape of a woman or copulation with a woman while she was unconscious.[51] This provision covers only part of delictual actions.

Section 28(3) is supplemented by Section 28(4) providing that an action for the damage inflicted to the property may also be brought based on the location where such damage was inflicted.[52] This rule is ambivalent. Under the restrictive interpretation, it would apply only to tangible objects that have been damaged or destroyed. Under the more extensive interpretation, it could likewise apply to any non-private delict with patrimonial effects. Such a reading might be justified because in the Latvian-language version, the provision does not refer to property, but uses the term '*manta*' which can mean both the object (usually tangible) or the whole patrimony of a person. Under the second reading, this jurisdictional heading could apply to a plethora of delicts that negatively affect patrimonial status of the victim, eg, if the person has suffered reduction of patrimony (damages) due to unfair competition. However, as with most other rules mentioned herein, the scarce case law and lack of scholarly analysis prevent drawing any definite conclusions.

[49] All in rem actions on immovable property are subject to exclusive jurisdiction under Section 29(1) CPL, which states that: 'An action for the ownership rights or any other property rights to immovable property or accessories thereof, or an action for registration of such rights in the Land register or extinguishment of such rights and exclusion of property from the inventory statement shall be brought based on the location of the property'. It follows from this provision that contractual actions do not fall within the scope of exclusive jurisdiction. However, there is no court practice known to the authors where this distinction would have been analysed.

[50] Section 28(3): 'A plaintiff may bring an action arising from private delicts (Sections 1635, 2347–2353 of the Civil Law) also based on his or her declared place of residence or the location where the delicts were inflicted'.

[51] See Articles 2347–2353 LCL.

[52] Section 28(4) CPL: 'An action for the damage inflicted to the property of a natural or legal person may also be brought based on the location where such damage was inflicted'.

(c)

The CPL contains one jurisdictional rule that is similar to that of Art 8(1) Brussels Ia. According to Section 28(7) 'an action against several defendants who reside at or are located in various places may be brought based on the declared place of residence or legal address of one defendant'.[53] However, this provision has an important distinction from Art 8(1) Brussels Ia. In the Brussels Ia Regulation this concentration of actions is subject to the qualifier that 'the claims are so closely connected that it is expedient to hear and determine them together to avoid the risk of irreconcilable judgments resulting from separate proceedings'. The CPL does not contain such a qualifier.

(d)

The CPL does not contain special jurisdictional rules for consumers and parties to the insurance contract. However, there is a special rule for employment relations. Section 28(9) establishes an additional jurisdiction for employment relations: an action may be brought based on the declared place of residence or place of work of the plaintiff.[54] This provision requires a few remarks. Commentators have observed that the provision allows the employee to bring an action at his/her DPR or place of the place of work.[55] This seemingly implies that employers cannot rely on this provision. There might be at least three arguments in favour of such interpretation. Firstly, a teleological argument states that the provision was probably meant to protect the employee (not the employer). Secondly, the provision implies that the plaintiff is the working party that has the place of work. Thirdly, the provision refers to the DPR of the plaintiff, implying that he/she is a natural person. Objectively, the majority of employers are legal persons without the DPR. However, it is not absolutely clear whether, eg, an employer who is a natural person could not try to base his/her actions against the employee on this provision and bring the action at his/her DPR.

[53] The word 'located' is meant to cover legal persons who have legal address, but never have place of residence (domicile).

[54] Section 28(9) CPL: 'An action arising from employment legal relations may also be brought based on the declared place of residence or place of work of the plaintiff'. However as with all jurisdictional rules in Section 28 CPL that refer to the DPR of the plaintiff, if the plaintiff does not have a DPR, he/she can rely on his/her place of residence (Section 28(10) CPL).

[55] K Torgāns (ed), *Civilprocesa likuma komentāri. I daļa (1.-28.nodaļa)*, 110.

Lithuania

KATAŽYNA BOGDZEVIČ AND GIEDRIUS OŽIŪNAS

Question 1

(a)

Matters of jurisdiction are primarily governed by the Republic of Lithuania Code of Civil Procedure (hereafter – Code of Civil Procedure; orig. *Lietuvos Respublikos civilinio proceso kodeksas*) of 2002 in Arts 781 to 787 and bilateral international treaties.[1] Such treaties have been concluded with Armenia, Azerbaijan, Belarus, China, Estonia, Moldova, Latvia, Poland, Russia, Turkey, Ukraine, Kazakhstan, and Uzbekistan.

The Code of Civil Procedure establishes an extremely wide jurisdiction for Lithuanian courts.[2] The rules of international jurisdiction in civil cases are established in Part VII of the Code of Civil Procedure. The structure for the international jurisdiction rules may seem confusing at first glance since it follows a peculiar and somewhat inconsistent pattern. Assessment of jurisdiction is established in Part VII Chapter LIX of the Code of Civil Procedure, which is composed of five Sections: Section 1 'General provisions', Section 2 'General national jurisdiction rules', Section 3 'National jurisdiction rules in disputes', Section 4 'National jurisdiction rules in extraordinary legal proceedings' and Section 5 'Cases for which Lithuanian courts do not have jurisdiction'.

At first glance, one could expect that Part VII Chapter LIX Section 1 and 2 of the Code of Civil Procedure (Arts 783–786) should list the general rules for international jurisdiction. Yet, contrary to the titles, these rules establish only special or exclusive rules of international jurisdiction rather than the general rule.

The general rule for international jurisdiction is found in Part VII Chapter LIX Section 3 Art 787 of the Code of Civil Procedure. However, it is identified and titled as a principle and that may be somewhat misleading. This minimalistic article essentially incorporates most of the main rules for international jurisdiction – the general rule, special rules, and prorogation of jurisdiction.

Under Art 787, the plaintiff may seise a Lithuanian court if the defendant is in Lithuania or has a permanent residence or resides there at the time of service of the

[1] V Mikelėnas, 'Reform of private international law in Lithuania' (2005) 7 *Yearbook of private international law*, 161–81.

[2] V Mikelėnas, 'Reform of private international law in Lithuania', 181.

claim,[3] the defendant owns property in Lithuania or owns property rights,[4] the subject matter of the dispute is an object in Lithuania, an inheritance in Lithuania or an obligation which has arisen or is to be performed in Lithuania.[5] The purpose of these criteria is to determine the State with which the claim is most closely connected.[6] Article 787 also provides for the possibility of prorogation of jurisdiction.[7]

Compared to the rules in Brussels Ibis, Art 787 of the Code of Civil Procedure is far more expansive, yet due to minimalistic and vague definition, it is also entirely reliant on the case-law of the courts, of which is there is not much.[8] Moreover, while the 1968 Brussels Convention and the Brussels I Regulation had clear general rules for international jurisdiction and special jurisdiction for contracts and damages (torts), Art 787 of the Code of Civil Procedure essentially merged all the different grounds for jurisdiction into a single article. Thus Art 787 of the Code of Civil Procedure encompasses the general rule and the special (alternative) jurisdictional rules.

(b)

Matters of jurisdiction in the Republic of Lithuania are regulated twofold: establishing national territorial jurisdiction rules and international jurisdiction. National territorial jurisdiction rules apply irrespective of the dispute, while international jurisdiction rules are applied only when an international element is present in a case. Under this regime, the seised court will first consider whether the Republic of Lithuania courts have jurisdiction to hear the case with an international element at all (assessment of international jurisdiction)[9] and, further on, which court by law should hear the case (assessment of national territorial jurisdiction).[10] The latter consists of not only determining the territory but also the competent court in that territory. Such twofold assessment is based primarily due to the peculiarities of the court system in the Republic of Lithuania and the legal system itself. It is worth noting that the *lis pendens* rule does not apply. Pursuant to Art 781(2) if the Lithuanian courts have jurisdiction to hear civil cases in accordance with the rules of jurisdiction established in the Code of Civil Procedure, this competence shall not disappear when the same case is heard in a court of a foreign state.

The system of courts, their competence, organisation and administration, and other issues related to the judicial activities, are primarily regulated by the Constitution of the Republic of Lithuania and the Republic of Lithuania Law of Courts (orig *Lietuvos Respublikos teismų įstatymas*). The court system of the Republic of Lithuania consists of courts of general jurisdiction and courts of special jurisdiction. The Supreme Court of Lithuania, the Court of Appeal of Lithuania, regional courts, and district courts are

[3] Art 787(1)(1).
[4] Art 787(1)(2).
[5] Art 787(1)(3).
[6] Lithuanian Court of Appeal, 30 January 2014, no°2-72/2014; 19 July 2018, no°e2-889-516/2018.
[7] Art 787(2).
[8] Since its inception in 2002, the Supreme Court of Lithuania ruled on this article only 12 times and most of this case law also deals with this article only indirectly.
[9] Art 782 Code of Civil Procedure (*Code of Civil Procedure*; COCP).
[10] Chapter IV COCP.

courts of general jurisdiction hearing civil and criminal cases. District courts also hear cases of administrative offences coming within their jurisdiction by law. The Supreme Administrative Court of Lithuania and regional administrative courts are courts of special jurisdiction hearing disputes arising from administrative legal relations.

Thus, in the Republic of Lithuania, the same territory (for example, the capital city of Vilnius) has three first instance courts (District Court of Vilnius City, Vilnius Regional Court, Vilnius Regional Administrative Court), two of which are for civil and commercial cases and one for administrative cases.

The rules of national territorial jurisdiction in civil cases are established in Chapter IV of the Code of Civil Procedure. Articles 27–28 in Chapter IV of the Code of Civil Procedure deal with national territorial jurisdiction. Regional courts, as the first instance courts, shall hear the following civil and commercial cases: in which the amount of the claim exceeds 40,000 euros, except in cases of family and employment legal relations and cases for non-pecuniary damages,[11] on non-pecuniary copyright legal relations,[12] civil public tender legal relationships,[13] where one of the parties is a foreign country or state,[14] compulsory selling of shares (dividends, interest),[15] also only Vilnius Regional Court can be the first instance court for all claims based on the Republic of Lithuania Law on Licensing (orig *Lietuvos Respublikos patentų įstatymas*) and Republic of Lithuania Law on Trademarks (orig *Lietuvos Respublikos prekių ženklų įstatymas*).[16] Other laws may also designate Vilnius Regional Court as the court of the first instance. Article 783 in Part VII Chapter LIX of the Code of Civil Procedure repeats the special rule for national territorial jurisdiction where one of the parties is a foreign country or state.

(c)

The Code of Civil Procedure does not directly extend the jurisdictional rules of the Brussels Regime (ie, the 1968 Brussels Convention, the Brussels I Regulation, and the Brussels Ibis Regulation) either by reference or incorporation to cases where the Brussels Ibis Regulation applies only to non-EU defendants. None of the *travaux preparatoires* of the Code of Civil Procedure support the notion that at its inception (2002), either the 1968 Brussels Convention or the Brussels I Regulation was of any significance to the legislator. The same conclusion could be reached by glancing at the main jurisdictional provisions in the Code of Civil Procedure. Scholars (or even lawmakers) have not considered the possibility of (further) extending the personal scope of those rules. The lack of legislative interest in this field may be explained by the fact that jurisdictional disputes are rare, and the application of international jurisdictional rules in the Code of Civil Procedure is even more so. The current model seems to rely entirely on the Brussels regime, without extending it, or bilateral treaties with third parties.

[11] Art 27(1) COCP.
[12] Art 27(2) COCP.
[13] Art 27(3) COCP.
[14] Art 27(5) COCP.
[15] Art 27(6) COCP.
[16] Art 28(1) and Art 28(2) COCP.

(d)

The information notified by Republic of Lithuania pursuant to Art 76(1) Brussels Ibis Regulation is exhaustive.

Question 2

Being an expression of a person's relationship with the state or part of its territory, domicile of a natural person shall be that state or its part, in which he permanently or ordinarily (habitually) resides, regarding that state or its part to be the seat of his personal, social and economic interests.[17]

A natural person is deemed to be domiciled in the Republic of Lithuania when of his own will, he establishes and maintains the only or principal residence, intending to make it a seat of his personal, social, and economic interests. This intention, among other things, may manifest itself by a person's actual presence on the territory of the Republic of Lithuania as well as the establishment of personal or business relations between him and the persons of the Republic of Lithuania or by some other criteria.[18] A natural person may have only one domicile. A person called to a temporary or revocable public office shall retain his domicile.[19] Domicile of a natural person shall be deemed unchanged until he changes it to another domicile.[20] Domicile of a married person shall not depend on the domicile of his spouse, although the domicile of the spouse is the fact which has to be taken into consideration in establishing the domicile of the other spouse.[21]

The residence of a person shall be the place where he ordinarily resides.[22] Where a person has more than one residence, the seat of his principal establishment (where the person has property or a significant part of the property, where he has his job, or where he lives the longest) shall be deemed his principal residence. In such case a person's principal residence shall be taken into consideration in establishing his domicile.[23] A person whose domicile cannot be determined with certainty in accordance with the criteria laid down in Art 2.12 of the Civil Code shall be deemed to be domiciled at the place of his residence. This rule is also applied to refugees from the state, which was their domicile unless they were domiciled in the Republic of Lithuania according to Art 2.12 of the Civil Code.[24]

In determining the place of residence of a natural person, an account shall be taken of the duration and continuity of the person's actual residence in that place, of the person's place of residence in public registers, and the person's public statements about

[17] Art 2.12(1) COCP.
[18] Art 2.12(2) COCP.
[19] Art 2.12(3) COCP.
[20] Art 2.12(4) COCP.
[21] Art 2.12(5) COCP.
[22] Art 2.16(1) COCP.
[23] Art 2.16(2) COCP.
[24] Art 2.16(3) COCP.

his place of residence.[25] Where the place of residence of a natural person is unknown or cannot be determined, the place of residence of such person shall be deemed to be his last known place of residence. In addition, a natural person must notify the counterparty in writing and his creditors or debtors of a change of residence.[26] If a person fails to comply with this obligation, the counterparty and the creditors have the right to send notices and take other action at the last known place of residence of the person known to them.[27]

Domicile of a legal person is the registered office which is the place where its permanent governing body is situated. The registered office of a legal person is described by giving the address of the premises where the registered office is located.[28] The registered office must be registered in the Register of Legal Entities, as well as stated in the articles of incorporation of the legal entity and in all other documents of the legal entity, which it uses in relation with other entities (letters, invoices, commercial documents, etc).[29] If the registered office of a legal person specified in the Register of Legal Entities or a transaction and the location of its permanent management body do not coincide, third parties shall have the right to consider the location of the permanent management body as the registered office of the legal person.[30] Although the place of business of a legal person is presumed to be where it has its registered office, the registered office could also be considered at its actual place of business.[31]

Question 3

Article 787 of the Code of Civil Procedure essentially goes beyond the notion of domicile in Art 4 of Brussels Ibis. It provides for jurisdiction based on the defendant's mere presence in the country at the time of service of the suit. Unfortunately, this ground for jurisdiction has never been comprehensively analysed either in legal scholars' works or relevant case law.

This jurisdictional ground is based on the fact that each state has jurisdiction over the persons in its territory, and the court has jurisdiction over the proper service of procedural documents.[32] By all accounts, this jurisdictional ground seems like a fusion of common law and continental law systems. Whether such an approach is more favourable to the plaintiff is highly debatable. One could argue that proof-wise such a rule makes it far easier for the plaintiff to establish grounds for jurisdiction, as opposed to, for example, proof of domicile, especially in cases where the plaintiff has very little access to the permanent residence of the defendant or the defendant is simply avoiding any proceedings by relocating constantly. Thus the only concern for the plaintiff is the service of documents. However, not only does this upset the balance between the

[25] Art 2.17(1) COCP.
[26] Art 2.17(2) COCP.
[27] Art 2.17(3) COCP.
[28] Art 2.49(1) COCP.
[29] Art 2.44(1)(3), Art 2.47(1)(3), Art 2.66(1)(4) COCP.
[30] Art 2.49(2) COCP.
[31] Supreme Court of Lithuania, 13 February 2012, no°3K-3-24/2012.
[32] G Bužinskas, 'Nepagrįstos jurisdikcijos problema tarptautiniame civiliniame procese' (2005) 57 *Teisė* 21.

general and special jurisdiction rules,[33] but the plaintiff gains very little, if anything, since the existence of domicile in itself proves a substantial connection with Lithuania, and thus any plaintiff can reasonably expect for the defendant to be present. The mere presence, in this case, gives no assurance of either further stay or proof of any intermittent interests of the defendant. Thus, the alternative general rule based on permanent residence seems to be a more reliable way to establish jurisdiction, while mere presence seems to be more like a last desperate measure to bring a defendant to court when there are no other grounds.[34]

Another ground for general jurisdiction is owning property or property rights in Lithuania. There is no distinction in this case on what kind of property (for example, movable or immovable) the defendant might possess. In the case law of the courts, this is a rarely seen jurisdictional ground, since just like the presence of the defendant, this may expand jurisdictional grounds to an absurd scope, where there would be no connection between the dispute and the country, except for some (unrelated to the dispute) possessions of the defendant. Given that the courts take into account the connection of the case with the Republic of Lithuania, it could be argued that mere possession of property or brief presence in the country might not be enough to justify the jurisdiction of the courts. These jurisdictional grounds would be interpreted narrowly since the purpose of the criteria defined in Art 787(1)(1–3) is to define the state with which the claim is most closely connected.[35] Yet, whether the current case law of the courts could be considered a shift from a very wide and formal interpretation of Art 787 is still a matter of debate.[36]

Domestic law does not provide for other general rules on jurisdiction in matters regulated by the Brussels Ibis Regulation based on other connecting factors (eg the citizenship of the claimant or defendant).

Question 4

Domestic law (including case law) does not envisage a *forum necessitatis* in any form.

Question 5

(a) and (b)

The following is an answer for both (a) and (b) due to the peculiarities of domestic law.

Matters relating to contract and tort, delict or quasi-delict fall within the most complex and convoluted ground for jurisdiction – when the subject of the dispute is

[33] Where general rules favour the defendant and the special ones provide alternative grounds, favourable to the plaintiff.

[34] G Bužinskas, J Grigienė, *Teismingumas tarptautiniame civiliniame procese* (Teisinės informacijos centras, 2007) 86.

[35] For example, Lithuanian Court of Appeal, 19 July 2018, no°e2-889-516/2018.

[36] Compare, for example, with Lithuanian Court of Appeal, 22 September 2015, no°2A-289-180/2015 where case concerned loan retrieval and jurisdiction was seized by the simple fact that the defendant had property rights in Lithuania, which were not connected to the loan in any way.

an obligation that has arisen or must be fulfilled in Lithuania. This jurisdiction ground loosely resembles Arts 7(1) and 7(2) but could not be considered a meaningful extension of these jurisdictional grounds.

The case law clarifies that within the meaning of Art 787(1)(3) of the Code of Civil Procedure, the peculiarity of an obligation that has arisen or is to be fulfilled in Lithuania is that this criterion determines two separate elements to determine jurisdiction: (i) the place where the obligation in question arose or (ii) the place of its performance. Therefore, in deciding which element is applicable, the court must assess which is closer to the nature of the obligation from which the plaintiff's claims arise.[37]

The complexity of this provision stems from the fact that instead of defining jurisdictional rules for delicts or contracts, the rule essentially became all-encompassing, as, in the Lithuanian legal system, an obligation may arise from a contract, tort or unjust enrichment or savings.[38] Thus, as opposed to Art 7(1)(b) of Brussels Ibis and its designation of an autonomous and straightforward assessment of jurisdictional grounds, Art 787(1)(3) first involves an in-depth assessment of the claim, determining the obligation in question and the nature of the obligation, followed by an assessment which criteria would lead to a state with which the claim is most closely connected.[39] The fact that there are no clearly defined elements that establish a connection between the claim and the state for jurisdictional purposes means that the courts essentially do have some discretion, based on their inner belief, to balance the place of performance with the place giving rise to the obligation. The main principle for assessment seems to be whether the court and the parties to the case would have direct access to evidence relevant to the dispute.

In legal contracts, Art 787(1)(3) does not make any effort to separate different types of contracts or set a protective jurisdiction. Instead, assessment of a contractual obligation as a jurisdictional ground is based on the general notion that obligations arising from a contract are characterised by the fact that the party has a civil legal relationship and the plaintiff must provide sufficient proof about the existence of a contract and its contents.[40]

The place of performance of a contractual obligation is usually straightforward, and jurisdiction is assessed according to it.[41] Place of performance is determined by Art 6.52 of Civil Code, which states that the obligation shall be performed at the place specified in the contract or law or determined by the nature of the obligation.[42] If the place of performance of the obligation is not specified, the obligation to transfer an object described according to individual characteristics – at the place where the object is located at the moment of the occurrence of the obligation;[43] the obligation to transfer immovable property – at the place where the property is located;[44] the obligation to

[37] Lithuanian Court of Appeal, 19 July 2018, no°e2-889-516/2018, para 38.

[38] As established in Art 6.2, Art 6.242, and Art 6.245 COCP.

[39] For example, Lithuanian Court of Appeal, 18 February 2021, no°e2A-67-464/2021; 19 July 2018, no°e2-889-516/2018.

[40] Lithuanian Court of Appeal, 3 May 2018, no°e2-570-516/2018.

[41] Supreme Court of Lithuania, 23 December 2015, in civil case no e3K-3-692-706/2015; 29 December 2016, no°3K-3-551-915/2016.

[42] Art 6.52(1) COCP.

[43] Art 6.52(2)(1) COCP.

[44] Art 6.52(2)(2) COCP.

transfer the object described according to the characteristics of the type – at the place of residence or business of the debtor;[45] pecuniary obligation – at the creditor's place of residence or business at the moment of maturity of the obligation. If the creditor's place of residence or business has changed after the obligation has arisen and, as a result, the debtor has incurred additional costs in performing the obligation, the creditor must reimburse the debtor for these costs. At the creditor's request, the pecuniary obligation may also be performed in another territory of the state where the creditor is domiciled or established at the time of payment, or in the territory of the state where the creditor was domiciled at the time the obligation arose. However, if such a creditor's claim would substantially aggravate the debtor's situation, the debtor may refuse to satisfy the creditor's claim and perform the obligation at the creditor's place of residence or business at the time the obligation arises;[46] all other obligations – at the place of residence or business of the debtor after the term to perform the obligation.[47]

While the place of performance is the usual jurisdictional ground for contractual claims, there is also the possibility to base jurisdiction on the place where the obligation arose. That possibility stems from the fact that Art 787(1)(3) does not designate the place of performance as a singular ground for contractual claims. For example, in cases where a party contests the validity of a contract signed in a foreign country, that might be the deciding element due to the proximity of the evidence.

Meanwhile, the obligation arising from a delict is not related to the contractual relationship, except when the law provides that the non-contractual liability also arises from the damage related to the contractual relationship.[48] According to Art 6.246 of the Civil Code, civil liability arises from non-fulfilment of an obligation established by law or a contract (illegal omission) or from acts prohibited by law or contract (illegal activity) or from a general obligation to act diligently. Paragraph 1 of Art 6.263 of the Civil Code stipulates that every person must follow the rules of such conduct so that his actions (actions, omissions) do not cause harm to another person. Damage caused to a person, property, and, in cases established by law, non-pecuniary damage, must be fully compensated by the responsible person (Paragraph 2 of Art 6.263 of the Civil Code). This is a special norm of non-contractual liability, which, together with the general norm of Article 6.246(1) of the Civil Code, establishes the so-called general tort, the essence of which is to ensure the main function of civil liability – to compensate the victim for damage caused by the violation of his rights.[49]

For jurisdictional purposes, the nature of delicts means that the obligation arises at the place where the damage occurred. The place where the damage occurred is assessed by localising the defendant's actions and the damaged property.[50] In this respect, while there is a theoretical possibility of relying on the place of performance to compensate damages at the creditor's place of residence or business, that would doubtfully be consistent with the nature of the obligation and the purpose of the criteria that define the state with which the claim is most closely connected.[51]

[45] Art 6.52(2)(3) COCP.
[46] Art 6.52(2)(4) COCP.
[47] Art 6.52(2)(5) COCP.
[48] Art 6.245(4) COCP.
[49] Supreme Court of Lithuania, 19 December 2019, no°e3K-3-393-916/2019.
[50] Lithuanian Court of Appeal, 18 February 2021, no°e2A-67-464/2021.
[51] For example, Lithuanian Court of Appeal, 19 July 2018, no°e2-889-516/2018.

For jurisdictional purposes, the nature of unjust enrichment means that the obligation arises at the place where the benefit received at the expense of the creditor occurred. There is a theoretical possibility of relying on the place of performance to return the unjustly gained benefits at the creditor's place of residence or business, that, however, would doubtfully be consistent with the nature of the obligation and the purpose of the criteria that define the state with which the claim is most closely connected.

(c)

Domestic law (including case law) does not provide jurisdiction based on a close connection between defendants in any form.

(d)

The 1968 Brussels Convention and the Brussels I Regulation had little effect on the reform of private international law in Lithuania. Thus, no special or protective jurisdiction over consumer, employment, and insurance contracts (cf Arts 10–23 Brussels Ibis Regulation) emerged. Those contracts are governed by general or special rules (ie Art 787(1)(3) of the Code of Civil Procedure) governing jurisdiction.

Malta

IOANNIS REVOLIDIS

Question 1

(a)

Maltese courts can claim jurisdiction on seven grounds, all of which are included in Art 742(1)(a)–(g) of the Code of Organisation and Civil Procedure[1] (hereinafter COCP). This provision reads as follows:

> 742. (1) Save as otherwise expressly provided by law, the civil courts of Malta shall have jurisdiction to try and determine all actions, without any distinction or privilege, concerning the persons hereinafter mentioned:
>
> (a) citizens of Malta, provided they have not fixed their domicile elsewhere;
> (b) any person as long as he is either domiciled or resident or present in Malta;
> (c) any person, in matters relating to property situate or existing in Malta;
> (d) any person who has contracted any obligation in Malta, but only in regard to actions touching such obligation and provided such person is present in Malta;
> (e) any person who, having contracted an obligation in some other country, has nevertheless agreed to carry out such obligation in Malta, or who has contracted any obligation which must necessarily be carried into effect in Malta, provided in either case such person is present in Malta;
> (f) any person, in regard to any obligation contracted in favour of a citizen or resident of Malta or of a body having a distinct legal personality or association of persons incorporated or operating in Malta, if the judgment can be enforced in Malta;
> (g) any person who expressly or tacitly, voluntarily submits or has agreed to submit to the jurisdiction of the court.

As it can be inferred from the text of Art 742(1)(a)–(g) COCP, Maltese law does not follow the structure of the Brussels jurisdictional regime.[2] The latter recognises a basic jurisdictional rule, namely the domicile of the defendant, while it also provides for special jurisdictional regimes: there are specific rules for exclusive jurisdiction, rules on the prorogation of jurisdiction, special protective regimes for socioeconomically weaker parties and, finally, special rules on concurrent jurisdictional bases. All of them compete

[1] Chapter 12 of the Laws of Malta.

[2] For a general appraisal of the Brussels Ia jurisdictional regime, see among many others B Hess, *Europäisches Zivilprozessrecht* 2nd edn (De Gruyter, 2020) 340–42.

with one another for the allocation of jurisdiction within the EU, depending on their scope of application. Maltese law, on the other hand, does not follow such distinctions. There are not, for example, rules on exclusive jurisdiction or rules that offer special jurisdictional protection to socioeconomically weaker parties. The jurisdictional grounds of Art 742(1) of the COCP retain equal status and can be applied in all cases. On the face of it, they represent a rather traditional approach to the allocation of jurisdiction, as many well established jurisdictional bases, such as domicile (Art 742(1)(a) of the COCP), residence and presence (Art 742(1)(b) of the COCP), forum contractus (Art 742(1)(d) and (e) of the COCP) and prorogation of jurisdiction (Art 742(1)(g) of the COCP) are available. On the other hand, there are important omissions, such as a lack of a dedicated *forum delicti* or of a traditional *forum rei sitae*, while the interpretation of classic jurisdictional concepts, such as that of domicile for example, by local jurisprudence comes with strong particularities. From a systematic point of view, one could classify the jurisdictional bases of Art 742(1)(a) and (b) COCP as the general rules, while the bases of 742(1)(c)–(g) COCP as special jurisdictional grounds, which, by virtue of their specific nature, will take precedence over the general rules. Nonetheless, Maltese courts will examine all seven jurisdictional bases of Art 742(1) in a given case and will try to claim jurisdiction on at least one of these. It must be noted, finally, that the current form of Art 742 of the COCP was introduced after an important overhaul of its predecessor, namely Art 793 of the COCP, in 1995. The 1995 amendments intended to expand the jurisdictional claims of Maltese courts and, therefore, one could argue that the Maltese system of international jurisdiction has obtained a rather exorbitant character after the 1995 amendments.

(b)

Domestic Maltese civil procedural law establishes that the concepts of 'jurisdiction' and 'competence' are clearly separated.[3] While 'jurisdiction' refers to the ability of the Maltese courts to adjudicate over a case with foreign elements, 'competence' refers to the allocation of adjudicatory powers between Maltese courts, when it is clear that a case shall be judged in Malta, either because it is a purely domestic one (displaying no international elements) or because it falls in the jurisdiction of the Maltese courts according to Art 742(1) COCP. In that sense, Art 742(1) of the COCP applies only to transnational disputes.

(c)

Malta has not followed Italy[4] in extending the Brussels jurisdictional regime to parties from non-EU countries. In cases where the foreign element is located in a non-EU

[3] Art 741 of the COCP is very illustrative of fact; it reads as follows: '… 741. It shall be lawful to plead to the jurisdiction of the court – (a) when the action is not one within the jurisdiction of the courts of Malta; (b) when the action, although one within the jurisdiction of the courts of Malta, is brought before a court different from that by which such action is cognizable; …'.

[4] For the extension of the Brussels Ibis jurisdictional rules on non-EU litigants under Italian law see A Bonomi and T Ballarino, 'National Report: Italy' in Jürgen Basedow, Giesela Rühl, Franco Ferrari and Pedro de Miguel Asensio (eds), *Encyclopedia of Private International Law* (Edward Elgar, 2017) 2208.

country, Maltese nationals (irrespective of their procedural position, namely irrespective of whether they are plaintiffs or defendants) and third-country defendants fall exclusively under domestic Maltese Law, namely Art 742 of the COCP, and Maltese courts will exercise or decline jurisdiction on the basis of that provision only. Malta has never considered the possibility of extending the Brussels Regime to non-EU parties and, in addition, Maltese courts have not, so far, interpreted Art 742 of the COCP in the light of the Brussels Regime. For the time being at least, Maltese Law has isolated cases related to non-EU parties from the Brussels Regime and prefers to regulate them under its own domestic jurisdictional framework, namely Art 742 of the COCP.

(d)

On 9 January 2015 the EU Commission published the information shared by the Member States in accordance with Art 76(1) Brussels Ibis.[5] This was followed by an update on 24 November 2015.[6] In essence, Art 76(1) Brussels Ibis refers mainly to information previously included in Annex I of the Brussels I Regulation regarding the so-called exorbitant jurisdictional bases located in the domestic laws of the Member States.

In this context, Malta has included its entire jurisdictional regime in the information requested under Art 76(1) of the Brussels Ibis Regulation, which is an indirect recognition of its exorbitant character, especially after the 1995 amendments. According to the information shared by Malta, both Art 742 and Art 743–744[7] of the COCP are included in the list of Art 76(1) of the Brussels Ibis Regulation. Taking into account that these are the only domestic Maltese provisions that cover the subject matter of the Brussels Ibis Regulation, the information shared by Malta with the EU Commission is exhaustive.

Question 2

Domicile is an important jurisdictional basis under Art 742(1)(a) and (b) of the COCP. The Maltese legislator borrowed the jurisdictional basis of domicile from Italian law. Nonetheless, Maltese courts have consistently been interpreting the concept of domicile according to the jurisprudence of UK courts. In that sense, UK and native Maltese case law provide the basic guidance in defining 'domicile' in Maltese jurisdictional law.

Maltese courts generally recognise three different types of domicile for natural persons:[8] the domicile of origin, the domicile of choice and the domicile of dependence. All three of them will qualify Maltese courts to exercise jurisdiction according to Art 742(1)(a) and (b) COCP.

[5] Notices from Member States, The information referring to Article 76 of Regulation (EU) No 1215/2012.

[6] Notices from Member States, First update of the information referring to Article 76 of Regulation (EU) No 1215/2012.

[7] Art 743 and 744 of the COCP provide for jurisdictional rules in relation to counter-claims. They are, in a way, the Maltese equivalents to Art 8 para 3 of the Brussels Ibis Regulation.

[8] Maltese courts have been heavily influenced by the 1983 'Report on Domicile and Habitual residence as Connecting Factors in the Conflict of Laws (LRC 7-1983)' of the UK Law Reform Commission.

Domicile of origin is considered as self-evident in Maltese law and Maltese jurisprudence. Maltese courts accept that no person can exist without a domicile and that a domicile must be obtained as soon as one is born. In that sense, the domicile of origin is the domicile of one's father at the time of one's birth. This is clearly illustrated in *Loreto Camilleri v Avv Dr George DeGiorgio et ne*,[9] where the court stated that:

> Every person has a domicile, and shall obtain one as soon as possible, namely at birth; this is the domicile of origin, which can never be abandoned, but only supplanted in favor of the domicile of one's choice. No person can have more than one domicile simultaneously.[10]

Simply put, according to Maltese law everybody is assigned his/her father's domicile at birth, which is the domicile to determine one's jurisdictional fate.

The aforementioned decision in the case of *Loreto Camilleri v Avv Dr George DeGiorgio* has introduced, nonetheless, one of the most mystifying concepts of Maltese private international law: the concept of the domicile of choice. The domicile of choice can be viewed as the opposite of the domicile of origin, in the sense that one needs to abandon one's domicile of origin in order to obtain a domicile of choice, eg a person born in Malta assigned with Malta as its domicile of origin at birth, must take active steps and meet a very high threshold in order to be deemed domiciled elsewhere. The same applies to foreigners: a person born outside of Malta, is assigned, under Maltese jurisdictional law, with its country of birth as its domicile; such a person must meet a very high threshold in order to be deemed domiciled in Malta. But what will amount to a domicile of choice under Maltese law?

In accordance with prevalent UK literature[11] and jurisprudence,[12] Maltese courts understand domicile of choice as a concept consisting of two elements: an external and an internal one. The external element refers to the legal and social relationships as well as the activities of a person, which showcase the relationship of this person with a sovereign state. The internal element refers to the will of a person to establish a new domicile in a country other than the country of its birth. In deciding whether a person has abandoned its domicile of origin for a domicile of choice, Maltese courts take a factual approach. They weigh all possible indications that showcase both the external and the internal relationship of a person with a country.[13] It shall be noted, however, that Maltese courts interpret the notion of domicile of choice very strictly, namely they

[9] First Hall Civil Court, 16 March 1949, *Camilleri v Avv Dr G DeGiorgio et ne.*

[10] The original passage of the decision reads as follows: 'Kull persuna gnandhajkollha domicilju, u gnandha d-domicilju tagnha malli titwieled, li huwa dak ta' l-origini, u Ii ma jista' qatt jigi abbandunat imma hiss potitivament soppjantat favur ta' domicilju ienor Ii jkun id-domicilju talghatzla. U lebda persuna ma jista' jkollha aktar minn domicilju wiened simultaneament'.

[11] Most notably *Cheshire, North and Fawcett, Private International Law* 15th edn (OUP, 2017).

[12] Maltese courts cite UK case law as early as eg *Udny v Udny* [1869] Lr 1 Sc & Div 441.

[13] Such as: (a) a long period of residence in the new territory; (b) the acquisition there of a permanent home; (c) residential accommodation of reasonably substantial value for occupation; (d) the acquisition of citizenship and passport of the new territory; (e) the making of a new will subject to the laws of the new territory; (f) the acquisition there of a burial plot; (g) the exercise of political (eg voting) rights; (h) the payment of local and state taxes; (i) development of local business interests, eg directorships; (j) membership of local clubs and associations; (k) establishment of local banking and financial facilities; (l) establishment of local business contacts; (m) whether the individual has maintained strong links with the other jurisdiction (ie strong family ties, property and assets in the other jurisdiction and so on); (n) whether the individual has retained his or her foreign nationality.

have raised the threshold to establish a domicile of choice to quite impossible heights.[14] It is thus very difficult under current Maltese case law to abandon one's domicile of origin in order to establish a domicile of choice.[15] It must also be noted that the Maltese courts put strong emphasis on the internal element. To be satisfied that a person has opted for a domicile of choice they must be able to discern that a person has decided to cut ties to its domicile of origin and establish a life in the chosen domicile, without being willing to return to the domicile of origin. This strong emphasis on the internal element of domicile of choice was established in the seminal case of *C Grech v Pl J Busuttil*,[16] which has been followed by all Maltese courts ever since.

Lastly, Maltese law also recognises the concept of domicile of dependence. This is devised for minors and persons of diminished capacity. Such persons are considered to be domiciled at the place of their legal guardian, which for minors, will usually be their parents.

When it comes to legal persons, Maltese courts once again follow closely UK literature and jurisprudence.[17] They consider legal persons to be domiciled in the place where their central management and control is located.

Question 3

Next to domicile, Maltese law recognizes two further connecting factors that provide for general jurisdiction: 'residence' and 'presence'; 'residence' is mentioned in Art 742(1)(f) of the COCP, while 'presence' in Art 742(1)(b), (d) and (e).

The concepts of residence and presence obtained jurisdictional status equal to that of domicile under the 1995 amendments. In reality, though, it is presence that takes the lion's share in determining jurisdiction. Due to the wide nature of the concept of presence, Maltese courts are usually satisfied with this jurisdictional criterion and only rarely, if ever, resort to residence. The main focus, therefore, of this section will be the jurisdictional basis of presence under Maltese law. What is the meaning of 'presence' that qualifies Maltese courts to exercise jurisdiction over a given case?

[14] The most characteristic example is the case of L-Avukat Dr Alex Perrici Calascione bhala mandatarju specjali ghan-nom u in in rappresentanza tas-societa estera *Banca Agricola Etna Spa v George Rizzo* First Hall Civil Court, 27 June 2002. In this case George Rizzo, the defendant, claimed that he had changed his domicile, namely that despite being a Maltese citizen, he was no longer domiciled in Malta and, therefore, the Maltese courts shall not claim jurisdiction over him. He presented the following facts: he had been living in Italy for a period of 15 years together with his family and children and had established both his residence and business in Italy. He was registered with the Italian tax authorities and was paying his taxes in Italy, not in Malta. The defendant also claimed that he wanted to cut all ties with Malta and had no intention of returning to live there. The court, nonetheless, and despite all the aforementioned factual elements, came to the conclusion that George Rizzo was still domiciled in Malta, because he still owned a house there, he had children and a wife in Malta, even though he was de facto separated from her, and also had some shares in a couple of businesses. The court held that according to the defendant's behaviour, he did not have the intention to terminate all ties he had with Malta up to the point where he would never return.

[15] It is, in other words, difficult in the eyes of the Maltese courts to establish that a Maltese person is no longer domiciled in Malta, while it is equally difficult to convince Maltese courts that a non-Maltese citizen has made Malta its domicile of choice.

[16] *C Grech v Pl J Busuttil* (1953) 37 I 397 Court of Appeal (civil).

[17] Quite notably UK jurisprudence as early as *Cesena Sulphur Co v Nicholson* [1876] I Ex D 428.

In answering this question, Maltese case law has taken a rather wide approach. Any presence, even transient, will suffice. This is clearly demonstrated by the characteristic case of *Angelo Cutajar and Sons Company Ltd v Cremona Anthony Dott*,[18] where the Court held that the term 'presence' in Art 742(1)(b) of the COCP shall be interpreted widely, so as to even encompass a situation where a non-Maltese party has not even been physically present in Malta, but has been represented in the Maltese Islands by a third person.[19] It, therefore, becomes clear that the threshold to be met in order to be 'present' in Malta within the context of Art 742(1)(b) COCP is extremely low. There need be no minimum contacts with the Maltese Islands; any distant, remote or trivial connection with this jurisdiction, eg a fly-by through Malta's airspace, is enough. In essence, 'presence' is mainly understood as in UK law. The basic reasoning behind presence as a jurisdictional basis is the classic common law idea that: 'whosoever is present within the realm, citizen or foreigner, owes allegiance to the sovereign'.[20]

Taking into account that exorbitant jurisdictional bases have lost their appeal in recent years, it is, at first sight, surprising that the Maltese legislator decided to establish mere presence as a jurisdictional basis in 1995. In reality, though, one must look at the jurisdictional history of Malta in order to understand the rationale of this choice: up until 1995 domicile used to be the only jurisdictional basis both for Maltese nationals and for non-Maltese nationals. As mentioned in question two, nonetheless, Maltese courts have borrowed the strict interpretation of the concept of domicile from UK jurisprudence. While establishing that Maltese nationals were domiciled in Malta was fairly easy, on the contrary, by adopting the UK jurisprudence on domicile of choice, it has been almost impossible for Maltese courts to assert jurisdiction over non-Maltese nationals, in the sense that it was difficult for them to establish Malta as one's domicile of choice under the high threshold established in *Dr Alex Perice Calascione v George Rizzo*[21] and *C Grech v Pl J Busuttil*.[22] This is what prompted the Maltese legislator to effectively abandon domicile and opt for presence, especially when it comes to non-Maltese nationals.[23]

At the same time, though, the Maltese legislature has established a balancing mechanism to the exorbitant jurisdictional basis of Art 742(1)(b) of the COCP. Inspired by the common law institution of forum conveniens/forum non conveniens,[24] Art 742(2) COCP awards a discretionary power to Maltese courts to either declare the defendant to

[18] Civil Court, 16 October 2003, *Angelo Cutajar and Sons Company Limited v Anthony Cremona Dott Et noe*. First Hall.

[19] The Court noted: '... bi presenza' wiehed ma jifhimx biss presenza attwali u fizika, imma jinkludi fiha wkoll presenza permezz ta' persuna rapprezentanti taghha ...', which roughly translates to '... presence does not only entail actual and physical presence within the jurisdiction, but also includes in it the case where somebody is represented by another person within the jurisdiction ...'.

[20] P Diwan, *Private International Law* 2nd edn (Deep and Deep Publications, 1988) 18.

[21] L-Avukat Dr A Perrici Calascione bhala mandatarju specjali ghan-nom u in in rappresentanza tas-societa estera *Banca Agricola Etna Spa v George Rizzo*.

[22] *C Grech v Pl J Busuttil* (1953) 37 I 397 Court of Appeal (civil).

[23] See the case of Court of Appeal, 7 October 1997, *Dr L Cassar Pullicino nom v A Xuereb*.

[24] The doctrine has penetrated a wide range of common law countries. Historically it is first traced in 19th century Scottish case law and, especially, in Lord Kinnear's opinion in *Sim v Robinow* [1892] 19 R 665: '... the plea can never be sustained unless the court is satisfied that there is some other tribunal, having competent jurisdiction, in which the case may be tried more suitably for the interests of all the parties and for the ends of justice ...'. It emigrated a century later in English case law, most notably in *Spiliada Maritime Corporation v Consulex Ltd* [1987] AC 460 and also in Hong Kong as evidenced by *The Owners of Cargo lately laden on board the Ship or Vessel 'Adhiguna Meranti' v The Owners of the Ships or Vessels 'Adhiguna Harapan'*

be non-suited or stay their proceedings on the ground that if an action were to continue in Malta it would be vexatious, oppressive or unjust to the defendant. While Art 742(2) is indeed the Maltese equivalent to the UK institution of forum conveniens/forum non conveniens, it must nonetheless be noted that Maltese law has created a *sui generis* mechanism with distinctive differences to the classic UK forum conveniens/forum non conveniens as established in *Spiliada*:[25] on the one hand, Maltese courts will only exercise their discretionary power and stay their proceedings if a court in a third country is also seised of the same case. In other words, *lis pendens* and parallel proceedings in a third country is a precondition in Malta,[26] while it is not in the UK, where UK courts might stay proceedings based on forum conveniens/forum non conveniens even if a foreign court merely has concurrent jurisdiction but is not seised of the same case. On the other hand, Maltese courts will only stay their proceedings if an action were to continue in Malta that would be vexatious, oppressive or unjust to the defendant. It is not the better suitability of the foreign court, as in traditional common law, that leads to a stay of proceedings, but foul play and elements of misuse of the procedure in Malta that justify such a stay.[27]

Question 4

After the 1995 amendments, Malta has refrained from creating a provision that expressly provides for a *forum necessitatis*.[28] Article 742(1) of the COCP guarantees that people in need of judicial protection will be able to bring their cases before the Maltese courts,

[1987] HKLR 904. Australia was more reluctant and adopted a *sui generis forum conveniens/forum non conveniens* test in *Voth v Manildra Flour Mills Pty Ltd* [1990] 171 CLR 538. The principle is well established also in the United States, see for example P Blair, 'The doctrine of forum non conveniens in Anglo-American Law' (1929) *Colum L Rev* 1; EL Barrett, Jr, 'The Doctrine of Forum Non Conveniens' (1947) *Cal L Rev* 380: R C Casad, 'Long Arm and Convenient Forum' (1971) *Kan L Rev* 1, D Berger, 'Zuständigkeit und forum non conveniens im amerikanischen Zivilprozess' (1977) *RabelsZ* 39. Canada also applies its own version of the form conveniens/forum non conveniens doctrine, see in that regard St G A Pitel, 'The Canadian Codification of Forum Non Conveniens' (2011) *JPrIL* 251. For a nice and recent comparative analysis of the doctrine of forum conveniens/forum non conveniens between different common law jurisdictions see DJ Svantesson, *Private International Law and the Internet* 4th edn (Wolters Kluwer, 2021) 212–35.

[25] *Spiliada Maritime Corp v Cansulex Ltd* [1986] UKHL 10, [1987] AC 460, House of Lords (UK).

[26] In that regard see the seminal case of *Patrick Pillon għan-nom u in rappreżentana tal-bank BNP Paribas [Suisse] S.A. u b'nota tal-15 ta' Marzu 2004 Dr Carmel Chircop assuma l-atti bħala mandatarju speċjali ta' BNP Paribas (Suisse) S.A. minflok Patrick Pillon v Smarta Navigation Ltd* [C29236], First Hall Civil Court, per Mr Justice N Cuschieri, 28 October 2005.

[27] In that sense, the Maltese variant of the forum conveniens/forum non conveniens doctrine seems to be closer to the test applied in Australia after *Voth v Manildra Flour Mills Pty Ltd* [1990] 171 CLR 538. For an insightful comparison between the classic *Spiliada forum conveniens/forum non conveniens* and the Australian *Voth forum conveniens/forum non conveniens* test see Peter Brereton, 'Forum Non Conveniens in Australia: A Case Note on *Voth v Manildra Flour Mills*' (1991) *ICLQ* 895, 897. It must be stated, nonetheless, that since the adoption of the doctrine in *Voth*, 'Australian Courts have been fine tuning its application': see in more detail, DJ Svantesson, 'In Defence of the Doctrine of Forum non Conveniens' (2005) *HKLJ* 395, 401–02.

[28] Prior to the 1995 amendments a *forum necessitatis* was made available under the predecessor of Art 742 of the COCP, namely Art 793 COCP. Art 793(1)(d) of the COCP used the following wording: 'Save as otherwise expressly provided by law, the Civil Courts of Malta shall have jurisdiction to try and determine all actions, without any distinction or privilege, concerning the persons hereinafter mentioned: … (d) any person who, having fled from the country in which he was domiciled, has not fixed his domicile elsewhere and is present in Malta …'. This provision reflected the tumultuous history of Italy in the first half of the 20th century, when political persecutions in Italy were frequent and many Italians sought refuge in Malta.

mostly on the basis of their mere presence in the Maltese Islands (see Art 742(1)(b) COCP). Even the mechanism of Art 742(2) COCP, namely the Maltese version of forum conveniens/forum non conveniens, will not be an obstacle in affording judicial protection to people in need of it, as it would be very difficult to claim before a Maltese court that judging a case in Malta for the sake of a person that otherwise has no access to justice, amounts to a vexatious, oppressive or unjust procedure for the defendant. In other words, Maltese courts will offer protection to those in need, in view of their wide default jurisdictional bases established in Art 742(1) of the COCP, while the mechanisms established in Maltese law to rationalise the jurisdictional claims of Maltese courts, will not result in denying someone the chance to obtain access to justice, especially if in dire need of it. After all, one of the reasons behind the 1995 amendments to the Maltese rules on jurisdiction has been to guarantee that nobody will remain without a forum that is eager to hear and adjudicate over one's case.

Question 5

(a)

Jurisdiction in contracts and torts is regulated by the fundamental provisions of Art 742(1) of the COCP. In fact, it can be noted that Art 742(1) COCP provides special jurisdictional treatment for obligations in general. In that sense, all kinds of obligations, namely both contractual and non-contractual, are treated under common heads of jurisdiction. Art 742(1) provides three jurisdictional grounds for obligations: the place of contract formation (Art 742(1)(d) COCP), the place of the performance of an obligation (Art 742(1)(e) COCP) and the place of the enforcement of an obligation (Art 742(1)(f) COCP).

When it comes to contractual disputes per se, the situation is comparable to the other EU Member States. If one were to compare Maltese law to the Brussels Ibis Regulation in terms of jurisdiction for contractual disputes, it becomes apparent that Art 742(1)(e) of the COCP, despite its complicated wording, is almost identical to Art 7 no 1 lit a of the Brussels Ibis Regulation. Both of them establish jurisdiction at the place of performance of the obligation in question. Similar to the methodology displayed in classic CJEU case-law on the Brussels Ibis Regulation,[29] the Maltese courts will follow the exact same path when applying Art 742(1)(e) of the COCP: they will first try to identify the *lex causae* and, through the *lex causae*, they will seek to identify the place of performance of the obligation in question. If Malta is the place of performance according to the *lex causae*, then they will exercise jurisdiction over a contractual dispute. If Malta is not the place of performance according to the *lex causae*, then they will refrain from exercising jurisdiction. The classic criticism expressed in the context of Art 7 no 1 lit a of the Brussels Ibis Regulation[30] applies, therefore, to Art 742(1)(e) of the COCP as well.

[29] Most notably case C-12/76 *Tessili*, paras 13–14, and C-14/76 *De Bloos*, para 15.

[30] See for example among many others A Lüderitz, 'Fremdbestimmte internationale Zuständigkeit? Versuch einer Neubestimmung von § 29ZPO, Art 5 Nr.1 EuGVÜ' in H Bernstein, U Drobnig and H Kötz (eds), *Festschrift für Konrad Zweigert* (Mohr Siebeck, 1981) 233.

It would be interesting to follow the methodology of Maltese courts if Maltese law would be the *lex causae* in a certain dispute. In such a case, in order to identify the place of performance one would have to look at the relevant provisions of the Maltese civil code,[31] namely Art 1159 of the latter, which provides four alternative places of performance. According to Art 1159(1) of the Maltese civil code, one must first look at the contract itself: if the contract specifies a place of performance then there shall be no further inquiry, the place designated by the parties will be the place of performance of the disputed obligation. In case such a choice is absent, Art 1159 of the Maltese civil code provides for alternatives, according to the nature and subject matter of the disputed obligation: according to Art 1159(2) of the Maltese civil code, if the obligation refers to the delivery of a material good, the place of performance is the place where the good to be delivered is located at the time of performance.[32] If the obligation is monetary, then the place of performance, according to Art 1159(3) of the Maltese civil code, is the place of the residence of the creditor. In all other cases, finally, the place of performance, according to Art 1159(4) of the Maltese civil code is the place of residence of the debtor.

Maltese law, nonetheless, goes a step further than Art 7 no 1 lit a1 of the Brussels Ibis Regulation, as it also establishes that contractual disputes can be brought before the courts of contract formation. There are no Maltese particularities as to the place of contract formation, that being the place where the proposal to form a contract is accepted.

Contrary to the Brussels Ibis Regulation, Maltese law provides for an additional jurisdictional basis for contracts, namely the place of enforcement of contractual obligations (Art 742(1)(f) of the COCP).

Two conditions must be met in order for Maltese courts to exercise jurisdiction under Art 742(1)(f): (a) the plaintiff must either be a Maltese national or have residence in Malta, and (b) Malta shall be the place of enforcement of the obligation for which the plaintiff seeks judicial protection. There are, therefore, two major problems of interpretation when it comes to the jurisdictional basis of Art 742(1)(f): what is the meaning of residence in Malta and what does it mean that an obligation can be enforced in Malta?

As regards the first problem, Maltese courts tend to interpret the term 'residence' in Art 742(1)(f), in very similar terms to the concept of mere presence, as identified in 742(1)(b).[33]

As regards the second problem, namely that Malta shall be the place of enforcement of the obligation, Maltese courts have established that the question of the place of enforcement must be related to the nature of the claims brought forward by the actions in question: if the subject matter of a case refers to the payment of a sum of money, one must prove that the defendant has money or other assets in Malta, so that the monetary claim can be satisfied through attachment proceedings in Malta.[34] On the contrary,

[31] Chapter 16 of the Laws of Malta.

[32] The wording of this provision is somewhat confusing, as the law uses the term 'payment', which implies a monetary obligation and not one on delivering a good. But this is a misnomer and the term 'payment' shall rather be understood as performance and not literally as payment.

[33] *Vassallo v Zammit Cutajar*, Commercial Court, 1931, where residence was equated to presence by a mere representative in Malta.

[34] Court of Appeal, 18 June 1928, *Coleiro v Dr C Parnis*.

if the obligation is non-monetary, then it is irrelevant whether money or assets exist in Malta. For non-monetary obligations to be enforceable in Malta, it suffices that the subject matter of the obligation is located in Malta.[35]

(b)

In what is a striking Maltese particularity, Maltese courts have consistently held that Art 742(1)(d) and (e) of the COCP do not refer only to contractual obligations but also cover non-contractual obligations.[36] In essence, Maltese law utilises the place of contract formation and the place of performance of the contract also for torts, delicts and quasi-delicts. This is a huge derogation from Art 7 no 2 of the Brussels Ibis Regulation and, therefore, there can be no comparison between them, save for the observation that Maltese law does not recognize a pure *lex loci delicti*.

Identifying the place where somebody has overtaken a non-contractual obligation or the place where somebody needs to perform a non-contractual obligation seems contradictory. Non-contractual obligations, especially torts, lack the voluntary element that characterises contractual obligations. It is not really the will of the parties that is essential to torts, but rather a behaviour of the tortfeasor that goes contrary to existing legislation. One could, of course, assume that maybe the place of 'contracting' a tortious obligation is the place where somebody has undertaken a behaviour that contradicts certain legal provisions. But then, when one tries to identify the place of performance of a tortious obligation the situation becomes complicated. One could assume that the nature of the tortious obligation shall define the place of its performance: if it is a monetary obligation, one could apply Art 1159(3) of the Maltese civil code. In such a case, the dispute will be jurisdictionally located at the place of the domicile of the creditor of the tortious obligation (that is, the victim). If the tortious obligation in question is non-monetary, then Art 1159(4) of the Maltese civil code will apply and the dispute will be decided by the courts of the domicile of the debtor, namely the tortfeasor. This methodology will, of course, be valid if two assumptions prove to be true: (a) that one is allowed to refer to the *lex causae* in order to find the place of the performance of the tortious obligation and (b) that such jurisdictional grounds will fit the unique nature of torts, delicts and quasi-delicts. Unfortunately, Maltese courts have very rarely applied the jurisdictional ground of Art 742(1)(d) and (e) in tort cases[37] and, therefore, there is not enough data to support these assumptions, which seem to be taken for granted nonetheless.

[35] Commercial Court, 12 November 1937, *Salamone v Mifsud Speranza*.

[36] See First Hall Civil Court, 11 January 1918, *GEC v Page*; First Hall Civil Court, 31 May 1931, *Darmanin v Despott*; Civil Court, First Hall Civil Court, 6 February 1957, *Domenico Spiteri v Leading Cook Graham Spencer*.

[37] There are two main cases in that regard, namely, First Hall Civil Court, 11 January 1918, *GEC v Page* and First Hall Civil Court, 31 May 1931, *Darmanin vs Despott*. In both cases, though, there has been no analysis on how to apply Art 742(1)(d) and (e) to torts, but it was rather stated as an obiter that the jurisdictional bases of Art 742(1)(d) and (e) apply not only to contractual but also to non-contractual obligations, including torts, delicts and quasi-delicts.

The explanation behind the rare application of Art 742(1)(d) and (e) in tort cases is Art 742(1)(b) of the COCP: by introducing the concept of mere presence as a basis of international jurisdiction the Maltese legislator has, in a way, undermined the jurisdictional bases of Art 742(1)(d) and (e) especially when it comes to torts. Instead of investing time in fine-tuning the special heads of jurisdiction in Art 742(1)(d) and (e) when applicable to torts, Maltese courts have routinely founded their jurisdiction in Art 742(1)(b) of the COCP (or even Art 742(1)(a) COCP). In addition, they have also made use of another Maltese particularity: Art 742(1)(f) of the COCP, namely the place where an obligation is enforced. Maltese courts have consistently held that Art 742(1)(f) of the COCP, namely the place of the enforcement of an obligation, covers every obligation, no matter its subject matter, namely also torts, delicts and quasi-delicts.[38] The place of enforcement of a tortious obligation is a unique jurisdictional ground and offers generous leeway to Maltese courts to establish their jurisdiction. If the tortious obligation is monetary, Malta will qualify as the place of enforcement, provided that the debtor has some assets (even minimal) in Malta. If the tortious obligation is non-monetary, then Malta will qualify as the place of enforcement, provided that the obligation can be carried out in Malta.[39] Maltese courts have been very generous when interpreting the place of enforcement of a tortious obligation. They have, in fact, gone as far as proclaiming that Malta is the place of enforcement when a car accident is committed outside of Malta and none of the parties has any connection to Malta, but the defendant has insured his/her vehicle with an insurance company that had assets in Malta: given that enforcement in car accidents can also be established against the insurer, Maltese courts were found to have jurisdiction as the place where the assets of the insurer were located.[40] It is obvious that the Maltese rules on international jurisdiction for torts, delicts and quasi-delicts are very different in comparison to the Brussels Regime and, also, that Maltese courts make rather exorbitant jurisdictional claims over non-contractual obligations.[41]

[38] See amongst others First Hall (Civil Court), 25 November, 1884, *A Annati v Dr F Sammut*, Vol X p 643; First Hall, 31 May 1901, *E Darmanin v Dr C Despott et nom*, Vol.XVIII.ii.179); First Hall, 26 March 1936, *M Tonna v Dr GM Speranza et ne*, Vol.XXIX.ii.1036); First Hall, 4 April 1946, *Maria Anna Tanti v Avv Paolo Borg Grech et ne*, Vol.X:XXIl.ii.301.); First Hall, 25 October 1955, *A Wells v Av Dr GB Olivier de Puget et ne*, Vol.XXXIX.ii.749); Court of Appeal, 11 March 1963, *C Fernandez v P Pace ne*, Vol.XLVIl.i.190.) amongst others.

[39] eg in a defamation case, it will be enough if Malta is the place where the distribution of the defamatory material must be stopped.

[40] This was the case in First Hall Civil Court, 6 February 1957, *Domenico Spiteri v Leading Cook Graham Spencer*.

[41] This underutilisation of the special jurisdictional grounds for obligations, which apart from torts has also influenced contractual disputes, is, nonetheless, not justified by the 1995 amendments. It is, of course, true that the 1995 amendments have been the major force behind the wide jurisdictional rules of Maltese law. At the same time, however, the Maltese legislature has also introduced a Maltese version of the *forum conveniens/forum non conveniens* institution. If anything, Arts 742(1)(b), (d), (e) and (f) of the COCP shall be interpreted in the light of the *forum conveniens/forum non conveniens* institution: the weaker the jurisdictional basis, the more plausible the stay of proceedings in favour of foreign courts that have stronger connections to a case; on the contrary, the stronger the connection of Malta to a dispute, the less plausible the stay of proceedings in favour of foreign courts. Seen in this light, Art 742(1)(b) shall not routinely justify the jurisdiction of Maltese courts over contractual or tortious disputes, as it establishes a rather weak jurisdictional bond between each given dispute and Malta. On the contrary, Art 742(1)(d) and (e) shall be interpreted as a form of a 'qualified presence', namely a presence within Malta so strong, as to make the stay of Maltese proceedings harder in view of *forum conveniens/forum non conveniens*. Applying such a yardstick on Art 742(1)(b), (d) and (e)

(c)

Article 742(1) of the COCP does not provide for any jurisdictional ground based on a close connection between defendants.[42] Such a jurisdictional basis is, therefore, unknown to Maltese law.

(d)

Article 742(1) of the COCP does not provide any special jurisdictional regime for consumer, employment or insurance contracts.

will afford some breathing space for the special jurisdictional grounds for obligations. The same applies to Art 742(1)(f) of the COCP, namely the jurisdictional basis of the place of enforcement of obligations, which, in certain situations, might prove to be an important addition to the jurisdictional grounds of Art 742(1)(d) and (e) COCP.

[42] On the contrary, Art 743 of the COCP provides a jurisdictional basis for counter-claims, resembling to a certain extent the provision of Art 8 no 3 of the Brussels Ibis Regulation).

Netherlands

TESS BENS

Question 1

(a)

The national rules that govern the international jurisdiction of the courts of the Netherlands can be found in Book 1, Title 1, Section 1 of the Dutch Code of Civil Procedure (*Wetboek van Burgerlijke Rechtsvordering*): Arts 1–14 DCCP. Article 1 DCCP reiterates that these national rules are applicable in the absence of a European regulation or an international convention that governs jurisdiction.[1] Articles 2 and 3 DCCP establish the general jurisdictional rules. In proceedings that are initiated by serving a writ of summons on the defendant, the courts of the Netherlands have jurisdiction on the basis of Art 2 DCCP if the defendant is domiciled or habitually resident in the Netherlands (*forum rei*). Article 3 DCCP instead applies to cases that are instituted by lodging a petition with the court, except in cases governed by Arts 4 and 5 DCCP, and principally bases the jurisdiction of the court on the domicile or habitual residence of the petitioner.[2]

Articles 6 and 6a DCCP provide additional grounds for jurisdiction for specific matters that may be applicable if the defendant or the petitioner is not domiciled in the Netherlands, including for contractual obligations (Arts 6(a) and 6a), employment and agency contracts (Arts 6(b) and (c)), consumer contracts (Art 6(d)), delictual obligations (Art 6(e)), rights in rem and tenancies (Art 6(f)), succession (Art 6(g)), corporate matters (Art 6(h)) and insolvency-related matters (Art 6(i)). Alternative bases of jurisdiction are established by Art 7 DCCP for cases involving multiple defendants (Art 7(1)), counter-claims and/or third-party proceedings (Art 7(2)). Article 8 DCCP establishes explicit rules on prorogation and derogation of jurisdiction on the basis of a choice of forum agreement, whereas Art 9(1) DCCP governs tacit prorogation.

[1] The precedence of European regulations and international conventions over national legislation is based on Arts 93–94 of the Dutch Constitution. Art 1 DCCP rather serves as a warning to avoid misunderstandings as to the nature of the national rules on international jurisdiction. See Kamerstukken II, 2 November 1999, 1999/00, no°26855, 3, 27.

[2] Arts 3–5 DCCP are not discussed in detail in this report, as these provisions generally concern matters of family law, rather than civil and commercial matters. However, it must be observed that the legislator explicitly decided against the adoption of separate regimes for proceedings initiated through serving a writ of summons and proceedings initiated through a petition; see Kamerstukken II, 2 November 1999, 1999/00, no°26855, 3, 26.

A *forum necessitatis* is envisaged by Art 9(b) and (c) DCCP. Article 10 DCCP provides that the courts have jurisdiction in cases envisaged by Art 767 DCCP, as well as in cases where the jurisdiction of the courts of the Netherlands derives from rules *other* than those that distribute internal competence in proceedings that are initiated through a writ of summons (Arts 99–110 DCCP) or through a petition (Arts 262–70 DCCP). Article 10 DCCP is a residual rule for establishing jurisdiction on a basis not mentioned in Arts 1–14 DCCP.[3] Article 767 DCCP allows the courts to establish jurisdiction on the basis of an attachment levied in the Netherlands (*forum arresti*); in the absence of another way to acquire an enforceable title in the Netherlands.[4] Articles 11–14 DCCP do not establish jurisdictional rules, but govern matters such as *lis pendens* and provisional measures.

(b)

Articles 1–14 DCCP govern the jurisdiction of the courts of the Netherlands in international cases, but do not govern their jurisdiction in interregional cases; ie cases exclusively involving (parties located in) different parts of the Kingdom of the Netherlands.[5] However, in the absence of rules governing interregional jurisdiction, the rules that govern the international jurisdiction of the courts of the Netherlands, including Arts 1–14 DCCP, ought to be applied by analogy.[6]

(c)

Articles 1–14 DCCP were introduced as part of a revision of the national rules of civil procedure over the course of the 1990s, the result of which entered into force on 1 January 2002.[7] Prior to the introduction of these national rules, the attribution of international jurisdiction was determined by distribution of internal competence amongst the courts.[8] As Polak and Van Rooij observed in 1987:

> One of the most striking features of Dutch non-conventional private international law is that, for the purposes of adjudicative jurisdiction, both domestic and international cases are

[3] Arts 1–14 DCCP are not exhaustive. More specific bases for jurisdiction may be found elsewhere in the DCCP, although recourse to the provisions that distribute internal competence is prevented; as these provisions have a specific function within the Dutch legal order; see Kamerstukken II, 2 November 1999, 1999/00, no°26855, 3, 43.

[4] Kamerstukken II, 2 November 1999, 1999/00, no°26855, 3, 44.

[5] Kamerstukken II, 2 November 1999, 1999/00, no°26855, 3, 22; the Kingdom comprises the Netherlands, Aruba, Curaçao and Sint Maarten as constituent countries, as well as Bonaire, Sint Eustasius and Saba as special municipalities of the Netherlands.

[6] Hoge Raad, 2 May 2014, ECLI:NL:HR:2014:1063, 3.6.2; in the light of the precedence of European regulations and international conventions over domestic law (cf Art 1 DCCP), the courts of the Netherlands must first determine whether a jurisdictional rule from such a regulation or convention can be applied by analogy to an interregional case, before resorting to analogous application of the national jurisdictional rules of Arts 1–14 DCCP.

[7] Law of 6 December 2001, *Stb* 2001, 580.

[8] The rule 'distribution determines attribution' (*distributie bepaalt attributie*) was formulated in Hoge Raad, 24 December 1915, NJ 1916/417 and remained in force until the introduction of Arts 1–14 DCCP, although its remnants remain visible in Art 10 DCCP.

> generally treated alike. In fact, most of the statutory provisions on 'jurisdiction' are merely aimed at internal situations. Nevertheless, these provisions have been extended in case law to cover international situations.[9]

The legislator considered this rule dated and obsolete; as it was conceived in a time where establishing international jurisdiction posed a less frequent problem and it mainly existed because of the absence of clear, codified national rules on international jurisdiction. The legislator explicitly acknowledged that (new) national rules would mainly be applicable in cases falling outside of the personal and/or material scope of the international conventions to which the Netherlands was a party. In order to promote uniformity and legal certainty, the legislator deemed it desirable to adapt these national rules to the rules on international jurisdiction in those conventions, in particular the Brussels Convention.[10] The jurisdictional rules of the Brussels Convention, as amended by the Brussels I Regulation,[11] have therefore been extended into the domestic law of the Netherlands through incorporation; although the extent of this incorporation varies per rule.[12]

Articles 6(a) and 6a DCCP are virtually identical to the jurisdictional rule for matters related to a contract (Art 7(1) Brussels Ibis Regulation), while 6(e) DCCP mirrors the jurisdictional rule for matters related to a tort, delict or quasi-delict (Art 7(2) Brussels Ibis Regulation). The preliminary rulings of the ECJ therefore serve as an important guideline for their interpretation, as will be further discussed in the answers to questions 5(a) and (b) below. Arts 6(d) (consumer contracts), 6(f) (rights in rem) and 6(h) (corporate matters) DCCP respectively incorporate elements of Arts 17–19, 24(1) and 24(2) of the Brussels Ibis Regulation, whereas Arts 6(b) and 6(c) DCCP (individual employment and agency contracts) deviate from the provisions of Arts 21–23 Brussels Ibis Regulation. The preliminary rulings of the ECJ may still serve as a source of inspiration in this context, albeit in a more limited role; which is discussed in the answer to question 5(d) below. The legislator deliberately refrained from incorporating other heads of jurisdiction that existed in Art 5 of the Brussels Convention, as amended by the Brussels I Regulation, that can presently be found in Art 7 Brussels Ibis Regulation.[13] Article 7 DCCP incorporates the derivative heads of jurisdiction of Art 8(1), (2) and (3) Brussels Ibis Regulation, although the rule of Art 7(1) DCCP that governs jurisdiction over multiple defendants is slightly broader than its European counterpart; as is discussed in the answer to question 5(c) below.

Articles 8(1) and (2) DCCP were modelled on (the predecessors) of Art 25 Brussels Ibis Regulation, although Art 8(2) DCCP explicitly mandates derogation of jurisdiction

[9] R van Rooij and MV Polak, *Private International Law in the Netherlands* (TMC Asser Instituut, 1987), 45.

[10] Kamerstukken II, 2 November 1999, 1999/00, no°26855, 22–25.

[11] Initially, a discrepancy existed between the national rules that entered into force on 1 January 2002 and the rules of the Brussels I Regulation, which entered into force on 1 March 2002. This discrepancy was fixed pursuant to the Law of 8 September 2005 (*Stb* 2005, 455), which entered into force on 15 October 2005. Kamerstukken II, 14 May 2003, 2002/03, no°28863, 3, 1.

[12] Such a review was already drafted by MV Polak, 'Inspiration From Above: Making and Interpreting Dutch Law on Jurisdiction in Civil and Commercial Matters in Light of European Law' in HJ Snijders and S Vogenauer (eds), *Content and Meaning of National Law in the Context of Transnational Law* (Otto Schmidt/De Gruyter, 2009), 113–31.

[13] Kamerstukken II, 2 November 1999, 1999/00, no°26855, 3, 33–34.

if a (valid) choice of forum was made for a foreign court. Articles 8(3) and (4) DCCP resemble Art 25(4) Brussels Ibis Regulation in the protection of consumers and employees. The requirements for the validity of a choice of forum are formulated in a less complicated manner than Art 8(5) Brussels Ibis Regulation. The separability requirement of Art 8(6) DCCP mirrors Art 25(5) Brussels Ibis Regulation.[14] The rule on tacit prorogation of Art 9(1) DCCP is similar to Art 26 Brussels Ibis Regulation, although the former rule allows the courts of the Netherlands to decline jurisdiction in the absence of a reasonable cause.[15] The rule on *lis pendens* of Art 12 DCCP is similar to Art 29 Brussels Ibis Regulation, in the sense that it is cast in European terminology, although a stay of proceedings is required if the decision of the foreign court first seised can be subject to recognition and enforcement in the Netherlands.[16] Lastly, the terminology of Art 13 DCCP on provisional and protective measures corresponds to Art 35 Brussels Ibis Regulation, which equally does not serve as a separate basis for jurisdiction.[17]

The possibility of (further) extending the personal scope of the jurisdictional rules of the Brussels Regime to non-EU defendants, through incorporation or by reference, is not considered by scholars or lawmakers.[18]

(d)

The legislator has observed that there are no (exorbitant) jurisdictional rules within the meaning of Art 5(2) Brussels Ibis Regulation in the Netherlands. Notifying the European Commission pursuant to Art 76(1)(a) Brussels Ibis Regulation was therefore considered unnecessary.[19] Consequently, the Netherlands has not notified the European Commission of any jurisdictional rule that falls within the scope of Arts 5(2) and 6(2) Brussels Ibis Regulation (Art 76(1)(a)), nor of any rules on third-party notice referred to in Art 65 Brussels Ibis Regulation (Art 76(1)(b)).[20]

One author recently voiced concerns over the exorbitant nature of the *forum arresti* created by Arts 10 and 767 DCCP.[21] However, it must be noted that a court is only allowed to base its jurisdiction on Arts 10 and 767 DCCP if (i) jurisdiction cannot be based on Arts 2–9 DCCP and (ii) the party that levied the attachment cannot procure an enforceable title through legal proceedings before a foreign court.[22] Whether this ground of jurisdiction should be notified to the European Commission appears debatable, as the jurisdictional rules of the Brussels Ibis Regulation clearly take precedence over the national rules on jurisdiction (cf Art 1 DCCP).

[14] Kamerstukken II, 2 November 1999, 1999/00, no°26855, 3, 38–39.
[15] Kamerstukken II, 2 November 1999, 1999/00, no°26855, 3, 40.
[16] Kamerstukken II, 2 November 1999, 1999/00, no°26855, 3, 45–46.
[17] Kamerstukken II, 2 November 1999, 1999/00, no°26855, 3, 46.
[18] The introduction of the Brussels Ia Regulation has not led the legislator to propose any changes to Arts 1–14 DCCP; see Kamerstukken II, 28 June 2013, 2012/13, no°33676, 3–5.
[19] Kamerstukken II, 28 June 2013, 2012/13, no°33676, 3–4.
[20] First update of the information referring to Art 76 of Regulation No 1215/2012.
[21] BFLM Schim, 'Enkele kritische gedachten over het forum arresti' (2019) *WPNR* 211, 220.
[22] Hoge Raad, 12 April 2019, ECLI:NL:HR:2019:566, 3.4.5; a valid choice of forum for a foreign court (Art 8(2) DCCP) also precludes recourse to Arts 10 and 767 DCCP. See also Hoge Raad, 9 November 2012, ECLI:NL:HR:2012:BX0331.

Question 2

In the Netherlands, the notion of domicile of natural and legal persons is defined in Book 1, Title 3 of the Dutch Civil Code (*Burgerlijk Wetboek*): Arts 1:10–1:15 DCC. These provisions define the notion of domicile for the purpose of substantive private law, as well as for jurisdictional purposes.

Article 1:10(1) DCC defines a natural person's domicile as their 'normal' place of residence (*woonstede*), ie the place within the Netherlands where that person is almost a permanent resident and with which they may be considered to be the most closely connected (eg for the service of writs). Factual circumstances are decisive to determine whether such a close connection exists.[23] In practice, a natural persons' normal place of residence will often correspond to the place of residence that is registered the Personal Records Database (*Basisregistratie Personen*);[24] although they may differ.[25] A natural person's normal place of residence does not change if that person is abroad for extended periods of time, provided that there is a clear intention to return to that place.[26] If a natural person does not have a normal place of residence in the Netherlands – or anywhere else in the world – their actual place of residence (*werkelijk verblijf*) may be considered as their domicile for the purpose of Art 1:10(1) DCCP. However, this residual rule must be interpreted restrictively and requires a certain prolonged presence at a certain place, rather than mere transient presence.[27]

Article 1:10(2) DCC defines the domicile of legal persons as the place where they have their statutory seat, ie the municipality identified as such in the articles of incorporation.[28] In addition, the legal person must register an office address with the Trade Register (*Handelsregister*) of the Chamber of Commerce.[29]

Article 1:14 DCC establishes an additional domicile for natural and legal persons at the place where they keep an office or branch in the Netherlands, for matters relating to that office or branch. Natural persons can therefore have concurrent domiciles, eg when they have an office separate from their normal place of residence,[30] although whether a natural person can have two or more normal places of residence that could each be characterised as domicile for the purpose of Art 1:10(1) DCC is questionable.[31] Likewise, a legal person can have concurrent domiciles, eg if the place of its registered office does

[23] R van Rooij and MV Polak, *Private International Law in the Netherlands*, 48. An alternative definition can be found in Hoge Raad 19 January 1880, *Weekblad van het Recht* 1880/4475 (the place where a natural person lives with his family and conducts his ordinary affairs or manages his property from, ie the place where a person departs from with a certain goal in mind and where he aims to return after its completion), although the assessment of domicile depends on facts rather than legal requirements. See WD Kolkman and FR Salomons, *Asser. 1-I. De persoon, afstamming en adoptie, gezag en omgang, levensonderhoud, bescherming van meerderjarigen* 2nd edn (Wolters Kluwer, 2020), para 83, 87.

[24] AC van Schaick, *Asser. Procesrecht. 2. Eerste aanleg* (Wolters Kluwer, 2016), para 20.

[25] Rechtbank Utrecht (District Court of Utrecht), 9 April 2008, ECLI:NL:RBUTR:2008:BD2164, 4.8.

[26] Hoge Raad, 21 December 2001, ECLI:NL:HR:2001:AD5829, Opinion of AG Strikwerda, para 13.

[27] Kamerstukken II, 2 November 1999, 1999/00, no°26855, 3, 28.

[28] MJ Kroeze, *Asser. 2-I. De Rechtspersoon* 10th edn (Wolters Kluwer 2021), para 237.

[29] MJ Kroeze, *Asser. 2-I. De Rechtspersoon*, para 267.

[30] WD Kolkman and FR Salomons (eds), *Asser 1-I De persoon, afstamming en adoptie, gezag en omgang, levensonderhoud, bescherming van meerderjarigen*, para 86.

[31] WD Kolkman and FR Salomons, *Asser 1-I De persoon, afstamming en adoptie, gezag en omgang, levensonderhoud, bescherming van meerderjarigen*, para 83.

not coincide with its statutory seat, although jurisdiction over corporate matters exclusively belongs to the court at the statutory seat. Legal persons that are incorporated outside of the Netherlands, but keep an office or branch in the Netherlands, are likewise considered to be domiciled there on the basis of Art 1:14 DCC for matters relating to that office or branch.[32]

Question 3

The courts of the Netherlands have general jurisdiction on the basis of Art 2 DCCP, provided that the defendant is domiciled or *habitually resident* in the Netherlands. The notion of 'habitual' place of residence (*gewone verblijfplaats*) in Art 2 DCCP is distinct from the notion of 'actual' place of residence' (*werkelijk verblijf*) that was discussed in the context of Art 1:10(1) DCC; the latter of which is a residual rule to establish domicile in exceptional cases where the defendant has no normal place of residence anywhere in the world and is present in the Netherlands.[33] The notion of habitual residence was rather inspired by similar notions in international conventions, including Art 5(2) of the Brussels Convention and Art 1 Hague Protection of Minors Convention,[34] and ought to be considered as a distinct concept of private international law; which presupposes a certain duration and intensity that transcends actual presence.[35]

Question 4

Article 9 DCCP envisages two different forms of *forum necessitatis*, which allow the courts of the Netherlands to establish jurisdiction if legal proceedings outside of the Netherlands appear impossible (Art 9(b)) or unduly burdensome for the claimant (Art 9(c)). The first form applies to proceedings initiated through a writ of summons, as well as to proceedings initiated through an application, and is referred to in legislative history as *forum necessitatis* in its 'purest' form.[36] This absolute *forum necessitatis* of Art 9(b) DCCP covers situations of legal impossibility (where no foreign court has jurisdiction to hear the case), as well as factual impossibility (where the foreign court that would have jurisdiction is inaccessible due to war, natural disasters, etc).[37] The second form only applies in proceedings initiated through a writ of summons and is referred to in legislative history as a 'weakened' form of *forum necessitatis*.[38] This relative *forum*

[32] MJ Kroeze, *Asser. 2-I. De Rechtspersoon*, para 246.
[33] Kamerstukken II, 2 November 1999, 1999/00, no°26855, 3, 28.
[34] Convention of 1961 Concerning the Powers of Authorities and the Law Applicable in Respect of the Protection of Infants (adopted on 5 October 1961, entered into force 4 February 1969) 1969 UNTS 145 (Hague Protection of Minors Convention).
[35] Kamerstukken II, 2 November 1999, 1999/00, no°26855, 3, 29.
[36] Kamerstukken II, 2 November 1999, 1999/00, no°26855, 3, 41–42.
[37] F Ibili, *Gewogen rechtsmacht in het IPR* (Vol 148, Recht and Praktijk Series, Wolters Kluwer, 2007), 112–119; L Strikwerda and S Schaafsma, *Inleiding tot het Nederlandse internationaal privaatrecht* 12th edn (Wolters Kluwer, 2019), 148.
[38] Kamerstukken II, 2 November 1999, 1999/00, no°26855, 3, 42–43.

necessitatis of Art 9(c) DCCP concerns situations where it is deemed unacceptable to require the claimant to submit the case to the jurisdiction of an otherwise competent foreign court. The wording of Art 9(c) DCCP was intentionally left vague to allow the courts to take into account the circumstances of the case, although the term 'unacceptable' must be interpreted restrictively to counterbalance this lenient formulation. In contrast to the absolute *forum necessitatis*, the relative form requires the case to have a sufficient connection with the legal order of the Netherlands as a prerequisite for establishing jurisdiction.[39]

Articles 9(b) and (c) DCCP are intended to serve as an *ultimum remedium* for exceptional cases where the claimant (or applicant) faces a potential denial of justice.[40] The drafting of Art 9 DCCP somewhat obscures the exceptional nature of these provisions; given that *forum necessitatis* was lumped together with tacit prorogation (Art 9(a)) and these grounds apply if the courts of the Netherlands lack jurisdiction on the basis or Arts 2–8 DCCP. Accordingly, tacit prorogation and *forum necessitatis* may appear as residual, rather than exceptional grounds for jurisdiction.[41] Jurisdiction on the basis of Art 9(b) DCCP has mainly been accepted in family law cases and barely appears to play a role in civil and commercial matters.[42] One recent example where jurisdiction was based on Art 9(c) DCCP concerns a claim for damages arising out of a breach of contract and tortious liability by the Dutch subsidiary of a Russian company (Chemix International BV) against the Republic of Turkmenistan, which pended before the District Court of Amsterdam. Chemix argued that it would be unacceptable to require it to submit to the jurisdiction of the courts of Turkmenistan, in support of which it relied on the human rights situation in Turkmenistan and the lack of an independent judicial authority, notwithstanding the existence of a choice of forum clause. The District Court deemed the case to be sufficiently connected to the legal order of the Netherlands, given that the statutory seat of Chemix was located in the Netherlands and upheld its jurisdiction.[43] Cases where jurisdiction is based on Arts 9(b) or (c) DCCP

[39] F Ibili, *Gewogen rechtsmacht in het IPR*, 120–34; L Strikwerda and S Schaafsma, *Inleiding tot het Nederlandse internationaal privaatrecht*, 148.

[40] Prior to 1 Januari 2002, the possibility of *forum necessitatis* was envisaged by case law. This possibility was intertwined with the *forum non conveniens* envisaged by Art 429c DCCP (old). In other words, the Dutch courts would refrain from exercising *forum non conveniens* where this would lead to a denial of justice. For example Hoge Raad, 20 January 1984, ECLI:NL:HR:1984:AG4737, NJ 1984/751 (*forum necessitatis* to establish probable death); Hoge Raad, 13 February 1987, ECLI:NL:HR:1987:AG5535, NJ 1987/1014 (*forum necessitatis* for revision of maintenance obligation to avoid denial of justice). See F Ibili, *Gewogen rechtsmacht in het IPR*, 108.

[41] F Ibili, *Gewogen rechtsmacht in het IPR*, 109–12. The perception of Arts 9(b) and/or (c) DCCP as residual provisions explains why *forum necessitatis* is frequently invoked, but rarely accepted as a basis for the jurisdiction of the courts of the Netherlands.

[42] See for example Hof Den Haag (Court of Appeal of The Hague), 21 December 2005, ECLI:NL:GHSGR:2005:AU9650 (impossibility to obtain a divorce in Malta); Rechtbank Den Haag (District Court of The Hague), 16 July 2019, ECLI:NL:RBDHA:2019:7701 (impossibility to adopt children in the United Arab Emirates); Rechtbank Den Haag, 18 March 2021, ECLI:NL:RBDHA:2021:2503 (impossibility to obtain a divorce in Thailand or Vietnam). One rare example where Art 9(b) DCCP was applied in a commercial case is Rechtbank Rotterdam (District Court of Rotterdam), 4 November 2003, *NIPR* 2004, 161 (impossibility to timely obtain protective measures under an arbitration agreement). However, the latter case is criticised for its improper use of Art 9(b) DCCP. See F Ibili, *Gewogen rechtsmacht in het IPR*, 119–20.

[43] Rechtbank Amsterdam (District Court of Amsterdam), 29 November 2017, ECLI:NL:RBAMS:2017:8984.

remain rare,[44] however, which underscores the exceptional and restrictive character of *forum necessitatis* in the Netherlands.[45]

Question 5

(a)

The courts of the Netherlands have jurisdiction over non-EU defendants in matters relating to a contract on the basis of Art 6(a) DCCP, provided that the obligation in question has been or must be performed in the Netherlands. Unless agreed otherwise, the place of performance is located in the Netherlands if – in the case of the sale of goods – the goods were delivered or should have been delivered in the Netherlands under the contract (Art 6a(a) DCCP), or – in the case of the provision of services – the services were provided or should have been provided in the Netherlands under the contract (Art 6a(b) DCCP). Arts 6(a) and 6a DCCP are an almost word-by-word copy of Art 5(1) of the Brussels Convention, as amended by the Brussels I Regulation (cf Art 7(1) of the Brussels Ibis Regulation).[46] The preliminary rulings of the ECJ serve as an important guideline for the interpretation of Arts 6(a) and 6a DCCP,[47] which in particular applies for the ECJ's ruling in *Tessili/Dunlop* to determine the place of performance under Art 6(a) DCCP.[48] In other words, the courts of the Netherlands may deviate from the preliminary rulings of the ECJ on Art 7(1) of the Brussels Ibis Regulation if necessary, but this seems to be the exception rather than the norm.[49]

The ECJ's ruling in *Car Trim/Keysafety*[50] has for example been used to interpret Art 6a(a) DCCP, in order to determine the place where, under the contract, the goods

[44] Jurisdiction on the basis of Art 9(c) DCCP has also been accepted in a case involving a claim for payment of letters of credit against a bank in Iraq by a chemical company domiciled in Rotterdam, in which proceedings were initiated prior to the invasion of the United States. See Rechtbank Rotterdam, 4 June 2003, *NIPR* 2004/158. One of the peculiar elements of this case is that the District Court neglected whether jurisdiction could be based on Art 6 (a) DCCP; see F Ibili, *Gewogen rechtsmacht in het IPR*, 119–20. The Court of Appeal of The Hague added that jurisdiction indeed could be based on Art 6(a) DCCP, given that the letters of credit were payable in the Netherlands, but did not strike out the District Courts' earlier ruling on the applicability of Art 9(c) DCCP; see Hof Den Haag 30 November 2010, ECLI:NL:GHSGR:2010:BO6529.

[45] F Ibili, *Gewogen rechtsmacht in het IPR*, 134–35.

[46] Art 6(a) DCCP entered into force on 1 January 2002 and was modelled on Art 5(1) of the Brussels Convention. Kamerstukken II, 2 November 1999, 1999/00, no°26855, 3, 34–35. Art 6a DCCP was introduced pursuant to the Law of 8 September 2005 (*Stb* 2005, 455), which entered into force on 15 October 2005, in order to adapt Art 6(a) DCCP to Art 5(1) of the Brussels I Regulation. Kamerstukken II, 14 May 2003, 2002/03, no°28863, 3, 5.

[47] Kamerstukken II, 2 November 1999, 1999/00, no°26855, 3, 33.

[48] Case 12/76 *Tessili/Dunlop*; Kamerstukken II, 2 November 1999, 1999/00, no°26855, 3, 35.

[49] The term 'matters relating to a contract' in Art 6(a) DCCP has for example been interpreted more extensively to also cover disputes arising out of agreements that concern marital property; which fall outside of the scope of the Brussels Regime. See Rechtbank Almelo (District Court of Almelo), 23 November 2011, ECLI:NL:RBALM:2011:BU7446; Rechtbank Gelderland (District Court of Gelderland), 27 July 2016, ECLI:NL:RBGEL:2016:4202; Rechtbank Overijssel (District Court of Overijssel), 22 March 2017, ECLI:NL:RBOVE:2017:1503.

[50] Case C-381/08, *Car Trim/KeySafety Systems*.

sold were delivered or should have been delivered.[51] The ECJ's ruling in *Krjeci/Ollbrich*[52] has been used in a similar vein, to interpret the term 'provision of services' for the purpose of applying Art 6a(b) DCCP,[53] whereas the ECJ's ruling in *Rehder/Air Baltic*[54] is generally used to determine the place where services were or should have been provided under the contract in flight delay cases against non-EU defendants.[55] The determination of the place of performance in accordance with the ECJ's ruling in *Tessili/Dunlop*, for the purpose of applying Art 6(a) DCCP, is only relevant for obligations that cannot be localised pursuant to Art 6a DCCP.[56] The manner in which Arts 6(a) and 6a DCCP are applied to non-EU defendants therefore hardly differs from the manner in which Art 7(1) of the Brussels Ibis Regulation is applied to EU defendants.

(b)

The courts of the Netherlands have jurisdiction over non-EU defendants in matters relating to tort, delict or quasi-delict on the basis of Art 6(e) DCCP, provided that the harmful event has occurred or may occur in the Netherlands. The legislative history of this provision highlights that Art 6(e) DCCP is an almost word-by-word copy of Art 5(3) Brussels Convention, as amended by the Brussels I Regulation (cf Art 7(2) Brussels Ibis Regulation).[57] The preliminary rulings of the ECJ serve as an important guideline for the interpretation and application of Art 6(e) DCCP,[58] which in particular applies for the ECJ's ruling in *Bier*.[59] The ECJ's ruling in *Bier* is consistently referenced to interpret the term 'place where the harmful event occurred' when applying Art 6(e) DCCP; often accompanied by references to rulings such as *Marinari*,[60] *Kronhofer*,[61] *Holterman*[62]

[51] Hof Arnhem-Leeuwarden (Court of Appeal Arnhem-Leeuwarden), 17 February 2015, ECLI:NL:GHARL:2015:1148, 5.7.

[52] Case C-469/12 *Krjeci/Ollbrich*.

[53] Rechtbank Rotterdam, 25 July 2018, ECLI:NL:RBROT:2018:6027, 4.6.2.

[54] Case C-204/08, *Rehder/Air Baltic*.

[55] Rechtbank Noord-Holland (District Court of Noord-Holland), 13 June 2018, ECLI:NL:RBNHO:2018:5006; Rechtbank Noord-Holland, 13 June 2018, ECLI:NL:RBNHO:2018:5007; Rechtbank Noord-Holland, 29 August 2018, ECLI:NL:RBNHO:2018:7482; Rechtbank Noord-Holland, 10 March 2021, ECLI:NL:RBNHO:2021:2288.

[56] Rechtbank Den Haag, 14 April 2011, ECLI:NL:RBSGR:2011:BQ2573, 4.10; Rechtbank Limburg (District Court of Limburg), 17 December 2014, 4.9; ECLI:NL:RBLIM:2014:11203; Hof Arnhem-Leeuwarden, 5 September 2017, ECLI:NL:GHARL:2017:7702, 5.4; Rechtbank Gelderland, 4 April 2018, ECLI:NL:RBGEL:2018:1874, 2.9.

[57] Art 6(e) DCCP entered into force on 1 January 2002 and was modelled on Art 5(3) of the Brussels Convention. Kamerstukken II, 2 November 1999, 1999/00, no°26855, 3 (Explanatory Memorandum), 36; Art 6(e) DCCP was amended pursuant to the Law of 8 September 2005 (*Stb* 2005, 455), which entered into force on 15 October 2005, in order to adapt its text to Art 5(3) of the Brussels I Regulation. Kamerstukken II, 14 May 2003, 2002/03, no°28863, 3, 5.

[58] Kamerstukken II, 2 November 1999, 1999/00, no°26855, 3, 33.

[59] Case 21/76 *Bier*. The legislator explicitly refrained from incorporation this preliminary ruling into the text of Art 6(e) DCCP to facilitate flexibility. See Kamerstukken II, 2 November 1999, 1999/00, no°26855, 3, 36.

[60] Case C-364/93 *Marinari*.

[61] Case C-168/02 *Kronhofer*.

[62] Case C-47/14 *Holterman*.

and/or *Universal*[63] to highlight that this term ought to be construed restrictively.[64] The District Court of The Hague has in this respect suggested that, in principle, there is no good reason to interpret Art 6(e) DCCP in a manner that deviates from the interpretation of Art 7(2) of the Brussels Ibis Regulation by the ECJ, absent an indication to the contrary.[65] The manner in which Art 6(e) DCCP is applied to non-EU defendants therefore barely differs from the manner in which Art 7(2) of the Brussels Ibis Regulation is applied to EU defendants.

(c)

In cases where a court of the Netherlands has jurisdiction over one of a number of defendants, that court may base its jurisdiction over the other (non-EU) defendant(s) on Art 7(1) DCCP, provided that the claims against the various defendants are so closely connected that, in the interest of efficiency, it is expedient to hear and determine them together. The text of this rule was inspired by Art 6(1) of the Brussels Convention and incorporated the preliminary rulings of the ECJ at the time of drafting;[66] although the addition 'in the interest of efficiency' derives from Dutch case law.[67] The preliminary rulings of the ECJ on Art 6(1) of the Brussels I Regulation and Art 8(1) of the Brussels Ibis Regulation serve as a guideline for the interpretation and application of Art 7(1) DCCP.[68] However, this guidance mainly concerns the requirement of a 'close connection' between the relevant claims. The courts in this respect frequently refer to the ECJ's preliminary rulings in cases such as *Roche*,[69] *Freeport*,[70] *Painer*[71] and/or *Solvay*[72] to determine whether the claims arise out of the same situation of fact and law, although an identical legal basis is not an indispensable requirement for establishing jurisdiction on the basis of Art 7(1) DCCP; provided that it was foreseeable by the defendants that they might be sued in the Netherlands.[73]

[63] Case C-12/15 *Universal*.

[64] Rechtbank Rotterdam, 18 April 2018, ECLI:NL:RBROT:2018:3300, 4.3-4.5; Rechtbank, 25 July 2018, ECLI:NL:RBROT:2018:6027, 4.10.2; Rechtbank Rotterdam, 17 April 2019, ECLI:NL:RBROT:2019:3033, 4.13; Rechtbank Den Haag, 9 September 2019, ECLI:NL:RBDHA:2019:10254, 5.9, 5.27; Hof Den Haag, 9 Oktober 2019; ECLI:NL:GHDHA:2018:2607, 24-26; Rechtbank Overijssel, 20 May 2020, ECLI:NL:RBOVE:2020:1808, 2.7.

[65] Rechtbank Den Haag, 27 February 2018, ECLI:NL:RBDHA:2018:2284, 4.3; see also Hof Den Bosch (Court of Appeal of Den Bosch), 7 October 2008, ECLI:NL:GHSHE:2008:BG2209, 4.3.2.

[66] Kamerstukken II, 2 November 1999, 1999/00, no°26855, 3, 37; Art 7(1) DCCP already incorporated Case 189/87 *Kalfelis*, in order to avoid the risk that jurisdiction on the basis of this provision would be considered exorbitant. Accordingly, the text of Art 7(1) DCCP did not have to be revised when *Kalfelis* was incorporated into the text of Art 6(1) of the Brussels I Regulation.

[67] Hoge Raad, 27 October 1978, NJ 1980/102, *Vierhout and Kreté/Crosland*; Hoge Raad, 16 May 1986, *NJ* 1987/456, *Stonestar/Javeri*.

[68] Kamerstukken II, 2 November 1999, 1999/00, no°26855, 3, 37; confirmed in Hoge Raad, 29 March 2019, ECLI:NL:HR:2019:443, 4.2.2.

[69] Case C-539/03 *Roche*.

[70] Case C-98/06 *Freeport*.

[71] Case C-145/10 *Painer*.

[72] Case C-616/10 *Solvay*.

[73] Hof Amsterdam (Court of Appeal of Amsterdam), 1 April 2008, ECLI:NL:GHAMS:2008:BD1246; 2.7-2.8; Rechtbank Arnhem (District Court of Arnhem), 26 October 2011, ECLI:NL:RBARN:2011:BU3546, 4.9;

Unlike Art 8(1) of the Brussels Ibis Regulation, Art 7(1) DCCP can be applied if the courts of the Netherlands have jurisdiction vis-à-vis one defendant; the exact basis for its jurisdiction being irrelevant.[74] In other words, jurisdiction over the anchor defendant on the basis of the Brussels Ibis Regulation or the DCCP equally suffice to establish jurisdiction over other (Non-EU) defendants on the basis of Art 7(1) DCCP.[75] A well-known example is *Milieudefensie/Shell*, which concerns claims for damages against Royal Dutch Shell and its Nigerian subsidiary due to oil spills in the Niger Delta.[76] Jurisdiction over Royal Dutch Shell was based on Art 2 of the Brussels I Regulation; whereas jurisdiction over its Nigerian subsidiary was based on Art 7(1) DCCP.[77]

(d)

The courts of the Netherlands have jurisdiction over consumer contracts in cases involving non-EU defendants on the basis of Art 6(d) DCCP, provided that the consumer is domiciled or habitually resident in the Netherlands and the contract was concluded with a person who pursues commercial or professional activities in the Netherlands or, by any means, directs such activities to the Netherlands, and the contract falls within the scope of such activities. The legislator incorporated elements of Arts 13–15 of the Brussels Convention, as amended by Arts 15–17 of the Brussels I Regulation (cf Arts 17–19 Brussels Ibis Regulation), into Arts 6(d) DCCP.[78] Article 8(c) DCCP specifies that this national jurisdictional rule cannot be derogated from by an agreement, unless it was entered into after the dispute has arisen or allows the consumer to bring proceedings in a foreign court (Art 8(d) DCCP); which denotes its protective nature.[79]

Rechtbank Rotterdam, 23 October 2013, ECLI:NL:RBROT:2013:8203, 4.11, 4.16; Rechtbank Rotterdam, 20 April 2016, ECLI:NL:RBROT:2016:3139, 3.11-3.15; Rechtbank Rotterdam, 5 February 2020, ECLI:NL:RBROT:2020:1031, 5.10-5.14.

[74] MV Polak, 'Inspiration From Above: Making and Interpreting Dutch Law on Jurisdiction in Civil and Commercial Matters in Light of European Law', in HJ Snijders and S Vogenauer (eds), *Content and Meaning of National Law in the Context of Transnational Law* (Otto Schmidt/De Gruyter, 2009) 120, 128.

[75] If a court has jurisdiction over a (non-EU) defendant on the basis of Art 7(1) DCCP, however, it cannot base its jurisdiction over yet another (non-EU) defendant on the mere fact that the claims against these defendants are closely connected; i.e. derivative jurisdiction on the basis of Art 7(1) DCCP cannot be chained in the absence of a 'proper' basis for jurisdiction. See Hoge Raad, 29 March 2019, ECLI:NL:HR:2019:443, 4.2.2.

[76] *Milieudefensie/Shell* is a short name for three joined cases, in which the paragraphs on jurisdiction are virtually identical. The rulings in first instance can be found in Rechtbank Den Haag, 14 September 2011, ECLI:NL:RBSGR:2011:BU3538; ECLI:NL:RBSGR:2011:BU3535; ECLI:NL:RBSGR:2011:BU3529. The rulings on appeal are found in Hof Den Haag, 18 December 2015, ECLI:NL:GHDHA:2015:3586, ECLI:NL:GHDHA:2015:3588; ECLI:NL:GHDHA:2015:3587.

[77] Elaborate analysis of the relevant rulings (in English) can be found elsewhere; see for example C de Groot, 'The 'Shell Nigeria Issue': Judgements by the Court of Appeal of The Hague, The Netherlands' (2016) 12 *ECL* 98.

[78] Art 6(d) DCCP entered into force on 1 January 2002 and was based on Arts 13–15 of the Brussels Convention. Kamerstukken II, 2 November 1999, 1999/00, no°26855, 3, 35-36. Art 6(d) DCCP was amended pursuant to the Law of 8 September 2005 (*Stb* 2005, 455), which entered into force on 15 October 2005, in order to adapt its text to Arts 15–17 of the Brussels I Regulation. Kamerstukken II, 14 May 2003, 2002/03, no°28863, 3, 5.

[79] Kamerstukken II, 2 November 1999, 1999/00, no°26855, 3, 38–39.

However, due to the universal scope of Art 18(1) Brussels Ibis Regulation, Arts 6(d) and 8(c)–(d) DCCP became virtually obsolete.[80]

The courts of the Netherlands have jurisdiction over individual contracts of employment and contracts of agency in cases involving non-EU defendants on the basis of Art 6(b) DCCP, provided that the employee or agent habitually carries out his work or lastly habitually carried out his work in the Netherlands or on a Dutch ship. The Dutch legislator deliberately refrained from using the special rules on jurisdiction over employment contracts in Arts 19–20 Brussels I Regulation (cf Arts 20–22 Brussels Ibis Regulation) and instead opted to retain its less detailed, less restricted approach;[81] for which inspiration was loosely drawn from Art 5(1) Brussels Convention.[82] However, due to the universal scope of Art 21(1)(b) of the Brussel Ibis Regulation, Arts 6(b) became virtually obsolete for cases in which a claim is brought by an employee.[83] Contracts of agency were explicitly added to the text of Art 6(b) DCCP in order to retain a previously existing jurisdictional rule, notwithstanding the absence of an explicit reference to contracts of agency in Art 5(1) Brussels Convention.[84] Article 6(c) DCCP also allows the court of the Netherlands to establish jurisdiction over individual contracts of employment for certain types of claims, provided that the employee temporarily carries out his work in the Netherlands.[85]

Article 8(c) DCCP does not allow a choice of forum for individual contracts of employment, unless the agreement was entered into after the dispute has arisen or allows the employee to bring proceedings in a foreign court (Art 8(d) DCCP, cf Art 23 Brussels Ibis Regulation); which denotes the protective nature of Arts 6(b) and (c) DCCP for employees.[86] However, Art 8(c) DCCP does not refer to contracts of agency.

[80] L Strikwerda and S Schaafsma, *Inleiding tot het Nederlandse internationaal privaatrecht*, 132. One peculiar aspect of Art 6(d) DCCP is that contracts of transportation are not explicitly excluded from its scope (cf Art 18(3) Brussels Ia Regulation), which appears to have led to some confusion in cases involving contracts of transportation that were concluded with a non-EU defendant. See Rechtbank Limburg, 20 September 2017, ECLI:NL:RBLIM:2017:9192, 4.5 (referred to Art 18(3) Brussels Ia Regulation in order to conclude that contracts of transportation were excluded from the scope of Art 6(e) DCCP); Rechtbank Gelderland, 10 January 2018, ECLI:NL:RBGEL:2018:125, 5.2 (applied Art 6(e) DCCP without considering if contracts of transportation ought to be considered as consumer contracts); Rechtbank Noord-Holland, 10 March 2021, ECLI:NL:RBNHO:2021:2288, 4.4 (dodged the bullet by ruling Art 6(a) DCCP is applicable).

[81] MV Polak, 'Inspiration From Above: Making and Interpreting Dutch Law on Jurisdiction in Civil and Commercial Matters in Light of European Law' in HJ Snijders and S Vogenauer (eds), *Content and Meaning of National Law in the Context of Transnational Law* (Otto Schmidt/De Gruyter, 2009) 119.

[82] Kamerstukken II, 2 November 1999, 1999/00, no°26855, 3, 35. Art 6(b) DCCP entered into force on 1 January 2002 and was amended pursuant to the Law of 8 September 2005 (*Stb* 2005, 455), which entered into force on 15 October 2005, in order to clarify that this provision also applies in disputes concerning a contract of employment that has already been terminated. Kamerstukken II, 14 May 2003, 2002/03, no°28863, 3, 5. The term habitually ought to be interpreted as 'predominantly' in accordance with Hoge Raad, 18 June 1920, NJ 1920/802 (*Scholte/De Jongh*), rather than by reference to the preliminary rulings of the ECJ.

[83] L Strikwerda and S Schaafsma, *Inleiding tot het Nederlandse internationaal privaatrecht* (12th edn, Wolters Kluwer 2019), 132

[84] Kamerstukken II, 2 November 1999, 1999/00, no°26855, 3, 35.

[85] Art 6(c) DCCP was introduced pursuant to the Law of 8 September 2005 (*Stb* 2005, 455), which entered into force on 15 October 2005. Directive 98/71/EC concerning the posting of workers had been implemented in Art 98(3) DCCP (old) in 1999, but the legislator overlooked its transposition into the revised DCCP that entered into force on 1 January 2002. Kamerstukken II, 14 May 2003, 2002/03, no°28863, 3, 5.

[86] Kamerstukken II, 2 November 1999, 1999/00, no°26855, 3, 38–39.

The reason for this 'omission' is that the Dutch legislator did not consider an extension of the protection afforded to consumers and employees to commercial agents necessary, as the latter were not regarded as structurally weaker parties.[87] Consequently, protective rules on jurisdiction in matters regulated by the Brussels Ibis Regulation that are applicable in cases involving parties other than consumers and employees do not exist in the Netherlands.

The jurisdiction of the courts of the Netherlands over contracts of insurance is not subject to special protective rules and instead governed by the ordinary rules for jurisdiction over contracts.

[87] Kamerstukken II, 2 November 1999, 1999/00, no° 26855, 3, 39; see Rechtbank Den Haag, 16 November 2016, ECLI:NL:RBDHA:2016:14210, para 5.12 (Choice of forum clause in agency agreement between non-EU parties upheld).

Poland

ANNA WYSOCKA-BAR

Question 1

(a)

In Poland, provisions on international civil procedure, including rules on direct jurisdiction, are contained in the Code of Civil Procedure.[1] It entered into force on 1 January 1965. The Code is divided into parts. The part currently numbered as Part Four 'Provisions on International Civil Procedure' was subject to substantive amendments, which entered into force as of 1 July 2009 (Amendment 2009).[2] As underlined in the Explanatory Note,[3] the main aim of the Amendment 2009 was to adapt the provisions of the Code of Civil Procedure to the laws of European Union, in particular Brussels I Regulation.[4]

Part Four is divided into five books, where Book 1 'Jurisdiction' contains rules on direct jurisdiction. This Book (Articles 1097–1110[4]) is in turn divided into four titles, as follows: Title I – General Provisions, Title III – Jurisdiction in contentious proceedings, Title IV – Jurisdiction in non-contentious proceedings, Title V – Jurisdiction with respect to provisional and execution measures. In order to apply an adequate rule on jurisdiction, which might be located either in Title III or Title IV, the judge must first decide in which type of proceeding (contentious or non-contentious) the case will be handled with. The matters, which might be classified as 'civil and commercial' within the meaning of Brussels Ia Regulation, might be decided in both types of proceedings.

The Code of Civil Procedure is an instrument which is applied as the 'last resort' when assessing whether courts in Poland are competent. It applies only if no EU

[1] Ustawa z 17 XI 1964 r Kodeks postępowania cywilnego [Act of 17 November 1964 – Code of Civil Procedure] Dz U 2021 poz 1805. All Polish legislation might be located in the official journal (Dziennik Ustaw) by year, numer [nr] and position [poz] or – starting from 2012 – year and position [poz] only. *Dziennik Ustaw* is available online at www.isap.sejm.gov.pl.

[2] Ustawa z 5 XII 2008 r o zmianie ustawy – Kodeks postępowania cywilnego oraz niektórych innych ustaw [Act of 5 December 2008 on the amendment to the act – Code of civil procedure and some other acts] Dz U 2008 nr 234 poz 1571.

[3] Explanatory Note to Amandment 2009 is available at www.orka.sejm.gov.pl/Druki6ka.nsf/wgdruku/949; see also: M Wójcik 'Comments to Art 1103' in A Jakubecki (ed) *Kodeks postępowania cywilnego Tom II Komentarz do art. 730–1217* (Wolters Kluwer, 2017) 602.

[4] Regulation No 44/2001.

Regulation or international agreement (bilateral or multilateral) is applicable to a given case. Some bilateral agreements to which Poland and a third state are contracting parties contain rules on direct jurisdiction in civil and commercial matters. Such agreements are in place with Belarus,[5] Bosnia and Herzegovina, Montenegro, North Macedonia, Serbia,[6] Russia,[7] Ukraine[8] and Vietnam.[9] There are also multilateral agreements, to which Poland is a contracting party containing rules on direct jurisdiction in matters, which might be classified as civil and commercial. This is the case, for example, of the CMR Convention,[10] Montreal Convention[11] and Athens Convention.[12]

The rules on direct jurisdiction of the Code of Civil Procedure are as follows. Pursuant to Art 1103^8 § 1 Code of Civil Procedure, cases involving immovable property rights and possession of immovable property located in Poland, as well as cases arising from a lease or rental relationship or other relationship involving the use of such immovable property, except cases involving rent and other charges related to using or benefitting from such immovable property, fall under exclusive jurisdiction. Also, cases other than those listed above fall under exclusive jurisdiction insofar as their adjudication concerns property rights or possession or use of immovable property located in Poland (Art 1103^8 § 2 Code of Civil Procedure).[13] It is submitted that this provision is of a very limited practical importance because of Art 24(1) Brussels Ibis Regulation.[14] It is not entirely clear whether *a contrario* to Art 1103 § 1 Code of Civil Procedure, there is no jurisdiction in similar cases with respect to immovable property located abroad.[15]

[5] Umowa między Rzecząpospolitą Polska a Republiką Białorusi o pomocy prawnej i stosunkach prawnych w sprawach cywilnych, rodzinnych, pracowniczych i karnych, sporządzona w Mińsku dnia 26 X 1994 r [Agreement between Poland and Belarus on legal aid and legal relations in civil, family, labor and criminal matters made in Minsk on 26 X 1994] Dz U 1995 nr 128 poz 619.

[6] Umowa między Polska Rzecząpospolitą Ludową a Federacyjną Ludową Republiką Jugosławii o obrocie prawnym w sprawach cywilnych i karnych, podpisana w Warszawie dnia 6 II 1960 [Agreement between Poland and Yugoslavia on judicial cooperation in civil and criminal matters signed in Warsaw on 6 II 1960] Dz U 1963 nr 27 poz 162. The agreement is binding on Bosnia and Herzegovina, Montenegro, North Macedonia, Serbia following succession.

[7] Umowa między Rzecząpospolitą Polska a Federacja Rosyjska o pomocy prawnej i stosunkach prawnych w sprawach cywilnych i karnych, sporządzona w Warszawie dnia 16 IX 1996 [Agreement between Poland and Russia on legal aid and legal relations in civil and criminal matters made in Warsaw on 16 IX 1996] Dz U 2002 r nr 83 poz 750.

[8] Umowa między Rzecząpospolitą Polska a Ukraina o pomocy prawnej i stosunkach prawnych w sprawach cywilnych i karnych sporządzona w Kijowie dnia 24 V 1993 [Agreement between Poland and Ukraine on legal aid and legal relations in civil and criminal matters made in Kiev on 24 V 1993] Dz U 1994 r nr 96 poz 465.

[9] Umowa między Rzecząpospolitą Polska a Socjalistyczna Republika Wietnamu o pomocy prawnej i stosunkach prawnych w sprawach cywilnych, rodzinnych i karnych, sporządzona w Warszawie dnia 22 III 1993 [Agreement between Poland and Vietnam on legal aid and legal relations in civil, family and criminal matters made in Warsaw on 22 III 1993] Dz U 1995 nr 55 poz 289.

[10] Konwencja o umowie międzynarodowego przewozu drogowego towarów [Convention on the Contract for the International Carriage of Goods by Road (CMR)] Dz U 1962 nr 49 poz 238.

[11] Konwencja o ujednoliceniu niektórych prawideł dotyczących międzynarodowego przewozu lotniczego [Convention for the Unification of Certain Rules for International Carriage by Air] Dz U 2007 nr 37 poz 235.

[12] Konwencja ateńska w sprawie przewozu morzem pasażerów i ich bagażu [Convention relating to the Carriage of Passengers and their Luggage by Sea] Dz U 1987 nr 18 poz 108.

[13] Similar rules are contained in Art 1107^1 and Art 1110^2 Code of Civil Procedure which concern cases handled in non-contentious proceeding.

[14] T Ereciński 'Comments to Art 1103' in T Ereciński (ed) *Kodeks postępowania cywilnego Komentarz Tom VI Międzynarodowe Postępowanie Cywilne Sąd polubowny* (arbitrażowy) (Wolters Kluwer, 2017) 127.

[15] On one hand, before the Amendment 2009, Art 1102 § 2 Code of Civil Procedure stated clearly that there is no jurisdiction in cases concerning rights in rem over immovable property and possession over immovable

Pursuant to Art 1109[1] § 1 Code of Civil Procedure exclusive jurisdiction encompasses also matters of registration proceedings concerning a register held in Poland. Similarly, exclusive jurisdiction exists with respect to cases concerning dissolution of a legal entity or an organisational unit without legal personality, if this legal entity or unit have their seat in Poland (Art 1109 § 2). Jurisdiction exists also with respect to other matters dealt with by registry courts, if the territorially competent court is located in Poland (Art 1109 § 3).

Pursuant to Art 1103 Code of Civil Procedure, jurisdiction exists if the defendant has his[16] place of domicile, habitual residence, or a seat in Poland. Additionally, pursuant to 1103[7] Code of Civil Procedure (in cases other than previously listed in Articles 1103[1]–1103[6], namely matters relating to matrimonial property, parental responsibility and maintenance, and matters relating to consumer, insurance, and employment contracts) jurisdiction exists if the case concerns: – obligations arising from an act in law which was performed or is or was to be performed in Poland (Art 1103[7](1)); obligations other than those arising from an act in law which were incurred in Poland (Art 1103[7](2)); operation of the defendant's branch or unit located Poland, (Art 1103[7](3)); claims involving property rights, if the defendant has his property in Poland or is entitled to property rights in Poland of major value compared to the value of the matter at dispute (Art 1103[7](4)); an object of the dispute, which is located in Poland (Art 1103[7](5)).

Prorogation and submission in favour of Polish courts is possible. Code of Civil Procedure distinguishes between prorogation agreements in favour of Polish courts (1104 § 1) and derogation agreements in favour of foreign courts in cases which normally fall under jurisdiction of Polish courts (Art 1105). Submission is possible even if a derogation agreement is in place (Art 1104 § 2). Prorogation agreement (and submission) is admissible in cases which are decided in contentious proceedings and concern property rights. When it comes to cases which are decided in non-contentious proceeding, prorogation agreement (and submission) is possible only with respect to cases concerning management related to co-ownership and dissolution of co-ownership (Art 1110[1]). Derogation agreement cannot relate to cases, where jurisdiction of Polish courts is exclusive. Both kinds of agreements must be in writing (Art 1104 § 1 and Art 1105) or in a form perceived as equivalent (Art 1105[1] Code of Civil Procedure). It is submitted that exchange of e-mail correspondence is sufficient.[17] Jurisdictional agreement might also be included in general terms of contract if the document in writing (or in equivalent form) refers to these general terms.[18]

property located aboard. This provision was deleted by the Amendment 2009, however Explanatory Note to Amendment 2009 explains that this rule might be deleted as its existence is obvious and might be deducted from the general principle of international law, namely sovereignty of a state over its territory. Hence, the Explanatory Note suggests that the rule is still in place. This is also confirmed in: T Ereciński 'Comments to Art 1103', 128. On the other hand, taking into account contemporary developments in international civil procedure, one might observe that exceptions to this rule become frequent (see for example: jurisdictional rules included in the Regulation No 650/2012 or in the Council Regulation 2016/1103. The deletion of the rule from the Code of Civil Procedure after decencies of its existence might be interpreted as bringing change in law. Compare also: M Wójcik 'Comments to Art 1103', 625–26.

[16] Please note that Code of Civil Procedure itself uses the masculine form only.

[17] M Wójcik 'Comments to Art 1105', 633.

[18] M Wójcik 'Comments to Art 1103', 634.

In accordance with Art 1103[10] § 1 Code of Civil Procedure, if the original case falls under jurisdiction, counter-complaints also fall under the jurisdiction of Polish courts. If a case involves substantial joint participation and jurisdiction exists as to one joint participant, the case falls under jurisdiction with respect to all the joint participants (Art 1103[10] § 2 Code of Civil Procedure).

There are also separate jurisdictional rules with respect to consumer, insurance and employment contracts. Please note that these rules provide for an additional basis of jurisdiction of Polish courts in addition to the jurisdiction resulting from general rules listed above (for example, Art 1103 Code of Civil Procedure). This conclusion follows from the fact that the below provisions indicate that a certain matter falls 'also' under the jurisdiction of Polish courts. These rules are inspired by Brussels I Regulation.[19]

(b)

The Code of Civil Procedure does not provide any guidance as to which case could be classified as 'international' and which could be classified as 'purely domestic'. At the same time, the lack of jurisdiction constitutes one of the premises of the nullity of the civil proceeding (Art 1099 § 2 Code of Civil Procedure). Lack of jurisdiction is examined ex officio by the court at each stage of the proceeding and requires the court to reject the claim or application (Art 1099 § 1 Code of Civil Procedure). Additionally, rules on jurisdiction contained in Code of Civil Procedure, in general, do not indicate which court in Poland is competent to hear a case. Code of Civil Procedure provides separately for rules concerning material and territorial competence. These rules are scattered in different parts of the Code depending on the type of case. There are no separate rules on material and territorial competence provided for international cases. Hence, even though the rules on jurisdiction are contained in the part of the Code of Civil Procedure titled 'Provisions on International Civil Procedure', rules on jurisdiction, just like the ones on material and territorial competence, should apply equally to international and purely domestic cases.[20]

(c)

The jurisdictional rules in place previously, namely before the Amendment 2009 entered into force, were less specific than the ones currently in force. Article 1102 § 1 Code of Civil Procedure provided for the exclusive jurisdiction with respect to claims concerning rights in rem and possession of an immovable property located in Poland, as well as relating to tenancy and lease of such immovable property, except claims concerning rent. The exclusive jurisdiction existed also with respect to other cases insofar as their adjudication concerned immovable property located in Poland. Art 1103 (1)–(3) Code of Civil Procedure provided that other cases, adjudicated in contentious proceedings,

[19] K Weitz 'Comments to Art 1103', 100.
[20] See also: M Wójcik 'Comments to Art 1097', 602.

fall under jurisdiction of Polish courts if the defendant is resident or domiciled or had its seat in Poland at the time of service of the claim; if the defendant has assets or property rights in Poland or if the case concerns an object of the dispute located in Poland or an obligation, which was incurred in Poland or was supposed to be performed in Poland. Art 1104 Code of Civil Procedure provided for the jurisdictional agreements in favour of Polish courts in cases concerning property rights resulting from a particular legal relation. Article 1105 § 1 Code of Civil Procedure provided for derogation agreements, but excluded such agreements in cases where jurisdiction of Polish courts was exclusive.

As already mentioned, the above rules were subject to significant change by the Amendment 2009. This amendment has not directly extended the 'Brussels regime' to non-EU defendants either by reference or by incorporation. Please note, however, that the very aim of the Amendment 2009 was to adapt the provisions of the Code of Civil Procedure to EU laws, in particular the Brussels I Regulation.[21] The Explanatory Note refers to 'Brussels regime' on different occasions. It explains that the aim of adapting the Code of Civil Procedure to EU law concerns, inter alia, rules on jurisdiction.[22] The proposed connecting factors serving as the basis for jurisdiction are inspired by the ones used in the EU law.[23] The Explanatory Note underlines, however, that adapting the Code of Civil Procedure does not mean the 'mechanical' incorporation of EU law. The Amendment 2009 considers the fact that the Code of Civil Procedure will be applied in relations with third states, namely with states from outside the EU, with which Poland is not bound by international agreements. That is the reason why the respective provisions of the Code of Civil Procedure differ from the rules provided for in the 'Brussels regime'.[24]

When it comes to specific provisions added by the Amendment 2009, the Explanatory Note provides the following. The jurisdictional rules with respect to employment contracts are aimed at implementing Art 6 of the Posted Workers Directive.[25] Rules on insurance contracts (Art 1103^5 Code of Civil Procedure) and employment contracts (Art 1103^6 Code of Civil Procedure) are modelled after the Brussels I Regulation.[26] New connecting factors serving as a basis for jurisdiction are added, namely place of performance for the purpose of obligations arising from an act in law (Art 1103^7(1) Code of Civil Procedure), place, where the obligation was incurred for obligations other than those arising from an act in law (Art 1103^7(2) Code of Civil Procedure), operations of the branch and unit (Art 1103^7(3) Code of Civil Procedure). With respect to the last one, the Explanatory Note directly refers to Art 5(5) Brussels I Regulation.[27] A rule modelled on Art 22(2) Brussels I Regulation is added (Art 1103^9 Code of Civil Procedure). Submission, modelled after Art 24 of the Brussels I Regulation, is a new feature in the Code of Civil Procedure. The Explanatory Note underlines, however, that the Code of Civil Procedure, as opposed to Brussels I Regulation, requires that the

[21] Explanatory Note (n 3), 2.
[22] Explanatory Note (n 3), 3.
[23] Explanatory Note (n 3), 3.
[24] Explanatory Note (n 3), 3.
[25] Explanatory Note (n 3), 7.
[26] Explanatory Note (n 3), 7–8.
[27] Explanatory Note (n 3), 8–9.

defendant raises an argument as to the merits of the case in order for the court to gain jurisdiction.[28] Rules on exclusive jurisdiction with respect to entries into public registers are 'partly consistent' with Art 22(2) and Art 22(3) of Brussels I Regulation.[29]

Works on the recast of Brussels I Regulation and the idea of extending its rules to defendants domiciled in third states, were commented in Poland. The idea was perceived as welcomed and needed to achieve consistency with respect to jurisdictional rules applied in Member States of the EU. At the same time, it was underlined that the rules on jurisdiction contained in the Code of Civil Procedure are already allowing for suing defendants from third states and therefore potential changes to the 'Brussels regime' would not bring substantial revolution to rules on jurisdiction already applied in Poland.[30] Adoption of the Brussels Ibis Regulation has not resulted in any amendments to the rules on jurisdiction included in the Code of Civil Procedure. On this occasion scholars have not advocated in favour of extending the 'Brussels regime' to defendants domiciled in third states via amendment to the Code of Civil Procedure.[31]

(d)

The notification made by Poland pursuant to Art 76(1)(a) Brussels Ibis Regulation indicates Art 1103^7 Code of Civil Procedure and Art 1110 Code of Civil Procedure 'insofar as they provide for jurisdiction for the Polish courts exclusively on the basis of one of the following circumstances concerning the applicant: Polish citizenship, domicile, habitual residence or registered office in Poland'.[32] Considering that pursuant to Art 76(1)(a) Brussels Ibis Regulation, Member States are supposed to notify of the rules of jurisdiction referred to in Arts 5(2) and 6(2), namely exorbitant rules of jurisdiction, which may not be applicable as against the persons domiciled in a Member State, the above list seems not exhaustive. The notification does not mention all grounds of jurisdiction listed in Art 1103^7Code of Civil Procedure, for example, jurisdiction concerning property rights, where the defendant has assets in Poland or property rights in Poland of significant value when compared with the value at dispute or in case the object of the dispute is located in Poland.

Question 2

The general rule stated in Art 1103 Code of Civil Procedure provides for jurisdiction of Polish courts if the defendant has his place of domicile, habitual residence, or a seat in Poland. The notion of domicile is understood as in Arts 25–28 Civil Code.[33] Pursuant

[28] Explanatory Note (n 3), 10.
[29] Explanatory Note (n 3), 13.
[30] K Weitz 'Projektowane zmiany rozporządzenia nr 44/2001' in P Grzegorczyk and K Weitz, *Europejskie prawo procesowe cywilne i kolizyjne* (Lexis Nexis, 2012) 28–34.
[31] B Trocha 'Uwagi na tle częściowego rozszerzenia zakresu podmiotowego rozporządzenia Bruksela Ibis na pozwanych z państw trzecich' [2013] *Polski Proces Cywilny* 2, 194–212.
[32] e-Justice Portal www.e-justice.europa.eu/350/EN/brussels_i_regulation_recast?POLAND&member=1.
[33] M Wójcik 'Comments to Art 1103', 612.

to Art 25 Civil Code[34] it is the place where a natural person resides with the intention of remaining. There are separate rules concerning domicile of a child (Art 26 Civil Code) and of a person under guardianship (Art 27 Civil Code). In accordance with Art 28 Civil Code, one may have only one domicile.

When it comes to legal persons the Code of Civil Procedure uses the connecting factor of a seat. The notion of a seat is understood as in Art 41 Civil Code, namely unless a legal act or the articles of association provide otherwise, the seat of a legal person is a place where its managing body has the seat.[35]

Question 3

Apart from domicile and seat, Art 1103 Code of Civil Procedure uses the connecting factor of habitual residence in Poland. Additionally, Art 1103^7 Code of Civil Procedure uses the following circumstances as basis for jurisdiction: location in Poland of property or property rights of a significant value when compared to the value of the object of dispute, if the claim concerns property rights (Art 1103^7(4) Code of Civil Procedure) and location of the object of the dispute in Poland (Art 1103^7(5) Code of Civil Procedure). Nationality of either of the parties has no influence on the existence of jurisdiction of Polish courts in civil and commercial matters.[36]

Habitual residence is understood as a place in which a person habitually resides. It is perceived as an interim category between domicile and short-term residence. It is the place of the main centre of the existence of a person. Hence, personal and professional circumstances should be considered. The time element is less important. When assessing the habitual residence, factual circumstances should be considered. The intention or plans of a person are not decisive.[37]

Location of property or property rights in Poland was used as a basis of jurisdiction also before the Amendment 2009. The Amendment 2009 added the requirement that the property or property rights should be of significant value when compared to the value of the object of a dispute. The notion of property is not defined. It is submitted that only actives (and not passives) should be considered.[38] The object of the dispute located in Poland means that the object of the dispute should physically be in Poland or that rights being object of the dispute are exercised in Poland.

It should be noted that in case Polish courts have jurisdiction in accordance with rules provided for in the Code of Civil Procedure, it is not possible to decline jurisdiction on the ground that the courts of another state would be better placed to hear the case. Hence, there is no institution similar to the common law *forum non conveniens*.

[34] Ustawa 24 IV 1964 Kodeks cywilny [Act of 24 April 1964 – Civil Code] Dz U 2020 poz 1740.

[35] M Wójcik 'Comments to Art 1103', 613.

[36] Nationality does infludence the existence of jurisdiction of Polish courts in other kind of cases, for example in a case concerning establishment of parenthood, jurisdiction of Polish courts exist if the claimant and the defendant are both Polish nationals (Art 1103 § 1(4) Code of Civil Procedure).

[37] K Weitz 'Comments to Art 1103', 87.

[38] T Ereciński 'Comments to Art 1103^7', 122.

Question 4

There is a general provision on *forum necessitatis* in the Code of Civil Procedure. It provides that if there are no grounds for jurisdiction in a given case and it is impossible to conduct proceedings or to request proceedings to be conducted before a court or another authority of a foreign state, the case falls under jurisdiction if it demonstrates a sufficient connection to the Polish legal order (Art 1099^1 § 1 Code of Civil Procedure). Additionally, in accordance with Art 1099^1 § 2 Code of Civil Procedure, if the court finally decides that a ruling of a court or another authority of a foreign state may not be recognised in Poland, the case in which that ruling was issued falls under jurisdiction of Polish courts, even if there are no grounds to justify that jurisdiction, provided that the case demonstrated a sufficient connection to the Polish legal order.

The provision on *forum necessitatis* was added to Code of Civil Procedure by the Amendment 2009. The existence of *forum necessitatis* was pronounced before that in the jurisprudence of the Supreme Court (*Sąd Najwyższy*) in succession matters, in cases where the deceased did not have Polish nationality, which could serve as basis for jurisdiction with respect to movables located in Poland.[39]

We are not aware of any case relating to civil and commercial matters, where the jurisdiction of the Polish court would be established based on Art 1099^1 Code of Civil Procedure. Usually, this provision is discussed when the plaintiff argues the existence of *forum necessitatis*, whereas the court explains why it is not applicable (for example, because the courts of other states have jurisdiction in accordance with the Brussels I Regulation[40] or Lugano II Convention).[41] Jurisprudence has also explained that 'impossibility' of conducting a proceeding abroad should be associated with lack of jurisdiction resulting from rules in place in the given country or other circumstances of general character (for example state of war or terrorist attacks directed at foreigners).[42] It was also explained that the financial situation of the plaintiff, the fact that foreign court would have to apply foreign law or that documents would have to be translated does not itself justify the existence of *forum necessitatis* in Poland.[43]

[39] See: Uchwała Sądu Najwyższego 31 V 1975 [Resolution of the Supreme Court of 31 May 1975] III CZP 78/75; uchwała Sądu Najwyższego 19 XI 1977 [Resolution of the Supreme Court of 19 November 1977] III CZP 76/77, postanowienie Sądu Najwyższego z 5 VIII 1999 [Decision of the Supreme Court of 5 August 1999] II CKN 444/99.

[40] Postanowienie Sądu Apelacyjnego w Katowicach 24 V 2018 [Decision of the Court of Appeal in Katowice of 24 May 2018] V AGz 290/18.

[41] Postanowienie Sądu Apelacyjnego w Szczecinie 30 XI 2012 [Decision of the Court of Appeal in Szczecin of 30 November 2012] I ACz 813/12; wyrok Sądu Okręgowego w Łodzi 25 X 2017 [Decision of the District Court in Łódź of 25 October 2017] III Ca 1334/17.

[42] Postanowienie Sądu Apelacyjnego w Szczecinie 30 XI 2012 [Decision of the Court of Appeal in Szczecin of 30 November 2012] I ACz 813/12.

[43] Postanowienie Sądu Apelacyjnego w Katowicach 24 V 2018 [Decision of the Court of Appeal in Katowice of 24 May 2018] V AGz 290/18.

Question 5

(a)

Apart from jurisdiction resulting from Art 1103 Code of Civil Procedure (based on the domicile, habitual residence, or seat in Poland of the defendant), pursuant to 1103^7 (1) Code of Civil Procedure, in matters relating to obligations arising from an act in law (including contract), jurisdiction of Polish courts exists if an obligation was performed or is or was to be performed in Poland. As opposed to the Brussels Ibis Regulation, the Code of Civil Procedure does not provide any guidance as to how this notion could be understood. In the jurisprudence it was explained that the place of performance should be assessed based on the law applicable to the given case (*lex causae*) designated by the rules of private international law of the forum.[44] In the legal literature it was also suggested that the notion of the 'place of performance' might be understood taking into account the jurisprudence of Court of Justice of the EU on Art 7(1)(b) Brussels Ibis Regulation.[45] Additionally, as mentioned above, jurisdiction of the Polish court may result from other circumstances, for example, the defendant's property of significant value being located in Poland (Art 1103^7(4) Code of Civil Procedure). Jurisdiction may also result from prorogation (Art 1104 § 1) and submission (Art 1104 § 2).

(b)

Apart from jurisdiction resulting from Art 1103 Code of Civil Procedure, pursuant to its Art 1103^7(2), in the case of obligations other than those arising from an act in law (including delicts and quasi-delicts) the jurisdiction of Polish courts exists if these obligations were incurred in Poland. It is submitted that the place where the obligation was incurred should be assessed based on the law applicable (*lex causae*) designated by the rules of private international law of the forum.[46] In the legal literature it was also suggested that the jurisprudence of the Court of Justice of the EU on Art 7(2) Brussels Ibis Regulation may serve as inspiration.[47] Additionally, as mentioned above the jurisdiction of the Polish court may result from other circumstances, for example, the defendant's property of significant value being located in Poland (Art 1103^7(4) Code of Civil Procedure). Jurisdiction may also result from prorogation (Art 1104 § 1) and submission (Art 1104 § 2).

[44] Postanowienie Sądu Najwyższego 5 I 2001 [Decision of the Supreme Court of 5 January 2001] I CKN 1180/00; postanowienie Sądu Najwyższego 19 VI 2007 [Decision of the Supreme Court of 19 June 2007] III CSK 444/06; see also: M Wójcik 'Comments to Art 1103', 623.

[45] T Ereciński 'Comments to Art 1103', 120.

[46] M Wójcik 'Comments to Art 1103', 623.

[47] T Ereciński 'Comments to Art 1103', 120.

(c)

Pursuant to Art 1103[10] § 1 Code of Civil Procedure, if the original case falls under the jurisdiction of Polish courts, Polish courts are competent also with respect to the counter-complains. If a case involves substantial joint participation and jurisdiction exists as to one joint participant, the case falls under the jurisdiction of Polish courts with respect to all the joint participants (Art 1103[10] § 2 Code of Civil Procedure). The notion of 'substantial joint participation' is characteristic to Polish civil procedure and pursuant to Art 72 § 1(1) Code of Civil Procedure exists provided that the matter at issue are rights or obligations common to plaintiffs or defendants or which are based on the same factual and legal grounds. It is submitted that this article has a wider scope than Art 8(1) Brussels Ibis Regulation, as is not limited to cases when jurisdiction results from the domicile of the defendant.[48]

(d)

There are specific jurisdictional rules relating to consumer, employment, and insurance contracts. As already mentioned, these rules provide for an additional basis of jurisdiction of Polish courts in addition to the jurisdiction resulting from general rules listed above (for example, Art 1103 Code of Civil Procedure). This conclusion follows from the fact that the below provisions indicate that a certain matter falls 'also' under the jurisdiction of the Polish courts. These rules are inspired by the Brussels I Regulation.[49] They are as follows.

Pursuant to Art 1103[4] § 1 Code of Civil Procedure, cases concerning labour law in which the plaintiff is an employee also fall under the jurisdiction of Polish courts if the work is, was or was supposed to be habitually carried out in Poland. Actions brought by a worker and related to ensuring employment conditions in accordance with the Law on the Posting of Workers in the Framework of the Provision of Services[50] fall under the jurisdiction also when the worker is or was posted to work in Poland by an employer having their registered office in an EU Member State (Art 1103[4] § 2 Code of Civil Procedure). It applies accordingly if an employee was posted to work in Poland by an employer with a seat outside of the EU (Art 1103[4] § 3 Code of Civil Procedure). It is submitted that Art 1103[4] § 2 and § 3 give to the posted worker additional grounds of jurisdiction to those provided for in Articles 20–23 of the Brussels Ibis Regulation. This is possible because of Art 67 of the Brussels Ibis Regulation, which provides that it does not prejudice the application of provisions governing (among others) jurisdiction

[48] T Ereciński 'Comments to Art 1103', 131.

[49] See, for example: K Weitz 'Comments to Art 1103[4]' in T Ereciński (n 160) 100.

[50] Ustawa 10 VI 2016 r. o delegowaniu pracowników w ramach świadczenia usług [Act of 10 June 2016 on the posting of workers in the framework of the provision of services] Dz U 2021 poz. 1140. It constitutes the implementation into Polish law of the Directive 2014/67/EU of the European Parliament and of the Council of 15 May 2014 on the enforcement of Directive 96/71/EC concerning the posting of workers in the framework of the provision of services and amending Regulation (EU) No 1024/2012 on administrative cooperation through the Internal Market Information System [2014] OJ L 159/11.

in specific matters which are contained in EU instruments or in national legislation harmonised pursuant to such instruments.[51]

In accordance with Art 1103^5 § 1(1)–(3) Code of Civil Procedure, cases against an insurer involving an insurance relationship also fall under the jurisdiction of Polish courts if one of the following requirements is met. First, the plaintiff has his place of domicile in Poland. Second, a case against the principal insurer falls under the jurisdiction of the Polish court, and the defendant is a joint insurer. Third, an event which caused damage took place in Poland and the case involves civil liability insurance, immovable property insurance or immovable and movable property insurance affected by the same event. In accordance with Art 1103^5 § 2 Code of Civil Procedure, in the above cases, an insurer is treated as if he had a place of domicile or seat in Poland if he has his branch or unit in Poland and the case involves the operation of that branch or unit.

Pursuant to Art 1103^6 § 1 Code of Civil Procedure, cases arising from agreements in which the plaintiff is a consumer also fall under the jurisdiction of the Polish courts if the consumer has his domicile or habitual residence in Poland and if the actions necessary to conclude an agreement were taken in Poland. Additionally, in cases indicated in Art 1103^6 § 1 Code of Civil Procedure, the other party to an agreement with a consumer is treated as having habitual residence or seat in Poland (for the purpose of applying grounds of jurisdiction of Art 1103 Code of Civil Procedure), if he has his branch or unit in Poland and the agreement with the consumer involves the operation of that branch or unit (Art 1103^6 § 2 Code of Civil Procedure).[52] The expressions 'branch and unit' should be interpreted as synonyms of 'branch, agency or establishment' used in Art 17(2) of the Brussels Ibis Regulation.[53] The above provisions refer to all kinds of consumer contracts (as opposed to Art 17(1)(a), (b) and (c) of the Brussels Ibis Regulation). If a consumer concludes an insurance contract, provisions on insurance should have priority.[54] The requirement that 'the actions necessary to conclude an agreement were taken in Poland' is inspired by Art 13(1)(3)(b) of the Brussels Convention and jurisprudence of the Court of Justice of the EU in *Rudolf Gabriel* (case C-96/00).[55]

[51] K Weitz 'Comments to Art 1103', 107.
[52] K Weitz 'Comments to Art 1103^4', 116–17.
[53] K Weitz 'Comments to Art 1103^4', 117.
[54] K Weitz 'Comments to Art 1103^4', 118.
[55] K Weitz 'Comments to Art 1103^4', 118.

Spain

MARÍA ASUNCIÓN CEBRIÁN SALVAT AND
ANNA MARIA RUIZ MARTÍN

1. Spanish International Jurisdiction Regime: Sources and Features

1.1. Sources

The exercise of judicial authority by Spanish courts is self-limited in two directions: inwards ('límites internos de la jurisdicción') and outwards ('límites territoriales de la jurisdicción'). Inward limits are related to the fact that jurisdiction in Spain is not exclusive but organised by 'matters'. Outward limits are relating to the idea that the world is divided into States and that each of them has got a judiciary power.

Spanish rules which have established both kinds of limits are enshrined in the Ley Orgánica 6/1985, del Poder Judicial (Spanish Organic Law on the Judiciary, OLJ).[1] The first version of this law was enacted in 1985 but amended in 2015.[2] The OLJ represents the general Spanish body of law dealing with the hierarchy and organisation of the Spanish courts and with the exercise of judicial authority in Spain. Therefore, the OLJ is the main legal body governing the issue of the subject-matter jurisdiction ('jurisdicción por razón de la materia') and of the international jurisdiction ('competencia judicial internacional') in Spain.

Likewise, a reference shall be also made to the Ley 29/2015 de Cooperación jurídica internacional en materia civil (Spanish Act on International legal cooperation in civil matters, AILC).[3] The AILC was enacted for the first time in 2015. It does not contain any specific *fora* or jurisdictional rule as the rules of the OLJ, but some rules on the functioning of international jurisdiction, such as the regulation of the international *lis pendens* when the OLJ is of application, complementing the function of the jurisdictional rules as of this year.[4]

[1] Organic Law 6/1985 of 2 July on the Judiciary Power (Official State Gazette, 157 [BOE]), www.legislationline.org/download/id/6791/file/Spain_law_juidiciary_1985_am2016_en.pdf.

[2] Organic Law 7/2015 modifying Organic Law 6/1985 on the Judiciary Power (Official State Gazette [BOE], 22 July 2015).

[3] Law 29/2015 on International Legal Cooperation in Civil Matters (Spanish Official Gazette 182 [BOE] of 31 July), www.global-regulation.com/translation/spain/615829/law-29-2015%252c-july-30%252c-of-international-legal-cooperation-in-civil-matters.html.

[4] Further details, A Font Segura, 'Título Preliminar' in GP Moreno and FP Méndez González (eds), *Comentarios a la Ley de Cooperación jurídica civil internacional* (Tirant Lo Blanch, 2017) 16–28; A Rodríguez

1.2. Features

Suffice it to say that the Spanish legislator utilised a system of incorporation of the 1968 Brussels Convention since the first OLJ was enacted in 1985.[5] Hence, the Spanish lawmaker copied the whole system of jurisdictional grounds of the said Convention and transformed its multilateral rules into unilateral rules.[6] This legislative technique produced a *totum revolutum*, mainly taking into consideration the nature of the Spanish rules as unilateral and attributive rules. Albeit there were some amendments in 2015 to the rules of the OLJ,[7] these amendments have implied minor changes with regard to the *fora* system in civil and commercial matters and have not solved the many problems that these rules have when they are applied, let alone the interpretative problems, as will be mentioned in this Report.[8]

2. Role of the Spanish International Jurisdiction Rules in Transnational and Domestic Claims

2.1. Spanish *Fora* Structure as a Dualist System

Prior to explaining the Spanish *fora* structure, it is necessary to clarify some of its particularities: the Spanish system is a dualist system of rules from a procedural approach. The international jurisdiction rules of the Spanish regime have a different nature than the procedural rules on territorial jurisdiction.[9] Regarding this feature, to hear a transnational case, a Spanish court shall not only have international and subject-matter jurisdiction conferred by the OLJ rules, but it shall also have territorial jurisdiction over the case. These rules on territorial jurisdiction deal with the allocation of cases among all the courts that are distributed according to the cited jurisdictional orders and are located in a different body of law. For civil matters, this law is the Ley 1/2000 de

Benot, 'La Ley de Cooperación jurídica internacional en materia civil' (2016) 8 *CDT*, 234–59; PA De Miguel Asensio, 'Coordinación de la Ley de Cooperación jurídica internacional en materia civil con la legislación especial' (2016) 68 *AEDIPr*, 99–108; M Gardeñes Santiago, 'Procedimientos paralelos en España y en el extranjero: El Título IV de la Ley 29/2015 (art. 37-40)' (2016) 68 *REDI*, 109–19.

[5] AL Calvo Caravaca and J Carrascosa González, *Tratado de Derecho internacional privado I* (Valencia, Tirant lo Blanc, 2021), 371–76; JC Fernández Rozas and S Sánchez Lorenzo, *Derecho internacional privado* 7th edn (Cizur Menor, Thomson Reuters, 2013) 54–62; FJ Garcimartín Alférez, *Derecho international privado* (Thomson Reuters, 2019), 86; A Nuyts, 'Study on Residual Jurisdiction: Review of the Member States' Rules concerning the residual jurisdiction of their courts in Civil and Commercial Matters pursuant to the Brussels I and II Regulations, General Report' (2007) *General Report* 156, 32.

[6] AL Calvo Caravaca and J Carrascosa González, *Tratado de Derecho internacional privado I*, 375; JC Fernández Rozas and S Sánchez Lorenzo, *Derecho internacional privado*, 104.

[7] The amendments were incorporated by the Organic Law 7/2015 of the 21 June 2015.

[8] See especially, Section 4.

[9] E Castellanos Ruiz and J Rodríguez Rodrigo, 'Comentarios a la Ley de Enjuiciamiento Civil: De la extensión y los límites de los tribunales civiles (arts. 36 a 39 LEC)' (2006) *InDret* 3–23; C Esplugues Mota, 'Aspectos de Derecho internacional privado de la nueva Ley de Enjuiciamiento civil, de 7 de enero de 2000', www.uv.es/revista-dret/archivo/num1/pdf/cesplugues.pdf.

Enjuiciamiento Civil (Spanish Civil Procedure Act, CPA). These rules will be applied together with the OLJ.[10]

It is important to emphasise the fact that these provisions of the CPA do not govern nor attribute international jurisdiction in civil and commercial matters to the Spanish courts, unlike other domestic regimes. They deal with 'territorial competence' itself, which is just one step below the international jurisdiction established by the OLJ jurisdictional rules which have a general scope only for cross-border cases.

2.2. Different Jurisdictional Levels

Spanish jurisdiction rules are not complemented with others relating to any specific legislation of the whole Spanish regime. The Spanish *fora*, which are all gathered in the same OLJ, can be differentiated depending on the subject-matter of the case. In this sense, the Spanish OLJ recognises four different subject matters, each of them having their own international jurisdiction rules and territorial rules under the CPA. These subject-matters are categorised in the Spanish regime as jurisdictional orders ('órdenes jurisdiccionales'): civil, criminal, contentious-administrative, labour and military.

In relation to the civil jurisdictional order, which embodies both civil and commercial matters, rules on international jurisdiction are located in Arts 22 to 22 *nonies* of the OLJ. For labour matters, included in the scope of Brussels Ia, there is a different rule located in Art 25 OLJ. Some of these articles were included in the OLJ amendment of 2015 though, as will be explained, most of them remain unchanged since 1985.

Besides, there are also some special civil and commercial laws enacted by the Spanish legislator that contain particular rules on international jurisdiction. The most relevant are located in the Real Decreto Legislativo 1/2020, por el que se aprueba el texto refundido de la Ley Concursal (Spanish Insolvency Law), Arts 45–49.[11] However, insolvency matters are out of the scope of Brussels Ia and these rules will not be addressed in the present report.

As the Spanish system is a dualist one, Spanish jurisdictional rules of the OLJ will apply exclusively to determine the international competence of the Spanish courts in transnational disputes or civil and commercial disputes with a foreign element when the Brussels Ia Regulation or 2007 Lugano Convention cannot be applied according to Art 21(1) OLJ, where the hierarchy of international and European rules concerning its application and of the Spanish rules is established (hierarchy sources system).[12]

[10] Law 1/2000 on Civil Procedure, (Spanish Officials Gazettes 90-180 [BOE], 7 January 2000) www.mjusticia.gob.es/es/AreaTematica/DocumentacionPublicaciones/Documents/Law%201-2000%20of%207%20January.pdf.

[11] Royal Legislative Decree 1/2020 of 5 May, passing the revised text of the Insolvency Law 22/2003, 9 July on Insolvency, *Official State Gazette* 127 [BOE].

[12] Art 21 OLJ reads as follows: 'Spanish Civil Courts will hear claims that arise within Spanish territory in accordance with the stipulations of the international conventions and treaties to which Spain is a party, the regulations of the European Union and Spanish laws'; Auto Audiencia Provincial de Madrid, 16 May 2006, no°318/2006, Sec.11, [ECLI:ES:APM:2006:5016A] FJ 3: 'El sistema español de competencia judicial internacional se inicia con una remisión general a los tratados y convenios internacionales en los que España sea parte (art. 21.1 LOPJ)'.

The rules of the CPA which govern territorial jurisdiction are the ones that are applied to domestic disputes, as well as to transnational disputes, but only once the rules of the OLJ have been applied in the first place.

2.3. Extension of Brussels Ia Rules

Concerning the possibility of extending some of the Brussels Ia rules, in Spain there has not been any legislative reform envisaging this option which can displace the domestic rules explained in this report. During the amendment process of the OLJ, Spanish academia was contributing with reports to the legislature, but in order to correct the wording of these rules, fitting them into their unilateral and attributive nature. Besides, there was a debate considering the application of some Brussels Ia rules by analogy to non-EU defendants when the Brussels recast was due to come, in connection with the debate whether the Brussels Ia rules should be extended when domestic rules could not be applied.

From the case law approach, Spanish courts are quite reluctant to do an extension of the EU PIL Regulations when the Spanish rules cover the same subject matter and those are of application to the case, following the hierarchy sources system at hand as explained.[13]

2.4. Information Provided by Spain to the European Commission: Art 76(1) Brussels Ia

According to the webpage *European Judicial Network*, the information provided by Spain to the European Commission concerning what is required under Art 76(1) Brussels Ia was exhaustive.[14]

3. Spanish General Rules of Jurisdiction

3.1. Domicile of Natural Persons

On the one hand, the general rule for natural persons is stated under Art 22 *ter* OLJ that: 'an individual will be understood to be domiciled in Spain where his or her habitual

[13] See Section 5; B Campuzano Díaz, 'Las normas de Competencia judicial internacional del Reglamento 1215/2012 y los demandados fuera de la UE: Análisis de la reforma' (2014) 28 *REEI*, 1–35; MA Cebrián Salvat, 'La Competencia judicial international residual en materia contractual en España' (2017) 9 *CDT* 127–150; FJ Garcimartín Alférez and S Sánchez, 'El nuevo Reglamento Bruselas I: qué ha cambiado en la Competencia judicial' (2013) 48 *REDE*, 9–35; Auto de la Audiencia Provincial de Barcelona, Sec 18, 15 September 2020, no°6151/2020, [ECLI:ES:APB:2020:6151A], esp. FJ 4.1.

[14] The information published in the OJ of 9 January 2015 has been confronted with the latest updated Spanish Compilation of Private International Law: AL Calvo Caravaca and J Carrascosa González et al (eds), *Kodex: Materiales de Derecho internacional privado europeo y español. Legislación y jurisprudencia* (Digitum, 2021), 201.

residence is in this country'. This rule portrays the *actor sequitur forum rei* in the Spanish regime. According to the scholars as well as to recurrent case law on the issue, the definition of domicile itself as a mere legal assumption, must be linked to the concept of habitual residence in the Spanish regime. It means that when applying Art 22 *ter* OLJ it shall be interpreted in accordance with the Art 40 of the Código Civil (Spanish Civil Code).[15] This provision refers to the 'physical place', ie the 'dwelling', a concrete place. Therefore, if the habitual residence of a person is where this person has his/her dwelling, then it will be regarded as his/her domicile.[16]

Nevertheless, if the defendant is domiciled in Spain according to Art 40 Spanish Civil Code, then Brussels Ia will supersede Art 22 *ter* OLJ, because the defendant would be domiciled in Spain being a Member State as it is known.

3.2. Domicile of Legal Persons

On the other hand, the general rule for determining the domicile of legal persons was also included in the same provision, Art 22(2) *ter* para 2: 'a legal entity will be understood to be domiciled in Spain where its business headquarters, administrative centre, central administration or the centre where it carries out its main activity is found in this country'.

This Spanish rule contains the same solution given by Art 63 Brussels Ia. Yet this copy has been criticised by Spanish academia, as the wording of the Brussels regime rule is more precise than the Spanish rule. It has been analysed by these scholars that if the copy of Art 22 *ter* OLJ had been more exact, this would have avoided some coordination and interpretative problems between the European and the domestic provisions.[17] Moreover, in contrast with the treatment given to the domicile for natural persons which applies in coordination with Art 40 Spanish Civil Code, for legal persons, Art 41 Spanish Civil Code, which contains the definition of domicile for legal persons, is not of application.

The only difference with the general jurisdiction rules of the Brussels regime is – as mentioned above – that the concept of domicile set forth in the Spanish regime is on the same level as the concept of 'habitual residence' according to Art 40 of the Spanish Civil Code.[18]

[15] Sentencia de la Audiencia Provincial de Málaga, Sec. no. 5, 28 March 2007, [ECLI:ES:APMA:2007:817], related to the property and temporal residence in Spain of a German national; Sentencia de la Audiencia Provincial de Bilbao, of 24 June 1993, (1994) *REDI*, 293–95; Resolución de la Dirección General de Registros y Notariado [RDGRN] 2nd, (2007) 2045 *BIMJ*, 3585–87; Resolución de la Dirección General de Registros y Notariado [RDGRN] 1st, (2007) 2045 *BIMJ*, 3592–94.

[16] AL Calvo Caravaca and J Carrascosa González, *Tratado de Derecho internacional privado I*, 402; M Virgós Soriano and FJ Garcimartín Alférez, *Derecho procesal civil internacional. Litigación internacional* (Thomson-Civitas, 2007), 158; FJ Garcimartín Alférez, 'La competencia judicial internacional en la reforma de la Ley Orgánica del Poder Judicial' (2015) 8614 *Diario la Ley* 1, 7.

[17] AL Calvo Caravaca and J Carrascosa González, *Tratado de Derecho internacional privado I*, 368–70; A Durán Ayago, 'Ley Orgánica 7/2015, de 21 de julio, por la que se modifica la Ley Orgánica 6/1985, de 1 de julio, del Poder Judicial [BOE nº 174, 22-VII-2015]: Competencia judicial internacional en materia civil y mercantil' (2016) 4 *Arts Iurs Salmaticensis*, 284, 286.

[18] AL Calvo Caravaca and J Carrascosa González, *Tratado de Derecho internacional privado I*, 398–404; C Salvat, 'La Competencia judicial international residual en materia contractual en España', 141.

3.3. Other Connecting Factors

The Spanish jurisdiction rules of the OLJ do not provide different connecting factors other than the ones established under the rules of the Brussels Ia to deal with civil and commercial matters. As was mentioned, these Spanish rules were a copy of the Brussels Regime primitive rules, namely of the 1968 Brussels Convention rules. Only a few significant changes to them were introduced during the amendment process of the OLJ in 2015, but these were not related to their connecting factors.

In addition, unlike other jurisdictional systems, the Spanish regime does not have either an exorbitant forum based on the nationality of the parties, or a forum based on temporary stay or situation of property (*forum arresti*). Apart from that, the doctrine of *forum non conveniens* is not usually applied by the Spanish courts as this is contrary to the fundamental procedural principle of the judge predetermined by the law enshrined under Art 24 Spanish Bill of Rights.[19]

However, according to the analysis of some Spanish scholars, the Spanish Constitutional Court has not entirely rejected its application. The Spanish Constitutional Court has recognised in its case law that via exception and provided this possibility will not infringe the constitutional rights, the *forum non conveniens*, even if it is a foreign doctrine, might be of application. What is prohibited in the Spanish legal system when considering as an exception the application of phenomena such as the *forum non conveniens* is the 'arbitrariness', rather than the requisite of extending the jurisdiction of the Spanish courts in cases of real necessity. These considerations are very related to what explained in the next Section 3.4 of the *forum necessitatis*.[20]

3.4. Forum Necessitatis

With the amendment of the OLJ in 2015, the Spanish legislator incorporated for the first time in the Spanish regime a specific *forum necessitatis* rule, under Art 22 *octies* para 2 OLJ.[21]

To date, there is no seminal case law on its interpretation, because it has not been invoked yet, at least for civil and commercial law matters.[22] This provision attributes

[19] I Diez-Picazo Jiménez, 'El derecho fundamental al juez ordinario predeterminado por la ley' (1991) 31 *REDE*, 75–124; M Amores Conradi, 'La nueva estructura del sistema español de competencia judicial internacional en el orden civil: Art. 22 LOPJ' (1989) *REDI*, 113–56; MJ Sánchez Cano, 'Reflexiones prácticas sobre la competencia judicial internacional y la filiación', (2021) 13 *CDT*, 1095–1105.

[20] C Otero García Castrillón, 'Problemas de aplicación de las normas de Competencia judicial internacional en el Derecho español y comunitario: Reflexiones en torno al *forum non conveniens*' (2000) 94 *RFUDC*, 99–128; AL Calvo Caravaca and J Carrascosa González, *Tratado de Derecho internacional privado I*, 347–48.

[21] This provision reads as follows: 'Spanish Courts cannot abstain or refuse their competence where the matter in litigation has links to Spain and the Courts of the various States connected to the matter have refused their competence. Nor may they do so in relation to the recognition and enforcement of judicial rulings, arbitration decisions and mediation agreements issued by foreign Courts'.

[22] Auto de la Audiencia Provincial de Barcelona, Sec. 18, 15 September 2020, no°6151/2020, [ECLI:ES:APB: 2020:6151A]; Auto de la Audiencia Provincial de Barcelona, Sec. 18, 9 December 2016, no°4160/2016 [ECLI:ES:APB: 2016:4160A]; this recent case law on the *forum necessitatis* set forth in the article 22 *octies* is usually connected to family law issues and EU Family PIL regulations.

international jurisdiction to the Spanish courts when the case has a connection with the Spanish courts and with other States courts with international jurisdiction to hear the case but *have refused* to do so, or these courts had no competence at all attributed by the EU PIL rules or by their domestic rules on jurisdiction. It may be said that the requirement of 'having been refused' by the courts of other States connected to the case, despite having attributed jurisdiction by their regimes, has been heavily criticised by Spanish academia as a disputed issue.[23]

It is likely that Spanish courts may not demand of the parties the requirement of *refusal of jurisdiction* needed to trigger this forum. The circumstance of the lack of international jurisdiction of the courts with alleged jurisdiction over the matter might be considered as sufficient by the Spanish Courts to consider they have international jurisdiction to hear the case.[24] This is justified because the Spanish regime is built – as the procedural regime of the EU Member States – by certain fundamental values protected under relevant Human Rights Conventions and under the EU Treaties of formation and functioning, such as access to justice.

3.5. Role of the Spanish Courts

Spanish lower and higher courts (viz, Spanish Supreme Court) mention in their case law the overriding principles enshrined under the Brussels Ia Regulation and of EU Law, according to the most seminal CJEU case law, when implementing Spanish rules on jurisdiction. Normally, reference to the doctrines rendered by the CJEU in its preliminary rulings is made to justify and explain the application of the Spanish rules instead of the Brussels Ia and other treaties' rules, eg the 2007 Lugano Convention or other treaties.[25]

4. Spanish Special Rules of Jurisdiction Over Contractual and Non-Contractual Obligations

4.1. Main Characteristics

Special jurisdiction or rules on contractual and extra contractual liability matters can be found under Art 22 *quinquies* lit a (correspondingly, with Art 7(1) lit a, b, c, d Brussels

[23] FJ Garcimartín Alférez, 'La competencia judicial internacional en la reforma de la Ley Orgánica del Poder Judicial', 7.

[24] AL Calvo Caravaca and J Carrascosa González, *Tratado de Derecho internacional privado I*, 379.

[25] Inter alia, as the latest resolutions handled down by the Spanish Supreme Court, Civil division (Tribunal Supremo, Sala de lo civil) on the implementation of Art 22 LOPJ which mention the principles enshrined under Brussels Ia Regulation: Sentencia del Tribunal Supremo, Sala 1ª, 27 July 2021, no°3188/2021, [ECLI:ES:TS:2021:3188]; Sentencia del Tribunal Supremo, Sala 1ª, 20 July 2020, no°2492/2020, [ECLI:ES:TS:2020:2492]; Sentencia del Tribunal Supremo, Sala 1ª, 6 July 2020, no°2282/2020, [ECLI:ES:TS:2020:2282]; Sentencia de la Audiencia Provincial de Zaragoza, Sec. 2ª, 28 December 2017, no°00844/2017, [ECLI:ES:APZ:2017:2813].

Ia); and Art 22 *quinquies* lit b jurisdiction in matters relating to tort, delict, or quasi-delict (in relation to Art 7(2) Brussels Ia).

These rules have a special and additional or supplementary procedural nature, as practically do the rest of the jurisdiction rules set out in the Art 22 OLJ. On the one hand, these rules are considered as 'special' because, in the same vein as Art 7 Brussels Ia, they are only addressed for covering specific matters/subjects.

However, these rules do not bestow territorial jurisdiction, as the rules of the Brussels Ia Regulation do when applied.[26] Territorial jurisdiction is conferred to the Spanish Courts under the rules of the CPA.[27] On the other hand, its 'additional or supplementary' nature is related to the hierarchy of *fora* that exists in the Spanish jurisdictional system in the same vein as in Brussels Ia. These rules have an ancillary position from the rules over choice-of-court agreements and submission by appearance (Art 22 *bis* OLJ) and from the general rule-forum of the domicile of the defendant (Art 22(1) *ter* OLJ).[28] This *fora* hierarchy between the special *fora* (contractual and extra-contractual claims) and the general rule of the domicile of the defendant as well as prorogation of jurisdiction *fora* is still established at the beginning of the wording of Art 22(1) *quinquies*: '(…) in the absence of express or tacit submission …'.[29]

With regard to the precedent on special jurisdiction *fora* and as was mentioned above under Section I and II about the OLJ rules structure on civil and commercial matters,[30] this has been heavily criticised by Spanish scholars.[31] With regard to these special jurisdiction rules, criticism was always made of the wording and of the hierarchy these rules have taken with the Brussels regime. While the nature of Spanish rules is *attributive* and unilateral rules enacted by a domestic lawmaker, the nature of the Brussels regime rules is *distributive* and bilateral enacted by the European lawmaker.[32] Bearing in mind this idea, the hierarchy and wording of the Brussels regime rules follow their own logic and principles that should not be copied by the national legislators without any change. As with the amendment of the OLJ, the Spanish legislator did not change these rules, fitting them into their attributive nature. Moreover, it appeared to have widened the scope of the application of these rules for EU defendants (mostly for companies) rather than for non-EU defendants.[33] Therefore the problem, which

[26] FJ Garcimartín Alférez, *Derecho international privado*, 109 et seq.; AL Calvo Caravaca and J Carrascosa González, *Tratado de Derecho internacional privado I*, 385.

[27] See above Section 2.1.

[28] See n 26.

[29] AL Calvo Caravaca and J Carrascosa González, *Tratado de Derecho internacional privado I*, 351; see below, n 37.

[30] See above Section 1.

[31] FJ Garcimartín Alférez, 'La competencia judicial internacional en la reforma de la Ley Orgánica del Poder Judicial', www.almacendederecho.org/la-competencia-judicial-internacional-en-la-reforma-de-la-lopj; AL Calvo Caravaca and J Carrascosa González, *Tratado de Derecho internacional privado I*, 335–79; A Durán Ayago, 'Ley Orgánica 7/2015, de 21 de julio, por la que se modifica la Ley Orgánica 6/1985, de 1 de julio, del Poder Judicial [BOE nº 174, 22-VII-2015]: Competencia judicial internacional en materia civil y mercantil', 284–288; PA de Miguel Asensio, 'La cuestionable revisión de las normas de competencia judicial internacional (LO 7/2015 de reforma de la LOPJ)' (*Pedro de Miguel Asensio blog*, 2015), www.pedrodemiguelasensio.blogspot.com/2015/07/la-cuestionable-revision-de-las-normas.html.

[32] ibid.

[33] FJ Garcimartín Alférez, 'La competencia judicial internacional en la reforma de la Ley Orgánica del Poder Judicial', www.almacendederecho.org/la-competencia-judicial-internacional-en-la-reforma-de-la-lopj.

still relies on their wording, is essentially that the Spanish rules are at odds with their attributive or unilateral procedural nature.[34] As a consequence, this situation has led to a series of problems of interpretation for legal practitioners when these rules came to be applied instead of the rules of Brussels Ia.[35] Additionally, since the OLJ was enacted in 1985, there have been problems of coordination between the international rules of the OLJ and some of the territorial jurisdiction rules of the CPA, which remain unsolved.[36]

4.2. Rule on Contractual Matters

The Spanish rule on contractual matters, encompassing contracts and contractual obligations, is Art 22 *quinquies* lit a OLJ. This provision reads as follows:

> (1) Furthermore, in the absence of express or tacit submission to them, and although the defendant is not domiciled in Spain, Spanish Courts will be competent:
>
> a) In matters relating to contractual obligations, where the obligation to which the lawsuit relates has been fulfilled or must be fulfilled in Spain.

According to this provision, Spanish courts will be seised in contractual matters when the following conditions are met:

First. – Considering the hierarchised nature of the Spanish *fora* in the same vein as the Brussels Regime rules, the forum will be triggered in the absence of any choice of court agreement or of any submission by appearance (Art 22 *bis* and *ter* OLJ – prorogation of jurisdiction).[37]

Second. – The defendant must be domiciled outside the EU, otherwise the Brussels Ia Regulation will be of application. In addition, considering that no other treaties are of application to the case.[38]

[34] AL Calvo Caravaca and J Carrascosa González, *Tratado de Derecho internacional privado I*, 337.

[35] See n 5; S Álvarez González, 'Jurisprudencia española y comunitaria de Derecho internacional privado' (2007) LIX *REDI*, 261; see case law cited at n 12.

[36] MJ Sánchez Cano, 'Reflexiones prácticas sobre la competencia judicial internacional y la filiación', 1101; AL Calvo Caravaca and J Carrascosa González, *Tratado de Derecho internacional privado I*, 349–350; 'Un convenio internacional perdido y hallado en las Islas Baleares: Reflexiones sobre el control de oficio de la competencia judicial internacional y las fuentes del Derecho internacional privado español', (2017) 9 *CDT*, 366–382; as example of this confusion in the Spanish case law, among the function of the jurisdictional and territorial rules, Auto de la Audiencia Provincial de Zaragoza, Sec. 5ª, 18 June 2020, no.°1115/2020, [ECLI:ES:APZ:2020:728A].

[37] However, the hierarchised or alternative nature of this rule with the prorogation of jurisdiction forum is very contested and it has not been clarified at all by the Spanish courts, as the Spanish academia cited in this report have analysed in detail. It is interesting to note what the Spanish scholars have analysed on the relationship between these *fora*: over contractual matters and choice of court agreements, B Campuzano Díaz, 'La *Derogatio Fori* en la Ley Orgánica del Poder Judicial' (2018) 70 *REEI*, 155–179; P Jiménez Blanco, 'La *Derogatio Fori* después de la reforma de la Ley Orgánica del Poder Judicial' (2017) XVII *AEDIPr*, 473–506; JM Espinar Vicente, 'Análisis y valoración crítica de la regulación de la sumisión a la jurisdicción Española antes y después de la reforma de la Ley Orgánica del Poder Judicial (LO 7 2015)' (2016) XVI *AEDIPr*, 199–247; 'Los riesgos de la incorrecta adaptación de las normas de la Unión Europea. La sumisión de las partes a la jurisdicción española tras la reforma de la Ley Orgánica del Poder Judicial de 2015' (2015) 31 *La Ley Unión Europea*, 6900/2015; FF Garau Sobrino, 'Los acuerdos atributivos de jurisdicción en Derecho procesal civil internacional español' (2010) 2 *CDT*, 52–91.

[38] See below Section 6.

Third. – When the contractual obligation or the contract must be, or it was, performed in Spain. Before the OLJ amendment of 2015, this article established that the contract itself had to be signed or entered into in Spain. Currently, it is only needed that the performance of the contract has been done in Spain.

4.2.1. Characterisation of Contractual Obligations and Contracts

Albeit Art 22 *quinquies* (1) is a copy of former Art 5(1) 1968 Brussels Convention, there are some differences in their wording.

In the first place, the Spanish rule does not make any consideration of the different kind of contracts and contractual obligations, such as sales or provision of contracts, as Art 7(1) Brussels Ia establishes in its lit a, b and c. Thus, all contractual obligations, and civil and commercial contracts of every kind, are included in its wording, with the exception of consumer, employment and insurance contracts, which have specific rules of jurisdiction in the OLJ.[39] The outcome of this is that Spanish courts have developed a sort of jurisprudential solution in their case law, explaining and interpreting the extension of Art 22 *quinquies* a OLJ to all kinds of civil and commercial contracts and contractual obligations.[40]

In the second place, this rule does not provide an autonomous concept of what has to be understood as the 'place of performance' nor of what is understood in the Spanish regime as a 'contractual obligation'. Consequently both concepts (contractual obligation and place of performance) are normally characterised according to the *lex fori*, the Spanish substantive law of obligations, instituted in the Spanish Civil Code,[41] though Spanish courts have occasionally considered a *lex causae* characterisation when the Spanish regime is of application. And also, a characterisation according to the CJEU case law on the interpretation of contractual obligation, understanding that the 'place of performance' of the contractual obligation is Spain when the Art 22 rule is of application.

Thus, there will be a contractual obligation when among the parties exists a contract/contractual obligation, and that damage was done as a consequence of this contract.

Last, the Spanish legislator has not incorporated in this rule the conflictual solutions given by Art 7(1) lit b Brussels Ia Regulation, in connection with the conflict of law rules of Regulation Rome I.[42]

4.2.2. Other Contractual Parties

For contractual parties such as agents or middlemen in commercial contracts, there are no special jurisdiction rules foreseen under the jurisdiction rules of the OLJ. Although,

[39] See below Section 5.

[40] FJ Garcimartín Alférez, *Derecho international privado*, 110.

[41] Sentencia de la Audiencia Provincial de La Coruña, Sec. 6ª, 15 June 2006, no°168/2005; Sentencia de la Audiencia Provincial de Barcelona, Sec. 6ª, 8 April 2004, no°190/2004; M Virgós Soriano, *Lugar de la celebración y de ejecución en contratación internacional* (Tecnos, 1989) 33; AL Calvo Caravaca & J Carrascosa González, *Curso de contratación internacional* (Colex, 2003) 29; M Virgós Soriano and FJ Garcimartín Alférez, *Derecho procesal civil internacional. Litigación internacional*, 158.

[42] AL Calvo Caravaca and J Carrascosa González, *Tratado de Derecho internacional privado I*, 405–07.

concerning agency contracts, the Ley 12/1992 sobre Contrato de Agencia (Spanish Act on Agency Contracts),[43] includes a territorial jurisdictional rule which can determine the international jurisdiction when the defendant is not domiciled in the EU but in agency contracts where the parties incorporated a choice of court agreement. Parties must previously confer jurisdiction to the Spanish courts with the inclusion of a choice of court agreement to activate this special rule of territorial jurisdiction on agency contracts, which 'seems' to also attribute international jurisdiction despite being a territorial jurisdiction rule.[44]

Nevertheless, this requirement has also been contested, because Art 25 Brussels Ia is of application regardless of the domicile of the contractual parties. Consequently, the rules of the Brussels Ia Regulation on prorogation of jurisdiction are superseding domestic rules since its entry into force.

4.3. Rule on Extracontractual Matters

Article 22 *quinquies* lit b, the Spanish rule over extracontractual matters, reads as follows:

> b) In matters relating to extra-contractual obligations, where the detriment occurred in Spanish territory.

This special forum is triggered under the following conditions:

First. – This forum is only functional when the defendant is domiciled outside the EU.

Second. – When the harmful event (*hecho dañoso*: detriment) occurred or when its effects were spread over the Spanish territory (only in Spain). The requirement of habitual residence in Spain for the victim and the tortfeasor was removed from the previous wording of Art 22 OLJ 1985. This result actually leads to the automatic application of the Brussels Regime once the tortfeasor has its domicile in Spain.

Third. – In cases where the damage ought to be characterised as a particular kind of damage, eg nuclear damages, this forum will not operate, since there are specific treaties and EU regulations which contain specific rules on jurisdiction for these type of damages.[45]

[43] Disposición adicional segunda (Second Additional Provision) de la Ley 12/1992, de 27 de mayo sobre el contrato de Agencia, (1992) *Official State Gazette [BOE]* 129; CI Cordero Alvárez, 'Algunas reflexiones sobre la autonomía jurisdiccional en el sistema autónomo español de competencia judicial tras la reforma de la LOPJ' https://tinyurl.com/2dh85r3x; H Aguilar Grieder, 'Sumisión de las partes a los tribunales belgas en el marco de un contrato internacional de agencia comercial: comentario a la sentencia de la Audiencia Provincial de Barcelona (Sección 1ª) de diciembre de 2018' (2019) 11 *CDT*, 380–87, 385–86.

[44] See Section 2.1 and 2.2.

[45] There are specific conventions and EU Regulations tailored for certain kinds of damages, which Spain has signed and ratified being in force. The application of these instruments supersedes the application of the Brussels Ia, and of the Spanish regime, eg: Convention on Third Party Liability in the Field of Nuclear Energy of 29 July 1960, as amended by the Additional Protocol of 28 January 1964 and by the Protocol of 16 November 1982; Sentencia del Tribunal Supremo, Sala 1ª, 15 March 2021, no°807/2021 [ECLI:ES:TS:2021:807].

Fourth. – In the same vein as Brussels Ia and Rome II Regulation, this forum also shelters *culpa in contrahendo* matters according to the Spanish Supreme Court case law, despite the contested nature of these kind of obligations under the Spanish Civil Doctrine and Law.[46]

4.3.1. Differences with Art 7(2) Brussels Ia

At first glance, one of the core differences with the wording of Art 7(2) Brussels Ia is that under the Spanish rule there is no mention of the *prospective* damage, ie it was not drafted with the expression 'may occur'. Consequently, some kind of remedies that might be requested by the parties when Art 7(2) Brussels Ia is of application, as the injunction relief and negative declarative actions, are not available when this Spanish rule has to be applied. Notwithstanding, it has been construed by the Spanish courts as a kind of solution which gives room to invoke these remedies, also established in the Spanish procedural system.

4.3.2. Characterisation of Extracontractual Obligation

This provision above cited has not included any concept in its wording of what is considered as an extracontractual obligation under the Spanish regime. Subsequently, the characterisation of the obligation will be determined by the Spanish courts according to the *lex fori*.

In this sense, to characterise the tort, Art 1089 has to be applied in connection with Art 1092 (general rule of tortious liability) of the Spanish Civil Code.[47] Additionally, the Spanish courts have also interpreted the concept according to the CJEU case law on the extracontractual obligation concept, that is, using a negative approach to the concept of extracontractual liability in line with Case C-189/87 *Kalfelis* CJEU case law onwards.[48] However, the concept has been interpreted with certain constraints and caveats, especially bearing in mind that Spanish rules cannot be applied *mutatis mutandis* as the Brussels regime rules. Therefore, it is difficult to find differences with the interpretation of the CJEU on it, as Spanish courts are applying in many cases the parameters of the CJEU case law.[49] Notwithstanding this, the Supreme Court has recognised, unlike the

[46] Sentencia del Tribunal Supremo, Sala 1ª, 16 May 1988, no 405/1988; Sentencia del Tribunal Supremo, Sala 1ª, 16 December 1999, no°1091/1999; L Díez Picazo, *Fundamentos de Derecho Civil Patrimonial* I, (Civitas, 1993), 311–325; R Arenas García, 'La distinción entre obligaciones contractuales y obligaciones extracontractuales en los instrumentos comunitarios de Derecho internacional privado' (2006) VI *AEDIPr*, 403–25.

[47] Art 1089 Spanish Civil Code; 'Obligations arise from the law, from contracts, and quasi contracts, and from unlawful acts or omissions or those in which there is any kind or fault or negligence'; Art 1902: 'A person who, as a result of an action or omission, causes damage to another through his fault or negligence shall be obliged to repair the damaged caused'. Spanish Civil Code, www.mjusticia.gob.es/es/AreaTematica/DocumentacionPublicaciones/Documents/Spanish%20Civil%20Code.pdf.

[48] R Arenas García, 'La distinción entre obligaciones contractuales y obligaciones extracontractuales en los instrumentos comunitarios de Derecho internacional privado', 406.

[49] ibid; E Roca Frías and M Navarro Michel, *Derecho de daños* (Valencia, Tirant lo Blanch, 2011), 46.

CJEU case law, the possibility to interpret that this forum also includes both actions: contractual and extracontractual.[50]

4.4. Close Connection Between Defendants or Joinder Rule

The Spanish autonomous system included with the OLJ amendment of 2015 a special jurisdictional rule on a close connection between defendants in Art 22(3) *ter*. This novelty solved this loophole of the Spanish regime. The provision is in connection with the Spanish procedural rule on joinder, Art 72 CPA (subjective joinder of actions).[51] However, the Spanish legislator did not include in this provision the other rules of joinder, as Art 8 Brussels Ia did.[52] Moreover, in comparison to Art 8(1) Brussels Ia, the Spanish rule does not specify what might be understood as a 'close connection' to seize Spanish courts as the proper courts to hear the claim. To determine what is understood as a 'close connection', one needs to link Art 22(3) *ter* to Art 72 CPA.

Requirements to trigger this forum are the following:[53]

First, at least one of the defendants must be domiciled in Spain (anchor defendant).

Second, none of the defendants (joinder) can be domiciled in any of the Member States of the EU, otherwise, Art 8 (1) Brussels Ia will be the rule to determine the jurisdiction in joinder cases.

5. Special Protection Rules: Consumers, Insurance and Employment Contracts

5.1. Consumer Contracts

Article 22 *quinquies* lit d contains the rule over cross-border consumer contracts.[54] The only condition to invoke this rule by the claimant is based on *rationae personae* grounds: the domicile of the consumers and of the professionals must be in Spain. Consumers

[50] Sentencia del Tribunal Supremo, Sala 1ª, 22 December 2008, no°1135/2008, [ECLI:ES:TS:2008:7354]; Spanish Supreme Court has named this doctrine as the 'principio de unidad de culpa civil', Sentencia del Tribunal Supremo, Sala 1ª, 7 October 2010, no°607/2010 [ECLI:ES:TS:2010:4860].

[51] Article 72 CPA: 'Actions may be joined and simultaneously brought against several or single defendants, as long as such actions have some sort of link or grounds based on a title or the causes of plea. It shall be construed that the title or grounds are identical or connected where the actions are grounded in the same facts'.

[52] FJ Garcimartín Alférez, 'La competencia judicial internacional en la reforma de la Ley Orgánica del Poder Judicial', www.almacendederecho.org/la-competencia-judicial-internacional-en-la-reforma-de-la-lopj.

[53] Art 22(3) *ter* OLJ: 'Where more than one defendant exists, the Spanish Courts will be competent where at least one of them is domiciled in Spain, providing that a single action is brought, or several that are interconnected by a nexus in view of the title or motive for the action, whereby a joinder is advisable'.

[54] Art 22 *quinquies* OLJ lit d: 'In matters relating to contracts entered into by consumers, they may go to law in Spain if their habitual residence lies in Spanish territory or where the habitual residence of the other contracting party is in Spanish territory; the latter may only go to law in Spain where the consumer's habitual residence lies in Spanish territory'.

might seize Spanish courts when they or the professionals have their domicile or habitual residence in Spain (in connection with the last paragraph of Art 22 *quinquies*).

This rule, according to Spanish academia views – which widely diverge on its interpretation – is not displaced by the rules over consumer contracts of the Brussels Ia Regulation when professionals as defendants are domiciled in third countries. According to these academia views, the extension of Spanish jurisdiction even to parties domiciled in third countries is ultimately a *de minimis* rule. Yet, it is advisable that – as Garcimartín highlights – Spanish courts interpret this rule narrowly, to avoid the unnecessary extension of *forum actoris*.[55]

The Spanish jurisdiction rule does not distinguish, as Art 17 Brussels Ia does, certain conditions or requirements to bring the actions before Spanish courts over contractual claims, such as, for instance, the necessity of a contract characterised as a consumer contract of any kind (supply of goods and services, loans, and so on) between the parties to the contract.

In contrast to Art 17 Brussels Ia Regulation, the Spanish rule has not specified or included the concept of 'consumer contracts', 'consumers' and 'professionals'. As a result, these concepts are characterised in accordance with the Spanish substantive sectorial bodies of law on consumer protection, such as the Real Decreto 1/2007, 16 de noviembre, por el que se aprueba el Texto Refundido de la Ley General para la Defensa de los Consumidores y Usuarios y otras leyes complementarias (TRLGDCU),[56] and Ley 7/1998, de 13 de abril sobre Condiciones Generales de la Contratación,[57] among others. Since all these Spanish consumer rules have implemented the EU secondary law on consumer protection, the CJEU case law on the concept of consumers and professionals is of application by the Spanish courts when they are seized to hear these cross-border consumer contractual disputes, either applying Arts 17 to 19 of Brussels Ia or the Spanish rule.[58] Even so, the concept of 'consumer' has been considered wider than the concept rendered by the EU consumer rules.[59]

5.2. Insurance Claims

Under the Art 22 *quinquies* lit e the forum for insurance claims is found.[60] Requirements for activating this forum are the same as in consumer contracts. In cases of 'liability

[55] FJ Garcimartín Alférez, *Derecho international privado*, 136.

[56] *Official State Gazzette* [BOE] 287 of 20 November 2007.

[57] *Official State Gazzette* [BOE] 89 of 14 April 1998.

[58] For instance, Sentencia del Tribunal Supremo, Sala 1ª, 20 July 2021, no°3073/2021 [ECLI:TS:2021:3073]; Sentencia del Tribunal Supremo, Sala 1ª, 6 March 2018, no°711/2018 [ECLI:ES:TS:2018:711]; Sentencia del Tribunal Supremo, Sala 1ª, 5 April 2017, no°1385/2017 [ECLI:ES:TS:2017:1385]; Sentencia del Tribunal Supremo, Sala 1ª, 20 July 2021, no°554/2021, [ECLI:ES:TS:2021:3073].

[59] Art 3 TRLGDCU; C Salvat, 'La Competencia judicial international residual en materia contractual en España', 145; A Espiniella Menéndez, *Abogacía Internacional. La protección de los consumidores* (Rasche, 2016) 10–20; S Cámara Lapuente, `El concepto legal de consumidor en el Derecho privado europeo y el Derecho español: aspectos controvertidos o no resueltos', (2011) 3 *CDT*, 84–117; F Esteban de la Rosa, *La protección de los consumidores en el mercado interior europeo* (Granada, Comares, 2003), 44–70.

[60] Art 22 *quinquies* OLJ lit e: 'In matters relating to insurance, where the insured party, policy holder or beneficiary of the insurance is domiciled in Spain; the insurance company can also have action brought against it before the Spanish Courts where the detriment occurs in Spanish territory and it involves a liability

insurances' – eg, liability insurance contracts, real estate insurances and so on – the insured parties or policy holders may seize the Spanish courts provided the damage or harmful event occurred in Spain, regardless of the domicile of the parties ('… where the detriment [sic]harmful event occurs in Spanish territory …'). In this sense, this rule includes in the same paragraph those cases that Brussels Ia has distributed under Chapter II, Section 3 (Jurisdiction in matters relating to Insurance).

For both insurance and consumer contracts there is an additional paragraph in Art 22 *quinquies, in fine* when protected parties (consumers and insured parties or policy holders) have agreed an ex-post (after the controversy arises) choice-of-court agreement with the professionals to bring actions before Spanish courts, similarly to Art 19 and Art 15 of Brussels Ia.[61]

5.3. Employment Contracts

For employment contracts, the rule was separated in a different rule of the OLJ. This forum was not amended in 2015 and its wording has remained the same from the enactment of the OLJ in 1985.

Analogously to consumer and insurance contracts, it is of residual application, pondering that the Brussels Ia special protection rules have broadened the scope to the professionals as defendants domiciled in third countries. As a matter of fact, the wording of Art 25(1) OLJ confers competence on the Spanish courts when an employment contract was entered into in Spain, regardless of the domicile of the parties and in the absence of other connecting factors linked to the Spanish territory. Nonetheless, opposed to the consumer and insurance contracts *for a*, which follow similar wording to the Brussels Ia rules, this article does not follow the same outline as Arts 20 to 23 Brussels Ia. Neither article has developed any definition of 'employment' contracts. In addition, the different connecting factors established in the article are not hierarchised at all. Thus these connecting factors have an alternative nature among them.[62]

The Spanish legislator has included three situations or factual conditions to ascribe international jurisdiction to the Spanish courts in the event Brussels Ia and other bilateral-multilateral treaties will not be of application over employment cases before Spanish courts.[63]

insurance contract or insurance relating to property, or, in the case of civil liability insurance, where the Spanish Courts are competent to hear the action initiated by the injured party against the insured party by virtue of the stipulations of letter b) of this article'.

[61] Art 22 *quinquies* OLJ last para: '(…) With regards to the cases envisaged in letters d) and e), the Spanish Courts will also be competent where the consumer, insured party or policy holder is the plaintiff and the parties have agreed to submit to the Spanish Courts subsequent to the initiation of the dispute, or were both parties to the contract were domiciled in Spain when they entered into the contract or where the plaintiff is the consumer, insured party or policy holder'.

[62] CE Mota, JL Iglesias Buhiges and GP Moreno, *Derecho internacional privado* (Valencia, Tirant Lo Blanch, 2015) 166–167; ME Zábalo Escudero, 'La competencia judicial internacional de los tribunales españoles en materia de contrato de trabajo. El artículo 25.1 de la Ley Orgánica del Poder Judicial de 1985' (1986) 38 *REDI* 613–629; FF Garau Sobrino, 'Competencia judicial internacional de los tribunales españoles para conocer de los litigios sobre relaciones laborales' (2018) XVIII *AEDIPr* 457–66; A Todolí Signes, 'La competencia judicial internacional del contrato individual de trabajo' (2016) 1 *Revista de información laboral*, 21–47.

[63] Art 25 OLJ reads as follows: 'In labour matters, the Spanish Courts and Tribunals will be competent in the following cases: (1) Rights and obligations stemming from employment contracts when the services have

Subsequently, paragraph 1 confers competence on the Spanish courts when the contract was entered into in Spain (territorial criteria); when the defendant is domiciled in Spain or has a branch, agency, subsidiary or any analogous establishment which represents the company; or if the professional and the employee both are Spanish, regardless of where the provision of services was performed (*rationae personae* criteria); for sea-workers if the employment offer was made in Spain (so-called in Spanish, *embarque).* Paragraph 2 attributes competence to the Spanish courts in cases of General Collective Agreements and conflicts thereof, when these Collective Agreements among employers and employees or the conflicts have occurred in Spain. And paragraph 3 comprises claims relating to the Sistema de Seguridad Social español (Spanish Social Security Insurance system) against any company incorporated (statutory seat) or which has its branches, agencies, or any analogous establishments, in Spain.

been rendered in Spain or when the contract has been executed in the Spanish territory; when the defendant is domiciled in the territory of Spain or an agency, branch or representative office in Spain; when the worker and the employer are Spanish nationals regardless of the place where the services were rendered or the employment contract was executed; and additionally in the event of sea-workers if prior to the contract an offer was made in Spain to a Spanish worker; (2) Compliance with the law of collective wage agreements executed in Spain and any claims arising from labour disputes that take place in the territory of Spain: (3) Social Security claims against Spanish companies or entities which have a registered address, branch, office, or any other representation in Spain'.

Sweden

LYDIA LUNDSTEDT

Question 1

(a)

In general, the Swedish legal system does not contain comprehensive statutory rules on international jurisdiction over non-EU defendants for matters regulated by the Brussels Ia Regulation.[1] Instead, the source of the Swedish rules on international jurisdiction over these matters is case law from the Supreme Court and legal scholarship. According to Supreme Court case law and legal scholarship, Swedish international jurisdiction exists when there is a Swedish interest in the administration of justice (*rättsskipningsintresse*).[2] A Swedish interest in the administration of justice generally exists if the dispute or one of the parties has some connection to Sweden giving Sweden an interest in the adjudication of the dispute.[3] An important source for determining whether such an interest exists

[1] Sweden has statutory rules on international jurisdiction for some specific situations. See eg Act (No°152 of 1978) on the Competence of Swedish Courts in Certain Cases in the field of Patent Law, etc (*Lag* (1978:152) *om svensk domstols behörighet i vissa mål på patenträttens område m.m.*).

[2] See in particular E Sinander, 'Svenskt rättskipningsintresse' (2019) *SvJT* 932. For Swedish Supreme Court practice, see eg Högsta domstolen (Swedish Supreme Court), 12 November 2010, (2010) *NJA* 508, para 2 ('The first question to be decided is whether there is a Swedish interest in the administration of justice and Swedish jurisdiction over the case'); Högsta domstolen, 13 November 2015, (2015), *NJA* 798, para 9 ('It follows from the territorial limitation that there is a Swedish interest in the administration of justice and Swedish jurisdiction when it comes to a Swedish trademark protection'); Högsta domstolen, 15 July 2016, (2016), *NJA* 779, para 10 ('When it is decided in which cases Swedish jurisdiction exists, *inter alia*, if the provisions of Chapter 10 of the Judicial Code are to be applied by analogy, consideration shall be given to the extent to which there is a Swedish interest in the administration of justice'); Högsta domstolen, 29 March 2017, (2017) *NJA* 168, para 9, Mahr ('Swedish jurisdiction is normally considered to exist when the dispute or one of the parties has some connection to Sweden. It can also be expressed as that there must be a Swedish interest in the administration of justice in order for there to be Swedish jurisdiction'). In legal scholarship see S Dennemark, 'Svensk rättspraxis. Internationell privaträtt 1941–1948' (1950) *Svensk Juristtidning* 35, 38; S Dennemark, *Om domstols behörighet i internationellt förmögenhetsrättsliga mål* (PA Norstedt & Söners Förlag, 1961) 175; H Eek, *Lagkonflikter i tvistemål* (PA Norstedt & Söners Förlag 1972, reprinted 1978) 118; H Karlgren, *Kortfattad lärobok i internationell privat-och processrätt* 5th edn (Gleerup, 1974) 158; L Pålsson, *Svensk rättspraxis i internationell processrätt* (Norstedts, 1989) 54; L Lundstedt, *Territoriality in Intellectual Property Law* (Stockholm University, 2016) 135; E Sinander, *Internationell kollektivavtalsreglering: En studie i internationell privaträtt av den svenska modellen för reglering av anställningsvillkor* (Stockholms universitet, 2017) 48, 119–20; M Bogdan and M Hellner, *Svensk internationell privat- och processrätt* 9th edn (Norstedts Juridik, 2020) 329.

[3] Högsta domstolen, 29 March 2017, (2017) *NJA* 168, para 9, Mahr. See also M Jänterä-Jareborg, *Svensk domstol och utländsk rätt, En internationellt privat- och processrättslig studie* (Iustus Förlag, 1997) 33, who,

is Chapter 10 of the Swedish Code of Judicial Procedure) (*10 kapitlet rättegångsbalken*, (SFS 1942:740); Judicial Code). Chapter 10 of the Judicial Code contains internal venue rules that allocate the territorial jurisdiction between the Swedish courts. These rules can be applied *ex analogia* to determine international jurisdiction where appropriate.[4] The fact that a court in Sweden is competent pursuant to an internal venue rule suggests that Sweden may have a sufficient connection to the case so that international jurisdiction should also be deemed to exist.[5] There is, however, no longer any principle of strict parallelism between the internal venue rules and international jurisdiction in the sense that jurisdiction automatically exists if there is an applicable venue rule and jurisdiction does not exist if a venue is lacking.[6] Indeed, the internal venue rules are not to be automatically applied but instead it must be determined in each specific case, taking into consideration the legislative history and the policy objectives underlying each rule and determining whether the rule is relevant in the context of international jurisdiction, which has somewhat different objectives and interests.[7]

As there is no longer a principle of strict parallelism, it is not fatal for the determination of jurisdiction that there is no applicable rule in the Judicial Code that can be applied *ex analogia*. A Swedish interest in the administration of justice can nevertheless exist.[8] More recently, the Supreme Court has focused more on the requirement of a Swedish interest in the administration of justice rather than on applying a provision in the Judicial Code *ex analogia*.[9] The Supreme Court has found international jurisdiction to exist where there was a close connection to Sweden, even when there was no Judicial Code provision that could be analogously applied. For instance, the Supreme Court found that there was international jurisdiction over a dispute where a defendant was sued by a Swedish bank on a guarantee that the defendant had given for a loan to a Swedish limited liability company and the loan agreement otherwise had a strong

while focusing primarily on the field of family law, maintains that the possibility of having a matter decided by a Swedish court is largely seen as a form of community service for the parties and that this service has been offered as soon as there is a practical need or a reasonable interest in the matter being tried by a Swedish court, even if there is in itself a stronger connection to another state.

[4] See eg Högsta domstolen, 15 July 2016, (2016) *NJA* 779, para 7 ('according to established case law, guidance may be sought in the internal Swedish venue rules, primarily Chapter 10 of the Code.').

[5] M Bogdan and M Hellner, *Svensk internationell privat- och processrätt*, 325.

[6] See, in particular S Dennemark, *Om domstols behörighet i internationellt förmögenhetsrättsliga mål*, 61 et seq who demonstrated in his doctoral thesis that strict parallelism does not exist in Swedish law. See also H Eek, *Internationell privaträtt: metod och material* (PA Norstedt & Söners Förlag, 1967) 89 (with references to older legal scholarship maintaining the view of strict parallelism between international jurisdiction and local venue); H Eek, *Lagkonflikter i tvistemål*, 115–16; H Karlgren, *Kortfattad lärobok i internationell privat- och processrätt*, 156; L Pålsson, *Svensk rättspraxis i internationell processrätt*, 48; C Saf, 'Ingen generell analog tillämpning av Bryssel I-förordningen' (2007–2008) *Juridisk Tidskrift vid Stockholms universitet* 920, 921; E Sinander, 'Svenskt rättskipningsintresse', 933; M Bogdan and M Hellner, *Svensk internationell privat- och processrätt*, 326.

[7] See eg C Saf, 'Ingen generell analog tillämpning av Bryssel I-förordningen', 921; E Sinander, 'Svenskt rättskipningsintresse', 936; M Bogdan and M Hellner, *Svensk internationell privat- och processrätt*, 327–28. See also L Lundstedt, 'Jurisdiction and enforcement outside of the Brussels System with a focus on IPR' (2007) 4 *NIR* 348, 353–63 (discussing jurisdiction over foreign intellectual property disputes under Swedish national rules on jurisdiction).

[8] S Dennemark, *Om domstols behörighet i internationellt förmögenhetsrättsliga mål*, 57–58, 63; H Eek, *Lagkonflikter i tvistemål*, 112; E Sinander, 'Svenskt rättskipningsintresse', 936.

[9] E Sinander, 'Svenskt rättskipningsintresse', 933; M Bogdan and M Hellner, *Svensk internationell privat- och processrätt*, 329.

connection to Sweden.[10] The court did not specifically state what the 'strong connection' otherwise consisted of but it can be noted that Swedish law was applicable to the loan agreement and the defendant was a Swedish citizen (albeit with habitual residence in Monaco).[11] This method of making an overall assessment of the facts has been compared to the individualising method which is primarily used to establish applicable law.[12] In other cases, a single but significant connection has been found to be sufficient for international jurisdiction to exist. For instance, the Supreme Court held that it was implicit from the fact that a Swedish trademark was territorially limited to (only) Sweden that the Swedish courts had international jurisdiction over disputes concerning an infringement of Swedish trademarks on the Swedish territory.[13] In another case, the Supreme Court found that the fact that the parties had agreed upon Sweden as the seat of arbitration meant that the Swedish courts had international jurisdiction over a declaratory action to determine the competence of an arbitrator.[14] Bogdan and Hellner are somewhat hesitant about placing too much focus on the nebulous concept of 'an interest in the administration of justice' because it makes jurisdiction under the Swedish rules unpredictable.[15]

(b)

As noted above, the internal venue rules in the Judicial Code may be applied *ex analogia* to transnational disputes. It is not completely clear, however, whether at least some of the rules in the Judicial Code directly determine international jurisdiction and not only local territorial jurisdiction.[16] Indeed, some of the internal venue rules apply specifically to transnational disputes and the legislative history indicates that they were intended to be used as jurisdiction rules as well venue rules.[17] For instance, the rules on *forum*

[10] Högsta domstolen, 15 July 2016, (2016) *NJA* 779.

[11] Högsta domstolen, 15 July 2016, (2016) *NJA* 779, para 1, 14.

[12] C Saf, 'Ingen generell analog tillämpning av Bryssel I-förordningen', 928; E Sinander, 'Svenskt rättskipningsintresse', 939–40; M Bogdan and M Hellner, *Svensk internationell privat- och processrätt*, 455.

[13] Högsta domstolen, 13 November 2015, (2015) *NJA* 798, para 9.

[14] Högsta domstolen, 12 November 2010, (2010) *NJA* 508. See also Högsta domstolen, 18 April 1989, (1989) *NJA* 143 (holding that Swedish jurisdiction existed over a dispute concerning the validity of an arbitral award when the arbitration proceedings took place in Sweden, despite the fact that neither the case nor the parties were connected to Sweden). But see Svea hovrätt (Svea Court of Appeal), 28 February 2005, RH 2005:1 (holding that the Swedish courts did not have international jurisdiction over a dispute concerning the validity of an arbitral award where there was no arbitration agreement designating Sweden as the place of arbitration (although the award itself stated that Sweden was the seat)). According to Art 1(2)(d) Brussels Ia Regulation, arbitration falls outside the scope of the regulation.

[15] M Bogdan and M Hellner, *Svensk internationell privat- och processrätt*, 329.

[16] M Bogdan and M Hellner, *Svensk internationell privat- och processrätt*, 325 (observing that the situation is unclear).

[17] See Chapter 10, Section 1, paragraph 5; Chapter 10, Section 3, paragraph 1 and Chapter 10, Section 4 of the Judicial Code (which are applicable to persons who do not have a known domicile in Sweden and the first rule is applicable to persons who do not have a known domicile anywhere). See also U Maunsbach, 'Kan domännamn utgöra domsrättsgrundande egendom?', 361 (referring to the legislative history); E Sinander, 'Svenskt rättskipningsintresse', 933 ('When the Code of Judicial Procedure was written, the legislator's intention was that the international jurisdiction should follow the local jurisdiction'); M Bogdan and M Hellner, *Svensk internationell privat- och processrätt*, 330–33 (stating that the legislative history indicates that Chapter

arresti and *forum rei sitae* in Chapter 10, Section 3 of the Judicial Code are applicable specifically to persons who do not have a known domicile in Sweden. A few commentators maintain that such rules are directly applicable rules to international jurisdiction and have a double function in that they determine both international jurisdiction and venue.[18] The fact that the rules are directly applicable would suggest that the courts would not need to exercise the same caution that they otherwise exercise when applying rules *ex analogia*.[19] Other commentators maintain, however, that one should not draw far-reaching conclusions from the fact that such rules are applicable to international situations.[20] They maintain that even if a forum exists pursuant to these rules, international jurisdiction may be lacking due to rules on immunity or because the subject matter of the dispute is considered to be of such a nature that a Swedish court would lack jurisdiction (eg validity of a foreign patent).[21] This latter view seems to be the understanding of the Supreme Court, which has repeatedly expressed the view that 'there are no directly applicable legal provisions [on international jurisdiction], and guidance must … be sought in internal Swedish venue rules, primarily Chapter 10 of the Code'.[22] This question does not seem to have much practical significance, however, as even those commentators who maintain that the rules can be directly applied, nevertheless reject a strict parallelism between the venue rules and the rules on international jurisdiction.[23]

(c)

The jurisdictional rules of the Brussels Regime have not been generally extended to non-EU defendants. In 2007, the Supreme Court stated that there was no general principle according to which the jurisdiction rules of the Brussels Regime would apply by analogy to non-EU defendants.[24] That said, the Supreme Court also stated that these rules can constitute an important basis for determining jurisdiction under Swedish law.[25] Indeed, in previous cases, the court has expressed the view that the rules on jurisdiction in the Brussels Regime are internationally accepted rules and has interpreted the Swedish rules on international jurisdiction against the background of the rules in

10, Section 3, paragraph 1 and Chapter 10, Section 4 of the Judicial Code were intended to be used also as rules on jurisdiction).

[18] See in particular C Saf, 'Ingen generell analog tillämpning av Bryssel I-förordningen', 920–30. See also H Karlgren, *Kortfattad lärobok i internationell privat-och processrätt*, 159 (stating that the rule on *forum arresti* in Chapter 10, Section 3 of the Judicial Code is 'a directly applicable international procedural law rule'); U Maunsbach, 'Kan domännamn utgöra domsrättsgrundande egendom?', 361 (stating that the legislative history indicates that the *forum arresti* rule and the *forum rei sitae* in Chapter 10, Section 3 of the Judicial Code are directly applicable rules on jurisdiction).

[19] U Maunsbach, 'Kan domännamn utgöra domsrättsgrundande egendom?', 361–62.

[20] S Dennemark, *Om domstols behörighet i internationellt förmögenhetsrättsliga mål*, 56–58; H Eek, *Internationell privaträtt: metod och material*, 114–15.

[21] S Dennemark, *Om domstols behörighet i internationellt förmögenhetsrättsliga mål*, 57.

[22] Högsta domstolen, 15 July 2016, (2016) *NJA* 779, para 7. This view has also been expressed by the Swedish Labour Court. See Arbetsdomstolen (Swedish Labour Court), 4 October 1995, AD 1995 no°120 ('The domestic Swedish rules on international jurisdiction have not been codified by statute but are based on case law').

[23] See C Saf, 'Ingen generell analog tillämpning av Bryssel I-förordningen', 921.

[24] Högsta domstolen, 15 June 2007, (2007) *NJA* 482.

[25] Högsta domstolen, 15 June 2007, (2007) *NJA* 482.

the Brussels Regime.[26] For instance, in one case the Supreme Court reasoned that the fact that the rule in the Lugano Convention on exclusive jurisdiction over proceedings concerned with the registration or validity of foreign patents did not encompass disputes concerning the right to a foreign patent application supported the argument that a Swedish court would not either lack jurisdiction over such a dispute pursuant to its national Swedish rules.[27] In another case, the court found that the fact that the Lugano Convention does not accept jurisdiction based on the place of contracting (*forum contractus*) supported a restrictive application of the Swedish rule in Chapter 10, Section 4 of the Judicial Code on the place of contracting.[28] In addition, in a case before the Labour Court, that court applied *ex analogia* the rule on jurisdiction over individual employment contracts that exists in both the Brussels and Lugano Conventions in a dispute where these conventions were not directly applicable because Sweden was bound by the Lugano Convention but not by the Brussels Convention, and Denmark was bound by the Brussels Convention but not by the Lugano Convention.[29]

The Supreme Court declined, however, to apply *ex analogia* the rule in the Brussels Regime on jurisdiction in matters relating to insurance.[30] First, the court found that it was doubtful whether the plaintiff fell within the rule's personal scope of application because the plaintiff was not the original policy holder and was not a weak party. The court also stated that the rule was designed primarily for standard insurance contracts and not the type of contract in the case at hand. In addition, the court stated that it was necessary to take into consideration (when considering an analogous application of the rules in the Brussels Regime) that the Brussels Regime not only contains provisions on jurisdiction but also provisions on the recognition and enforcement of judgments with the objective of facilitating the functioning of the common market. Thus, the court found that the special rule on jurisdiction in insurance disputes in the Brussels Regime could not be applied *ex analogia* in this case.

In a case concerning jurisdiction over an action for recovery brought by a Swedish bankruptcy estate against a Norwegian company, the court found that there was Swedish jurisdiction despite a lack of support in the Judicial Code.[31] The court rejected the proposition that the EU Insolvency Regulation could generally provide support for Swedish jurisdiction in relation to non-EU states. The court observed that the purpose of the Insolvency Regulation is to ensure efficient and flexible insolvency proceedings in order to facilitate the proper functioning of the internal market. The court noted further that the Insolvency Regulation contains provisions on jurisdiction, rules on the recognition and enforcement of judgments, and on applicable law. In this specific case, however, the court found that the reasons underlying the Insolvency Regulation justified Swedish

[26] See Högsta domstolen, 23 February 1994, (1994) *NJA* 81; (2001) *NJA* 800. See also Arbetsdomstolen, 4 October 1995, AD 1995 no°120.

[27] Högsta domstolen, 23 February 1994, (1994) *NJA* 81.

[28] Högsta domstolen, 28 November 2001, (2001) *NJA* 800. The court found, however, that the rule in Chapter 10, Section 4 of the Judicial Code could be applied in this specific case.

[29] Arbetsdomstolen, 4 October 1995, AD 1995 no°120 (Labour Court).

[30] Högsta domstolen, 15 June 2007, (2007) *NJA* 482.

[31] Högsta domstolen, 31 January 2013, (2013) *NJA* 22. Pursuant to Art 1(2)(b), bankruptcy and analogous proceedings are outside the scope of Brussels Ia.

jurisdiction in the case because Norway was part of the EU's internal market, there was a Nordic treaty pursuant to which Nordic rules on jurisdiction would be respected and Nordic judgments would be recognised and enforceable, and Swedish law would be applicable to the recovery action.[32]

In general, scholars are positive to the possibility of extending the personal scope of jurisdiction rules in the Brussels Regime to non-EU defendants.[33] For instance, Maunsbach maintains that the rules in the Brussels Regime are more appropriate than the rules in the Judicial Code because the rules in the Brussels Regime are based on generally accepted principles and are therefore more likely to be enforced abroad.[34] Linton suggests that the rules in the Brussels Regime may be a more appropriate basis for analogies than the rules in the Judicial Code because the former are explicitly designed to deal with international situations, whereas most of the rules in the Code only deal with domestic situations.[35] That said, scholars observe that when considering an analogous application of the rules in the Brussels Regime, one needs to consider the interests and policies underlying Swedish international jurisdiction and not the policies underlying the Brussels Regime.[36] In particular, there is a need for additional rules not existing in the Brussels Regime.

The prevailing view is that the rules in the Brussels Regime should not limit the courts from applying the rules in the Judicial Code *ex analogia* in situations where the rules in the Brussels Regime do not have an applicable rule.[37] In particular, scholars note that in light of the fact that Sweden has a restrictive view on the enforcement of foreign judgments (outside of the Brussels Regime), the rules in the Judicial Code, not least the rule on *forum arresti*, should continue to play a role.[38] Maunsbach, for instance,

[32] See also Högsta domstolen, 31 January 2013, (2013) *NJA* 31 (finding no support in the Insolvency Regulation in this case where the defendants were from St. Kitts and Nevis. Sweden does not have any international treaties with these States on the recognition and enforcement of judgments. The Court ultimately found that there was Swedish jurisdiction, although it is not at all clear which, if any rule in the Judicial Code it applied or on what connection to Sweden the jurisdiction was based). See M Bogdan, 'Svensk och EU-domstolens rättspraxis i internationell privat- och processrätt 2015–2016' (2017) *SvJT* 521, 618.

[33] See U Maunsbach, 'Kan domännamn utgöra domsrättsgrundande egendom?', (2002) 4 *Nordiskt immateriellt rättsskydd* 357, 359–62; M Bogdan, 'Användning av allmänt förmögenhetsforum med avseende på papperslösa aktier i svenska aktiebolag' (2005) *Juridisk Tidskrift vid Stockholms universitet* 674, 675–76; U Maunsbach, *Svensk domstols behörighet vid gränsöverskridande varumärkestvister – särskilt om Internetrelaterade intrång*, 206–208; C Saf, 'Ingen generell analog tillämpning av Bryssel I-förordningen', 929; M Linton, *Konsumentens skydd i handels över landsgränserna* (Iustus Förlag, 2013) 45–46.

[34] U Maunsbach, *Svensk domstols behörighet vid gränsöverskridande varumärkestvister – särskilt om Internetrelaterade intrång*, 206–08.

[35] M Linton, Konsumentens skydd i handels över landsgränserna, 45.

[36] C Saf, 'Ingen generell analog tillämpning av Bryssel I-förordningen', 922.

[37] U Maunsbach, *Svensk domstols behörighet vid gränsöverskridande varumärkestvister – särskilt om Internetrelaterade intrång* (Juridiska fakulteten Lund, 2005) 361; P Lindskoug, *Domsrätt och lagval vid elektronisk handel* (Juridiska fakulteten Lund, 2004) 77; M Bogdan, 'Användning av allmänt förmögenhetsforum med avseende på papperslösa aktier i svenska aktiebolag', 675–76; C Saf, 'Ingen generell analog tillämpning av Bryssel I-förordningen', 929–30 (maintaining that the rule in Art 7(1)(b) could be applied by analogy. Saf observes that the Swedish legislator had rejected the *locus solutionis* rule in favour of the locus contractus rule in 10:4 of the Judicial Code because it believed there could be difficulties trying to determine the place of performance. She maintains that *locus solutionis* in Art 7(1)(b) is hardly more arbitrary or difficult to apply than the locus contractus rule.); M Bogdan and M Hellner, *Svensk internationell privat- och processrätt*, 328–29. Cf E Sinander, 'Svenskt rättskipningsintresse' (maintaining that the *locus contractus* rule is nowadays obsolete and unsuitable to apply *ex analogia* to determine the jurisdiction).

[38] M Bogdan and M Hellner, *Svensk internationell privat- och processrätt*, 328–29; E Sinander, 'Svenskt rättskipningsintresse', 938.

maintains therefore that the Brussels Regime rules should be applied first if possible, and only if there is no relevant rule in the Brussels Regime, that the rules in the Code be applied *ex analogia*, albeit with some caution.[39]

In contrast, Pålsson maintains that it would be 'appropriate and desirable' if the Swedish jurisdiction rules (as well as the corresponding rules in the other Member States and Contracting States) were adapted as far as possible to the rules on jurisdiction in the Brussels Regime.[40] He argues that the Brussels Regime rules should not only be used to expand national jurisdiction rules but also to restrict them.[41] In particular, Pålsson is critical of the use of the rule on *forum arresti* in cases where the property on which jurisdiction is based does not have any market value.[42] In one specific case, he criticised the Supreme Court for holding that jurisdiction could be based on property that had been used to secure a debt when the value of the debt significantly exceeded the value of the property.[43] Still, many scholars who are in favour of maintaining the rule nonetheless maintain that it should be interpreted in light of its objective of facilitating the enforcement of the judgment.[44] This view is also reflected in the Supreme Court's more recent case law.[45]

(d)

Pursuant to Art 76(1) Brussels Ia, the Member States are to notify the Commission of their national rules on jurisdiction, which, due to the Brussels Regime, may not be used against persons domiciled in the EU. The list contains rules that are generally considered to be exorbitant, and therefore '[i]n particular' are not applicable against such persons.[46] Sweden has notified the rule on *forum arresti* in Chapter 10, Section 3, first sentence, to the Commission. This rule is described in question 3 below. Sweden has not notified the Commission of any other rules.

Sweden has a few other rules on international jurisdiction that do not have any corresponding rule in the Brussels Regime, namely, *forum contractus*, *forum rei sitae* and *forum deprehensionis*. Of these rules, the rule on *forum contractus* is considered by at least one scholar to be exorbitant.[47]

[39] U Maunsbach, 'Kan domännamn utgöra domsrättsgrundande egendom?', 361.

[40] L Pålsson, *Bryssel I-förordningen jämte Bryssel och Luganokonventionerna* 2nd edn (Norstedts Juridik, 2008) 73.

[41] L Pålsson, 'Svensk rättspraxis: Internationell privat- och processrätt 1996–2000' (2001) *Svensk Juristtidning* 770, 796 (maintaining that because these are internationally accepted rules, they should 'rub off' ('smittoeffekt') on the interpretation of the Swedish rules).

[42] L Pålsson, 'Svensk rättspraxis: Internationell privat- och processrätt, 770, 796 (criticising the Supreme Court in (1999) *NJA* 16).

[43] (1999) *NJA* 16.

[44] E Sinander, 'Svenskt rättskipningsintresse', 937; M Bogdan and M Hellner, *Svensk internationell privat- och processrätt*, 332.

[45] Högsta domstolen, 15 July 2016, (2016) *NJA* 779, para 10 ('If the only connection to Sweden is that the defendant has an asset here that is of such limited value that in practice it is irrelevant from the point of view of execution, Swedish jurisdiction should not be considered to exist.').

[46] Art 5(2) Brussels Ia Regulation.

[47] See H Karlgren, *Kortfattad lärobok i internationell privat-och processrätt*, 160.

The *forum rei sitae* rule on international jurisdiction is based on the venue rule in Chapter 10, Section 3, second sentence, of the Judicial Code. This venue rule is explicitly applicable to international situations. Pursuant to this rule, for disputes concerning movable property, a person who does not have a known domicile within the realm may be sued where the property is located. This rule is not generally considered to be exorbitant because it is limited to disputes that directly concern the property that forms the basis for jurisdiction. In more recent history, the rule was successfully invoked to obtain jurisdiction over a United States company in a negative declaratory action alleging that the plaintiff's activity would not fall within the scope of the US company's European patent with effect in Sweden.[48]

The rule on the *forum deprehensionis* is described below in question 3 and the rule on *forum contractus* is described below in question 5a.

Sweden does not have any rules of jurisdiction referred to in Art 6(2) Brussels Ia nor any rules on third party notice as referred to in Art 65. The list of Conventions referred to in Art 69 is complete.

Question 2

There is no directly applicable statutory definition of domicile for jurisdictional purposes in matters regulated by the Brussels Ia Regulation. There is a statutory definition of domicile for natural persons in the area of family law that is used by analogy for these matters.[49] Pursuant to this definition, 'a person who is resident in a particular state shall be deemed to be domiciled there, if the residence may be considered permanent with regard to the duration of the stay and the circumstances in general'.[50] The concept of domicile under Swedish law is made up of an objective component, that the person is actually resident in Sweden, and a subjective component, that the person has an intention to remain there.[51] The subjective component is tested, however, against an objective standard of what an average person's intentions would be in the same situation taking into consideration all the relevant circumstances, such as place of residence, employment, family situation, etc.[52] There is a statutory definition of domicile in the Judicial Code that determines the proper venue.[53] This rule states: 'When the defendant has civil

[48] Högsta domstolen, June 2006, (2006) *NJA* 354.

[49] M Bogdan and M Hellner, *Svensk internationell privat- och processrätt*, 131–32. See also P Lindskoug, *Domsrätt och lagval vid elektronisk handel*, 43; E Sinander, *Internationell kollektivavtalsreglering: En studie i internationell privaträtt av den svenska modellen för reglering av anställningsvillkor*, 115. For an in-depth discussion of the Swedish definition of domicile in the area of family law see K Örtenhed, *Bosättningsanknytningar i gränsöverskridande familjerättsförhållanden: En internationellt privat- och processrättslig studie* (Iustus Förlag 2006) 166–252.

[50] See Chapter 7, Section 2 Act (No 26 of 1904) on Certain International Legal Relations Concerning Marriage and Guardianship) (*Lag* (1904:26 s.1) *om vissa internationella rättsförhållanden rörande äktenskap och förmynderskap*); Chapter 6, Section 2 of the Act (No 234 of 2019) on Spouses' and Cohabitants' Property Relations in International Situations (*Lag* (2019:234) *om makars och sambors förmögenhetsförhållanden i internationella situationer*).

[51] M Bogdan and M Hellner, *Svensk internationell privat- och processrätt*, 132; Örtenhed 173.

[52] M Bogdan and M Hellner, *Svensk internationell privat- och processrätt*, 133–34.

[53] Chapter 10, Section 1, paragraph 2 Judicial Code.

registration in Sweden, the place where he was registered on the first of November of the preceding year shall be considered to be his residence'. This rule is, however, not determinative of jurisdiction, although it may be one of several factors to consider.[54] Unlike in the field of family law, the definition of domicile for natural persons does not seemed to have given rise to difficulties in practice.[55]

For legal persons, the courts have been guided by the definition of domicile in the Judicial Code:[56] 'A corporation, partnership, cooperative, association or similar society, foundation or similar institution is considered to reside at the place where the board has its seat or, if the board has no permanent seat or there is no board, at the place from which the administration is carried out. This rule also applies to municipalities or similar public authority'.[57] Lindskoug maintains that the definition of domicile in the Brussels Regime should be applied by analogy instead of the definition in the Judicial Code in order to avoid 'incoherence' between the two rules.[58] As the Brussels Regime supplies its own EU autonomous definition of domicile for legal persons, the Swedish definition is relevant only for matters outside the scope of the Brussels Regime.[59]

Question 3

Sweden has a rule on *forum arresti* that is based on an application *ex analogia* of the venue rule in Chapter 10, Section 3, first sentence of the Judicial Code. This rule states: 'In disputes concerning debt obligations, a person with no known residence in the Realm may be sued where property he owns is located'. Three criteria must be satisfied for the rule to apply: the dispute concerns a debt obligation; the defendant is domiciled outside of Sweden (and States bound by the Brussels Regime); and the defendant owns property that is located in Sweden. The justification for the rule is to provide a creditor with an opportunity to sue a debtor at the place where the property is located so that the judgment can be directly enforced against that property.[60] Jurisdiction in Sweden is necessary in order to obtain an enforceable judgment in light of the fact that Sweden does not enforce foreign judgments coming from states outside of the Brussels Regime.

Concerning the first criterion, the dispute must concern a debt obligation. The debt obligation may be contractual or have arisen through tort or delict.[61] The debt obligation

[54] M Bogdan and M Hellner, *Svensk internationell privat- och processrätt*, 133 (with further references). See also L Pålsson, *Svensk rättspraxis i internationell processrätt*, 57 (stating that it is not relevant); P Lindskoug, *Domsrätt och lagval vid elektronisk handel*, 44; M Linton, Konsumentens skydd i handels över landsgränserna, 94–96.

[55] L Pålsson, *Svensk rättspraxis i internationell processrätt*, 58. Judging from the paucity of case law in this area, it seems that the situation has not changed much since Pålsson made his statement in 1989.

[56] L Pålsson, *Svensk rättspraxis i internationell processrätt*, 59; P Lindskoug, *Domsrätt och lagval vid elektronisk handel*, 50–53.

[57] Chapter 10, Section 1, para 3 Judicial Code.

[58] P Lindskoug, *Domsrätt och lagval vid elektronisk handel*, 50–53.

[59] See Article 63 Brussels Ia Regulation. See U Maunsbach, *Svensk domstols behörighet vid gränsöverskridande varumärkestvister – särskilt om Internetrelaterade intrång*, 208–09 (stating that the Swedish rule on domicile for legal persons has 'played out its role' for matters regulated by the Brussels Regime).

[60] S Dennemark, *Om domstols behörighet i internationellt förmögenhetsrättsliga mål*, 145–46 (discussing the legislative history).

[61] S Dennemark, *Om domstols behörighet i internationellt förmögenhetsrättsliga mål*, 149.

can have arisen in Sweden or abroad. Disputes concerning property ownership or the possibility of obtaining an injunction (eg to stop the use of a patented invention), are outside the scope of the rule.[62] In addition, the prevailing view is that negative declaratory actions concerning debt obligations are outside the scope of the rule.[63]

Concerning the second criterion, it is explicit from the text of the rule that the defendant must be domiciled outside of Sweden as the venue rule was specifically designed to apply in international cases. This rule may not be applied if the defendant is domiciled in States bound by the Brussels Regime. The question whether the defendant is domiciled in Sweden will be determined under Swedish law as discussed above in question 2. The question whether the defendant is domiciled in a Member State or contracting state will be determined pursuant to that state's national law.[64] The domicile of the plaintiff is not relevant and neither is the nationality of any of the parties.

Concerning the third criterion, the connecting factor is the presence of the defendant's property in Sweden. Any kind of property having a market value – tangible or intangible – can be a basis for jurisdiction.[65] There is no absolute minimum value but the property must have more than mere symbolic value.[66] In a fairly recent case, the Supreme Court held that a bank account with 888 crowns (approximately 89 euros) could not be the basis for jurisdiction over a dispute concerning debt of 40 million crowns (approximately 4 million euros) because the value was so limited that it had no practice significance from enforcement perspective.[67] In addition, the court observed that the value was insignificant in relation to the value of the debt.[68]

Is not clear whether a defendant's private, personal property can form a basis for jurisdiction.[69] The reason for this is that this type of property may be exempt from seizure and therefore the judgment will not be able to be enforced against it, which is the justification for the rule.[70] In one case, the Supreme Court held that a Swedish court could not base jurisdiction on property that the defendant had with him for his personal use during a temporary stay in Sweden.[71] Bogdan and Hellner observe however that exemptions for private, personal property are taken into consideration later on at the

[62] S Dennemark, *Om domstols behörighet i internationellt förmögenhetsrättsliga mål*, 149.

[63] S Dennemark, *Om domstols behörighet i internationellt förmögenhetsrättsliga mål*, 148–52; M Bogdan and M Hellner, *Svensk internationell privat- och processrätt*, 331.

[64] See Article 62(2) Brussels Ia; Article 59(2) Lugano Convention.

[65] S Dennemark, *Om domstols behörighet i internationellt förmögenhetsrättsliga mål*, 153 (referring to the legislative history). See U Maunsbach, 'Kan domännamn utgöra domsrättsgrundande egendom?', 2002 (concluding that a domain name can be a basis for jurisdiction, provided it is 'located' in Sweden).

[66] See eg Högsta domstolen, 15 September 1988, (1988) *NJA* 440 (holding that a bill of lading for goods that had already been delivered lacked market value); Högsta domstolen, 10 June 1998, (1998) *NJA* 361 (holding that an unprivileged claim in bankruptcy could found jurisdiction unless the defendant can show that the claim is obviously worthless because there will not be any distribution); Högsta domstolen, 30 December 2010, (2010) *NJA* 734 (holding that the fact that the value of the asset that formed the basis for jurisdiction depended on the outcome of the claim did not prevent that asset from being a basis for jurisdiction, where the action does not appear to be unfounded).

[67] Högsta domstolen, 15 July 2016, (2016) *NJA* 779, para 10.

[68] Högsta domstolen, 15 July 2016, (2016) *NJA* 779, para 11.

[69] M Bogdan and M Hellner, *Svensk internationell privat- och processrätt*, 332–33.

[70] See S Dennemark, *Om domstols behörighet i internationellt förmögenhetsrättsliga mål*, 158.

[71] Högsta domstolen, 15 February 1981, (1981) *NJA* 386.

enforcement stage, and by then, the circumstances that may potentially have given rise to the exemption may have changed.[72]

Questions can arise concerning the localisation of, in particular, intangible property. The Judicial Code explicitly states that negotiable instruments are located where the instrument is kept, non-negotiable claims are located where the debtor resides, and if a debt is secured by property, the place where that property is kept may be deemed to be the location of the debt.[73]

In one case, the Supreme Court held that shares in a Swedish limited liability company could not be the basis for jurisdiction in Sweden.[74] The company had not issued any physical certificates for the shares. Instead, the shares were registered in a share account, which as the court observed, is the norm today for publicly traded shares. The court found that the rule on non-negotiable instruments, which would have supported jurisdiction in Sweden at the location of the Swedish company (the debtor), was not applicable because account-based shares were by definition negotiable. The court also declined to localise the account-based shares at the place where the account was managed and where changes could be made in the registration because this would subject many persons to Swedish jurisdiction who had not been so in the past. The court stated that such a drastic change would have to be made by the legislator.

Professor Bogdan has criticised this decision because he claims that it creates an 'asset asylum' for such shares, which may represent considerable value.[75] He explains that as a result of the decision, the plaintiff cannot sue in Sweden, even though the shares could be seized here. Even though the plaintiff can most likely sue in the country where the defendant is domiciled, Bogdan observes that that judgment cannot be enforced against the shares there (because they can only be seized in Sweden) and the foreign judgment cannot be enforced in Sweden either because Sweden does not enforce third state judgments.

Questions may arise also concerning the localisation of intellectual property rights. A prerequisite for localisation is that the intellectual property right is capable of being seized.[76] Assuming that seizure is possible, Swedish intellectual property rights should be localised in Sweden, ie, the country of protection.[77] EU intellectual property rights are likely to be localised in Sweden if the right holder has its domicile, or failing that, an establishment in Sweden.[78] Domain names are likely localised in Sweden if they are administered and controlled from Sweden.[79]

[72] M Bogdan and M Hellner, *Svensk internationell privat- och processrätt*, 333.

[73] Chapter 10, Section 3, paragraph 2.

[74] Högsta domstolen, 30 december 2004, (2004) *NJA* 891.

[75] M Bogdan, 'Användning av allmänt förmögenhetsforum med avseende på papperlösa aktier i svenska aktiebolag', (2004/05) 3 *Juridisk tidskrift* 674, 676–79.

[76] M Bogdan and M Hellner, *Svensk internationell privat- och processrätt*, 414. See also M Levin and Å Hellstadius, *Lärobok i immaterialrätt* (Norstedts Juridik, 2019) 122, 304, 375, 446 (stating that patents, designs and trademarks are capable of being seized, but that the possibility to seize copyright is more limited).

[77] Högsta domstolen, June 2006, (2006) *NJA* 354 (holding that a European patent that is valid for Sweden was located in Sweden); M Bogdan and M Hellner, *Svensk internationell privat- och processrätt*, 414.

[78] See Art 27 Regulation No 6/2002; Art 19 Regulation 2017/1001; Art 7 Regulation No 1257/2012.

[79] See U Maunsbach, 'Kan domännamn utgöra domsrättsgrundande egendom?', 377–78. See also Högsta domstolen, 21 December 2017, (2017) *NJA* 1070 (holding that a domain name that was administered and controlled by The Swedish Internet Foundation (*Stiftelsen för Internetinfrastruktur*) could be confiscated because it was used in aid of a crime).

Another rule on general jurisdiction is the *forum deprehensionis* rule based on Chapter 10, Section 1, fifth paragraph of the Judicial Code. This rule states: 'A person with no known residence in or outside Sweden may be sued at the place where he is sojourning (ie temporality staying). If he is a Swedish citizen and sojourning outside the Realm or at an unknown place, he may be sued at the place within the Realm where he last resided or sojourned'. Two criteria must be satisfied for the rule to apply: the defendant's residence must be unknown; the defendant must be sojourning in Sweden. If the defendant is a Swedish citizen, the defendant may be sued at the place where he last resided or sojourned, even if he is not sojourning there at the time the case is filed. This rule overlaps partly with the rules on jurisdiction in the Brussels Regime and will not be applicable if the defendant is an EU citizen who had their last known domicile in a Member State.[80]

The Swedish courts do not apply the doctrine of *forum non conveniens*, at least not in the traditional sense.[81] Some Swedish legal scholarship equates, however, the analysis concerning whether there is a basis for jurisdiction because an interest in the administration of justice exists, with the doctrine of *forum non conveniens*, whereby a court having jurisdiction over a case may dismiss it because the convenience of the parties and the interest of justice would be better served if the case were brought in another forum.[82] That said, it is not apparent from the Supreme Court's case law that a court should balance the public and private interests to arrive at a conclusion whether a foreign forum would be a more appropriate, but the court has focused instead on whether the requirements for Swedish jurisdiction exist in the first place.[83]

Question 4

There is no statutory rule on *forum necessitatis*. Nevertheless, the Supreme Court has approved the exercise of jurisdiction to avoid *déni de justice*, at least when the dispute has some connection to Sweden. In a case concerning a dispute between two persons domiciled in Sweden about the ownership of buildings located in Åland, one of the parties had previously sued the other in Finland but the case was dismissed for lack of jurisdiction.[84] In Finland, buildings on freehold land are not equated with immovable property for the purpose of jurisdiction. Finland does not therefore claim exclusive jurisdiction over these cases and the general rules on jurisdiction apply. Pursuant to Swedish rules, however, a Swedish court would not normally have jurisdiction over a dispute concerning the ownership of a building on freehold land situated abroad because they are equated with immovable property for the purpose of jurisdiction.[85] The Supreme

[80] See C-327/10 *Hypoteční banka*; C-292/10 *G*.

[81] See L Pålsson, *Svensk rättspraxis i internationell processrätt*, 54–56; C Saf, 'Brysselkonventionens tillämpningsområde', (2005/06) 1 *Juridisk Tidskrift JT* 158, 164.

[82] S Dennemark, *Om domstols behörighet i internationellt förmögenhetsrättsliga mål*, 67, 173–78, 190; H Eek, *Lagkonflikter i tvistemål*, 118–19; M Bogdan and M Hellner, *Svensk internationell privat- och processrätt*, 330.

[83] C Saf, 'Brysselkonventionens tillämpningsområde', 164.

[84] Högsta domstolen, 12 May 1985, (1985) *NJA* 832.

[85] Chapter 10, Section 10, 12 of the Judicial Code.

Court reasoned, however, that an exception could be made in this case in order to fulfil the parties' need for an enforceable judgment and to avoid *déni de justice*. Sinander maintains that the fact that the plaintiff does not have access to court will usually satisfy the requirement of an interest in the administration of justice in Sweden.[86] He notes that if the case has some minimum connection to Sweden, Sweden might be obligated under international law to exercise jurisdiction over the case.[87] Eek maintains that Sweden might have jurisdiction even if it is not obligated under international law.[88]

Question 5

(a)

Sweden has a rule on international jurisdiction that is based on an application *ex analogia* of the *forum contractus* venue rule in Chapter 10, Section 4 of the Judicial Code. Section 4 states: 'A person with no known residence within the Realm who has entered into an obligation or otherwise incurred a debt in the Realm may be sued in a dispute concerning the same at the place where the obligation was created or the debt incurred'. Three criteria must be satisfied for this rule to apply: the defendant is domiciled outside of Sweden (and States bound by the Brussels Regime); the obligation was entered into or the debt was incurred in Sweden; and the dispute concerns this obligation or debt.

Concerning the first criterion, it is explicitly stated that the defendant must not be domiciled in Sweden as the venue rule was specifically designed to apply in international cases. Whether the defendant is domiciled in Sweden will be determined under Swedish law as discussed above in question 2. Whether the defendant is domiciled in a Member State or contracting state will be determined pursuant to that state's national law.[89] The domicile of the plaintiff is not relevant and neither is the nationality of any of the parties.

Unlike the rule on *forum arresti*, this rule is not limited to monetary debt obligations (arising from contractual or non-contractual claims) but also covers disputes about the transfer of ownership or a security interest in property and declaratory judgments about the existence of an obligation.[90] A prerequisite for the rule's application is that the obligation was created or the debt was incurred 'within the realm'. The Supreme Court has interpreted this criterion strictly so as not to cover obligations and debts created or incurred via letter, fax, e-mail, or telephone.[91] The rule was designed to cover those

[86] E Sinander, 'Svenskt rättskipningsintresse', 939. See also S Dennemark, *Om domstols behörighet i internationellt förmögenhetsrättsliga mål*, 176; H Eek, *Lagkonflikter i tvistemål*, 121–22.

[87] E Sinander, 'Svenskt rättskipningsintresse', 939 (with further references).

[88] H Eek, *Lagkonflikter i tvistemål*, 121–22.

[89] See Art 62(2) Brussels Ia; Art 59(2) Lugano Convention.

[90] S Dennemark, *Om domstols behörighet i internationellt förmögenhetsrättsliga mål*, 189–190; M Bogdan and M Hellner, *Svensk internationell privat- och processrätt*, 334.

[91] M Larsson, *Konsumentskyddet över gränserna- särskilt inom EU: En studie i internationell privat- och processrätt*, 120 (stating that it is likely that contracts entered into via internet will be treated the same way); M Bogdan and M Hellner, *Svensk internationell privat- och processrätt*, 333–34 (with further references).

situations where a foreign defendant or its authorised agent actually visits Sweden.[92] The Supreme Court has held that an obligation is considered entered into in Sweden even if the authorised agent of the foreign defendant has left the country before their offer was accepted by the Swedish party.[93] Due to the rule's restrictive interpretation, it does not have much practical application today.

The scope of application for this rule partially overlaps with the scope of application of rule in Art 7(1) Brussels Ia in that both cover disputes about contractual obligations. The Swedish rule is broader as it covers also non-contractual obligations. Importantly, the two rules utilise different connecting factors. The connecting factor for Art 7(1) Brussels Ia is the place of performance of the obligation in question whereas the connecting factor for the Swedish rule is the place where the obligation was created or the debt incurred.

As noted above, in interpreting the Swedish rule, the Supreme Court has referred to the Brussels Regime and the fact that it rejects such a rule as a reason to interpret the Swedish rule restrictively.[94]

(b)

Sweden has a rule on international jurisdiction that is based on an application *ex analogia* of the *forum delicti* venue rule in Chapter 10, Section 8 of the Judicial Code.[95] Section 8 states:

> An action regarding injurious actions may be instituted in the court at the place where the act was done or the injury occurred. When the act was done or the injury occurred in two or more court districts, the action may be instituted in any of those districts.

Two criteria must be satisfied for the rule to apply: the action must concern an injurious action; and the act or its effect must take place/occur in Sweden. It is not necessary for the application of the rule that the defendant is domiciled outside of Sweden. As noted, this venue rule was not specifically designed with international cases in mind. The domicile of the plaintiff is not relevant and neither is the nationality of any of the parties.

The scope of application of the Swedish rule is actions 'regarding' injurious actions, which indicates that it is not limited to actions against the person causing the damage.[96] Like Art 7(2) Brussels Ia, the Swedish rule may cover third parties, such as insurance companies who may be liable for the damage.[97] Unlike Art 7(2) Brussels Ia, however, the

[92] L Pålsson, *Svensk rättspraxis i internationell processrätt*, 77; M Bogdan and M Hellner, *Svensk internationell privat- och processrätt*, 334.

[93] Högsta domstolen, 28 November 2001, (2001) *NJA* 800.

[94] Högsta domstolen, 28 November 2001, (2001) NJA 800.

[95] S Dennemark, *Om domstols behörighet i internationellt förmögenhetsrättsliga mål*, 191–93; H Eek, *Lagkonflikter i tvistemål*, 114; L Pålsson, *Svensk rättspraxis i internationell processrätt*, 82; M Bogdan and M Hellner, *Svensk internationell privat- och processrätt*, 334–35.

[96] See L Pålsson, *Svensk rättspraxis i internationell processrätt*, 82; U Maunsbach, *Svensk domstols behörighet vid gränsöverskridande varumärkestvister – särskilt om Internetrelaterade intrång*, 242; M Bogdan and M Hellner, *Svensk internationell privat- och processrätt*, 334–35.

[97] See Högsta domstolen, 9 July 2019, (2019) *NJA* 622 (holding that the district court in the place where the damaging act was committed or the damage occurred was competent to try a case for compensation under the Traffic Injuries Act, even if the action is brought against the plaintiff's own traffic insurance company).

Swedish rule does not explicitly state that it is applicable to preventive actions concerning damage that 'may occur' nor is there any support in the legislative history or the legal scholarship for interpreting the Swedish rule to cover such actions. Maunsbach argues that support for preventive actions should be based on Art 7(2) Brussels Ia *ex analogia*.[98] Unlike Art 7(2) Brussels Ia, it is not clear whether the Swedish rule may possibly encompass claims for contractual damages.[99] The view expressed in the legal scholarship is that it is limited to non-contractual damages.[100] In a case before a court of appeal, however, the court held that claims for contractual damages were covered by the rule.[101] The court found that the wording 'actions regarding injurious action' gave no indication that the scope of the provision would be limited to only non-contractual claims for damages and that there was nothing in the case law or legislative history to support an application contrary to its wording and that the legal scholarship did not discuss this question in depth. This case involved the direct application of the venue rule. Thus, it may not be indicative of how the courts will interpret the rule *ex analogia* for the purpose of international jurisdiction.

The connecting factor for the Swedish rule is either 'where the act was done' or where 'the injury occurred'. Unlike the rule in Art 7(2) Brussels Ia, it is explicit from the provision that it contains two alternative connecting factors, ie the act or the damage.[102] The Supreme Court has not yet interpreted these connecting factors for the purpose of jurisdiction. Maunsbach maintains that it is likely the court will interpret the damage head in the same way that the CJEU has interpreted Art 7(2) Brussels Ia to be limited to damage arising in Sweden.[103] It is submitted that the Supreme Court should also interpret the act head similarly to the case law of the CJEU to cover all damage arising from the injurious act, that is, even damage occurring outside of Sweden.[104]

In a case concerning the application of the rule for venue purposes concerning copyright infringement on the internet, a court of appeal found that economic damage may be considered to have occurred in the venue where the plaintiff had his assets, which the court assumed was where the claimant was domiciled.[105] This is in contrast to established CJEU case law, where the CJEU has held that damage to the claimant's financial assets is not a basis for jurisdiction.[106] In addition, the CJEU has specifically held that damage arising from an infringement of copyright on the internet occurs where the website is accessible within the court's territorial jurisdiction and that court has jurisdiction only to rule on the damage caused in the Member State within which the court

[98] U Maunsbach, *Svensk domstols behörighet vid gränsöverskridande varumärkestvister – särskilt om Internetrelaterade intrång*, 244.

[99] Concerning the delineation between Art 7(1) and Art 7(2) Brussels Ia see eg Case *Wikingerhof*, C-59/19, paras 32–33.

[100] See S Dennemark, *Om domstols behörighet i internationellt förmögenhetsrättsliga mål*, 191-192; L Pålsson, *Svensk rättspraxis i internationell processrätt*, 82; M Bogdan and M Hellner, *Svensk internationell privat- och processrätt*, 334.

[101] See Svea hovrätt (Svea Court of Appeal), 13 April 2010, RH 2010: 21.

[102] Cf Case 21-76 *Bier*; Case C-68/93 *Shevill*.

[103] U Maunsbach, *Svensk domstols behörighet vid gränsöverskridande varumärkestvister – särskilt om Internetrelaterade intrång*, 243.

[104] See L Lundstedt, *Territoriality in Intellectual Property Law* (Stockholm University, 2016) 171–73.

[105] Svea hovrätt (Svea Court of Appeal), 18 October 2007, RH 2007:54.

[106] See Case C-364/93 *Marinari/Lloyd's Bank*.

is situated.[107] That said, due to the different interests and policies involved when determining venue as compared to international jurisdiction, and not least the principle of territoriality of IP rights that refers to the country of protection, it is submitted that this part of the decision would not be indicative of how a Swedish court would rule when it comes to international jurisdiction. Similar to the case law of the CJEU, however, the court in this case held that damage to the claimant's moral rights occurred in the place where the plaintiff was habitually resident and had his main circle of acquaintances.[108]

(c)

As a general rule, Sweden does not have a rule on international jurisdiction based on a close connection between defendants. The prevailing view in the Swedish legal scholarship is that the provision on multiple defendants in Chapter 10, Section 14, first sentence, of the Judicial Code cannot be used as a rule on international jurisdiction and there must be an independent basis for jurisdiction over the foreign defendant.[109] Section 14, first sentence states: 'Claims based on essentially the same ground against several defendants, when brought simultaneously, may be instituted in the court in which any defendant is required to respond under the preceding provisions in this chapter'. Three criteria must be satisfied for the rule to apply: the court must be the proper venue for the claim against at least one of the defendants, the claims against the other defendant(s) must be based on essentially the same ground, and the claims must be brought simultaneously.

Chapter 10, Section 14 of the Judicial Code, like Art 8(1) Brussels Ia, deals with cumulation of claims against two or more defendants. Unlike Art 8(1) Brussels Ia, the dispute does not have to be brought in the venue where the anchor defendant is domiciled. Pursuant to Section 14, it can be any venue where any defendant is required to respond under law. If a defendant agrees to submit to a particular venue, eg on the basis of a forum agreement, this does not apply to other defendants.[110] The criterion in Section 14 that the claims are 'based on essentially the same ground' is similar to the requirement in Art 8(1) Brussels Ia that 'the claims are so closely connected that it is expedient to hear and determine them together to avoid the risk of irreconcilable judgments resulting from separate proceedings;'.[111] Unlike Art 8(1) Brussels Ia, however, Section 14 contains an explicit requirement that the claims must be brought

[107] See C-441/13 *Hejduk*; C-170/12 *Pinckney*.

[108] Cf Joined Cases C-509/09 and C-161/10 *eDate and Martinez*.

[109] S Dennemark, *Om domstols behörighet i internationellt förmögenhetsrättsliga mål*, 220–26; L Pålsson, *Svensk rättspraxis i internationell processrätt*, 92–93; U Maunsbach, *Svensk domstols behörighet vid gränsöverskridande varumärkestvister – särskilt om Internetrelaterade intrång*, 245–47; M Bogdan and M Hellner, *Svensk internationell privat- och processrätt*, 328.

[110] See C Thornefors, Lagkommentar Rättegångsbalk (Karnov 2018) 1942:740.

[111] U Maunsbach, *Svensk domstols behörighet vid gränsöverskridande varumärkestvister – särskilt om Internetrelaterade intrång*, 245–46; Högsta domstolen, 8 June 2001, (2001) *NJA* 386 (comparing Art 6(1) Lugano to Chapter 10, Section 14 of the Judicial Code). See also Chapter 13, Section 3, paragraph 1. and Chapter 14, Sections 1–2 of the Judicial Code.

simultaneously.[112] For this requirement to be satisfied, the lawsuits do not necessarily have to be filed through the same lawsuit.[113]

As noted, the starting point is that this rule cannot be applied *ex analogia* and that there should normally be an independent basis for jurisdiction against the defendant.[114] Exceptionally, the rule can be applied if the reasons of procedural economy outweigh the inconvenience for the defendant.[115] In one case, the Supreme Court found that Swedish jurisdiction could be based on the rule when the defendant was domiciled in a third state but was a Swedish citizen, a foreign representative of a Swedish company and spent three months a year in Sweden.[116]

(d)

In general, there are no protective rules on international jurisdiction governing jurisdiction over consumer, employment and insurance contracts.[117] To the extent that such disputes are not covered by the Brussels Ia Regulation,[118] the disputes are regulated in the same way as other disputes against non-EU defendants in matters regulated by the Brussels Ia Regulation, ie by determining in each specific case whether an interest in the administration of justice exists.

Sweden has a *lex specialis* venue provision for consumer disputes in Chapter 10, Section 8a of the Judicial Code. There is no case law where this provision has been applied *ex analogia* nor is there any support in the legal scholarship for this.[119] The rule states: 'In disputes between consumers and commercial enterprises concerning goods, services, or other commodities offered mainly for personal use, an action against the commercial enterprise may be instituted in the court for the place where the consumer resides. However, this rule shall apply only in cases presumptively qualifying for adjudication by a single legally qualified judge, pursuant to Chapter 1, Section 3d'.[120]

[112] See Svea hovrätt (Svea Court of Appeal), 30 September 1997, RH 1999: 53 (finding that even if Art 6(1) Lugano Convention gives a Swedish court jurisdiction to hear cases against several defendants, Swedish law on the joining of cases (cumulation) may impede such proceedings when the action against the defendants is not brought simultaneously).

[113] C Thornefors, Lagkommentar Rättegångsbalk, 1942:740.

[114] S Dennemark, *Om domstols behörighet i internationellt förmögenhetsrättsliga mål*, 220; U Maunsbach, *Svensk domstols behörighet vid gränsöverskridande varumärkestvister – särskilt om Internetrelaterade intrång*, 245–47.

[115] S Dennemark, *Om domstols behörighet i internationellt förmögenhetsrättsliga mål*, 220; U Maunsbach, *Svensk domstols behörighet vid gränsöverskridande varumärkestvister – särskilt om Internetrelaterade intrång*, 245–47; C Thornefors, Lagkommentar Rättegångsbalk, 1942:740.

[116] Högsta domstolen, 12 December 1986, (1986) *NJA* 729.

[117] There are *lex specialis* rules for certain specific situations. See Section 49, second paragraph of the Posting of Workers Act (No 678 of 1999) (*Lag* (1999:678) *om utstationering av arbetstagare*); Section 75 Seamen's Act (No 282 of 1973) (*Sjömanslag* (1973:282))

[118] Unlike Regulation No 44/2001, the Brussel Ia Regulation is applicable to consumer and employee disputes against third state defendants. See Art 18(1) and 21(2) Brussels Ia.

[119] See M Larsson, *Konsumentskyddet över gränserna- särskilt inom EU: En studie i internationell privat- och processrätt* (Iustus Förlag, 2002) 118; M Bogdan and M Hellner, *Svensk internationell privat- och processrätt*, 328.

[120] These are cases where the value of the claim does not clearly exceed half of the base amount according to the National Insurance Act (1962:381), which in 2021 is 23,800 Swedish crowns.

Two criteria must be satisfied for the rule to apply: the plaintiff must be a 'consumer' and the value of the claim must be under a certain ceiling (ie a 'small claim'). It is submitted that the concept of consumer is likely to be interpreted consistently with Art 17 Brussels Ia, at least for cases where a Swedish court is exercising jurisdiction on the basis of a rule on international jurisdiction in the Brussels Regime. Unlike Art 17 Brussels Ia, however, Section 8a does not contain any explicit requirement that there is a contract between the parties. Section 8a does not either contain any of the qualifying criteria in Art 17(1)(a)–(c) on, for instance, directing activities to the consumer's Member State of domicile. In contrast, Art 17 Brussels Ia does not contain any maximum ceiling as does Section 8a.

As noted there is no support for applying this rule *ex analogia*. Saf had suggested, however, that Art 15(1)(c) of the (old) Brussels I might be used to support jurisdiction pursuant to Chapter 10, Section 4 of the Judicial Code.[121] As noted, Chapter 10, Section 4 has been given a restrictive interpretation. Saf maintains that if a trader established in a third state directs its activities towards the Swedish market in the manner set out in Art 15, this might justify a finding under Chapter 10, Section 4 of the Judicial Code that the contract has been entered into in Sweden.[122] Saf's solution is no longer necessary, however, because pursuant to the Brussels Ia Regulation, the weaker party rules for the protection of consumers are now applicable to defendants domiciled in third states.[123]

There are also *lex specialis* venue rules for disputes regarding employment contracts in the Labour Disputes (Judicial Procedure) Act (No 371 of 1974) (*Lag* (1974:371) *om rättegången i arbetstvister*). These rules are not intended to regulate international jurisdiction and there is no support in the case law or legal scholarship for applying them *ex analogia*.[124]

Chapter 2, Section 1 of the Labour Disputes Act states that the Labour Court is the proper venue for certain disputes (eg disputes concerning collective agreements). It goes without saying that the fact that the Labour Court's jurisdiction extends throughout Sweden cannot be extended by analogy to lead to the conclusion that Swedish jurisdiction exists for all labour disputes throughout the world.[125]

Chapter 2, Section 2 of the Labour Disputes Act states that the district court in the place where the employee resides is competent to adjudicate disputes related to employment contracts.[126] This venue rule also may not be used as a rule on international jurisdiction. Bogdan maintains that the mere fact that an employee is domiciled in Sweden should not be sufficient to give him or her the right to bring an action against

[121] See Regulation No 44/2001.

[122] C Saf, 'Ingen generell analog tillämpning av Bryssel I-förordningen', 930.

[123] See Art 18(1) Brussels Ia Regulation.

[124] M Bogdan, 'Den svenska internationella arbetsrättens grunder', (1979) *SvJT* 81, 86; Arbetsdomtolen, 31 August 1983, AD 1983 no.°121 (stating that Chapter 2, Section 2, third paragraph, of the Labour Disputes (Judicial Procedure) Act (1974: 371) is not relevant for the question of international jurisdiction); M Bogdan and M Hellner, *Svensk internationell privat- och processrätt*, 328.

[125] M Bogdan, 'Den svenska internationella arbetsrättens grunder', 86–87; L Pålsson, *Svensk rättspraxis i internationell processrätt*, 52; M Bogdan and M Hellner, *Svensk internationell privat- och processrätt*, 327.

[126] The provision in the Labour Disputes Act is thus not exclusive and the employee may bring action in other venues pursuant to Chapter 10 of the Judicial Code.

the employer in Sweden.[127] Sinander maintains that for employment disputes an interest in the administration of justice should normally exist if the dispute has a connection to employee protection on the Swedish labour market, if there is a rule in the Judicial Code or in Brussels Ia that can be applied *ex analogia*, if Swedish labour law is applicable or if there is a risk for *deni de justice*.[128] In a case before the Labour Court, the court found that the fact that the employee worked in Sweden meant that Sweden had a sufficient connection to the dispute for international jurisdiction to lie in Sweden.[129] The Brussels Ia Regulation now extends its weaker party rules for employment disputes to third state defendants.[130]

There are no *lex specialis* statutory venue provisions for insurance or distribution contracts. These matters are subject to the venue provisions in Chapter 10 of the Judicial Code, which may be applied *ex analogia* as described above.[131]

[127] M Bogdan, 'Den svenska internationella arbetsrättens grunder', 87 (giving an example of an immigrant from Yugoslavia who otherwise would be allowed to bring an action against his former Yugoslav employer concerning disputes arising from the time before the move to Sweden); L Pålsson, *Svensk rättspraxis i internationell processrätt*, 52; M Bogdan and M Hellner, *Svensk internationell privat- och processrätt*, 328, fn 139.

[128] E Sinander, *Internationell kollektivavtalsreglering: En studie i internationell privaträtt av den svenska modellen för reglering av anställningsvillkor*, 120.

[129] Arbetsdomtolen, 31 August 1983, AD 1983 no.°121.

[130] See Art 21(2) Brussels Ia.

[131] Concerning insurance contracts, see Högsta domstolen, 15 June 2007, (2007) *NJA* 482.

IV.

The European Perspective

Ratione Materiae Reciprocity as a Head of Jurisdiction in View of the Extension of the Brussels Ia Regulation to Non-EU Defendants

MARGHERITA SALVADORI

I. Introduction

The legal framework on the exercise and potential limitations by judicial discretion of jurisdiction have remained unchanged in recent times within the EU. In fact, the Brussels Ia Regulation,[1] similarly to its predecessors (the Brussels I Regulation,[2] and the 1968 Brussels Convention),[3] provides that the uniform rules on jurisdiction contained therein only apply in cases involving defendants domiciled in the EU, whereas national rules on jurisdiction of the Member State apply in cases involving defendants domiciled outside the EU. Admittedly, only a limited number of jurisdictional rules of Brussels Ia apply also to defendants domiciled outside the EU.[4] However, as mentioned, pursuant to Art 6(1) Brussels Ia, jurisdiction *vis-à-vis* defendants domiciled outside the EU is governed by national rules on jurisdiction of the Member State of the court seized. Therefore, when EU-uniform rules on jurisdiction are applicable, national courts have no discretion: they are bound to apply those rules. In fact, the rules in question hold to

[1] Regulation No 1215/2012.

[2] Regulation No 44/2001.

[3] On the basis of Art 220 of the 1957 Treaty of Rome, the 1968 Brussels Convention was negotiated by six Member States: France, Germany, Italy, Belgium, the Netherlands and Luxembourg; a few years later, in 1971, a protocol was added, the Protocol Concerning the Interpretation by the Court of Justice of the Convention of September 27, 1968 on Jurisdiction and the Enforcement of Judgments in Civil and Commercial Matters, signed at Luxembourg, [1975] OJ L 204/28. In the following years the 1968 Brussels Convention was renegotiated when the international organisation was enlarged in 1978, 1982, 1989 and 1996, upon the accession of the United Kingdom, Ireland and Denmark, Greece, Spain and Portugal, and most recently Austria, Finland and Sweden, respectively. The Protocol was also subsequently ratified by the new Member States, see [1978] OJ L 304/1, [1982] OJ L 388/1, [1989] OJ L 285/1, [1987] OJ C 15/1. The consolidated text of the 1968 Brussels Convention is published at [1998] OJ C 27/28.

[4] This is the case of protective rules concerning consumer and employment disputes (Arts 18(1), 21(2) Brussels Ia), in cases of exclusive jurisdiction (Art 24 Brussels Ia) and in cases of choice-of-court agreements (Art 25 Brussels Ia).

a hard-and-fast logic based on the principles of legal certainty and predictability, refusing any flexibility based on convenience, fairness or justice. In turn, national rules on jurisdiction and grounds for declining jurisdiction in favour of non-EU courts, may vary considerably from one Member State to the other. Furthermore, as of today, the decision by the ECJ in the *Owusu* case has not been overruled.[5]

The difference between each Member State's rules on jurisdiction may result in unequal situations among claimants.[6] Some may be able to 'attract' defendants domiciled in third States more easily than others. What is more, a further distortion may occur when the judgment rendered on the basis of the national rules on jurisdiction is recognised and enforced in another Member State; in fact, even such a judgment may circulate under the simplified EU regime – rather than under the stricter national rules – and thus be eligible to unfold its effects throughout the territory of the EU.[7]

Considering that the 2019 Hague Convention has been signed (even if not in force yet),[8] it seems quite unrealistic that, in the near future, issues of jurisdiction might

[5] Case C-281/02, *Owusu v Jackson*. On that case, even prior to the CJEU's decision, see R Fentiman, National Law and the European Jurisdiction Regime, in A Nuyts and N Watt (eds), *International Civil Litigation in Europe and Relations with Third States* (Bruylant, 2005) 83, 98, 105, 126.

[6] See A Bonomi, 'European Private International Law and Third States' (2017) *IPRax* 184–86 on disparities to ensuring equal access to justice.

[7] Part of the legal scholarship has argued in favour of extending EU-uniform jurisdictional rules to non-EU defendants. See, inter alia, DP Fernández Arroyo, 'Compétence Exclusive et Compétence Exorbitante dans les Relations Privées Internationales', in *Collected Courses of The Hague Academy of International Law*, vol 323 (Brill Nijhoff, JC Leiden, 2006) 13–198.

[8] The 2019 Hague Conventions has been signed, but not yet ratified, by Costa Rica, Israel, Russian Federation, Ukraine, United States of America, Uruguay. Most recently, the EU has signed and ratified the 2019 Hague Convention (see Council Decision (EU) 2022/1206 of 12 July 2022, concerning the accession of The European Union to the Convention on the Recognition and Enforcement of Foreign Judgement in Civil or Commercial Matters [2022] OJ L187/1. The entry into force of the 2019 Hague Convention is governed by Art 28, which reads: '[1] This Convention shall enter into force on the first day of the month following the expiration of the period during which a notification may be made in accordance with Art 29(2) with respect to the second State that has deposited its instrument of ratification, acceptance, approval or accession referred to in Art 24. [2] Thereafter this Convention shall enter into force (…)'. The EU Decision mentioned above states in Art 3 that: 'When depositing the instrument, the Union shall make the following declaration in accordance with Art 27(1) of the Convention: The European Union declares, in accordance with Art 27(1) of the Convention, that it exercises competence over all the matters governed by this Convention. Its Member States will not sign, ratify, accept or approve the Convention, but shall be bound by the Convention by virtue of the accession of the European Union. For the purposes of this declaration, the term "European Union" does not include the Kingdom of Denmark by virtue of Articles 1 and 2 of Protocol No 22 on the position of Denmark, annexed to the Treaty on European Union and the Treaty on the Functioning of the European Union'. According to para 2 of Art 27, headed 'Regional Economic Integration Organisation as a Contracting Party without its Member States', of the 2019 Hague Convention: 'In the event that a declaration is made by a Regional Economic Integration Organisation in accordance with paragraph 1, any reference to a "Contracting State" or "State" in this Convention shall apply equally, where appropriate, to the Member States of the Organisation'. In light of these provisions, when the EU's decision to ratify the 2019 Hague Convention will be deposited, this will determine the formal entry into force of the 2019 Hague Convention for 26 EU Member States: as a result, if any other contracting States will ratify, the Convention will be not applied in *intra*-EU relations and the recognition and enforcement of European judgments will continue to be governed by Brussels Ia, in accordance with Art 23 para 4 of the same Convention. The latter provision reads: 'This Convention shall not affect the application of the rules of a Regional Economic Integration Organisation that is a Party to this Convention as concerns the recognition or enforcement of a judgment given by a court of a Contracting State that is also a Member State of the Regional Economic Integration Organisation where – (a) the rules were adopted before this Convention was concluded; or (b) the rules were adopted after this Convention was concluded (…)'.

successfully be addressed in an additional treaty-instrument. If this prediction comes true, the question will have to be tackled once more by the EU institutions unilaterally.[9]

This solution was clearly addressed by the European Group for Private International Law (GEDIP/EGPIL) at the virtual meeting of 2022 on the possible accession of the European Union to the 2019 Hague Convention. On that occasion the GEDIP stressed that: 'If the European Union wishes to ensure recognition and enforcement of judgments given by its courts under the Convention, it should ensure that its courts exercise jurisdiction regarding those defendants based on the rules of EU law'.[10] Moreover, in this chapter I will only deal with the main subject matter of the May 2022 Dubrovnick Conference: 'Jurisdiction Over Non-EU Defendants – Should the Brussels Ia Regulation be Extended?'

II. Solutions Considered During the Recast of Brussels I

The following issue of legal policy arises in the context of the EU-uniform legal framework on jurisdiction: why should the application of exorbitant heads of jurisdiction be rejected in cases involving defendants not domiciled in a Member State, but in a third State, without the assurance that the latter third State will also reject similar exorbitant heads of jurisdiction?

In order to address that policy issue, at the time of the recast of Brussels I, the Commission[11] underlined two related aspects concerning the functioning of Art 4 Brussels I (now Art 6 Brussels Ia) and the reference contained therein to the national rules of jurisdiction of the Member States. The first aspect was that the mechanism underlying Art 4 Brussels I was liable to create distortions of competition in that

[9] See again A Bonomi, 'European Private International Law and Third States', 184–85 ('As is well known, this problem is made even worse by the existing 'asymmetry' in scope between the rules on jurisdiction and those on recognition of the Regulation. Member States' judgments given against a defendant domiciled in a non-Member State benefit from the mutual recognition system, even when they are based on unreasonable jurisdictional bases. This ensues from the prohibition under the Brussels Instruments to review the jurisdiction of the rendering court, combined with the impossibility of applying public policy to the rules relating to jurisdiction'). And also R Luzzatto, 'On the Proposed Application of Jurisdictional Criteria of Brussels I Regulation to Non-Domiciled Defendants,' in F Pocar, I Viarengo, FC Villata (eds), *Recasting Brussels I* (Padova, 2012) 111; M Fallon, T Kruger, 'The Spatial Scope of the EU's Rules on Jurisdiction and Enforcement of Judgments: From Bilateral Modus to Unilateral Universality?' (2012/2013) *Yearbook of Private International law* 1–15.

[10] These Observations are published on the web site of the GEDIP/EGPIL, www.gedip-egpil.eu/wp-content/uploads/2020/08/DOC-Jugements-ENG-Final.pdf, particularly relevant is the para 9: 'In the opinion of the Group, the accession to the Judgments Convention should be an opportunity to restart the process of extending the rules of the Regulation 1215/2012 to third States, a process that had been only partially brought about by the 2012 recast. In line with its 2010 proposal, the Group calls for the inclusion of a set of uniform European rules on the recognition and enforcement in the Member States of third-country judgments. It also recommends the replacement of current Article 6 of that Regulation by jurisdictional rules applicable to defendants domiciled in third countries (in line with the approach followed in all most recent EU regulations). Indeed, there is a discrepancy between the design of the jurisdictional filters in the Judgments Convention, which largely build on the existing rules of the Regulation 1215/2012, and the non-application of most of these rules to defendants domiciled in a third State'.

[11] On 14 December 2010, the Commission published its Proposal to recast Regulation No 44/2001, COM (2010) 748 final.

companies from Member States with restrictive rules of jurisdiction would usually incur higher business risk and legal costs than companies based in other Member States granting broader access to national courts.[12] The second aspect was that, the absence in many Member States of a right for weaker parties (consumers, employees or insured) to sue in their home jurisdiction created an additional burden for those parties and would have been likely to deprive them of the protection granted by mandatory EU legislation. Considering that, in the cases mentioned above, access to nationals courts could have been prevented in many Member States, the Commission envisaged two possible solutions: either to keep in force the national rules on jurisdiction in cases involving defendants domiciled outside the EU, or to introduce in the same Regulation two additional heads of jurisdiction, namely a subsidiary head of jurisdiction at the place where moveable assets belonging to the defendant are located and a head of jurisdiction based on *forum necessitatis*.[13] The first solution was ultimately adopted and implemented in Brussels Ia. The solution adopted is all but 'innovative': it is the same as that implemented by Brussels I and, previously, by the 1968 Brussels Convention.[14]

The issue of the application of Brussels I to so-called 'external situations' was also addressed by the European Group for Private International Law (GEDIP/EGPIL), first during the Hamburg Session (2007). On that occasion, a statement was issued on the possibility of extending the Regulation to defendants domiciled outside the EU. One year later, after the Bergen Meeting (2008), that statement developed into a specific proposal.[15] That proposal consisted in amending Art 4 Brussels I, in order to allow the Regulation to apply to any dispute, regardless of the defendant's domicile. The proposal also entailed amendments to a number of articles of the Regulation – among which those providing for special and protective heads of jurisdiction – in order to adapt them to cases involving defendants whether or not domiciled in a Member State. In particular, the GEDIP proposed to re-word Art 4 Brussels I as follows: 'Persons not domiciled in any Member States may be sued in the courts of a Member State only by virtue of the rules set out in Sections 2 to 8'. The set of rules referred to in the proposed Art 4 included those additional heads of jurisdiction envisaged also by the Commission: the subsidiary head of jurisdiction at the place where moveable assets belonging to the defendant are located, and the head of jurisdiction based on *forum necessitatis*.[16]

[12] The impact assessment of the Commission stressed that being unable to sue in their 'home' court, companies from Member States had to litigate in a foreign, unfamiliar legal system with the risk that they may not get a fair trial, particularly in countries where the judiciary cannot be considered to be independent or is riven by corruption; see SEC (2010) 1547 final.

[13] See RA Brand, 'Transaction Planning Using Rules on Jurisdiction and the Recognition and Enforcement of Judgments', in *Collected Courses of The Hague Academy of International Law*, vol 358 (Brill Nijhoff, JC Leiden, 2013) 27–46.

[14] Even if the Commission's proposal to include jurisdictional rules of universal application was not accepted by the European Parliament (European Parliament Resolutions of September 2010, paras 15–18, and of 23 November 2010), protective grounds based on the consumer's or employee's domicile, and the provision on choice-of-court agreements, have been made applicable regardless of the parties' domicile. See A Layton, 'The Brussels I Regulation in the International Legal Order: Some Reflections on Reflectiveness', in E Lein (ed), *The Brussels I Review Procedure Uncovered* (BIICL, 2012) 75–77.

[15] A Borras, 'La XVIII Session del Gruppo Europeo de Derecho internacional privado' (2008) *Revista Espanola de Derecho Internacional* 716–17.

[16] A Borras, 'Application of the Brussels I Regulation to External Situations. From Studies Carried Out by the European Group for Private International Law (EGPIL/GEDIP) to the Proposal for the Revision of the Regulation' (2010) *Yearbook of Private International Law* 333–50.

As pointed out, the jurisdictional rules of the Brussels Ia Regulation, where combined with those on recognition and enforcement, may place non-EU defendants in an invidious position.[17]

In addition, it is worth recalling that the CJEU clarified, in its Opinion 1/03,[18] that the national grounds referred to in Art 4(1) Brussels I (today Art 6(1) Brussels Ia) are incorporated by reference into the Regulation. In particular, the ECJ stated that: 'The purpose of that regulation (…) is to unify the rules on jurisdiction in civil and commercial matters, not only for intra-Community disputes but also for those which have an international element';[19] and that: 'That regulation contains a set of rules forming a unified system which apply not only to relations between different Member States (…) but also to relations between a Member State and a non-member country'.[20]

In conclusion, Brussels Ia, subject to some minor adjustments, mainly maintained the status quo: uniform rules on jurisdiction apply in cases involving defendants domiciled in the EU and national rules on jurisdiction of the Member States in cases involving defendants domiciled outside the EU. As previously mentioned, that Regulation is, however, applicable to non-EU defendants in few situations concerning consumer and employment contracts, cases of exclusive jurisdiction and of disputes prorogued by agreement.

III. Reciprocity as a Head of Jurisdiction: Former Art 4 No 4 of the Italian Code of Civil Procedure

With a view to the future recast of the Brussels Ia Regulation it might be useful to identify a different and new solution as compared to those previously envisaged and mentioned above, in order to allow a further extension of the Regulation to cases involving defendants domiciled outside the EU. Any solution should take into account two elements. The first element is the need to increase the efficiency and the level of protection granted by the EU-uniform rules on judicial cooperation in civil and commercial matters. The second element is that of adequately addressing the interests of the single EU Member States.

With these two elements in mind, a possible solution would be that of adopting the criterion of reciprocity. The latter is a method that comes into play when it is not possible to regulate international relations through cooperative methods and international conventions, that is to say the traditional method used by the national legislators of the single Member States before the establishment of judicial cooperation in civil and commercial matters within (what is today) the EU.

[17] See A Dickinson, 'Surveying the Proposed Brussels I bis Regulation: Solid Foundations but Renovation Needed' (2010) *Yearbook of Private International Law* 247–72.

[18] See, ECJ, Opinion 1/03 on the competence of the Community to conclude the new Lugano Convention on jurisdiction and the recognition and enforcement of judgments in civil and commercial matters, EU:C:2006:81.

[19] Opinion 1/03, para 143.

[20] Opinion 1/03, para 144.

Apparently, nowadays, national rules on jurisdiction of the Member States do not, or do no longer, adopt the method of reciprocity. Before 1995,[21] in Italy, Art 4 no 4 CPC (*Codice di procedura civile*; Code of Civil Procedure) provided that, on a subsidiary basis, a foreign defendant could be sued in Italy, on condition of reciprocity, that is to say when, in similar cases, an Italian citizen could have been sued in the foreign defendant's home country.[22] In particular, the Italian provision was worded as follows: 'The foreigner may be sued before the judges of the [Italian] Republic, if, in the reciprocal case, the judge of the State to which the foreigner belongs may hear claims brought against an Italian citizen'.[23] Italian scholars and courts noted that the provision in question was aimed at protecting Italian citizens against foreign rules which excessively extended the jurisdiction of the respective foreign courts.[24] Moreover, it was believed that through the method of reciprocity foreign countries would be encouraged to reject exorbitant heads of jurisdiction.[25] In fact, rather than that of discriminating against foreigners, the purpose of Art 4 no 4 CPC was that of dissuading foreign countries from applying exorbitant heads of jurisdiction against Italian defendants.[26] Art 4 no 4 CPC was appropriately abrogated by the Italian reform of private international law,[27] which

[21] Namely, before Law 31 May 1995 no 218, 'Reform of the Italian system of private international law', which abrogated, among others, Art 4 CPC.

[22] The main idea underlying Art 4 CPC, was that all disputes involving an Italian citizen were always relevant for the Italian legal order; jurisdiction over the citizen was thus unlimited both *ratione personae* and *materiae* (see F Carnelutti, 'Intorno al principio della pienezza della giurisdizione', *Rivista di diritto processuale civile* (Cedam, 1942), 222). This choice was criticised by many scholars, including *Quadri*, who pointed out that Art 4 CPC 'insofar as it governs Italian jurisdiction over foreigners and foreigners only, cannot be regarded as an exceptional rule which stands in relation to a general principle that sanctions the unlimitedness of jurisdiction (…) this rules on jurisdiction, while assuming in principle a diversity of treatment of the citizen and of the foreigners, does not make it possible to determine in what such treatment consists'. See R Quadri, 'La giurisdizione sul cittadino nel nuovo codice di procedura civile', in R Quadri (ed), *Studi critici di diritto internazionale. Diritto internazionale privato*, vol 1 (Giuffrè, 1958), 301–07.

[23] The original text of Art 4 no 4 CPC was: '*Lo straniero può essere convenuto davanti ai giudici del Regno: (…) 4) se, nel caso reciproco, il giudice dello stato al quale lo straniero appartiene può conoscere delle domande proposte contro un cittadino italiano*'. After the entry into force of the Italian Constitution, on 1 January 1948, the word 'Regno' (Kingdom) was replaced with the word Repubblica Italiana (Italian Republic).

[24] As highlighted by *Vitta*, reciprocity is aimed at protecting Italian citizens from legislative provisions of foreign Sates excessively extending their jurisdiction. With this in mind, jurisdiction based on reciprocity could be established only in cases where the claimant was an Italian citizen and the defendant a foreigner, and not in cases involving two foreigners. See, E Vitta, *Corso di diritto internazionale privato e processuale* (UTET, 1983) 12.

[25] See Corte di cassazione, 21 July 1967, n°1890, Foro it. 1967, I, 2042; Corte di cassazione, 2 July 1969, n°2427, Foro it., I, 1, 574; Corte di cassazione, 4 March 1975, n°809, Riv. dir. internaz. 1976, 581.

[26] It is worth underlining that in Art 4 no 4 of the former CPC, reciprocity allows the claimant, absent other heads of jurisdiction, to sue the foreign claimant before the Italian judge if it is ascertained that the foreign judge could hear a similar claim brought against the Italian citizen. See G Campeis and A De Pauli, *Il processo civile italiano e lo straniero, Lineamenti di diritto processuale civile internazionale* (Giuffrè, 1986) 68. It is further worth underlining that the procedural rule on reciprocity of Art 4, no 4 former CPC is different from that contained in Art 16 of the Preliminary Provisions to the Italian Civil Code. The first provision concerned a procedural aspect, namely jurisdiction, whereas the latter a substantive aspect, namely the exercise of (civil law) rights. On Art 16 Preliminary Provisions to the Italian Civil Code, see, most recently, E Piovesani, 'Article 16 of the Preliminary Provisions to the Italian Civil Code and Brexit', in A Fernández Pérez (ed), *Ciudadanía, asilo e inmigración en la Unión Europea* (I Foro europeo de Derecho internacional private, Iprolex, 2020) 235 et seq.

[27] Law 31 May 1995 no 218. See, in this book, the Italian Report by E Piovesani and S Dominelli.

aimed at governing the subject-matter in an organic manner.[28] More generally, reciprocity clauses based on nationality, such as that contained in the provision in question, became incompatible with the fundamental principle of EU law of non-discrimination based on nationality, in the context of civil judicial cooperation between Member States, in *intra*-EU relations.[29]

IV. *Ratione Materiae* Reciprocity: A Connecting Factor in Cases Involving Non-EU Defendants

Rather than maintaining the reference to national rules on jurisdiction, or introducing additional heads of jurisdiction in the future recast of Brussels, it could be envisaged that, on a subsidiary basis (that is to say, when there is no jurisdiction based on other heads of jurisdiction of the same Regulation), a person domiciled outside the EU can be sued before the seized courts of the given Member State, when, in the reciprocal case, a person domiciled in the EU could be sued in the third State where the former is domiciled. It is very important to emphasise that this solution does not entail an extension of the *ratione personae* jurisdiction, but rather the application of a *ratione materiae* method, since it concerns only specific kinds of disputes exorbitantly regulated by the system of the non-EU country. In other words, the scope of the condition of reciprocity is determined by the foreign system, and should apply only in those cases defined by that system to establish the jurisdiction of a Member State court.

The operation of a rule based on the method of reciprocity is only apparently simple. In fact, issues arise when it comes to assessing whether reciprocity is actually established. Some scholars have defined reciprocity as a 'legal chemistry' in relation to the functioning of private international law treaties in relation to civil law.[30] Other scholars have emphasised the functioning of reciprocity in the development of international law, along with State characterisation.[31] More recently, reciprocity has been deducted as a means in itself unwelcome due to its indirect nature, which necessarily leads to injustice: the State that sets the condition of reciprocity claims to exercise pressure on a foreign

[28] Art 4 no 4 former CPC was being applied by the Italian court at the time of the 1968 Brussels Convention, until the entry into force of Law 218 of 1995, which repealed the provision and introduced Art 3.2 that extends, by reference, the personal scope of application of specific jurisdictional criteria set forth in the 1968 Brussels Convention.

[29] Incidentally, from a comparative perspective, a similar development concerned also other Member States, eg Germany, where § 110 ZPO (Code of Civil Procedure – *Zivilprozessordnung*: ZPO) – on *cautio iudicatum solvi* – is no longer based on nationality, but rather on domicile.

[30] See JP Niboyet, 'La notion de réciprocité dans les traités diplomatiques de droit international privé', in *Collected Courses of The Hague Academy of International Law*, vol 52 (Brill Nijhoff, JC Leiden, 1935) 259–320, where the author analyses the combination of the various reciprocity processes in the light of a kind of transition that seems to bring the theory of obligation, as regards diplomatic reciprocity, towards the initial bases of the law of obligations, that is to say towards the civil law.

[31] See M Virally, 'Le principe de réciprocité dans le droit international contemporain', in *Collected Courses of The Hague Academy of International Law*, vol 122 (Brill Nijhoff, JC Leiden, 1967) 5–59, where it is held that reciprocity acts, depending on the case, as an incentive or, on the contrary, as an instrument of dissuasion, which pushes States to negotiate, to make concessions or to limit their claims and to control their behaviour; indeed, reciprocity also has a strong ethical character.

State by disrupting the normal and just solution of purely private law issues.[32] If this evaluation can be reasonable on the perspective of a single State, it might not be the same in the light of an international organisation such as the EU, where States cooperate (and 'share' jurisdiction) within the European Judicial Area and need to face relations with third States.

In order to clarify the notion of reciprocity, three different situations may be identified: diplomatic, legislative or *de facto* reciprocity.[33] In the first case a diplomatic treaty must have been concluded between the State of the forum and the foreign State guaranteeing the legal solution which is at stake in the reciprocity.[34] In the second case, it is sufficient that this solution results from the foreign law; in this situation reciprocity leads to refusing jurisdiction when the seized court ascertains that the *lex fori* of the foreign court rejects exorbitant rules of jurisdiction. *De facto* reciprocity is met if exorbitant heads of jurisdiction are concretely applied by the courts of the given third State; this poses evidentiary problems when proof of legislative reciprocity is adduced, but that such reciprocity does not in fact exist.

Furthermore, *ratione materiae* reciprocity requires an ascertainment of foreign law: in other words, the one considered here is the case of legislative reciprocity anchored on the individual foreign statutory provision that must be ascertained by the court of the Member State concerned on its own motion. It is important to stress that the burden of proof concerning the content of foreign law cannot be left to the non-EU defendant: this to ensure his right of access to justice and to a fair trial before the jurisdiction of a Member State court.[35]

It is crucial to know whether and to what extent courts will apply conflict of laws and foreign law *suo moto*, and how they will ascertain it. The treatment of foreign law is distinguished from that of domestic law, as the principle of *jura novit curia* does not always apply to the former.[36] While most civil law jurisdictions provide for the *ex officio* application of foreign law, the establishment and review of foreign law often encounter restrictions. Common law jurisdictions, for example, require parties to prove the content of foreign law.[37] The treatment of foreign law in court proceedings is key to the

[32] See P Lagarde, 'La réciprocité en droit international privé', in *Collected Courses of The Hague Academy of International Law*, vol 154 (Brill Nijhoff, JC Leiden, 1977) 105 et seq, where a significant statement is also made at p 162 'Le résultat est détestable. L'Etat du for accepte de consacrer une solution injuste dans un litige individuel en raison d'une circonstance totalement extérieure à ce litige. Non seulement il est injuste que le plaideur étranger soit pénalisé en raison de l'attitude de son Etat national, mais il est encore plus contraire à l'équité que le national du for ait la bonne fortune de pouvoir profiter de cette détérioration des relations entre l'Etat du for et l'Etat étranger' (trans. 'The result is detestable. The forum State accepts an unjust solution to an individual dispute because of a circumstance totally external to that dispute. Not only is it unfair that the foreign litigant should be penalised because of the attitude of his national State, but it is even more unfair that the national of the forum should have the good fortune to be able to profit from this deterioration in relations between the forum State and the foreign State').

[33] See again P Lagarde, 'La réciprocité en droit international privé', 105–66.

[34] As is the case with the 2005 Hague Convention on Choice of Court Agreements.

[35] A reference should be made to Art 47 EU Charter of Fundamental Rights and to Art 6 European Convention on Human Rights.

[36] The *iura novit curia* principle applies in the Italian legal system, but it is expressly provided that the judge may appoint an expert on foreign law (see Art 14 Law 218/1995).

[37] In common law jurisdiction foreign law being a question of fact, it must be proved by the evidence of witness expert in the foreign law. See P Le Gay Breton, 'AM, RFD, Conclusion', in M Douglas, V Bath, M Keyes and A Dickinson (eds), *Commercial Issues in Private International Law. A common law Perspective*

functioning of private international law, but it is reasonable to assume that the courts of the EU states may be prepared to use the criterion of reciprocity *ratione materiae* as a head of jurisdiction.

This is simply a proposal for an intermediate solution. It must be said that the method of reciprocity, may appear to be innovative, because, on the one hand, it would solve the problem of maintaining several national exorbitant heads of jurisdiction and, on the other hand, it would avoid the need to provide for specific ones at an EU level. But in the end, it would be no more than 'old wine in a new bottle', in the European Judicial Area.

(Hart, 2019), 313–26 ('evidence of a statute (including of delegated legislation) of a foreign country may be adduced by producing a book or pamphlet containing the statute, that purports to have been printed by the government (…). Moreover, evidence of the unwritten or common law of a foreign country may be adduced by producing a book containing reports of judgments of courts of the country, if the book is or would be used in the courts of the country to inform them about the unwritten or common law of the country and evidence of the interpretation of a statute of a foreign country may be adduced by producing a book containing reports of judgments of courts of the country if the book is or would be used in the courts of the country to inform the courts about the interpretation of the statute').

V.

The Global Perspective

Jurisdiction Over Non-EU Defendants: The Brussels I Article 79 Review

RONALD A BRAND

I. Introduction

Article 79 of the Brussels I (Recast) Regulation requires that the European Commission report in 2022 on the possible application of the direct jurisdiction rules of the Regulation to all defendants and not just to defendants domiciled in EU Member States.[1] This issue was set aside in the Recast of the Brussels I Regulation in 2011, when the Commission recommendation for such a change was rejected by the Parliament and Council. As a result, the Recast Regulation continues to allow each Member State to discriminate by applying otherwise prohibited bases of jurisdiction to cases involving non-EU defendants. Article 79 provides the opportunity to revisit the matter with the benefit of a decade of experience under the Recast Regulation. It also provides the opportunity to address the manner in which the Recast Regulation discriminates as well in it its rules on recognition and enforcement of judgments.

In this chapter I consider the possible extension of the internal direct jurisdiction rules to external defendants from a perspective external to the European Union. In doing so, I consider developments both within and outside of Europe in the law of jurisdiction and the recognition of foreign judgments. I begin with background on the 2009 Commission proposal to apply the direct jurisdiction rules of the Brussels I (Recast) Regulation to all defendants. I then provide the context for my own thoughts based on the evolution of EU competence for matters of private international law, discussion of related developments in jurisdiction and judgments recognition law in the United States, and consideration of the global negotiations on jurisdiction and the recognition of judgments at the Hague Conference on Private International Law. I use this context in order to consider whether matters have changed in ways that might justify a different rule in 2022 than in 2012 for the European Union. I conclude with thoughts about whether any EU changes in this regard should come internally by Regulation, or externally through multilateral treaty negotiations. I focus this part on the ways in which such changes can

[1] Art 79: By 11 January 2022 the Commission shall present a report to the European Parliament, to the Council and to the European Economic and Social Committee on the application of this Regulation. That report shall include an evaluation of the possible need for a further extension of the rules on jurisdiction to defendants not domiciled in a Member State, taking into account the operation of this Regulation and possible developments at international level. Where appropriate, the report shall be accompanied by a proposal for amendment of this Regulation.

properly eliminate discrimination against non-EU defendants in Member State courts in both jurisdiction and the recognition and enforcement of judgments.

II. Article 79[2]

Article 5(1) of the Brussels I (Recast) Regulation states that '[p]ersons domiciled in a Member State may be sued in the courts of another Member State only by virtue of the rules set out in Sections 2 to 7 of this Chapter'. Thus, the Regulation provides an exhaustive set of jurisdiction rules for suits brought in the courts of a Member State against defendants who are domiciled in another Member State. No other bases of jurisdiction are available in such cases.

Article 8(1) provides that '[i]f the defendant is not domiciled in a Member State, the jurisdiction of the courts of each Member State shall, subject to Article 18(1), Article 21(2) and Articles 24 and 25, be determined by the law of that Member State'. Thus, as a general rule, except when there is exclusive jurisdiction under Art 25, or a choice of court agreement under Art 26, jurisdiction over a person not domiciled in a Member State is determined under a Member State's law excluding the Regulation.

In the Recast process, the European Commission published a proposal[3] for revision of the Brussels I Regulation.[4] One of the significant changes recommended in the proposal was in the original Art 4(2) (now Art 3(2)), where the Commission Proposal would have provided that '[p]ersons not domiciled in any of the Member States may be sued in the courts of a Member State only by virtue of the rules set out in Sections 2 to 8 of this Chapter'. This would have applied the jurisdictional rules of the Brussels I Regulation to all defendants in EU Member State courts, and not just to defendants domiciled in another Member State,[5] making them the complete and exhaustive set of rules of direct jurisdiction for defendants domiciled outside the forum state.

The Commission Proposal was reviewed by a Committee of the European Parliament in early 2011,[6] resulting in a June 2012 'proposal as proposed by the Presidency as a compromise with a view to the adoption of a general approach by the Council (Justice and Home Affairs)'.[7] That proposal was endorsed by the Council at its meeting on June 7–8, 2012.[8]

[2] For a more detailed discussion of related issues, see RA Brand, 'Transaction Planning Using Rules on Jurisdiction and the Recognition and Enforcement of Judgments' (2013) 358 *Recueil des cours of the Hague Academy of International Law* 13, 45–48.

[3] Proposal for a Regulation of the European Parliament and of the Council on jurisdiction and the recognition and enforcement of judgments in civil and commercial matters (Recast), (COM (2010) 748/3 final, 14.12.2010).

[4] Regulation No 44/2001, as amended by Regulations Nos 1496/2002, 1791/2006 and 1103/2008.

[5] Commission Proposal (n 3), Art 4(2).

[6] Committee on Legal Affairs of the European Parliament, 'Draft Report on the proposal for a regulation of the European Parliament and of the Council on jurisdiction and the recognition and enforcement of judgments in civil and commercial matters (recast)' (COM(2010)0748 – C7-0433/2010–2010/0383(COD), Rapporteur: Tadeusz Zwiefka, 28.6.2011) ['Legal Affairs Committee Report'].

[7] Proposal for a Regulation of the European Parliament and of the Council on jurisdiction and the recognition and enforcement of judgments in civil and commercial matters (Recast) – First reading, (10609/12 JUSTCIV 209 CODEC 1495, 1.6.2012) ['President's Compromise Proposal'].

[8] Council of the European Union, Press Release, 3172nd Council meeting, Justice and Home Affairs, Brussels, (7 and 8 June 2012, 10760/12, PR CO 34), 17.

The President's Compromise Proposal, as endorsed by the Council, rejected the position in the Commission proposal that would have extended the jurisdiction rules in the Brussels I Regulation to application in cases against defendants domiciled outside the European Union. Instead, it selectively extended certain of the Regulation's jurisdictional rules to cases involving defendants not domiciled in the European Union. These changes to the Regulation included:

1) The Art 18(1) rule that a consumer may bring a suit in the consumer's home state against a party to a contract *no matter where that party is domiciled.*
2) The Art 19(2) rule that an employee may bring a suit against their employer in the state in which the employee carries out their work *no matter where the employer is domiciled.*
3) The Art 22 rule providing that all of the bases for exclusive jurisdiction apply to all defendants, *no matter where they are domiciled.*
4) The Art 25(1) rule now extending jurisdiction to all parties to an agreement choosing a court within a Member State, and not just to agreements that include a party who is domiciled in a Member State.

Notably, the President's Compromise Proposal continued the discrimination against defendants not domiciled in the European Union which is maintained in Art 6 by allowing additional bases of jurisdiction under national law to be applied against non-EU defendants.

III. The Context for Article 79

In order to understand the review required under Art 79, it is helpful to understand three other matters: (1) the evolution of EU competence for matters of private international law; (2) the corresponding evolution of the jurisprudence on jurisdiction and judgments recognition in the United States; and (3) the history of multilateral negotiations on issues of jurisdiction and judgments recognition at the Hague Conference of Private International Law. These matters overlap in time, particularly from the beginning of the jurisdiction and judgments project at the Hague Conference to the current time, with each having impact on the others. Both the European Union and the United States have played major roles in the Hague Conference negotiations.

(a) The Evolution of Private International Law in Europe[9]

(1) Competence for Rules of Private International Law

When the six original Member States created the European Economic Community in 1957, they understood that private international law was important to the free

[9] For a more detailed discussion of this issue, see RA Brand, 'Of Magnets and Centrifuges: The US and EU Federal Systems and Private International Law' in: N Ringe and JJM Spoon (eds), *Comparative Regional Integration and Multilevel Governance: The European Union and Beyond, Essays in Honor of Alberta Sbragia*, (ECPR Press, 2020), www.papers.ssrn.com/sol3/papers.cfm?abstract_id=3505601; see also

movement of goods, services, capital, and people.[10] They demonstrated this when they included Art 220 in the original Treaty of Rome, declaring that the Member States of the Community should negotiate a further treaty on the mutual recognition of judgments.[11] Acting on this provision, in 1968 the Member States concluded the Convention on jurisdiction and the recognition and enforcement of judgments in civil and commercial matters (Brussels Convention).[12]

The conclusion of the Treaty of Amsterdam in 1997 effectively moved competence for private international law matters from the Member States to the institutions of the European Community.[13] This was accomplished in its Art 61 (providing that 'the Council shall adopt … measures in the field of judicial cooperation in civil matters as provided for in Article 65'),[14] and Art 65 (stating that such authority would cover service of process, taking of evidence, the recognition of judgments, rules of conflict of laws and jurisdiction, and rules of civil procedure).[15] Those institutions responded by moving the sources of private international law from the Member States – largely found in codes of private international law – to the EU institutions, using regulations and directives in order to govern these matters through centralised EU law.[16]

While there originally were questions about the extent to which the Treaty of Amsterdam moved competence from Member States to the EU institutions, the matter was settled in 2003 with the *Lugano Convention* opinion of the European Court of Justice.[17] The Opinion presented questions regarding a challenge to the competence of

RA Brand, 'External Effects of Internal Developments: A US Perspective on Changing Competence for Private International Law in Europe' in S Bariatti and G Venturini (eds), *Liber Amicorum Fausto Pocar: New Instruments of Private International Law* (Giuffrè, 2009) 163–79.

[10] For a discussion of the rationale for including private international law rules under the rubric of a trade law regime, see RA Brand, 'Recognition of Foreign Judgments as a Trade Law Issue: The Economics of Private International Law' in J Bhandari and AO Sykes (eds), *Economic Dimensions in International Law* (CUP, 1998), 592.

[11] Treaty Establishing the European Community, Art 293 (ex Art 220) (calling for the Member States to 'enter into [further] negotiations with each other with a view to securing for the benefit of their nationals … the simplification of formalities governing the reciprocal recognition and enforcement of judgments of courts or tribunals and of arbitration awards').

[12] European Convention on Jurisdiction and Enforcement of Judgments in Civil and Commercial Matters, ('Brussels Convention', 27 September 1968, 41 OJ Eur Comm C 27/1, 26 January 1998), consolidated and updated version of the 1968 Convention and the Protocol of 1971, following the 1996 accession of the Republic of Austria, the Republic of Finland and the Kingdom of Sweden.

[13] Treaty of Amsterdam, signed on 2 October 1997, and entered into force on 1 May 1999.

[14] TEC (n 11), Art 61 (ex Art 73i).

[15] TEC (n 11), Art 65 (ex Art 73m).

[16] The centralisation of European private international law after the Treaty of Amsterdam has been dramatic, both in regard to the internal law of the EU and in regard to external legal developments. Regulations have been adopted establishing rules on insolvency; recognition and enforcement of judgments in civil and commercial matters; taking of evidence; judicial cooperation; recognition and enforcement of family law judgments; uncontested claims; common payment procedures; small claims procedure; applicable law for non-contractual obligations; service of documents; applicable law for contractual obligations; jurisdiction, applicable law, and recognition of judgments in maintenance obligation matters; applicable law for divorce and separation; and matters of succession, among others.

[17] Opinion 1/03, Request by the Council of the European Union for an Opinion pursuant to Art 300(6), EC Official Journal C 101/1 26 April 2003, [2006] E.C.R. I-1145; see A Borrás, 'The Effect of the Adoption of Brussels I and Rome I on the External Competences of the EC and the Member States' in J Meeusen, M Pertegás and G Straetmans (eds), *Enforcement of International Contracts in the European Union* (Intersentia, 2004), 99–100.

the European Community to enter into a treaty with EFTA Member States (the Lugano Convention) that would parallel the rules the then-recent Brussels I Regulation had established for jurisdiction and the recognition of judgments when a case involved a defendant from another Member State. In the *Lugano Convention* Opinion, the Court followed the 1999 Opinion of the European Council Legal Service, which had stated that 'once the Community has exercised its internal competences adopting positions by which common rules are fixed [pursuant to Art 65 of the TEC], the Community competence becomes exclusive, in the sense that the Member States lose the right to contract, individually and even collectively, obligations with third countries which affect the said rules'.[18] Based on the 1971 *ERTA/AETR* decision,[19] as further developed in the *Open Skies* judgments of 2002,[20] the court stated that 'whenever the Community has included in its internal legislative acts provisions relating to the treatment of nationals of non-member countries or expressly conferred on its institutions powers to negotiate with non-member countries, it acquires an exclusive external competence in the spheres covered by those acts',[21] and '[t]he same applies, even in the absence of any express provision authorising its institutions to negotiate with non-member countries, where the Community has achieved complete harmonisation in a given area'.[22] Thus, '[t]he conclusion of the new Lugano Convention on jurisdiction and the recognition and enforcement of judgments in civil and commercial matters … falls entirely within the sphere of exclusive competence of the European Community'.[23]

The *Lugano Convention* Opinion laid to rest any claim of remaining competence with the Member States for external relations on matters of jurisdiction and the recognition and enforcement of judgments. This evolution of EU competence for private international law affects both internal and external competence. The development of external competence was reflected on the international level when, in 2005, the Statute of the Hague Conference on Private International Law was amended to allow membership by a Regional Economic Integration Organization (REIO), ie, by the European Union.[24] EU Membership in the Hague Conference became effective on 4 March 2007.[25] This external competence of the European Union has been explicitly claimed as well through EU Regulations dealing with procedures for external negotiation regarding matters

[18] See A Borrás, 'The Effect of the Adoption of Brussels I and Rome I on the External Competences of the EC and the Member States', 99–100.

[19] Case 22/70 *European Rail Transport Agreement*.

[20] Cases C-467/98, C-468/98, C-469/98, C-471/98, C-472/98, C-475/98, and C-476/98 *Open Skies*.

[21] Case C-467/98 *Open Skies*, para 82.

[22] ibid.

[23] ibid.

[24] Hague Conference on Private International Law, Final Act, C, approved by Members on 30 September 2006 and entered into force on 1 January 2007, amending Art 3(1) of the Statute to provide that 'The Member States of the Conference may, at a meeting concerning general affairs and policy where the majority of Member States is present, by a majority of the votes cast, decide to admit also as a Member any Regional Economic Integration Organisation which has submitted an application for membership to the Secretary General. References to Members under this Statute shall include such Member Organisations, except as otherwise expressly provided. The admission shall become effective upon the acceptance of the Statute by the Regional Economic Integration Organisation concerned'.

[25] See Hague Conference on Private International Law Membership Status, www.hcch.net/index_en.php?act=conventions.status&cid=29.

such as applicable law,[26] and procedures for external negotiation regarding jurisdiction and the recognition of judgments in family law matters.[27] It has also been demonstrated in negotiations at the Hague Conference generally, where the EU speaks on behalf of all Member States in the negotiation of new multilateral instruments.

(2) Jurisdiction

Of course, in the area of direct jurisdiction in the courts of EU Member States, the transition from the 1968 Brussels Convention, to the 2001 Brussels I Regulation, to the 2012 Brussels I (Recast) Regulation, demonstrates both the evolutionary process of moving from Member State to EU competence and the way in which judicial jurisdiction has been structured in a formal manner intended to create as much predictability as possible. With the rule of general jurisdiction focused on the domicile of the defendant in Art 4(1) of the Brussels I (Recast) Regulation, and the special jurisdiction rules found principally in Art 7, the structure is basically clear.

A defendant domiciled in an EU Member State may always be sued in that state, for any matter arising anywhere in the world. In addition, that defendant may be sued in the courts of another Member State if the criteria of one of the provisions of Art 7(1)–(7) are met. While the rule of general jurisdiction is based entirely on the strength of the connection between the forum state and the defendant, the rules of special jurisdiction found in Art 7 are based primarily on a relationship between the forum state and the claim (eg, the place of performance of a contract under Art 7(1), and the place 'where the harmful event occurs' for torts under Art 7(2)). In some cases, those special jurisdiction rules require no other connection between the forum state and the defendant. This sets up particularly interesting comparisons with the corresponding development of the law of judicial jurisdiction in the United States.[28]

The aspect of the Brussels I (Recast) Regulation that plays an important role in the Art 79 requirement of a review is the manner in which the Regulation discriminates against defendants not domiciled in EU Member States. Art 5 of the Regulation limits the available bases of jurisdiction when suing a defendant domiciled in a Member State to those found in Chapter II of the Regulation. It also (by reference to an Annex) specifically prohibits suit on bases of jurisdiction that exist in Member States but are considered to be exorbitant under European Union law. Art 6 then operates to discriminate against defendants domiciled outside the European Union by specifically allowing jurisdiction based on those exorbitant national law bases of jurisdiction, and by extending them to all plaintiffs domiciled in the state in which the action is brought.

Article 79 of the Brussels I (Recast) Regulation brings into question whether it is appropriate to engage in the type of jurisdictional discrimination that would have been removed by the 2011 Proposal of the European Commission. As noted below, that discrimination contrasts with the personal jurisdiction rules applicable in US courts,

[26] Regulation No 662/2009, 25–30.
[27] Regulation No 664/2009, 46–51.
[28] See below notes 34–72 and accompanying text.

which provide protection to defendants from outside the forum state, whether those defendants are from other US states or from foreign States.[29]

What Article 79 does not do is require any consideration of the rules of recognition and enforcement of judgments found in the Brussels I (Recast Regulation). But those rules as well provide for discrimination in favour of defendants from other Member States as compared with defendants from outside the European Union. It is thus useful to think about whether those rules should also be reconsidered in the Art 79 review process.

(3) *Judgments Recognition*

Article 36 of the Brussels I (Recast) Regulation provides that '[a] judgment given in a Member State shall be recognised in the other Member States without any special procedure being required'. Article 45 then provides for limited bases for non-recognition. Except for judgments in certain consumer, employment, and insurance cases, Art 45(3) prevents the recognising court from reviewing the jurisdiction of the court of origin.

Article 5(3) of the Regulation, by reference to Art 75(1), determines jurisdictional provisions in the Member States that go beyond the list of bases specifically authorised in the Regulation 'shall not be applicable as against' persons domiciled in a Member State. Because the exercise of such a jurisdictional basis against a defendant domiciled in another Member State is prohibited, no further provision is required to prevent the recognition of a judgment based on such jurisdiction. The Regulation thus addresses condemned bases of jurisdiction in a direct manner in the originating court, rather than in an indirect manner in the recognising court. A review of the substance of the original decision by the recognising court is prohibited, and the reviewing court is bound by the findings of fact in the originating court, including those on which jurisdiction was based.

Article 6 allows a defendant not domiciled in a Member State to be subject to suit based on otherwise prohibited national grounds of jurisdiction. Such a judgment rendered against a non-EU defendant is required to be recognised and enforced in all other Member States under the basic Art 36 rule.

The Brussels I (Recast) Regulation does not contain rules governing the recognition and enforcement of judgments from courts outside the European Union. Absent the benefits of a treaty or an EU Regulation, such a foreign judgment is governed by national rules of recognition and enforcement. This usually means that a new action must be brought on the judgment in order to obtain recognition (*exequatur*), with the resulting local judgment of recognition being the one for which enforcement is sought.[30] The prerequisites for judgment recognition generally are statutorily regulated.

[29] ibid.

[30] A significant change in the internal European recognition of judgments resulting from the 2012 Recast Regulation is the abolishment of the requirement of an *exequatur* (declaration of enforceability). Rather than require such a separate declaration by the recognising court prior to enforcement, the Recast provides that '[a] judgment given in a Member State which is enforceable in that State shall be enforceable in another Member State without the need for a declaration of enforceability being required', Art 39. With the Recast, it is up to the party against whom recognition and enforcement is sought to seek refusal of recognition of the judgment, Art 45(1).

While the Brussels I (Recast) Regulation does not have rules for the recognition and enforcement of judgments from courts in non-EU Member States, its jurisdictional rules do affect non-EU defendants in the process of recognition and enforcement. A judgment from another EU Member State is not subject to jurisdictional review because the jurisdictional analysis when an EU-domiciled defendant is involved must occur in the court of origin under the Brussels I (Recast) Regulation, and any contest of jurisdiction must occur in that court (subject to ultimate review by the Court of Justice of the European Union).[31] For non-EU-domiciled defendants, there simply is no such jurisdictional protection in EU Member State courts because other national law bases of jurisdiction may still apply, but the resulting judgment is subject to the requirement for recognition and enforcement in other Member State courts under Art 36. This discrimination in recognition and enforcement would, of course, change if the rules of direct jurisdiction in the Regulation applied to *all* defendants in Member State courts. Thus, the Art 79 Review does affect recognition and enforcement as well as direct jurisdiction.

In applying the *exequatur* process in national courts to judgments from courts outside the European Union, there are two basic approaches in national law. Each of these approaches generally provides for non-recognition based on a list of concerns similar to those found in Art 45 of the Brussels I (Recast) Regulation (public policy, lack of proper notice, fraud, inconsistent judgments subject to recognition, etc). The difference lies in the approach to indirect jurisdiction – ie, the way in which the reviewing court considers the original (direct) jurisdiction of the court of origin. In the first approach, Member States, such as Germany and Italy, make no distinction between the rules of direct and indirect jurisdiction.[32] This means that a foreign judgment is tested (indirect jurisdiction) by the same rules as apply to bring an action brought originally in the recognising court (direct jurisdiction).

A second approach involves a separate set of rules of indirect jurisdiction by which the judgment from a foreign court is tested, with that set of rules generally being much narrower than the direct jurisdiction rules in the state of the recognising court.[33] This results in a type of discrimination by which a foreign judgment in which the facts in the court of origin would have satisfied a recognising state basis of direct jurisdiction (ie, the case could have been brought in the courts of the recognising state under similar jurisdictional facts) will be denied recognition and enforcement because it does not meet the narrower test of the rules of indirect jurisdiction. This 'jurisdiction gap' results in clear discrimination against judgments from outside the European Union.

[31] Brussels I (Recast) Regulation, Art 45(3).

[32] See, eg section 328(I) of the German Code of Civil Procedure ('The judgment of a foreign court shall not be recognized (1) if the courts of the State to which the foreign court belongs have no jurisdiction under German law'), translation from IP Weems, Enforcement of Money Judgments Abroad FRG-29 (1993) and Article 64(1)(a) of Law 218/1995, Italy ('the authority rendering the judgement had jurisdiction pursuant to the criteria of jurisdiction in force under Italian law').

[33] For further discussion of such jurisdiction gaps, with specific reference to the law of the United Kingdom, see RA Brand, 'The Hague Judgments Convention in the United States: A "Game Changer" or a New Path to the Old Game?' (2021) 82 *U Pitt L Rev* 847, 866–74.

(b) The Evolution of US Law on Jurisdiction and Judgments Recognition

(1) Jurisdiction

The type of jurisdiction governed in the European Union by the Brussels I Regulation is known in US jurisprudence as personal or *in personam* jurisdiction. Most often, personal jurisdiction in US courts is obtained by demonstrating a relationship between the forum state, the defendant, and the cause of action.[34] Like in Europe, when the relationship between the forum state and the defendant is strong (ie, when the defendant's domicile is in the forum state), then the relationship to the claim can be weaker (or even non-existent). On the other hand, when the relationship between the forum state and the defendant is not continuous and systematic such that it makes the defendant 'at home', then the relationship with the claim becomes more significant. Nonetheless, as explained below, a relationship with the defendant must still be present because jurisdiction in US courts is a matter of federal Constitutional law based on due process protections of the person – in this case, the defendant – against actions by the state.

Whether a case is brought in state or federal court, analysis of personal jurisdiction in U.S. courts generally involves a two-step process. The first step is the application of the state 'long-arm statute', to determine whether statutory jurisdiction *in personam* jurisdiction exists.[35] These statutes differ, but generally can be categorised as list-type provisions, providing specific bases of jurisdiction,[36] and the constitutional limits statutes, providing that a court in the state can exercise *in personam* jurisdiction to the limits of the Due Process Clause.[37]The process of applying a list-type long-arm statute is similar to the application of the jurisdictional rules of the Brussels I Regulation.

The second step in the United States is the constitutional analysis by which it is determined whether the exercise of jurisdiction allowed by state statute in the particular case is within the limits of the Due Process Clause. Because it usually is a state long-arm statute that is being considered, it is the Fourteenth Amendment with which courts are most often concerned.

The Due Process Clauses of both the Fifth and Fourteenth Amendments are written as limitations on the federal and state governments.[38] As such, they protect all persons

[34] For a more detailed discussion, see RA Brand, 'Transaction Planning Using Rules of Jurisdiction and the Recognition and Enforcement of Judgments' (2013) 358 *Hague Academy Collected Course* 12, 49–95.

[35] Jurisdiction in the federal courts is governed by Rule 4(k) of the Federal Rules of Civil Procedure. This Rule provides three principal jurisdictional authorisations: (1) Rule 4(k)(1)(A) authorises a district court to borrow the jurisdictional powers of state courts in the state where it is located; (2) Rule 4(k)(1)(D) confirms the availability of any applicable federal statute granting personal jurisdiction; and (3) Rule 4(k)(2) grants district courts personal jurisdiction to the limits of the [Fifth Amendment] due process clause in certain federal question cases. See GB Born and PB Rutledge, *International Civil Litigation in US Courts* 4th edn (Aspen, 2007) 193. This most often results in the federal court 'borrowing' the state statute under Rule 4(k)(1)(A): ibid at 172–97.

[36] See, eg, 42 Pa Cons Stat Ann § 5322.

[37] See, eg, Cal CivProc. Code Ann § 410.10.

[38] US Const amends V & XIV. The Fifth Amendment, ratified on 15 December 1791, provides a limitation on the federal government, stating that 'No person shall be … deprived of life, liberty, or property, without due process of law'. The Fourteenth Amendment, ratified on 9 July 1868, provides a limitation on state governments, stating that 'No State shall … deprive any person of life, liberty, or property, without due process of law'.

(and not just citizens or those domiciled in the United States) from excessive exercises of governmental authority. In their application to judicial jurisdiction, this means the Due Process Clauses restrict the extent to which courts may exercise jurisdiction over a defendant. Because the plaintiff is considered to have consented to jurisdiction by bringing the case, it is the defendant who is entitled to due process in any determination affecting their life, liberty, or property. Thus, unlike the Brussels I (Recast) Regulation, these protections exist for *all* defendants, and not just for defendants domiciled in the United States. The resulting protections for defendants have been developed through the jurisprudence of the United States Supreme Court applying concepts of due process to judicial jurisdiction.

Soon after the ratification of the Fourteenth Amendment with its Due Process Clause, in the 1877 case of *Pennoyer v Neff*,[39] the Supreme Court applied a territorial approach to jurisdiction over a defendant,[40] looking for the presence of the defendant within the territory, stating that 'every State possesses exclusive jurisdiction and sovereignty over persons and property within its territory', and 'no State can exercise direct jurisdiction and authority over persons or property without its territory'.[41] This territorial approach follows a defendant domiciled in a forum state, even when they are outside the territory of that state. Thus, in *Milliken v Meyer*,[42] the court held that a defendant domiciled in Wyoming who was served personally in Colorado, was properly subject to the jurisdiction of the courts of Wyoming on the basis of domicile.[43] This established a principle similar to the general jurisdiction rule found in Art 4 of the Brussels I (Recast) Regulation, that a defendant will always be subject to jurisdiction at his or her domicile.

When the Supreme Court responded over time to concerns about modern methods of communication and transportation, and to the development of corporations as legal persons, there was an appearance that they were expanding concepts of jurisdiction within the Due Process framework. Thus, in *International Shoe Co v Washington*,[44] an action was brought in a Washington State court, by the State of Washington Office of Unemployment Compensation, to collect delinquent contributions from a Delaware corporation which had its offices in Missouri. Drawing on both *Pennoyer v Neff* and *Milliken v Meyer*, the court emphasised the importance of a nexus between the defendant and the forum state.[45] While *Pennoyer* represented the historical focus on the presence of the defendant within the jurisdiction as a 'prerequisite to its rendition of

[39] 95 US 714 (1877). Rightly or wrongly, *Pennoyer v Neff* linked American jurisdictional law with the Fourteenth Amendment's Due Process Clause, and however questionable that linkage may be, it has become part of American conventional wisdom'. FK Juenger, 'Constitutionalizing German Jurisdictional Law' (1996) *American Journal of Comparative Law* 521 (book review).

[40] 'The authority of every tribunal is necessarily restricted by the territorial limits of the State in which it is established. Any attempt to exercise authority beyond those limits would be deemed in every other forum, as has been said by this court, in illegitimate assumption of power, and be resisted as mere abuse'. 95 US at 720.

[41] ibid at 722.

[42] 311 US 457 (1940).

[43] ibid at 462 ('Domicile in the state is alone sufficient to bring an absent defendant within the reach of the state's jurisdiction for purposes of a personal judgment by means of appropriate substituted service. Substituted service in such cases has been quite uniformly upheld where the absent defendant was served at his usual place of abode in the state … as well as where he was personally served without the state'.)

[44] 326 US 310 (1945).

[45] ibid at 316.

a judgment personally binding him',[46] *Milliken* demonstrated that something less was necessary. In *International Shoe*, the court developed this line further, stating that due process requires only that in order to subject a defendant to a judgment *in personam*, if he be not present within the territory of the forum, he have certain minimum contacts with it such that the maintenance of the suit does not offend 'traditional notions of fair play and substantial justice'.[47]

The need for rules accommodating the fiction of the corporate personality led the court to focus on the conduct of those acting on behalf of the corporation.[48] It noted two variables in determining the constitutionality of jurisdiction over non-resident defendants. The first is the extent and intensity of the defendant's activities in the forum state, and the second is the connection between those activities and the cause of action.[49] 'Continuous and systematic' activity supports general jurisdiction over a defendant, allowing a court to consider actions against the defendant whether or not they arise out of those activities.[50] A 'single isolated' contact, on the other hand, will (at most) support only specific jurisdiction, and the action must arise out of the contact. Finding that the activities of the defendant in the State of Washington were 'systematic and continuous', and resulted 'in a large volume of interstate business, in the course of which appellant received the benefits and protection of the laws of the state', and that the obligation sued upon 'arose out of those very activities',[51] the court found it to be 'evident that these operations establish sufficient contacts or ties with the state of the forum to make it reasonable and just according to our traditional conception of fair play and substantial justice' to permit jurisdiction.[52]

The distinction in the United States between general and specific jurisdiction was first explicitly suggested by Professors Arthur T von Mehren and Donald T Trautman, in their 1966 article, 'Jurisdiction to Adjudicate: A Suggested Analysis'.[53] That distinction was then developed judicially by the Supreme Court in *Helicopteros Nacionales de Colombia, SA v Hall*.[54] In a wrongful death action brought in Texas state court against a Colombian corporation, when a helicopter crash in Peru resulted in the deaths of four US citizens, Justice Blackmun's opinion for the court stated that, '[w]hen a controversy is related to or "arises out of" a defendant's contacts with the forum, the court has said that a "relationship among the defendant, the forum, and the litigation" is the essential foundation of *in personam* jurisdiction'.[55] Thus, specific jurisdiction required that the cause of action in litigation 'arise out of', and thus be directly related to, the activities of the defendant within the forum state.[56] The court expressed the alternative general

[46] ibid (citing *Pennoyer v Neff*, 95 US 714, 733 (1877)).
[47] ibid at 313 (quoting from *Milliken v Meyer*, 311 US 457, 463 (1940)).
[48] ibid at 316.
[49] ibid at 316–20.
[50] ibid at 317.
[51] 326 US at 320.
[52] ibid.
[53] 79 Harv L Rev 1121, 1144–1164 (1966).
[54] 466 U.S. 408 (1984).
[55] 466 US at 414.
[56] ibid at 415.

jurisdiction by stating that, '[e]ven when the cause of action does not arise out of or relate to the foreign corporation's activities in the forum State, due process is not offended by a State's subjecting the corporation to its *in personam* jurisdiction when there are sufficient contacts between the State and the foreign corporation'.[57] Under general jurisdiction, so long as the contacts are 'continuous and systematic', they may support jurisdiction even though the cause of action does not 'arise out of' the contacts.[58] The *Helicopteros* court found the cause of action at issue not to have arisen out of the contacts with Texas, thereby avoiding a discussion of specific jurisdiction. It then ruled that general jurisdiction did not exist under the Due Process Clause.[59]

Throughout this development of the application of the Due Process Clauses to personal jurisdiction, it was generally assumed that certain corporations are so ubiquitous that general jurisdiction existed over them in every US state because those corporations were engaged in continuous and systematic activity everywhere. This was true in *World-Wide\Volkswagen Corp v Woodson*,[60] a products liability lawsuit brought in Oklahoma based on an automobile accident which occurred in that state when an automobile sold in New York to New York residents was being driven through Oklahoma. The plaintiff sued both the New York regional distributor and the New York retail dealer from whom the car had been purchased. Both of these defendants successfully challenged the jurisdiction of the Oklahoma court. The plaintiffs also sued the manufacturer and Audi NSY Auto Union Aktiengesellschaft, but those defendants did not challenge the issue of jurisdiction on appeal, apparently because they assumed the existence of general jurisdiction through continuous and systematic activity in or directed at Oklahoma.[61]

The assumption of widespread general jurisdiction over multinational corporations met an abrupt change in 2011 with the decision in *Goodyear Dunlop Tires Operations, SA v Brown*.[62] A products liability action was brought in a North Carolina state court, based on an accident in France injuring North Carolina residents, against Goodyear Tire and Rubber Company (Goodyear USA), and three of its subsidiaries, located in Turkey, France, and Luxembourg.[63] All three foreign subsidiaries moved to dismiss for lack of jurisdiction. Because the accident took place in France, and the tires involved were manufactured and sold outside the United States, there was no specific jurisdiction. The only question was whether there was general jurisdiction over the foreign subsidiaries.[64] Justice Ginsburg, writing for a unanimous court, used language seeming to draw upon the Brussels I Regulation and its general jurisdiction rule based on domicile:

[57] ibid at 414.
[58] ibid at 414–15 (discussing *Perkins v Benguet Consolidated Mining Co*, 342 US 437 (1952), and *Keeton v Hustler Magazine, Inc*, 465 US 770, 779–80 (1984)).
[59] ibid at 418–19.
[60] 444 US 286 (1980).
[61] 444 US at 288 n 3.
[62] 564 US 915 (2011).
[63] 564 US at 918.
[64] 564 US at 919–20.

> *International Shoe* distinguished from cases that fit within the 'specific jurisdiction' categories, 'instances in which the continuous corporate operations within a state [are] so substantial and of such a nature as to justify suit against it on causes of action arising from dealings entirely distinct from those activities.' Adjudicatory authority so grounded is today called 'general jurisdiction.' For an individual, the paradigm forum for the exercise of general jurisdiction is the individual's domicile; for a corporation, it is an equivalent place, one in which the corporation is fairly regarded as at home.[65]

The court found the three European defendants not to be sufficiently 'at home' in North Carolina.[66] *Goodyear* thus brought a dramatic limitation to the concept of general jurisdiction as it had previously been applied in US courts.[67]

On the same day that *Goodyear* was decided, the court also decided *J McIntyre Machinery Ltd v Nicastro*,[68] a case dealing with specific jurisdiction. Justice Ginsburg, writing in dissent this time, suggested an expansion of US concepts of specific jurisdiction that would be comparable to the corresponding special jurisdiction rules in the Brussels I Regulation.[69] Her opinion implied that such a result would properly accompany the severe restriction of general jurisdiction brought about by the *Goodyear* decision by having less severe limitations on specific jurisdiction. A combination of opinions that makes it difficult to discern a clear rule going forward resulted in a majority of the court holding that jurisdiction did not exist in New Jersey for injury to a New Jersey resident caused by a metal-shearing machine manufactured by an English company in England, when that company did not sell its product directly in the United States, but rather through an independent distributor. Justice Ginsburg specifically referred to the Brussels I Regulation in her dissenting opinion, noting that the decision of the 'splintered majority' set the rules of jurisdiction in the United States at odds with the example of the approach taken in much of the rest of the world. The result, she noted, 'puts United States plaintiffs at a disadvantage in comparison to similarly situated complainants elsewhere in the world',[70] specifically when compared to Art 7(2) of the Brussels I Regulation, which allows jurisdiction at the place of injury.[71] The Supreme Court has addressed personal jurisdiction three more times after *Goodyear* and *Nicastro*, but those decisions have not altered the general thrust of the 2011 decisions.[72]

(2) Judgments Recognition

Like the European Union, in the United States judgments from courts within the United States (both federal and state courts) circulate rather freely. This results from the Full

[65] 564 US at 924.
[66] ibid.
[67] For a representative discussion of this shift, see M Gardner, PK Bookman, AD Bradt, ZD Clopton and DT Rave, 'The False Promise of General Jurisdiction' (2022) *Alabama Law Review* 455.
[68] 564 US 873 (2011).
[69] 564 US at 909 n 16 (Ginsburg, J, dissenting).
[70] ibid.
[71] See Case 21/76 *Bier*, defining the place where the harmful event occurred as either 'the place where the damage occurred' or 'the place of the event which gives rise to and is at the origin of that damage'.
[72] *Ford Motor Co v Montana Eighth Judicial District Court*, 141 S Ct 1017, (2021); *Bristol-Myers Squibb Co v Superior Court of California*, 137 S Ct 1773 (2017); *Daimler AG v Bauman*, 571 US 117 (2014).

Faith and Credit clause in Article IV of the United States Constitution and the federal full faith and credit statute.[73] For judgments from outside the United States, whether the recognition action is brought in state or federal court, it generally is state law that governs. Nonetheless, that law is relatively uniform, with most states having adopted either the 1962 Uniform Foreign Money-Judgments Recognition Act[74] or the updated 2005 Uniform Foreign-Country Money Judgments Recognition Act.[75] Other states follow similar rules by applying common law principles, generally consistent with the interpretation found in the Restatement. The provisions of the Third Restatement on judgments recognition[76] were updated in the Fourth Restatement,[77] and basically now track the Uniform Acts.

Both the Uniform Acts and the Restatement make the United States a quite liberal country for the purposes of recognition and enforcement of foreign judgments. The basic structure for the analysis is as follows:

(a) A court will recognize a foreign country judgment that grants or denies recovery of a sum of money if the judgment is final, conclusive and enforceable in the state in which it was rendered.[78]

(b) A court must deny recognition if

  (1) the judgment was rendered under a judicial system that does not provide impartial tribunals or procedures compatible with the requirements of due process of law;

  (2) the foreign court did not have personal jurisdiction over the defendant; or

  (3) the foreign court did not have jurisdiction over the subject matter.[79]

(c) A court may discretionarily deny recognition if

  (1) the defendant in the proceeding in the foreign court did not receive notice of the proceeding in sufficient time to enable the defendant to defend;

  (2) the judgment was obtained by fraud that deprived the losing party of an adequate opportunity to present its case;

  (3) the judgment or the [cause of action] [claim for relief] on which the judgment is based is repugnant to the public policy of this state or of the United States;

  (4) the judgment conflicts with another final and conclusive judgment;

  (5) the proceeding in the foreign court was contrary to an agreement between the parties under which the dispute in question was to be determined otherwise than by proceedings in that foreign court;

  (6) in the case of jurisdiction based only on personal service, the foreign court was a seriously inconvenient forum for the trial of the action;

[73] 28 USC § 1738.
[74] Uniform Foreign Money-Judgments Recognition Act ('1962 Recognition Act').
[75] Uniform Foreign-Country Money Judgments Recognition Act, ('2005 Recognition Act').
[76] Restatement (Third) Foreign Relations Law §§ 481–83 (1987).
[77] Restatement (Fourth) Foreign Relations Law §§ 481–89 (2018).
[78] 2005 Recognition Act (n 75), § 3(a); Restatement (Fourth) (n 77) § 481.
[79] 2005 Recognition Act (n 75), § 4(b); Restatement (Fourth) (n 77) § 483.

(7) the judgment was rendered in circumstances that raise substantial doubt about the integrity of the rendering court with respect to the judgment; or
(8) the specific proceeding in the foreign court leading to the judgment was not compatible with the requirements of due process of law.[80]

Most notably, the mandatory ground for non-recognition based on personal jurisdiction requires that the court apply the same jurisdictional analysis to the foreign judgment (indirect jurisdiction) as it would apply to a case being brought originally in its own court (direct jurisdiction). Thus, there is no jurisdiction gap, and no resulting discrimination that limits the acceptable bases of jurisdiction in the foreign court of origin. The rules of direct jurisdiction for the purposes of bringing a case are the same as the rules of indirect jurisdiction by which a foreign judgment is tested for recognition purposes.[81]

(c) Negotiations at the Hague Conference on Private International Law

The Jurisdiction and Judgments Project at the Hague Conference on Private International Law provides the global context for understanding the impact of differing rules on jurisdiction for EU and non-EU defendants in the courts of the EU Member States. This too is helpfully developed in a chronological manner, keeping in mind that the developments already highlighted for the European Union and the United States had an impact on the Hague negotiations both because each of them was a major player in those negotiations and because other States involved in the Hague negotiations have similar approaches to questions of jurisdiction and the recognition and enforcement of judgments.

In May of 1992, the United States proposed that the Hague Conference consider preparing a multilateral convention on the recognition and enforcement of judgments.[82] The matter was placed on the agenda of the Hague Conference in October 1996,[83] resulting in a Preliminary Draft Convention text in October 1999.[84] That text was revised again at the first part of a split Diplomatic Session in June 2001. An Interim Text created at that 2001 Session fared no better than the 1999 Preliminary Draft text.[85] Thus, in April 2002 it was decided to consider a more limited convention, including only those jurisdictional provisions on which substantial consensus existed, with the result

[80] 2005 Recognition Act (n 75), § 4(c); Restatement (Fourth) (n 77), § 484.

[81] Such a jurisdictional challenge in a judgment recognition action is the same for judgments from outside the United States as it is for judgments from inside the United States.

[82] Letter of 5 May 1992 from ED Williamson, Legal Advisor, US Department of State, to G Droz, Secretary General, The Hague Conference on Private International Law, distributed with Hague Conference document Lc ON No 15 (92).

[83] 'Final Act of the Eighteenth Session of the Hague Conference on Private International Law', 19 October 1996, at 21.

[84] Informational note on the work of the informal meetings held since October 1999 to consider and develop drafts on outstanding items, drawn up by the Permanent Bureau, Hague Conference on Private International Law, Prel Doc No 15 (May 2001) (containing the text of the Preliminary Draft Convention).

[85] Hague Conference on Private International Law, Commission II, Jurisdiction and Foreign Judgments in Civil and Commercial Matters, Summary of the Outcome of the Discussion in Commission II of the First Part of the Diplomatic Conference 6–20 June 2001, Interim Text.

being a March 2003 Draft Text for a Convention on Choice of Court Agreements.[86] A further Special Commission considered that text, and the Convention on Choice of Court Agreements was concluded at a Diplomatic Session in June of 2005.[87]

The Hague Convention on Choice of Court Agreements came into effect for Mexico and the European Union (for 27 of its Member States) on October 1, 2015;[88] for Singapore on October 1, 2016; for Montenegro on August 1, 2018, and for Denmark on September 1, 2018.[89] The United Kingdom has given notice that it remains in effect for the United Kingdom subsequent to Brexit.[90] Israel, the People's Republic of China, the Republic of North Macedonia, Ukraine, and the United States have signed, but have not ratified, the Convention.[91] There is no indication that the United States will be able to move soon to ratification and implementation.[92]

The Choice of Court Convention contains three basic rules: Art 5 provides that a court chosen in an exclusive choice of court agreement shall have exclusive jurisdiction; Art 6 provides that a court not chosen shall defer to the chosen court; and Art 8 provides that the courts of all contracting states shall recognise and enforce judgments from a court chosen in an exclusive choice of court agreement, subject to an explicit list of bases for non-recognition found in Art 9.[93] Thus, the 2005 Convention is both a jurisdiction convention (limited to one basis of jurisdiction: consent to exclusive dispute settlement in the courts of one state) and a judgments convention (providing for circulation of judgments from cases based on exclusive choice of court agreements).

In October 2011, an Experts' Group was established to consider a resumption of the project in order to deal with those issues not addressed in the Choice of Court Convention.[94] The jurisdiction and judgments elements of the project were split in 2012, with a Working Group established to prepare proposals for a judgments convention and an Experts' Group directed to give further study to a separate jurisdiction convention.[95] The Working Group completed a Proposed Draft Text of a judgments convention in 2016, and Special Commission meetings were held in June 2016, February 2017, November 2017, and May 2018, with the Experts' Group instructed to move

[86] 'Preliminary Result of the Work of the Informal Working Group on the Judgments Project', Hague Conference on Private International Law, Prel Doc No 8 (March 2003) (corrected) for the attention of the Special Commission of April 2003 on General Affairs and Policy of the Conference.

[87] The text of the Final Act of the Twentieth Session, and a documentary history of the Choice of Court Convention project, are available on the Hague Conference website at: www.hcch.net/index_en.php?act=conventions.text&cid=98.

[88] On 31 January 2020, the United Kingdom notified the Depositary that 'the United Kingdom and the European Union have signed, ratified and approved a Withdrawal Agreement', which entered into force on 1 February 2020 (the 'Withdrawal Agreement'). The Withdrawal Agreement includes provisions for a transition period to start on the date the Withdrawal Agreement enters into force and end on 31 December 2020 (the 'transition period'). In accordance with the Withdrawal Agreement, during the transition period, European Union law, including the Agreement, will continue to be applicable to and in the United Kingdom. See status table www.hcch.net/index_en.php?act=conventions.status&cid=98.

[89] ibid.

[90] ibid.

[91] ibid.

[92] SB Burbank, 'A Tea Party at The Hague?' (2012) *Southwestern Journal of International Law* 101.

[93] For a more complete discussion of the Choice of Court Convention, see RA Brand and P Herrup, *The 2005 Hague Convention on Choice of Court Agreements* (CUP, 2008).

[94] www.hcch.net/en/projects/legislative-projects/judgments.

[95] ibid.

forward on a jurisdiction convention only after the judgments convention text would be concluded.[96] A Diplomatic Session adopted the 2019 Convention on Jurisdiction and the Recognition and Enforcement of Foreign Judgments in Civil or Commercial Matters as its Final Text.[97] Costa Rica, Israel, the Russian Federation, Ukraine, the United States, and Uruguay have signed the Convention, but none has yet ratified.[98]

The basic structure of the Judgments Convention text is rather simple, but is then made complex through the set of connecting factors (some of which are similar to indirect bases of jurisdiction) by which a court is to determine whether a judgment may circulate under the Convention. Articles 1–3 set forth the scope of the Convention and provide definitions.[99] Art 4(1) provides the operative rule of the Convention, which requires that each Contracting State shall recognise and enforce judgments from other Contracting States and permits refusal only on those grounds expressly set out in the Convention. Article 5 then determines which judgments are 'eligible for recognition and enforcement' under the Convention by providing a list of bases of jurisdiction on which a judgment may have been founded. Thus, the court addressed for purposes of recognition and enforcement indirectly considers the connection on which the court of origin directly founded its judgment (or could have done so). Article 7 provides the general bases for non-recognition of a judgment, even if that judgment meets the requirements of Art 5. This list tracks closely the grounds for non-recognition found in the 2005 Hague Choice of Court Convention.[100]

Like the Choice of Court Convention, the Judgments Convention did not exhaust the set of issues originally presented in the jurisdiction and judgments project. Thus, the Experts Group on jurisdiction continued its work and, in February 2021 recommended to the Council on General Affairs and Policy (CGAP) of the Hague Conference that a Working Group be established 'to develop draft provisions on matters related to jurisdiction in civil or commercial matters, including rules for concurrent proceedings'.[101] The recommendation included that the Working Group have 'an initial focus on developing binding rules for concurrent proceedings (parallel proceedings and related actions or claims)',[102] and 'explore how flexible mechanisms for judicial coordination and cooperation can support the operation of any future instrument on concurrent proceedings and jurisdiction in transnational civil or commercial litigation'.[103] CGAP followed the Expert's Group recommendation and, in October 2021, mandated that a Working Group be created on the bases recommended by the Expert's Group. An online Working Group meeting was held in February 2022, followed by a hybrid meeting in September 2022, at which initial drafting of a Convention on Parallel Proceedings was begun. Both the European Union and the United States remained important parties in these efforts.

[96] ibid.
[97] Convention of 2 July 2019 on the Recognition and Enforcement of Foreign Judgments in Civil or Commercial Matters, www.hcch.net/en/instruments/conventions/specialised-sections/judgments.
[98] www.hcch.net/en/instruments/conventions/status-table/?cid=137.
[99] Hague Judgments Convention (n 97), Arts 1–3.
[100] Hague Convention on Choice of Court Agreements (n 87), Art 9.
[101] Aide-Mémoire of the Fifth (Online) Meeting of the Expert's Group on the Jurisdiction Project, February 2021, 39.
[102] ibid.
[103] ibid.

IV. Concluding Thoughts

Article 79 of the Brussels I (Recast) Regulation directs the Commission to answer only one question: whether it is now appropriate to apply the closed system of direct jurisdiction in the courts of EU Member States to all defendants, and not just to defendants domiciled in other EU Member States. The above discussion suggests that the review should address two other important issues:

(1) whether changes should also be made in the Regulation in order to extend its rules on the recognition and enforcement of judgments to external judgments, and
(2) if such changes are recommended on either or both of the rules on jurisdiction and judgments recognition, whether those changes occur through internal EU legislation or through global negotiations at the Hague Conference on Private International law.

Much has changed in both the European Union and the United States on the law of jurisdiction and judgments recognition since the initial consideration of these matters at the Hague Conference in the early 1990s. Competence for private international law has shifted fully from the EU Member States to the EU institutions. That law is now centralised, coordinated, and comprehensive. This is best demonstrated in the evolution from the Brussels Convention to the Brussels I Regulation to the Brussels I (Recast) Regulation.

In the United States, the law on jurisdiction over foreign defendants changed dramatically in 2011 with the Supreme Court's *Goodyear* decision. The move from broad-based general jurisdiction founded on continuous and systematic presence through corporate conduct to very limited general jurisdiction only where a corporation is 'at home' places the United States squarely in line with the rules of general jurisdiction in the Brussels I system.

While rules of general jurisdiction have moved closer together, however, that has not happened to rules of special/specific jurisdiction. The *Nicastro* decision made clear that a contraction of US general jurisdiction would not be accompanied by a corresponding expansion of concepts of specific jurisdiction. Thus, US jurisdictional reach is much more limited than is EU jurisdictional reach, even if only the direct jurisdiction rules applicable to defendants domiciled in EU Member States are applied. When the additional national law bases of jurisdiction are included in the EU Member State courts as available against defendants from non-EU Member States, the differences between the US and EU systems remain rather dramatic.

The difference in special/specific jurisdiction rules results largely from the US focus on due process rights of the defendant; rights that are available to all persons, both domestic and foreign, and both natural and legal. The EU special jurisdiction rules that focus almost solely on the connection between the court and the claim provide a very different result, and tip the balance significantly in favour of plaintiffs (perhaps enhancing concepts of access to justice) while providing much less protection for defendants (limiting the availability of due process – something rather different from access to justice).

An amendment to the Brussels I (Recast) Regulation that unifies the jurisdiction rules by making them applicable to all foreign defendants, and not just those domiciled in another Member State, would be a positive development in removing the discrimination that now exists against defendants domiciled outside the European Union. It would effectively extend due process to all defendants by removing the use of bases of jurisdiction the Member States themselves have determined to be unacceptable within the EU.

The opportunity should not be lost, however, to remove discrimination in judgments recognition law as well. As noted above,[104] the original Rome Treaty creating the European Economic Community, in its Art 220, clearly recognised the importance of unified rules on judgments recognition to the effective free movement of goods, services, capital, and people. Moreover, by combining rules on judgments recognition with rules on jurisdiction, the resulting Brussels Convention demonstrated a clear recognition of the importance of coordinating rules of jurisdiction and the recognition and enforcement of judgments. The further development of the European Union as a cohesive federal system for purposes of private international law makes it not only appropriate but important to take the next step in what has been a natural and organic evolutionary process.[105]

While much has happened at the Hague Conference on Private International Law, with the completion of the 2005 Convention on Choice of Court Agreements and the 2019 Convention on the Recognition and Enforcement of Judgments in Civil or Commercial Matters, the differences existing on a global basis, and particularly between the European Union and the United States, make the possibility of a global treaty on jurisdiction no more likely than was the case in 2001 when the transition away from that part of the goal was made. Had the rest of the US Supreme Court in 2011 followed Justice O'Connor's lead in *Nicastro* as they did in *Goodyear*, it may be that US and EU jurisdictional rules would be ready for coordination on a global stage. Unfortunately, that is not the case and any global possibilities on this front remain rather distant at best. This means it is most appropriate for the European Union to take those steps on rules for both jurisdiction and the recognition and enforcement of judgments internally. Article 79 of the Brussels I (Recast) Regulation provides that opportunity. It is an opportunity to remove discriminatory practices built into the Regulation and present a strengthened common front and example to the rest of the world.

[104] n 11 and accompanying text.

[105] See RA Brand, 'Recognition of Foreign Judgments as a Trade Law Issue: The Economics of Private International Law'.

Serbian Perspective on the Proposed Changes of the Brussels I Recast Regulation

MARKO JOVANOVIĆ

1. Introduction

Any changes of the European Union (EU) legislation concern not only the Member States (which are directly affected by such changes once they enter into force) but the candidate countries as well. This is because the candidate countries have a general obligation to harmonise their legal systems with the EU *acquis* prior to becoming the members of the Union. Although these harmonisation efforts may sometimes resemble the attempts to catch the train which is already leaving the station, they may be facilitated to a great extent if the candidate countries are included in the discussions regarding the legislative changes at their early stage and thus given sufficient time to fully understand the nature and ambit of such changes so that they can adapt to them in the best possible way.

The strategies for harmonisation of the Western Balkans countries with the EU international civil procedure rules have been studied for more than a decade. Local experts in private international law maintained constant and close contacts with their colleagues from the EU in order to enable smooth adaptation to and harmonisation with the EU rules of private international law. An illustration of the efforts to keep an eye on the developments of EU private international law is the Seventh annual regional conference on private international law held in Novi Sad (Serbia) in 2009. That conference was dedicated to the analysis of potential enlargement of the European Judicial Area to CEFTA countries and one of the papers presented at that conference focused specifically on various possible methods of harmonisation in the area of international civil procedure.[1] The examination of possibilities for a common regional approach to that issue was justified by the fact that the starting point for all the countries of the former Socialist Federative Republic of Yugoslavia (SFRY) was the same – up until the

[1] I Kunda, 'The Question of an Appropriate Method: Incorporation of the Brussels I Regulation, Invitation to Join the Lugano Convention or a New Convention?' in B Bordaš and M Stanivuković (eds), *VII Private International Law Conference – Enlargement of the European Judicial Area to CEFTA Countries* (Pravni fakultet u Novom Sadu, 2010), 47–69.

end of the 1990s, ie almost a full decade after the breakup of SFRY, they all applied the 1982 Yugoslav Private International Law Act (PILA) in its original version. The first country to introduce some substantive changes was Slovenia in 1999,[2] but the changes that the Slovenian legislator brought to the 1982 text were minor and primarily aimed at modernising the codification, while the structure and the 'spirit' of the 1982 Yugoslav PILA remained intact.

Although it concluded the Stabilization and Association Agreement with the EU and its Member States[3] and is advancing in the accession process, Serbia is not yet a member of the EU, so it still has an outsider's look on the changes of the EU legislation. Nevertheless, there is a strong interest in analysing the proposed changes to the Regulation No 1215/2012 on jurisdiction and the recognition and enforcement of judgments in civil and commercial matters (Brussels I Recast). In order to present the Serbian perspective regarding the possible changes of the Brussels I Recast Regulation, this report will first explain the current state of legislation in the field of private international law. It will then discuss the possibilities of harmonisation of Serbian law with the changes of EU private international law rules and, finally, analyse the potential impact of the changes.

2. Current State of Private International Law Legislation in Serbia

Serbia still applies the (almost) unaltered version of the 1982 Yugoslav PILA, which has been in force since 1 January 1983.[4] That act was the result of a dedicated work of the most renowned Yugoslav experts in private international law who conducted a comprehensive study of the modern comparative legislative tendencies at the time on the basis of which they drafted a modern, pragmatic and ideologically neutral codification. Shortly after the 1982 Yugoslav PILA entered into force, the English,[5] French[6] and German[7] translations of the act were published in leading international scientific journals, so that the foreign researchers and practitioners who are not familiar with the languages spoken in SFRY could discover its content.

After the breakup of SFRY, Serbia continued to apply the original version of the 1982 Yugoslav PILA with almost no modifications. For example, the reference to Yugoslavia and Yugoslav citizens still remains in PILA and the legislator never replaced those parts of the Act with references to Serbia and Serbian citizens. The only substantive amendment to the Serbian PILA came in 2006, when the Arbitration Act entered into force

[2] Obviously, all the former SFRY countries had to adopt some formal changes that reflected the status aspects of breakup of the Yugoslav federation.

[3] This Agreement entered into force on 1 September 2013.

[4] PILA was modified on two occasions: in 1996 and in 2006. The changes adopted in 1996 were of a merely formal nature, while the changes in 2006 only repealed some of the provisions that became superfluous due to the enactment of new sectorial legislation.

[5] See (1983) *Netherlands International Law Review* 222 et seq.

[6] See (1983) *Revue critique DIP* 353 et seq.

[7] See (1985) *RabelsZ* 544 et seq.

repealing Arts 97–100 PILA.[8] These provisions governed the recognition of foreign arbitral awards so they were no longer necessary once the Arbitration Act entered into force.

Serbian private international law is not fully codified in PILA. Some conflict of laws rules and rules on jurisdiction are contained in sectorial legislation, such as the Bill of Exchange Act,[9] the Commercial Shipping Act,[10] etc. Nevertheless, both in terms of its content and in terms of its practical use, PILA remains the most important source of Serbian private international law.

Apart from the national sources of private international law, Serbia is bound by numerous international conventions in this matter. More than 25 bilateral conventions govern various aspects of mutual legal assistance and recognition of judgments. As far as the multilateral conventions are concerned, Serbia is a party to 13 instruments drafted under the auspices of The Hague Conference on Private International Law. Some provisions of the PILA were modelled upon the solutions contained in The Hague conventions (eg Art 31 of the Serbian PILA, containing conflict of laws rules for formal validity of wills, was modelled upon the 1961 Convention on the Conflicts of Laws Relating to the Form of Testamentary Dispositions) and some conventions even practically replaced (if not formally repealed) the corresponding provisions of the PILA (eg conflict of laws rules for maintenance obligation are now superseded by the 2007 Protocol on the Law Applicable to Maintenance Obligations).

The Serbian PILA is a relatively short act – it has 109 articles divided into six chapters. These chapters were:

1. General provisions;
2. Rules on determining the applicable law;
3. Rules on jurisdiction and international civil procedure;
4. Rules on recognition and enforcement of foreign decisions;
5. Special provisions (rules on the competences of the Serbian consular officers regarding the conclusion of marriages between Serbian citizens abroad, the guardianship, drafting last wills of Serbian citizens abroad, legalization of documents and signatures and issuing the *certificats de coutume*);
6. Transitory and final provisions.

The basic rule on general jurisdiction in the Serbian PILA is quite common: the Serbian court shall have general jurisdiction when the defendant is domiciled in Serbia.[11] If the defendant is a legal person, the criterion for establishing general jurisdiction is the place of its registered seat.[12] This basic rule on general jurisdiction has several modifications.

First, if the defendant is a person without a domicile, the Serbian courts shall hold general jurisdiction if that person resides in Serbia. It should be noted that the Serbian PILA, having been drafted in the late 70s and early 80s, does not refer to the habitual

[8] See Arbitration Act (*Official Gazette RS* 46/06), Art 69(2).

[9] Bill of Exchange Act (*Official Gazette FPRY* 104/46, *Official Gazette SFRY* 16/65, 54/70, 57/89, *Official Gazette FRY* 46/96, *Official Gazette SM* 1/03), Arts 94–100.

[10] Commercial Shipping Act (*Official Gazette RS* 96/15, 113/17), Arts 759–783.

[11] Serbian PILA, Art 46(1).

[12] ibid.

residence in the sense of modern private international law acts. Rather, the notion of domicile should be interpreted in light of the relevant national provisions contained in the Law on domicile and residence[13] (in case that the defendant is a Serbian national) or the Law on foreigners[14] (if the defendant is not a Serbian national).

If both parties to the proceedings are Serbian nationals and the defendant resides in Serbia, the Serbian court shall have general jurisdiction even if the defendant is domiciled abroad.[15] Although this modification to the basic rule of general jurisdiction is justified by the intensity of connection between the litigants and the forum,[16] it might potentially lead to a conflict of general jurisdictions between the Serbian court and the court of the domicile of the defendant. If such a problem indeed occurs, it could be resolved through the rules on coordination of international jurisdiction (*lis pendens*), but this situation certainly calls for caution and attention. The caution is warranted by the fact that some situations of conflict of general jurisdictions might escape the default rule on coordination of jurisdictions which is based on the principle of *prior tempore*. Namely, the Serbian provision on *lis pendens* requires several conditions to be fulfilled in order for the request for stay of proceedings to be granted.[17] One of those conditions is the requirement of reciprocity between Serbia and the country of the other court seised in terms granting requests for stay of proceedings. If this requirement is not met, the request for stay of proceedings shall be denied by the Serbian court even though all other conditions are fulfilled, and the conflict of jurisdictions would not be resolved – both courts would continue to act in parallel.

Somewhat similar to the previous situation is the one which may happen on the basis of Art 52 of the Serbian PILA. Pursuant to this provision, the Serbian court shall have (general) jurisdiction over the defendant who is a Serbian national but who lives abroad because s/he is sent to work there by a State organ, company or other legal person, on the condition that such person had a domicile in Serbia immediately prior to being sent abroad. In this case, the conflict of general jurisdictions could emerge if the Serbian national living abroad fulfills the conditions for general jurisdiction in the country of residence, eg if s/he acquires domicile in that country or complies with any other ground of general jurisdiction that may exist in that country.

As far as the rules on special jurisdiction are concerned, the Serbian PILA remains consistent with its general conceptual approach of using broad categories, so it classifies them into rather large groups. As far as the matters governed by Brussels I Recast are concerned, the Serbian PILA distinguishes only four grounds of special jurisdiction. These are: (1) pecuniary claims; (2) claims for obligations presenting specific contacts with Serbia; (3) torts; (4) rights *in rem*; (5) rights *in rem* concerning an aircraft or a

[13] *Official Gazette RS* 87/11.

[14] *Official Gazette RS* 24/2018 and 31/2019.

[15] Serbian PILA, Art 46(3).

[16] M Dika, G Knežević, S Stojannović, *Komentar Zakona o međunarodnom privatnom i procesnom pravu* (Nomos, 1991) 170.

[17] Pursuant to Art 80 of the Serbian PILA, aside from the basic prerequisite of identity of the disputes, this condition includes the requirements that the foreign court was first seised, that the Serbian court does not have exclusive jurisdiction over the subject matter of the dispute and reciprocity.

vessel. The rest of the jurisdictional provisions apply to the disputes in family, inheritance and personal status matters, so they remain outside the scope of the issues covered by Brussels I Recast.

The provision on special jurisdiction for pecuniary claims is modelled upon the original version of the German provision of Art 23 of the German Code of Civil Procedure (*Zivilprozessordnung*). Namely, Art 54(1) of the Serbian PILA provides that the Serbian court shall have jurisdiction over a pecuniary claim if the defendant has assets in Serbia (irrespective of the relation between the value of the claim and the value of the assets) or if the object requested by the claim is located in Serbia. In absence of any requirement of correlation between the value of the claim and the value of the assets located in Serbia, Art 54(1) should be deemed to represent an example of exorbitant jurisdiction, since no additional connection between the parties and the forum is required.

The Serbian court may establish jurisdiction for claims regarding the obligations created while the defendant was present in Serbia,[18] or the obligations created in Serbia on the condition that the defendant has also a business representation in Serbia.[19] Likewise, the Serbian court would be competent for disputes over obligations performed or to be performed in Serbia, but again on the condition that the defendant has a business representation in Serbia.[20]

As far as the special jurisdiction for torts is concerned, by virtue of Art 53(1) PILA the Serbian court may be competent if the damage occurred in Serbia. However, seeing that this is a special ground of jurisdiction, the competence of the Serbian court shall, in this case, extend only to the damage localised in Serbia. Claim for compensation of damage incurred outside Serbia can only be lodged with the Serbian court if the Serbian court has general jurisdiction.

Several provisions of the Serbian PILA deal with jurisdiction over rights *in rem*. As noted earlier, if the plaintiff requests to be handed over a certain object, the Serbian court shall hold special jurisdiction if that object is located in Serbia.[21] The reasoning behind this solution is evident and it lays in enabling an easy enforcement of the decision if the claim is granted. In case of disputes caused by prevention of enjoyment of property rights on movables, the Serbian court shall hold jurisdiction if the prevention occurred on the territory of Serbia.[22] Finally, it comes as no surprise that in case of disputes over the rights *in rem* on immovable property, the special jurisdiction of the Serbian court shall be exclusive if the immovable property is situated in Serbia.[23]

In case of disputes over the rights *in rem* concerning an aircraft or a vessel, the special jurisdiction of the Serbian court shall exist if the aircraft or the marine or river vessel is listed in a registry maintained by Serbian organs, ie if it bears the Serbian flag.[24] It is worth noting, though, that despite the fact that the legal status of aircrafts and vessels under Serbian law is largely similar to the status of immovable property, the special

[18] Serbian PILA, Art 54(2).
[19] Serbian PILA, Art 55.
[20] ibid.
[21] Serbian PILA, Art 54(1).
[22] Serbian PILA, Art 57.
[23] Serbian PILA, Art 56.
[24] Serbian PILA, Art 58.

jurisdiction of the Serbian court in this case would not be exclusive. The exclusive jurisdiction would be triggered only in cases of some disputes concerning State vessels.[25]

As it can be seen, the currently applicable Serbian rules on international jurisdiction in civil and commercial matters show certain similarities to the rules contained in Brussels I Recast. Nevertheless, numerous differences in structure and content are obvious. Seeing the perspective of Serbian accession to the EU, legal scholars have examined the possibilities for harmonization of the Serbian private nternational law with the EU *acquis* for more than a decade.

3. Possibilities and Strategies for Harmonisation of Serbian Private International Law with EU Acquis

Different possibilities of harmonisation of private international law systems of former SFRY countries have been in focus of the attention so far. In particular, a very thorough analysis was presented at the aforementioned Seventh regional private international law conference by Professor Ivana Kunda (University of Rijeka, Croatia), who identified three possible methodological approaches:

1. Incorporation of the EU private international law instruments prior to the accession to the EU;
2. Accession to the Lugano Convention as a 'preparation' for integration into the European Judicial Area;
3. Adoption of a new regional convention unifying private international law rules among the candidate States.[26]

As far as the application of these solutions in practice is concerned, the situation is rather heterogeneous. Some former SFRY countries opted for incorporating certain elements of EU private international law into their national codifications. That was the case of Montenegro[27] and North Macedonia.[28]

Although praised in the doctrine,[29] the option of acceding to the Lugano Convention did not seem to attract a particular attention of the legislators in the region. A potential reason for the lack of interest for this option might be the fact the accession to this Convention is subject to the fulfilment of certain criteria and requires a unanimous consent by the current State Parties to the Convention.[30]

[25] See Commercial Shipping Act, Art 780.

[26] For detailed presentation and evaluation of these approaches see I Kunda, 'The Question of an Appropriate Method: Incorporation of the Brussels I Regulation, Invitation to Join the Lugano Convention or a New Convention?', 47–68.

[27] More on the modifications of private international law codification in Montenegro see M Kostić-Mandić, *Međunarodno privatno pravo* (Pravni fakultet Univerziteta Crne Gore, 2017), 37–38.

[28] More on the modifications of private international law codification in North Macedonia see T Deskoski, V Dokovski, *Megunarodno privatno pravo* (Praven fakultet "Justinijan Prvi", 2021), 83–85.

[29] M Stanivuković, 'Umesto zaključka – o potrebi pristupanja Luganskoj konvenciji' in B Bordaš and M Stanivuković (eds), *VIII Private International Law Conference – Enlargement of the European Judicial Area to CEFTA Countries* (Pravni fakultet Univerziteta u Novom Sadu, 2010) 91.

[30] See Lugano Convention, Arts 70–72.

On the other hand, the possibilities for adopting a special regional convention parallel to the Lugano Convention appeared to be a more appealing solution. In 2011 the Republic of Slovenia proposed the idea of adopting a convention aimed at unification of rules on jurisdiction and recognition and enforcement of foreign judgments within Central European Free Trade Association (CEFTA). That project was called the Sarajevo Convention. At the very outset, the negotiators were faced with the dilemma whether to transpose the full text of the Brussels I Regulation (Regulation No 44/2001, which was in force at the time) or to work towards drafting a shorter, more concise text. The decision was taken to transpose the Brussels I Regulation and to open the possibilities for modifying the text of the convention with the forthcoming changes of the Regulation, seeing that the work on the Brussels I Recast was ongoing at the time when the Sarajevo Convention was negotiated.[31] However, as the time went by, the political interest within CEFTA for the adoption of the Sarajevo Convention was gradually declining. In this moment, there are no indications that the Sarajevo Convention project would be revived in near future.[32]

Beside the options elaborated by Professor Kunda, there seems to be yet another approach for the modernisation of private international law rules in the Western Balkans. As noted in the introduction to this report, that approach was taken by Slovenia as early as in 1999 (ie 5 years prior to its accession to the EU) and it consists in certain substantive modifications of the existing codification, while keeping the structure, most of the original provisions and the general underlying idea of the 1982 Yugoslav PILA. The modifications were aimed at keeping the old Yugoslav codification up-to-date with modern tendencies in comparative private international law and at correcting some shortcomings identified in practice. For example, the Slovenian PILA now includes the rules on jurisdiction for disputes concerning patents and trademarks[33] or status of legal persons,[34] and these provisions were modelled upon the solutions contained in the Brussels regime. Also, the exorbitant ground of jurisdiction for pecuniary claims that still exists in Art 54(1) of the Serbian PILA is now restrained in the Slovenian codification through the introduction of two additional jurisdictional requirements: not only is it necessary that the defendant has assets on the territory of Slovenia, but it is also required that the plaintiff has its domicile or seat in Slovenia and manages to prove the likelihood of enforcement of the claim on those assets (which actually represents the requirement of correlation between the value of the plaintiff's claim and the value of the defendant's assets).[35] Strictly speaking, the Slovenian approach to the reform of private international law does not lead to the harmonisation of the private international law of the candidate country with the EU *acquis* in the pre-accession phase, but it only

[31] That goal was supposed to be achieved by way of the Protocol No 3 to the Sarajevo Convention, by which the Contracting Parties would agree to align the provisions of the Convention with the future changes of the Brussels regime.

[32] More on the Sarajevo Convention Project see J Alihodžić, Z Meškić, A Duraković, 'Accepting EU Private International Law Standards into the Legal System of Bosnia and Herzegovina: What Can Be Done While Waiting for Godot?' (2019) *Lexonomica* 166–67.

[33] Slovenian PILA, Art 62.

[34] Slovenian PILA, Art 60.

[35] Slovenian PILA, Art 58(2).

allows a national codification to keep the pace with current global tendencies of the development of private international law. Leaving aside the question of whether such approach is useful and efficient, it certainly confirms that it is feasible to move towards the accession to the EU without (fully) aligning with the *acquis* in the field of private international law.

Almost all the options and strategies described above were considered at some point by the Serbian legislator. In early 2009 the Ministry of Justice of the Republic of Serbia convened the leading Serbian academics and practitioners and entrusted them with the task of reforming the Serbian PILA. Quite logically, the group was first faced with the conceptual choice whether to move towards drafting a completely new codification or to simply 'update' the existing PILA following the Slovenian model. Both options had their partisans and the initial discussions on the orientation that the work should take were rather heated. Eventually, the opinion in favour of completely new codification prevailed. Thus, the group proceeded to conducting a comprehensive study of the leading comparative normative solutions. This was done in an attempt to come up with the text that would represent the 'state-of-the-art' at the time of drafting. The special attention was naturally given to the solutions of the Brussels regime and they were widely reflected in the text of the draft. It should be noted that the work of the group was very transparent: all interested academics and practitioners were always welcome at the meetings, irrespective of whether they were officially appointed members of the working group or not and the chair of the working group, Professor Mirko Živković (University of Niš, Serbia), constantly maintained a close contact with experts from the EU. The laborious task of preparing a new, modern text was completed by summer 2014 and the draft of the new codification was delivered to the Ministry of Justice.[36] The draft had 199 articles divided into 4 parts: general provisions (Arts 1–45), special provisions (Arts 46–181), provisions on recognition and enforcement of foreign judgments (Arts 182–193) and transitory and final dispositions (Arts 194–199). Contrary to the 1982 Yugoslav PILA, which placed all the conflict of laws rules in one section and then all the rules on jurisdiction in the other, the 2014 draft Serbian PILA contained sections organised by subject matters, each section starting with the rules on jurisdiction and then continuing with conflict of laws rules for the subject matter concerned.

Despite the remarkable energy, enthusiasm and knowledge invested into drafting the new Serbian codification of private international law, the parliamentary procedure for the enactment of the 2014 draft PILA has not yet been initiated. The reasons for this unusual delay have never been officially disclosed. Seeing that almost a decade passed since the submission of the draft to the Ministry of Justice, it seems highly unlikely that it would ever be adopted in the current form and content. Broadly speaking, three options can be envisaged. If the legislator eventually decides to adopt the 2014 draft, this text would have to be reviewed and brushed up, so that it indeed represents the 'state-of-the-art' at the time of enactment. If the Ministry decides to dismiss that draft, it can either form a new working group and instruct it to prepare a completely new draft, or decide to embrace the Slovenian approach and introduce only the most necessary changes to

[36] The Serbian version of the draft and the statement of reasons for its enactment are available at www.mpravde.gov.rs/obavestenje/6274/konacna.

the currently applicable Serbian PILA. Bearing in mind that almost all Serbian experts on private international law participated in the preparation of the 2014 draft, it seems rather unlikely that they would be now willing to accept to start the whole work from scratch and agree to come up with a completely new draft.

The array of solutions that the Ministry of Justice could adopt would therefore come down to two: either to 'revive' the 2014 draft or to proceed to 'face-lifting' of the currently applicable Serbian PILA. It remains to be seen what will be the eventual decision of the Serbian legislator.

4. Potential Impact of Changes of the Brussels Regime to the Defendants Domiciled in Serbia

Even though Serbia is not yet a member of the EU, it is a part of the European continent and, due to the geographical proximity to the EU, Serbian national or persons domiciled in Serbia frequently engage in private law relations, civil or commercial, with EU citizens or persons domiciled in the EU.[37] The downside of the frequency of these relations is the increased likelihood of disputes. Depending on the facts of each particular case and the applicable rules on jurisdiction, these disputes might potentially lead to an overlap or lack of adequate coordination between the EU and Serbian procedural systems. It is therefore necessary to examine the effect of potential changes of the Brussels regime to the Serbian international civil procedure rules.

Indeed, the previous changes have confirmed that the interest in the external effects of reforms of the Brussels regime is justified. That was the case, for example, with the amendments to Art 23 of the Brussels I Regulation that led to the abandonment of the request that one of the parties to a prorogation agreement had to be domiciled in the EU so that the validity of the agreement on choice of jurisdiction of an EU Member State court would be governed by the rules of the Brussels regime. This change improved the position of the persons domiciled in third States in the way that two parties domiciled in a third State can now opt for the jurisdiction of an EU Member State court as a neutral forum and benefit from a greater predictability and legal certainty as to the conditions for validity of their agreement, since that question is no longer governed by the national rules of the place of forum but by the unified and certainly more easily accessible EU rules.

The practical advantages of these amendments are not just abstract, but they can easily be illustrated from the standpoint of Serbian rules on validity of choice of court agreements. Namely, pursuant to Art 49(1) of the Serbian PILA, the parties may derogate from the jurisdiction of the Serbian court as long as (at least) one of them is a foreign national and the subject matter of the dispute does not fall under the exclusive jurisdiction of the Serbian court. It should be noted that the parties may choose

[37] As far as the commercial relations are concerned, this is confirmed by the statistics. According to the data available for 2021, 6 out of 10 biggest Serbian trading partners were EU Members States (Germany, Italy, Hungary, Romania, Poland and the Czech Republic).

any national court they perceive as desirable, since there is no requirement of connexity between the place of the court chosen, nationality or domicile of the parties to the prorogation agreement or any other territorial element of the legal relation giving rise to the dispute.[38] Obviously, Serbian procedural rules can only govern the conditions for the validity of derogation from the jurisdiction of Serbian courts and, due to their unilateral nature, they cannot set any criteria for assessing validity that would bind the court chosen. Under such circumstances, the parties to a prorogation agreement would be expected to consider whether their prorogation agreement would be valid from the perspective of *lex fori prorogati*. If, hypothetically, during the time of applicability of the Brussels I Regulation a party domiciled in Serbia and a party domiciled in Montenegro concluded a complex prorogation agreement in favour of a court in Croatia, Hungary or Greece at the choice of claimant, it would be advisable that they establish whether such agreement would be valid from the standpoint of each of the three countries concerned prior to concluding such an agreement. This would obviously require time, energy and specific knowledge of each of the three procedural systems concerned. Since the entry into force of Brussels I Recast, this issue would fall under the unified jurisdictional regime and the parties to the prorogation agreement could rather easily detect whether, based on the *Meeth v Glacetal* jurisprudence[39] and the cases that followed, the court in any of the three countries named would uphold the validity of their agreement provided that all conditions laid down in Art 25 of the Brussels I Recast are fulfilled.

Similar benefits might be expected from the potential expansion of the scope of application of Brussels I Recast to the defendants not domiciled in the EU. Even though it could be argued that any extension brought to the scope of application of the rules on jurisdiction is more likely to have an effect on the recognition and enforcement of judgments, it is nevertheless possible to envisage some effects on the coordination of jurisdictions as well. At a very general level, it could be anticipated that the announced amendments to Brussels I Recast would lead to an even better solution of the problem of the 'reflexive effect' of the grounds of exclusive jurisdiction. This would certainly lead to more efficient, more predictable and more reliable settlement of disputes. But apart from those general considerations, one might envisage some more concrete developments.

In that sense, the first provision that comes to mind is Art 48 of the Serbian PILA. This provision reads:

> If the court of a foreign country can establish jurisdiction in the proceedings against Serbian citizens on the basis of a criterion that does not exist among the grounds of jurisdiction of Serbian courts, such criterion shall be applicable for establishing jurisdiction of the Serbian court in the proceedings where the defendant is the citizen of that foreign country.

Former Yugoslav and Serbian doctrine generally considered this provision to enable the 'jurisdiction based on retorsion'.[40] The documented examples of application of this

[38] M Dika, G Knežević, S Stojannović, *Komentar Zakona o međunarodnom privatnom i procesnom pravu*, 179.

[39] Case 23/78 *Meeth v Glacetal* [1978].

[40] T Varadi, B Bordaš, G Knežević, V Pavić, *Međunarodno privatno pravo* (University of Belgrade Faculty of Law, 2019), 499.

provision are rather scarce, but they generally show that the application of Art 48 of the Serbian PILA was triggered by an exorbitant ground of jurisdiction existing in the law of the country of the defendant,[41] which is an argument in favour of considering this provision as a rule that enables jurisdictional 'retaliation'. However, it seems worth noting that the text of Art 48 of the Serbian PILA does not speak about the exorbitant character or the scope of the foreign rule on jurisdiction as a precondition to its applicability. It merely requires that the relevant ground of jurisdiction 'does not exist among the grounds of jurisdiction of Serbian courts'. Therefore, it can be concluded that the purpose of Art 48 of the Serbian PILA is not to 'correct' Serbian rules on jurisdiction in cases where foreign law would simply have a different ground of jurisdiction than the Serbian law for the same subject matter of the dispute, as long as that foreign ground of jurisdiction is familiar to the Serbian PILA. Rather, the scope of application of this provision is limited to the situations where the foreign ground of jurisdiction is completely unknown to Serbian law, meaning that the Serbian PILA never uses it (eg nationality of the plaintiff).

Therefore, it seems possible to argue that Art 48 of the Serbian PILA may also represent the tool for modernisation of the Serbian codification by enabling the transposition of a novel, modern ground of jurisdiction which does not exist among the heads of jurisdiction used by the PILA. In the context of Brussels I Recast, such ground of jurisdiction may be eg in case of disputes over individual contracts of employment, the place where the employer habitually carries out his work or the last place where he did so. This ground of jurisdiction is not used anywhere in the Serbian PILA, which might point to the conclusion that the criterion of extraneousness to Serbian law could be deemed fulfilled in this case.

It should be noted that the possibility of transposing the modern grounds of jurisdiction into the Serbian international civil procedure exists even today and that it will not be launched by the extension of the scope of application of the Brussels regime. This is because the personal connecting factor that triggers the application of Art 48 of the Serbian PILA is the nationality and not the domicile of the defendant. Therefore, a Serbian citizen domiciled in an EU Member State would even now fall under the Brussels regime if sued before a court in a Member State. However, with the extension of the scope of application of Brussels I Recast to the defendants not domiciled in the EU, the array of possibilities where a Serbian defendant could hypothetically fall under the Brussels jurisdictional rules would become larger, since the requirement of domicile would no longer be required. Consequently, the call for application of Art 48 of the Serbian PILA would become more obvious, assuming that it is accepted that it can transpose not only exorbitant but all grounds of jurisdiction unknown to the Serbian PILA.

It might be interesting to examine whether the method of interaction between the EU and Serbian rules of jurisdiction that we have just suggested might be used in the sphere of disputes in contractual matters, where the cross-border disputes are relatively frequent. With the suppression of the requirement that the defendant is domiciled in

[41] M Dika, G Knežević, S Stojannović, *Komentar Zakona o međunarodnom privatnom i procesnom pravu*, 177–78.

the EU, a court in a Member State would be able to establish its jurisdiction whenever the place of performance of the obligation in question is located in that Member State. This would represent a broader and more flexible solution than the one retained by the Serbian PILA, according to which the Serbian court can assume special jurisdiction if the obligation was created during the defendant's sojourn in the Republic of Serbia (Art 54(2) of the Serbian PILA) or if the obligation in question was created or is to be performed in Serbia *and* the defendant has its business representation in Serbia (Art 55 of the Serbian PILA). However, it seems that this hypothetical example would represent the case of 'correction' of the Serbian jurisdictional rules, rather than transposition of a criterion that is unknown to the Serbian PILA. This is because the place of performance of the obligation in question as such is not extraneous to the Serbian PILA. The Serbian legislator only considers that this connecting factor alone is not sufficient to justify the jurisdiction of the domestic court so it requires additional points of contact, such as the existence of business representation in Serbia. Accordingly, it should be assumed that Art 48 of the Serbian PILA could not be used to expand the scope of jurisdiction of Serbian courts in contractual disputes. Nevertheless, this potential dilemma will be finally resolved once the case law based on Art 48 of the Serbian PILA becomes richer and the courts offer their interpretation of this provision.

5. Conclusion

Potential extension of the scope of application of Brussels I Recast to the defendants not domiciled in the EU shall certainly have an impact on the candidate countries. This is for at least two reasons. First, the candidate countries are obliged to harmonise their legal systems with the EU *acquis*. Second, the volume and frequency of personal and business relations between persons domiciled in the EU and candidate countries raise the likelihood of disputes, which in turn calls for more careful coordination of jurisdictions between the EU Member States and candidate countries. With the extension of the scope of application of Brussels I Recast, it is conceivable that the cases of potential overlap become even more numerous than they are now and that gives rise to the need for ever better coordination of the systems.

As far as the first reason is concerned, it appears that the obligation of harmonisation of the rules of private international law is not that strict as it may be in some other spheres, in the sense that it precisely entails the transposition of the EU rules into the national legal system of the candidate country. Nevertheless, even in absence of a strict formal obligation, it would be prudent for the candidate countries, including Serbia, to closely monitor the developments in EU private international law and adjust the domestic systems so that the adaptation to the Brussels regime, once they become members, runs as smoothly as possible. Serbia has not yet amended its 40-year-old codification of private international law, so the review of Brussels I Recast will provide even more food for thought to the Serbian legislator.

Concerning the second reason, we have tried to identify and illustrate some cases of potential direct interaction between the EU and Serbian procedural systems, which might be expected to become even more frequent if the scope of application of Brussels I

Recast is indeed expanded. These cases call for close attention and require solutions on at least three levels: jurisdictional rules themselves, rules on coordination of jurisdictions and rules on recognition and enforcement of foreign judgments. This task will indeed be complex, but if performed successfully, it will certainly confirm the motto of the European Union – united in diversity.

Extending the Brussels Ia Regulation to Third State Defendants – Cui Bono?

A Third State Perspective from the UK

JOHANNES UNGERER*

I. Introduction

When the Brussels Ia Regulation[1] was enacted in 2012 as a recast of the Brussels I Regulation,[2] there was no consensus over following the European Commission's proposal to unify the rules on international jurisdiction applicable to defendants not domiciled in a Member State. It was however agreed to revisit the issue a decade later. Now, it is high time to reconsider the arguments for and against unifying the rules for Third State defendants by extending the Regulation's rules to them. Instead of simply assuming that the unification by extension is an end worthwhile pursuing in itself, the question has to be raised whether and, most importantly, for whom the extension would be beneficial.[3] While several scholars from within the EU have argued in favour of the extension,[4] this chapter will advocate a more cautious approach by showing that the extension would not be of greater benefit to the EU and its Member States, but rather Third States. To illustrate this, the perspective of the UK will be taken, which due to Brexit has joined the ranks of Third States and now competes with the EU over international litigation and the profits for the legal services industry. In the light of this change of circumstances

* Dr Johannes Ungerer, Erich Brost Lecturer in German Law and EU Law, Faculty of Law and St Hilda's College, University of Oxford, johannes.ungerer@law.ox.ac.uk.

[1] Regulation (EU) No 1215/2012.

[2] Council Regulation (EC) No 44/2001.

[3] Similarly R Fentiman, 'Brussels I and Third States: Future Imperfect?' (2010) 13 *Cambridge Yearbook of European Legal Studies* 65, 69.

[4] A Bonomi, 'European Private International Law and Third States' [2017] *Praxis des Internationalen Privat- und Verfahrensrechts* 184, 185 et seq.; B Hess, *Europäisches Zivilprozessrecht* 2nd edn (De Gruyter, 2020) para 5.24; T Lutzi and FM Wilke, 'Brüssel Ia extendenda est?' (2022) 86 *Rabels Zeitschrift für ausländisches und internationales Privatrecht* 841; R Luzzatto, 'On the Proposed Application of Jurisdictional Criteria of Brussels I Regulation to Non-Domiciled Defendants' in F Pocar, I Viarengo and FC Villata (eds), *Recasting Brussels I* (Cedam, 2012); J Weber, 'Universal Jurisdiction and Third States in the Reform of the Brussels I Regulation' (2011) 75 *Rabels Zeitschrift für ausländisches und internationales Privatrecht* 619; also see U Magnus and P Mankowski, 'The Proposal for the Reform of Brussels I' (2011) 110 *Zeitschrift für Vergleichende Rechtswissenschaft* 252, 262 et seq.; M Poesen, 'Civil litigation against Third-Country defendants in the EU: effective access to justice as a rationale for European Harmonization of the law of international jurisdiction' (2022) 59 *Common Market Law Review* 1597.

since the extension was discussed a decade ago, it will be demonstrated that the EU would do itself a disservice if it were to unify the jurisdictional rules on Third State defendants by extending the Regulation to them while the EU Member States actually wish to win over litigation from London and other popular hubs overseas.

II. Status Quo

Under the status quo of the Brussels Ia Regulation, the EU unification of the rules on jurisdiction is limited to proceedings with a sufficient connection to the territory of the Member States (or, the EU Single Market).[5] This means that Third State defendants are presently not covered by the ordinary Brussels Ia rules, for instance Art 7 which determines jurisdiction over EU defendants in matters such as contract and tort. Instead, the autonomous rules of Member States govern jurisdiction of Member State courts over defendants from Third States in principle.[6] Consequently, in cases against Third State defendants, Member State courts can still employ autonomous rules which are exorbitant in the sense that those rules are internationally unusual and are based on a fairly tenuous connection of the defendant with the forum.[7] Exposing Third State defendants in this way is discriminatory in comparison to how EU defendants are treated:[8] EU defendants are protected from the autonomous rules of other Member States, especially exorbitant rules, because EU defendants may only be sued in another Member State according to the unified Brussels Ia rules.[9]

The discriminatory effect of the Brussels Ia Regulation is worsened by the fact that autonomous exorbitant rules of any Member State which only apply to nationals of that Member State are made available by the Regulation to all claimants domiciled in that Member State regardless of their nationality.[10] This is relevant in particular with regard to Art 14 of the French Civil Code, so that any claimant domiciled in France can sue a Third State defendant there.[11]

In addition, Third State defendants are discriminated against by the Brussels Ia Regulation when it comes to recognition and enforcement of Member State courts' judgments in other Member States. Even if a Member State's jurisdiction over a Third State defendant is based on the autonomous exorbitant rules of the respective Member

[5] Recital 13 Brussels Ia Regulation; also see Case C-281/02 *Owusu*.

[6] Recital 14 and Art 6(1) Brussels Ia Regulation.

[7] D Childress, 'Jurisdiction, Limits under International Law' in J Basedow and others (eds), *Encyclopedia of private international law* (Elgar, 2017) 1054.

[8] This has been criticised since the times of the Brussels Convention, see for instance F Juenger, 'Judicial Jurisdiction in the United States and in the European Communities: A Comparison' (1984) 82 *Michigan Law Review* 1195, 1211; P Grolimund, *Drittstaatenproblematik des europäischen Zivilverfahrensrechts* (Mohr Siebeck, 2000) para 601 et seq. More recently, TC Hartley, *International Commercial Litigation: Text, Cases and Materials on Private International Law* 3rd edn (Cambridge University Press, 2020) 22, 191; SC Symeonides, 'The Brussels I Regulation and Third Countries' in *Libro homenaje al Profesor Eugenio Hernández-Bretón*, (Editorial Jurídica Venezolana, 2019). It is also described by B Hess, T Pfeiffer and P Schlosser, *The Brussels I-Regulation (EC) No 44/2001: The Heidelberg Report on the Application of Regulation Brussels I in 25 Member States (Study JLS/C4/2005/03)* (CH Beck, 2008) para 156.

[9] Art 5 Brussels Ia Regulation.

[10] Art 6(2) Brussels Ia Regulation.

[11] For a recent application of Art 14 French Civil Code in conjunction with Art 6(2) Brussels Ia Regulation, see Cour de cassation, ECLI:FR:CCASS:2022:C100536 and ECLI:FR:CCASS:2022:C100616.

State, the resulting judgment of this Member State court can nonetheless move freely across the EU due to the Brussels Ia Regulation,[12] which thus EU-wide multiplies the exorbitant effect of the autonomous rules.[13]

There are three limited instances under the status quo where the Brussels Ia rules apply instead of the autonomous rules of the Member States against Third State defendants; these instances are thus not subject to any further reform decisions about extending or not extending the Brussels Ia Regulation. First, the special protective rules of the Brussels Ia Regulation apply instead of the Member States' autonomous rules to consumer and employment disputes,[14] and to a varied extent to insurance disputes.[15] Secondly, the Brussels Ia rules apply in cases of exclusive jurisdiction, such as disputes about rights *in rem*.[16] Thirdly, the autonomous rules of the Member States are superseded in cases of a choice of court,[17] although the Brussels Ia Regulation itself is superseded in turn by the 2005 Hague Convention on Choice of Court Agreements if the case is covered by the Convention.[18] The latter is highly relevant for exclusive prorogation agreements between EU and British commercial parties since both the EU and the UK are Contracting States of the Convention. Apart from these three instances, however, the autonomous rules of the Member States apply to Third State defendants under the status quo. As indicated above, this pertains to common commercial disputes, such as about contracts or torts, where no valid prorogation has been agreed upon; for such disputes, any reform decision about extending the Brussels Ia rules to Third State defendants would matter.

III. Full Extension of the Regulation to Third State Defendants

Fully extending the Brussels Ia Regulation to Third State defendants would mean that the rules on jurisdiction of the Regulation, which so far are only applicable to EU defendants, such as Art 7, would become applicable to Third State defendants as well. Treating EU and Third State defendants alike in this way by removing all differentiation in the Regulation was the Commission's proposal in 2010 for the recast of the Brussels I Regulation,[19] but it was not adopted in the Brussels Ia Regulation. The reason was that,

[12] Art 36 et seq. Brussels Ia Regulation. However, see the exception in Art 72.

[13] Criticised for instance by A Taylor von Mehren, 'Recognition and Enforcement of Foreign Judgments: General Theory and the Role of Jurisdictional Requirements' (1980) 167 *Recueil des cours* 9, 98 et seq regarding the Brussels Convention; K Takahashi, 'Review of the Brussels I Regulation: A Comment from the Perspectives of Non-Member States (Third States)' (2012) 8 *Journal of Private International Law* 1, 2.

[14] Art 18(1), 21(2) Brussels Ia Regulation.

[15] Art 11(2) Brussels Ia Regulation; cf P Vlas, 'Article 6' in U Magnus and P Mankowski (eds), *European Commentaries on Private International Law: Brussels Ibis Regulation* (Vol 1, Otto Schmidt, 2016) para 2.

[16] Art 24 Brussels Ia Regulation.

[17] Art 25 Brussels Ia Regulation.

[18] Art 71 Brussels Ia Regulation.

[19] European Commission, 'Proposal for a Regulation of the European Parliament and of the Council on Jurisdiction and the Recognition and Enforcement of Judgments in Civil and Commercial Matters (Recast)' (COM(2010) 748 Final, 14.12.2010) www.eur-lex.europa.eu/LexUriServ/LexUriServ.do?uri=COM:2010:0748:FIN:EN:PDF.

in the Legal Affairs Committee of the European Parliament, it was felt that 'it would be premature to take [the step of removing all differentiation in the Regulation] without wide-ranging consultations and political debate'.[20] Since it was agreed though in the adopted text of the Brussels Ia Regulation to re-evaluate the situation in January 2022,[21] assessment of whether the Commission's proposal is worth reviving or not is now overdue. Several scholars support the unification by full extension.[22]

IV. Consequences of a Full Extension

At first sight, it might seem beneficial and desirable for the EU and its Member States to unify the rules for Third State defendants by fully extending the Regulation's rules to them.[23] Indeed, it would at least increase the simplicity and clarity of the rules which Member State courts have to apply, because they would not have to potentially apply other rules to Third State defendants than to EU defendants.[24] However, it will be demonstrated that the rule unification by extension would ultimately be detrimental for the EU and its Member States and rather beneficial for Third States, such as the UK.

Insofar, the verdicts of benefit and detriment are based on the assumption that a State, as a matter of principle, prefers to have its own courts affirm international jurisdiction wherever reasonable instead of rejecting it and leaving it to foreign courts. This assumption of self-interest of States to attract international litigation domestically is understandable in the context of the international competition of the various legal systems. The motivation for seeking to affirm jurisdiction and to attract litigation can,

[20] European Parliament (Committee on Legal Affairs, Rapporteur: Tadeusz Zwiefka), 'Draft Report on the Proposal for a Regulation of the European Parliament and of the Council on Jurisdiction and the Recognition and Enforcement of Judgments in Civil and Commercial Matters (Recast)' (PE467.046v01-00, 28.6.2011) www.europarl.europa.eu/meetdocs/2009_2014/documents/juri/pr/869/869709/869709en.pdf, 8, 47.

[21] Art 79 Brussels Ia Regulation required the Commission to present a report by 11 January 2022.

[22] For instance A Bonomi, 'European Private International Law and Third States', 186–87; J Weber, 'Universal Jurisdiction and Third States in the Reform of the Brussels I Regulation', 623 et seq; also see F Horn, 'Note – The Proposal for a Regulation of the European Parliament and of the Council on Jurisdiction and the Recognition and Enforcement of Judgments in Civil and Commercial Matters (Recast)' (DATE) www.europarl.europa.eu/RegData/etudes/STUD/2011/453202/IPOL-JURI_NT(2011)453202_EN.pdf, 17; ML Niboyet, 'Note – Proposal for a Regulation of the European Parliament and of the Council on Jurisdiction and the Recognition and Enforcement of Judgments in Civil and Commercial Matters (Recast)' (DATE) www.europarl.europa.eu/RegData/etudes/IDAN/2011/453204/IPOL-JURI_NT(2011)453204_EN.pdf, 14.

[23] This has also been alleged by the European Commission, 'Impact Assessment – Accompanying Document to the Proposal for a Regulation of the European Parliament and of the Council on Jurisdiction and the Recognition and Enforcement of Judgments in Civil and Commercial Matters (Recast)', (SEC(2010) 1548 Final, 14.12.2010), www.eur-lex.europa.eu/LexUriServ/LexUriServ.do?uri=SEC:2010:1547:FIN:EN:PDF, 26: 'The full extension of the Regulation's rules on jurisdiction to third country defendants would increase the possibilities for EU companies to litigate in the EU rather than abroad'.

[24] This was one of the main arguments for the reform by the European Commission, ibid 20. Cf A Nuyts, 'Study on Residual Jurisdiction (Review of the Member States' Rules Concerning the "Residual Jurisdiction" of Their Courts in Civil and Commercial Matters Pursuant to the Brussels I and II Regulations)' (European Commission, 2007) para 147. Similarly L Mari and I Pretelli, 'Possibility and Terms for Applying the Brussels I Regulation (Recast) to Extra-EU Disputes' (2013) XV *Yearbook of Private International Law* 211, 243; and I Pretelli and others, 'Study – Possibility and Terms for Applying Brussels I Regulation (Recast) to Extra-EU Disputes' (European Parliament, 2014) www.europarl.europa.eu/RegData/etudes/STUD/2014/493024/IPOL-JURI_ET(2014)493024_EN.pdf, 39.

on the moral high ground, arise from the State's conviction that only its own courts are capable of administering justice in the best way possible. Yet the motives can also be of political and pecuniary nature if the State, its court system, and the national legal services industry profit from adjudicating cases and from advising and representing the parties. These motives certainly matter for commercial litigation hubs, such as London, in the world of Common Law. With regard to Continental Europe and Civil Law, the relevance of these motives might be questioned because the litigation ambitions of the States on the Continent might be considered to be neutral and not-for-profit. However, the EU Member States' eager determination to win over litigation from the UK post-Brexit is evident from their ambitions to establish special commercial courts handling cases in English.[25] Similar intentions on the part of the EU are apparent from the fact that, acting with exclusive competence on behalf of its Member States, it rejected the UK's application post-Brexit to join the 2007 Lugano Convention, which would have been the closest available replacement for the UK departing from the EU jurisdictional system of the Brussels Ia Regulation.[26]

(a) Detriment to the EU and its Member States

If affirming jurisdiction and attracting litigation is the inclination of States, then it is counterproductive for the EU and its Member States to unify the jurisdictional rules for Third State defendants by extending the Regulation's rules to them. The reason is that this unification by extension is only imaginable if it is attained at the expense of displacing the autonomous exorbitant rules of the Member States, as the Commission admitted in its proposal.[27] In other words, the extension would, by virtue of the EU supremacy doctrine,[28] prevent that Member States could apply their autonomous exorbitant rules against Third State defendants any longer, who would then receive the same protection as EU defendants. Then, lacking their traditional exorbitant grounds of jurisdiction, the courts of the Member States would less often be able to affirm their jurisdiction compared to the situation without EU rule extension.[29]

[25] See, for instance, MR Isidro, 'International Commercial Courts in the Litigation Market' (2019) 9 *International Journal of Procedural Law* 4; X Kramer and J Sorabji, 'International Business Courts in Europe and Beyond: A Global Competition for Justice?' (2019) 12 *Erasmus Law Review* 1; SA Kruisinga, 'Commercial Courts in the Netherlands, Belgium, France and Germany – Salient Features and Challenges' [2019] *Praxis des Internationalen Privat- und Verfahrensrechts* 277; G Rühl, 'Settlement of International Commercial Disputes Post-Brexit, or: United We Stand Taller' in JA Kämmerer and HB Schäfer (eds), *Brexit: Legal and Economic Aspects of a Political Divorce* (Elgar, 2021) 195; M Witkamp, 'Internationalizing Domestic Courts in Europe' in SL Brekoulakis and G Dimitropoulos (eds), *International commercial courts* (Cambridge University Press, 2022) 278.

[26] For the reasons, see European Commission, 'Communication from the Commission to the European Parliament and the Council: Assessment on the Application of the United Kingdom of Great Britain and Northern Ireland to Accede to the 2007 Lugano Convention' (COM (2021) 222 Final, 4.5.2021) www.ec.europa.eu/info/sites/default/files/1_en_act_en.pdf.

[27] European Commission, 'Impact Assessment', 24. Cf T Lutzi and FM Wilke, 'Brüssel Ia extendenda est?', 845; A Nuyts, 'Study on Residual Jurisdiction', para 147; U Magnus and P Mankowski, 'The Proposal for the Reform of Brussels I', 263 and 266 have to concede this, too.

[28] Case C-26/62 *Van Gend en Loos*; Case C-6/64 *Costa v ENEL*; Case C-10/97 *Ministero delle Finanze v IN.CO.GE.*

[29] A Nuyts, 'Study on Residual Jurisdiction', para 166 referred to it as a 'paradoxical' consequence.

In full awareness of this, it is surprising that the Commission tried to gain support for its reform proposal in 2010 by arguing that, due to the divergence of the autonomous rules across Member States, EU claimants have unequal access to justice in cases against Third State defendants, and that this would be remedied by extending the uniform Regulation's rules to Third State defendants.[30] Strangely, the Commission tried to illustrate its point by reference to the example of Italy which has autonomously chosen to extend the unified rules of the Brussels Convention to Third State defendants in its courts.[31] The Italian autonomous extension (and the absence of any autonomous exorbitant rule) has indeed led to instances where the claimant could not sue in Italy. The Commission contrasted the Italian dilemma with the French situation, where a claimant would most likely have been able to sue in France. Yet the Commission omitted the clarification that this discrepancy was due to the autonomous Brussels regime extension in Italy, in contrast to the claimant's ability in France to rely on the autonomous exorbitant rule of Art 14 of the French Civil Code.[32]

The Commission is right about the discrepancy and inequality, but the comparison and conclusion are flawed. It is true that claimants in some Member States are in a better position to sue Third State defendants there than claimants in other Member States. Yet being better off in the former Member States than in the latter is due to the ability of the claimants being able or unable to rely on autonomous exorbitant rules of the respective Member State. If the autonomous exorbitant rules of the former Member States, such as France, were to be removed by flattening them off to level with the Brussels rules, such as in Italy, equality would be established. Then, however, access to justice in the EU would be reduced for all claimants in all Member States.[33] Being denied access to justice across the EU on 'equal' terms can surely not be regarded as a benefit for EU claimants worth striving for by EU law reform.

Therefore, the EU Member States should in their own interest maintain the status quo by refraining from the temptation to unify the rules on Third State defendants on the EU level. Claimants in some Member States, such as France, will continue to be better off than in others; however, at least all claimants domiciled in the EU can benefit from such preferential autonomous exorbitant rules, as pointed out above.[34] Member States can also choose, as Italy has done, to change their autonomous rules; they can amend their rules autonomously and discreetly, it does not have to be done through unification by the EU. The national choice may depend on whether the respective Member State actually wants to attract litigation or is quite happy not to. It is a corollary for those

[30] European Commission, 'Impact Assessment', 20. Previously addressed by B Hess, T Pfeiffer and P Schlosser, *The Brussels I-Regulation*, para 157 et seq; similarly A Bonomi, 'European Private International Law and Third States', 185–86.

[31] A Nuyts, 'Study on Residual Jurisdiction', para 15.

[32] European Commission, 'Impact Assessment', 20–21.

[33] See similarly A Dickinson, 'The Revision of the Brussels I Regulation: Surveying the Proposed Brussels Ibis Regulation – Solid Foundations but Renovation Needed' (2010) XII *Yearbook of Private International Law* 247, 278; A Dickinson, 'Note – The Proposal for a Regulation of the European Parliament and of the Council on Jurisdiction and the Recognition and Enforcement of Judgments in Civil and Commercial Matters (Recast)' (2011) www.europarl.europa.eu/RegData/etudes/STUD/2011/453200/IPOL-JURI_NT(2011)453200_EN.pdf, 14; also R Fentiman, 'Brussels I and Third States: Future Imperfect?', 73–74.

[34] See above section II. on Art 6(2) Brussels Ia Regulation.

Member States who want to attract litigation that they ask more of their own courts by requiring the judges to apply different rules to EU than to Third State defendants; yet this complexity is the only detriment of the status quo for an EU Member State.[35]

(b) Benefit for the UK and other Third States

Unifying the rules in the EU for Third State defendants by extending the Regulation's rules to them would in fact be rather beneficial for Third States, such as the UK. In essence, the reason is that it would become easier for Third States, especially when they determine jurisdiction with Common Law methods, to affirm their own jurisdiction and it would let them attract more litigation. This would become possible for them because jurisdiction in EU Member States could no longer be established on the basis of autonomous exorbitant rules, which would be disabled by the Regulation's extension.

Exploring this more closely by reference to English law, the ultimately crucial question for determining jurisdiction of an English court is whether England is the proper place to bring the claim,[36] *forum conveniens*. This requires the claimant to show clearly and distinctly, when seeking permission for service out of the jurisdiction, that England is the 'natural forum' in which the case can be most suitably tried in the interest of the parties and for the ends of justice, which is negated if there is another more appropriate forum to adjudicate the claim. Also, in the other direction, if the defendant wants the English court to stay the proceedings, it has to be shown inversely that the English court is *forum non conveniens* because there is another more appropriate forum to hear the claim.[37] One can characterise these English autonomous rules as exorbitant because they provide English courts with plenty of discretion to exercise 'long-arm' jurisdiction.

For assessing whether there is another more appropriate forum than in England, for instance in an EU Member State, this depends in the first place on whether an EU Member State court would be able to affirm its jurisdiction. Where an EU Member State court, for instance in France, is able to affirm its jurisdiction based on the autonomous exorbitant rule of Art 14 of the French Civil Code under the status quo, the French court would be unable to do so if the Brussels Ia rules were to be extended and the autonomous exorbitant rules of the Member States were to be displaced. The French court in this situation would then have no jurisdiction, similar to an Italian court currently, as illustrated above.

So if the Regulation were to be extended, it would mean for the assessment of whether England is the appropriate forum in this situation that there would not be another, potentially more appropriate, (French) forum available. Thus, the English forum would, being left without any competition, be the only forum to hear the case. In other words, abolishing autonomous exorbitant rules through EU unification would

[35] The Commission, 'Impact Assessment', 22 and 25, had to concede that the detriment of the status quo is hard to quantify, which is of course not the same as saying it is hardly quantifiable, but perhaps it demonstrates that there is no real urgency and suffering.

[36] Civil Procedure Rules, r 6.37(3); cf for an overview A Briggs, *The Conflict of Laws* 4th edn (Oxford University Press, 2019) 108 et seq; J Hill and MN Shúilleabhái, *Clarkson & Hill's Conflict of Laws* 5th edn (Oxford University Press, 2016) para 2.150 et seq.

[37] *Spiliada Maritime Corp v Cansulex Ltd* [1986] UKHL 10; *VTB Capital plc v Nutritek International Corp* [2013] UKSC 5; *Vedanta Resources plc v Lungowe* [2019] UKSC 20.

reduce the chances that an EU forum is available and, in turn, this would make it more likely that England would be regarded as the natural forum. The underlying reason is that, in contrast to EU Member States giving up their autonomous exorbitant rules if the Regulation were to be extended, the UK can employ its 'long-arm' autonomous exorbitant rules. Due to Brexit and non-accession to the Lugano Convention, the UK has been able to reactivate its autonomous exorbitant rules again and can use them against EU Member States, which was prevented under the Brussels regime during the UK's period of EU membership. It has also to be borne in mind that the EU forwent the chance to bring the UK's autonomous exorbitant rules under control when it chose to reject the UK's application for accession to the Lugano Convention.

Accordingly, unifying the rules in the EU for Third State defendants by extending the Regulation's rules to them would drive litigation towards Third States and away from the EU. Similar predictions had already been made in respect of the Commission's proposal in 2010,[38] but the issue has become a lot more critical since Brexit with regard to the UK. As a consequence, the litigation service industry in England would benefit from extending the Regulation, at the expense of the service providers in the EU and to the detriment of European initiatives launched in the Brexit aftermath.[39]

V. Other Reform Options

In addition or as an alternative to unifying the rules for Third State defendants by extending the Regulation's rules to them, which has been discussed so far, it is advisable to consider three other reform options. If they were to be introduced into the Regulation, they could – potentially – be suitable ways to meet the need in the EU for increased simplicity and clarity without driving litigation away from the EU. Yet, as will be shown, this would most likely not be achievable.

(a) Adding Exorbitant Rules to the Regulation

If the Regulation were to be reformed to cover Third State defendants, one could consider the idea of additionally introducing some exorbitant rules into the Regulation.[40] These uniform exorbitant rules could be modelled on autonomous exorbitant rules of Member States. For instance, the Commission proposed in 2010 to introduce a 'mildly' exorbitant rule into the Regulation which 'grants jurisdiction to the court of the Member State where assets of the defendant are situated'.[41] Adding exorbitant rules to the Regulation seems to ensure uniformity and greater simplicity within the EU than having various autonomous ones in Member State laws. Most importantly, these benefits seem to be

[38] From within the EU pre-Brexit: A Dickinson, 'The Revision of the Brussels I Regulation', 277; Dickinson, 'Note', 14.

[39] See above, n 24.

[40] For an upheld proposal to introduce 'one or two' uniform exorbitant rules, see for instance H Schack, *Internationales Zivilverfahrensrecht: mit internationalem Insolvenzrecht und Schiedsverfahrensrecht* (8th edn., CH Beck 2021) para 111.

[41] European Commission, 'Impact Assessment', 24, 27.

achievable without running the risk that the EU and its Member States would be losing litigation: at least some exorbitant rules would be saved by transferring them from the autonomous regimes into the Regulation.

However, this would elevate the discrimination of the exorbitant rules to the EU level.[42] It would then be the EU instead of the Member States which would discriminate against Third States, and the EU would do it outrightly and intentionally in a uniform manner. The Member States might have got away with their sporadic autonomous exorbitant rules as relicts predating modern reforms, but there would be no excuse for the EU to take such action nowadays after decades of consideration. Adopting truly exorbitant rules in the Regulation would potentially be harmful to the EU's external relations on the global level.[43] In addition, within the EU, it would be difficult to decide which exorbitant rules from the autonomous laws of the Member States are so common that they should be transferred into the Regulation and are worth the potential diplomatic disaster. Not even the 'mildly' exorbitant rule basing jurisdiction on the location of the defendant's assets, which the Commission had in mind, is sufficiently common among all Member States.[44] If, nonetheless, a fairly common exorbitant rule were to be adopted into the Regulation, it would neither be easy, given the divergence among autonomous laws, to agree within the EU on the criteria according to which this uniform rule should be applicable, ie how tenuous a connection of the defendant with the forum would be deemed acceptable. Moreover, if an antiquated exorbitant rule of common Member State heritage were to be transposed nowadays in an effective manner into the Regulation, determining the scope would be a vital and equally uneasy task especially in the light of its exorbitant character; for instance, in the case of a rule relating to assets, this would be tricky in today's world of intangible and digital assets.[45] Hence, neither the flattening off of the exorbitant rules, as discussed for the full extension of the Regulation's rules to Third State defendants, nor the idea of levelling up the exorbitant rules by copying them into the Regulation are viable options for unification on the EU level.

What might seem like another possible alternative in order to avoid the intensification of Third State discrimination would be to introduce exorbitant rules into the Brussels regime which would, however, be applicable to EU and Third State defendants equally. Yet this is completely unimaginable because this would mean taking disputes within the EU back to the situation before any unification, ie pre-1968 and before the Brussels Convention.

(b) Adding a Forum Necessitatis

Instead of adding specific exorbitant rules to the Regulation, which would untenably intensify Third State discrimination, one might consider simply introducing a rule for

[42] A Nuyts, 'Study on Residual Jurisdiction', para 173 considered this option as likely to prove 'very controversial'.

[43] Conceded by European Commission, 'Impact Assessment', 27.

[44] A Nuyts, 'Study on Residual Jurisdiction', para 77; see also A Dickinson, 'The Revision of the Brussels I Regulation', 278–79; A Dickinson, 'Note', 14–15.

[45] A Dickinson, 'The Revision of the Brussels I Regulation', 279; A Dickinson, 'Note', 15; also K Takahashi, 'Review of the Brussels I Regulation', 8.

establishing jurisdiction of a Member State court out of necessity in cases in which jurisdiction cannot be established otherwise. This would still somewhat resemble a rule of exorbitant character, but it might seem less problematic internationally. In the 2010 Commission proposal for such a *forum necessitatis*, it was suggested that a court of a Member State may assume jurisdiction for the purposes of offering a fair trial and granting access to justice 'if proceedings cannot reasonably be brought or conducted or would be impossible in a Third State with which the dispute is closely connected'.[46] If the rule were to be adopted in a reform of the Brussels Ia Regulation, it would seem as if it would become harder for English courts to deny the availability of an EU forum. The particular attractiveness of introducing it might be seen in the fact that the reasonableness requirement for an EU *forum necessitatis* resembles the appropriateness requirement of the English *forum conveniens*. So, perhaps, a *forum necessitatis* rule would be the best way for the EU to beat Common Law jurisdictions in their own game; however, in fact, the resemblance with the *forum conveniens* doctrine is the Achilles' heel of the *forum necessitatis* rule.

If adopted, the EU *forum necessitatis* rule would not be capable of neutralising or softening the effects of extending the Regulation's rules to Third State defendants because it would not change the jurisdiction assessment and affirmation by an English court. When determining under English rules whether a more appropriate forum exists than the English one, as discussed above, the English court would consider whether there is an EU forum, and this EU forum could be based on an EU *forum necessitatis* rule if introduced in the Brussels Ia Regulation. As part of this exercise by the English court to determine whether it has jurisdiction, the English court would, in order to determine the existence of an EU forum, look through the glasses of the EU *forum necessitatis* rule. When doing so, however, the English court would not act in complete self-denial: the English court would not find that the English proceedings, which are closely connected with England, could not be reasonably brought in England and that, thus, an EU *forum necessitatis* should be affirmed. In consequence, the English court looking through the EU glasses would not conclude that the EU *forum necessitatis* exists in the case at hand, and that the (in fact denied) EU forum is distinctly and clearly the more appropriate forum than the English forum.

Therefore, the introduction of an EU *forum necessitatis* rule would still be beneficial only for the UK and other Third States, but detrimental to the EU Member States. In addition, the *forum necessitatis* rule would not even achieve the most basic goal of the reform, namely increasing simplicity and clarity for the courts of Member States when dealing with Third State defendants. On the contrary, it would impose complex and uncomfortable questions on the courts of Member States,[47] as they would have to assess whether the claimant has sufficiently demonstrated the necessity for an EU forum because the Third State, to which the dispute is connected, for instance the UK, cannot

[46] European Commission, 'Proposal', Art 26 (p 34). Supported by A Bonomi, 'European Private International Law and Third States', 186, 188; ML Niboyet, 'Note', 15–16; also see T Lutzi and FM Wilke, 'Brüssel Ia extendenda est?', 871; A Nuyts, 'Study on Residual Jurisdiction', para 179; European Group for Private International Law (GEDIP/EGPIL), 'Proposed Amendment of Regulation 44/2001 in Order to Apply It to External Situations' [2009] *Praxis des Internationalen Privat- und Verfahrensrechts* 283, Art 22 bis.

[47] A Dickinson, 'Revision of the Brussels I Regulation', 280; A Dickinson, 'Note', 15; R Luzzatto, 'On the Proposed Application of Jurisdictional Criteria of Brussels I Regulation to Non-Domiciled Defendants', 115.

offer a fair trial and grant access to justice. At least as long as the respective Third State belongs to the Council of Europe and the European Convention on Human Rights, which provides for a fair trial and access to justice,[48] it is hard to believe how a court of an EU Member State could conclude that fairness and justice would be unavailable there. A *forum necessitatis* is helpful and important in cases where no other jurisdiction is willing to offer a fair trial and to grant access to justice, but it is not useful for the EU Member States as a tool to mitigate the fallout of disabling the autonomous exorbitant rules by extending the Regulation's rules to Third State defendants.

(c) Permitting Reflexive Effect

A way of partially extending the Regulation's rules to Third States might be the doctrine of reflexive effect (*effet réflexe*).[49] The doctrine posits that in cases of exclusive jurisdiction, for instance over rights *in rem* in a Third State, a Member State court could decline any jurisdiction it might have under other Brussels Ia rules; it would do so by reflexively giving effect to the Brussels Ia rules on exclusive jurisdiction in favour of the Third State court. The rationale of reflexive effect is to respect the spirit of exclusive jurisdiction. The underlying idea resembles the flexibility under the Common Law approach to jurisdiction and the *forum non conveniens* doctrine. However, the reflexive effect doctrine does not fit with the Brussels Ia Regulation's rigid and mandatory nature according to which Member State courts do not have discretion to decline jurisdiction in favour of Third State courts.[50] The discretion of the doctrine of reflexive effect would also create a risk of arbitrariness when Member State courts were free to decline or not to decline their otherwise existing jurisdiction.[51] Moreover, if the discretion were to be bound insofar as it would require the Member State court to determine whether the Third State court would provide a fair trial and access to justice,[52] it would impose the same complex and uncomfortable questions on Member State courts as a *forum necessitatis* rule.

In any case, the doctrine of reflexive effect would not be suitable to mitigate the fallout from extending the Regulation's rules to Third State defendants considering the way the doctrine operates. Due to the reflexive effect, Member State courts would further limit their jurisdiction by declining their otherwise existing jurisdiction in favour of Third State courts, albeit discretionary and in individual cases only. If paired with extending the Regulation's rules to Third State defendants, this would in fact aggravate the detriment to EU Member States' jurisdiction.

[48] Art 6(1), 13 ECHR.

[49] Originally devised by GAL Droz, *Compétence judiciaire et effets des jugements dans le Marché commun (étude de la Convention de Bruxelles du 27 septembre 1968)* (Dalloz, 1972) para 164 et seq. Recommended for instance by European Group for Private International Law (GEDIP/EGPIL), 'Proposed Amendment of Regulation 44/2001', Art 24 bis; ML Niboyet, 'Note', 15; J Weber, 'Universal Jurisdiction and Third States in the Reform of the Brussels I Regulation', 630, 632–33, 644; also see A Nuyts, 'Study on Residual Jurisdiction', para 180 et seq.

[50] Case C-281/02 *Owusu v Jackson*, para 37; Case C-420/07 *Apostolides v Orams*, opinion of AG Kokott, para 86 with reference to the Lugano Opinion 1/03; also see *T Kruger, Civil Jurisdiction Rules of the EU and Their Impact on Third States* (Oxford University Press 2008) para 3.19, 5.118.

[51] Similarly Pretelli and others, 'Possibility and Terms for Applying the Brussels I Regulation (Recast) to Extra-EU Disputes', 19.

[52] For this suggestion see B Hess, *Europäisches Zivilprozessrecht*, para 5.17.

So the remaining question is whether the doctrine of reflexive effect would at least be, if not a mitigation strategy, a suitable alternative to fully extending the Regulation's rules to Third State defendants. In other words, would it be overall possible and better for the EU and its Member States to 'unify' the rules on Third State defendants by simply introducing an express provision on reflexive effect into the Regulation? Certainly, the general problems of this discretionary doctrine and the corollary of risking unequal exercise of discretion across Member States would persist and would undermine the very unification effort, which aims at guaranteeing equal access to justice across the EU. The main problem is, however, that the doctrine of reflexive effect can only cover selected cases, such as of exclusive jurisdiction, and can only be used in a negative way by Member State courts, namely to decline their jurisdiction in favour of Third State courts.[53] By contrast, reflexive effect is incapable of offering ways for Member States' courts to affirm their jurisdiction over Third State defendants. In fact, establishing jurisdiction (at least in the first place, subject to possibly declining it subsequently) would still be left to the autonomous rules of the Member States. This means in essence that the EU 'unification' by introducing a reflexive effect rule into the Brussels regime would be plagued by problems of discretionary application, and would be limited to a narrow range of applicable cases. Most importantly, the reflexive effect rule would be operating in the same disadvantageous direction as the full extension of the Regulation's rules to Third State defendants. Reflexive effect is unsuitable to create a beneficial uniform framework for establishing jurisdiction of EU Member State courts over Third State defendants.

VI. Conclusion

The current regime of the Brussels Ia Regulation discriminates against Third State defendants because, in contrast to EU defendants, they are not protected from autonomous exorbitant rules of Member States in principle. If the uniform rules of the Brussels Ia Regulation applicable to EU defendants were to be extended to Third States, the discrimination would be remedied.

Based on the understanding that States seek to affirm their own jurisdiction and to attract litigation, it has been shown that unifying the rules for Third State defendants by fully extending the Regulation to them has, however, greater benefits for Third States than the EU and its Member States. While the unification by extension would simplify jurisdictional issues for Member State courts, these courts would less often be able to affirm their jurisdiction compared to the current situation where they can rely on their autonomous exorbitant rules. For the UK as a Third State, conversely, the EU rule unification by extension would make it easier to conclude that, for instance, England is *forum conveniens* instead of concluding that there is a potentially more appropriate forum in the EU available under autonomous exorbitant rules of a Member State.

Since the unification by full extension of the Regulation's rules cannot be recommended, three other options for reforming the Brussels Ia Regulation have been considered,

[53] Therefore approving the idea: K Takahashi, 'Review of the Brussels I Regulation', 10.

but none of them is a realistic option for the EU either. First, transposing some exorbitant rules common among the autonomous laws of the Member States into the Regulation could be harmful to the EU's external relations, and it would be difficult for the Member States to agree on which rule design is worth the trouble. Secondly, introducing a uniform rule on *forum necessitatis* would not help prevent that an English court would affirm its own jurisdiction as *forum conveniens*. Thirdly, enacting the doctrine of reflexive effect would not be helpful for Member States courts because it would only allow them to decline their jurisdiction in favour of Third State courts.

So, after all, how severe would the consequences be if the status quo with the different rules for EU defendants and Third States defendants were maintained? For Member States, whose courts have managed the practical application for the past decades, it is not a huge problem to continue business as usual. Admittedly, the discrimination against Third States would remain, which is not ideal, but at least it would not be worsened. If Member States genuinely intended to reduce this discrimination, they could always autonomously choose to extend for their courts the Brussels Ia regime to Third State defendants and thereby give up their autonomous exorbitant rules, following the example of Italy; each Member State can make this decision to reduce its share of international litigation and to promote international fairness. Consequently, it seems neither necessary nor recommendable to reform the Brussels Ia Regulation by uniformly extending its rules to cover Third State defendants. It would be self-contradictory to do so while also trying to win over litigation from the UK post-Brexit.

VI.

Outlook

The Resumed HCCH Jurisdiction Project

NING ZHAO*

For decades, the Hague Conference on Private International Law (HCCH) has been undertaking the development of international instruments on jurisdiction and recognition and enforcement of foreign judgments, key components of private international law. Undoubtedly, its recent endeavours have borne important fruit: the HCCH 2005 Choice of Court Convention and the HCCH 2019 Judgments Convention were successfully adopted on 30 June 2005[1] and on 2 July 2019,[2] respectively. Notwithstanding these monumental achievements, the HCCH has not stopped there, continuing to fulfil its mandate for 'the progressive unification of the rules of private international law'[3] which includes many of the rules on international jurisdiction analysed in the research project led by the editors of this book and discussed in its previous chapters. Since the adoption of the 2019 Judgments Convention, the HCCH resumed the Jurisdiction Project, which has reached the stage of Working Group negotiations. Despite what its name may suggest, the Jurisdiction Project has at the time of writing shifted its focus towards the development of uniform rules for the treatment of concurrent proceedings in multiple jurisdictions with the aim of providing efficient solutions to such cumbersome reality. Against this background, the present chapter provides readers with a holistic overview of the HCCH's endeavour in the area of jurisdiction since its inception, offering up-to-date information on the current status of the Jurisdiction Project, all while shedding some light on its future perspective.

* The views and opinions expressed in this chapter are the personal views of the author and do not reflect the official policy or position of the Hague Conference on Private International Law (HCCH), nor its Secretariat (the Permanent Bureau).

[1] HCCH, 'Convention of 30 June 2005 on Choice of Court Agreements', (HCCH, 2005, Choice of Court Convention). It entered into force on 1 October 2015, and, at the time of writing, binds 32 Members: Mexico, the European Union (EU), all EU Member States, Singapore, Montenegro and the UK. More information about the Convention is available at www.net/en/instruments/specialised-sections/choice-of-court.

[2] HCCH, 'Convention of 2 July 2019 on the Recognition and Enforcement of Foreign Judgments in Civil or Commercial Matters', (HCCH, 2019, Judgments Convention). The Convention will enter into force on 1 September 2023, following the joining of the EU and Ukraine on 29 August 2022. At the time of writing, Uruguay, Costa Rica, Israel, Russia and the USA are signatories to the Convention. More information about the Convention is available at www.hcch.net/en/instruments/conventions/specialised-sections/judgments.

[3] Art 1 of the Statute of the HCCH.

I. Introduction

The need for regulating jurisdiction and recognition and enforcement was raised 150 years ago, three decades prior to the first diplomatic conference of the HCCH, which took place in 1893. The learnt scholar and diplomat, Mr Tobias Asser, 1911 Nobel Prize winner for his work in the field of private international law (including his achievements in establishing the HCCH), considered the need to harmonise the rules of international procedural law so as to secure the free circulation of judicial decisions throughout Europe. He advocated for the establishment of a legal framework under which States should maintain some fundamental legal principles while making concessions to one another in this regard.[4] In Asser's view, a treaty containing uniform rules on jurisdiction and procedural law between neighbouring countries would be the best way forward.[5]

As envisioned by Asser, the HCCH has been actively working on enhancing efficient and effective transnational dispute resolution since its establishment, through the development of conventions.[6] Particularly in the past several decades, the HCCH's endeavours to regulate jurisdiction and recognition and enforcement have borne fruit under the framework of the Judgments Project, as exemplified by the adoption of the HCCH 2005 Choice of Court Convention and the HCCH 2019 Judgments Convention. Now that recognition and enforcement of foreign judgments are covered by these two Conventions,[7] work on jurisdiction was resumed at the HCCH in 2020, as mandated by its governing body – the Council on General Affairs and Policy (CGAP),[8] and so far the Project has progressed to the Working Group level. In order to yield a better understanding of the Jurisdiction Project, this chapter begins by providing a historical background of the Project in Part II, including a brief description of the most salient phases of the development of the Project. Part III then illustrates the current status of the Jurisdiction Project and the progress hitherto made. Finally, the chapter concludes with an outlook of the Jurisdiction Project, underscoring its main challenges and the key principles that ought to underlie a successful framework for cross-border parallel proceedings.

II. Historical Background of the Jurisdiction Project

The Jurisdiction Project is the second limb of the prolonged Judgments Project that has expanded for several decades. Thus, to understand the Jurisdiction Project and its outlook, it is useful to begin this chapter with an overview of the history of the project.

[4] A Eyffinger, *T.M.C.Asser, In quest of liberty, justice and peace* (Volume I, Brill Nijhoff, 2019) 636; T Asser, 'Private International Law and uniform law' (1869) *Revue de droit international et législation comparée* 1–17.

[5] A Eyffinger, *T.M.C.Asser, In quest of liberty, justice and peace*, 527 and 637.

[6] General information about the Jurisdiction Project is available at www.hcch.net/en/projects/legislative-projects/jurisdiction-project/.

[7] As it will be explained in part II of this chapter, the 2005 Choice of Court Convention deals with one limited jurisdictional ground – exclusive choice of court agreements made by the parties.

[8] At the time of writing, a Working Group on matters related to jurisdiction in transnational civil or commercial litigation was established to 'develop draft provisions on matters related to jurisdiction in civil or commercial matters, including rules for concurrent proceedings, to further inform policy considerations and

The inception of the Judgments Project can be traced back to 1992, when the United States of America came up with a proposal for a project to deal with the recognition and enforcement of foreign judgments in civil and commercial matters.[9] Initially, efforts of the Judgments Project were aimed towards a mixed convention on jurisdiction and recognition and enforcement. As developed by Professor Arthur von Mehren, the mixed Convention would include three categories of jurisdictional bases and corresponding recognition rules, namely:[10] (1) permitted grounds (white list) of jurisdiction, and judgments that are given based on these grounds must be recognised and enforced in all Contracting States; (2) prohibited grounds (black list) of jurisdiction, and judgments given based on these grounds will not be recognised and enforced; (3) and the 'grey area' grounds of jurisdiction, and judgments based on these grounds would not be entitled to recognition and enforcement under that Convention, but left to the respective Contracting State to decide whether to recognise them or not.

The negotiations at the Nineteenth Session of the HCCH in 2001, unfortunately, did not achieve the desired result:[11] instead of leading to the adoption of a Convention, they produced the 2001 Interim Text – a summary of the outcome of the discussions that took place during the Session.[12] The main reason for such outcome was linked to the different core values and philosophies in relation to jurisdiction that underpinned either side of the Atlantic.[13] The US jurisdictional system is based on constitutional

decisions in relation to the scope and type of any new instrument focusing on regulating parallel litigation'. See, in this regard, The Council on General Affairs and Policy, 'Conclusions and Decisions (C&D)', 2021, C&D No 9(a).

[9] A Letter from the US Department of State to the Permanent Bureau (PB) dated 5 May 1992, see Prel Doc No°17 of May 1992, 'Some reflections of the Permanent Bureau on a general convention on enforcement of judgments', in *HCCH Proceedings of the Seventeenth Session* (1993), Tome I, Miscellaneous matters 230–239 (Prel Doc No 17 of May 1992), para 18.

[10] See A von Mehren, 'Theory and Practice of Adjudicatory Authority in Private International Law: A Comparative Study of the Doctrine, Policies and Practices of Common- and Civil-Law Systems' (1996) *Recueil des cours* 404–425.

[11] Out of the six major areas of the difficulties that were identified (the Internet and e-commerce; activity-based jurisdiction; consumer and employment contracts; IP rights; the relationship with other instruments; and bilateralisation), four related to jurisdiction issues. See Prel Doc No°16 of February 2002, 'Some Reflections on the Present State of Negotiations on the Judgments Project in the context of the Future Work Programme of the Conference', for the attention of Commission I (CGAP) of the Nineteenth Diplomatic Session – April 2002, in *HCCH Proceedings of the Nineteenth Session* (2001/2002), Tome I, Miscellaneous matters, para 5.

[12] Permanent Bureau and the Co-Reporters, 'Summary of the Outcome of the Discussion in Commission II of the First Part of the Diplomatic Conference 6–20 June 2001 – Interim Text', in *HCCH Proceedings of the Twentieth Session* (2005), Tome II, Judgments, 2013, 621, (2001 Interim Text).

[13] See generally JJ Barceló III and KM Clermont (eds), *A Global Law of Jurisdiction and Judgments: Lessons from The Hague*, (Kluwer Law International, 2002); GP Calliess, 'Value-added Norms, Local Litigation, and Global Enforcement: Why the Brussels-Philosophy failed in The Hague' (2004) *German Law Journal* 1489; WE O'Brian Jr, 'The Hague Convention on Jurisdiction and Judgments: The Way Forward' (2003) *Modern Law Review*, 491–509; Y Oestreicher, 'We're on a Road to Nowhere – Reasons for the Continuing Failure to Regulate Recognition and Enforcement of Foreign Judgments' (2008) *The International Lawyer* 59 (61); J Regan, 'Recognition and Enforcement of Foreign Judgments – A Second Attempt in The Hague?' (2015) *Rich J Global L & Bus,* 64–71; RA Brand, 'Jurisdictional Developments and the New Hague Judgments Project' in *A Commitment To Private International Law: Essays In Honour Of Hans Van Loon* (Intersentia, 2013), 91 et seq; A Bonomi, 'Courage or Caution? A critical overview of the Hague Preliminary Draft on Judgments' (2015/2016) *YPIL* 1–31.

limitations focusing on the relationship between defendants and the forum,[14] whereas in the EU, jurisdiction rules aim at facilitating 'sound administration of justice' and predictability and legal certainty, thus putting the emphasis on the relationship between the subject matter of the dispute and the forum.[15]

Subsequently, the Judgments Project turned its focus to jurisdiction agreed upon by the parties under exclusive choice of court agreements, which led to the adoption of the HCCH 2005 Choice of Court Convention on 30 June 2005. The need for a global framework on jurisdiction and recognition and enforcement was, however, not forgotten. Since 2011, the Judgments Project resumed in two parallel tracks: an Experts' Group was tasked with identifying possible areas for further work;[16] and a Working Group was mandated to prepare proposals on the recognition and enforcement of foreign judgments.[17] For the sake of efficient management of the Project, as well as a response to policy concerns that certain States had with regard to the negotiation of the jurisdiction issue at the international level, it was decided to develop a Convention solely focused on the recognition and enforcement of foreign judgments by the Working Group, leaving jurisdictional matters to be dealt with by the Experts' Group once the work of the Working Group was finalised.[18] Following many years of negotiations and intense efforts, the HCCH 2019 Judgments Convention was successfully concluded on 2 July 2019.

Given the emphasis of this book on international jurisdiction and non-Contracting States (or third States, the equivalent term in the EU context), this section briefly introduces the two HCCH Conventions and their crucial role in transnational litigation. The essence of both Conventions, concluded under the umbrella of the Judgments Project, is discussed alongside their implications for the aforementioned area and the possibility of their application, if any, to non-Contracting States. By the same token, the general principles followed during the development of the 2019 Judgments Convention are also explored in view of their relevance for understanding the current state of affairs of the Jurisdiction Project.

[14] L J Silberman, 'Judicial Jurisdiction and Forum Access – The Search for Predictable Rules' in F Ferrari and DP Fernandez Arroyo (eds), *Private International Law: Contemporary Challenges and Continuing Relevance* (Cheltenham, 2019), 332.

[15] Regulation No 1215/2012.

[16] Conclusions and Recommendations (C&R) of CGAP 2011, para 15; C&R of CGAP 2012, para 18.

[17] C&R of CGAP 2012, para 17.

[18] 'Process Paper on the Continuation of the Judgments Project' of August 2013; in 2016, CGAP mandated that matters relating to direct jurisdiction be put for consideration to the Experts' Group soon after a Special Commission had drawn up the draft Judgments Convention, see C&R of CGAP 2016, para 13, C&R of CGAP 2017, para 7. In 2018, CGAP mandated that the Experts' Group resume its work once the Diplomatic Session was concluded, see C&R of CGAP 2018, para 5. In 2019, CGAP tasked the Permanent Bureau with making preparations for the Experts' Group meeting in February 2020, see C&R of CGAP 2019, para 5. In 2021, CGAP endorsed the recommendations of the Experts' Group and mandated the establishment of a Working Group on matters related to jurisdiction in transnational civil or commercial litigation, see C&D of CGAP 2021, paras 8 and 9.

(a) HCCH 2005 Choice of Court Convention[19]

The 2005 Convention gives effect to choice-of-court agreements between the parties, by ensuring that the will of the parties regarding to the chosen court will be respected by courts and that judgments given by the chosen courts will be recognised and enforced in other Contracting Parties. Along these lines, the Convention sets up three main rules: the chosen court should hear the disputes (Art 5); non-chosen courts should decline or suspend the case in favour of the chosen court (Art 6), and judgments given by the chosen court should be recognised and enforced in other Contracting Parties (Art 8). This simple but effective framework is subject only to narrow exceptions.[20]

The 2005 Choice of Court Convention contains only one jurisdiction rule – exclusive choice of court agreements. Its relevance may, however, be extended to non-Contracting Parties, as the Convention only requires the chosen court to be located in a Contracting Party, irrespective of the nationalities of the parties or their places of habitual residence.

The Convention addresses parallel proceedings as well, but it does so from the perspective of reinforcing parties' choice of court agreements: it prohibits the chosen courts from declining to exercise jurisdiction on the grounds[21] that another court is a more appropriate forum *(forum non conveniens)*[22] or that it has been seised first in proceedings involving the same cause of action between the same parties *(lis pendens)*.[23]

(b) HCCH 2019 Judgments Convention[24]

The 2019 Convention establishes an international framework under which judgments in civil or commercial matters can be circulated among Contracting Parties. Its application does not extend to non-Contracting Parties.

The Convention requires that a judgment given by a court of a Contracting Party that fulfils the conditions for the recognition and enforcement be recognised and enforced in other Contracting Parties.[25] One of these conditions is the fulfilment of jurisdictional filters (indirect jurisdiction rules) contained in Arts 5 or 6 of the Convention.

[19] For a better understanding of the Convention, see the Explanatory Report prepared by T Hartley and M Dogauchi (Hartley/Dogauchi Report).

[20] Art 5(1), Art 6 and Art 9 of the Convention.

[21] Art 5(2) of the Convention.

[22] Hartley/Dogauchi Report, para 132.

[23] ibid para. 133.

[24] For a better understanding of the Convention, see the Explanatory Report drafted by F Garcimartín and G Saumier (Garcimartín/Saumier Report). See also in this regard: N Zhao, 'Completing a long-awaited puzzle in the landscape of cross-border recognition and enforcement of judgments: An overview of the HCCH 2019 Judgments Convention' (2020) *SRIEL* 345.

[25] Art 4(1) of the Convention. It should also be stressed that the Convention does not prevent the recognition and enforcement of judgments in a Contracting State under national law or under other treaties, with the one exception of Art 6 (relating to an exclusive base for recognition and enforcement for a judgment that ruled on rights *in rem* in immovable property). Thus, the Convention, which is based on the principle of *favor recognitionis*, only sets a floor (with some minimum standards), rather than a ceiling, for the recognition and enforcement of foreign judgments.

Such filters, applied by the court addressed, assess whether there was a sufficient connection between the judgment and the State of origin that certifies the eligibility of the judgment for circulation under the Convention. The basis on which the court of origin originally established its jurisdiction is thus not relevant for the operation of the Convention. Therefore, the Convention does not regulate international (direct) jurisdiction and does not purport to amend States' national law on international jurisdiction.

Both the 2005 and 2019 Conventions pursue the same objectives. They aim to promote access to justice for all and to facilitate multilateral trade and investment, as well as mobility.[26] They do so by providing greater predictability and certainty in relation to the effectiveness of exclusive choice of court agreements and the global circulation of foreign judgments, through enhanced judicial cooperation mechanisms. With a view to developing a parallel convention in the field of transnational litigation, the negotiators of the 2019 Judgments Convention have followed the general principles that the Convention should complement the 2005 Choice of Court Convention,[27] as well as be consistent and compatible with the 2005 Convention, and that any departure from it can only be made with justified reasons.[28]

III. Jurisdiction Project

(a) Experts' Group

Work on the Jurisdiction Project was resumed after the adoption of the 2019 Judgments Convention. Between February 2020 and February 2021, three Experts' Group meetings were held to consider the necessity, desirability and feasibility of developing an international instrument relating to jurisdiction, including parallel proceedings. During the discussions, the Experts' Group generally agreed on the objectives of the future instrument, which, similar to those of the 2005 and 2019 Conventions, aim to enhance legal certainty, predictability and access to justice, and to reduce risks and costs associated with the multiplicity of proceedings and prevent inconsistent judgments in international civil or commercial litigation.[29]

The Experts' Group also considered the relationship between the future instrument and the 2005 and 2019 Conventions. It was agreed that the future instrument

[26] Preamble 1 of the 2019 Judgments Convention and Preamble 1 of the 2005 Choice of Court Convention.

[27] Preamble 3 of the 2019 Judgments Convention.

[28] The consistency, complementarity and compatibility of the two Conventions should be stressed when the interpretation of the Conventions is concerned. Any contradictory interpretation would hinder the operation and the application of the Conventions.

[29] Prel Doc No°3 of February 2021, 'Report on Jurisdiction Project', for the attention of CGAP 2021, (Prel Doc No°3 of February 2021); Annex I, '*Aide-mémoire* of the fifth meeting (online) of the Experts' Group on the Jurisdiction Project' (*Aide-mémoire* of the fifth Experts' Group meeting), para 7.

should avoid any conflict or overlap with the other two Conventions, and that it should complement them and be in line with them to avoid confusion, inconsistency or *a contrario sensu* interpretations. Such is the case for exclusive choice of court agreements, as they are covered by the 2005 Choice of Court Convention and should therefore not be dealt with by the future Convention. With these founding principles and having the same goals to pursue, the three instruments would offer a full package of HCCH Conventions on transnational litigation to facilitate international trade, business and investment.

The core discussions taking place at the Experts' Group concerned the scope and the nature of the future instrument, two topics that are often intertwined. Particularly, they hinged on whether the future instrument should cover issues relating to direct jurisdiction, and if so, how and to what extent.[30] In this respect, the jurisdictional concerns flagged two decades ago still remained at the crossroads. Some considered that harmonising direct jurisdiction rules was unrealistic and encroached onto State sovereignty; while others considered that there was a need to unify jurisdiction rules at the international level, particularly as work carried out in the last few decades might form a good basis for future work.

Views were therefore divided on how the Jurisdiction Project should proceed. The alternatives were generally the following: (1) developing a hard-law instrument on direct jurisdiction, including parallel proceedings; (2) developing a hard-law instrument focusing on only parallel proceedings; (3) developing a hard law instrument on parallel proceedings and a soft-law instrument on direct jurisdiction; or (4) developing soft-law instruments on both.[31] Being aware of the importance of the prospect of acceptance of the future instrument, the Experts' Group generally agreed to consider option II, ie, regulating parallel proceedings[32] in a hard-law instrument. With a view to further advancing the work, CGAP, as recommended by the Experts' Group, mandated the establishment of a Working Group, and determined that, among others, the Working Group 'proceed in an inclusive and holistic manner, with an initial focus on developing binding rules for concurrent proceedings (parallel proceedings and related actions or claims), and acknowledging the primary role of both jurisdictional rules and the doctrine of *forum non conveniens*, notwithstanding other possible factors, in developing such rules'; and 'explore how flexible mechanisms for judicial coordination and cooperation can support the operation of any future instrument on concurrent proceedings and jurisdiction in transnational civil or commercial litigation'.[33]

[30] For details, see ibid, Annex I; N de Araujo and M De Nardi, 'International Jurisdiction in Civil or Commercial Matters: HCCH's New Challenge', in M Pfeiffer, J Brodec, P Bríza and M Zavadilová (eds), *Liber Amicorum Monika Pauknerová* (Wolters Kluwer, 2021), 3 et seq.

[31] See '*Aide-mémoire* of the fifth Experts' Group meeting', paras 10 et seq.

[32] With a view to facilitating the work of the Experts' Group, the Permanent Bureau circulated a 'Questionnaire on Parallel Proceedings and Related Actions in Court-to-Court Cases' to collect information on how parallel proceedings, including issues pertaining to related actions or claims, are addressed under the laws of each HCCH Member. The Summary of Responses is available in Prel Doc No°3 of February 2021 (n 29), Annex II (Summary of Questionnaire Responses 2021).

[33] C&D of CGAP 2021, para 9.

(b) Working Group[34]

The Working Group, which consists of over 60 participants from 28 HCCH Members and two Observer Organisations representing different legal traditions and geographic diversity, commenced working on the development of draft provisions on parallel proceedings in court-to-court cases, with a view to further informing policy considerations and decisions in relation to the scope and type of any new instrument. In its meetings, held in October 2021 and February 2022 respectively, the Working Group generally agreed that the future Convention needed to contain rules on parallel proceedings, related claims/actions and coordination and cooperation mechanisms.

The Working Group focused its discussion on parallel proceedings first and faced two challenging issues in this regard. The first concerned the role of jurisdictional reference in parallel proceedings: some members of the Working Group suggested including indirect jurisdictional rules in the future Convention, which is a similar approach to the one adopted in the 2019 Judgments Convention, while others preferred making no reference to jurisdiction rules at all. The other challenging issue was to address the diverging practices in civil law and common law traditions on parallel proceedings. As already reflected in the Working Group discussion (also to some extent in the Experts' Group discussion), some members suggested adopting the first-in-time rule, as it provides legal certainty and predictability, whilst others proposed introducing the *forum non conveniens* doctrine so as to give discretion to courts to better deal with the particular facts of individual cases.

The Working Group was presented with different approaches.[35] Mindful of the fact that the discussion is still ongoing, this section refers to the approach documented at the end of the second Working Group meeting,[36] which can generally be summarised as a 'two-steps' test aimed at identifying which court has priority. It consists of a jurisdictional 'connection' test, followed by the 'more appropriate court' test.

Reference to jurisdictional 'connections' of courts in parallel proceedings was discussed during the second Working Group meeting. Similar to the functions of the jurisdictional filters adopted in Arts 5 and 6 of the 2019 Judgments Convention, the 'connections' would serve as indirect jurisdictional criteria to be applied by all courts involved for the purposes of prioritising the parallel proceedings under the future Convention. Assessing the applicability of the 'connections' would not evaluate how other courts have established competence in their ongoing proceedings, which would remain to be determined by domestic law.

As to the contents of the 'connections', the Working Group agreed that Arts 5 and 6 of the 2019 Judgments Convention would be a starting point for the consistency consideration, partly due to these two provisions having been thoroughly deliberated during

[34] The discussion of the Working Group can be found in Prel Doc No°7 of February 2022, 'Report of the Working Group on Jurisdiction', for the attention of CGAP 2022, (Prel Doc No°7 of February 2022), (Chair's Report 2022).

[35] An approach is described in P Herrup and RA Brand, 'A Hague Convention on Parallel Proceedings: Architecture and Features' (2022) University of Pittsburgh Legal Studies Research Paper No 2021–23.

[36] See Annex II (Basic Structure of the Possible Future Convention) to Annex I of the Chair's Report 2022 (Flowchart).

the negotiation of the Judgments Convention, entailing that they would be more easily accepted in the Jurisdiction Project. Along these lines, the Group agreed on giving primacy to the court where the immovable property is located in cases concerning rights *in rem* over immovable property. The result of this rule is that said court should proceed with the proceedings and other courts should suspend or dismiss their proceedings.[37] This connection rule is in line with Art 6 of the 2019 Judgments Convention, the sole exclusive jurisdictional filter present in that Convention.

By referring to the 'connections', the Working Group further considered distinguishing three scenarios for parallel proceedings and providing solutions for each of them:[38]

- Scenario One: when only one of the court proceedings has at least one of the connections, the court that has said connection should have priority and proceed with the proceedings;
- Scenario Two: when none of the court proceedings has the connection, parallel court proceedings would be dealt with by domestic law;
- Scenario Three: when more than one court proceedings has one of the connections, the second phase of the 'two-step' test would come into play.

The Working Group considered it necessary to further calibrate whether, and if adequate, how exceptions or safeguards should be introduced for the first two scenarios. By way of example, in Scenario One, a safeguard may be necessary for cases where the proceedings before the court having a connection have not started within a reasonable timeframe since the moment when the court proceedings which do not have a connection had commenced the proceedings.[39] Another instance of the need for an exception may be found in Scenario Two, regarding whether to provide negative priority connections.[40]

The test of finding a 'more appropriate court' would be relevant in Scenario Three, where more than one court has a connection. At this stage of the test, party autonomy (which constitutes a so-called 'priority connection') would need to be checked first, followed by the timeline of the proceedings. In absence of party autonomy and any potential issues relating to the timeline of proceedings, a 'more appropriate court' test (in the words of the current draft provisions), based on *forum non conveniens* criteria, would then be conducted by all the courts involved which have initiated their proceedings within a reasonable timeframe. If all courts reach the same result as to which constitutes a more appropriate court, said court will proceed with hearing the case. On the other hand, in those cases where diverging outcomes of the test are reached among the different courts, the court which first instituted the case would have priority and proceed with it. Particularly at this stage, coordination and/or cooperation among courts for a more efficient referral or transfer of cases, or for the swift exchange of information, would be needed and has to be analysed in more depth.[41]

[37] Chair's Report 2022, para 14.

[38] See the Flowchart.

[39] Chairs' Report 2022, para 25.

[40] A negative priority rule means that a court of a Contracting State which only has a connection listed as a negative priority in the future Convention should give way to courts of other Contracting States where the parallel proceedings are pending, see ibid, para 24.

[41] ibid, para 22.

It should be stressed that the discussions carried out by the Working Group are still ongoing. This means that more details about this approach, including the criteria to be employed, or even the possibility of adopting a different approach, remain to be considered by the Working Group, which will, as mandated by CGAP, meet twice more before the CGAP's meeting in March 2023.

IV. Outlook

Although it is still named the 'Jurisdiction Project', the project is now focussing on the development of a hard-law instrument dealing with concurrent proceedings, including parallel proceedings, related actions and claims, and cooperation and coordination mechanisms. Being mindful that the discussion of the Project is still ongoing, its current direction suggests that the future instrument, in its present form, would not provide direct jurisdiction rules applied to determine the competence of a court in transnational cases.

This suggests a pragmatic and realistic approach taken thus far by the Working Group with the purpose of developing a meaningful and widely acceptable instrument that aims to solve real problems pervading transnational litigation.

As shown during the Experts' Group and Working Group discussions, the views on the treatment of direct jurisdiction were so divided that it might have been unlikely to conclude a convention regulating direct jurisdiction.[42] The history of the Judgments Project also suggests that the fundamental differences regarding direct jurisdiction in each legal system could not have easily been harmonised,[43] in certain contrast to the situation within the EU, as explained in the previous chapters of this book.

The need for an instrument dealing with parallel proceedings has been referred to in the past,[44] and the focus on parallel proceedings in the Jurisdiction Project echoes such need.[45] In cross-border dealings, as long as there are multiple grounds of jurisdiction available to litigants, there is always a risk of proceedings being brought in multiple fora simultaneously. Such practices are costly and burdensome for the parties, especially those who have fewer financial means. And they tend to result in delays and uncertainties in litigation as well as potential conflicting judgments. Nowadays, in a world increasingly interconnected through globalisation and the use of technology, more venues or fora before which parties may bring their disputes are available, further hindering the situation.

[42] See Chair's Report 2021; for discussion, see P Herrup and RA Brand, 'A Hague Convention on Parallel Proceedings' (2022) *Harvard International Law Journal* 1.

[43] P Herrup and RA Brand (n 35), 1 et seq; A Bonomi and CM Mariottini, 'A Game Changer in International Litigation? Roadmap to the 2019 Hague Judgments Convention' in A Bonomi and GP Romano (eds), *YPIL* (Vol XX, 2018/2019), 539; G Cuniberti, 'Signaling the Enforceability of the Forum's Judgments Abroad' (2020) *Rivista di diritto internazionale privato e processuale* 33; A Bonomi, 'Courage or Caution? A critical overview of the Hague Preliminary Draft on Judgments' (2015/2016) *YPIL* 3.

[44] Permanent Bureau for the attention of Experts' Group, 'Note 2: Issues Paper on Matters of Jurisdiction (including parallel proceedings', January 2013, paras 28–41.

[45] Herrup and Brand (n 35), 3–4; N Zhao (n 24), 366.

Most States recognise the potential risks associated with parallel proceedings and have developed their own rules for the courts to decide on how to deal with these situations. Broadly, there are two general approaches.[46] Most civil law jurisdictions adopt the first-in-time (*lis alibi pendens*) rule, which requires the court second seised to suspend or dismiss the proceedings. Although this approach provides certainty, its disadvantages are also obvious, eg, having the risks of leading to a race to the court, forum shopping, or strategic litigation by requesting negative declaratory judgments. In common law jurisdictions, the existence of parallel proceedings is dealt with through the doctrine of *forum non conveniens*, for which the existence of parallel proceedings is one factor to be taken into account when determining the most appropriate forum.

As described in section three, the Working Group has made progress in sketching the basic structure of the future Convention on parallel proceedings. Yet, manifold issues remain to be further considered in the upcoming meetings, such as:

- the material scope and geographical reach of the future Convention. In particular, for the geographical application, the Working Group still needs to consider whether to extend the application of the future Convention to non-Contracting States,[47] for example, in the situation where the 'more appropriate court' analysis leads to a court of a non-Contracting State;
- the definition of parallel proceedings and related actions/claims, eg, whether it would cover interim measures.

If the 'two-steps' test is the preferred approach for the future Convention, the Working Group needs to further:

- develop the 'connections' rules: what connections should be included in the future Convention, for instance, how to deal with exclusive jurisdictions under national laws;[48] the categories and hierarchy of these connections, including the role of party autonomy as a priority connection,[49] or protection of weaker parties, like consumers and employees;[50]
- lay down the criteria to be employed for identifying a 'more appropriate court'. In this context, the Group should consider how to bridge the first-in-time rule and the *forum non conveniens* doctrine, and whether and how the prognosis of the recognition and enforcement of the judgments will play a role;
- design the coordination and/or cooperation mechanisms:[51] consideration should be given to its nature and operation, like whether the mechanism would be mandatory; whether it should operate directly among courts, central authorities,

[46] See 'Summary of Questionnaire Responses', 2021 (n 32).

[47] See de Araujo and De Nardi (n 30), 5. To facilitate the discussion at the Experts' Group, the Permanent Bureau prepared a note on 'Assuming or transferring jurisdiction to non-Contracting States'.

[48] See N de Araujo and M De Nardi (n 30), 8–9.

[49] It was agreed by the Working Group that choice of court agreements which are not covered by the 2005 Choice of Court Convention will be dealt with by the future Convention. See Chair's Report 2022, para 7.

[50] See N de Araujo and M De Nardi (n 30), 4.

[51] Chair's Report 2022, para 22. It was also suggested that the future Convention works on establishing cooperation/coordination mechanism, see Herrup and Brand (n 35), 3–4.

> or a combination of both; who should raise the existence of parallel proceedings, the parties or *ex officio*; and some other practical elements, for instance, how to remove language barriers so as to ensure an efficient and effective operation of the mechanism. The existing direct judicial communication models could be used as inspirations in this regard.[52]

While these rules for the future Convention need to be further developed, several founding principles should continue to be taken into account throughout its discussion and development. Among these, the compatibility, consistency and complementarity with the 2005 Choice of Court and 2019 Judgments Conventions, stand out as particularly relevant ones, especially with regard to the development of 'connections', the scope of the Convention and the definition of parallel proceedings. Likewise, the practical operation of the future Convention and how efficiently parallel proceedings can be managed remain as key considerations, in particular when all courts involved in parallel proceedings need to conduct the 'two-step' test and communicate with each other. Furthermore, the future Convention, which aims at enhancing access to justice, should not contain rules that might cause a denial of justice for the parties; so it may also need to accommodate certain situations where parallel proceedings might be allowed to continue (subject to specific criteria) in the interest of justice and efficiency.[53]

It is evident from the foregoing matters that developing an international framework addressing parallel proceedings and its necessary cooperative mechanism for communication constitutes a challenging task. The future success of the Jurisdiction Project, in its current form, will largely depend on the creativity of its negotiators in reaching a pragmatic solution. That solution will have to bridge the diverse practices among States in the treatment of parallel proceedings, including the formidable task of finding an approach that balances the first-in-time and the *forum non conveniens* doctrines. Nonetheless, surmounting similar obstacles is of no novelty to the HCCH and the avid negotiators in charge of the discussion, as evidenced by the success of many of its previous Conventions. Once more, as it has been demonstrated throughout the negotiation of the 2019 Judgments Convention, the cooperative spirit and constructive flexibility that the committed members of the Working Group have shown will be crucial. I, myself, remain particularly hopeful that these experts will gather their intellectual minds to prepare the core provisions of the future Convention on parallel proceedings, which is to be submitted for negotiation at the Special Commission in a not-too-distant future.

[52] Such as the International Hague Network of Judges within the HCCH, the 1997 UNCITRAL Model Law on Cross-Border Insolvency (Chapter IV, Arts 25–27), ILA Resolution 1/2000, at para 5.2. To facilitate the discussion at the Experts' Group, the Permanent Bureau prepared a 'Survey of Mechanisms for Judicial Coordination and Cooperation'.

[53] Chair's Report 2022, para 23.

INDEX

www.ingramcontent.com/pod-product-compliance
Ingram Content Group UK Ltd.
Pitfield, Milton Keynes, MK11 3LW, UK
UKHW020234290926
15470UKWH00002B/530